1980

S0-AHX-599

3 0301 00075047 7

# Elementary Algebra
## Third Edition

**ROBERT G. MOON**
Fullerton College

**ROBERT D. DAVIS**
Fullerton College

LIBRARY
College of St. Francis
JOLIET, ILL.

CHARLES E. MERRILL PUBLISHING COMPANY
*A Bell & Howell Company*
Columbus    Toronto    London    Sydney

*to Marilyn and to Jan*

Published by Charles E. Merrill Publishing Co.
*A Bell & Howell Company*
Columbus, Ohio 43216


This book was set in Times Roman
Production Editor: Charles Robinson
Cover design by Graphic House, Inc.

Copyright© 1980, 1975, 1970, by Bell & Howell Company. All rights reserved. No part of this book may be reproduced in any form, electronic or mechanical, including photocopy, recording, or any information storage and retrieval system, without permission in writing from the publisher.

Library of Congress Catalog Card Number: 79-90159
International Standard Book Number: 0–675–08158–0
Printed in the United States of America
1 2 3 4 5 6 7 8 9 10—85 84 83 82 81 80

**ITEM CHARGED**

on:             Joyce Mary Gamagami Craig

on Barcode:
                2 0 3 0 1 0 0 0 1 4 5 5 7 1

on Group:       Distance Students

Date:           7/23/2010  05.00 PM

                College algebra [by] M. Richardson.
or:             Richardson, Moses, 1911-1968.
Number:         512 R534
neration:
hnology:

Barcode:        |
                3 0 3 0 1 0 0 0 1 9 9 2 9 5

patron has permission to remove this item from the
ry

**ITEM CHARGED**

on:             Joyce Mary Gamagami Craig
on Barcode:
                2 0 3 0 1 0 0 0 1 4 5 5 7 1

on Group:       Distance Students

Date:           7/23/2010  05:00 PM

                Elementary algebra / Robert G. Moon.
                Robert D. Davis.
or:             Moon, Robert G.
Number:         512 M819
neration:
nology:

Barcode:        |
                3 0 3 0 1 0 0 0 7 5 0 4 7 7

patron has permission to remove ... item from the
ry

# ...he Third Edition

...f *Elementary Algebra* were created and tested over a
...llege, Fullerton, California. The authors wished to
...xt and audio tapes whereby students could become
...gebra. The response to this program has been highly

...nally conceived as an "integrated" approach, with the
...nd tapes simultaneously, many students and instructors
...xt. Therefore we have *redesigned* this *third edition* so
...itable for the integrated approach, the text is now
...audio support materials may be used, if desired.

...ed format of the earlier editions has been eliminated.
...ntinue to use both tapes and text, the symbol, □,
...llcate the beginning of each new discussion on the
...parentheses in the right margin is likewise used to
...HESE SYMBOLS APPEAR SOLELY FOR THE
...RENCING.

... is to develop understanding of and computational skill
...ebra. The following features are included:

...arting with the simplicity of the whole numbers in
...ssing step-by-step through the integers in Module 2 and
...onal numbers, and real numbers in Module 3.
...g polynomial and rational expressions are developed in
...with radicals and exponents. Graphing skills, systems
...s, the function concept, and functional notation are

...lems are heavily emphasized throughout.
...us examples, study exercises, and review exercises,
...olutions.

...supplementary problems, graded from the simple to
...s to the odd-numbered supplementary problems are
...book. Answers to the even-numbered problems are
...'s *Manual* available from the publisher.

...there is a set of review problems with answers.
...ged to study these before a module test. Also, they
...w for the final examination.

...st and second editions are as follows:

...zed and used only where it enhances the explanation.
...properties of whole numbers have been condensed to

...hortened by one unit allowing students to reach the
...lving earlier.

Calculator problems have been included in the Supplementary Problems. No attempt, however, has been made to teach the operation of the electronic calculator, due to the diversity of models. The teacher should discuss the operational techniques in the classroom and use the included problems for practice.

Unit 21, "Solving Inequalities" now solves inequalities using division rather than multiplication by the reciprocal.

Unit 23, "Introduction to Radicals and Rational Exponents" now proceeds further by discussing rational exponents of the form $m/n$.

Unit 27, "Graphing Linear and Quadratic Equations" now introduces the slope of a straight line.

A new unit has been included—Unit 29—entitled "Linear Inequalities and Systems of Linear Inequalities."

The authors would like to express their appreciation to the many fine people who helped with the publication of this book; in particular, Professor Robert A. Yawin, Springfield Technical Community College, and Professor Don Hostettler, Mesa College, for their thoughtful reviews. We are also indebted to Andrea Posner of Charles E. Merrill. And special thanks to Charles Robinson, our Production Editor. His many contributions were invaluable.

January 1980

Robert G. Moon

Robert D. Davis

# A Word about Using This Program...

The *Elementary Algebra, Third Edition* program has two components: a text and a set of audio tapes. These components make the program suitable for both classroom and self-paced modes of instruction. In the classroom, you will want to use the text by itself. In a mathematics laboratory, or learning resource center, you may wish to supplement the text with the accompanying audio tapes in one of two ways: either by listening to the tapes selectively for help with more difficult topics, or by working through the text and tapes together. If you are using the text and tapes together, remember to use the symbol, □, appearing in the left-hand margin of the text with the corresponding reference number in the right-hand margin to match your place in the text with the correct place on the tape. When you come to a *study* or *review exercise*, turn off the recorder. Work the exercises and check your answers before you turn the recorder on again. In most cases, detailed solutions are provided. Be sure to compare your work carefully with the details of these solutions. Many of your mistakes can be corrected in this manner.

Immediately following the solutions to the review exercises is a section of supplementary problems. The answers to odd-numbered supplementary problems are given in Appendix 3. You are encouraged to try as many of these problems as you wish. Remember, in mathematics, practice is the key to success.

## STUDY TECHNIQUES

1. The recorder may be stopped at any time to give more time for analysis of a concept.
2. The recorder may be reversed to review a particular portion of a unit.
3. Module review problems with answers are spaced periodically throughout the text. These review problems cover several units and should be worked prior to each examination, since they contain questions similar to those you will encounter on the examination itself.
4. Before an examination, review all of the units involved, examine the review exercises, and work the module review problems.
5. Before the final examination, you should review the text and rework the review exercises and module review problems.
6. Mathematics pyramids; that is, it builds on itself. Don't get behind. In fact, it is a good idea to try to stay a unit ahead.
7. Many students have indicated that a "constant review" was extremely successful; that is, constantly going back and redoing earlier units.
8. Several units are closely related. If you are having difficulty with:

## A Word About Using This Program...

| Unit | Then Review Units |
|------|-------------------|
| 9    | 5, 7, 8           |
| 15   | 5, 9              |
| 16   | 4, 9, 15          |
| 17   | 10, 16            |
| 18   | 12, 13            |
| 19   | 14                |
| 20   | 10, 12, 16, 17, 19 |
| 21   | 10, 17, 20        |
| 22   | 5                 |
| 25   | 10, 16, 17, 20    |
| 27   | 26                |
| 30   | 26, 27            |

# Contents

Contents

# MODULE 4 • OPERATIONS WITH POLYNOMIAL AND RATIONAL EXPRESSIONS

# MODULE 5 • EXPONENTS AND RADICALS

# Whole Numbers— Operations and Properties

# Sets and Whole Numbers

## ☐ Objectives       (1)

By the end of this unit you should be able to define the following terms:

- set
- one-to-one correspondence
- whole numbers
- member or element
- matching sets
- natural numbers
- equal sets
- subset

You should also be able to perform the following operations with sets:

- union
- intersection

And, you should be able to use the "greater than" and "less than" signs.

## ☐ Set       (2)

In mathematics, the word *set* is used to describe a group or a collection of objects. The objects contained in a set are called *elements* or *members*.

**Example 1:** The set consisting of the first four letters of the English alphabet. The elements or members are $a$, $b$, $c$, and $d$.

**Example 2:** The set of counting numbers between 5 and 9. The elements or members are 6, 7, and 8.

**Example 3:** The set of letters used to spell the word *chair*. The elements or members are $c$, $h$, $a$, $i$, and $r$.

## ☐ Set Notation       (3)

Sets may be specified two ways: by *word statements* or by the *roster method*. In a word statement, the set is specified by a descriptive sentence. In the roster method, the set is specified by listing the elements and enclosing them within braces.

**Example 1:** Word statement. The set consisting of the first four letters of the English alphabet.
Roster method. $\{a, b, c, d\}$

**Example 2:** Word statement. The set of counting numbers between 5 and 9.
Roster method. $\{6, 7, 8\}$

**Example 3:** Word statement. The set of letters used to spell the word *chair*.
Roster method. $\{c, h, a, i, r\}$

## ☐ Order of Elements       (4)

In the roster method of specifying a set, the order of the elements is irrelevant.

**Example:** Word statement. The set consisting of the last three letters of the English alphabet.
Roster method: $\{x, y, z\}$ or $\{z, x, y\}$

## ☐ Repetition of Elements       (5)

In the roster method, elements should not be repeated.

**Example:** Word statement. The set of letters used to spell the word *mathematics*.
Roster method: $\{m, a, t, h, e, i, c, s\}$
Incorrect method: $\{\overline{m, a, t, h, e, m, a, t, i, c, s}\}$

## ☐ The Empty Set       (6)

The following sets contain no elements.

**Example 1:** The set of women who have been president of the United States before 1980.

**Example 2:** The set of counting numbers between 5 and 6.

☐ **(7)**

A set which contains no elements is called the *null* set or the *empty* set, and it is symbolized by either { } or $\varnothing$. It is incorrect to symbolize the empty set by $\{\varnothing\}$.

☐ *Study Exercise One* **(8)**

A.  Use the roster method to specify the following sets.
1.  The set consisting of the first six letters of the English alphabet.
2.  The set of counting numbers between 15 and 22.
3.  The set of letters used to spell the word *arithmetic*.
4.  The set of counting numbers between 9 and 10.

B.  Write a word statement to describe each of the following sets.
5.  $\{q, r, s, t, u, v, w, x, y, z\}$        6.  $\{7, 8, 9\}$

C.  Do as directed.
7.  Which of the following is an incorrect way of specifying this set: The set of letters used to spell the word *ball*.
    (a)  $\{b, a, l\}$      (b)  $\{a, l, b\}$      (c)  $\{b, a, l, l\}$
8.  Write the preferred symbol representing the null set.
9.  Why does this symbol, $\{\varnothing\}$, fail to represent the null set?

☐ **Equal Sets** **(9)**

Sets are said to be *equal* providing they contain identically the same elements.

**Example 1:** $\{a, b, c\} = \{a, b, c\}$

**Example 2:** $\{3, 4, 5, 6\} = \{5, 6, 3, 4\}$

**Example 3:** $\{a, b\} \neq \{a, b, c\}$

☐ Uppercase letters may be assigned to represent sets. **(10)**

**Example 1:** Let $S$ represent the set consisting of the letters used to spell the word *happy*.

    **Solution:** $S = \{h, a, p, y\}$

**Example 2:** Let $A$ represent the set of counting numbers between 10 and 16.

    **Solution:** $A = \{11, 12, 13, 14, 15\}$

**Example 3:** Let $A = \{e, f, g, h\}$ and $B = \{h, g, f, e\}$. Then $A = B$.

☐ **One-to-One Correspondence** **(11)**

Two sets can be placed into a *one-to-one correspondence* provided their respective elements can be paired one-to-one with no elements left unpaired in either set.

**Example 1:** These sets can be placed into a one-to-one correspondence.

$$\{a, \quad b, \quad c\} \qquad \text{or} \qquad \{a, \quad b, \quad c\}$$
$$\{\square, \quad \triangle, \quad \bigcirc\} \qquad\qquad \{\square, \quad \triangle, \quad \bigcirc\}$$

**Example 2:** These sets cannot be placed into a one-to-one correspondence.

$$\{w, \quad x, \quad y, \quad z\}$$
$$\{1, \quad 2, \quad 3\}$$

☐ **Another Example** **(12)**

Let $A$ represent the set of letters used to spell the word *soothe*. Let $B$ represent the set of counting numbers between 8 and 14. Sets $A$ and $B$ can be placed into a one-to-one correspondence.

$$A = \{s, \quad o, \quad t, \quad h, \quad e\,\}$$
$$\updownarrow \quad \updownarrow \quad \updownarrow \quad \updownarrow \quad \updownarrow$$
$$B = \{9, \quad 10, \quad 11, \quad 12, \quad 13\}$$

## ☐ Matching Sets (13)

Sets are said to be *matching* provided they can be placed into a one-to-one correspondence. Matching sets are the same size.

**Example 1:** These sets are matching sets because they can be placed into a one-to-one correspondence.

$$\{3, \quad 6, \quad 9, \quad 12\}$$
$$\updownarrow \quad \updownarrow \quad \updownarrow \quad \updownarrow$$
$$\{a, \quad c, \quad d, \quad g\,\}$$

**Example 2:** These sets are not matching sets because they cannot be placed into a one-to-one correspondence.

$$\{m, \quad n, \quad p, \quad k, \quad t\}$$
$$\updownarrow \quad \updownarrow \quad \updownarrow$$
$$\{a, \quad b, \quad k\}$$

## ☐ Another Example (14)

Which of the following sets are matching sets?

$A = \{\square, \triangle, \bigcirc\}$
$B = \{3, 5, 7, 9\}$
$C = \{1, 2, 3\}$
$D = $ The set of letters used to spell the word *seek*.
$E = $ The set of letters used to spell the word *some*.

## ☐ Solution (15)

$A$, $C$, and $D$ are matching sets: $\quad A = \{\square, \triangle, \bigcirc\}$
$\qquad\qquad\qquad\qquad\qquad\qquad\quad C = \{1, 2, 3\}$
$\qquad\qquad\qquad\qquad\qquad\qquad\quad D = \{s, e, k\}$

$B$ and $E$ are matching sets: $\quad B = \{3, 5, 7, 9\}$
$\qquad\qquad\qquad\qquad\qquad\qquad\quad E = \{s, o, m, e\}$

## ☐ Study Exercise Two (16)

1. Using arrows, illustrate two ways in which the following sets may be placed into a one-to-one correspondence:

$$A = \{a, t, k\} \qquad B = \{1, 5, 9\}$$

2. Separate the following into groups of matching sets.
   $A = \{3, 4, 5, 6, 7\}$
   $B = \{a, b, c, d\}$
   $C = $ The set of letters used to spell the word *class*.
   $D = $ The set of letters used to spell the word *smooth*.
   $E = $ The set of counting numbers between 5 and 10.
   $F = $ The set consisting of the first four letters of the alphabet.
   $G = $ The set of counting numbers between 20 and 22.
   $H = \{a\}$
3. Which sets in problem 2 are equal sets?
4. True or false: If two sets are equal then they will also be matching sets.
5. True or false: If two sets are matching then they are not necessarily equal sets.

## ☐ Subsets  (17)

Set $A$ is said to be a *subset* of set $B$ if every element of set $A$ is also an element of set $B$. The symbol for subset is $\subseteq$.

**Example 1:**  $A = \{a, b\}$ and $B = \{a, b, c, d\}$. $A$ is said to be a subset of $B$, or $A \subseteq B$.

**Example 2:**  $S = \{3, 5, 7\}$ and $T = \{1, 2, 3, 4, 5, 6, 7\}$. $S$ is said to be a subset of $T$, or $S \subseteq T$. →

**Example 3:**  $C = \{x, y, z\}$ and $D = \{z, y, x\}$. $C$ is said to be a subset of $D$, or $C \subseteq D$.

**Example 4:**  $H = \{3, 5\}$ and $J = \{1, 3, 7\}$. $H$ is not a subset of $J$.

## ☐ Union  (18)

The *union* of two sets is the single set containing all those elements which are in either set. Union is symbolized by $\cup$.

**Example 1:**  $\{a, b\} \cup \{c, d, e\} = \{a, b, c, d, e\}$

**Example 2:**  $\{1, 2, 3\} \cup \{3, 4\} = \{1, 2, 3, 4\}$

**Example 3:**  $\{c, d, e, f\} \cup \{c, d, e, f\} = \{c, d, e, f\}$

**Example 4:**  $\varnothing \cup \{a, b, c\} = \{a, b, c\}$

## ☐ Intersection  (19)

The *intersection* of two sets is the single set containing only those elements which are common to both sets. The symbol for intersection is $\cap$.

**Example 1:**  $\{a, b, c\} \cap \{c, d, e\} = \{c\}$        **Example 2:**  $\{3, 6, 7, 9\} \cap \{7, 9, 11\} = \{7, 9\}$

**Example 3:**  $\{e, f, g\} \cap \{e, f, g\} = \{e, f, g\}$        **Example 4:**  $\{1, 2, 3\} \cap \{7, 8\} = \varnothing$

**Example 5:**  $\varnothing \cap \{5, 10, 15\} = \varnothing$

## ☐  *Study Exercise Three*  (20)

Given these sets,

$$B = \{m, n, p\} \qquad C = \{p, t, k\} \qquad D = \{m, n, p, j\} \qquad E = \{t, k, x, y\}$$

find the following.

1.  $B \cup C$        2.  $B \cap C$        3.  $B \cup D$        4.  $B \cap D$
5.  $D \cup E$        6.  $D \cap E$        7.  $\varnothing \cup B$        8.  $\varnothing \cap B$
9.  True or false:  $B \subseteq E$        10.  True or false:  $B \subseteq D$        11.  True or false:  $D \subseteq B$

## ☐ Associating Numbers with Sets  (21)

Numbers may be associated with certain sets by simply counting the elements contained in the set.

**Example 1:**  $A = \{a, b, c\}$. The number associated with set $A$ is 3.

**Example 2:**  $B = \{c, d, x, y, z, m\}$. The number associated with set $B$ is 6.

**Example 3:**  The number associated with the null set is zero.

**Example 4:**  If $A = \{a, b\}$ and $B = \{c, d, e\}$, the number associated with $A \cup B$ is 5. $A \cup B = \{a, b, c, d, e\}$.

**Example 5:**  If $A = \{a, b\}$ and $C = \{b, c, e\}$, the number associated with $A \cup C$ is 4. $A \cup C = \{a, b, c, e\}$.

## ☐ Whole Numbers  (22)

The whole numbers are all of the numbers which can be associated with sets.

$$0, 1, 2, 3, 4, 5, 6, 7, 8, 9, 10, 11, 12, \ldots$$

☐ **Natural Numbers** **(23)**

The *natural* numbers are all of the whole numbers except 0.

$$1, 2, 3, 4, 5, 6, 7, 8, 9, 10, 11, 12,\ldots$$

The first natural number is one.

The first whole number is zero.

The natural numbers are a subset of the whole numbers.

☐ *Study Exercise Four* **(24)**

A.  Give the whole number which is associated with each of the following sets.

1.  $\{a, b, c, d, e, f, g, h, i\}$      2.  $\{c, k, l\}$      3.  $\{b\}$      4.  $\varnothing$
5.  The set of letters used to spell the word *spoon*
6.  The set of counting numbers between 38 and 39
7.  $A \cup B$ where $A = \{x, y, z\}$ and $B = \{m, o, t, p\}$
8.  $S \cup R$ where $S = \{a, c, e\}$ and $R = \{a, c, m, o\}$
9.  $\varnothing \cup D$ where $D = \{m, n\}$

B.  True or False

10.  The first whole number is one.
11.  The whole numbers are a subset of the natural numbers.

☐ **Comparing Whole Numbers** **(25)**

There are three important symbols which allow us to compare two whole numbers.

1.  The equal sign, $=$
2.  The less than sign, $<$
3.  The greater than sign, $>$

☐ **The Equal Sign** **(26)**

The equal sign states that two symbols represent the same number.

**Example:**  $2 + 3 = 5$

☐ **Less Than—Greater Than Signs** **(27)**

The less than and greater than signs state that two symbols represent different numbers. These symbols must always point to the smaller number.

**Example 1:**  $5 < 8$                **Example 2:**  $12 > 4$

☐ *Study Exercise Five* **(28)**

A.  Insert the correct symbol to make the statement true.

1.  $0 \underline{\hspace{1cm}} 5$          2.  $15 \underline{\hspace{1cm}} 4$          3.  $6 + 1 \underline{\hspace{1cm}} 7$

4.  $1 \underline{\hspace{1cm}} 0$          5.  $3 \underline{\hspace{1cm}} 5 + 2$          6.  $7 + 2 \underline{\hspace{1cm}} 4 + 5$

B.  True or False

7.  $0 > 5$          8.  $100 > 10$          9.  $0 + 5 = 5$

## REVIEW EXERCISES

A.  Fill in the blanks.
    1.  A group of objects is called a _____.
    2.  The objects contained in a set are called _____.
    3.  A set which contains no elements is called the _____ set.

B.  Use the roster method to specify the following sets.
    4.  The set of counting numbers between 10 and 15.
    5.  The set of letters used to spell the word *college*.

C.  Given these sets,

$$A = \{a, b, c, d\} \qquad B = \{\square, \triangle, \bigcirc\} \qquad C = \{d, c, b, a\}$$
$$D = \text{the set of letters used to spell the work } peek$$
$$E = \text{the set of counting numbers between 20 and 25}$$

answer the following.

    6.  Using arrows, illustrate two ways in which set $B$ may be placed into a one-to-one correspondence with set $D$.
    7.  Which of the above sets are matching sets?
    8.  Which of the above sets are equal sets?

D.  Given these sets,

$A = \{c, d, e\}, B = \{m, n, o\}, C = \{a, b, c, d, e\}, D = \{m, n, x, y\}$

find the following.

|   |   |   |   |
|---|---|---|---|
| 9.  $A \cup B$ | 10. $A \cap B$ | 11. $A \cup C$ | 12. $A \cap C$ |
| 13. $B \cup D$ | 14. $B \cap D$ | 15. $\varnothing \cup C$ | 16. $\varnothing \cap C$ |

    17. True or false:  $A \subseteq C$     18. True or false:  $C \subseteq A$     19. True or false:  $B \subseteq D$

E.  Give the whole number which is associated with each of the following sets.

    20. $\{r, s, t, u, v, w, x, y, z\}$     21. $\{o, n, p, t\}$          22. $\{a\}$
    23. The set of letters used to spell the word *sitting*
    24. The set of counting numbers between 18 and 19
    25. $A \cup B$ where $A = \{e, f, g\}$ and $B = \{h, i, j, k\}$
    26. $S \cup T$ where $S = \{a, b\}$ and $T = \{a, b, c, d\}$

F.  True or False

    27.  $17 < 14$       28.  $0 > 5$          29.  $3 + 2 < 6$          30.  $4 + 7 = 11$

### Solutions to Review Exercises

A.  1.  set           2.  elements or members           3.  null or empty

B.  4.  $\{11, 12, 13, 14\}$                      5.  $\{c, o, l, e, g\}$

C.  6.  Any two of the following:

    7.  $A$, $C$, $E$ are matching sets and $B$, $D$ are also matching sets.          8.  $A = C$

## Solutions to Review Exercises, Contd.

D.  9.  $A \cup B = \{c, d, e, m, n, o\}$     10.  $A \cap B = \emptyset$     11.  $A \cup C = C$
    12.  $A \cap C = A$     13.  $B \cup D = \{m, n, o, x, y\}$     14.  $B \cap D = \{m, n\}$
    15.  $\emptyset \cup C = C$     16.  $\emptyset \cap C = \emptyset$     17.  True
    18.  False     19.  False

E.  20.  9     21.  4     22.  1     23.  5     24.  0     25.  7     26.  4

F.  27.  False     28.  False     29.  True     30.  True

## SUPPLEMENTARY PROBLEMS

A.  Use the roster method to specify the following sets.

    1.  The set of letters used to spell the word *night*
    2.  The set of letters used to spell the word *pool*
    3.  The set of letters used to spell the word *Mississippi*
    4.  The set of counting numbers between 1 and 10
    5.  The set of counting numbers between 5 and 7

B.  Given these sets,

$$A = \{x, y, z, w\} \quad B = \{y, z, x, w\} \quad C = \{c, d, e\}$$
$$D = \text{The set of letters used to spell the word } tea$$
$$E = \text{The set of letters used to spell the word } week$$

do the following.

    6.  Using arrows, illustrate three ways in which set $C$ may be placed into a one-to-one correspondence with set $D$.
    7.  Which of the above sets are matching sets?
    8.  Which of the above sets are equal sets?

C.  Given these sets,

$$A = \{f, g, h\} \quad B = \{h, i, j\} \quad C = \{k, m\} \quad D = \{k, m, n, o\}$$

find the following.

    9.  $A \cup B$     10.  $A \cup C$     11.  $C \cup D$     12.  $A \cap B$     13.  $B \cap C$
    14.  $C \cap D$     15.  $A \cup A$     16.  $A \cap A$     17.  $\emptyset \cap A$     18.  $\emptyset \cup B$
    19.  True or false:  $C \subseteq D$     20.  True or false:  $D \subseteq C$
    21.  True or false:  $A \subseteq B$     22.  True or false:  $A = B$

D.  Give the whole number which is associated with each of the following sets.

    23.  $\{d, e, f, g, h, i, j, k\}$     24.  $\{a, k, t\}$     25.  $\{t\}$     26.  $\emptyset$
    27.  The set of letters used to spell *day*     28.  The set of letters used to spell *algebra*
    29.  $A \cup B$ where $A = \{k, t, p\}$ and $B = \{a, b, c, d, e\}$
    30.  $C \cup D$ where $C = \{a, b, c, d, e, f\}$ and $D = \{d, e, f, g, h\}$
    31.  The set of counting numbers between 30 and 31

E.  True or False

    32.  $23 > 15$     33.  $0 > 9$     34.  $6 + 2 < 10$     35.  $2 = 1 + 1$
    36.  One is the first whole number.     37.  Zero is a natural number.
    38.  $\{\emptyset\}$ is a symbol representing the empty set.
    39.  Ten is a whole number, but it is not a natural number.
    40.  If $A = \{1, 3, 5\}$ and $B = \{3, 1, 5\}$, then $A = B$
    41.  If two sets are equal, then they must also be matching sets.
    42.  If two sets are matching, then they must also be equal sets.

☐ **Solutions to Study Exercises** **(8A)**

## Study Exercise One (Frame 8)

A.  1.  $\{a, b, c, d, e, f\}$    2.  $\{16, 17, 18, 19, 20, 21\}$    3.  $\{a, r, i, t, h, m, e, c\}$    4.  $\varnothing$

B.  5.  The set consisting of the last ten letters of the English alphabet.
    6.  The set of counting numbers between 6 and 10.

C.  7.  (c)    8.  $\varnothing$    9.  Because the set contains one element, namely, this symbol: $\varnothing$.

☐ **(16A)**

## Study Exercise Two (Frame 16)

1.  Any two of the following:

2.  $A, D$ are matching; $B, C, E, F$ are matching; $G, H$ are matching.
3.  $B = F$    4.  True    5.  True

☐ **(20A)**

## Study Exercise Three (Frame 20)

1.  $B \cup C = \{m, n, p, t, k\}$    2.  $B \cap C = \{p\}$    3.  $B \cup D = \{m, n, p, j\}$, or $D$
4.  $B \cap D = \{m, n, p\}$, or $B$    5.  $D \cup E = \{m, n, p, j, t, k, x, y\}$    6.  $D \cap E = \varnothing$
7.  $\varnothing \cup B = \{m, n, p\}$, or $B$    8.  $\varnothing \cap B = \varnothing$    9.  False
10.  True    11.  False

☐ **(24A)**

## Study Exercise Four (Frame 24)

A.  1.  9    2.  3    3.  1    4.  0    5.  4    6.  0    7.  7    8.  5    9.  2

B.  10.  False; the first whole number is zero.    11.  False; the natural numbers are a subset of the whole numbers.

☐ **(28A)**

## Study Exercise Five (Frame 28)

A.  1.  $0 < 5$    2.  $15 > 4$    3.  $6 + 1 = 7$

    4.  $1 > 0$    5.  $3 < 5 + 2$    6.  $7 + 2 = 4 + 5$

B.  7.  False    8.  True    9.  True

# Operations on Whole Numbers

□ Objectives     **(1)**

By the end of this unit you should be able to define the following terms:

- addend, sum
- dividend, divisor, quotient
- numeral expression
- minuend, subtrahend, difference
- binary operation
- simplify completely

You should also be able to:

- show the interrelationships of addition, subtraction, multiplication, and division.
- use the order of operations agreement.
- use grouping symbols.
- classify expressions as basic sums, differences, products, or quotients.

□ Basic Vocabulary: Numerals and Equality     **(2)**

*Numerals* are symbols which represent numbers. The following are the common numerals which represent whole numbers:

$$0, 1, 2, 3, 4, 5, 6, 7, 8, 9, 10, 11, 12, \ldots$$

The equal sign or equality states that two numerals represent the same number.

**Example 1:** seven = 7         **Example 2:** $3 + 2 = 5$

**Example 3:** $8 + 2 = 7 + 3$

□ The Fundamental Operations with Whole Numbers     **(3)**

1. Addition: $12 + 8$
2. Subtraction: $10 - 6$
3. Multiplication: $5 \times 8$ or $5 \cdot 8$ or $(5)(8)$
4. Division: $15 \div 3$ or $\dfrac{15}{3}$

In the next few frames we will see how the four fundamental operations are interrelated. We will show that subtraction is related to addition, that multiplication is also related to addition, and that division is related to multiplication.

□ The Operation of Addition     **(4)**

Addition is described by +, the plus sign. It is used to denote the total of two numbers.

**Example:** $3 + 5 = 8$

□ Terms to Remember     **(5)**

$$\begin{array}{ccccc} 3 & + & 5 & = & 8 \\ \uparrow & & \uparrow & & \uparrow \\ addend & & addend & & sum \end{array}$$

Since $3 + 5$ names the same number as the numeral 8, $3 + 5$ may also be called the sum.

**Example:** Given the equality, $7 + 3 = 10$,

1. 7 is called an *addend*.
2. 3 is called an *addend*.
3. 10 is called the *sum*.
4. $7 + 3$ is called the *sum*.

□ The Operation of Subtraction     **(6)**

**Example:** $5 - 3 = ?$

Subtraction is really an addition problem with a missing addend. We think: what number when added to 3 produces 5? The answer is 2, because $2 + 3 = 5$.

☐ Terms to Remember (7)

$$5 \quad - \quad 3 \quad = \quad 2$$
↑         ↑         ↑
*minuend*   *subtrahend*   *difference*

Since $5 - 3$ names the same number as the numeral 2, $5 - 3$ may also be called the difference.

**Example:** Given the equality, $16 - 7 = 9$,

1. 16 is called the *minuend*.
2. 7 is called the *subtrahend*.
3. 9 is called the *difference*.
4. $16 - 7$ is called the *difference*.

☐ (8)

Subtraction is related to addition as follows: The difference when added to the subtrahend must equal the minuend.

$$8 - 2 = 6, \text{ because } 6 + 2 = 8$$

☐ *Study Exercise One* (9)

A. Given the equality $8 + 13 = 21$, then:

     1. 8 is called an _____.
     2. 13 is called an _____.
     3. 21 is called the _____.
     4. $8 + 13$ is called the _____.

B. Given the equality $25 - 9 = 16$, then:

     5. 25 is called the _____.
     6. 9 is called the _____.
     7. 16 is called the _____.
     8. $25 - 9$ is called the _____.

C. Check the following subtraction exercises by adding the difference to the subtrahend to produce the minuend.

     9. $12 - 7 = 5$, because _____ + _____ = _____.
     10. $6 - 0 = 6$, because _____ + _____ = _____.
     11. $5 - 5 = 0$, because _____ + _____ = _____.
     12. $4628 - 2199 = 2429$, because _____ + _____ = _____.

☐ The Operation of Multiplication (10)

**Example 1:** $2 \cdot 3$ means to use 3 as an addend two times. So, $2 \cdot 3$ means $3 + 3$, or 6.

**Example 2:** $4 \cdot 8$ means to use 8 as an addend four times. So, $4 \cdot 8$ means $8 + 8 + 8 + 8$, or 32.

**Example 3:** $3 \cdot 0$ means to use 0 as an addend three times. So, $3 \cdot 0 = 0 + 0 + 0$, or 0.

Multiplication of whole numbers is related to addition in that multiplication is repetitive addition.

☐ Terms to Remember (11)

$$3 \quad \cdot \quad 6 \quad = \quad 18$$
↑      ↑       ↑
*factor*   *factor*    *product*

Since $3 \cdot 6$ names the same number as the numeral 18, $3 \cdot 6$ may also be called the *product*.

**Example:** Given the equality, $5 \cdot 9 = 45$,

1. 5 is called a *factor*.
2. 9 is called a *factor*.
3. 45 is called the *product*.
4. $5 \cdot 9$ is called the *product*.

☐ The Operation of Division (12)

Division is related to multiplication in the same manner as subtraction is to addition.

**Example:** $5 - 3 = 2$ because $2 + 3 = 5$.
$18 \div 3 = 6$ because $6 \cdot 3 = 18$.

## ☐ More Examples of Division (13)

**Example 1:** $10 \div 2 = 5$ because $5 \cdot 2 = 10$. 　　**Example 2:** $\dfrac{20}{5} = 4$ because $4 \cdot 5 = 20$.

**Example 3:** $7 \div 7 = 1$ because $1 \cdot 7 = 7$. 　　**Example 4:** $\dfrac{0}{4} = 0$ because $0 \cdot 4 = 0$.

## ☐ Terms to Remember (14)

$$\underset{\uparrow}{18} \div \underset{\uparrow}{3} = \underset{\uparrow}{6} \qquad\qquad \overset{\text{dividend}}{\dfrac{18}{3}} = 6 \leftarrow quotient$$

$$dividend \quad divisor \quad quotient \qquad\qquad divisor$$

Since $18 \div 3$ and $\dfrac{18}{3}$ name the same number as the numeral 6, then $18 \div 3$ or $\dfrac{18}{3}$ may also be called the quotient.

## ☐ Example 1: Given the equality, $20 \div 4 = 5$, (15)

1. 20 is called the *dividend*. 　　　　　2. 4 is called the *divisor*.
3. 5 is called the *quotient*. 　　　　　4. $20 \div 4$ is called the *quotient*.

**Example 2:** Given the equality, $\dfrac{12}{3} = 4$,

1. 12 is called the *dividend*. 　　　　　2. 3 is called the *divisor*.

3. 4 is called the *quotient*. 　　　　　4. $\dfrac{12}{3}$ is called the *quotient*.

Remember, division is related to multiplication as follows: The quotient when multiplied by the divisor must equal the dividend.

**Example:** $24 \div 6 = 4$ or $\dfrac{24}{6} = 4$ because $4 \cdot 6 = 24$.

## ☐ Division by Zero (16)

*Case 1: Dividing a natural number by zero.*

**Example 1:** $7 \div 0$ does not represent a number because no number times zero produces 7.

**Example 2:** $\dfrac{12}{0}$ does not represent a number because no number times zero produces 12.

**Example 3:** $4 \div 0 =$ no answer 　　　　　**Example 4:** $\dfrac{25}{0} =$ no answer

## ☐ *Case 2: Dividing zero by zero.* (17)

**Example 1:** $0 \div 0 = 0$ since $0 \cdot 0 = 0$. 　　**Example 2:** $0 \div 0 = 1$ since $1 \cdot 0 = 0$.

**Example 3:** $\dfrac{0}{0} = 2$ since $2 \cdot 0 = 0$. 　　**Example 4:** $\dfrac{0}{0} = 48$ since $48 \cdot 0 = 0$.

Conclusion: $0 \div 0$ or $\dfrac{0}{0}$ is indeterminate because it does not represent a unique number. Remember, never use zero as a divisor. Therefore, each of the following has no answer:

$$6 \div 0, \qquad \dfrac{13}{0}, \qquad 0 \div 0, \qquad \dfrac{0}{0}$$

☐ Properties of Division                                                                                    **(18)**

1.  Any number divided by 1 produces the original number.

**Example:**  $12 \div 1 = 12$ or $\frac{12}{1} = 12$

2.  The divisor may never be zero.

**Examples:**  $3 \div 0 =$ no answer. $\frac{3}{0} =$ no answer. $\frac{0}{0} =$ no answer.

3.  If the dividend is zero and the divisor is not zero, then the quotient is zero.

**Example:**  $0 \div 17 = 0$ or $\frac{0}{17} = 0$

☐ Analysis of the Four Basic Operations                                                        **(19)**

1.  Addition and multiplication are known as the *primary* operations.
2.  Subtraction and division are known as the *secondary* operations.
3.  All four operations are called *binary* operations, because each operation acts on exactly two numbers to produce exactly one answer.

☐ Multiple Operations                                                                                **(20)**

When more than one operation is performed in a single problem, each operation refers to exactly two numbers. The same number of operations must be performed as there are symbols of operations.

**Example:**  $2 + 3 + 4$

  **Solution:**   There are two operation symbols, so there are exactly two additions to perform.

$$
\begin{array}{c}
\underbrace{2 + 3} + 4 \\
\underbrace{5 + 4} \\
9
\end{array}
$$

☐                                         *Study Exercise Two*                                          **(21)**

A.  Write the meaning for each multiplication problem.

  1.  $3 \cdot 6$ means _____.                   2.  $2 \cdot 0$ means _____.
  3.  $3 \cdot 1$ means _____.                   4.  $2 \cdot 100$ means _____.

B.  In the equality $8 \cdot 9 = 72$,

  5.  8 is called a _____.                         6.  9 is called a _____.
  7.  72 is called the _____.                     8.  $8 \cdot 9$ is called the _____.

C.  In the equality $30 \div 6 = 5$,

  9.  30 is called the _____.                    10.  6 is called the _____.
  11.  5 is called the _____.                     12.  $30 \div 6$ is called the _____.

D.  In the equality $\frac{27}{3} = 9$,

  13.  27 is called the _____.                   14.  3 is called the _____.
  15.  9 is called the _____.                     16.  $\frac{27}{3}$ is called the _____.

E.  Check the following division problems by multiplying the quotient times the divisor to produce the dividend.

    17.  $48 \div 6 = 8$      18.  $5 \div 5 = 1$      19.  $\frac{12}{1} = 12$      20.  $\frac{0}{7} = 0$

F.  Which of the following represents a number? (Answer yes or no.)

    21.  $0 \div 9$      22.  $\frac{0}{6}$      23.  $15 \div 0$

    24.  $\frac{11}{0}$      25.  $0 \cdot 9$      26.  $9 \cdot 0$

## ☐ Numeral Expressions     (22)

A *numeral expression* is a phrase containing numerals and at least one symbol of operation. The phrase must also represent a number.

**Example 1:** $2 + 4$ is a numeral expression.      **Example 2:** $2 \cdot 3 + 4$ is a numeral expression.

**Example 3:** $5 \cdot 2 + 6 \div 3$ is a numeral expression.      **Example 4:** $6$ is not a numeral expression.

**Example 5:** $7 \div 0$ is not a numeral expression.

**Example 6:** $8 + 2 \div 0 + 6$ is not a numeral expression.

## ☐ Simplifying Numeral Expressions     (23)

A numeral expression is said to be *evaluated* or *simplified completely* when it is represented by exactly one numeral and no symbols of operation.

    1.  $5 + 2 = 7$      2.  $6 - 2 = 4$      3.  $18 \div 9 = 2$      4.  $3 \cdot 6 = 18$      5.  $0 \div 9 = 0$

## ☐                 *Study Exercise Three*     (24)

A.  Which of the following are numeral expressions? (Answer yes or no.)

    1.  $5 + 2$      2.  $6 \div 0$      3.  $\frac{0}{6}$      4.  $\frac{0}{0}$

    5.  $18$      6.  $2 + 3 \cdot 5 - 4$      7.  $5 + 6 \cdot 2 + 8 \div 0$

B.  Simplify completely the following numeral expressions.

    8.  $10 \div 2$      9.  $\frac{4}{4}$      10.  $2 \cdot 12$      11.  $0 \div 5$      12.  $0 \cdot 5$      13.  $32 - 14$

## ☐ Combining the Operations     (25)

**Example:** Evaluate $5 \cdot 2 + 6$.

   **Solution 1:** $5 \cdot 2 + 6$
                 $\downarrow$
          $5 \cdot \quad 8$
        $\downarrow$
        $40$

   **Solution 2:** $5 \cdot 2 + 6$
          $\downarrow$
         $10 + 6$
            $\downarrow$
          $16$

When an expression is evaluated, there should be only one answer.

## ☐ The Order of Operations Agreement (26)

Unless specified otherwise:

*Step (1):* Do all multiplications and divisions in the order they appear in the problem from left to right.

*Step (2):* Do all additions and subtractions in the order they appear in the problem from left to right.

## ☐ **Example 1:** $8 \div 2 \cdot 3$ (27)

**Solution:**

*Step (1):* $8 \div 2 \cdot 3$
↓
$4 \quad \cdot 3$
↓
$12$

*Step (2):* There is no addition or subtraction, so the answer is 12.

$$\overset{①}{8} \div \overset{②}{2} \cdot 3$$

## ☐ **Example 2:** $23 - 10 - 5$ (28)

**Solution:**

*Step (1):* There is no multiplication or division, so proceed to Step (2).

*Step (2):* $23 - 10 - 5$
↓
$13 \quad - \quad 5$
↓
$8$

$$23 \overset{①}{-} 10 \overset{②}{-} 5$$

## ☐ **Example 3:** $3 \cdot 8 \div 2 + 7 - 4 \div 2$ (29)

**Solution:**

*Step (1):* Do multiplications and divisions in the order they appear in the problem from left to right.

*line (a)* $3 \cdot 8 \div 2 + 7 - 4 \div 2$
↓
*line (b)* $24 \div 2 + 7 - 4 \div 2$
↓
*line (c)* $12 + 7 - 4 \div 2$
↓
*line (d)* $12 + 7 - 2$

*Step (2):* Do all additions and subtractions in the order they appear in the problem from left to right.

*line (e)* $12 + 7 - 2$
↓
*line (f)* $19 - 2$
↓
*line (g)* $17$

$$\overset{①}{3} \cdot \overset{②}{8} \div 2 \overset{④}{+} 7 \overset{⑤}{-} 4 \overset{③}{\div} 2$$

## ☐ *Study Exercise Four* (30)

Evaluate each of the following using the order of operations agreement.

1. $36 \div 3 \cdot 2$       2. $4 \cdot 7 + 5$       3. $12 - 3 \cdot 2$

4. $3 \cdot 4 + 2 \cdot 5 - 2 \cdot 0$    5. $16 \div 2 \cdot 3 + 8 - 10 \div 2$

□                                                                                    **(31)**

By the order of operations agreement, $6 \cdot 4 + 3 = 27$. Suppose we wrote the expression $6 \cdot 4 + 3$, intending that 4 and 3 be added first, then multiplied by 6. How would we indicate this in order to obtain an answer of $6 \cdot 7$, or 42?

□ **Grouping Symbols**                                                                **(32)**

$$6 \cdot (4 + 3)$$

Grouping symbols indicate to "do this first."

$$6 \cdot (4 + 3)$$
$$\downarrow$$
$$6 \quad \cdot \quad 7$$
$$\downarrow$$
$$42$$

$$\overset{②}{6} \cdot (\overset{①}{4 + 3})$$

□ **Commonly Used Grouping Symbols**                                                 **(33)**

$$( \quad ) \quad [ \quad ] \quad \{ \quad \}$$

Grouping symbols take precedence over the order of operations agreement.

□ **Evaluating Expressions Containing Grouping Symbols**                              **(34)**

**Example 1:** Evaluate $(8 - 2) \cdot 3$.

   **Solution:**

   *line (a)*  $(8 - 2) \cdot 3$
   $$\downarrow$$
   *line (b)*  $\quad 6 \cdot 3$
   $$\downarrow$$
   *line (c)*  $\quad 18$

$$(\overset{①}{8} - 2) \overset{②}{\cdot} 3$$

□ **Example 2:** Evaluate $(5 - 2) \cdot (3 + 4)$.                                     **(35)**

   **Solution:**

   *line (a)*  $(5 - 2) \cdot (3 + 4)$
   $$\downarrow \qquad \downarrow$$
   *line (b)*  $\quad 3 \quad \cdot \quad 7$
   $$\downarrow$$
   *line (c)*  $\quad 21$

$$(\overset{①}{5} - 2) \overset{③}{\cdot} (\overset{②}{3 + 4}) \quad \text{or} \quad (\overset{②}{5} - 2) \overset{③}{\cdot} (\overset{①}{3 + 4})$$

□ **Example 3:** Evaluate $3 \cdot [22 - (4 - 1) \cdot 5]$.                            **(36)**

We begin on the inside.

20

**Solution:**

*line (a)*  $3 \cdot [22 - (4 - 1) \cdot 5]$
                          $\downarrow$

*line (b)*  $3 \cdot [22 - \quad 3 \quad \cdot 5]$
                               $\downarrow$

*line (c)*  $3 \cdot [22 \quad - \quad 15]$
                       $\downarrow$

*line (d)*  $3 \quad \cdot \quad 7$
                  $\downarrow$

*line (e)*  $21$

$$\overset{④}{\phantom{3}}\overset{③}{\phantom{3}}\overset{①}{\phantom{3}}\overset{②}{\phantom{3}}$$
$$3 \cdot [22 - (4 - 1) \cdot 5]$$

☐ ***Study Exercise Five***   **(37)**

A. Insert grouping symbols so that each of the following is true.

   1. $5 \cdot 8 + 2 = 50$        2. $6 + 8 \div 2 = 7$        3. $4 + 5 - 6 - 1 = 4$

B. Evaluate each of the following.

   4. $(20 - 8) \cdot 2$        5. $4 \cdot [7 - (5 - 2)]$        6. $3 \cdot (8 - 1) + 5 \cdot (2 + 6)$

☐ **Classifying Expressions**   **(38)**

Every expression can be classified as exactly one of the following:

   1. Basic Sum       2. Basic Difference       3. Basic Product       4. Basic Quotient

☐ To classify an expression:   **(39)**

   *Step (1):* Determine the order of operations in the expression.
   *Step (2):* Find the last operation. It classifies the expression.

☐ **Example 1:** Classify $4 \cdot 5 + 7 \cdot 8$.   **(40)**

   $\overset{①}{\phantom{4}}\overset{③}{\phantom{5}}\overset{②}{\phantom{7}}$
   *Step (1):* $4 \cdot 5 + 7 \cdot 8$
   *Step (2):* Addition is the last operation. The expression is a basic sum.

**Example 2:** Classify $2 \cdot (3 + 5) - 6$.

   $\overset{②}{\phantom{2}}\overset{①}{\phantom{3}}\overset{③}{\phantom{5}}$
   *Step (1):* $2 \cdot (3 + 5) - 6$
   *Step (2):* Subtraction is the last operation. The expression is a basic difference.

**Example 3:** Classify $3 \cdot (6 - 2)$.

   $\overset{②}{\phantom{3}}\overset{①}{\phantom{6}}$
   *Step (1):* $3 \cdot (6 - 2)$
   *Step (2):* Multiplication is the last operation. The expression is a basic product.

**Example 4:** Classify $(12 - 3) \cdot 2 \div 6$.

   $\overset{①}{\phantom{1}}\overset{②}{\phantom{2}}\overset{③}{\phantom{6}}$
   *Step (1):* $(12 - 3) \cdot 2 \div 6$
   *Step (2):* Division is the last operation. The expression is a basic quotient.

☐ ***Study Exercise Six***   **(41)**

Classify each of the following as basically a sum, difference, product, or quotient.

   1. $7 + 2 \cdot 9$        2. $(7 + 2) \cdot 9$        3. $(4 + 3) \cdot (7 - 2)$
   4. $6 \div 3 \cdot 2$        5. $5 - (2 + 3)$        6. $[8 \div 2 + 5) - 7] \div 2$

## REVIEW EXERCISES

A. Check the following subtraction problems by using addition.

    1. $10 - 3 = 7$         2. $6 - 0 = 6$         3. $15 - 15 = 0$

B. Write the meaning of the following multiplication problems by using addition.

    4. $3 \cdot 2$         5. $2 \cdot 0$         6. $1 \cdot 5$

C. Check the following division problems by using multiplication.

    7. $35 \div 5 = 7$     8. $\dfrac{36}{12} = 3$     9. $0 \div 5 = 0$     10. $\dfrac{8}{8} = 1$

D. Which of the following represent a number? (Answer yes or no.)

    11. $0 \div 0$     12. $\dfrac{0}{128}$     13. $\dfrac{128}{0}$     14. $0 \div 12$     15. $9 \cdot 0$

E. In the addition problem $96 + 112 = 208$,

    16. The addends are _____ and _____.     17. The sum is _____ or _____.

F. In the subtraction problem $42 - 28 = 14$,

    18. The minuend is _____.     19. The subtrahend is _____.
    20. The difference is _____ or _____.

G. In the division problem $72 \div 9 = 8$ or $\dfrac{72}{9} = 8$,

    21. The dividend is _____.     22. The divisor is _____.
    23. The quotient is _____ or _____ or _____.

H. Fill in the blanks.

    24. The primary operations are _____ and _____.
    25. The secondary operations are _____ and _____.
    26. An operation which acts on exactly two elements to produce exactly one result is said to be a _____ operation.

I. Which of the following are numeral expressions? (Answer yes or no.)

    27. $2 \cdot 3 + 8$     28. $4 + 7 \cdot 0$     29. $6 \cdot 8 \div 0 + 3$     30. $2 \cdot 10 + 0 \div 5$

J. Simplify completely each of the following.

    31. $15 - 2 \cdot 3$                 32. $8 \cdot 6 - 5$
    33. $30 \div 6 - 1 \cdot 3 + 8 \cdot 3 \div 2$     34. $24 \div 3 \cdot 2 - 8 \div 2 + 5$
    35. $(7 - 2) \cdot (8 - 4)$           36. $3 \cdot (6 + 12)$
    37. $5 \cdot \{22 - [(13 - 2) - 4]\}$

K. Classify each of the following as basically a sum, difference, product, or quotient.

    38. $5 + 7 - 2$     39. $6 \cdot (7 - 5)$     40. $15 \div 3 \cdot (5 - 2) \cdot 3$     41. $(24 - 4) \div (3 + 2)$

L. Insert grouping symbols to make the following true.

    42. $8 - 2 \cdot 3 + 1 = 24$     43. $8 - 2 \cdot 3 + 1 = 19$     44. $8 - 2 \cdot 3 + 1 = 3$

### Solutions to Review Exercises

A.  1. $7 + 3 = 10$       2. $6 + 0 = 6$       3. $0 + 15 = 15$

B.  4. $2 + 2 + 2 = 6$      5. $0 + 0 = 0$       6. $5$

C.  7. $7 \cdot 5 = 35$     8. $3 \cdot 12 = 36$     9. $0 \cdot 5 = 0$     10. $1 \cdot 8 = 8$

## Solutions to Review Exercises, Contd.

D.  11.  No          12.  Yes          13.  No          14.  Yes          15.  Yes

E.  16.  96 and 112          17.  208 or 96 + 112

F.  18.  42          19.  28          20.  14 or 42 − 28

G.  21.  72          22.  9          23.  8 or 72 ÷ 9 or $\dfrac{72}{9}$

H.  24.  addition and multiplication          25.  subtraction and division          26.  binary

I.  27.  Yes          28.  Yes          29.  No          30.  Yes

J.  31.  9          32.  43          33.  14          34.  17          35.  20          36.  54          37.  75

K.  38.  $\overset{①}{5} + \overset{②}{7} - 2$    Basic difference          39.  $\overset{②}{6} \cdot (\overset{①}{7} - 5)$    Basic product

40.  $\overset{②}{15} \div \overset{③}{3} \cdot (\overset{①}{5} - 2) \cdot \overset{④}{3}$    Basic product          41.  $(\overset{①}{24} - 4) \div (\overset{③}{3} + \overset{②}{2})$    Basic quotient

L.  42.  $(8 - 2) \cdot (3 + 1) = 24$          43.  $(8 - 2) \cdot 3 + 1 = 19$

44.  $8 - 2 \cdot 3 + 1 = 3$    No grouping symbols needed.

## SUPPLEMENTARY PROBLEMS

A.  Check the following subtraction problems by using addition.

1.  12 − 7 = 5          2.  13 − 2 = 11          3.  7 − 0 = 7          4.  9 − 9 = 0

B.  Write the meaning of the following multiplication problems by using addition.

5.  2·1          6.  4·3          7.  5·0          8.  1·8

C.  Check the following division problems by using multiplication.

9.  24 ÷ 6 = 4          10.  $\dfrac{32}{4} = 8$          11.  0 ÷ 13 = 0          12.  $\dfrac{0}{1} = 0$          13.  11 ÷ 11 = 1

D.  Which of the following represent a number? (Answer yes or no.)

14.  0 ÷ 12          15.  $\dfrac{0}{7}$          16.  $\dfrac{0}{0}$          17.  $\dfrac{19}{0}$          18.  0 ÷ 19          19.  4·0          20.  0·4

E.  In the addition problem 31 + 22 = 53,

21.  The addends are _____ and _____.          22.  The sum is _____ or _____.

F.  In the subtraction problem 18 − 6 = 12,

23.  The minuend is _____.          24.  The subtrahend is _____.

25.  The difference is _____ or _____.

G.  In the division problem 54 ÷ 6 = 9 or $\dfrac{54}{6} = 9$,

26.  The dividend is _____.          27.  The divisor is _____.

28.  The quotient is _____ or _____ or _____.

H.  Which of the following are numeral expressions? (Answer yes or no.)

29.  7          30.  8 + 2          31.  9 + 4 − 3

32.  6 + 0 ÷ 7 − 1          33.  6 + 7 ÷ 0 − 1          34.  8 + 2 ÷ (5 − 5)

35.  (5 + 7·2 − 1)·0

I.  Simplify completely each of the following. (Evaluate.)

36.  3·4 + 2          37.  3·(4 + 2)          38.  3·4 + 3·2

39.  20·2 + 3 − 2·7          40.  20·(2 + 3) − 2·7          41.  20·2 + (3 − 2)·7

42.  20·[2 + 3 − 2]·7          43.  10 − 4 − 3          44.  (10 − 4) − 3

## SUPPLEMENTARY PROBLEMS, Contd.

45. $10 - (4 - 3)$
46. $40 \div 4 \div 2$
47. $(40 \div 4) \div 2$
48. $40 \div (4 \div 2)$
49. $0 \div 3 + 6 \cdot 2 \div 3 - 2$
50. $2 \cdot 6 \div 3 \cdot 2$
51. $(9 - 3) + (6 - 4)$
52. $2 \cdot (7 + 3) - 3 \cdot (7 - 6)$
53. $25 \div 5 \cdot (6 - 5)$

J.  Classify each of the following as basically a sum, difference, product, or quotient.

54. $3 + 9 - 4$
55. $2 \cdot [3 + 6 - (1 + 2)]$
56. $8 \div 2 + 1$
57. $3 \cdot (7 - 4)$
58. $16 \div 2 - 12 \div 2$
59. $15 \div 3 \cdot (5 - 2) \cdot 3$
60. $5 \cdot \{22 - [(13 - 2) - 4]\}$

K.  Insert grouping symbols to make the following true.

61. $3 \cdot 2 + 2 \cdot 5 = 60$
62. $3 \cdot 2 + 2 \cdot 5 = 36$
63. $3 \cdot 2 + 2 \cdot 5 = 16$
64. $6 \cdot 5 - 4 \div 2 = 3$
65. $6 \cdot 5 - 4 \div 2 = 18$
66. $60 - 3 + 4 \cdot 8 \div 2 = 244$
67. $60 - 3 + 4 \cdot 8 \div 2 = 73$
68. $60 - 3 + 4 \cdot 8 \div 2 = 2$

 L.  Calculator problems. With your instructor's approval, evaluate each of the following using a calculator.

69. $236 \cdot 41 + 369$
70. $191 \cdot 54 + 121 \cdot 73$
71. $163 \cdot 75 + 1692 - 41 \cdot 17$
72. $1226 \div 2 + 116 \cdot 24 - 163$
73. $561(778 - 123)$
74. $650 \div 50 \cdot (820 - 769) \cdot 12$
75. $105 \cdot \{86 + [(132 - 94) + 121]\}$

## ☐ Solutions to Study Exercises                                    (9A)

### Study Exercise One (Frame 9)

A.  1. addend
    2. addend
    3. sum
    4. sum
B.  5. minuend
    6. subtrahend
    7. difference
    8. difference
C.  9. $5 + 7 = 12$
    10. $6 + 0 = 6$
    11. $0 + 5 = 5$
    12. $2429 + 2199 = 4628$

## ☐                    Study Exercise Two (Frame 21)              (21A)

A.  1. $6 + 6 + 6$
    2. $0 + 0$
    3. $1 + 1 + 1$
    4. $100 + 100$
B   5. factor
    6. factor
    7. product
    8. product
C.  9. dividend
    10. divisor
    11. quotient
    12. quotient
D.  13. dividend
    14. divisor
    15. quotient
    16. quotient
E.  17. $8 \cdot 6 = 48$
    18. $1 \cdot 5 = 5$
    19. $12 \cdot 1 = 12$
    20. $0 \cdot 7 = 0$
F   21. Yes, $0 \div 9 = 0$
    22. Yes, $\dfrac{0}{6} = 0$
    23. No
    24. No
    25. Yes, $0 \cdot 9 = 0$
    26. Yes, $9 \cdot 0 = 0$

## ☐                    Study Exercise Three (Frame 24)            (24A)

A.  1. Yes
    2. No, cannot divide by zero.
    3. Yes
    4. No, cannot divide by zero.
    5. No, must contain a symbol of operation.
    6. Yes
    7. No, cannot divide by zero.
B.  8. 5
    9. 1
    10. 24
    11. 0
    12. 0
    13. 18

## ☐                    Study Exercise Four (Frame 30)             (30A)

1. 24
2. 33
3. 6
4. 22
5. 27

## Solutions to Study Exercises, Contd.

☐             *Study Exercise Five (Frame 37)*             **(37A)**

A.   1.   $5 \cdot (8 + 2) = 50$      2.   $(6 + 8) \div 2 = 7$      3.   $(4 + 5) - (6 - 1) = 4$

B.   4.   24                    5.   16                    6.   61

☐             *Study Exercise Six (Frame 41)*             **(41A)**

1.   $\overset{②}{7} + \overset{①}{2 \cdot 9}$    Basic sum      2.   $\overset{①}{(7 + 2)} \cdot \overset{②}{9}$    Basic product      3.   $\overset{①}{(4 + 3)} \cdot \overset{③}{(7} \overset{②}{- 2)}$    Basic product

4.   $\overset{①}{6} \div \overset{②}{3 \cdot 2}$    Basic product      5.   $\overset{②}{5} - \overset{①}{(2 + 3)}$    Basic difference

6.   $[(\overset{①}{8} \div \overset{②}{2} + \overset{③}{5}) - 7] \div \overset{④}{2}$    Basic quotient

91180

LIBRARY
College of St. Francis
JOLIET, ILL.

# Variables, Variable Expressions, and Equations

## ☐ Objectives (1)

By the end of this unit you should be able to:

- define *variable*, *constant*, and *variable expression*.
- evaluate variable expressions.
- use variable expressions to describe patterns.
- use variable expressions as mathematical models for word statements.
- classify variable expressions as basic sums, differences, products, or quotients.
- classify equations as identities or as conditionals.
- solve simple equations by inspection.
- identify the five fundamental properties of equations.

## ☐ Variable (2)

A *variable* is a symbol which represents any number from a given replacement set. The replacement set is sometimes called the domain of the variable and must contain more than one number. The following are common symbols used for variables:

$$x, y, a, b, \square, \triangle, \bigcirc$$

## ☐ Examples Using Variables (3)

**Example 1:** If $x$ is a variable and its replacement set or domain is $\{1, 2, 6\}$, then $x + 10$ represents:

*line (a)*   $1 + 10$
*line (b)*   $2 + 10$
*line (c)*   $6 + 10$
*line (d)*   ~~$7 + 10$~~   (Incorrect)

**Example 2:** If $\square$ is a variable and its replacement set or domain is $\{10, 15, 20\}$, then $3 \cdot \square + \square$ represents:

*line (a)*   $3 \cdot 10 + 10$
*line (b)*   $3 \cdot 15 + 15$
*line (c)*   $3 \cdot 20 + 20$
*line (d)*   ~~$3 \cdot 10 + 15$~~   (Incorrect)

**Example 3:** If $a$ and $b$ are variables and their replacement set or domain is the set of whole numbers, then $2 \cdot a + 5 \cdot b$ represents:

*line (a)*   $2 \cdot 0 + 5 \cdot 1$
*line (b)*   $2 \cdot 35 + 5 \cdot 20$
*line (c)*   $2 \cdot 12 + 5 \cdot 12$

## ☐ Constant (4)

A *constant* is any symbol which has exactly one number in its replacement set.

**Example 1:** Any numeral is a constant such as 5, 2, and 10.

**Example 2:** $\pi$ is a constant since it represents approximately 3.14.

**Example 3:** If $c$ has a replacement set of $\{6\}$, then $c$ is a constant.

## ☐ Variable Expression (5)

A *variable expression* is any phrase containing one or more variables and one or more symbols of operation. Also, it must represent a number for every element of its replacement set. Each of the following is a variable expression for a replacement set of whole numbers.

28

**Example 1:** $\square + 8$  **Example 2:** $6 \cdot x + 3$

**Example 3:** $10 \cdot x - x$  **Example 4:** $3x + 2y + 5z$

## ☐ Phrases Which Are Not Variable Expressions (6)

For replacement sets of whole numbers, the following are not variable expressions.

**Example 1:** $x$  **Example 2:** $+y$

**Example 3:** $3 + 2 \cdot (4 - 1)$  **Example 4:** $2 \cdot x + y \div 0$

**Example 5:** $a \div a$

## ☐ Evaluating Variable Expressions (7)

Variable expressions may be evaluated by substituting from the replacement set and simplifying completely the resulting numeral expression.

Evaluate the following when $x = 5$ and $y = 2$.

**Example 1:** $\begin{aligned} 2 \cdot x &= 2 \cdot 5 \\ &= 10 \end{aligned}$  **Example 2:** $\begin{aligned} x + y &= 5 + 2 \\ &= 7 \end{aligned}$

**Example 3:** $\begin{aligned} 3 \cdot (x + y) &= 3 \cdot (5 + 2) \\ &= 3 \cdot 7 \\ &= 21 \end{aligned}$  **Example 4:** $\begin{aligned} 3 \cdot x + 3 \cdot y &= 3 \cdot 5 + 3 \cdot 2 \\ &= 15 + 6 \\ &= 21 \end{aligned}$

## ☐ Classifying Variable Expressions (8)

A variable expression can be classified as a basic sum, difference, product, or quotient.

**Example 1:** $3 \cdot x + 4 \cdot y$

  **Solution:** $3 \cdot x \overset{①}{+} 4 \cdot y$  Basic sum

**Example 2:** $5 \cdot (a + b) - c$

  **Solution:** $5 \cdot (a + b) - c$  Basic difference

**Example 3:** $x \cdot (y + 2)$

  **Solution:** $x \cdot (y + 2)$  Basic product

**Example 4:** $(m + 3) \cdot n \div 2$

  **Solution:** $(m + 3) \cdot n \div 2$  Basic quotient

## ☐ Three Agreements (9)

1. If a variable's replacement set is not given, we will assume that it is the last set of numbers we have studied. At this time it would be the set of whole numbers.
2. If an operation symbol is obviously missing in an expression, then this operation is assumed to be multiplication.

**Example 1:** $2x$ means $2 \cdot x$.  **Example 2:** $3(x + y)$ means $3 \cdot (x + y)$.

3. If the same variable is present more than once in an expression, then the same number must be substituted for them all.

**Example 1:** $3x + 2x = 3 \cdot 0 + 2 \cdot 0$ (Correct)  **Example 2:** $3x + 2x = 3 \cdot 4 + 2 \cdot 4$ (Correct)

**Example 3:** $3x + 2x = 3 \cdot 4 + 2 \cdot 6$ (Incorrect)

☐                        *Study Exercise One*                             **(10)**

A.   Which of the following are variable expressions for replacement of whole numbers? (Answer yes or no.)

    1.  $3x$                   2.  $a \div 0$                 3.  $y$

    4.  $6y + 3$            5.  $7x + 3y + 2$       6.  $8 \div b$

B.   Evaluate each of the following variable expressions by letting $x = 5$, $y = 2$, and $z = 0$.

**Example:**  $3x + y = 3 \cdot 5 + 2$
                              $= 17$

    7.  $x + 3$             8.  $y - 1$             9.  $xz$

   10.  $5x - 2y$        11.  $xy + z$        12.  $2(x + y) - 3z$

   13.  $(x + 3)(y + 4)$    14.  $3x - y + z$    15.  $3 \cdot [x - (x + z)] + 5 \cdot y$

C.   Classify each of the following as a basic sum, difference, product or quotient.

   16.  $\square - \triangle$           17.  $3a + b$           18.  $3xy$

   19.  $(x + 2)(x + 3)$    20.  $5(a + b)$       21.  $5a + 5b$

## ☐ Mathematical Models                                          **(11)**

A *mathematical model* is an expression which describes a written or a verbal situation.

## ☐ Variable Expressions Used as Mathematical Models    **(12)**

**Example 1:**   Word phrase:   The sum of a number and 12
                  Mathematical model:  $n + 12$

**Example 2:**   Word phrase:   5 more than twice a certain number
                  Mathematical model:  $2n + 5$

**Example 3:**   Word phrase:   6 less than 3 times a certain number
                  Mathematical model:  $3x - 6$

**Example 4:**   Word statement: The number of cents in $x$ dimes.
                  Mathematical model:   $10x$

**Example 5:**   Word statement:   A wire 3 feet long is cut into two pieces. If one piece is $y$ feet long, the other is _____ feet long.
                  Mathematical model: $3 - y$

☐                        *Study Exercise Two*                             **(13)**

Give a variable expression representing each of the following word statements.

1.  The sum of a certain number and 10.       2.  15 less than seven times a certain number.
3.  7 more than three times a certain number.   4.  The number of cents in $x$ quarters.
5.  The number of cents in $(n + 5)$ dollars.
6.  A 25-foot rope is cut into two pieces. If one piece is $y$ feet long, how long is the other?

## ☑ Equations                                                **(14)**

When numerals, numeral expressions, variables, or variable expressions are connected with an equal sign, we have an *equation*.

**Example 1:**  $6 + 2 = 8$                    **Example 2:**  $6 + 2 = 9$

**Example 3:**  $x = 5$                        **Example 4:**  $3x + 1 = 2(x + 3)$

**Example 5:**  $x + 1 = x + 1$

☐ **Parts of an Equation** **(15)**

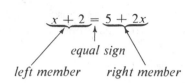

$$\underbrace{x + 2}_{} = \underbrace{5 + 2x}_{}$$

*equal sign*

*left member*     *right member*

Each member of an equation must represent a number.

☐ **Solving Equations** **(16)**

An equation containing a variable may be solved by finding all replacements that make the equation true.

**Example:**  Solve $3x = 12$

**Solution:**  Three times what whole number produces 12? Choose 4. Then $3x = 12$ will generate the true equation, $3 \cdot 4 = 12$.

The solution of the equation is 4. It may also be called a root.

☐ **Solving Equations by Inspection** **(17)**

**Example 1:**  $5x = 15$

**Solution:**  {5 times 3 produces 15. The solution is 3.

**Example 2:**  $y - y = 0$

**Solution:**  {Every whole number when subtracted from itself produces zero. Therefore, each whole number is a root of the equation.

**Example 3:**  $\dfrac{x}{x} = 1$

**Solution:**  {Every natural number when divided by itself will produce one. Therefore, each natural number is a solution of the equation.

**Example 4:**  $m + 1 = m$

**Solution:**  {This equation always gives a false result. There are no solutions.

☐  *Study Exercise Three* **(18)**

Solve each of the following equations by inspection. The replacement set for each variable is the set of whole numbers.

1.  $2x = 6$          2.  $7x = 21$          3.  $m + 3 = 8$          4.  $8n = 8$
5.  $9a = 0$          6.  $0 \cdot y = 0$          7.  $y = y$          8.  $x \cdot x = 4$
9.  $0 + x = x$          10.  $n + 3 = n$          11.  $2(x + 3) = 14$          12.  $3m + 1 = 10$

☐ **Identities** **(19)**

Some equations are true for every permissable value of the variable. When this occurs the equation is called an identity.

**Example 1:**  $x = x$

**Example 2:**  $y + 1 = 1 + y$

**Example 3:**  $1 \cdot x = x$

**Example 4:**  $\dfrac{m}{m} = 1$, where $m$ is any natural number

□ **(20)**

Identities will be used in subsequent units to describe various properties of whole numbers. For example, we know that any whole number times zero is zero. This property can be symbolized by the following identity:

$$x \cdot 0 = 0$$

□ **Conditional Equations** **(21)**

An equation which is false for at least one value of the variable's replacement set is called a conditional equation.

**Example 1:** $3x = 12$; true when $x$ is 4 but false for all other values.

**Example 2:** $y - 7 = 0$; true when $x$ is 7 but false for all other values.

**Example 3:** $5(m + 1) = 20$; true when $x$ is 3 but false for all other values.

□ *Study Exercise Four* **(22)**

A. Classify each equation as either an identity or a conditional equation.

1. $3x = 12$
2. $y + 3 = 3 + y$
3. $8m = 16$
4. $0 \cdot x = 0$
5. $1 \cdot a = a$
6. $3(x + 2) = 12$

B. Write an identity which describes each of the following statements concerning whole numbers.

7. Any whole number when subtracted from itself produces zero.
8. Zero when added to any whole number produces the original whole number.
9. One when multiplied times any whole number produces the original whole number.

□ **The Five Fundamental Properties of Equations** **(23)**

1. Reflexive:   For every number $a$, $a = a$.
2. Symmetric:   If $a = b$ then $b = a$.
3. Substitution:   If $a = b$, then $b$ may be replaced for $a$ in any expression.
4. Addition:   If $a = b$, and $c$ represents any number, then $a + c = b + c$.
5. Multiplication:   If $a = b$, and $c$ represents any number, then $a \cdot c = b \cdot c$.

□ **Examples of the Fundamental Properties** **(24)**

**Example 1:** $2 = 2$.   (Reflexive)

**Example 2:** If $2x = 8$, then $8 = 2x$.   (Symmetric)

**Example 3:** If $x = y$, and the variable expression $2x + x$ is given, then we may write $2y + y$ for the same expression. (Substitution)

**Example 4:** If $3x = 15$, then $3x + 2 = 15 + 2$.   (Addition)

**Example 5:** If $x = 2$, then $x \cdot 3 = 2 \cdot 3$.   (Multiplication)

□ **Some Vocabulary** **(25)**

1. The inequality symbol, $\neq$, means "not equal."

**Example 1:** $2 \neq 3$         **Example 2:** $x \neq 0$

2. Remember, if a replacement set is not given for a variable, we will assume that it is the last set of numbers we have studied. At this time it would be the set of whole numbers.

**Example 1:** $3x = 9$         **Example 2:** $y \div y = 1, y \neq 0$

□ *Study Exercise Five* **(26)**

Name the fundamental property of equations which justifies each of these statements.

1. If $y = 5$, then $5 = y$.

2. $6 = 6$
3. If $7 + 8 = 15$, then $15 = 7 + 8$.
4. If $a = b$, and the variable expression $5a + 2$ is given, then we may write $5b + 2$ for the same expression.
5. $9 + 2 = 9 + 2$
6. If $x = 5$, then $x \cdot 3 = 5 \cdot 3$.
7. If $x = 5$, then $x + 2 = 5 + 2$.
8. If the left and right members of an equation are interchanged, we have used the _____ property of equations.

## REVIEW EXERCISES

A. Define the following terms.

　　1.  Variable　　　　　　　2.  Constant　　　　　　　3.  Variable expression

B. Which of the following are variable expressions? (Answer yes or no.)

　　4.  $2 \cdot x + y$　　　　　5.  $3(x + y) + 4x$　　　　　6.  $y$

　　7.  $(a + b) \div c$　　　　8.  $2 + 3 \cdot (4 + 5)$　　　　9.  $\dfrac{2m + n}{3}$

C. Evaluate each of the following variable expressions by letting $a = 3$, $b = 10$, and $c = 0$. Show both the substitution and the answer.

　　10.  $7a - b$　　　　　11.  $2ab + ac$　　　　　12.  $a \cdot (a + b)$

D. Evaluate each of these variable expressions by letting $x = 5$, $y = 2$, and $z = 0$.

　　13.  $xy + z$　　　　　14.  $(x + 3)(y + 4)$　　　　　15.  $3[x - (x + z)] + 5y$

E. Classify each of the following as a basic sum, difference, product, or quotient.

　　16.  $\square \div \triangle$　　　　　17.  $2rs + t$　　　　　18.  $3(a + b)$

F. Give a variable expression representing each of the following word statements.

　　19.  Three less than five times a certain number
　　20.  The number of cents in $n$ dimes

G. Solve the following equations by inspection.

　　21.  $2x = 20$　　　　　22.  $y = y$　　　　　23.  $\dfrac{a}{a} = 1, a \neq 0$
　　24.  $3x = 3$　　　　　25.  $y + 6 = y$　　　　　26.  $m = 2$
　　27.  $n - 5 = 0$　　　　28.  $2x + 3 = 7$　　　　29.  $3(y + 1) = 18$

H. Classify each equation as either an identity or a conditional equation.

　　30.  $a + 7 = 7 + a$　　　　31.  $m + 3 = 8$　　　　32.  $3y = y + y + y$

　　33.  $2x = 4$　　　　　34.  $2(x + 1) = 6$　　　　35.  $\dfrac{0}{n} = 0, n \neq 0$

　　36.  $3y + 2 = 5$　　　　37.  $0 \cdot x = 0$　　　　38.  $5 \cdot y = y \cdot 5$

I. Name the fundamental property of equations which justifies each of these statements.

　　39.  $2 + 13 = 2 + 13$　　　　　　40.  If $3x = 18$, then $3x + 5 = 18 + 5$.
　　41.  If $4(x + 1) = 24$, then $24 = 4(x + 1)$.　　42.  If $n = 3$, then $n \cdot 2 = 3 \cdot 2$.
　　43.  If $a = 5$, then $2a + 3$ may be written as $2 \cdot 5 + 3$.

## Solutions to Review Exercises

A.  1. See Frame 2.　　　　2. See Frame 4.　　　　3. See Frame 5.

B.  4. Yes　　　　　　　　5. Yes　　　　　　　　6. No

　　7. No, $c$ could represent zero.　8. No, it is a numeral expression.　9. Yes

C.  10. $7 \cdot 3 - 10 = 11$　　11. $2 \cdot 3 \cdot 10 + 3 \cdot 0 = 60$　　12. $3 \cdot (3 + 10) = 39$

D.  13. $5 \cdot 2 + 0 = 10$　　14. $(5 + 3)(2 + 4) = 48$　　15. $3[5 - (5 + 0)] + 5 \cdot 2 = 10$

E.  16. Basic quotient　　　17. Basic sum　　　　　18. Basic product

F.  19. $5x - 3$　　　　　　20. $10n$

G.  21. 10　　　　　　　　22. All whole numbers　　23. All natural numbers
　　24. 1　　　　　　　　25. No solutions　　　　26. 2
　　27. 5　　　　　　　　28. 2　　　　　　　　　29. 5

H.  30. Identity　　　　　　31. Conditional　　　　32. Identity
　　33. Conditional　　　　34. Conditional　　　　35. Identity
　　36. Conditional　　　　37. Identity　　　　　38. Identity

I.  39. Reflexive　　40. Addition　　41. Symmetric　　42. Multiplication　　43. Substitution

## SUPPLEMENTARY PROBLEMS

A.  Which of the following are variable expressions? (Answer yes or no.)

　　1. $5x$　　　　　2. $3 + x$　　　　3. $a \div 0$　　　　4. $2 \cdot x + 3 \cdot y$

　　5. $7m \div m$　　6. $\dfrac{8m + 4}{1}$　　7. $4(a + b)$　　8. $4a + 4b$

　　9. $x + (y + 3)$　　10. $0 \div (x + z)$　　11. $+a$　　　　12. $-b$

B.  Evaluate each of the following variable expressions by letting $x = 4$, $y = 2$, and $z = 0$.

　　13. $x + y$　　　　　　　14. $3x + 2y$　　　　　　15. $5x - 3y + z$
　　16. $3(x + y)$　　　　　　17. $3x + 3y$　　　　　　18. $(x + y)(y + z)$
　　19. $2x + 3y + 4z$　　　　20. $3x(2y - x)$　　　　　21. $5 \cdot [x + 2(y - z)]$
　　22. $(x + y)(y + z)(x - y)$　　23. $2(x + y) - 3z$　　　24. $z(3x - 4y)$
　　25. $x[(x + y) - (y + z)] + 3y$　　26. $6[x - (x + z)] + 5y - 4z$

C.  Classify each of the following as a basic sum, difference, product, or quotient.

　　27. $m + 8$　　　　　　　28. $x - y$　　　　　　　29. $2 \cdot x \cdot y$
　　30. $5(z + w)$　　　　　　31. $6x + 2y - 1$　　　　32. $5(x + y - z)$
　　33. $(x + 4)(x + 5)$　　　34. $7a(b + c)$　　　　　35. $7ab + 7ac$

D.  Give a variable expression representing each of these word statements.

　　36. The sum of a number and 3　　　37. Six less than some number
　　38. Five more than six times a certain number　　39. Ten less than twice a certain number
　　40. The number of cents in $n$ nickels
　　41. A wire 7 feet long is cut into two pieces. If one piece is $x$ feet long, how long is the other?

E.  Solve the following equations by inspection.

　　42. $3x = 12$　　　　　　43. $a + 1 = 1 + a$　　　　44. $2x = 10$
　　45. $m + 5 = 12$　　　　　46. $b = b + 1$　　　　　47. $6 - x = x$
　　48. $5n = 0$　　　　　　　49. $2x + 1 = 13$　　　　　50. $3x - 1 = 2$
　　51. $2(m + 1) = 2$　　　　52. $3(n + 3) = 15$　　　　53. $a \cdot 1 = a$

F.  Classify each equation as either an identity or a conditional equation.

　　54. $a = a$　　　　　　　55. $m = 1$　　　　　　　56. $7 + x = x + 7$
　　57. $2x = x + x$　　　　　58. $0 \cdot y = 0$　　　　　59. $3x = 21$

## SUPPLEMENTARY PROBLEMS, Contd.

60. $a + 0 = a$  61. $5x + 1 = 11$  62. $2(x + 3) = 14$

G. Name the fundamental property of equations which justifies each of these statements.

63. If $a = 6$, then $6 = a$.  64. $2 = 2$
65. If $5 = 3 + 2$, then $3 + 2 = 5$.  66. If $x = 4$ and $2x = 8$, then $2 \cdot 4 = 8$.
67. If $x = y$, then $2x + x$ can be written as $2y + y$.
68. If $m = 3$, then $m \cdot 2 = 3 \cdot 2$
69. If $x + 1 = 8$, then $(x + 1) + 4 = 8 + 4$.
70. If $a = 3$, then $5a = 5 \cdot 3$.

H. Calculator problems. With your instructor's approval, use a calculator to evaluate the following variable expressions when $x = 236$, $y = 1054$, and $z = 561$.

71. $x(y + z)$  72. $(x + y)(y + z)$  73. $3y - 2x + 4z$
74. $5 \cdot [x + 2(y - z)]$  75. $(y - x) \cdot [y - (z - x)]$

## □ Solutions to Study Exercises   (10A)

### Study Exercise One (Frame 10)

A. 1. Yes
   3. No, there is no symbol of operation.
   5. Yes

   2. No, cannot divide by zero.
   4. Yes
   6. No, $b$ could represent zero.

B. 7. $x + 3 = 5 + 3$
       $= 8$

   8. $y - 1 = 2 - 1$
       $= 1$

   9. $xz = 5 \cdot 0$
       $= 0$

   10. $5x - 2y = 5 \cdot 5 - 2 \cdot 2$
        $= 21$

   11. $xy + z = 5 \cdot 2 + 0$
        $= 10$

   12. $2(x + y) - 3z = 2(5 + 2) - 3 \cdot 0$
        $= 14$

   13. $(x + 3)(y + 4) = (5 + 3)(2 + 4)$
        $= 48$

   14. $3x - y + z = 3 \cdot 5 - 2 + 0$
        $= 13$

   15. $3 \cdot [x - (x + z)] + 5 \cdot y = 3 \cdot [5 - (5 + 0)] + 5 \cdot 2$
        $= 10$

C. 16. Basic difference  17. Basic sum  18. Basic product  19. Basic product
   20. Basic product  21. Basic sum

### □ Study Exercise Two (Frame 13)   (13A)

1. $x + 10$  2. $7x - 15$  3. $3x + 7$  4. $25x$  5. $100(n + 5)$  6. $25 - y$ feet

### □ Study Exercise Three (Frame 18)   (18A)

1. 3  2. 3  3. 5  4. 1
5. 0  6. Every whole number  7. Every whole number  8. 2
9. Every whole number  10. No solutions  11. 4  12. 3

### ☑ Study Exercise Four (Frame 22)   (22A)

A. 1. Conditional  2. Identity  3. Conditional
   4. Identity  5. Identity  6. Conditional
B. 7. $x - x = 0$  8. $x + 0 = x$  9. $1 \cdot x = x$

### □ Study Exercise Five (Frame 26)   (26A)

1. Symmetric  2. Reflexive  3. Symmetric
4. Substitution  5. Reflexive  6. Multiplication
7. Addition  8. Symmetric

# Properties of Whole Numbers

## ☐ Objectives (1)

This unit develops the following properties of whole numbers:

- Closure properties of addition and multiplication.
- Commutative properties of addition and multiplication.
- Associative properties of addition and multiplication.
- Additive and multiplicative identity properties.
- Multiplication by zero property.
- Distributive property of multiplication with respect to addition.

By the end of this unit you should be able to:

- write an identity describing each property.
- recognize the properties when used in true equations.
- correctly spell the names of the properties and know their abbreviations.
- use the distributive property to change basic products to basic sums.
- use the reverse of the distributive property to change basic sums to basic products.

## ☐ Axioms or Properties (2)

An axiom or a property is a statement which we assume to be true. They are the foundation of algebra. In other words, they are the rules of the game.

We will study these properties in two parts:
Part 1.   Properties of Addition
Part 2.   Properties of Multiplication

## ☐ Part 1: Properties of Addition (3)

The following properties involving addition will be explained and illustrated.

1.   The Closure Property of Addition
2.   The Commutative Property of Addition
3.   The Associative Property of Addition
4.   The Additive Identity Property

## ☐ The Closure Property of Addition (4)

If $x$ and $y$ represent any two whole numbers, then their sum, denoted by $x + y$, is also a whole number.

**Example:**   $12 + 60 = 72$

When two whole numbers are added the result is also a whole number. The closure property of addition will be abbreviated clpa.

## ☐ The Commutative Property of Addition (5)

If $x$ and $y$ represent any two whole numbers, then $x + y = y + x$.

**Example:**   $3 + 5 = 5 + 3$

Interchanging or reversing the positions of the addends has no effect on the sum. The commutative property of addition will be abbreviated cpa.

## ☐ More Illustrations of cpa (6)

**Example 1:**   $13 + 21 = 21 + 13$

**Example 2:** $a + 2b = 2b + a$

**Example 3:** $3(m + n) = 3(n + m)$

**Example 4:** $2a + 3b + c = 3b + 2a + c$

☐ The commutative property does not hold true for subtraction and division. Consider these examples: **(7)**

**Example 1:** $8 - 3 \neq 3 - 8$ **Example 2:** $\dfrac{10}{2} \neq \dfrac{2}{10}$

☐ **The Associative Property of Addition** **(8)**

If $x$, $y$, and $z$ represent whole numbers, then $(x + y) + z = x + (y + z)$.

**Example:** $\underbrace{(2 + 3)} + 4 = 2 + \underbrace{(3 + 4)}$

$\qquad\quad \underbrace{5 + 4} \;\; = \;\; \underbrace{2 + 7}$

$\qquad\qquad\quad 9 \;\;\; = \;\;\; 9$

The sum of three or more numbers is the same no matter how the numbers are "associated" in groups. The associative property of addition will be abbreviated apa.

☐ **More Illustrations of apa** **(9)**

**Example 1:** $(0 + 5) + 2 = 0 + (5 + 2)$

**Example 2:** $(2a + 3b) + c = 2a + (3b + c)$

**Example 3:** $(1 + 3 + 2) + 5 = (1 + 3) + (2 + 5)$

**Example 4:** $5x + (y + 3) = (5x + y) + 3$

☐ The associative property does not hold true for subtraction and division. **(10)**

**Example 1:** $\underbrace{(8 - 5)} - 2 \neq 8 - \underbrace{(5 - 2)}$      **Example 2:** $\underbrace{(36 \div 6)} \div 2 \neq 36 \div \underbrace{(6 \div 2)}$

$\qquad\quad \underbrace{3 - 2} \;\; \neq \;\; \underbrace{8 - 3} \qquad\qquad\qquad\qquad\qquad \underbrace{6 \div 2} \;\; \neq \;\; \underbrace{36 \div 3}$

$\qquad\qquad 1 \;\;\; \neq \;\;\; 5 \qquad\qquad\qquad\qquad\qquad\qquad\quad 3 \;\;\; \neq \;\;\; 12$

☐ **The Additive Identity Property** **(11)**

If $x$ represents any whole number, then $0 + x = x$ and $x + 0 = x$.

**Example 1:** $0 + 10 = 10$ **Example 2:** $5m + 0 = 5m$

The sum of zero and any whole number equals the same whole number. Zero when added leaves the identity of the original whole number unchanged. The additive identity property will be abbreviated add. ident.

☐                                 *Study Exercise One* **(12)**

Each of the following is an example of one of the properties of addition. State the property. You may use the abbreviations.

1. $7 + 10 = 10 + 7$
2. $(3 + 6) + 1 = 3 + (6 + 1)$
3. $2 \cdot (8 + 0) = 2 \cdot 8$
4. $192 + 856$ is a whole number
5. $x + 2 = 2 + x$
6. $(3a + 4) + 6 = 3a + (4 + 6)$
7. $5(2m + 3n) = 5(3n + 2m)$
8. $a(b + 0) = ab$
9. $(a + 2b + c) + 4d = (a + 2b) + (c + 4d)$
10. $3x + 0 = 3x$

## ☐ Combining the Commutative and Associative Properties (13)

In combination, cpa and apa allow us to interchange addends and regroup any way we desire.

**Example:** The numeral expression $1 + 3 + 5$ can be rewritten any of the following ways. Each of these expressions will produce the same answer, 9.

| | | |
|---|---|---|
| $(3 + 1) + 5$ | $(1 + 5) + 3$ | $5 + (1 + 3)$ |
| $(3 + 5) + 1$ | $(1 + 3) + 5$ | $5 + (3 + 1)$ |
| $(5 + 1) + 3$ | $3 + (1 + 5)$ | $1 + (5 + 3)$ |
| $(5 + 3) + 1$ | $3 + (5 + 1)$ | $1 + (3 + 5)$ |

## ☐ More Illustrations (14)

**Example 1:** $1 + 2 + 5 + 4 = (2 + 1) + (4 + 5)$

**Example 2:** $2a + (3b + 4a) = (2a + 4a) + 3b$

## ☐ *Study Exercise Two* (15)

A. Use the commutative and associative properties of addition to evaluate the following expressions two ways.

**Example:** Evaluate $2 + 5 + 1 + 8$

**Solution (a):** $\begin{aligned} 2 + 5 + 1 + 8 &= (2 + 8) + (5 + 1) \\ &= \quad 10 \quad + \quad 6 \\ &= \qquad 16 \end{aligned}$

**Solution (b):** $\begin{aligned} 2 + 5 + 1 + 8 &= (8 + 5 + 1) + 2 \\ &= \quad 14 \quad + \quad 2 \\ &= \qquad 16 \end{aligned}$

1. $6 + 0 + 3$
2. $2 + 6 + 4 + 7$
3. $8 + 10 + 2 + 11 + 4$
4. $2 \cdot [4 + 1 + 6]$

B. Use the commutative and associative properties to correctly fill in the blanks.
5. $(a + b) + c = (b + \underline{\qquad}) + a$
6. $3x + 4y + z + 5w = (3x + 5w) + (z + \underline{\qquad})$
7. $5(2x + 3y + 7z) = 5(3y + 2x + \underline{\qquad})$

## ☐ Part 2: Properties of Multiplication (16)

The following properties involving multiplication will be explained and illustrated.

1. The Closure Property of Multiplication
2. The Commutative Property of Multiplication
3. The Associative Property of Multiplication
4. The Multiplicative Identity Property
5. The Multiplication by Zero Property

## ☐ The Closure Property of Multiplication (17)

If $x$ and $y$ represent any two whole numbers then their product, denoted by $xy$, is also a whole number.

**Example:** $(23)(351) = 8,073$

When two whole numbers are multiplied the result is also a whole number. The closure property of multiplication will be abbreviated clpm.

☐ **The Commutative Property of Multiplication** **(18)**

If $x$ and $y$ represent any two whole numbers, then $x \cdot y = y \cdot x$.

**Example:** $3 \cdot 8 = 8 \cdot 3$

Interchanging or reversing the position of the factors has no effect on the product. The commutative property of multiplication will be abbreviated cpm.

☐ **More Illustrations of cpm** **(19)**

**Example 1:** $6 \cdot 9 = 9 \cdot 6$ **Example 2:** $2(ab) = 2(ba)$

**Example 3:** $a(b + c) = (b + c)a$

☐ **The Associative Property of Multiplication** **(20)**

If $x$, $y$ and $z$ represent whole numbers, then $(x \cdot y) \cdot z = x \cdot (y \cdot z)$.

**Example:** $(2 \cdot 3) \cdot 7 = 2 \cdot (3 \cdot 7)$

$\phantom{Example:} 6 \cdot 7 = 2 \cdot 21$

$\phantom{Example:} 42 = 42$

The product of three or more numbers is the same no matter how the factors are "associated" in groups. The associative property of multiplication will be abbreviated apm.

☐ **More Illustrations of apm** **(21)**

**Example 1:** $3 \cdot 5 \cdot 2 = 3 \cdot (5 \cdot 2)$
**Example 2:** $(a \cdot 2) \cdot 3 = a \cdot (2 \cdot 3)$
**Example 3:** $(2 \cdot m \cdot 3) \cdot n = (2 \cdot m) \cdot (3 \cdot n)$

☐ **The Multiplicative Identity Property** **(22)**

If $x$ represents any whole number, then $1 \cdot x = x$ and $x \cdot 1 = x$.

**Example 1:** $1 \cdot 15 = 15$ **Example 2:** $1 \cdot (5x + 2) = 5x + 2$

The product of one and any whole number equals that same whole number. The number 1, when multiplied, leaves the identity of the original whole number unchanged. The multiplicative identity property will be abbreviated mult. ident.

☐ **The Multiplication by Zero Property** **(23)**

If $x$ represents any whole number, then $0 \cdot x = 0$ and $x \cdot 0 = 0$.

**Example 1:** $0 \cdot 12 = 0$ **Example 2:** $(2a + b) \cdot 0 = 0$

The product of zero and any whole number is zero. The multiplication by zero property will be abbreviated mult. by 0.

☐ *Study Exercise Three* **(24)**

Each of the following is an example of one of the properties of multiplication. State the property. You may use the abbreviations.

1. $(9 + 7) \cdot 0 = 0$      2. $m \cdot (n \cdot 1) = m \cdot n$
3. $(3 \cdot x \cdot y) \cdot z = (3 \cdot x) \cdot (y \cdot z)$      4. $a \cdot (b + 2) = (b + 2) \cdot a$

5.  $6 \cdot (x \cdot 1) = 6 \cdot x$
6.  $a \cdot 1 + 0 = 1 \cdot a + 0$
7.  $a \cdot 1 + 0 = a + 0$
8.  $(2 \cdot x) \cdot y = y \cdot (2 \cdot x)$
9.  $(x + y) \cdot 1 = x + y$
10.  $(3 + a) \cdot x \cdot y = (3 + a) \cdot (x \cdot y)$

## ☐ Combining the Commutative and Associative Properties (25)

In combination, cpm and apm allow us to interchange factors and regroup any way we desire.

**Example:** The numeral expression $2 \cdot 4 \cdot 5$ can be rewritten any of the following ways. Each of these expressions will produce the same answer, 40.

| | | |
|---|---|---|
| $(4 \cdot 2) \cdot 5$ | $(2 \cdot 5) \cdot 4$ | $5 \cdot (2 \cdot 4)$ |
| $(4 \cdot 5) \cdot 2$ | $(2 \cdot 4) \cdot 5$ | $5 \cdot (4 \cdot 2)$ |
| $(5 \cdot 2) \cdot 4$ | $4 \cdot (2 \cdot 5)$ | $2 \cdot (4 \cdot 5)$ |
| $(5 \cdot 4) \cdot 2$ | $4 \cdot (5 \cdot 2)$ | $2 \cdot (5 \cdot 4)$ |

## ☐ More Illustrations (26)

**Example 1:**  $2 \cdot 3 \cdot 5 \cdot 4 = (2 \cdot 5) \cdot (4 \cdot 3)$

**Example 2:**  $3 \cdot a \cdot 2 \cdot b = (3 \cdot 2) \cdot (a \cdot b)$

## ☐ Study Exercise Four (27)

A.  Use the commutative and associative properties of multiplication to evaluate the following expressions two ways.

**Example:**  Evaluate  $2 \cdot 4 \cdot 1 \cdot 5$

**Solution (a):**
$$2 \cdot 4 \cdot 1 \cdot 5 = (2 \cdot 5) \cdot (4 \cdot 1)$$
$$= 10 \cdot 4$$
$$= 40$$

**Solution (b):**
$$2 \cdot 4 \cdot 1 \cdot 5 = (2 \cdot 4 \cdot 5) \cdot 1$$
$$= 40 \cdot 1$$
$$= 40$$

1.  $8 \cdot 0 \cdot 4$
2.  $8 \cdot 2 \cdot 4 \cdot 5$
3.  $4 + (2 \cdot 1 \cdot 6)$
4.  $(3 \cdot 2 \cdot 4) + (1 \cdot 8 \cdot 3)$

B.  Use the commutative and associative properties of multiplication to correctly fill in the blanks.

5.  $2 \cdot a \cdot b = a \cdot (2 \cdot \underline{\hspace{1cm}})$
6.  $3xyz = (3x) \cdot (z \cdot \underline{\hspace{1cm}})$
7.  $3a + 6bc = 3a + c(b \cdot \underline{\hspace{1cm}})$
8.  $5 \cdot (b \cdot a) + 7 \cdot (f \cdot e) = 5 \cdot a \cdot \underline{\hspace{1cm}} + 7 \cdot e \cdot \underline{\hspace{1cm}}$

## ☐ The Distributive Property of Multiplication with Respect to Addition (28)

We now study a special property which involves both multiplication and addition. It states the following:

If $x$, $y$, and $z$ represent whole numbers, then $x(y + z) = xy + xz$ and $(y + z)x = yx + zx$.

**Example:**  $2 \cdot (3 + 4) = 2 \cdot 3 + 2 \cdot 4$

This property will be abbreviated dpma.

## ☐ More Illustrations of dpma (29)

The distributive property states that when a number is multiplied times a sum, it must be distributed or shared with each addend.

**Example 1:**  Evaluate $3 \cdot (2 + 5)$ by applying the distributive property.

  **Solution:**  Distribute the multiplier, 3, to each addend.

$$3 \cdot (2 + 5) = 3 \cdot 2 + 3 \cdot 5$$
$$= 6 + 15$$
$$= 21$$

**Example 2:**  Evaluate $(3 + 4) \cdot 5$ by applying the distributive property.

  **Solution:**  Distribute the multiplier, 5, to each addend.

$$(3 + 4) \cdot 5 = 3 \cdot 5 + 4 \cdot 5$$
$$= 15 + 20$$
$$= 35$$

□                                                                                    **(30)**

The distributive property of multiplication with respect to addition can also be applied to certain variable expressions. It will change a basic product into a basic sum.

$$2 \cdot (a + b) = 2 \cdot a + 2 \cdot b$$

Basic       Basic<br>Product     Sum

□ **More Illustrations**                                                              **(31)**

**Example 1:**  $5 \cdot (x + y) = 5x + 5y$       **Example 2:**   $(y + 7) \cdot 2 = y \cdot 2 + 14$

**Example 3:**  $2a(b + c) = 2ab + 2ac$

□                              ***Study Exercise Five***                              **(32)**

A.  Evaluate the following numeral expressions using dpma. Show your work.

    1.  $5 \cdot (6 + 1)$            2.  $(2 + 6) \cdot 4$            3.  $10 \cdot (4 + 3)$

    4.  $(8 + 2) \cdot 7$            5.  $1 \cdot (6 + 9)$            6.  $(9 + 12) \cdot 0$

B.  Use dpma to write each of the following as a basic sum.

    7.  $6(m + n)$            8.  $3(a + 5)$            9.  $(m + 4) \cdot 7$

  10.  $3a(b + c)$          11.  $(a + b) \cdot c$          12.  $8(b + 1)$

### Reversing the Distributive Property                                              **(33)**

The distributive property of multiplication can be reversed to change certain basic sums into basic products. This procedure is called factoring. The number common to both addends is "undistributed" and multiplied times the remaining group.

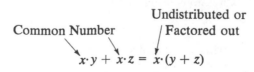

$$\text{Common Number} \qquad \text{Undistributed or Factored out}$$
$$x \cdot y + x \cdot z = x \cdot (y + z)$$

□ **More Illustrations of Factoring**                                                **(34)**

**Example 1:**  $3x + 3y = 3(x + y)$       **Example 2:**   $5m + 15 = 5(m + 3)$

**Example 3:**  $4y + 4 = 4(y + 1)$

43

☐ *Study Exercise Six* **(35)**

Use the reverse of dpma to factor the following:

1.  $2m + 2n$
2.  $5x + 5y$
3.  $6a + 6$
4.  $7x + 7$
5.  $6m + 24$
6.  $4ab + abc$

☐ **Summary: Properties of the Whole Numbers** **(36)**

If $x$, $y$, and $z$ represent whole numbers, then each of the following is true:

1.  Closure Property of Addition (clpa): $x + y$ is a whole number.
2.  Closure Property of Multiplication (clpm): $x \cdot y$ is a whole number.
3.  Commutative Property of Addition (cpa): $x + y = y + x$.
4.  Commutative Property of Multiplication (cpm): $x \cdot y = y \cdot x$
5.  Associative Property of Addition (apa): $(x + y) + z = x + (y + z)$.
6.  Associative Property of Multiplication (apm): $(x \cdot y) \cdot z = x \cdot (y \cdot z)$.
7.  Additive Identity Property (add. ident.): $0 + x = x$ and $x + 0 = x$.
8.  Multiplicative Identity Property (mult. ident.): $1 \cdot x = x$ and $x \cdot 1 = x$.
9.  Multiplication by Zero Property (mult. by 0): $0 \cdot x = 0$ and $x \cdot 0 = 0$.
10. Distributive Property of Multiplication with Respect to Addition (dpma): $x(y + z) = xy + xz$ or $(y + z)x = yx + zx$.

## REVIEW EXERCISES

A.  Each of the following is an example of one of the properties of whole numbers. Name the property by giving its abbreviation.

1.  $x \cdot 2 = 2 \cdot x$
2.  $3 \cdot (x + 0) = 3 \cdot x + 3 \cdot 0$
3.  $3 \cdot (x + 0) = 3 \cdot x$
4.  $(x + 2) + y = x + (2 + y)$
5.  $(5 \cdot x) \cdot 0 = 0$
6.  $(5 \cdot x) + 0 = 5x$
7.  $(5 \cdot x) \cdot 1 = 1 \cdot (5 \cdot x)$
8.  $(5 \cdot x) \cdot 1 = 5 \cdot x$
9.  $2 \cdot x \cdot 4 = 4 \cdot (2 \cdot x)$
10. $4 \cdot (2 \cdot x) = (4 \cdot 2) \cdot x$
11. $(123) \cdot (2046)$ is a whole number.
12. $402 + 856$ is a whole number.
13. $[(x + 2) \cdot (x + 3)] \cdot (x + 4) = (x + 2) \cdot [(x + 3) \cdot (x + 4)]$
14. $(a + 2b + c) + 4d = (a + 2b) + (c + 4d)$
15. $ab + c = c + ab$
16. $2x + y + 3z = y + 2x + 3z$
17. $9x + 9 = 9(x + 1)$
18. $0 \cdot (a + b) = 0$

B.  Use the commutative and associative properties of addition or multiplication to evaluate the following expression in two ways. Show your work.

19. $2 + 5 + 8 + 3$
20. $3 \cdot 2 \cdot 1 \cdot 5$

C.  Evaluate the following numeral expressions using dpma.

21. $6 \cdot (5 + 2)$
22. $(12 + 4) \cdot 3$

D.  Use dpma to write each of the following as a basic sum.

23. $2(a + b)$
24. $5(x + 1)$
25. $(x + 3) \cdot 2$
26. $(m + 4) \cdot 7$
27. $2x(y + z)$
28. $5a(b + c)$

E.  Reverse dpma to factor each of the following.

29. $4x + 4y$
30. $8a + 8b$
31. $xy + xt$
32. $4ab + 4ac$

## REVIEW EXERCISES, Contd.

33. $7a + 7$

34. $5m + 20$

35. $6n + 3$

36. $8a + 4b$

## Solutions to Review Exercises

A.  1. cpm
    4. apa
    7. cpm
    10. apm
    13. apm
    16. cpa

    2. dpma
    5. mult. by 0
    8. mult. ident.
    11. clpm
    14. apa
    17. dpma

    3. add. ident.
    6. add. ident.
    9. cpm
    12. clpa
    15. cpa
    18. mult. by 0

B.  19. 18

    20. 30

C.  21. $6 \cdot (5 + 2) = 6 \cdot 5 + 6 \cdot 2$
    $$= 30 + 12$$
    $$= 42$$

    22. $(12 + 4) \cdot 3 = 12 \cdot 3 + 4 \cdot 3$
    $$= 36 + 12$$
    $$= 48$$

D.  23. $2a + 2b$
    25. $x \cdot 2 + 6$
    27. $2xy + 2xz$

    24. $5x + 5$
    26. $m \cdot 7 + 28$
    28. $5ab + 5ac$

E.  29. $4(x + y)$
    31. $x(y + t)$
    33. $7(a + 1)$
    35. $3(2n + 1)$

    30. $8(a + b)$
    32. $4a(b + c)$
    34. $5(m + 4)$
    36. $4(2a + b)$

## SUPPLEMENTARY PROBLEMS

A.  Each of the following is an example of one of the properties of whole numbers. Name the property by giving its abbreviation.

1. $(x + 2) + 3 = x + (2 + 3)$
2. $3x + 4 = 4 + 3x$
3. $78 \cdot 95$ is a whole number
4. $7 \cdot (3 + 4) = 7 \cdot 3 + 7 \cdot 4$
5. $18 \cdot 1 = 18$
6. $0 \cdot (3a + 1) = 0$
7. $n = 1 \cdot n$
8. $ab + 0 = ab$
9. $ab + 0 = 0 + ab$
10. $3(b + c) = 3(c + b)$
11. $3(b + c) = (b + c) 3$
12. $3(b + c) = 3b + 3c$
13. $(3a)b = b(3a)$
14. $(3a)b = 3(ab)$
15. $[3x(9y + 4z)] \cdot 0 = 0$
16. $1023 + 4695$ is a whole number.
17. $8a + 8 = 8(a + 1)$
18. $3 + x + y + 7 = (3 + x) + (y + 7)$
19. $(3x + 2y + 7z) \cdot 1 = 3x + 2y + 7z$
20. $[(a + 5) \cdot (a + 10)] \cdot (a + 1) = (a + 5) \cdot [(a + 10) \cdot (a + 1)]$

B.  Use the commutative and associative properties of addition to multiplication to evaluate the following expressions in two ways. Show your work.

21. $3 + 1 + 4$
22. $8 \cdot 3 \cdot 2$
23. $2 + 1 + 0 + 5$
24. $2 \cdot 6 \cdot 3 \cdot 4$
25. $2 \cdot 5 + 3 \cdot 2 + 1 \cdot 4$
26. $4 \cdot [2 \cdot 3 + 8 \cdot 1 + 5 \cdot 2]$

C.  Evaluate the following numeral expressions using dpma.

27. $3 \cdot (6 + 2)$
28. $5 \cdot (4 + 7)$

## SUPPLEMENTARY PROBLEMS, Contd.

29. $(10 + 13) \cdot 3$　　　　　　　　　　30. $(6 + 1) \cdot 7$
31. $12 \cdot (3 + 1)$　　　　　　　　　　32. $11 \cdot (5 + 0)$

D. Use dpma to write each of the following as a basic sum.

33. $3(x + z)$　　　　　　　　　　34. $8(t + s)$
35. $(y + 2) \cdot 6$　　　　　　　　36. $(n + 7) \cdot 3$
37. $3x(y + w)$　　　　　　　　　38. $6a(b + c)$
39. $7(t + 1)$　　　　　　　　　　40. $(n + 5) \cdot 6$

E. Reverse dpma to factor each of the following.

41. $3m + 3n$　　　　　　　　　　42. $7x + 7y$
43. $ab + ac$　　　　　　　　　　44. $2ax + 2ay$
45. $9m + 9$　　　　　　　　　　46. $4m + 20$
47. $6t + 18$　　　　　　　　　　48. $5xy + 15y$
49. $12y + 8$　　　　　　　　　　50. $4x + 16xy$

## ☐ Solutions to Study Exercises　　　　　　　　　　　　　　　　(12A)

### Study Exercise One (Frame 12)

| | | | |
|---|---|---|---|
| 1. cpa | 2. apa | 3. add. ident. | 4. clpa |
| 5. cpa | 6. apa | 7. cpa | 8. add. ident. |
| 9. apa | 10. add. ident. | | |

☐　　　　　　　　　　　　**Study Exercise Two (Frame 15)**　　　　　　　　　　(15A)

A. 1. 9　　　　　　2. 19　　　　　　3. 35　　　　　　4. 22
B. 5. $(a + b) + c = (b + c) + a$
6. $3x + 4y + z + 5w = (3x + 5w) + (z + 4y)$
7. $5[2x + 3y + 7z] = 5(3y + 2x + 7z)$

☐　　　　　　　　　　　　**Study Exercise Three (Frame 24)**　　　　　　　　(24A)

| | | | |
|---|---|---|---|
| 1. mult. by 0 | 2. mult. ident. | 3. apm | 4. cpm |
| 5. mult. ident. | 6. cpm | 7. mult. ident. | 8. cpm |
| 9. mult. ident. | 10. apm | | |

☐　　　　　　　　　　　　**Study Exercise Four (Frame 27)**　　　　　　　　(27A)

A. 1. 0　　　　　　2. 320　　　　　3. 16　　　　　4. 48

B. 5. $2 \cdot a \cdot b = a \cdot (2 \cdot b)$　　　　　　6. $3xyz = (3x) \cdot (z \cdot y)$
7. $3a + 6bc = 3a + c(b \cdot 6)$　　　8. $5 \cdot (b \cdot a) + 7 \cdot (f \cdot e) = 5 \cdot a \cdot b + 7 \cdot e \cdot f$

☐　　　　　　　　　　　　**Study Exercise Five (Frame 32)**　　　　　　　　(32A)

A. 1. $5 \cdot (6 + 1) = 5 \cdot 6 + 5 \cdot 1$　　　　　2. $(2 + 6) \cdot 4 = 2 \cdot 4 + 6 \cdot 4$
　　　　　　　　$= 30 + 5$　　　　　　　　　　　　$= 8 + 24$
　　　　　　　　$=\quad 35$　　　　　　　　　　　　　$=\quad 32$

3. $10 \cdot (4 + 3) = 10 \cdot 4 + 10 \cdot 3$　　　　4. $(8 + 2) \cdot 7 = 8 \cdot 7 + 2 \cdot 7$
　　　　　　　　$=\quad 40 + 30$　　　　　　　　　　$= 56 + 14$
　　　　　　　　$=\quad 70$　　　　　　　　　　　　$=\quad 70$

## Solutions to Study Exercises, Contd.

5. $1 \cdot (6 + 9) = 1 \cdot 6 + 1 \cdot 9$
   $= 6 + 9$
   $= 15$

6. $(9 + 12) \cdot 0 = 9 \cdot 0 + 12 \cdot 0$
   $= 0 + 0$
   $= 0$

B. 7. $6(m + n) = 6m + 6n$
   9. $(m + 4) \cdot 7 = m \cdot 7 + 28$
   11. $(a + b) \cdot c = ac + bc$

8. $3(a + 5) = 3a + 15$
10. $3a(b + c) = 3ab + 3ac$
12. $8(b + 1) = 8b + 8$

□

## *Study Exercise Six (Frame 35)*                    **(35A)**

1. $2m + 2n = 2(m + n)$
3. $6a + 6 = 6(a + 1)$
5. $6m + 24 = 6(m + 4)$

2. $5x + 5y = 5(x + y)$
4. $7x + 7 = 7(x + 1)$
6. $4ab + abc = ab(4 + c)$

# Whole Numbers Used as Exponents

☐ **Objectives** **(1)**

By the end of this unit you should be able to:

- understand the use of whole numbers as exponents.
- identify the base and the exponent in an exponential expression.
- change certain products to exponential notation.
- evaluate exponential expressions.
- use the following properties of exponents:
  - (a) The Zero Power Property.
  - (b) The Addition Property of Exponents.
  - (c) The Subtraction Property of Exponents.
  - (d) The Power to a Power Property.
  - (e) The Distributive Property of Exponents.
- multiply and divide exponential expressions.

☐ *Factors* are numbers which are related by the operation of multiplication. **(2)**

$$3 \cdot 12 \qquad 4ab \qquad 6(x + 12)$$

factors   factors   factors

☐ One number may be used as a factor several times. **(3)**

**Example 1:** $3 \cdot 3 \cdot 3 \cdot 3 \cdot 3 \cdot 3$    **Example 2:** $a \cdot a \cdot a$    **Example 3:** $(a + b)(a + b)(a + b)(a + b)$

☐ **A Simpler Notation** **(4)**

**Example 1:** $3 \cdot 3 \cdot 3 \cdot 3 \cdot 3 \cdot 3 = 3^6$    **Example 2:** $a \cdot a \cdot a = a^3$

**Example 3:** $(a + b)(a + b)(a + b)(a + b) = (a + b)^4$

☐ **Exponential Notation** **(5)**

$$3^6$$

base   exponent or power

The base 3 is used as a factor six times. The exponent or power indicates the number of times the base is used as a factor.

☐ **(6)**

$$(a + b)^4$$

base    exponent or power

The exponent 4 indicates that the base $(a + b)$ is used as a factor four times.

☐ **Reading Exponential Expressions** **(7)**

**Example 1:** $4^2$ is read "4 to the second" or "4 squared."

**Example 2:** $5^3$ is read "5 to the third" or "5 cubed."

**Example 3:** $x^4y^5$ is read "$x$ to the fourth times $y$ to the fifth."

**Example 4:** $(a + b)^{10}$ is read "the group $(a + b)$ to the tenth."

☐ **Study Exercise One** **(8)**

A. Indicate the base and the exponent for each of the following.

1. $2^5$      2. $(x + y)^2$      3. $(4x)^3$      4. $(ab)^6$

B. Write a word statement describing how each of the following would be read.

5. $7^2$       6. $a^3$       7. $(x + y)^6$       8. $x^5y^{12}$

## ☐ Changing to Exponential Notation          (9)

1. $3 \cdot 3 = 3^2$            2. $3 = 3^1$
3. $(a + b)(a + b)(a + b) = (a + b)^3$     4. $5 \cdot x \cdot x \cdot x \cdot x = 5^1 x^4$ or $5x^4$
5. $(xy)(xy)(xy)(xy) = (xy)^4$

## ☐ Evaluating Exponential Expressions         (10)

**Example 1:**   $2^3$

   **Solution:**

     *line (a)*   $2^3 = 2 \cdot 2 \cdot 2$

     *line (b)*   $2^3 = 4 \cdot 2$

     *line (c)*   $2^3 = 8$

**Example 2:**   $(2^3)(3^2)$

   **Solution:**

     *line (a)*   $(2^3)(3^2) = (2 \cdot 2 \cdot 2) \cdot (3 \cdot 3)$

     *line (b)*   $(2^3)(3^2) = 8 \cdot 9$

     *line (c)*   $(2^3)(3^2) = 72$

**Example 3:**   $(5 \cdot 2)^4$

   **Solution:**

     *line (a)*   $(5 \cdot 2)^4 = (5 \cdot 2) \cdot (5 \cdot 2) \cdot (5 \cdot 2) \cdot (5 \cdot 2)$

     *line (b)*   $(5 \cdot 2)^4 = 10 \cdot 10 \cdot 10 \cdot 10$

     *line (c)*   $(5 \cdot 2)^4 = 100 \cdot 100$

     *line (d)*   $(5 \cdot 2)^4 = 10,000$

**Example 4:**   $(4 + 3)^2$

   **Solution:**

     *line (a)*   $(4 + 3)^2 = (4 + 3)(4 + 3)$

     *line (b)*   $(4 + 3)^2 = 7 \cdot 7$

     *line (c)*   $(4 + 3)^2 = 49$

## ☐ Trouble Spots               (11)

**Example 1:**   $2 \cdot 3^2 = 2 \cdot (3 \cdot 3)$        **Example 2:**   $(3 + 4)^2 = (3 + 4)(3 + 4)$
           $2 \cdot 3^2 \neq (2 \cdot 3)(2 \cdot 3)$                 $(3 + 4)^2 \neq 3^2 + 4^2$

## ☐             *Study Exercise Two*           (12)

A. Change each of the following to exponential notation.

1. $4 \cdot 4 \cdot 4$      2. $5$      3. $3 \cdot x \cdot x \cdot x \cdot x$      4. $a \cdot a \cdot a \cdot b \cdot b$
5. $(rs)(rs)(rs)$                   6. $(m + n)(m + n)(m + n)(m + n)$

B. Evaluate each of the following.

7. $3^2$      8. $5^3$      9. $10^2$      10. $8^1$
11. $(2 \cdot 5)^3$      12. $2 \cdot 5^3$      13. $(3 + 5)^2$      14. $(4 \cdot 5)^2$

## ☐ A Base to the Zero Power (13)

**Example 1:** Consider descending powers of 3.

$$3^3 = 27$$
$$3^2 = 9$$ divide by 3
$$3^1 = 3$$ divide by 3
$$3^0 = ?$$ divide by 3

Therefore, $3^0$ means $3 \div 3$ or 1.

**Example 2:** Consider descending powers of 10.

$$10^3 = 1000$$
$$10^2 = 100$$ divide by 10
$$10^1 = 10$$ divide by 10
$$10^0 = ?$$ divide by 10

Therefore, $10^0$ means $10 \div 10$ or 1.

### The Zero Power Property (14)

Any number, except zero, when raised to the zero power is 1. The *zero power* means the base is divided by itself; therefore, $0^0$ does not represent a number because division by zero is impossible.

$$a^0 = 1 \quad \text{where} \quad a \neq 0$$

## ☐ *Study Exercise Three* (15)

Simplify the following completely (evaluate).

1. $6^0$    2. $0^0$    3. $(3 \cdot 5)^0$    4. $3 \cdot 5^0$    5. $(6 - 6)^0$    6. $7 \cdot x^0$ where $x \neq 0$

## ☐ Multiplying Exponential Expressions (16)

**Example 1:** $3^2 \cdot 3^4 = \underbrace{(3 \cdot 3) \cdot (3 \cdot 3 \cdot 3 \cdot 3)}$
$3^2 \cdot 3^4 = \phantom{(3 \cdot 3)} 3^6$

**Example 2:** $x^3 \cdot x^2 = \underbrace{(x \cdot x \cdot x) \cdot (x \cdot x)}$
$x^3 \cdot x^2 = \phantom{(x \cdot x)} x^5$

## ☐ Addition Property of Exponents (17)

To multiply exponential expressions with identical bases, add the exponents.

For every whole number $m$ and $n$:

$$a^m \cdot a^n = a^{m+n}$$

**Example 1:** $10^3 \cdot 10^4 = 10^7$

**Example 3:** $a^3 \cdot a^4 = a^7$

**Example 2:** $x \cdot x^2 = x^3$

**Example 4:** $(x + y)^2 \cdot (x + y)^4 = (x + y)^6$

## ☐ *Study Exercise Four* (18)

Simplify the following according to the addition property of exponents.

**Example:** $2^5 \cdot 2^3 = 2^8$

1. $3^2 \cdot 3^3$    2. $x^3 \cdot x^5$    3. $(a^2 \cdot a^3) \cdot (b^4 \cdot b^2)$    4. $a^2 \cdot b^4 \cdot a^3 \cdot b^2$
5. $a^3 \cdot a^6 \cdot a^2$    6. $x^0 \cdot x^5$    7. $(x + y)^3 (x + y)^5$    8. $(3a^2)(2a^5)$

## ☐ Dividing Exponential Expressions (19)

**Example 1:** $3^5 \div 3^2 = (3 \cdot 3 \cdot 3 \cdot 3 \cdot 3) \div (3 \cdot 3)$
$3^5 \div 3^2 = 3^3$

**Example 2:** $\dfrac{x^5}{x^2} = \dfrac{x \cdot x \cdot x \cdot x \cdot x}{x \cdot x}$

$\dfrac{x^5}{x^2} = x \cdot x \cdot x$

$\dfrac{x^5}{x^2} = x^3$

## ☐ Subtraction Property of Exponents (20)

To divide exponential expressions with identical bases, subtract the exponents.

For every whole number $m$ and $n$, where $m \geq n$ and $a \neq 0$:

$$a^m \div a^n = a^{m-n} \quad \text{or} \quad \frac{a^m}{a^n} = a^{m-n}$$

**Example 1:** $3^6 \div 3^2 = 3^4$  **Example 2:** $\dfrac{x^7}{x^2} = x^5$  **Example 3:** $\dfrac{(a + 2b)^5}{(a + 2b)^3} = (a + 2b)^2$

☐                             *Study Exercise Five*                             **(21)**

Simplify the following according to the subtraction property of exponents.

**Example:** $5^3 \div 5 = 5^2$

1. $10^3 \div 10^2$      2. $\dfrac{3^6}{3^2}$      3. $\dfrac{x^6}{x^2}$      4. $(a + b)^{10} \div (a + b)^7$      5. $\dfrac{6a^5}{2a^2}$      6. $\dfrac{m^3}{m^0}$

☐ **Raising a Power to a Power**                                             **(22)**

**Example 1:**    $(2^3)^2 = 2^3 \cdot 2^3$                            **Example 2:**    $(x^4)^3 = x^4 \cdot x^4 \cdot x^4$

                     $(2^3)^2 = \quad 2^6$                                           $(x^4)^3 = \quad x^{12}$

☐ **Power to a Power Property**                                           **(23)**

To raise a power to a power, multiply the exponents.

For every whole number $m$ and $n$:

$$(a^m)^n = a^{m \cdot n}$$

**Example 1:** $(3^4)^5 = 3^{20}$       **Example 2:** $(y^2)^0 = y^0$ or 1, where $y \neq 0$       **Example 3:** $(r^3)^5 = r^{15}$

☐                             *Study Exercise Six*                              **(24)**

Apply the power to a power property to each of the following.

**Example:** $(7^2)^3 = 7^6$

1. $(10^3)^2$      2. $(x^2)^4$      3. $(4^0)^5$      4. $(r^3)^5$      5. $[(x + y)^2]^5$    6. $[(a^2)^3]^4$

☐ **Sharing Exponents**                                                    **(25)**

**Example 1:**    $(xy)^2 = (xy)(xy)$                      **Example 2:**    $(a^2b^4)^3 = (a^2b^4)(a^2b^4)(a^2b^4)$

                   $(xy)^2 = (x \cdot x)(y \cdot y)$                              $(a^2b^4)^3 = (a^2 \cdot a^2 \cdot a^2)(b^4 \cdot b^4 \cdot b^4)$

                   $(xy)^2 = x^2y^2$                                       $(a^2b^4)^3 = a^6b^{12}$

**Example 3:**    $(x^5y^2)^4 = x^{20}y^8$

☑ **The Distributive Property of Exponents**                            **(26)**

An exponent may be shared, then multiplied times each exponent of a basic product.

For every whole number $m$, $n$, and $p$:

$$(a^m \cdot b^n)^p = a^{m \cdot p} \cdot b^{n \cdot p}$$

**Example 1:**    $(2x)^3 = 2^3x^3$ or $8x^3$

**Example 2:**    $(a^4b^2)^4 = a^{16}b^8$

**Example 3:**    $(3x^3y^5)^2 = 3^2x^6y^{10}$ or $9x^6y^{10}$

**Example 4:**    $(2 + 3)^2 \neq 2^2 + 3^2$      [Incorrect, $25 \neq 13$.]

**Example 5:**    $(x^2 - y^3)^3 \neq x^6 - y^9$      [Incorrect]

*Remember*, an exponent must never be distributed over a basic sum or a basic difference.

*Study Exercise Seven* **(27)**

A.  Apply the distributive property of exponents to each of the following.

**Example:** $(3x^4)^2 = 9x^8$

1. $(2a^5)^2$        2. $(x^2y^4)^3$        3. $(3m^2n^3)^3$        4. $(2x^3y^5z)^3$

B.  Which of the following are incorrect uses of the distributive property of exponents?

5. $(2m^2)^3 = 2m^6$        6. $(3x^4)^2 = 9x^8$        7. $(x+y)^2 = x^2 + y^2$
8. $(x^3 - y^2)^4 = x^{12} - y^8$        9. $(a^2b^3c)^4 = a^8b^{12}c^4$        10. $(x^4y^3)^2 = x^6y^5$

## Properties of Whole Number Exponents                                (28)

1.  **The Zero Power Property:** Any number, except zero, when raised to the zero power is one.

$$x^0 = 1 \quad \text{where} \quad x \neq 0$$

2.  **Addition Property of Exponents:** To multiply exponential expressions with identical bases, add the exponents.

$$a^m \cdot a^n = a^{m+n}$$

3.  **Subtraction Property of Exponents:** To divide exponential expressions with identical bases, subtract the exponents.

$$a^m \div a^n = a^{m-n} \quad \text{or} \quad \frac{a^m}{a^n} = a^{m-n}$$

4.  **Power to a Power Property:** To raise a power to a power, multiply the exponents.

$$(a^m)^n = a^{m \cdot n}$$

5.  **Distributive Property of Exponents:** An exponent may be shared, then multiplied times each exponent of a basic product.

$$(a^m \cdot b^n)^p = a^{m \cdot p} \cdot b^{n \cdot p}$$

## Multiplication and Division of Exponential Expressions                (29)

**Example 1:** $(2a^3) \cdot (3a^4)$

  **Solution:** Use **cpm** and **apm.**

  *line (a)*  $(2a^3) \cdot (3a^4) = (2 \cdot 3) \cdot (a^3 \cdot a^4)$
  *line (b)*  $\qquad\qquad = 6a^7$

**Example 2:** $(2a^3) \cdot (3a^4)$     [A shortcut]

  **Solution:** Multiply numerical coefficients and add the exponents which appear on identical bases.

  Multiply numerical coefficients.

  *line (a)*  $(2a^3) \cdot (3a^4) = 6a^7$

  Add exponents.

## More Examples                                                         (30)

**Example 1:** Multiply $(4x^2y) \cdot (3xy^3)$.

  Multiply numerical coefficients.

  **Solution:** 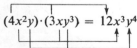 $(4x^2y) \cdot (3xy^3) = 12x^3y^4$

  Add exponents on identical bases.

**Example 2:** Divide $(10a^5) \div (5a^2)$.

Divide numerical coefficients

**Solution:** $(10a^5) \div (5a^2) = 2a^3$

Subtract exponents on identical bases

**Example 3:** Divide $\dfrac{20a^4b^2}{10a^2b}$.

**Solution:** $\dfrac{20a^4b^2}{10a^2b} = 2a^2b$

**Example 4:** Multiply $(2x^3yz)\cdot(6x^2y^4)$.

**Solution:** $(2x^3yz)\cdot(6x^2y^4) = 12x^5y^5z$

**Example 5:** Divide $\dfrac{8m^5n^2}{4m^2n^2}$.

**Solution:** $\dfrac{8m^5n^2}{4m^2n^2} = 2m^3n^0$ or $2m^3$

### Study Exercise Eight (31)

Multiply or divide the following expressions.

1. $3(2a)$
2. $(3x)(4x)$
3. $(2a^2)(5a^3)$
4. $(3x^2y)(2xy^3z)$
5. $(12m^3) \div (3m)$
6. $\dfrac{6x^3}{2x}$
7. $\dfrac{15a^3b^2c}{3ab}$
8. $\dfrac{9m^5n^2}{3m^2n^2}$

## REVIEW EXERCISES

A. Indicate the base and the exponent for each of the following.

1. $3^5$  2. $x^2$  3. $2^x$  4. $3a^4$  5. $(3a)^4$  6. $(x+2y)^3$

B. Write a word statement describing how each of the following would be read.

7. $m^2$  8. $n^3$  9. $(x+y)^5$

C. Change each to exponential notation.

10. $7\cdot7\cdot7\cdot7\cdot7\cdot7$  11. $7\cdot7$  12. $7$
13. $x\cdot x\cdot x\cdot x$  14. $(2a)(2a)(2a)$  15. $2\cdot a\cdot a\cdot a$
16. $x\cdot x\cdot y\cdot y\cdot y$  17. $a\cdot a\cdot b\cdot b\cdot c\cdot c$  18. $(x+3y)(x+3y)(x+3y)$

D. Simplify the following completely (evaluate).

19. $10^0$  20. $3\cdot5^0$  21. $(3\cdot5)^0$  22. $2^3$  23. $(3+5)^2$  24. $3^2+5^2$

E. Apply one of the properties of exponents on each of the following. Identify the property you use.

**Example:** $(2x^3)^2 = 4x^6$ [Distributive Property of Exponents]

25. $a^5\cdot a^4$  26. $x^7 \div x^2$  27. $\dfrac{m^{10}}{m^2}$
28. $b^0$, where $b \neq 0$  29. $(x^3)^5$  30. $(mn)^2$
31. $(x^2y^3)^4$  32. $(x+2)^3\cdot(x+2)^2$

## REVIEW EXERCISES, Contd.

F.　Multiply or divide the following.

| | | | |
|---|---|---|---|
| 33. $5(2x)$ | 34. $(3a)(2a)$ | 35. $(2x^3)(5x^2)$ | 36. $(2a^2b^3c)(4ab^2)$ |
| 37. $10a \div 2$ | 38. $\dfrac{15x}{3}$ | 39. $(8a^2) \div (4a)$ | 40. $\dfrac{12m^2}{3m^2}$ |
| 41. $\dfrac{21x^4y^3z}{7x^2yz}$ | 42. $\dfrac{6mn}{6mn}$ | | |

## Solutions to Review Exercises

A.　1.　Base is 3; exponent is 5.　　2.　Base is $x$; exponent is 2.　　3.　Base is 2; exponent is $x$.
　　4.　Base is $a$; exponent is 4.　　5.　Base is $(3a)$; exponent is 4.　　6.　Base is $(x + 2y)$; exponent is 3.

B.　7.　"$m$ squared" or "$m$ to the second"　　　　　　8.　"$n$ cubed" or "$n$ to the third"
　　9.　"the group $(x + y)$ to the fifth"

C.　10.　$7^6$　　　　11.　$7^2$　　　　12.　$7^1$　　　　13.　$x^4$　　　　14.　$(2a)^3$
　　15.　$2a^3$ or $2^1a^3$　　16.　$x^2y^3$　　　　17.　$a^2b^2c^2$　　18.　$(x + 3y)^3$

D.　19.　1　　　　20.　3　　　　21.　1　　　　22.　8　　　　23.　64　　　　24.　34

E.　25.　$a^9$; Addition Property of Exponents　　　　26.　$x^5$; Subtraction Property of Exponents
　　27.　$m^8$; Subtraction Property of Exponents　　　28.　1; Zero Power Property
　　29.　$x^{15}$; Power to a Power Property　　　　　30.　$m^2n^2$; Distributive Property of Exponents
　　31.　$x^8y^{12}$; Distributive Property of Exponents　32.　$(x + 2)^5$; Addition Property of Exponents

F.　33.　$10x$　　　　34.　$6a^2$　　　　35.　$10x^5$　　　36.　$8a^3b^5c$　　　37.　$5a$
　　38.　$5x$　　　　39.　$2a$　　　　40.　$4m^0$ or 4　　41.　$3x^2y^2z^0$ or $3x^2y^2$　42.　1

## SUPPLEMENTARY PROBLEMS

A.　Indicate the base and the exponent for each of the following.

　　1.　$y^6$　　　2.　$6^y$　　　3.　$5x^2$　　　4.　$(5x)^2$　　　5.　$(x + 4)^5$　　6.　$(3m)^7$

B.　Write a word statement describing how each of these expressions would be read.

　　7.　$y^2$　　　　　　　　8.　$z^3$　　　　　　　9.　$(a + 2b)^6$

C.　Change each to exponential notation.

　　10.　$x \cdot x$　　　　　　11.　$y \cdot y \cdot y \cdot y$　　　　　12.　$3 \cdot 3 \cdot 3 \cdot 3 \cdot 3$
　　13.　$(a + 2)(a + 2)$　　14.　$a \cdot a \cdot a \cdot b \cdot b$　　15.　$(xy)(xy)(xy)$
　　16.　$x \cdot x \cdot y \cdot y \cdot y \cdot z \cdot z$　　17.　$(x + 5y)(x + 5y)$　　18.　$4 \cdot b \cdot b \cdot b \cdot b \cdot b$

D.　Simplify the following completely (evaluate).

　　19.　$5^1$　　　　　　　　20.　$6^0$　　　　　　　21.　$2 \cdot 6^0$
　　22.　$(2 \cdot 6)^0$　　　　　23.　$2^2$　　　　　　　24.　$3^2$
　　25.　$2^3$　　　　　　　　26.　$(2 + 3)^2$　　　　　27.　$2^2 + 3^2$

E.　Each of the following is an identity. Name the property of exponents which each illustrates.

　　28.　$y^0 = 1$, where $y \neq 0$　　　　　　29.　$x^2 \cdot x^4 = x^6$
　　30.　$\dfrac{m^5}{m^2} = m^3$, where $m \neq 0$　　　　31.　$(ab)^3 = a^3b^3$
　　32.　$(2x^2y^3z)^3 = 8x^6y^9z^3$　　　　　　33.　$(a^3)^5 = a^{15}$

F.　Apply one of the properties of exponents on each of the following. Identify the property you use.

**Example:**　$m^5 \cdot m^6 = m^{11}$ [Addition Property of Exponents]

　　34.　$y^9 \div y^2$　　　　　　　　　　　35.　$x^5 \cdot x^3$

## SUPPLEMENTARY PROBLEMS, Contd

36. $\dfrac{a^7}{a}$                      37. $9^0$

38. $(y^2)^6$                   39. $(2x)^3$

40. $(3x^4 \cdot y^5 \cdot z^2)^2$         41. $(m + 3n)^7 \cdot (m + 3n)^4$

G. Multiply or divide the following.

42. $2(3m)$           43. $(2n)(5n)$        44. $(3n^2)(2n^4)$

45. $(3x)(2x^3)(4x^2)$     46. $(2xy^2)(5xy^3)$    47. $(3a^2bc)(2a^4b^2)$

48. $(8m) \div 2$         49. $\dfrac{9x}{3}$            50. $(10a) \div (2a)$

51. $\dfrac{6r}{2r}$              52. $\dfrac{12a^3b^4}{2ab^2}$      53. $\dfrac{24x^5y^7z^4}{12x^2y^5z}$

54. $\dfrac{18m^2n^3}{6m}$        55. $\dfrac{10a^2b^3c^2}{2abc^2}$

H. Calculator Problems. With your instructor's approval, use a calculator to evaluate the following problems.

56. $3^8$              57. $2^{12}$            58. $125^2$

59. $325^3$           60. $3^{15}$           61. $4 \cdot 5^{10}$

62. $8 \cdot 9^4 - 3^5$       63. $(7 \cdot 31)^3$      64. $2 \cdot 4^5 + 3 \cdot 5^6$

65. $3^4 \cdot 2^3 + 5^3 \cdot 6^2$

☐ **Solutions to Study Exercises**                                        **(8A)**

### Study Exercise One (Frame 8)

A. 1. Base is 2; exponent is 5.         2. Base is $(x + y)$; exponent is 2.
    3. Base is $(4x)$; exponent is 3.        4. Base is $(ab)$; exponent is 6.

B. 5. "7 squared" or "7 to the second"     6. "a cubed" or "a to the third"
    7. "the group $(x + y)$ to the sixth"      8. "x to the fifth times y to the twelfth"

☐             ### Study Exercise Two (Frame 12)                **(12A)**

A. 1. $4^3$     2. $5^1$     3. $3x^4$     4. $a^3b^2$     5. $(rs)^3$     6. $(m + n)^4$

B. 7. 9     8. 125     9. 100     10. 8     11. 1000     12. 250
   13. 64     14. 400

☐             ### Study Exercise Three (Frame 15)              **(15A)**

1. $6^0 = 1$                             2. $0^0$ does not represent a number.
3. $(3 \cdot 5)^0 = 1$                      4. $3 \cdot 5^0 = 3 \cdot 1 = 3$
5. $(6 - 6)^0 = 0^0$, but this has no answer.     6. $7 \cdot x^0 = 7 \cdot 1 = 7$

☐             ### Study Exercise Four (Frame 18)                **(18A)**

1. $3^5$     2. $x^8$     3. $a^5b^6$     4. $a^5b^6$     5. $a^{11}$     6. $x^5$     7. $(x + y)^8$     8. $6a^7$

☐             ### Study Exercise Five (Frame 21)                 **(21A)**

1. $10^1$ or 10     2. $3^4$     3. $x^4$     4. $(a + b)^3$     5. $3a^3$     6. $m^3$

☐             ### Study Exercise Six (Frame 24)                 **(24A)**

1. $10^6$     2. $x^8$     3. $4^0$ or 1     4. $r^{15}$     5. $(x + y)^{10}$     6. $a^{24}$

## Solutions to Study Exercises, Contd.

☐                 *Study Exercise Seven (Frame 27)*             **(27A)**

A.   1.  $2^2 \cdot a^{10}$ or $4a^{10}$                                  2.  $x^6 y^{12}$

      3.  $3^3 \cdot m^6 \cdot n^9$ or $27m^6 n^9$                    4.  $2^3 \cdot x^9 \cdot y^{15} \cdot z^3$ or $8x^9 y^{15} z^3$

B.   5.  Incorrect, it should be $8m^6$.                 6.  Correct

      7.  Incorrect, do not share an exponent over a sum.     8.  Incorrect, do not share an exponent over a difference.

      9.  Correct                                  10.  Incorrect, it should be $x^8 y^6$.

☐                 *Study Exercise Eight (Frame 31)*                 **(31A)**

1.  $3(2a) = 6a$       2.  $(3x)(4x) = 12x^2$       3.  $(2a^2)(5a^3) = 10a^5$       4.  $(3x^2 y)(2xy^3 z) = 6x^3 y^4 z$

5.  $(12m^3) \div (3m) = 4m^2$       6.  $\dfrac{6x^3}{2x} = 3x^2$       7.  $\dfrac{15a^3 b^2 c}{3ab} = 5a^2 bc$       8.  $\dfrac{9m^5 n^2}{3m^2 n^2} = 3m^3 n^0$ or $3m^3$

# Module 1 Review Problems

Units 1–5

A.  For problems 1 through 5, use these sets:

   $A = \{a, b, c, d\}$     $B = \{5, 7, 9, 11\}$     $C = \{a, d, i, t, o, n\}$
   $D$ = The set of counting numbers between 1 and 15
   $E$ = The set of letters used to spell the word *addition*
   1.   Which of the above sets are matching?     2.   Which of the above sets are equal?
   3.   True or false: $B \subseteq D$                        4.   Find $A \cup C$.
   5.   Find $A \cap C$.                                 6.   Find $B \cap D$.
   7.   True or false: $C \subseteq A$

B.  Give the check for each of these problems.

   8.   $7 - 2 = 5$                 9.   $2 \cdot 6 = 12$                 10.   $12 \div 4 = 3$

C.  Fill in the blanks.

   11.   In the addition problem, $12 + 10 = 22$, the numbers 12 and 10 are called _____.
   12.   In the subtraction problem, $9 - 3 = 6$, the number 3 is called the _____.
   13.   In the division problem, $\dfrac{15}{3} = 5$, the number 3 is called the _____.

D.  Evaluate the following numeral expressions.

   14.   $24 \div 6 \cdot 2$                              15.   $40 \div 2 - 0 \cdot 5 + 6 \cdot 4 \div 2$
   16.   $5 \cdot (8 - 2)$                            17.   $(6 - 2) \cdot [10 - (8 - 3)]$

E.  Classify each of these numeral expressions as basically a sum, difference, product, or quotient.

   18.   $10 - 2 \cdot 3 + 4$                        19.   $(9 - 1) \cdot (4 + 5)$

F.  Insert grouping symbols to make the following true.

   20.   $12 - 4 \cdot 2 + 3 = 40$                   21.   $12 - 4 \cdot 2 + 3 = 19$

G.  Evaluate the following variable expressions by letting $x = 0$, $y = 5$, and $z = 8$.

   22.   $3x + y + 2z$                             23.   $y(z - x)$

H.  Give a variable expression representing each of these word statements.

   24.   four more than twice a certain number       25.   the number of cents in $x$ quarters

I.  Classify each of these equations as being either an identity or a conditional.

   26.   $3x = 18$            27.   $1 \cdot a = a$            28.   $2(x + 4) = 2x + 8$
   29.   $5x + 2 = 17$        30.   $2y = y + y$            31.   $a + 5 = 5 + a$
   32.   $5m = 0$

J.  Name the fundamental property of equations which justifies each of these statements.

   33.   If $x = 5$, then $5 = x$.                    34.   If $y = 3$, then $2 \cdot y = 2 \cdot 3$.
   35.   If $a = 4$, then $5a + 7$ may be written as $5 \cdot 4 + 7$.

## Module 1 Review Problems, Contd.

Units 1–5

K.  Solve the following equations by inspection.

    36.  $2x = 10$      37.  $x + 4 = 4 + x$      38.  $2n = 0$      39.  $5a + 4 = 14$

L.  Each of these equations illustrates one of the properties of whole numbers. Name the property by giving its abbreviation.

    40.  $3 \cdot (a + b) = 3 \cdot (b + a)$      41.  $3 \cdot (a + b) = (a + b) \cdot 3$
    42.  $(a + 2b) + 3c = a + (2b + 3c)$      43.  $(2x) \cdot 1 = 2x$
    44.  $2(a + b) = 2a + 2b$      45.  $3n + 0 = 3n$

M.  Each of these equations illustrates one of the properties of exponents. Name the property.

    46.  $x^2 \cdot x^5 = x^7$      47.  $(a^2)^4 = a^8$      48.  $\dfrac{m^8}{m^2} = m^6$      49.  $(3x^3y^2)^2 = 9x^6y^4$      50.  $6^0 = 1$

N.  Multiply or divide the following.

    51.  $(2a^3b^2c)(3ab^3)$      52.  $\dfrac{12m^5n^2}{3m^3n^2}$      53.  $(3x^2)(2xy)(5y^2)$      54.  $(6a^3) \div (3a^2)$

## ☐ Answers to Module 1 Review Problems

A.  1.  $A, B$, match and $C, E$ match.    2.  $C = E$        3.  True
    4.  $A \cup C = \{a, b, c, d, i, t, o, n\}$    5.  $A \cap C = \{a, d\}$      6.  $B \cap D = \{5, 7, 9, 11\}$ or $B$
    7.  False

B.  8.  $7 - 2 = 5$ because $5 + 2 = 7$.    9.  $2 \cdot 6 = 12$ because $6 + 6 = 12$.    10.  $12 \div 4 = 3$ because $3 \cdot 4 = 12$.

C.  11.  addends      12.  subtrahend      13.  divisor

D.  14.  8      15.  32      16.  30      17.  20

E.  18.  Basic sum      19.  Basic product

F.  20.  $(12 - 4) \cdot (2 + 3) = 40$      21.  $(12 - 4) \cdot 2 + 3 = 19$

G.  22.  21      23.  40

H.  24.  $2x + 4$      25.  $25x$

I.  26.  Conditional      27.  Identity      28.  Identity
    29.  Conditional      30.  Identity      31.  Identity
    32.  Conditional

J.  33.  Symmetric      34.  Multiplication      35.  Substitution

K.  36.  5      37.  All whole numbers      38.  0      39.  2

L.  40.  **cpa**      41.  **cpm**      42.  **apa**      43.  **Mult. ident.**      44.  **dpma**      45.  **Add. ident.**

M.  46.  Addition Property of Exponents      47.  Power to a Power Property
    48.  Subtraction Property of Exponents      49.  Distributive Property of Exponents
    50.  Zero Power Property

N.  51.  $6a^4b^5c$      52.  $4m^2n^0$ or $4m^2$      53.  $30x^3y^3$      54.  $2a$

# Integers—Operations, Properties, and Equation Solving

# The Integers

☐ **Objectives**  (1)

In this unit we shall develop a new set of numbers called the set of integers. By the end of this unit, you should know the following terms:

- integer.
- positive integer.
- nonnegative integer.

- opposite or additive inverse.
- negative integer.
- absolute value.

☐  (2)

There is no whole number $x$ such that $3 + x = 0$. Thus, for each whole number, $n$, we shall define an *opposite*, $-n$, such that $n + (-n) = 0$.

| $n$ | $-n$ | Sum |
|---|---|---|
| 0 | $-0$  or  0 | $0 + 0 = 0$ |
| 1 | $-1$ | $1 + (-1) = 0$ |
| 2 | $-2$ | $2 + (-2) = 0$ |
| 3 | $-3$ | $3 + (-3) = 0$ |
| 4 | $-4$ | $4 + (-4) = 0$ |
| 5 | $-5$ | $5 + (-5) = 0$ |

☐ **The Set of Integers**  (3)

$I = \{\ldots, -4, -3, -2, -1, 0, 1, 2, 3, 4, \ldots\}$

☐ **Positive Integers**  (4)

Natural numbers may also be called *positive integers*.
**Examples:**
1.  $1 = +1$   2.  $2 = +2$   3.  $68 = +68$

☐ **Negative Integers**  (5)

The opposites of the natural numbers may be called *negative integers*.
**Examples:**
1.  $-1$ is negative one.   2.  $-8$ is negative eight

☐ **Zero**  (6)

Zero is neither positive nor negative.
**Examples:**
1.  $-0$ is 0.   2.  $+0$ is 0.

☐ **Uses of Integers**  (7)

Integers can be used to represent concepts in many fields. For example, we may represent:

A temperature of 15° above zero as $+15°$ or simply 15°.
A temperature of 15° below zero as $-15°$.
A gain of 10 dollars as $+10$ dollars or simply 10 dollars.
A loss of 10 dollars as $-10$ dollars.
20 feet above sea level as $+20$ feet or simply 20 feet.
20 feet below sea level as $-20$ feet.

☐ **Summary** **(8)**

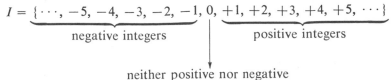

$$I = \{\cdots, -5, -4, -3, -2, -1, \underbrace{\phantom{x}}, 0, \underbrace{+1, +2, +3, +4, +5, \cdots}\}$$

negative integers        positive integers

neither positive nor negative

☐ **The Standard Number Line** **(9)**

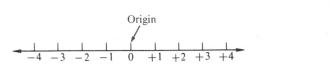

Positive is to the right. Negative is to the left.

☐ **Opposite of a Number** **(10)**

**Example 1:** $-(+3)$

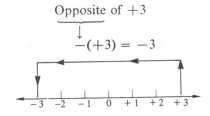

Opposite of $+3$

$$-(+3) = -3$$

**Example 2:** $-(-4)$

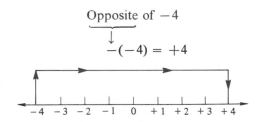

Opposite of $-4$

$$-(-4) = +4$$

☐ **More Examples** **(11)**

**Example 1:** Simplify $-(+8)$.        **Example 2:** Simplify $-(-23)$.

   **Solution:** $-(+8) = -8$          **Solution:** $-(-23) = +23$

**Example 3:** Simplify $+(-13)$.       **Example 4:** Simplify $-(-y)$.

   **Solution:** $+(-13) = -13$        **Solution:** $-(-y) = +y$ or $y$

☐ **Simplifying a Series of Minus Signs** **(12)**

**Example 1:** Simplify $-[-(-2)]$.      **Example 2:** Simplify $-\{-[-(-5)]\}$.

   **Solution:**                          **Solution:**

    *line (a)*   $-[-(-2)]$         *line (a)*   $-\{-[-(-5)]\}$

    *line (b)*   $-[+2]$            *line (b)*   $-\{-[+5]\}$

    *line (c)*   $-2$              *line (c)*   $-\{-5\}$

                                *line (d)*   $+5$

## ☐ Summary of Signs (13)

1. An odd number of minus signs will simplify to a minus sign.

**Example:** $-[-(-9)] = -9$

2. An even number of minus signs will simplify to a plus sign.

**Example:** $-\{-[-(-12)]\} = +12$

## ☐ *Study Exercise One* (14)

A. Fill in the blanks.
   1. The natural numbers may be called _____ integers.
   2. The opposites of the natural numbers may be called _____ integers.
   3. Zero is neither a _____ nor a _____ number.
   4. On the standard number line, positive numbers name points to the _____ of the origin, and negative numbers name points to the _____ of the origin.

B. Simplify the following:
   5. $-(+2)$        6. $-(-3)$        7. $-0$        8. $-(-52)$        9. $-[-(-2)]$

## ☐ The Opposite of a Variable (15)

Let the variable ☐ have the following replacement set: $\{-5, -3, -1\}$. What does $-$☐ represent?

1. $-\boxed{-5} = -(-5)$ or $+5$        2. $-\boxed{-3} = -(-3)$ or $+3$        3. $-\boxed{-1} = -(-1)$ or $+1$

## ☐ Let $x$ have a replacement set of $\{-4, -2, 0, +1, +3\}$. What does $-x$ represent? (16)

| $x$ | $-x$ |
|-----|------|
| $-4$ | $+4$ |
| $-2$ | $+2$ |
| $0$ | $0$ |
| $+1$ | $-1$ |
| $+3$ | $-3$ |

## ☐ An Important Point (17)

"$-x$" does not mean negative number. "$-x$" represents the opposite of whatever number $x$ represents.

**Example 1:** If the replacement set for $y$ is $\{-4, -3, -2, -1\}$, then $-y$ represents $+4, +3, +2,$ or $+1$.

**Example 2:** If the replacement set for $n$ is $\{-10, -5, 0, +2, +8\}$, then $-n$ represents $+10, +5, 0, -2,$ or $-8$.

## ☐ *Study Exercise Two* (18)

1. What numbers does $-x$ represent if the replacement set for $x$ is $\{-12, -9, -1\}$?
2. What numbers does $-y$ represent if the replacement set for $y$ is $\{-19, -6, 0, +1, +3\}$?
3. What numbers does $-z$ represent if the replacement set for $z$ is:
   (a) positive integers?
   (b) negative integers?
   (c) integers?

## ☐ Three Meanings for Minus Sign (19)

1. Subtraction:  $8 - 3$  or  $(+8) - (+3)$
2. Negative number:  $-5$
3. Opposite of:  $-x$

**Example:** $(-3) - (-x)$

$$(-3) \quad - \quad (-x)$$

negative $\downarrow$ opposite
number $\downarrow$ of $x$
subtraction

☐ **Three Meanings for Plus Sign** **(20)**

1. Addition: $8 + 3$ or $(+8) + (+3)$
2. Positive number: $+5$
3. Same as: $+x$ means $x$

**Example:** $(+5) + (+x)$

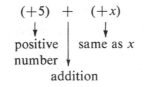

$$(+5) \quad + \quad (+x)$$

positive $\downarrow$ same as $x$
number $\downarrow$
addition

☐            *Study Exercise Three* **(21)**

Each of the signs in the following expressions is labeled above with a letter. Write the meaning for each sign after the corresponding letter.

      a    b    c
1. $(-9) - (-x)$
   (a) _____          (b) _____                 (c) _____       —

      a    b    c
2. $(+1) + (+y)$
   (a) _____          (b) _____                 (c) _____

      a    b
3. $-(-x)$
   (a) _____          (b) _____

      a
4. $x - y$
   (a) _____

      a    b
5. $x + (-y)$
   (a) _____          (b) _____

      a    b
6. $-5 - 6$
   (a) _____          (b) _____

☐ **The Additive Inverse Property (Add. Inv.)** **(22)**

For each integer, $x$, there exists a unique opposite, $-x$, called the *opposite* of $x$ or the *additive inverse* of $x$, such that:

$$x + (-x) = 0$$

Abbreviation: **add. inv.**

**Example 1:** $(+2) + (-2) = 0$          **Example 2:** $2 + (-2) = 0$

**Example 3:** $(-5) + [-(-5)] = 0$       **Example 4:** $-5 + (+5) = 0$

☐ **Ordering the Integers** **(23)**

The standard number line orders the integers.

$$-4 \quad -3 \quad -2 \quad -1 \quad 0 \quad +1 \quad +2 \quad +3 \quad +4$$

"Greater than" means "names a point to the right of . . . ."
"Less than" means "names a point to the left of . . . ."

☐ **Examples** **(24)**

| 1. $+6 > -1$ | 2. $0 > -8$ | 3. $-2 > -10$ |
|---|---|---|
| 4. $+8 < +10$ | 5. $0 < +5$ | 6. $-7 < -2$ |

Notice that the symbols always point towards the smaller number.

☐ **Some Vocabulary** **(25)**

Four statements involving a variable are used quite frequently in algebra, and it is important that you know their meaning:

1. $x > 0$:  read "$x$ is greater than zero."
2. $x \geq 0$:  read "$x$ is greater than or equal to zero."
3. $x < 0$:  read "$x$ is less than zero."
4. $x \leq 0$:  read "$x$ is less than or equal to zero."

☐ *Study Exercise Four* **(26)**

A.  Give the additive inverse or opposite for each of the following:

1. $+3$     2. $5$     3. $-16$     4. $0$     5. $x$     6. $+x$     7. $-x$

B.  Fill in the blank with the correct symbol, $>$ or $<$, to make each statement true.

8. $0$ _____ $+3$          9. $-5$ _____ $+6$          10. $-19$ _____ $-32$
11.  If $x$ represents a negative number, then $x$ _____ $0$.
12.  If $x$ represents a positive number, then $x$ _____ $0$.
13.  If $x$ represents a negative number or perhaps zero, then $x$ _____ $0$.

☐ **Distance** **(27)**

Distance between two points is given by a nonnegative number.

*Nonnegative:*  positive or zero

**(28)**

Origin

$$-4 \quad -3 \quad -2 \quad -1 \quad 0 \quad +1 \quad +2 \quad +3 \quad +4$$

1.  How far from the origin is the point named $+3$?
2.  How far from the origin is the point named $-3$?

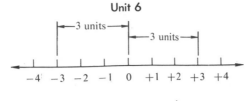

Unit 6

☐ **(29)**

Each point is three units away from the origin.

☐ **Absolute Value** **(30)**

|+3| is read "absolute value of positive three."
|−3| is read "absolute value of negative three."

☐ |+3| asks the question, How far from the origin is the point named by +3? **(31)**
|−3| asks the question, How far from the origin is the point named by −3?

☐ **Examples** **(32)**

1. |+3| = 3 or +3                    2. |−3| = 3 or +3

When evaluating an absolute value, the answer is a nonnegative number.

☐ *Study Exercise Five* **(33)**

A.  What questions do the following ask?
    1.  |+5|                    2.  |−5|                    3.  |0|

B.  Simplify the following completely (evaluate).

**Example:** |−4| = 4
    4.  |+6|          5.  |6|          6.  |−6|          7.  |−17|          8.  |0|

☐ **Some Facts Concerning Absolute Value** **(34)**

1.  The absolute value of a positive number is that number.
$$|+6| = +6$$
    no change

2.  The absolute value of zero is that number.
$$|0| = 0$$
    no change

3.  The absolute value of a negative number is the opposite of that number.
$$|-8| = +8$$
    opposites

☐ **Definition of Absolute Value** **(35)**

1.  $|x| = x$, if $x > 0$                    2.  $|x| = x$, if $x = 0$

3.  $|x| = -x$, if $x < 0$

    opposites                    *Note:*  Remember, $-x$ is a positive number when $x$ is negative.

69

# ☐ Properties of the Integers (36)

If $x$, $y$, and $z$ represent integers, then each of the following is true.

1. Closure Property of Addition (clpa): $x + y$ is an integer
2. Closure Property of Multiplication (clpm): $x \cdot y$ is an integer
3. Commutative Property of Addition (cpa): $x + y = y + x$
4. Commutative Property of Multiplication (cpm): $x \cdot y = y \cdot x$
5. Associative Property of Addition (apa): $(x + y) + z = x + (y + z)$
6. Associative Property of Multiplication (apm): $(x \cdot y) \cdot z = x \cdot (y \cdot z)$
7. Additive Identity Property (add. ident.): $0 + x = x$ and $x + 0 = x$
8. Multiplication Identity Property (mult. ident.): $1 \cdot x = x$ and $x \cdot 1 = x$
9. Additive Inverse Property (add. inv.): $x + (-x) = 0$
10. Multiplication by Zero Property (mult. by 0): $0 \cdot x = 0$ and $x \cdot 0 = 0$
11. Distributive Property of Multiplication With Respect to Addition (dpma): $x(y + z) = xy + xz$ or $(y + z)x = yx + zx$

## REVIEW EXERCISES

A. Give the opposite or additive inverse for each of the following.

| | | | | |
|---|---|---|---|---|
| 1. 3 | 2. $+3$ | 3. $-5$ | 4. 0 | 5. $-21$ |
| 6. $x$ | 7. $-a$ | 8. $6 \cdot 8$ | 9. $10 \div 2$ | 10. $0 \div 6$ |

B. Fill in the blanks so that each of the following is true.

11. $5 +$ _____ $= 0$          12. _____ $+ (-6) = 0$          13. $(-7) +$ _____ $= 0$
14. $|-12| =$ _____          15. $|+12| =$ _____          16. $|12| =$ _____
17. $-|-12| =$ _____          18. _____ $+ |-2| = 0$

C. Draw a standard number line and locate the points named by:

$-8$, $-1$, 5, $+3$, $|-3|$, $-|-4|$

D. Arrange the following in increasing order:

18, $+12$, $-21$, 0, $|-6|$, $-(-5)$

E. State the additive inverse property and give an example.

F. Solve these equation by inspection. The replacement set for each variable is the set of integers.

19. $x + (-3) = 0$          20. $3x + (-6) = 0$          21. $4x + (-12) = 0$
22. $|-4| = x$          23. $|x| = 6$          24. $|x| = -3$
25. $|x + (-18)| = 0$          26. $0 - x = -10$ (Use the subtraction check.)

G. The following are identities over the set of integers. Name the property each illustrates.

27. $(-5 + a) \cdot 0 = 0$          28. $a + (-a) = 0$
29. $-5(-3 + x) = (-5) \cdot (-3) + (-5) \cdot x$          30. $-a + 3 + x = -a + (3 + x)$
31. $-6(-2 + x) = (-2 + x) \cdot (-6)$          32. $[(-3) + (-4) + x] \cdot 1 = (-3) + (-4) + x$
33. $(-6 + a) + 0 = -6 + a$          34. $(-6 + a) + 0 = 0 + (-6 + a)$
35. $-x \cdot 2 + (-x) \cdot (-3) = -x[2 + (-3)]$          36. $(-8) \cdot (-10)$ is an integer.

## REVIEW EXERCISES, Contd.

H. In the following expression each sign is labeled with a letter. Give the meaning of each sign.

$$\overset{a\quad b\quad c\quad\quad d\quad\quad e\quad\quad f\quad\quad g\quad h}{-3 + (-x) - 5 - (+y) + (+3)}$$

I. True or False

37. $+3 = 3$
38. Each natural number is also a positive integer
39. $-(-6) = +6$
40. For every integer, $x$, $-(-x) = x$.
41. If $a < 0$, $|a| = a$.

## Solutions to Review Exercises

A. 1. $-3$    2. $-3$    3. $5$ or $-(-5)$    4. $0$    5. $+21$
   6. $-x$    7. $a$ or $-(-a)$    8. $-48$    9. $-5$    10. $0$

B. 11. $-5$   12. $+6$   13. $+7$   14. $+12$   15. $+12$   16. $+12$   17. $-12$   18. $-2$

C.

D. $-21, 0, -(-5), |-6|, +12, 18$

E. For each integer, $x$, there exists a unique opposite, $-x$, such that $x + (-x) = 0$.

**Example:** $5 + (-5) = 0$

F. 19. $3$    20. $2$    21. $3$    22. $4$    23. $6, -6$
   24. no solutions   25. $18$   26. $10$

G. 27. **mult. by 0**   28. **add. inv.**   29. **dpma**   30. **apa**   31. **cpm**
   32. **mult. ident.**   33. **add. ident.**   34. **cpa**   35. **dpma**   36. **clpm**

H. (a) negative or opposite   (b) addition   (c) opposite of   (d) subtract
   (e) subtract   (f) same as   (g) addition   (h) positive or same as

I. 37. True    38. True    39. True
   40. True    41. False, if $a < 0$, $|a| = -a$.

## SUPPLEMENTARY PROBLEMS

A. Classify the following integers as positive, negative, or neither.

1. $+8$
2. $-3$
3. $0$
4. $23$

B. Fill in the blanks.

5. If $+50$ means 50 miles north, then $-50$ means 50 miles _____.
6. If $+15$ means the temperature has increased 15 degrees, then $-15$ means the temperature has _____ 15 degrees.
7. If 25 means you have a gain of 25 dollars, then $-25$ means you have a _____ of 25 dollars.

C. On the standard number line below, several points are labeled with uppercase letters. Give the correct number that belongs at each letter.

8. Give the correct number for $A$.
9. Give the correct number for $B$.
10. Give the correct number for $C$.
11. Give the correct number for $D$.
12. Give the correct number for $E$.

SUPPLEMENTARY PROBLEMS, Contd.

D.   Write the additive inverse or opposite for each of the following.

13.   +2                 14.   −3                 15.   0                 16.   12

E.   Simplify each of the following expressions.

17.   $-(-7)$                18.   $-(+4)$                19.   $-(-1)$                20.   $-[-(-12)]$
21.   $-[-(+1)]$             22.   $-0$                   23.   $-(-a)$                24.   $-(+b)$
25.   $-\{-[-(-13)]\}$        26.   $(+2) + (-2)$          27.   $8 + (-8)$             28.   $0 + 0$
29.   $(-9) + [-(-9)]$        30.   $|-5|$                 31.   $|+12|$                32.   $|0|$
33.   $|23|$                 34.   $|a|$ if $a < 0$

F.   Complete the following table.

|      | If x equals: | Then −x equals: |
|------|--------------|-----------------|
| 35.  | +20          |                 |
| 36.  | 13           |                 |
| 37.  | 0            |                 |
| 38.  | −1           |                 |
| 39.  | −10          |                 |
| 40.  | −30          |                 |

G.   True or False

41.   $0 > -3$              42.   $0 < -16$             43.   $+5 > -6$             44.   $-14 > -10$
45.   $-200 > 100$          46.   $-1 = 1$              47.   $+8 = 8$               48.   $|-5| = -5$
49.   $|+8| = |-8|$
50.   If $y$ represents a negative number, then $y < 0$.
51.   If $b$ represents a positive number or possibly zero, then $b \geq 0$.
52.   $-x$ always represents negative numbers.

H.   Solve these equations by inspection. The replacement set for each variable is the set of integers.

53.   $x + (-7) = 0$          54.   $x + (-8) = -8$          55.   $x + 3 = 0$
56.   $|-6| = x$              57.   $|x| = 10$               58.   $|x + (-2)| = 0$
59.   $|x + 3| = 0$           60.   $5x + (-10) = 0$         61.   $6 \cdot x + (-12) = 0$
62.   $|x| = -8$

I.   In the following expression each sign is labeled with a letter. Give the meaning of each sign.

$$\overset{a}{-}x \overset{b}{+} (\overset{c}{-}2) \overset{d}{-} (\overset{e}{+}y) \overset{f}{+} (\overset{g}{+}5)$$

☐ Solutions to Study Exercises                                                        (14A)

### Study Exercise One (Frame 14)

A.   1.   positive              2.   negative              3.   positive, negative              4.   right, left
B.   5.   $-2$          6.   $+3$ or $3$          7.   0          8.   $+52$ or $52$          9.   $-2$

☐                        ### Study Exercise Two (Frame 18)                               (18A)

1.   $-x$ represents $\{+12, +9, +1\}$.                    2.   $-y$ represents $\{+19, +6, 0, -1, -3\}$.
3.   (a)   $-z$ represents negative integers.     (b)   $-z$ represents positive integers.     (c)   $-z$ represents integers.

## Solutions to Study Exercises, Contd.

### Study Exercise Three (Frame 21)         (21A)

1. (a) negative or opposite     (b) subtraction     (c) opposite of
2. (a) positive or same as     (b) addition     (c) same as
3. (a) opposite of     (b) opposite of
4. (a) subtraction
5. (a) addition     (b) opposite of
6. (a) negative or opposite     (b) subtraction

### Study Exercise Four (Frame 26)         (26A)

A. 1. $-3$     2. $-5$     3. $+16$ or $16$     4. $0$
   5. $-x$     6. $-x$     7. $+x$ or $x$

B. 8. $0 < 13$     9. $-5 < +6$     10. $-19 > -32$
   11. $x < 0$     12. $x > 0$     13. $x \leqq 0$

### Study Exercise Five (Frame 33)         (33A)

A. 1. How far from the origin is the point named by $+5$?
   2. How far from the origin is the point named by $-5$?
   3. How far from the origin is the origin?

B. 4. $+6$ or $6$     5. $+6$ or $6$     6. $+6$ or $6$     7. $+17$ or $17$     8. $0$

# Addition and Subtraction of Integers

☐ **Objectives**　　　　　　　　　　　　　　　　　　　　　　　　　　　　　**(1)**

By the end of this unit, you should be able to:

- add any two integers.
- convert basic differences to basic sums.
- subtract any two integers.
- show that addition and subtraction of integers are closed.

☐ Select any two integers, $a$ and $b$. Then exactly one of the following is true:　　**(2)**

1. At least one of the integers is zero.　　　2. The integers have the same sign.
3. The integers have opposite signs.

☐ **Three Major Cases for Adding Integers**　　　　　　　　　　　　　　　**(3)**

**Case 1:** $a + 0$, such as $(+3) + 0$
**Case 2:** $a + b$, where $a$ and $b$ have the same sign, such as $(+2) + (+3)$ or $(-2) + (-3)$
**Case 3:** $a + b$, where $a$ and $b$ have opposite signs, such as $(+5) + (-3)$ or $(-5) + (+3)$

☐ **Case One**　　　　　　　　　　　　　　　　　　　　　　　　　　　　　**(4)**

$$a + 0 \quad \text{where } a \text{ is any integer}$$

The additive identity property states that $a + 0 = a$, so:

1. $(+3) + 0 = +3$　　2. $(-3) + 0 = -3$　　3. $0 + (-5) = -5$　　4. $0 + 0 = 0$

☐　　　　　　　　　　　　　　*Study Exercise One*　　　　　　　　　　　　**(5)**

Perform the following additions:

1. $5 + 0$　　　　　2. $(+5) + 0$　　　　3. $(-5) + 0$　　　　4. $(-8) + 0$
5. $0 + (-19)$　　　6. $x + 0$　　　　　7. $-x + 0$

☐ **Case Two**　　　　　　　　　　　　　　　　　　　　　　　　　　　　　**(6)**

$$a + b \quad \text{where } a \text{ and } b \text{ have the same sign}$$

**Example 1:** $(+2) + (+3)$　　　　　　　　**Example 2:** $(-2) + (-3)$

☐ **Example 1:** Addition of $+2$ and $+3$ by the standard number line:　　　　**(7)**

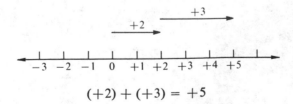

$$(+2) + (+3) = +5$$

☐ **Example 2:** Addition of $-2$ and $-3$ by the standard number line:　　　　**(8)**

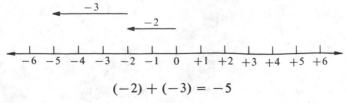

$$(-2) + (-3) = -5$$

76

☐ **(9)**

When adding two positive or two negative integers, add the absolute values and use the common sign.

1.  $(+8) + (+9) = +17$                    2.  $(-6) + (-12) = -18$

☐                                                    *Study Exercise Two*                                            **(10)**

Perform the following additions.

1.  $(+1) + (+3)$        2.  $1 + 3$        3.  $(+6) + 7$        4.  $(-8) + (-3)$        5.  $(-10) + (-5)$

☐ **Case Three**                                                                                            **(11)**

$$a + b \quad \text{where } a \text{ and } b \text{ have opposite signs}$$

**Example 1:**  $(+5) + (-3)$                              **Example 2:**  $(-5) + (+3)$

☐ **Example 1:**   Addition of $+5$ and $-3$ by the standard number line:                    **(12)**

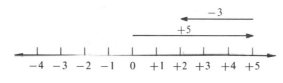

$$(+5) + (-3) = +2$$

The sum is positive, because $|+5| > |-3|$.

☐ **Example 2:**   Addition of $-5$ and $+3$ by the standard number line:                    **(13)**

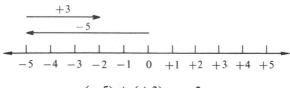

$$(-5) + (+3) = -2$$

The sum is negative, because $|-5| > |+3|$.

☐ To find the sum of two integers with opposite signs:                                        **(14)**

*Step (1):*   Find their absolute values.
*Step (2):*   Take the smaller absolute value from the larger absolute value.
*Step (3):*   Use the sign of the number having the greater absolute value.

☐ **Example:**  $(+5) + (-3)$                                                                    **(15)**

*Step (1):*   The absolute values are 5 and 3.
*Step (2):*   Take 3 from 5 to obtain 2.
*Step (3):*   The sum is positive, since $|+5| > |-3|$.
                   So, $(+5) + (-3) = +2$ or 2.

☐ **Example:**  $(-5) + (+3)$                                                                    **(16)**

*Step (1):*   The absolute values are 5 and 3.
*Step (2):*   Take 3 from 5 to obtain 2.
*Step (3):*   The sum is negative, since $|-5| > |+3|$.
                   So, $(-5) + (+3) = -2$.

☐ **Example:** $(+23) + (-68)$ **(17)**

*Step (1):* The absolute values are 23 and 68.
*Step (2):* Take 23 from 68 to obtain 45.
*Step (3):* The sum is negative, since $|-68| > |+23|$.

So, $(+23) + (-68) = -45$.

☐ *Study Exercise Three* **(18)**

Perform the following additions:

1. $(-8) + (+2)$　　2. $(-8) + 2$　　3. $(-1) + (+9)$　　4. $(+28) + (-16)$　　5. $(-36) + (+9)$

☐ **Review of the Rules for Addition of Integers** **(19)**

**Case 1:** $a + 0 = a$
**Case 2:** If the two integers have the same signs, add the absolute values and use the common sign.
**Case 3:** If the two integers have opposite signs, take the smaller absolute value from the larger and use the sign of the number with the greater absolute value.

☐ *Study Exercise Four* **(20)**

Perform the following additions:

1. $(-8) + 0$　　　2. $5 + 0$　　　3. $(+12) + (+15)$　　4. $(-18) + (-12)$
5. $(+15) + (-9)$　6. $(-15) + (+9)$　7. $(-62) + 12$　　8. $17 + (-5)$
9. $(+8) + (-15)$　10. $(-8) + (-15)$

☐ **Adding Expressions Containing More Than Two Addends** **(21)**

**Example 1:** $(-5) + (+8) + (-6)$

Method 1: By using the order of operations convention:
$$(-5) + (+8) + (-6)$$
$$\downarrow$$
$$+3 + (-6)$$
$$\downarrow$$
$$-3$$

Method 2: **Cpa** and **apa** allow you to add in any order:

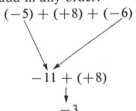

$$-11 + (+8)$$
$$\downarrow$$
$$-3$$

**Example 2:** $(-8) + (+4) + (+8) + (-4)$

Method 1: By using the order of operations convention:
$$(-8) + (+4) + (+8) + (-4)$$
$$\downarrow$$
$$(-4) + (+8) + (-4)$$
$$\downarrow$$
$$(+4) + (-4)$$
$$\downarrow$$
$$0$$

Method 2:   **Cpa** and **apa** allow you to add in any order:

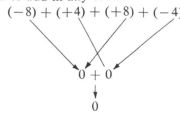

$$(-8) + (+4) + (+8) + (-4)$$

$$0 + 0$$

$$0$$

## ☐ An Important Point                                                                 (22)

When all operations are addition, the addition signs may be left out.

**Example 1:**   $(-12) + (+5) + (+12) + (-5)$        **Example 2:**   $(+8) + (-12) + (+7) + (-3)$

   **Solution:**   $-12 + 5 + 12 - 5 = 0$             **Solution:**   $8 - 12 + 7 - 3 = 0$

## ☐                                         *Study Exercise Five*                        (23)

Simplify completely by performing the following additions in any order you wish:

1. $(+3) + (-8) + (+1)$                     2. $3 + (-8) + 1$
3. $(-8) + (+2) + (-2) + (+8)$             4. $(+1) + (-15) + (-3) + (-6)$
5. $3 - 2 + 9 - 4$                          6. $-1 - 2 - 3 - 4 - 5$

## ☐ Subtraction of Integers                                                            (24)

We now wish to develop a method of subtracting two integers. We will do this by finding a pattern which will convert each subtraction problem into an addition problem. This will enable us to *use the rules of addition to work subtraction problems*.

## ☐                                                                                    (25)

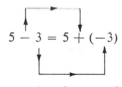

$$5 - 3 = 2 \qquad 5 + (-3) = 2$$

basic difference      basic sum

So, $5 - 3 = 5 + (-3)$.

## ☐                                                                                    (26)

difference to a sum

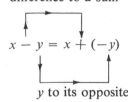

$$5 - 3 = 5 + (-3)$$

3 to its opposite

The minuend, 5, is not changed.

## ☐ The Pattern for Changing a Difference to a Sum                                      (27)

difference to a sum

$$x - y = x + (-y)$$

$y$ to its opposite

1. Subtraction is changed to addition.        2. The subtrahend is changed to its opposite.
3. The minuend is not changed.

☐ **Converting from a Difference to a Sum** **(28)**

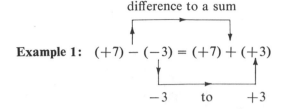

**Example 1:** $(+7) - (-3) = (+7) + (+3)$

$-3 \quad$ to $\quad +3$

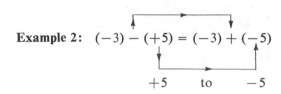

**Example 2:** $(-3) - (+5) = (-3) + (-5)$

$+5 \quad$ to $\quad -5$

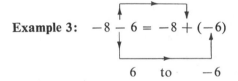

**Example 3:** $-8 - 6 = -8 + (-6)$

$6 \quad$ to $\quad -6$

**Example 4:** $8 - (-10) = 8 + 10$

$-10 \quad$ to $\quad 10$

☐ **The Subtraction Property** **(29)**

For every integer $a$, $b$:

$$a - b = a + (-b)$$

basic difference $\qquad$ basic sum

Subtraction means "add the opposite."

☐ **Proof** **(30)**

We will prove that $a - b = a + (-b)$ always generates true equations by showing that the answer, $a + (-b)$, added to the subtrahend, $b$, will produce the minuend, $a$.

1. $[a + (-b)] + b = a + [(-b) + b]$     **(apa)**
2. $\qquad\qquad\quad = a + 0$     **(add. inv.)**
3. $\qquad\qquad\quad = a$     **(add. ident.)**

Therefore,

$$[a + (-b)] + b = a$$

answer + subtrahend = minuend

80

Convert each of the following basic differences to basic sums:

1. $(+6) - (+2)$    2. $6 - 2$        3. $(-5) - (-4)$    4. $(+10) - (-12)$
5. $(-1) - (-7)$    6. $13 - 18$      7. $-3 - 10$        8. $x - y$
9. $r - (-w)$       10. $-t - y$

☐ To completely simplify a basic difference:                          (32)

*Step (1):*   Convert the difference to a sum.
*Step (2):*   Use the previous rules of addition.

☐ **Examples of Subtraction**                                          (33)

**Example 1:**   $(+6) - (+8)$

*Step (1):*   $(+6) - (+8) = +6 + (-8)$

*Step (2):*   $+6 + (-8) = -2$
So, $(+6) - (+8) = -2$.

**Example 2:**   $(-3) - (-12)$

*Step (1):*   $(-3) - (-12) = -3 + (+12)$

*Step (2):*   $-3 + (+12) = +9$
So, $(-3) - (-12) = +9$.

**Example 3:**   $-13 - 10$

*Step (1):*   $-13 - 10 = -13 + (-10)$

*Step (2):*   $-13 + (-10) = -23$
So, $-13 - 10 = -23$.

Simplify completely each of the following.

1. $(+5) - (+9)$    2. $5 - 9$        3. $(-8) - (-15)$    4. $-12 - 7$
5. $0 - (-2)$       6. $25 - (-32)$   7. $15 - 12$         8. $(-3) - 0$
9. $(+14) - 25$     10. $(-38) - (-2)$

☐ **Subtracting Expressions Containing More Than Two Terms**          (35)

**Example 1:**   $(-8) - (-2) - (+4)$
$$\downarrow \quad \downarrow \quad \downarrow \quad \downarrow$$
$$(-8) + (+2) + (-4)$$

Then add in any order, obtaining $-10$.

**Example 2:**   $(-11) - (+4) - (-8) - 6$
$$\downarrow \quad \downarrow \quad \downarrow \quad \downarrow$$
$$(-11) + (-4) + (+8) + (-6)$$

Then add in any order, obtaining $-13$.

☐                    *Study Exercise Eight*                    **(36)**

Simplify completely each of the following.

1. $(-5) - (-2) - (-1)$            2. $(+8) - (+6) - (-12) - (-1)$
3. $6 - 10 - (-5) - (-4)$            4. $0 - 3 - (-2) - 12 - 8 - (-13)$

## ☐ Expressions Involving Both Subtraction and Addition     **(37)**

**Example 1:** $(-3) - (-6) + (+4)$

Do not change signs of addends!

$(-3) + (+6) + (+4)$

Then add in any order to obtain $+7$.

**Example 2:** $5 + (-8) + (-2) - 6 + 8 - (-3)$

$5 + (-8) + (-2) + (-6) + 8 + (+3)$

Then add in any order to obtain $0$.

## ☐ A Useful Shortcut     **(38)**

Sometimes expressions are written with the positive signs omitted. For example, $2 - 5 + 6$ means $(+2) - (+5) + (+6)$:

$$2 - 5 + 6 = (+2) - (+5) + (+6)$$
$$= (+2) + (-5) + (+6)$$
$$= +3$$

However, by simply "thinking addition," the subtraction is automatically converted to addition:

think addition

$$2 - 5 + 6 = 2 \oplus -5 \oplus +6 \quad \left[ \begin{array}{c} \text{try to do this step} \\ \text{in your head} \end{array} \right]$$
$$= +3$$

## ☐ More Illustrations     **(39)**

**Example 1:** Evaluate $8 - 12$

**Solution:** "Think addition."

$$8 - 12 = 8 \oplus -12$$
$$= -4$$

**Example 2:** Evaluate $3 - 5 - 1 + 2$

**Solution:** "Think addition"; then add in any order.

$$3 - 5 - 1 + 2 = 3 \oplus -5 \oplus -1 \oplus +2$$
$$= -1$$

☐                    *Study Exercise Nine*                    **(40)**

A. Simplify the following completely. Do not use the shortcut.

1. $-8 - (-2) + (+4)$            2. $7 - (+3) + (-6) - (-2)$
3. $0 - 3 + 5 - 8 - (-2)$            4. $1 - 5 - 7 + 10 - 6$

B.  Simplify the following completely. You may use the shortcut.

5.  $8 - 5 - 7$

6.  $4 - 7 - 1 + 9$

7.  $5 + 6 - 5 - 6$

8.  $10 - 2 - 11 - 5 - 7$

## □ Important Points                                                      (41)

1.  Subtraction problems are converted to addition problems in order that the commutative and associative properties of addition may be used.
2.  Addition and subtraction are closed for the set of integers.
3.  The pattern, $a - b = a + (-b)$, which converts differences to sums, may also be used to convert sums to differences.

**Example 1:** $x + (-y) = x - y$          **Example 2:** $a + (-3) = a - 3$

**Example 3:** $4 + (-x) = 4 - x$          **Example 4:** $3x^2 + [-(2x)] = 3x^2 - 2x$

## REVIEW EXERCISES

A.  Using the standard number line, show that:

1.  $(+2) + (+3) = +5$

2.  $(-2) + (-3) = -5$

3.  $(+5) + (-3) = +2$

4.  $(-5) + (+3) = -2$

B.  State the three rules for adding any two integers.

C.  Perform the following additions. (Simplify completely.)

5.  $(-7) + 0$

6.  $(+8) + (+3)$

7.  $8 + 3$

8.  $(-9) + (-7)$

9.  $(-3) + (+9)$

10.  $(-8) + (+2)$

11.  $0 + (+2)$

12.  $(-2) + (+3) + (-3) + (+2)$

13.  $-1 + 5 - 3 + 4 - 8 - 3$

14.  $32 - 7 - 21 + 14 - 62$

D.  Using the pattern, $a - b = a + (-b)$, convert each basic difference to a basic sum. (Do not simplify.)

15.  $(+3) - (+8)$     16.  $3 - 8$     17.  $(-2) - (-3)$     18.  $x - y$     19.  $r - (-t)$

E.  Perform the following subtractions. (Simplify completely.)

20.  $(+3) - (+8)$

21.  $3 - 8$

22.  $(-2) - (-3)$

23.  $5 - (-7)$

24.  $13 - (-2)$

25.  $-9 - (+15)$

26.  $(-2) - (+4) - (-5) - (-6)$

27.  $0 - (-3) - 7$

28.  $4 - 8 - 9 - 1$

29.  $(-3) - (-2) - 5 - (+3) - 2$

F.  Simplify completely.

30.  $(-2) + (-6) - (-7) - (+8)$

31.  $3 - 8 + 9 - 10$

32.  $4 + (-10) + (-12) - (-12) - (-10) + (-4)$

33.  $-63 - 52 + (-16) - (-43)$

G.  Using the reverse of the pattern, $a - b = a + (-b)$, convert each basic sum to a basic difference.

34.  $x + (-5)$          35.  $(-r) + (-x)$          36.  $5x^2 + (-2x) + (-6)$

## REVIEW EXERCISES, Contd.

H.   True or False

   37.   $-5 + (+3)$ represents a negative number, because $|-5| > |+3|$.
   38.   Addition of positive integers is the same as addition of natural numbers.
   39.   Subtraction is usually converted to addition, in order that the commutative and associative properties may be used.

## Solutions to Review Exercises

A.   1.   See Frame 7.          2.   See Frame 8.          3.   See Frame 12.          4.   See Frame 13.

B.   See Frame 19.

C.   5.   $-7$          6.   $+11$ or 11          7.   $+11$ or 11          8.   $-16$          9.   $+6$ or 6
     10.   $-6$          11.   $+2$ or 2          12.   0          13.   $-6$          14.   $-44$

D.   15.   $(+3) + (-8)$          16.   $3 + (-8)$          17.   $-2 + (+3)$ or $-2 + 3$
     18.   $x + (-y)$          19.   $r + (+t)$ or $r + t$

E.   20.   $-5$          21.   $-5$          22.   $+1$ or 1          23.   $+12$ or 12          24.   $+15$
     25.   $-24$          26.   5          27.   $-4$          28.   $-14$          29.   $-11$

F.   30.   $-9$          31.   $-6$          32.   $0$          33.   $-88$

G.   34.   $x - (+5)$ or $x - 5$          35.   $-r - (+x)$ or $-r - x$
     36.   $5x^2 - [+(2x)] - (+6)$ or $5x^2 - 2x - 6$

H.   37.   True
     38.   True, positive integers are the same as natural numbers.
     39.   True, addition is commutative and associative, but subtraction is not.

## SUPPLEMENTARY PROBLEMS

A.   Use the standard number line to show:

   1.   $(+3) + (+4) = +7$          2.   $(-2) + (-7) = -9$
   3.   $(-3) + (+5) = +2$          4.   $(+3) + (-5) = -2$

B.   Simplify the following completely.

   5.   $(+3) + (+8)$          6.   $(-3) + (-8)$
   7.   $10 + (-2)$          8.   $(-10) + 2$
   9.   $(-6) - (-3)$          10.   $(+8) - (-10)$
   11.   $(-2) - (+3)$          12.   $18 - 24$
   13.   $2 + (-6) + (-8) - 10$          14.   $-6 + 7 - 13 + 1 - 0 + (-3)$
   15.   $-5 - 6 - 7 - 8$          16.   $(-2) + (+8) - (-2) - 8$
   17.   $0 - (-2) + (-3) - (+6) + (+3)$          18.   $-23 - 108 + 23 - 5 + 108$

C.   Convert each of the following differences to basic sums.

   19.   $x - y$          20.   $x - (-y)$          21.   $5x^2 - 3$          22.   $(-3a) - (-2a)$          23.   $6x^3 - 5x^3$

D.   Convert each of the following sums to basic differences.

   24.   $x + (-y)$          25.   $5x^2 + [-(2x)]$          26.   $3a + (-a) + (-4)$

E.   Complete each sentence.

   27.   If $x$ and $y$ represent positive integers, then $x + y$ represents a _____ integer.
   28.   If $x$ and $y$ represent negative integers, then $x + y$ represents a _____ integer.
   29.   If $x > 0$, $y < 0$, and $|y| > |x|$, then $x + y$ represents a _____ integer.
   30.   If $x$ and $y$ represent negative integers, and $|y| > |x|$, then $x - y$ represents a _____ integer.

## SUPPLEMENTARY PROBLEMS, Contd.

F.   Fill in the blanks with an integer, so that each is a true equation.

31.  _____ $+ 8 = -5$             32.  _____ $- 7 = 6$
33.  $-5 +$ _____ $= 11$          34.  $2 +$ _____ $= -8$
35.  $-5 -$ _____ $= 17$          36.  $2 + (-8) =$ _____
37.  $-5 - (-7) =$ _____          38.  _____ $- 3 + (-6) = 7$
39.  $-2 +$ _____ $- 5 = -14$     40.  $-6 - (-4 + 7) =$ _____

G.   Simplify the following completely.

41.  $(+8) + (-8)$                42.  $12 - 10 + 8 + 2 - 6 - 6$
43.  $0 + (-6)$                   44.  $(-2) - (-5)$
45.  $0 + 0$                      46.  $(+10) - (-3)$
47.  $(-5) + (-5)$                48.  $(+8) - (+4)$
49.  $(-2) + (-7)$                50.  $(+12) - (+20)$
51.  $(+10) + (-18)$              52.  $(-13) - (-12) - (-5)$
53.  $(+23) + (-5)$               54.  $(+5) - (-2) - (+4)$
55.  $(-6) + (-8) + (+7)$         56.  $(-6) + (+8) - (-10)$
57.  $(+1) + (-1) + (-2)$         58.  $(+1) - (-7) + (+12) - (-8)$
59.  $2 - 3 + 5 - 6$              60.  $-7 + 8 - 2 - 3 + 5$

H.   Calculator Problems. With your instructor's approval, use a calculator to evaluate the following expressions.

61.  $86 + (-295) + 624$
62.  $2,048 - 6,025 - 3,098$
63.  $-29,472 + 6,927 - 12,098 + 18,647$
64.  $8,095 - [12,604 + 16,908 - (24,899 - 9,087)]$
65.  $(20,647 - 82,912) - (62,498 - 104,297)$

□ Solutions to Study Exercises                                    (5A)

### Study Exercise One (Frame 5)

1.  $+5$ or $5$     2.  $+5$ or $5$     3.  $-5$     4.  $-8$     5.  $-19$     6.  $x$     7.  $-x$

□                         Study Exercise Two (Frame 10)              (10A)

1.  $+4$ or $4$     2.  $+4$ or $4$     3.  $+13$ or $13$     4.  $-11$     5.  $-15$

□                         Study Exercise Three (Frame 18)            (18A)

1.  $-6$     2.  $-6$     3.  $+8$ or $8$     4.  $+12$ or $12$     5.  $-27$

□                         Study Exercise Four (Frame 20)             (20A)

1.  $-8$     2.  $+5$ or $5$     3.  $+27$ or $27$     4.  $-30$     5.  $+6$ or $6$
6.  $-6$     7.  $-50$          8.  $+12$ or $12$      9.  $-7$      10.  $-23$

□                         Study Exercise Five (Frame 23)             (23A)

1.  $-4$     2.  $-4$     3.  $0$     4.  $-23$     5.  $+6$ or $6$     6.  $-15$

## Solutions to Study Exercises, Contd.

☐ *Study Exercise Six (Frame 31)* **(31A)**

1. $(+6) + (-2)$ or $6 + (-2)$    2. $6 + (-2)$    3. $-5 + (+4)$ or $-5 + 4$
4. $(+10) + (+12)$ or $10 + 12$    5. $-1 + (+7)$ or $-1 + 7$    6. $13 + (-18)$
7. $-3 + (-10)$    8. $x + (-y)$    9. $r + (+w)$ or $r + w$
10. $-t + (-y)$

☐ *Study Exercise Seven (Frame 34)* **(34A)**

1. $-4$    2. $-4$    3. $+7$    4. $-19$    5. $+2$
6. $57$    7. $3$    8. $-3$    9. $-11$    10. $-36$

☐ *Study Exercise Eight (Frame 36)* **(36A)**

1. $-2$    2. $15$    3. $+5$    4. $-8$

☐ *Study Exercise Nine (Frame 40)* **(40A)**

A. 1. $-2$    2. $0$    3. $-4$    4. $(-7)$
B. 5. $-4$    6. $5$    7. $0$    8. $-15$

# Multiplication and Division of Integers

☐ **Objectives** **(1)**

By the end of this unit, you should be able to:

- multiply any two integers.
- divide two integers, when the quotient is an integer.
- show that multiplication of integers is closed.
- show that division of integers is not closed.

☐ Select any two integers, $a$ and $b$. Then exactly one of the following is true: **(2)**
1. At least one of the integers is zero.   2.   The integers have opposite signs.
3. The integers have the same sign.

☐ **Three Cases for Multiplying Integers** **(3)**

**Case 1:** $a \cdot 0$, such as $(+5) \cdot 0$

**Case 2:** $a \cdot b$, where $a$ and $b$ have opposite signs, such as $(+3) \cdot (-2)$ or $(-4) \cdot (+2)$

**Case 3:** $a \cdot b$, where $a$ and $b$ have the same signs, such as $(+3) \cdot (+2)$ or $(-3) \cdot (-2)$

☐ **Case One** **(4)**

$$a \cdot 0 \quad \text{where } a \text{ is any integer}$$

The multiplication by zero property states that:

$$a \cdot 0 = 0$$

**Examples:**

1. $(+5) \cdot 0 = 0$      2. $(-5) \cdot 0 = 0$      3. $0 \cdot (-2) = 0$      4. $0 \cdot 0 = 0$

☐                   *Study Exercise One* **(5)**

Perform the following multiplications.

1. $(+7) \cdot 0$    2. $7 \cdot 0$    3. $(-7) \cdot 0$    4. $0 \cdot (-19)$    5. $0 \cdot 0$    6. $x \cdot 0$    7. $(-x) \cdot 0$

☐ **Case Two** **(6)**

$$a \cdot b \quad \text{where } a \text{ and } b \text{ have opposite signs}$$

**Example 1:** $(+3) \cdot (-2)$             **Example 2:** $(-4) \cdot (+2)$

☐ **Example 1:** Multiplication of $(+3) \cdot (-2)$ by the standard number line: **(7)**

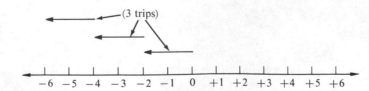

1. Start at the origin, 0.
2. Take three trips.
3. Each trip goes 2 units in the negative direction.

Hence, $(+3) \cdot (-2) = -6$.

**(8)**

**Example 2:** Multiplication of $(-4)\cdot(+2)$ by the standard number line. By **cpm**, $(-4)\cdot(+2) = (+2)\cdot(-4)$:

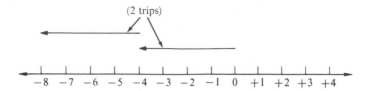

1. Start at the origin, 0.
2. Take two trips.
3. Each trip goes 4 units in the negative direction.

Hence, $(-4)\cdot(+2) = -8$

**(9)**

When multiplying a positive and a negative integer, multiply the absolute values and make the product negative.

**Example 1:** $(+6)\cdot(-3) = -18$          **Example 2:** $(-5)\cdot(+8) = -40$

*Study Exercise Two*      **(10)**

Perform the following multiplications:

1. $(+7)\cdot(-3)$     2. $7\cdot(-3)$     3. $(-10)\cdot(+3)$     4. $(-12)\cdot(+6)$     5. $4\cdot(-16)$

## Case Three **(11)**

$$a\cdot b \quad \text{where } a \text{ and } b \text{ have the same signs}$$

**Example 1:** $(+3)\cdot(+2)$          **Example 2:** $(-3)\cdot(-2)$

**Example 1:** Multiplication of $(+3)\cdot(+2)$ by the standard number line: **(12)**

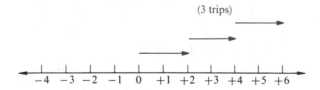

1. Start at the origin, 0.
2. Take three trips.
3. Each trip goes 2 units in the positive direction.

Hence, $(+3)\cdot(+2) = +6$.

**(13)**

**Example 2:** Multiplication of $(-3)\cdot(-2)$. The standard number line cannot be used to illustrate the product of two negative integers. Therefore, we will show that the product is positive by using the existing properties of integers.

## Using the Properties of Integers to Show That $(-3)\cdot(-2) = +6$ **(14)**

We will create an expression for which we know the answer. Inside the expression will be the product of $(-3)$ and $(-2)$.

$$-3 \cdot [(+2) + (-2)] = 0$$

because

$$-3 \quad \cdot \quad 0 \quad = \quad 0$$

But,

$$-3 \cdot [(+2) + (-2)] = (-3) \cdot (+2) + (-3) \cdot (-2) \qquad \text{by \textbf{dpma}}$$

Therefore,

$$(-3) \cdot (+2) + (-3) \cdot (-2) = 0$$

the product for which we wish
to find the answer

☐ *Step (1):*   $(-3) \cdot (+2) + (-3) \cdot (-2) = 0$ **(15)**

*Step (2):*   $-6 \quad + (-3) \cdot (-2) = 0$
*Step (3):*   $-6 \quad + \boxed{\phantom{XXXXX}} = 0$

$+6$ is the only number which can be added to $(-6)$ to produce a sum of zero.
*Step (4):*   Therefore, $(-3) \cdot (-2)$ is the opposite or additive inverse of $-6$. Hence, $(-3) \cdot (-2) = +6$.

In general, the product of two negative integers is a positive integer.

☐ **(16)**

When multiplying two positive integers or two negative integers, multiply the absolute values to produce a positive product.

**Example 1:**   $(+6) \cdot (+7) = +42$ **Example 2:**   $(-8) \cdot (-6) = +48$

☐ *Study Exercise Three* **(17)**

Perform the following multiplications:

1.  $(+2) \cdot (+8)$     2.  $2 \cdot 8$     3.  $(-5) \cdot (-7)$     4.  $(-10) \cdot (-12)$     5.  $(+6) \cdot 2$

☐ **Review of the Rules for Multiplication of Integers** **(18)**

**Case 1:**   $a \cdot 0 = 0$, where $a$ is any integer

**Case 2:**   If the two integers have opposite signs, multiply the absolute values, and make the product negative.

**Case 3:**   If the two integers have the same signs, multiply the absolute values, obtaining a positive product.

☐ *Study Exercise Four* **(19)**

Perform the following multiplications:

1.  $(-6) \cdot 0$     2.  $(-5) \cdot (-3)$     3.  $(+2) \cdot (-8)$     4.  $6 \cdot (-9)$
5.  $(+7) \cdot (+9)$     6.  $(-12) \cdot (-12)$     7.  $0 \cdot (+3)$     8.  $(+3) \cdot (-3)$
9.  $(-9) \cdot 4$     10.  $(-1) \cdot (-1)$

☐ **Multiplying Expressions Containing More Than Two Factors** **(20)**

**Example:**   $(-2) \cdot (-5) \cdot (-6)$

Method 1:   Using the order of operations convention:

$$(-2) \cdot (-5) \cdot (-6)$$
$$(+10) \cdot (-6)$$
$$-60$$

Method 2:  **Cpm** and **apm** allow you to multiply in any order:

$$(-2)\cdot(-5)\cdot(-6)$$

$$(+12)\cdot(-5)$$

$$\downarrow$$

$$-60$$

☐ **Example:**  $(-5)\cdot(+2)\cdot(-2)\cdot(+6)$                                    **(21)**

Method 1:   Using the order of operations convention:

$$(-5)\cdot(+2)\cdot(-2)\cdot(+6)$$

$$\downarrow$$

$$(-10)\quad\cdot(-2)\cdot(+6)$$

$$\downarrow$$

$$(+20)\quad\cdot(+6)$$

$$\downarrow$$

$$+120$$

Method 2:   **Cpm** and **apm** allow you to multiply in any order.

$$(-5)\cdot(+2)\cdot(-2)\cdot(+6)$$

$$(+10)\quad\cdot\quad(+12)$$

$$\downarrow$$

$$+120$$

☐ An even number of negative factors will produce a product which is positive.   **(22)**

**Example 1:**  $(-3)\cdot(-2) = +6$   [Two factors]

**Example 2:**  $(-1)\cdot(-5)\cdot(-2)\cdot(-3)$   [Four factors]

$$(+5)\quad\cdot\quad(+6)$$

$$\downarrow$$

$$(+30)$$

☐ An odd number of negative factors will produce a product which is negative.   **(23)**

**Example 1:**  $(-2)\cdot(-3)\cdot(-5)=-30$  [Three factors]

**Example 2:**  $(-1)\cdot(-3)\cdot(-2)\cdot(-5)\cdot(-2)$  [Five factors]

$$(+3)\quad\cdot\quad(+10)\quad\cdot\quad(-2)$$

$$(+30)\quad\cdot\quad(-2)$$

$$\downarrow$$

$$-60$$

☐                          *Study Exercise Five*                          **(24)**

Simplify completely by performing the following multiplications in any order you wish:

1.  $(-3)(-4)(-1)$          2.  $(-2)\cdot(-1)\cdot(-4)\cdot(-3)$          3.  $(-1)\cdot(+3)\cdot(-2)$
4.  $(+5)\cdot(-6)\cdot(-7)$          5.  $(-10)(+2)(+10)$          6.  $(-3)(-2)(+4)(+3)(-2)$

☐ **Division of Integers**                                              **(25)**

Remember the check for division.

**Example 1:**  $8 \div 2 = 4$, because $4\cdot2 = 8$.

91

**Example 2:** $\frac{10}{2} = 5$, because $5 \cdot 2 = 10$.

The quotient times the divisor must produce the dividend.

## ☐ Relating Division to Multiplication (26)

*Case (1):* Division of like signs.

**Example 1:** $(+8) \div (+2) = +4$, because $(+4) \cdot (+2) = +8$.

**Example 2:** $\frac{-10}{-5} = +2$, because $(+2) \cdot (-5) = -10$.

*Case (2):* Division of unlike signs.

**Example 1:** $(+12) \div (-3) = -4$, because $(-4) \cdot (-3) = +12$.

**Example 2:** $\frac{-15}{+5} = -3$, because $(-3) \cdot (+5) = -15$.

*Case (3):* Dividing a number into zero.

**Example 1:** $0 \div (+5) = 0$, because $0 \cdot (+5) = 0$.

**Example 2:** $\frac{0}{-7} = 0$, because $0 \cdot (-7) = 0$.

## ☐ Rules for Dividing Integers (27)

Dividing two integers follows the same pattern as multiplying two integers.
1. When dividing like signs, divide the absolute values and make the quotient positive.
2. When dividing unlike signs, divide the absolute values and make the quotient negative.
3. Zero divided by any number except zero will produce a quotient of zero.

## ☐ Using the Rules of Division (28)

**Example 1:** $(-30) \div (-6) = +5$      **Example 2:** $(+25) \div (-5) = -5$

**Example 3:** $\frac{-32}{+8} = -4$      **Example 4:** $\frac{0}{-3} = 0$

**Example 5:** $(-8) \div 0$ is impossible.

## ☐ Important Points (29)

1. Multiplication and division of integers have the same rules.
2. Division by zero is impossible.
3. Multiplication is closed for the set of integers.
4. Division is not closed for the set of integers; for example, $+3 \div (-2)$ does not represent an integer.

## ☐                  *Study Exercise Six* (30)

Divide the following.

1. $(-24) \div (-6)$    2. $(-12) \div (+3)$    3. $-12 \div 3$    4. $(+42) \div (-7)$

5. $(-21) \div 3$    6. $0 \div (-2)$    7. $(+7) \div 0$    8. $\frac{-100}{-10}$

9. $\frac{-1}{-1}$    10. $\frac{-8}{8}$    11. $\frac{+46}{-23}$    12. $\frac{0}{-6}$

☐ Powers of Integers  **(31)**

$$(-3)^2 \leftarrow \text{exponent}$$
$$\uparrow$$
$$\text{base}$$

$(-3)^2$ means $(-3)\cdot(-3)$. Therefore, $(-3)^2 = +9$.

☐ More Examples  **(32)**

**Example 1:** Evaluate $(-2)^3$.

**Solution:**
$$(-2)^3 = \underbrace{(-2)\cdot(-2)}\cdot(-2)$$
$$= \quad (+4) \quad \cdot \quad (-2)$$
$$= \qquad\qquad -8$$

**Example 2:** Evaluate $(-2)^4$.

**Solution:**
$$(-2)^4 = \underbrace{(-2)\cdot(-2)}\cdot\underbrace{(-2)\cdot(-2)}$$
$$= \quad (+4) \quad \cdot \quad (+4)$$
$$= \qquad\qquad +16$$

**Example 3:** Evaluate $(-1)^2$.

**Solution:**
$$(-1)^2 = (-1)\cdot(-1)$$
$$= \quad +1$$

**Example 4:** Evaluate $(-1)^5$.

**Solution:**
$$(-1)^5 = \underbrace{(-1)\cdot(-1)}\cdot\underbrace{(-1)\cdot(-1)}\cdot(-1)$$
$$= \quad (+1) \quad \cdot \quad (+1) \quad \cdot \quad (-1)$$
$$= \qquad\qquad -1$$

**Example 5:** Evaluate $(+3)^5$.

**Solution:**
$$(+3)^5 = \underbrace{(+3)\cdot(+3)}\cdot\underbrace{(+3)\cdot(+3)}\cdot(+3)$$
$$= \quad (+9) \quad \cdot \quad (+9) \quad \cdot \quad (+3)$$
$$\downarrow$$
$$= \qquad\qquad (+81) \quad \cdot \quad (+3)$$
$$\downarrow$$
$$= \qquad\qquad\qquad +243$$

☐ Some Observations  **(33)**

1. A negative base to an even power gives a positive answer.

**Example:** $(-2)^4 = +16$

2. A negative base to an odd power gives a negative answer.

**Example:** $(-2)^3 = -8$

3. A positive base to either an even or an odd power gives a positive answer.

**Examples:** $(+3)^2 = +9$, $(+2)^3 = +8$

4. Any base, except zero, to the zero power gives an answer of $+1$.

**Examples:** $(+3)^0 = +1$, because $(+3) \div (+3) = +1$.
$\qquad\qquad (-4)^0 = +1$, because $(-4) \div (-4) = +1$.

## ☐ An Agreement (34)

An exponent always applies only to the symbol on its immediate left unless there are grouping symbols which indicate otherwise.

**Example 1:** $-3^2$ means $-(3)(3)$ or $-9$.  **Example 2:** $(-3)^2$ means $(-3) \cdot (-3)$ or $+9$.

**Example 3:** $-5^2$ means $-(5)(5)$ or $-25$  **Example 4:** $(-5)^2$ means $(-5) \cdot (-5)$ or $+25$.

## ☐ *Study Exercise Seven* (35)

Evaluate each of the following.

1. $-6^2$    2. $(-6)^2$    3. $(-3)^3$    4. $(+2)^4$
5. $(+2)^5$    6. $0^3$    7. $(-1)^4$    8. $(-1)^5$
9. $(-1)^{234}$    10. $(-1)^{235}$    11. $(-9)^0$

## ☐ Evaluating Expressions Containing More Than One Operation (36)

Remember, to evaluate expressions containing exponents:

*Step (1):* Evaluate exponential expressions and groups.
*Step (2):* Apply the order of operations agreement.

## ☐ Example 1: Evaluate $(-2)^3 + [(-4)(-1) - 6]$. (37)

**Solution:**

*line (a)*  $(-2)^3 + [(-4)(-1) - 6]$
              ↓
*line (b)*  $-8 + [(-4)(-1) - 6]$
                      ↓
*line (c)*  $-8 + [+4 - 6]$
*line (d)*  $-8 + (-2)$
                  ↓
*line (e)*      $-10$

## ☐ Example 2: Evaluate $(-3 - 2)^2 + 3(-4)^0 \div (-3)$. (38)

**Solution:**

*line (a)*  $(-3 - 2)^2 + 3(-4)^0 \div (-3)$
*line (b)*  $(-5)^2 + 3(-4)^0 \div (-3)$
                ↓             ↓
*line (c)*  $(+25) + 3(+1) \div (-3)$
*line (d)*  $(+25) + (+3) \div (-3)$
*line (e)*  $(+25) + (-1)$
*line (f)*      $+24$

## ☐ *Study Exercise Eight* (39)

Evaluate each of the following.

1. $(-2)^3 \cdot (-3)^0$    2. $5(-3)^2 - 6(-3) - 7$
3. $(-1)^4 \div (-1)^5$    4. $(-3 + 1)^2 + (-5 + 5)^3$

## REVIEW EXERCISES

A.  Illustrate each of the following on the number line.

    1.  $(+3)(-2) = -6$        2.  $(-4)(+2) = -8$        3.  $(+3)(+2) = +6$

B.  Multiply the following.

    4.  $0 \cdot (-6)$      5.  $(-3) \cdot (-4)$      6.  $(+7) \cdot (-1)$      7.  $(-2) \cdot (-3) \cdot (-4)$

C.  Divide the following.

    8.  $(-28) \div (-14)$      9.  $0 \div (-2)$      10.  $\dfrac{-35}{-7}$

    11.  $\dfrac{+42}{-7}$      12.  $\dfrac{-12}{0}$

D.  Evaluate the following.

    13.  $(-4)^2$        14.  $-4^2$        15.  $(-7)^0$
    16.  $(-1)^{138}$      17.  $(-1)^{139}$      18.  $0^5$
    19.  $4(-6)^2 - 3(-6) - 4$      20.  $(-3)^2 \cdot (-2)^0$      21.  $(-5 + 1)^2 + (-3 + 3)^2$

E.  Fill in the blanks so that each of the following is true.

    22.  ____ $\cdot (-8) = +32$      23.  ____ $\cdot (-4) = 0$      24.  ____ $\div (-5) = -10$
    25.  $(-27) \div$ ____ $= +3$      26.  ____ $\div (-4) = 0$

F.  True or False

    27.  A negative number to an odd power gives a negative number.
    28.  A positive number to an even power gives a negative number.
    29.  A negative number to an even power gives a positive number.
    30.  It is impossible to divide a number by zero.
    31.  The set of integers is closed for the operation of division.
    32.  In a division problem the dividend should never be zero.
    33.  The only way a product can be zero is for at least one of the factors to be zero.
    34.  The only way a quotient can be zero is for the dividend to be zero.
    35.  Every time an integer is divided by itself, the quotient is $+1$.

## Solutions to Review Exercises

A.  1.  See Frame 7.        2.  See Frame 8.        3.  See Frame 12.

B.  4.  0        5.  $+12$      6.  $-7$      7.  $-24$

C.  8.  $+2$      9.  0      10.  $+5$      11.  $-6$      12.  Impossible

D.  13.  $+16$      14.  $-16$      15.  $+1$      16.  $+1$      17.  $-1$
    18.  0      19.  $+158$      20.  $+9$      21.  $+16$

E.  22.  $-4$      23.  0      24.  $+50$      25.  $-9$      26.  0

F.  27.  True      28.  False      29.  True      30.  True      31.  False
    32.  False      33.  True      34.  True      35.  False, $0 \div 0 \neq +1$

## SUPPLEMENTARY PROBLEMS

A.  Illustrate each of the following on the number line.

    1.  $(+2)(+5)$        2.  $(-3)(+4)$        3.  $(+2)(-6)$

B.  Multiply the following.

    4.  $0 \cdot (-8)$      5.  $(+7) \cdot 0$      6.  $(+4) \cdot (+5)$
    7.  $(-4) \cdot (+5)$      8.  $(-7) \cdot (-8)$      9.  $(-10) \cdot (+10)$

## SUPPLEMENTARY PROBLEMS, Contd.

10. $(-1)^2$      11. $(-1)^0$      12. $(-3)^4$

13. $(-3)^3$      14. $0^3$      15. $(-2) \cdot (-4) \cdot (-5) \cdot (-1)$

16. $(+4) \cdot (-1) \cdot (0) \cdot (+6)$      17. $(-1)(+2)(-1)(-3)(+4)(-2)$

C. Divide the following.

18. $(+8) \div (-4)$      19. $(-9) \div (+3)$      20. $(+54) \div (-6)$      21. $\dfrac{-81}{-9}$

22. $\dfrac{+20}{+5}$      23. $\dfrac{-15}{-15}$      24. $0 \div (-6)$      25. $(-6) \div 0$

26. $(+100) \div (-2) \div (-5) \div (+2)$      27. $(-18) \div (-3) \div (+2) \div (+1)$

D. Evaluate each of the following.

28. $(+3) \cdot (-6) \div (-2)$      29. $(-8) \div (-2) \div (-1)$

30. $(-1) \cdot (-1) \div (+1) \cdot (-9) \div (+3)$      31. $(-2)(-3)^2 + 3(-3) - 5$

32. $(-3 - 1)^2 + (-2 + 1)^5$

E. Fill in the blanks.

33. ___ $\cdot (+2) = -18$      34. $(-24) \div$ ___ $= +4$

35. $(-18) \div (+9) \cdot (-2) =$ ___      36. $(-100) \cdot$ ___ $= 400$

37. $(+3) \cdot$ ___ $\cdot (-6) = +36$      38. $(-10) \cdot$ ___ $= 0$

39. $(+2) \cdot$ ___ $\div (-4) = 4$      40. ___ $\div (-2) = 0$

F. Multiple Choice

41. If the product of two integers is negative and one of the integers is positive, then the other integer is _____.

     (a) positive      (b) zero      (c) negative

42. If the product of two integers is zero, then at least one of the factors is _____.

     (a) positive      (b) zero      (c) negative

43. If the quotient of two integers is zero, then the dividend is _____.

     (a) positive      (b) zero      (c) negative

44. If the quotient of two integers is negative, then the dividend is not _____.

     (a) positive      (b) zero      (c) negative

G. Calculator Problems. With your instructor's approval, use a calculator to evaluate the following expressions.

45. $(-23)(-15)$      46. $(-3)^7$

47. $(-251)(17)^2 - (161)(4)^5$      48. $(-47)(-13)^4 + 38(-13)^2 - 28{,}512$

49. $\dfrac{(-36)(47)}{(94)(-9)}$      50. $\dfrac{(15)(20)^3}{(12)(-5)^2}$

□ Solutions to Study Exercises      **(5A)**

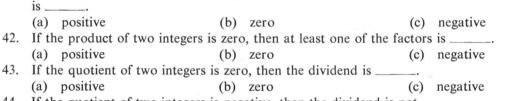

### Study Exercise One (Frame 5)

Zero is the correct answer for each problem.

□      **Study Exercise Two (Frame 10)**      **(10A)**

1. $-21$      2. $-21$      3. $-30$      4. $-72$      5. $-64$

□      **Study Exercise Three (Frame 17)**      **(17A)**

1. $+16$ or $16$      2. $+16$ or $16$      3. $+35$ or $35$      4. $+120$ or $120$      5. $+12$ or $12$

## Solutions to Study Exercises, Contd.

☐                            *Study Exercise Four (Frame 19)*             **(19A)**

| | | | | |
|---|---|---|---|---|
| 1. 0 | 2. $+15$ or $15$ | 3. $-16$ | 4. $-54$ | 5. $+63$ or $63$ |
| 6. $+144$ or $144$ | 7. 0 | 8. $-9$ | 9. $-36$ | 10. $+1$ or $1$ |

☐                            *Study Exercise Five (Frame 24)*             **(24A)**

| | | | | | |
|---|---|---|---|---|---|
| 1. $-12$ | 2. $+24$ | 3. $+6$ | 4. $+210$ | 5. $-200$ | 6. $-144$ |

☐                            *Study Exercise Six (Frame 30)*             **(30A)**

| | | | | | |
|---|---|---|---|---|---|
| 1 $+4$ | 2. $-4$ | 3. $-4$ | 4. $-6$ | 5. $-7$ | 6. 0 |
| 7. Impossible | 8. $+10$ | 9. $+1$ | 10. $-1$ | 11. $-2$ | 12. 0 |

☐                            *Study Exercise Seven (Frame 35)*            **(35A)**

1. $-36$ because $-6^2 = -(6)(6)$.               2. $+36$ because $(-6)^2 = (-6)(-6)$.

3. $-27$    4. $+16$    5. $+32$    6. 0     7. $+1$    8. $-1$    9. $+1$     10. $-1$     11. $+1$

☐                            *Study Exercise Eight (Frame 39)*            **(39A)**

1. $(-2)^3 \cdot (-3)^0 = (-8) \cdot (+1)$
$$= \quad -8$$

2. $5(-3)^2 - 6(-3) - 7 = 5 \cdot (+9) - 6(-3) - 7$
$$= (+45) - (-18) - 7$$
$$= (+45) + (+18) - 7$$
$$= +56$$

3. $(-1)^4 \div (-1)^5 = (+1) \div (-1)$
$$= \quad -1$$

4. $(-3 + 1)^2 + (-5 + 5)^3 = (-2)^2 + 0^3$
$$= (+4) + 0$$
$$= \quad +4$$

# Operations with
# Variable Expressions

☐ **Objectives** **(1)**

By the end of this unit you should be able to use the following properties:

- property one of multiplication: $(a)(-b) = (-a)(b) = -(a \cdot b)$.
- property two of multiplication: $(-a)(-b) = ab$.
- the distributive property of multiplication with respect to subtraction.
- extensions of the distributive properties.

You will also be able to perform the following operations:

- multiplication and division of variable expressions.
- addition and subtraction of variable expressions using either a horizontal or a vertical format.
- removing grouping symbols preceded by either a plus or a minus sign.

☐ **Property One of Multiplication** **(2)**

We learned in the preceding unit that the product of a positive number and a negative number is a negative number.

**Example 1:** $(+3)(-2) = -6$ **Example 2:** $(-3)(+2) = -6$

An analogous property can be stated for variables. This is called property one of multiplication:

$$(a)(-b) = (-a)(b) = -(a \cdot b)$$

☐ **Using Property One of Multiplication** **(3)**

**Example 1:** $(-3)(x) = -3x$ **Example 2:** $(2)(-b) = -2b$

**Example 3:** $(-a)(a) = -(a \cdot a)$ or $-a^2$

☐ **Property Two of Multiplication** **(4)**

We learned in the preceding unit that the product of two negative numbers is a positive number.

**Example:** $(-2)(-3) = 6$

An analogous property can be stated for variables. This is called property two of multiplication and is sometimes said to be the double opposite law:

$$(-a)(-b) = ab$$

☐ **Using Property Two of Multiplication** **(5)**

**Example 1:** $(-3)(-x) = 3x$ **Example 2:** $(-m)(-n) = mn$

**Example 3:** $(-a)(-a) = a \cdot a$ or $a^2$

☐ **Multiplying Variable Expressions** **(6)**

As we learned earlier, the commutative and associative properties of multiplication ~~enable~~ us to multiply variable expressions by multiplying the numerical coefficients and adding the exponents which appear on identical bases.

**Example 1:** Multiply $(3x^2)(5x^4)$.

Multiply numerical coefficients.

**Solution:** $(3x^2)(5x^4) = 15x^6$

Add exponents.

**Example 2:** Multiply $(-5a^2b)(3a^2b)$.

Multiply numerical coefficients.

**Solution:** $(-5a^2b)(3a^2b) = -15a^4b^2$

Add exponents.

☐ **More Examples** **(7)**

**Example 1:** $2(4x) = 8x$

**Example 2:** $(-2a)(3a) = -6a^2$

**Example 3:** $(-3x)(-xy) = 3x^2y$

**Example 4:** $(-4x^2)(-5x^2y) = 20x^4y$

**Example 5:** $(-3a^2b^3c)(2ab^2)(4a^2c^3) = -24a^5b^5c^4$

☐ **Division of Variable Expressions** **(8)**

As we learned earlier, we can divide variable expressions by dividing the numerical coefficients and subtracting the exponents which appear on identical bases.

**Example 1:** Divide $(10x^5) \div (2x^3)$.

Divide numerical coefficients.

**Solution:** $(10x^5) \div (2x^3) = 5x^2$

Subtract exponents.

**Example 2:** Divide $\dfrac{24a^2b^3}{-3ab} = -8ab^2$.

**Example 3:** Divide $\dfrac{-15x^3y^4z^2}{-5xy^2z^2} = 3x^2y^2z^0$ or $3x^2y^2$

☐                        *Study Exercise One* **(9)**

A. Multiply the following according to property one or property two of multiplication. Indicate the property used.

   1. $(-4)(-x)$         2. $(-a) \cdot c$         3. $(-y)(-y)$

   4. $(-m)(m)$         5. $(-2)(a)$          6. $(x)(-y)$

B. Multiply the following.

   7. $5 \cdot (3a)$               8. $(-2mn)(-5mn)$

   9. $(-2a^2b)(-3abc)$      10. $(-4x^2)(5x^2y)(2xy)$

C. Divide the following.

   11. $(-6x) \div 2$             12. $(-12a^4) \div (-6a^2)$

   13. $\dfrac{18m^3n^2}{-6mn^2}$           14. $\dfrac{-25x^3y^4z}{-5xy^2}$

☐ **Review of dpma** **(10)**

Remember, the distributive property of multiplication with respect to addition states the following:

$$a \cdot (b + c) = a \cdot b + a \cdot c$$

We now wish to show that multiplication is distributive with respect to subtraction, that is:

$$a \cdot (b - c) = a \cdot b - a \cdot c$$

This property will be abbreviated as **dpms.**

## ☐ Proof of dpms (11)

We will now prove that $a \cdot (b - c) = a \cdot b - a \cdot c$.

line (a)  $a \cdot [b - c] = a \cdot [b + (-c)]$
line (b)  $\qquad\qquad = a \cdot b + a(-c)$
line (c)  $\qquad\qquad = a \cdot b + [-(ac)]$
line (d)  $\qquad\qquad = a \cdot b - a \cdot c$

Therefore, $a \cdot (b - c) = a \cdot b - a \cdot c$.

## ☐ Examples of dpms (12)

**Example 1:**  $2(x - y) = 2x - 2y$ $\qquad\qquad$ **Example 2:**  $2a(a - b) = 2a^2 - 2ab$
**Example 3:**  $3x^2(2x - 3y) = 6x^3 - 9x^2y$

Observe that **dpms** will change a basic product to a basic difference.

## ☐ Extensions of the Distributive Properties (13)

The two distributive properties can be combined and extended to hold for any number of terms.

**Example 1:**  $2(a + b + c) = 2a + 2b + 2c$
**Example 2:**  $3(x - y - z) = 3x - 3y - 3z$
**Example 3:**  $5(a + b - c + d) = 5a + 5b - 5c + 5d$
**Example 4:**  $2x(3x^2 + 4xy - 3) = 6x^3 + 8x^2y - 6x$

## ☐ Study Exercise Two (14)

Multiply the following according to the distributive properties or their extensions.

1.  $2(3x - 4)$ $\qquad\qquad\qquad$ 2.  $3(2x + 3y - 4z)$
3.  $5ab(2a^2 - 3ab + b)$ $\qquad\qquad$ 4.  $4xy^2(2x^2y - 3xy^2 + 1)$
5.  $-4a(3a^2 - 2a + 1)$

## ☐ Basic Factoring (15)

A variable expression is said to be *factored* when it is written as a basic product by removing the common element. This is accomplished by reversing the distributive properties.

**Example 1:**  $ab + ac = a(b + c)$ $\qquad\qquad$ **Example 2:**  $2x - 2y = 2(x - y)$

$\qquad\qquad$ Common element is $a$. $\qquad\qquad\qquad\qquad$ Common element is 2.

**Example 3:**  $4x + 2y + 2 = 2(2x + y + 1)$

$\qquad\qquad$ Common element is 2.

## ☐ More Examples of Factoring (16)

**Example 1:**  $5a - 10 = 5(a - 2)$ $\qquad\qquad$ **Example 2:**  $4a^2 + 6a - 2 = 2(2a^2 + 3a - 1)$
**Example 3:**  $6x^2y - 3xy + 3x = 3x(2xy - y + 1)$

*Note:*  The largest common element should be removed when one is factoring.

## ☐ Study Exercise Three (17)

Factor each of the following using the reverse of the distributive properties.

1.  $2x + 6$ $\qquad\qquad$ 2.  $5m^2 + 5$ $\qquad\qquad$ 3.  $3a + 3b - 3c$
4.  $4x + 6y - 10z - 8w$ $\qquad$ 5.  $6m^2 + 12m - 3$ $\qquad$ 6.  $8a^2b - 4ab + 4a$

## ☐ Addition and Subtraction of Variable Expressions (18)

Using the concept of factoring, we can develop a method for adding and subtracting certain types of variable expressions.

**Example 1:**   Add $2x + 3x$.

   **Solution:**   Factor out the common element, $x$.

     *line (a)*   $2x + 3x = x \cdot (2 + 3)$
     *line (b)*   $\phantom{2x + 3x} = x \cdot 5$
     *line (c)*   $\phantom{2x + 3x} = 5x$

   Therefore, $2x + 3x = 5x$.

**Example 2:**   Combine $7a^2 + 8a^2 - 11a^2$.

   **Solution:**   Factor out the common element, $a^2$.

     *line (a)*   $7a^2 + 8a^2 - 11a^2 = a^2 \cdot (7 + 8 - 11)$
     *line (b)*   $\phantom{7a^2 + 8a^2 - 11a^2} = a^2 \cdot 4$
     *line (c)*   $\phantom{7a^2 + 8a^2 - 11a^2} = 4a^2$

   Therefore, $7a^2 + 8a^2 - 11a^2 = 4a^2$.

**Example 3:**   Combine $5x + 2y$.

   **Solution:**   There is no common element, so this expression cannot be combined.

**Example 4:**   Combine $5x^2 + 2x$.

   **Solution:**   Factor out the common element, $x$.

     *line (a)*   $5x^2 + 2x = \underbrace{x(5x + 2)}$
                      cannot be combined further

## ☐ Points to Remember   (19)

*Remember*, variable expressions may be added or subtracted only if the variables and exponents are identical. We can only combine like terms.

**Example 1:**   $5a + 3$ cannot be added.       **Example 2:**   $5a + 3b$ cannot be added.

**Example 3:**   $5a^2 - 3a$ cannot be subtracted.       **Example 4:**   $6x^2y - 4xy^2$ cannot be subtracted.

## ☐ The Shortcut   (20)

Variable expressions can be added or subtracted by combining their respective numerical coefficients, provided the variables and exponents are identical.

**Example 1:**   Add $2x + 3x$.

   **Solution:**   $2x + 3x = 5x$

     Add the numerical coefficients.

**Example 2:**   Subtract $5m^2 - 3m^2 - 6m^2$.

   **Solution:**   $5m^2 - 3m^2 - 6m^2 = -4m^2$

     Subtract the numerical coefficients.

**Example 3:**   Combine $4a^2b + 3ab^2 + 2a^2b - ab^2$.

   Add the numerical coefficients.

   **Solution:**   $4a^2b + 3ab^2 + 2a^2b - ab^2 = 6a^2b + 2ab^2$

     Subtract the numerical coefficients.

## ☐ More Examples   (21)

**Example 1:**   $3x + 5x - 10x = -2x$

**Example 2:**   $5x^2y + x^2y = 6x^2y$

**Example 3:** $7a^2b + 4ab^2 - 3a^2b - 5ab^2 = 4a^2b - ab^2$

**Example 4:** $-3a^2 + 2a - 8 + 9a^2 - 6a + 2 = 6a^2 - 4a - 6$

**Example 5:** $6x^2y^3 + 7x^3y^2 - 2x^2y^3 + x^3y^2 = 4x^2y^3 + 8x^3y^2$

☐            *Study Exercise Four*            **(22)**

A.   Which of the following cannot be combined by addition or subtraction? Justify your answer.

    1.   $3x + 5y$          2.   $4a^2 - 3a$          3.   $7m^2 + 2m^2$          4.   $6x + 2$

B.   Combine the following using addition or subtraction.

    5.   $7a + 4a$                             6.   $3x + 2x - x$

    7.   $4r^2t - 3r^2t$                    8.   $3x^3y + 2xy^3 + 4x^3y - xy^3$

    9.   $2a^2 - 3a + 4 + 3a^2 - 5a + 1$

☐ **Vertical Addition**                                                             **(23)**

Variable expressions may be added vertically if like terms are arranged in the same columns.

**Example 1:**   Add $(3x^2 - 5x + 2) + (7x^2 - 3x - 8)$.

    **Solution:**

       *Step (1):*   Arrange like terms in the same columns.

$$3x^2 - 5x + 2$$
$$\underline{7x^2 - 3x - 8}$$

       *Step (2):*   Add the terms in each column.

$$3x^2 - 5x + 2$$
$$\underline{7x^2 - 3x - 8}$$
$$10x^2 - 8x - 6$$

☐ **Example 2:**   Add $(6y^2 + 7y - 3) + (3y^2 - 5y) + (-y - 10)$.                    **(24)**

    **Solution:**

       *Step (1):*   Arrange like terms in the same columns.

$$6y^2 + 7y - 3$$
$$3y^2 - 5y$$
$$\underline{\phantom{3y^2} - y - 10}$$

       *Step (2):*   Add the terms in each column.

$$6y^2 + 7y - 3$$
$$3y^2 - 5y$$
$$\underline{\phantom{3y^2} - y - 10}$$
$$9y^2 + 1y - 13 \quad \text{or} \quad 9y^2 + y - 13$$

☐ **Vertical Subtraction**                                                            **(25)**

*Remember*, a subtraction problem is worked by converting it to a related addition problem. The rules for addition can then be used to obtain the answer.

**Example:**   $(-8) - (-2) = (-8) + (+2)$

1. The minuend is not changed.
2. Subtraction is changed to addition.
3. The subtrahend has its sign changed.

Therefore, variable expressions may be subtracted vertically, if each term in the subtrahend has its sign changed.

## ☐ Examples of Vertical Subtraction (26)

**Example 1:** Subtract $(5x^2 - 6x + 7) - (2x^2 + 3x - 9)$.

    **Solution:** Arrange vertically, change each sign in the subtrahend, then add each column.

$$\begin{array}{l} 5x^2 - 6x + 7 \\ 2x^2 + 3x - 9 \end{array} \quad \text{Change all signs.} \xrightarrow{\phantom{xxxx}} \quad \begin{array}{l} 5x^2 - 6x + 7 \\ -2x^2 - 3x + 9 \\ \hline 3x^2 - 9x + 16 \end{array}$$

**Example 2:** Subtract $(4m^2 + m - 5) - (2m^2 - 4m)$.

    **Solution:** Arrange vertically, change each sign in the subtrahend, then add each column.

$$\begin{array}{l} 4m^2 + m - 5 \\ 2m^2 - 4m \end{array} \quad \text{Change all signs.} \xrightarrow{\phantom{xxxx}} \quad \begin{array}{l} 4m^2 + m - 5 \\ -2m^2 + 4m \\ \hline 2m^2 + 5m - 5 \end{array}$$

## ☐ *Study Exercise Five* (27)

A. Combine the following by vertical addition.

    1. $(5x^2 + 2x - 7) + (6x^2 - 7x + 10)$      2. $(2m^2 + m - 5) + (3m^2 + 6) + (4m^2 - 2m)$

B. Combine the following by vertical subtraction.

    3. $(7x^2 - 2x + 3) - (2x^2 - 6x + 5)$      4. $(3a^2 - 4a + 1) - (5a^2 + 2a)$

## ☐ Removing Grouping Symbols Preceded by a Plus Sign (28)

A plus sign in front of grouping symbols does not change any signs within the group.

**Example 1:** $+(x - y) = x - y$

**Example 2:** $3x + (4y - 7) = 3x + 4y - 7$

**Example 3:** $(2x^2 + x) + (3y^2 - y) = 2x^2 + x + 3y^2 - y$

## ☐ Removing Grouping Symbols Preceded by a Minus Sign (29)

A minus sign in front of grouping symbols will change the sign of each term within the group.

**Example 1:** $-(-a + b) = +a - b$ or $a - b$

**Example 2:** $-(x - y) = -x + y$

**Example 3:** $3x - (2y + z) = 3x - 2y - z$

## ☐ Groups within Groups (30)

**Example 1:** $3a - [2b - (c + 5)]$

    **Solution:** Remove innermost grouping symbols first.

    *line (a)*    $3a - [2b - (c + 5)]$

    *line (b)*    $3a - [2b - c - 5]$

    *line (c)*    $3a - 2b + c + 5$

**Example 2:** $2x - \{3y + [2z - (-w + 2)]\}$

   **Solution:** Remove innermost grouping symbols first.

    *line (a)*   $2x - \{3y + [2z - (-w + 2)]\}$

    *line (b)*   $2x - \{3y + [2z + w - 2]\}$

    *line (c)*   $2x - \{3y + 2z + w - 2\}$

    *line (d)*   $2x - 3y - 2z - w + 2$

□                         *Study Exercise Six*                           **(31)**

Remove grouping symbols from each of the following.

1.   $+(3x - y)$                           2.   $-(3x - y)$
3.   $7a - (2b + 3)$                4.   $6x - [5y - (3z + 2)]$
5.   $3a - \{4b - [-3c + (d - 3) - 3e]\}$

□ **Simplifying Expressions Involving Grouping Symbols**            **(32)**

*Step (1):*   Remove grouping symbols.
*Step (2):*   Combine like terms by using addition.

□ **Example 1:**   Simplify $(5x + 2) + (3x - 8)$.                **(33)**

   **Solution:**

      *Step (1):*   Remove grouping symbols.
      *line (a)*   $(5x + 2) + (3x - 8)$
      *line (b)*   $5x + 2 + 3x - 8$

      *Step (2):*   Combine like terms by using addition.
      *line (c)*   $5x + 2 + 3x - 8$
      *line (d)*   $8x - 6$

□ **Example 2:**   Simplify $(3x - 7) - (4x + 2)$.               **(34)**

   **Solution:**

      *Step (1):*   Remove grouping symbols.
      *line (a)*   $(3x - 7) - (4x + 2)$
      *line (b)*   $3x - 7 - 4x - 2$

      *Step (2):*   Combine like terms by using addition.
      *line (c)*   $3x - 7 - 4x - 2$
      *line (d)*   $-1x - 9$
      *line (e)*   $-x - 9$

□ **Example 3:**   $5x - [8x - (4 + 2x)]$                    **(35)**

   **Solution:**

      *Step (1):*   Remove grouping symbols.
      *line (a)*   $5x - [8x - (4 + 2x)]$
      *line (b)*   $5x - [8x - 4 - 2x]$
      *line (c)*   $5x - 8x + 4 + 2x$

      *Step (2):*   Combine like terms by using addition.
      *line (d)*   $5x - 8x + 4 + 2x$
      *line (e)*   $-1x + 4$
      *line (f)*   $-x + 4$

Unit 9

Remove grouping symbols and simplify each of the following.

1. $(3a + 4) + (5a - 6)$
2. $(5m - 6) - (7m + 2)$
3. $7x - [8x + (x - 4)]$
4. $8a - [3a - (5 - 2a)]$

## REVIEW EXERCISES

A. Multiply the following according to property one or property two of multiplication. Indicate which property was used.

1. $(-a)(-a)$
2. $(-2)(x)$
3. $4 \cdot (-y)$

B. Multiply or divide the following.

4. $3 \cdot (4x)$
5. $(-2ab)(-3a)$
6. $(-2x^2y)(-3xy^3)(4x)$
7. $(-mn^2)(6m^2)(-m)$
8. $(-10a) \div 5$
9. $(-21x^5) \div (-7x^2)$
10. $\dfrac{18r^2t}{-3r}$
11. $\dfrac{-36x^2y^4z^3}{-3xy^2z^3}$

C. Multiply the following according to the distributive properties or their extensions.

12. $3(2x - 5)$
13. $2ab(3a^2 - 4a + 2)$
14. $-5m(m^2 - 3m + 1)$
15. $2x^2y(4x^3y^2 + 3x^2y - 5)$

D. Factor the following, using the reverse of the distributive properties.

16. $3a - 9$
17. $4x - 4y - 4z$
18. $2x^2 - 4x$
19. $6m^2n - 8mn - 2m$

E. Combine the following, using addition or subtraction. Use the shortcut.

20. $3x + 5x$
21. $6a - 3a + 2a$
22. $10m^2n - 7m^2n$
23. $2x^2y + 4xy^2 - x^2y + xy^2$

F. Why is it incorrect to combine the following by addition or subtraction of the numerical coefficients?

24. $3x + 5y$
25. $6x^2y - 2xy^2$

G. Combine the following, using vertical addition or subtraction.

26. $(6x^2 - 3x + 1) + (x^2 - 5x - 7)$
27. $(2y^2 + y - 7) + (3y^2 - 6y)$
28. $(7a^2 + 6a - 5) - (3a^2 - 2a + 4)$
29. $(x^2 - 3x + 1) - (2x + 5)$

H. Remove grouping symbols from the following.

30. $+(2x - 5y)$
31. $-(2x - 5y)$
32. $5a - (3b + 4)$
33. $8x - [4y - (2z + 3)]$

I. Remove grouping symbols and simplify the following.

34. $(2x + 3) + (4x - 7)$
35. $(6a - 2) - (2a + 1)$
36. $7m - [3m + (m - 2)]$
37. $4y - [2y - (6 - 5y)]$

## Solutions to Review Exercises

A. 1. $a^2$ [Property Two]  2. $-2x$ [Property One]  3. $-4y$ [Property One]

B. 4. $12x$  5. $6a^2b$  6. $24x^4y^4$  7. $6m^4n^2$
   8. $-2a$  9. $3x^3$  10. $-6rt$  11. $12xy^2z^0$ or $12xy^2$

C. 12. $6x - 15$  13. $6a^3b - 8a^2b + 4ab$  14. $-5m^3 + 15m^2 - 5m$  15. $8x^5y^3 + 6x^4y^2 - 10x^2y$

D. 16. $3(a - 3)$  17. $4(x - y - z)$  18. $2x(x - 2)$  19. $2m(3mn - 4n - 1)$

107

## Solutions to Review Exercises, Contd.

E.  20. $8x$     21. $5a$     22. $3m^2n$     23. $1x^2y + 5xy^2$ or $x^2y + 5xy^2$

F.  24. The variables are different.     25. The exponents are different.

G.  26. $7x^2 - 8x - 6$     27. $5y^2 - 5y - 7$     28. $4a^2 + 8a - 9$     29. $x^2 - 5x - 4$

H.  30. $2x - 5y$     31. $-2x + 5y$     32. $5a - 3b - 4$     33. $8x - 4y + 2z + 3$

I.  34. $(2x + 3) + (4x - 7) = 2x + 3 + 4x - 7$
$= 6x - 4$

35. $(6a - 2) - (2a + 1) = 6a - 2 - 2a - 1$
$= 4a - 3$

36. $7m - [3m + (m - 2)] = 7m - [3m + m - 2]$
$= 7m - 3m - m + 2$
$= 3m + 2$

37. $4y - [2y - (6 - 5y)] = 4y - [2y - 6 + 5y]$
$= 4y - 2y + 6 - 5y$
$= -3y + 6$

## SUPPLEMENTARY PROBLEMS

A.  Multiply the following according to property one or property two of multiplication. Indicate which property was used.

1. $(-x)(y)$     2. $(-3)(-x)$     3. $(-m)(m)$
4. $6(-a)$     5. $(-a)(-a)$     6. $(-7)(x)$

B.  Multiply or divide the following.

7. $4 \cdot (2x)$     8. $(-3)(-5a)$
9. $(-5x)(-7x)$     10. $(-3a^2)(2a^3)$
11. $(-4x^2y)(-3xy^2)$     12. $(2m^2n)(-6mn)(3mn^3)$
13. $(-4x^2y^3)(-2xyz)(-3y^3z^2)$     14. $(-4a^2) \div a$
15. $(-4a^2) \div 2$     16. $\dfrac{-9x^2}{3}$
17. $\dfrac{-9x^2}{3x}$     18. $\dfrac{10xy^3}{-10xy^3}$
19. $\dfrac{-20a^3b^2}{-10ab^2}$     20. $\dfrac{15x^5y^7z^3}{-3x^2y^4z}$
21. $2(x - 5)$     22. $-3a(7a^2 - 5)$
23. $-2mn(4m^2n - 5m + 2n)$     24. $2(a - 3b)$
25. $5x(x^2 - y)$     26. $2xy(3x + 4y - 3)$
27. $3mn(m^2 - 4m - 1)$     28. $-3x(2x^2 - x + 2)$

C.  Factor the following, using the reverse of the distributive properties.

29. $9x - 9y$     30. $mn + mp$
31. $3mn + 9mp$     32. $4a + 8$
33. $5x - 10$     34. $3y^2 - 3y$
35. $2x + 2y + 2z$     36. $2a - 4b + 6c$
37. $5x^2y^2 + 10x^2y - 5xy$     38. $6x^2 - 3xy + 9xy^2$

D.  Why is it incorrect to combine the following by addition or subtraction of the numerical coefficients?

39. $4a - 3b$     40. $6x + 2$     41. $2x^3y + 3xy^2$     42. $5x^2 - 4x$

E.  Combine the following, using addition or subtraction.

43. $5x + 2x$     44. $5x + x$
45. $3a - 5a$     46. $7b - 3b + 2b$
47. $11xy + 4xy$     48. $2mn - 5mn + mn$
49. $2m^2n - 3m^2n - 4m^2n$     50. $2x - 5y + 4x - 2y + 3y$
51. $6ab - 7a + 2b + 8mn$     52. $2m^3n^2 + 3m^2n^3 - 6m^3n^2 + 4m^2n^3$
53. $(2x^2 - 3x - 5) + (4x^2 - 7x + 2)$     54. $(2m^2 - 3m + 4) + (8m^2 + 2m - 3)$
55. $(6x^2 + 7x - 4) + (2x^2 - 3x + 2) + (5x^2 - 7x + 1)$

## SUPPLEMENTARY PROBLEMS, Contd.

56. $(4x^2 - 5x + 1) - (7x^2 - 2x - 8)$      57. $(3x^2 + x - 5) - (2x^2 + x + 7)$

58. $(a^2 - 2a + 1) - (3a^2 - 4a)$

F. Remove grouping symbols and simplify the following.

59. $2x + (4x + 3)$            60. $2x - (4x + 3)$

61. $3x - (5x - 6)$            62. $5a - (2 + a)$

63. $(6a + b) - (7a + b)$     64. $(m - 2n) - (3m + n)$

65. $4a - [2a - (3a - 4)]$     66. $-[3a - (2b - a)]$

67. $-(2a + 3b) - (5a - b)$     68. $3x - \{2x + [2z - (3z + 2x)]\}$

☐ Solutions to Study Exercises                                                    **(9A)**

### Study Exercise One (Frame 9)

A.   1. $4x$    [Property Two]      2. $-ac$    [Property One]      3. $y^2$    [Property Two]

     4. $-m^2$    [Property One]      5. $-2a$    [Property One]      6. $-xy$    [Property One]

B.   7. $15a$         8. $10m^2n^2$         9. $6a^3b^2c$         10. $-40x^5y^2$

C.   11. $-3x$         12. $2a^2$         13. $-3m^2n^0$ or $-3m^2$         14. $5x^2y^2z$

### Study Exercise Two (Frame 14)                    **(14A)**

1. $6x - 8$         2. $6x + 9y - 12z$         3. $10a^3b - 15a^2b^2 + 5ab^2$

4. $8x^3y^3 - 12x^2y^4 + 4xy^2$         5. $-12a^3 + 8a^2 - 4a$

### Study Exercise Three (Frame 17)                **(17A)**

1. $2(x + 3)$         2. $5(m^2 + 1)$         3. $3(a + b - c)$

4. $2(2x + 3y - 5z - 4w)$         5. $3(2m^2 + 4m - 1)$         6. $4a(2ab - b + 1)$

### Study Exercise Four (Frame 22)              **(22A)**

A.   1. Cannot be combined because the variables are different

     2. Cannot be combined because the exponents are different

     3. $9m^2$

     4. Cannot be combined because the variables are different

B.   5. $11a$               6. $4x$                         7. $1r^2t$ or $r^2t$

     8. $7x^3y + 1xy^3$ or $7x^3y + xy^3$      9. $5a^2 - 8a + 5$

### Study Exercise Five (Frame 27)              **(27A)**

A.   1. $\begin{aligned} 5x^2 + 2x - 7 \\ \underline{6x^2 - 7x + 10} \\ 11x^2 - 5x + 3 \end{aligned}$         2. $\begin{aligned} 2m^2 + m - 5 \\ 3m^2 \qquad + 6 \\ \underline{4m^2 - 2m} \\ 9m^2 - 1m + 1 \end{aligned}$ or $9m^2 - m + 1$

B.   3. $\begin{aligned} 7x^2 - 2x + 3 \\ \underline{-2x^2 + 6x - 5} \\ 5x^2 + 4x - 2 \end{aligned}$         4. $\begin{aligned} 3a^2 - 4a + 1 \\ \underline{-5a^2 - 2a} \\ -2a^2 - 6a + 1 \end{aligned}$

### Study Exercise Six (Frame 31)              **(31A)**

1. $+(3x - y) = 3x - y$      2. $-(3x - y) = -3x + y$      3. $7a - (2b + 3) = 7a - 2b - 3$

4. $6x - [5y - (3z + 2)] = 6x - [5y - 3z - 2]$

                              $= 6x - 5y + 3z + 2$

## Solutions to Study Exercises, Contd.

5. $3a - \{4b - |-3c + (d-3) - 3e]\} = 3a - \{4b - |-3c + d - 3 - 3e]\}$
$\qquad\qquad\qquad\qquad\qquad\qquad\quad = 3a - \{4b + 3c - d + 3 + 3e\}$
$\qquad\qquad\qquad\qquad\qquad\qquad\quad = 3a - 4b - 3c + d - 3 - 3e$

☐         *Study Exercise Seven (Frame 36)*         **(36A)**

1. $(3a + 4) + (5a - 6) = 3a + 4 + 5a - 6$
$\qquad\qquad\qquad\qquad\quad = 8a - 2$

2. $(5m - 6) - (7m + 2) = 5m - 6 - 7m - 2$
$\qquad\qquad\qquad\qquad\qquad = -2m - 8$

3. $7x - [8x + (x - 4)] = 7x - [8x + x - 4]$
$\qquad\qquad\qquad\qquad\quad = 7x - 8x - x + 4$
$\qquad\qquad\qquad\qquad\quad = -2x + 4$

4. $8a - [3a - (5 - 2a)] = 8a - [3a - 5 + 2a]$
$\qquad\qquad\qquad\qquad\qquad = 8a - 3a + 5 - 2a$
$\qquad\qquad\qquad\qquad\qquad = 3a + 5$

# Introduction to Equation Solving

## ☐ Objectives (1)

By the end of this unit you should be able to:

- classify equations as identities or as conditionals.
- define the term *equivalent equations*.
- define and use the four properties of equivalent equations.
- solve first degree equations and check their solutions.
- use equations to solve word problems.

## ☐ Parts of an Equation (2)

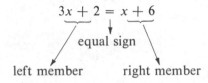

$$3x + 2 = x + 6$$

equal sign

left member    right member

## ☐ Solutions of an Equation (3)

A *solution* of an equation is any value from the variable's replacement set which makes the equation true.

**Example 1:** $-5$ is the solution of $3x = -15$, because $3 \cdot (-5) = -15$ is a true equation.

**Example 2:** 3 is the solution of $x + 7 = 10$, because $3 + 7 = 10$ is a true equation.

**Example 3:** 1 is not a solution of $6x = 12$, because $6 \cdot 1 \neq 12$.

Solutions may also be called *roots*.

## ☐ Solving an Equation (4)

To solve an equation means to find all of its solutions or roots.

**Example 1:** Solve $3y = -12$. The only solution is $-4$. This is sometimes written as $y = -4$.

**Example 2:** Solve $x^2 = 4$. The solutions are 2 and $-2$. This could be written as $x = 2$ and $x = -2$.

## ☐ *Study Exercise One* (5)

A. Indicate whether or not 5 is a solution for each of these equations. (Answer yes or no.)

1. $4x = 20$
2. $x - 5 = 0$
3. $2(y + 3) = 16$
4. $2y + 3 = 16$
5. $5m + 3 - m = 2m + 13$
6. $4(y - 5) = 4$

B. Each of these equations is followed by a set. Indicate whether or not the given set contains all of the correct solutions. Answer yes or no.

7. $3x = -21$    $\{-7\}$
8. $y + 4 = 0$    $\{-4\}$
9. $2(x - 1) = 0$    $\{0\}$
10. $x^2 = 9$    $\{3, 1\}$

## ☐ Types of Equations (6)

1. *Identities* or *identical equations* are true for all values of the variable's replacement set.

**Example 1:** $x + 1 = x + 1$      **Example 2:** $3(y + 2) = 3y + 6$

2. *Conditional equations* are true for only some value or values of the variable's replacement set.

**Example 1:** $2x = 6$      **Example 2:** $x^2 = 4$

*Note:* In this unit, unless otherwise specified, we will assume that, the variable's replacement set is the set of integers, i.e., $\{\ldots, -3, -2, -1, 0, 1, 2, 3, \ldots\}$.

☐ *Study Exercise Two* **(7)**

Classify each equation as either an identity or a conditional equation.

1. $3x = 12$
2. $x + 2 = 2 + x$
3. $7y = -14$
4. $2(y + 4) = 2y + 8$
5. $x - 3 = 0$
6. $3x + 4 = 2x + 5$

☐ **Equivalent Equations** **(8)**

Equations are said to be equivalent provided they each have exactly the same solutions.

**Example 1:** The following equations are equivalent because each has exactly the same solution, 2.

$$x = 2$$
$$3x = 6$$
$$x - 2 = 0$$

**Example 2:** The following equations are equivalent because each has exactly the same solution, −1.

$$y = -1$$
$$2y = -2$$
$$y + 1 = 0$$

**Example 3:** The following equations are not equivalent because they have different solutions.

$$2m = 6 \quad \text{[solution is 3]}$$
$$x + 5 = 9 \quad \text{[solution is 4]}$$
$$y^2 = 16 \quad \text{[solutions are 4 and } -4]$$

☐ **Properties of Equivalent Equations** **(9)**

We will discuss four properties that will enable us to solve equations:

1. The Addition Property
2. The Subtraction Property
3. The Multiplication Property
4. The Division Property

☐ **The Addition Property of Equivalent Equations [apee]** **(10)**

The same number or expression may be added to both sides of an equation, and the resulting equation is equivalent to the original.

**Example:** Original equation: $\quad x = 5$
Add 2 to each side: $\quad x + 2 = 5 + 2$
5 is the solution to both equations.

☐ **The Subtraction Property of Equivalent Equations [spee]** **(11)**

The same number or expression may be subtracted from both sides of an equation, and the resulting equation is equivalent to the original.

**Example:** Original equation: $\quad x + 3 = 5$
Subtract 3 from both sides: $\quad x + 3 - 3 = 5 - 3$, or $x = 2$
2 is the solution to all the equations.

☐ **The Multiplication Property of Equivalent Equations [mpee]** **(12)**

The same number or expression, other than zero, may be multiplied times both sides of an equation, and the resulting equation is equivalent to the original.

**Example:** Original equation: $\quad x = 4$
Multiply both sides by 2: $\quad 2 \cdot x = 2 \cdot 4$, or $2x = 8$
4 is the solution to all equations.

## ☐ The Division Property of Equivalent Equations [dpee] (13)

The same number or expression, other than zero, may be divided into each side of an equation, and the resulting equation is equivalent to the original.

**Example:** Original equation: $3x = 12$

Divide each side by 3: $\frac{3x}{3} = \frac{12}{3}$, or $x = 4$

4 is the solution to all equations.

## ☐ *Study Exercise Three* (14)

Identify the property of equivalent equations which has been applied in each of the following equations:

1. Original equation: $x + 5 = 12$
$$x + 5 - 5 = 12 - 5$$
$$x = 7$$

2. Original equation: $4x = 20$
$$\frac{4x}{4} = \frac{20}{4}$$
$$x = 5$$

3. Original equation: $3x + 1 = 2x + 7$
$$3x + 1 - 1 = 2x + 7 - 1$$
$$3x = 2x + 6$$

4. Original equation: $5x = 6 + 2x$
$$5x - 2x = 6 + 2x - 2x$$
$$3x = 6$$

5. Original equation: $x = 8$
$$2 \cdot x = 2 \cdot 8$$
$$2x = 16$$

6. Original equation: $x - 4 = 2$
$$x - 4 + 4 = 2 + 4$$
$$x = 6$$

## ☐ Solving Equations (15)

To solve an equation:

*Step (1):* Combine like terms.

*Step (2):* Use the properties of equivalent equations to obtain a form where the terms containing variables are on one side of the equal sign and the numbers are on the other.

*Step (3):* Use the division property of equivalent equations to obtain an equation of the form, $x = a$.

## ☐ Example 1: Solve $5x + 2x + 2 = 23$. (16)

*Step (1):* Combine like terms.
$$5x + 2x + 2 = 23$$
$$7x + 2 = 23$$

*Step (2):* Obtain an equation with variables on one side and numbers on the other.
line (a) $\qquad 7x + 2 = 23$
line (b) $7x + 2 - 2 = 23 - 2$ [spee]
line (c) $\qquad 7x = 21$

*Step (3):* Obtain an equation of the form, $x = a$.
line (d) $7x = 21$
line (e) $\frac{7x}{7} = \frac{21}{7}$ [dpee]
line (f) $x = 3$

The solution is 3.

## ☐ Checking the Solution (17)

The solution may be checked by replacing it for the variable in the original equation:

Original equation: $5x + 2x + 2 = 23$

114

**Solution:** 3

Check: $\underbrace{5 \cdot 3 + 2 \cdot 3 + 2}_{23} = 23$

☐ **Example 2:** Solve $4x + 3 + 2x = 3x + 9$. **(18)**

*Step (1):* Combine like terms.

$$4x + 3 + 2x = 3x + 9$$

$$6x + 3 = 3x + 9$$

*Step (2):* Obtain an equation with variables on one side and numbers on the other.

*line (a)*      $6x + 3 = 3x + 9$

*line (b)*   $6x + 3 - 3 = 3x + \underbrace{9 - 3}$    **[spee]**

*line (c)*      $6x = 3x + \;\; 6$

*line (d)*    $\underbrace{6x - 3x} = 3x + 6 - 3x$    **[spee]**

*line (e)*      $3x \;\;\; = 6$

*Step (3):* Obtain an equation of the form, $x = a$.

*line (f)*   $3x = 6$

*line (g)*   $\dfrac{3x}{3} = \dfrac{6}{3}$    **[dpee]**

*line (h)*    $x = 2$

The solution is 2.

☐ **Checking the Solution** **(19)**

Original equation:   $4x + 3 + 2x = 3x + 9$

**Solution:** 2

Check: $\underbrace{4 \cdot 2 + 3 + 2 \cdot 2}_{15} = \underbrace{3 \cdot 2 + 9}_{15}$

☐ **Example 3:** Solve $2(3x + 1) = 3(x - 5) - 1$. **(20)**

*Step (1):* Multiply and combine like terms.

*line (a)*   $2(3x + 1) = 3(x - 5) - 1$

*line (b)*     $6x + 2 = 3x - \underbrace{15 - 1}$

*line (c)*    $6x + 2 = 3x - \;\; 16$

*Step (2):* Obtain an equation with variables on one side and numbers on the other.

*line (d)*      $6x + 2 = 3x - 16$

*line (e)*   $6x + 2 - 2 = 3x - \underbrace{16 - 2}$    **[spee]**

*line (f)*      $6x = 3x - \;\; 18$

*line (g)*    $\underbrace{6x - 3x} = 3x - 18 - 3x$    **[spee]**

*line (h)*      $3x \;\;\; = -18$

*Step (3):* Obtain an equation of the form, $x = a$.

*line (i)*    $3x = -18$

*line (j)* $\dfrac{3x}{3} = \dfrac{-18}{3}$    **[dpee]**

*line (k)*    $x = -6$

The solution is $-6$.

☐ **Checking the Solution**    **(21)**

Original equation:   $2(3x + 1) = 3(x - 5) - 1$

**Solution:**   $-6$

Check:   $\underbrace{2[3 \cdot (-6) + 1]}_{-34} = \underbrace{3[-6 - 5] - 1}_{-34}$

☐    *Study Exercise Four*    **(22)**

Solve the following equations. Check your solutions.

1.  $3x = -12$                    2.   $-5x = 15$
3.  $y - 6 = 0$                   4.   $m + 2 = -10$
5.  $2x - 3 = 15$                 6.   $2y + 14 = 2$
7.  $7x - 2x + 4 = 3x + 6$        8.   $2(5y - 3) = 4(2y + 3) + 4$

☐ **A Shortcut**    **(23)**

**Example 1:**   Solve $x - 4 = 8$.

*line (a)*   $x - 4 = 8$

*line (b)*   $x - 4 = 8$
*line (c)*        $x = 8 + 4$     [Change to addition.]
*line (d)*        $x = 12$

The solution is 12.

**Example 2:**   Solve $x + 5 = 7$.

*line (a)*   $x + 5 = 7$

*line (b)*   $x + 5 = 7$
*line (c)*        $x = 7 - 5$     [Change to subtraction.]
*line (d)*        $x = 2$

The solution is 2.

☐    **(24)**

1.  If a term is added on one side of an equation, it may be placed on the other side and subtracted.
**Example:**  $3x = 10 + 2x$ becomes $3x - 2x = 10$.
2.  If a term is subtracted on one side of an equation, it may be placed on the other side and added.
**Example:**  $7x - 3 = 11$ becomes $7x = 11 + 3$.

☐ **More Examples**    **(25)**

**Example 1:**   Solve $4x - 3 = 2x + 7$.

**Solution:**

*line (a)*    $4x - 3 = 2x + 7$

*line (b)*   $4x - 2x = 7 + 3$

line (c)    $2x = 10$
line (d)    $x = 5$

The solution is 5.

**Example 2:** Solve $-5x - 2(3x + 1) = -7x - 22$.

**Solution:**

line (a)   $-5x - 2(3x + 1) = -7x - 22$
line (b)   $-5x - 6x - 2 = -7x - 22$

line (c)   $-11x - 2 = -7x - 22$
line (d)   $-11x + 7x = -22 + 2$
line (e)   $-4x = -20$
line (f)   $x = 5$

The solution is 5.

□                                   *Study Exercise Five*                                   **(26)**

Using the shortcut, solve the following equations.

1.  $5x - 3 = 17$
2.  $-2y + 1 = 4y - 17$
3.  $4m + 2 = 2m - 10$
4.  $3(5x + 4) = 6(x + 5)$

□ **Using Equations to Solve Word Problems**                                   **(27)**

*Step (1):*  Let some letter represent one of the unknowns.

*Step (2):*  Describe the other unknowns with variable expressions using the same letter.

*Step (3):*  Relate the variable expressions in terms of an equation using the information given in the problem.

*Step (4):*  Solve the equation.

*Step (5):*  Interpret the solution in terms of the original problem.

**(28)**

□ **Example 1:**  The sum of two numbers is 39. The larger number is 3 less than twice the smaller number. Find both numbers.

**Solution:**

*Step (1):*  Let $x$ represent the smaller number.

*Step (2):*  $2x - 3$ represents the larger number.

*Step (3):*  The sum of the two numbers is 39.
$x + 2x - 3 = 39$

*Step (4):*  Solve the equation.
$x + 2x - 3 = 39$
$3x - 3 = 39$
$3x = 42$
$x = 14$

*Step (5):*  If $x = 14$, then $2x - 3 = 25$. The smaller number is 14 and the larger number is 25.

☐ **(29)**

**Example 2:** A wire 22 inches long is cut into two parts. One piece is 6 inches longer than the other. How long is each piece?

**Solution:**

*Step (1):* Let $x$ represent the length of the shorter piece.

*Step (2):*

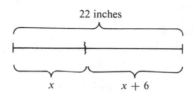

*Step (3):* The sum of the two pieces is 22 inches.
$$x + x + 6 = 22$$

*Step (4):* Solve the equation.
$$x + x + 6 = 22$$
$$2x + 6 = 22$$
$$2x = 16$$
$$x = 8$$

*Step (5):* If $x = 8$, then $x + 6 = 14$. The length of the shorter piece is 8 inches, and the length of the longer piece is 14 inches.

☐ **(30)**

**Example 3:** A water main has a flow capacity of 290 gallons per minute. The main separates into three branches. The second main has a capacity of 50 gallons per minute more than the first, and the third main has a capacity of twice the first. Find the capacity of each branch.

**Solution:**

*Step (1):* Let $x$ represent the capacity of the first branch.

*Step (2):*

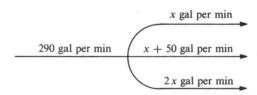

*Step (3):* The sum of the three branches is 290 gallons per minute.
$$x + x + 50 + 2x = 290$$

*Step (4):* Solve the equation.
$$x + x + 50 + 2x = 290$$
$$4x + 50 = 290$$
$$4x = 240$$
$$x = 60$$

*Step (5):* If $x = 60$, then $x + 50 = 110$ and $2x = 120$. The capacity of the first branch is 60 gallons per minute; the capacity of the second is 110 gallons per minute; and the capacity of the third is 120 gallons per minute.

□ **(31)**

**Example 4:** A collection of nickels and dimes has a value of $7. How many nickels and dimes are in the collection if there are 40 more dimes than nickels?

**Solution:**

*Step (1):* Let $x$ represent the number of nickels.

*Step (2):* $x + 40$ would represent the number of dimes.

*Step (3):*

| Value of nickels in cents | | Value of dimes in cents | | Value of collection in cents |
|---|---|---|---|---|
| $5x$ | $+$ | $10(x + 40)$ | $=$ | $700$ |

*Step (4):* Solve the equation.

$$5x + 10(x + 40) = 700$$
$$\underbrace{5x + 10x} + 400 = 700$$
$$15x + 400 = 700$$
$$15x = 300$$
$$x = 20$$

*Step (5):* If $x = 20$, then $x + 40 = 60$. There are 20 nickels and 60 dimes in the collection.

□ *Study Exercise Six* **(32)**

Solve each of the following problems.

1. The sum of two numbers is 66. The larger number is 6 more than three times the smaller number. Find both numbers.

2. A rope 50 feet long is cut into two pieces. One piece is 8 feet longer than the other. How long is each piece?

3. An electric current of 23 amperes is branched off into three circuits. The second branch carries three times the current of the first branch. The third branch carries 2 amperes less than the first branch. Find the amount of current carried in each branch.

4. A collection of dimes and quarters has a value of $10. How many dimes and quarters are in the collection if there are 12 fewer dimes than quarters?

X **REVIEW EXERCISES**

A. Indicate whether or not 6 is a solution for each of the following equations. (Answer yes or no.)

1. $3x = 18$
2. $3 + x = 18$
3. $2(y + 4) = 20$
4. $2y + 4 = 20$
5. $3y + 5 + y = 2y + 17$

B. Indicate whether or not 0 is a solution for each of the following equations. (Answer yes or no.)

6. $n + 7 = 7$
7. $3n - 3 = 0$
8. $5(x + 2) = 10$
9. $5x + 2 = 10$
10. $2(x + 3) + 4 = 4$

C. Classify each of the following as an identity or a conditional equation.

11. $2x = 10$
12. $2 \cdot x = x \cdot 2$
13. $3(n + 2) = 3n + 6$
14. $5x + 3 = 2x + 12$

D. In each of the following identify which property of equivalent equations has been applied.

15. Original equation:
$$y + 7 = 15$$
$$y + 7 - 7 = 15 - 7$$
$$y = 8$$

16. Original equation:
$$3x = 21$$
$$\frac{3x}{3} = \frac{21}{3}$$
$$x = 7$$

## REVIEW EXERCISES, Contd.

E.   Solve these equations.

17.  $2x = 16$                        18.   $-3x = 21$
19.  $6x = 42$                        20.   $-5y = -30$
21.  $5x = 5$                         22.   $-x = 3$
23.  $3x + 2 = 23$                    24.   $4m - 3 = 6m + 5$
25.  $6x - 4 = 26$                    26.   $2(3a + 1) = 5(a - 1)$
27.  $4x + 3 = 2x + 11$               28.   $2x + 3 + x = x + 3$
29.  $5x + 2 - 3x = x + 3$            30.   $8(x + 1) = 3(x + 2) + 12$

F.   Solve the following word problems.

31.  The sum of two numbers is 45. The larger number is five more than four times the smaller number. Find both numbers.

32.  A wire 20 inches long is cut into two pieces so that one piece is 6 inches longer than the other. How long is each piece?

33.  A collection of nickels and quarters is worth $5. How many nickels and quarters are in the collection if there are 10 more nickels than quarters?

## Solutions to Review Exercises

A.   1.  Yes          2.  No                3.  Yes          4.  No              5.  Yes
B.   6.  Yes          7.  No                8.  Yes          9.  No              10.  No
C.   11.  Conditional      12.  Identity              13.  Identity          14.  Conditional
D.   15.  Subtraction Property                16.  Division Property

E.   17.  $2x = 16$                    18.   $-3x = 21$                  19.  $6x = 42$
$$\frac{2x}{2} = \frac{16}{2}$$       $$\frac{-3x}{-3} = \frac{21}{-3}$$       $$\frac{6x}{6} = \frac{42}{6}$$
$x = 8$                          $x = -7$                      $x = 7$
The solution is 8.              The solution is $-7$.         The solution is 7.

20.  $-5y = -30$                 21.   $5x = 5$                   22.  $-x = 3$
$$\frac{-5y}{-5} = \frac{-30}{-5}$$   $$\frac{5x}{5} = \frac{5}{5}$$         $$\frac{-x}{-1} = \frac{3}{-1}$$
$y = 6$                          $x = 1$                       $x = -3$
The solution is 6.              The solution is 1.            The solution is $-3$.

23.  $3x + 2 = 23$               24.   $4m - 3 = 6m + 5$          25.  $6x - 4 = 26$
$3x = 23 - 2$                    $4m - 6m = 5 + 3$             $6x = 26 + 4$
$3x = 21$                        $-2m = 8$                     $6x = 30$
$x = 7$                          $m = -4$                      $x = 5$
The solution is 7.              The solution is $-4$.         The solution is 5.

26.  $2(3a + 1) = 5(a - 1)$      27.   $4x + 3 = 2x + 11$         28.  $2x + 3 + x = x + 3$
$6a + 2 = 5a - 5$               $4x - 2x = 11 - 3$            $3x + 3 = x + 3$
$6a - 5a = -5 - 2$             $2x = 8$                      $3x - x = 3 - 3$
$a = -7$                        $x = 4$                       $2x = 0$
The solution is $-7$.          The solution is 4.            $$\frac{2x}{2} = \frac{0}{2}$$
                                                             $x = 0$
                                                             The solution is 0.

29.  $5x + 2 - 3x = x + 3$       30.   $8(x + 1) = 3(x + 2) + 12$
$2x + 2 = x + 3$                $8x + 8 = 3x + 6 + 12$
$2x - x = 3 - 2$               $8x + 8 = 3x + 18$
$x = 1$                         $8x - 3x = 18 - 8$
The solution is 1.             $5x = 10$
                               $x = 2$
                               The solution is 2.

## Solutions to Review Exercises, Contd.

F.  31.  *Step (1):*   Let $x$ represent the smaller number.

      *Step (2):*   $4x + 5$ represents the larger number.

      *Step (3):*   The sum of the two numbers is 45.

$$x + 4x + 5 = 45$$

      *Step (4):*   Solve the equation.

$$\begin{aligned} x + 4x + 5 &= 45 \\ 5x + 5 &= 45 \\ 5x &= 40 \\ x &= 8 \end{aligned}$$

      *Step (5):*   If $x = 8$, then $4x + 5 = 37$. The smaller number is 8 and the larger number is 37.

  32.  *Step (1):*   Let $x$ represent the length of the smaller piece.

      *Step (2):*   The length of the larger piece is represented by $x + 6$.

      *Step (3):*   The sum of the two pieces is 20 inches.

$$x + x + 6 = 20$$

      *Step (4):*   Solve the equation.

$$\begin{aligned} x + x + 6 &= 20 \\ 2x + 6 &= 20 \\ 2x &= 14 \\ x &= 7 \end{aligned}$$

      *Step (5):*   If $x = 7$, then $x + 6 = 13$. The shorter piece is 7 inches and the longer piece is 13 inches.

  33.  *Step (1):*   Let $x$ represent the number of quarters.

      *Step (2):*   $x + 10$ represents the number of nickles.

      *Step (3):*

| Value of nickels in cents | | Value of quarters in cents | | Value of collection in cents |
|:---:|:---:|:---:|:---:|:---:|
| $5(x + 10)$ | $+$ | $25x$ | $=$ | $500$ |

      *Step (4):*   Solve the equation.

$$\begin{aligned} 5(x + 10) + 25x &= 500 \\ 5x + 50 + 25x &= 500 \\ 30x + 50 &= 500 \\ 30x &= 450 \\ x &= 15 \end{aligned}$$

      *Step (5):*   If $x = 15$, then $x + 10 = 25$. There are 15 quarters and 25 nickels in the collection.

## SUPPLEMENTARY PROBLEMS

A.  Indicate whether or not 7 is a solution for each of the following equations. (Answer yes or no.)

    1.  $7x = 49$         2.  $2(x - x) = 0$         3.  $3x + 2 = 19$

    4.  $3x + 2 = 23$       5.  $5(3y - 6) = 75$

B.  Indicate whether or not the number 1 is a solution for each of the following equations. (Answer yes or no.)

    6.  $n + 1 = 1$       7.  $2y = 2$         8.  $x - 1 = 0$

    9.  $2(x + 5) = 12$     10.  $5a - 3 + 2a = 11$

C.  Classify each of the following as either a conditional equation or an identity.

    11.  $2x = 10$       12.  $3 \cdot x = x \cdot 3$     13.  $x + 4 = 4 + x$

    14.  $7(2y + 3) = 14y + 21$     15.  $3(5m - 2) = 9$

D.  In each of the following identify which property of equivalent equations has been applied.

    16.  Original equation:       $m - 5 = 8$

$$\begin{aligned} m - 5 + 5 &= 8 + 5 \\ m &= 13 \end{aligned}$$

## SUPPLEMENTARY PROBLEMS, Contd.

17. Original equation:
$$3x + 4 = x + 10$$
$$3x + 4 - 4 = x + 10 - 4$$
$$3x = x + 6$$

18. Original equation:
$$-12x = 36$$
$$\frac{-12x}{-12} = \frac{36}{-12}$$
$$x = -3$$

19. Original equation:
$$3x = 24$$
$$2 \cdot (3x) = 2 \cdot 24$$
$$6x = 48$$

E. Solve these equations.

20. $-5x = 50$    21. $-3x = -9$    22. $12x = 48$    23. $2y = 2$
24. $11m = 55$    25. $3a = 0$    26. $x + 7 = -12$    27. $x + 15 = 10$
28. $n + 4 = 1$    29. $m - 5 = 4$    30. $y - 3 = 7$    31. $y + 12 = 0$
32. $3m + 6 = 12$    33. $5a + 6 = 21$    34. $8y + 20 = 4$    35. $6x + 7 = 73$
36. $3(a + 2) = 21$    37. $5(x - 4) = 5$
38. $4y + 3 - y = y + 13$    39. $10 + 2x + 5 = x + 20$
40. $13 + 4(2r - 3) = 2(r - 3) + 7$    41. $2(x + 3) + 3(4x - 1) = 4x + 13$
42. $5 + 2(a - 1) = 7 + a$    43. $10(x + 1) = 2(3x + 7)$

F. Solve the following word problems.

44. The sum of two numbers is 48. The larger number is three times the smaller. Find both numbers.

45. The sum of two numbers is 38. The larger number is 18 more than the smaller. Find both numbers.

46. The sum of two numbers is 46. The smaller number is 14 less than the larger. Find both numbers.

47. The sum of two numbers is 15. The larger number is 7 more than three times the smaller. Find both numbers.

48. The sum of two numbers is 25. The larger number is 7 more than 8 times the smaller. Find both numbers.

49. The sum of two numbers is 66. The larger number is 6 more than 3 times the smaller number. Find both numbers.

50. The sum of two numbers is 45. The larger number is 5 more than 4 times the smaller number. Find both numbers.

51. If twice a certain number is decreased by 3, the result is 9. Find the number.

52. If 10 is added to 3 times a number the result is 31. Find the number.

53. If 3 times the sum of a certain number and 5 is decreased by twice the number, the result is 20. Find the number.

54. If 5 times the sum of a certain number and 3 is decreased by 21, the result is twice the number. Find the number.

55. A wire 20 centimeters long is cut into two pieces so that one piece is 6 centimeters longer than the other. How long is each piece?

56. A rope 50 feet long is cut into two pieces. One piece is 8 feet longer than the other. How long is each piece?

57. A wire 24 inches long is cut into two pieces. The larger piece is 4 inches longer than the smaller. Find the length of both pieces.

58. A wire 48 inches long is cut into three pieces. The second piece is twice the length of the first, and the third piece is three times the length of the first. Find the length of each piece.

## SUPPLEMENTARY PROBLEMS, Contd.

59. Three resistors connected in series have a total resistance of 50 ohms. The second resistor has a resistance of 5 ohms more than the first, while the third resistor has a resistance of 12 ohms more than the first. Find the resistance of each resistor.

60. An electric current of 23 amperes is branched off into three circuits. The second branch carries 3 times the current of the first branch. The third branch carries 2 amperes less than the first branch. Find the amount of current carried in each branch.

61. The flow capacity of a pipeline is 800 liters per minute. The pipeline separates into three branches. The second branch has 3 times the capacity of the first, while the third branch has a capacity of 100 liters per minute more than the second. Find the capacity of each branch.

62. A coin collection consisting of nickels and dimes is worth $4.00. There are 10 more dimes than nickels. Find the number of nickels and dimes.

63. A coin collection consisting of nickels, quarters, and half dollars is worth $10. There are 6 times as many nickels as quarters and 1 less half dollar than quarters. Find the number of nickels, quarters, and half dollars.

64. In a basketball game one team made twice as many points as the other. The total number of points made by both teams was 87. How many points did each team score?

65. At a football game, the price of admission was $4.00 for regular seats and $6.00 for box seats. The total receipts were $75,600 for a total of 16,300 paid admissions. Find the number of regular seats and box seats that were sold.

66. A house and lot cost $66,000. The cost of the house is 10 times the cost of the lot. Fnd the cost of the house.

☐ **Solutions to Study Exercises** (5A)

### Study Exercise One (Frame 5)

A. 1. Yes 2. Yes 3. Yes 4. No 5. Yes 6. No
B. 7. Yes 8. Yes 9. No 10. No

☐ ### Study Exercise Two (Frame 7) (7A)

1. Conditional 2. Identity 3. Conditional 4. Identity 5. Conditional 6. Conditional

☐ ### Study Exercise Three (Frame 14) (14A)

1. Subtraction Property 2. Division Property 3. Subtraction Property
4. Subtraction Property 5. Multiplication Property 6. Addition Property

☐ ### Study Exercise Four (Frame 22) (22A)

1. $3x = -12$
$$\frac{3x}{3} = \frac{-12}{3}$$
$x = -4$
The solution is $-4$.

2. $-5x = 15$
$$\frac{-5x}{-5} = \frac{15}{-5}$$
$x = -3$
The solution is $-3$.

3. $y - 6 = 0$
$y - 6 + 6 = 0 + 6$
$y = 6$
The solution is 6.

## Solutions to Study Exercises, Contd.

4. 
$$m + 2 = -10$$
$$m + 2 - 2 = -10 - 2$$
$$m = -12$$
The solution is $-12$.

5. 
$$2x - 3 = 15$$
$$2x - 3 + 3 = 15 + 3$$
$$2x = 18$$
$$\frac{2x}{2} = \frac{18}{2}$$
$$x = 9$$
The solution is 9.

6. 
$$2y + 14 = 2$$
$$2y + 14 - 14 = 2 - 14$$
$$2y = -12$$
$$\frac{2y}{2} = \frac{-12}{2}$$
$$y = -6$$
The solution is $-6$.

7. 
$$7x - 2x + 4 = 3x + 6$$
$$5x + 4 = 3x + 6$$
$$5x + 4 - 4 = 3x + 6 - 4$$
$$5x = 3x + 2$$
$$5x - 3x = 3x + 2 - 3x$$
$$2x = 2$$
$$\frac{2x}{2} = \frac{2}{2}$$
$$x = 1$$
The solution is 1.

8. 
$$2(5y - 3) = 4(2y + 3) + 4$$
$$10y - 6 = 8y + 12 + 4$$
$$10y - 6 = 8y + 16$$
$$10y - 6 + 6 = 8y + 16 + 6$$
$$10y = 8y + 22$$
$$10y - 8y = 8y + 22 - 8y$$
$$2y = 22$$
$$\frac{2y}{2} = \frac{22}{2}$$
$$y = 11$$
The solution is 11.

☐ ### Study Exercise Five (Frame 26) (26A)

1. 
$$5x - 3 = 17$$
$$5x = 17 + 3$$
$$5x = 20$$
$$x = 4$$
The solution is 4.

2. 
$$-2y + 1 = 4y - 17$$
$$-2y - 4y = -17 - 1$$
$$-6y = -18$$
$$y = 3$$
The solution is 3.

3. 
$$4m + 2 = 2m - 10$$
$$4m - 2m = -10 - 2$$
$$2m = -12$$
$$m = -6$$
The solution is $-6$.

4. 
$$3(5x + 4) = 6(x + 5)$$
$$15x + 12 = 6x + 30$$
$$15x - 6x = 30 - 12$$
$$9x = 18$$
$$x = 2$$
The solution is 2.

☐ ### Study Exercise Six (Frame 32) (32A)

1. *Step (1):* Let $x$ represent the smaller number.

   *Step (2):* $3x + 6$ represents the larger number.

   *Step (3):* The sum of the two numbers is 66.
   $$x + 3x + 6 = 66$$

   *Step (4):* Solve the equation.
   $$x + 3x + 6 = 66$$
   $$4x + 6 = 66$$
   $$4x = 60$$
   $$x = 15$$

   *Step (5):* If $x = 15$, then $3x + 6 = 51$. The smaller number is 15, and the larger number is 51.

2. *Step (1):* Let $x$ represent the shorter piece.

   *Step (2):* $x + 8$ represents the longer piece.

   *Step (3):* The sum of the two lengths is 50 feet.
   $$x + x + 8 = 50$$

   *Step (4):* Solve the equation.
   $$x + x + 8 = 50$$
   $$2x + 8 = 50$$
   $$2x = 42$$
   $$x = 21$$

   *Step (5):* If $x = 21$, then $x + 8 = 29$. The shorter piece is 21 feet long, and the longer piece is 29 feet long.

## Solutions to Study Exercises, Contd.

3.  *Step (1):*  Let $x$ represent the amount of current carried by the first branch.

    *Step (2):*  $3x$ represents the amount of current carried by the second branch, and $x - 2$ represents the amount of current carried by the third branch.

    *Step (3):*  The sum of the currents is 23 amperes.
    $$x + 3x + x - 2 = 23$$

    *Step (4):*  Solve the equation.
    $$x + 3x + x - 2 = 23$$
    $$5x - 2 = 23$$
    $$5x = 25$$
    $$x = 5$$

    *Step (5):*  If $x = 5$, then $3x = 15$ and $x - 2 = 3$. The first branch carries 5 amperes. The second branch carries 15 amperes, and the third branch carries 3 amperes.

4.  *Step (1):*  Let $x$ represent the number of quarters.

    *Step (2):*  $x - 12$ represents the number of dimes.

    *Step (3):*

    | Value of quarters in cents | + | Value of dimes in cents | = | Value of collection in cents |
    |---|---|---|---|---|
    | $25x$ | + | $10(x - 12)$ | = | $1000$ |

    *Step (4):*  Solve the equation.
    $$25x + 10(x - 12) = 1000$$
    $$25x + 10x - 120 = 1000$$
    $$35x - 120 = 1000$$
    $$35x = 1120$$
    $$x = 32$$

    *Step (5):*  If $x = 32$, then $x - 12 = 20$.  There are 32 quarters and 20 dimes in the collection.

# Module 2 Review Problems

Units 6–10

A. Give the opposite (additive inverse) for each of the following.

1. $+6$      2. $0$      3. $-4$      4. $x$      5. $-y$

B. Simplify each of the following.

6. $-(-3)$      7. $-[-(-4)]$      8. $-[-(+8)]$

9. $|+3|$      10. $|-7|$      11. $|0|$

C. Insert $>$, $<$, or $=$ to make the following true.

12. $-3$ ____ $-1$      13. $-4$ ____ $-6$      14. $|-3|$ ____ $|+3|$

D. Each of these equations illustrates one of the properties of integers. Name the property by giving its abbreviation.

15. $m + (-m) = 0$      16. $-2 \cdot (x + y) = (-2)x + (-2)y$

17. $(-a + 3) \cdot 0 = 0$      18. $(-2a + 4c) + 3d = -2a + (4c + 3d)$

E. Simplify the following completely (evaluate).

19. $(+6) + (-6)$      20. $(-8) + (+2)$      21. $(-3) + (+5)$

22. $-2 + 5 - 7$      23. $6 - 7 - 10$      24. $(-3) - (-2)$

25. $(+1) - (-5) - (+8)$      26. $(-2)(+3)$      27. $(-5)(-4)$

28. $(-20) \div (-2)$      29. $\dfrac{-15}{+3}$      30. $\dfrac{0}{-2}$

31. $(-3)(+2)(-4)$      32. $(-1)(-3)(-6)(-2)$      33. $(-3)^2$

34. $-3^2$      35. $(-1)^{158}$      36. $(-1)^{159}$

F. True or False

37. A negative number raised to an even power produces a negative answer.

38. If a negative integer is subtracted from a positive integer, the result is a positive integer.

39. The product of three negative integers is a positive integer.

G. Combine the following variable expressions, using addition or subtraction.

40. $3x + 5x$      41. $2a^2 + 3a - a^2 + 4a$

42. $3a^2b + 2ab^2 - 5a^2b - ab^2$      43. $(2a^2 + 3a - 5) + (3a^2 - 5a - 1)$

44. $(6m^2 - m + 2) - (3m^2 + 4m - 6)$

H. Multiply or divide the following variable expressions.

45. $(-3)(-a)$      46. $(2a^2b)(-3ab^3c)(4ab)$      47. $5(3a + 2b - 1)$

48. $2x(3x^2 + x - 5)$      49. $\dfrac{12m^3n^2}{-4mn^2}$

## Module 2 Review Problems, Contd.

Units 6–10

I.   Remove grouping symbols and combine like terms.

    50.  $-(2a + 3b)$           51.  $3x - (5x + 2)$         52.  $(3a - b) - (4a + 3b)$

J.   Solve the following equations.

    53.  $-7y = 21$           54.  $3x + 5 = -10$       55.  $3(x + 1) = 15$
    56.  $5x + 3 = 6x + 5$      57.  $2m + 3 = 3$         58.  $2(3a - 1) = 3(a + 5) + 1$

K.   Solve the following word problems. Give both the equation and the answer.

    59.  The sum of two numbers is 16. The larger number is four less than three times the smaller number. Find both numbers.

    60.  A rope 48 inches long is cut into two parts. One piece is 12 inches longer than the other. Find the length of each piece.

## Answers to Module 2 Review Problems

A.   1.  $-6$     2.  0     3.  4     4.  $-x$     5.  $y$

B.   6.  3     7.  $-4$     8.  8     9.  3     10.  7     11.  0

C.   12.  $-3 < -1$     13.  $-4 > -6$     14.  $|-3| = |+3|$

D.   15.  add. inv.     16.  dpma     17.  mult. by zero     18.  apa

E.   19.  0     20.  $-6$     21.  2     22.  $-4$     23.  $-11$     24.  $-1$     25.  $-2$     26.  $-6$     27.  20
    28.  10     29.  $-5$     30.  0     31.  24     32.  36     33.  9     34.  $-9$     35.  1     36.  $-1$

F.   37.  False     38.  True     39.  False

G.   40.  $8x$     41.  $a^2 + 7a$     42.  $-2a^2b + ab^2$     43.  $5a^2 - 2a - 6$     44.  $3m^2 - 5m + 8$

H.   45.  $3a$     46.  $-24a^4b^5c$     47.  $15a + 10b - 5$     48.  $6x^3 + 2x^2 - 10x$   49.  $-3m^2$

I.   50.  $-2a - 3b$     51.  $-2x - 2$     52.  $-a - 4b$

J.   53.  $x = -3$     54.  $x = -5$     55.  $x = 4$
    56.  $x = -2$     57.  $m = 0$     58.  $a = 6$

K.   59.  $x + (3x - 4) = 16$; the smaller number is 5 and the larger number 11.
    60.  $x + (x + 12) = 48$; one piece is 18 inches and the other piece is 30 inches.

# Real Numbers—Rational Numbers, Irrational Numbers, and Fractional Expressions

# Rational Numbers, Irrational Numbers, and Real Numbers

## ☐ Objectives (1)

In this unit we shall develop the final set of numbers to be used in this course — the set of real numbers. By the end of this unit you should be able to define the following terms:

- rational number.
- irrational number.
- real number.

You should be able to write decimal names for rational numbers and indicate whether they are terminating or repeating.

A new property will be developed, the multiplicative inverse property. You should be able to define this property and be able to write the multiplicative inverse of any real number except zero.

Most of the properties of real numbers have been developed in previous units. However, they will be reviewed, and you should be able to apply them to various exercises.

## ☐ Sets of Numbers (2)

1. Natural numbers: $N = \{1, 2, 3, 4, 5, \ldots\}$
2. Whole numbers: $W = \{0, 1, 2, 3, 4, 5, \ldots\}$
3. Integers: $I = \{\cdots, -3, -2, -1, 0, +1, +2, +3, \ldots\}$

The *natural* numbers are a subset of the *whole* numbers, and the whole numbers are a subset of the *integers*.

$$N \subseteq W \subseteq I$$

## ☐ Quotients of Integers (3)

We will now develop a new set of numbers where each element is formed from a quotient of two integers. This set is called the *set of rational numbers*.

**Example 1:** $1 \div 2$ or $\dfrac{1}{2}$ is a rational number.

**Example 2:** $1 \div (-2)$ or $\dfrac{1}{-2}$ is a rational number.

**Example 3:** $2 \div 3$ or $\dfrac{2}{3}$ is a rational number.

**Example 4:** $(-2) \div 3$ or $\dfrac{-2}{3}$ is a rational number.

**Example 5:** $6 \div 1$ or $\dfrac{6}{1}$ or $6$ is a rational number.

**Example 6:** $0 \div 1$ or $\dfrac{0}{1}$ or $0$ is a rational number.

## ☐ Definition of the Set of Rational Numbers (4)

The set of rational numbers is composed of all numbers which can be written in the form $a \div b$ or $\dfrac{a}{b}$ where $a$ and $b$ are integers and $b \neq 0$. The set of rational numbers will be represented by an uppercase $Q$. Examples of elements belonging to set $Q$:

$$Q = \left\{ \cdots, \frac{-8}{5}, \frac{-3}{2}, \frac{-2}{1}, \frac{-1}{1}, \frac{0}{1}, \frac{1}{2}, \frac{2}{3}, \frac{1}{1}, \frac{4}{3}, \frac{2}{1}, \cdots \right\}$$

☐ **Subsets of the Rational Numbers** **(5)**

1. Natural numbers are also rational, because every natural number may be symbolized by a quotient of two integers.

$$N = \left\{ \frac{1}{1}, \frac{2}{1}, \frac{3}{1}, \frac{4}{1}, \cdots \right\}$$

2. Whole numbers are also rational, because every whole number may be symbolized by a quotient of two integers.

$$W = \left\{ \frac{0}{1}, \frac{1}{1}, \frac{2}{1}, \frac{3}{1}, \frac{4}{1}, \cdots \right\}$$

3. Integers are also rational, because every integer may be symbolized by a quotient of two integers.

$$I = \left\{ \cdots, \frac{-3}{1}, \frac{-2}{1}, \frac{0}{1}, \frac{+1}{1}, \frac{+2}{1}, \frac{+3}{1}, \cdots \right\}$$

Natural numbers, whole numbers, and integers are subsets of the rational numbers.

☐ Rational Numbers: **(6)**

$$\frac{-9}{5}, \frac{-3}{2}, \frac{-2}{1}, \frac{0}{1}, \frac{1}{2}, \frac{5}{2}, \frac{3}{1}$$

↑

Integers: $\cdots, -3, -2, -1, 0, +1, +2, +3, \cdots$

↑

Whole Numbers: $0, 1, 2, 3, 4, \cdots$

↑

Natural Numbers $1, 2, 3, 4, \cdots$

☐ **Multiplicative Inverse Property (Mult. Inv.)** **(7)**

For each rational number $x$, except zero, we define a number $\frac{1}{x}$ such that $x \cdot \frac{1}{x} = 1$.

$\frac{1}{x}$ is called the multiplicative inverse of $x$.

**Abbreviation: mult. inv.**

*Note:* The multiplicative inverse of a number is sometimes referred to as the *reciprocal* of the number.

☐ **Examples of the Multiplicative Inverse Property** **(8)**

1. The multiplicative inverse of 2 is $\frac{1}{2}$, and $2 \cdot \frac{1}{2} = 1$.

2. The multiplicative inverse of $-2$ is $\frac{1}{-2}$, and $(-2) \cdot \frac{1}{-2} = 1$.

3. The reciprocal of 6 is $\frac{1}{6}$, and $6 \cdot \frac{1}{6} = 1$.

4. The multiplicative inverse of $\frac{2}{3}$ is $\frac{1}{\frac{2}{3}}$, and $\frac{2}{3} \cdot \frac{1}{\frac{2}{3}} = 1$.

5. The multiplicative inverse of zero does not exist. The symbol $\frac{1}{0}$ does not represent a number.

## ☐ Comparing the Multiplicative Inverse and Additive Inverse Properties (9)

The multiplicative inverse property is analogous to the additive inverse property.

1. **add. inv.:** $x + (-x) = 0$

A number plus its additive inverse produces the additive identity.

2. **Mult. inv.:** $x \cdot \dfrac{1}{x} = 1$

A number times its multiplicative inverse produces the multiplicative identity.

## ☐ Study Exercise One (10)

A. True or False

1. $3 \div 2$ is a rational number.
2. $\dfrac{-4}{5}$ is a rational number.
3. 2 is an integer.
4. $\dfrac{3}{4}$ is an integer.
5. $I \subseteq Q$
6. $W \subseteq Q$
7. $Q \subseteq N$
8. The product of a number and its multiplicative inverse is one.

B. Give the multiplicative inverse for each of the following.

9. 4    10. $-3$    11. 1    12. $-1$    13. 0    14. $\dfrac{3}{5}$

## ☐ Writing Rational Numbers as Decimals (11)

Since every rational number may be symbolized as $\dfrac{a}{b}$ or $a \div b$, where $a$ and $b$ are integers and $b \neq 0$, we can divide $a$ by $b$ to obtain a decimal numeral.

## ☐ Example 1: Given the rational number $\dfrac{3}{4}$, we can divide 3 by 4 and write it as a decimal. (12)

$$
\begin{array}{r}
.75 \\
4\overline{)3.00} \\
\underline{2\,8}\phantom{0} \\
20 \\
\underline{20} \\
0
\end{array}
$$

Hence, $\dfrac{3}{4} = 0.75$. This result is a *terminating* decimal.

## ☐ Example 2: Given the rational number $\dfrac{12}{99}$, we can divide 12 by 99 and write it as a decimal. (13)

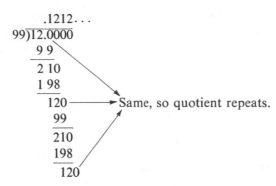

Hence, $\frac{12}{99} = 0.121212\ldots$ This result is a *repeating* decimal.

## ☐ Equivalent Notation for Repeating Decimals (14)

A bar is sometimes placed above the repetitive pattern, thereby eliminating the three dots.

**Example 1:** $0.121212\ldots = 0.\overline{12}$      **Example 2:** $0.713713713\ldots = 0.\overline{713}$

**Example 3:** $0.2474747\ldots = 0.2\overline{47}$      **Example 4:** $3.7040404\ldots = 3.7\overline{04}$

## ☐            *Study Exercise Two* (15)

Using the operation of division, write each of the following rational numbers as a decimal. If the decimal repeats, use the bar. (Do not round off.)

1. $1 \div 2$    2. $\frac{4}{5}$    3. $\frac{14}{99}$    4. $\frac{11}{7}$    5. $\frac{-2}{9}$    6. $\frac{7}{1000}$

## ☐ Alternate Definition of Rational Number (16)

We have seen that a rational number can be written as either a terminating or a repeating decimal. In more advanced courses it can be proved that every terminating or repeating decimal is indeed a rational number.

*Alternate definition:* A number is said to be rational provided it can be symbolized as either a terminating or a repeating decimal.

## ☐ Examples: Each of the following numbers is rational. (17)

1. $0.35$    2. $0.\overline{61}$    3. $5.2\overline{34}$    4. $-8.041$    5. $9$    6. $-3$    7. $0$

## ☐ The Set of Irrational Numbers (18)

We are now in a position to find some numbers that are not rational. Real numbers which are not rational are called *irrational*. The set of irrational numbers will be denoted by an uppercase $H$.

*Definition:* An irrational number is a number whose decimal numeral is nonterminating and nonrepeating

**Example:** $.20200200020000200000 2\ldots$

Zeros increase by one.

This numeral does not terminate and does not have a repetitive pattern. Therefore, it represents an irrational number.

## ☐ Other Examples of Irrational Numbers (19)

1. $0.313113111311113\ldots$
2. $-6.5252252225\ldots$
3. $0.12345678910111213\ldots$
4. $0.919293949596979899109119129139\ldots$
5. $\pi = 3.14159\ldots$

*Note:* No number can be both rational and irrational at the same time.

$$Q \cap H = \varnothing$$

## ☐ *Study Exercise Three* (20)

Classify each of the following numbers as being either rational or irrational.

1. $.125$
2. $1.6$
3. $0.\overline{516}$
4. $0.313113111311113\ldots$
5. $0.\overline{31}$
6. $0$
7. $5.010203040506\ldots$
8. $\dfrac{-5}{8}$
9. $-2$
10. $2.3$

## ☐ The Set of Real Numbers (21)

The *set of real numbers* is defined to be the union of the rationals with the irrationals. The set of real numbers is symbolized by an uppercase *R*.

$$R = Q \cup H$$

A *real number* is any number which can be symbolized by a decimal.

## ☐ Examples of Real Numbers (22)

1. $2.36$
2. $5.\overline{41}$
3. $0.2020020002\ldots$
4. $2 \div 3$
5. $\dfrac{-4}{5}$
6. $0$
7. $-3$
8. $23$

## ☐ (23)

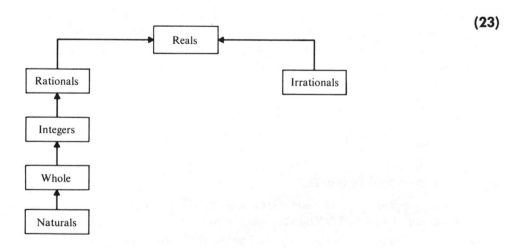

## ☐ The Standard Real Number Line (24)

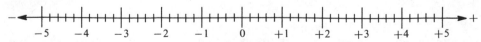

There exists a one-to-one correspondence between the set of real numbers and the set of points on a line.

## ☐ Basic Properties or Axioms of the Set of Real Numbers (25)

Given the set of real numbers, $R$, the equality relationship, $=$, and the two binary operations $+$ and $\cdot$, then the following properties are assumed to be true.

1. The Reflexive Property of Equality: $a = a$
2. The Symmetric Property of Equality: If $a = b$, then $b = a$.
3. The Substitution Property of Equality: If $a = b$, then $b$ may be replaced for $a$ in any expression.
4. The Addition Property of Equality: If $a = b$, then $a + c = b + c$.
5. The Multiplication Property of Equality: If $a = b$, then $a \cdot c = b \cdot c$.
6. The Closure Property for Addition [**clpa**]: If $a$ and $b$ are real numbers, then $a + b$ also represents a real number.
7. The Closure Property for Multiplication [**clpm**]: If $a$ and $b$ are real numbers, then $a \cdot b$ also represents a real number.
8. The Commutative Property of Addition [**cpa**]: $a + b = b + a$
9. The Commutative Property of Multiplication [**cpm**]: $a \cdot b = b \cdot a$
10. The Associative Property of Addition [**apa**]: $(a + b) + c = a + (b + c)$
11. The Associative Property of Multiplication [**apm**]: $(a \cdot b) \cdot c = a \cdot (b \cdot c)$
12. The Distributive Property of Multiplication with Respect to Addition [**dpma**]: $a \cdot (b + c) = a \cdot b + a \cdot c$ and $(b + c) \cdot a = b \cdot a + c \cdot a$
13. The Additive Identity Property [**add. ident.**]: There exists a unique number, 0, such that $a + 0 = a$ and $0 + a = a$.
14. The Multiplicative Identity Property [**mult. ident.**]: There exists a unique number, 1, such that $a \cdot 1 = a$ and $1 \cdot a = a$.
15. The Additive Inverse Property [**add. inv.**]: For each real number, $a$, there exists a unique opposite, $-a$, such that $a + (-a) = 0$.
16. The Multiplicative Inverse Property [**mult. inv.**]: For each real number, $a$, where $a \neq 0$, there exists a unique multiplicative inverse, $\dfrac{1}{a}$, such that $a \cdot \dfrac{1}{a} = 1$.
17. The Multiplication by Zero Property [**mult. by 0**]: $a \cdot 0 = 0$ and $0 \cdot a = 0$

## ☐ Other Properties Which Are True for the Set of Real Numbers (26)

1. The Order of Operations Convention: Unless specified otherwise, first do multiplication and division from left to right in the order they appear. Second, do addition and subtraction in the order they appear from left to right.
2. Grouping Symbols: Grouping symbols take precedence over the order of operations convention. They indicate to "do this first."
3. "Less Than" and "Greater Than" Symbols: They must point toward the symbol representing the smaller number. "Less than" means "names a point to the left of . . . ." "Greater than" means "names a point to the right of . . . ."
4. Whole Numbers Used as Exponents:
   (a) Definition: $a^n = \underbrace{a \cdot a \cdot a \cdots a}_{n \text{ factors}}$

   (b) Zero Power Property: $a^0 = 1$ where $a \neq 0$
   (c) Addition Property of Exponents: $a^m \cdot a^n = a^{m+n}$
   (d) Subtraction Property of Exponents: $a^m \div a^n = \dfrac{a^m}{a^n} = a^{m-n}$
   (e) Power to a Power Property: $(a^m)^n = a^{m \cdot n}$
   (f) Distributive Property of Exponents: $(a^m \cdot b^n)^x = a^{mx} \cdot b^{nx}$
5. Relation of Subtraction to Addition: $a - b = a + (-b)$

6. Properties of Multiplication:
   (a) $(a)(-b) = (-a)(b) = -ab$
   (b) $(-a)(-b) = ab$
7. The Distributive Property of Multiplication with Respect to Subtraction: $a \cdot (b - c) = a \cdot b - a \cdot c$
8. Extensions of the Distributive Properties: $a \cdot (b - c + d - e) = a \cdot b - a \cdot c + a \cdot d - a \cdot e$
9. Removing Grouping Symbols:
   (a) $+(a + b) = a + b$
   (b) $-(a + b) = -a - b$
10. Definition of Absolute Value:
    (a) If $x$ is either a positive real number or zero, then $|x| = x$.
    (b) If $x$ is a negative real number, then $|x| = -x$.

## ☐ Replacement Sets for the Remainder of the Course (27)

Throughout the remainder of this course, if the replacement set for a variable is not given, we will assume that it is the set of real numbers.

## ☐ *Study Exercise Four* (28)

A. True or False

1. A real number is any number that can be symbolized by a decimal.
2. The set of real numbers can be considered to be the union of the rational numbers with the irrational numbers.

B. Each of the following identities is an example of one of the "Basic Properties of Real Numbers" (Frame 25). Name the property by giving the abbreviation.

3. If $x - 5 = 8$, then $x - 5 + 5 = 8 + 5$.
4. $(2 \cdot x) \cdot y = 2 \cdot (x \cdot y)$
5. $3(a + b) = 3a + 3b$
6. $(x + 2) \cdot 1 = x + 2$
7. $6 \cdot \dfrac{1}{6} = 1$

C. Each of the following identities is an example of one of the "Other Properties of Real Numbers" (Frame 26). Name the property associated with each exercise.

8. $x^4 = x \cdot x \cdot x \cdot x$
9. $y^2 \cdot y^5 = y^7$
10. $(m^2 n)^3 = m^6 n^3$
11. $5(x - y) = 5x - 5y$
12. $2(a + b - c + d) = 2a + 2b - 2c + 2d$
13. $x - (y + 2) = x - y - 2$

## REVIEW EXERCISES

A. True or False

1. $2 \div 5$ is a rational number.
2. $\dfrac{-4}{7}$ is a rational number.
3. $1.63$ is a rational number.
4. $3.\overline{57}$ is an irrational number.
5. $0$ is an irrational number.
6. $0.303003000300003\ldots$ is an irrational number.
7. $-6$ is an integer.
8. $5$ is a whole number.
9. $2.56$ is a real number.
10. $-12$ is a real number.
11. $Q \subseteq H$
12. $I \subseteq Q$
13. $Q \cup H = R$

B. Give the multiplicative inverse (reciprocal) for each of the following.

14. $5$    15. $-3$    16. $1$    17. $-1$    18. $0$    19. $8$    20. $-10$    21. $\dfrac{5}{7}$

## REVIEW EXERCISES, Contd.

22. $a$, where $a \neq 0$           23. $-x$, where $x \neq 0$

C. Using the operation of division, write each of these rational numbers as a decimal. If the decimal repeats, use the bar. (Do not round off.)

24. $\dfrac{1}{5}$      25. $\dfrac{3}{8}$      26. $\dfrac{35}{100}$      27. $\dfrac{13}{11}$      28. $\dfrac{-4}{9}$

D. Classify each of these numbers as being rational or irrational.

29. $\dfrac{4}{7}$          30. 0          31. 0.616116111611116...

32. 0.63          33. $2.\overline{53}$          34. $-1.07007000700007...$

E. Each of the following identities is an example of one of the "Basic Properties of Real Numbers" (Frame 25). Name the property by giving the abbreviation.

35. If $m = 7$, then $2m = 2 \cdot 7$.      36. $(a + b) \cdot 2 = 2 \cdot (a + b)$

37. $(x^2 + 2x) + 3 = x^2 + (2x + 3)$      38. $y \cdot 1 = y$

39. $4(a + b) = 4a + 4b$      40. $m \cdot \dfrac{1}{m} = 1$, where $m \neq 0$

41. $x + (-x) = 0$      42. $\dfrac{2}{3} \cdot 0 = 0$

F. Each of the following identities is an example of one of the "Other Properties of Real Numbers" (Frame 26). Name the property associated with each exercise.

43. $\dfrac{x^5}{x^2} = x^3$, where $x \neq 0$      44. $(a^3b)^4 = a^{12}b^4$      45. $(-3)^0 = 1$

46. $-(x + y - 2) = -x - y + 2$      47. $|-7| = 7$

G. Answer the following.

48. Give a diagram illustrating the subset relationships among natural numbers, whole numbers, integers, rational numbers, irrational numbers, and real numbers.

49. State the two definitions of the set of rational numbers.

50. State the multiplicative inverse property.

## Solutions to Review Exercises

A.  1. True    2. True    3. True    4. False    5. False    6. True
    7. True    8. True    9. True    10. True    11. False    12. True
    13. True

B. 14. $\dfrac{1}{5}$    15. $\dfrac{1}{-3}$    16. $\dfrac{1}{1}$ or 1    17. $\dfrac{1}{-1}$ or $-1$    18. Does not exist.

   19. $\dfrac{1}{8}$    20. $\dfrac{1}{-10}$    21. $\dfrac{1}{\frac{5}{7}}$    22. $\dfrac{1}{a}$    23. $\dfrac{1}{-x}$

C. 24. 0.2    25. 0.375    26. 0.35    27. $1.\overline{18}$    28. $-0.\overline{4}$

D. 29. Rational    30. Rational    31. Irrational    32. Rational    33. Rational    34. Irrational

E. 35. Multiplication property of equality
   36. **cpm**         37. **apa**         38. **mult. ident.**         39. **dpma**
   40. **mult. inv.**      41. **add. inv.**      42. **mult. by zero**

F. 43. Subtraction property of exponents      44. Distributive property of exponents
   45. Zero power property      46. Removing grouping symbols preceded by a minus sign
   47. Definition of absolute value

G. 48. See Frame 23.      49. See Frames 4 and 16.      50. See Frame 7.

## SUPPLEMENTARY PROBLEMS

A. True or False
   1. Every rational number can be written as a terminating decimal.
   2. Every integer is also a rational number.
   3. Every rational number is also an integer.
   4. A real number can be thought of as any number which can be represented by a decimal.
   5. $(-3) \div (-7)$ is a rational number.
   6. $\frac{4}{5}$ is an irrational number.
   7. Zero is a real number.
   8. 2.303003000300003... is a rational number.
   9. $\frac{2}{5}$ is an integer.
   10. $-3$ is a rational number.
   11. The multiplicative inverse of zero is zero.
   12. The terms *multiplicative inverse* and *reciprocal* have the same meaning.
   13. $N \subseteq W$               14. $I \subseteq R$               15. $R \subseteq H$

B. Give the multiplicative inverse (reciprocal) for each of the following.

   16. 3          17. $-8$          18. $-1$          19. 1          20. 0          21. $\frac{2}{7}$

   22. $m$, where $m \neq 0$                    23. $-n$, where $n \neq 0$

C. Use the operation of division to write each of these rational numbers as a decimal. If the decimal repeats, use the bar. (Do not round off.)

   24. $\frac{7}{10}$          25. $\frac{5}{100}$          26. $\frac{1}{7}$          27. $\frac{11}{5}$          28. $\frac{-17}{9}$

D. Classify each of these numbers as being rational or irrational.

   29. $\frac{1}{2}$                    30. $\frac{3}{5}$                    31. $\frac{-2}{3}$
   32. 0                    33. $-6$                    34. 5.707007000700007...
   35. $\pi$                    36. $2.\overline{61}$                    37. 0.123456789101112...

E. Each of the following identities is an example of one of the "Basic Properties of Real Numbers" (Frame 25). Name the property by giving the abbreviation.
   38. $2 \cdot (x + y) = (x + y) \cdot 2$          39. $2 \cdot (x + y) = 2 \cdot (y + x)$
   40. $(2 \cdot x) \cdot y = 2 \cdot (x \cdot y)$          41. If $r = s + 3$, then $s + 3 = r$.
   42. If $x = 7$, then $x + 1 = 7 + 1$.          43. $5 + (-5) = 0$
   44. $6 \cdot \frac{1}{6} = 1$          45. $3(m + n) = 3m + 3n$
   46. $(2x + 5y) \cdot 1 = 2x + 5y$          47. $(2x + 5y) \cdot 0 = 0$
   48. $(5a) \cdot \frac{1}{5a} = 1$, where $a \neq 0$          49. $(2.635)(-4.967)$ is a real number.
   50. $(5x + 3y) + 2y = 5x + (3y + 2y)$

F. Each of the following identities is an example of one of the "Other Properties of Real Numbers" (Frame 26). Name the property associated with each exercise.

   51. $a^2 \cdot a^5 = a^7$          52. $\frac{m^6}{m^2} = m^4$          53. $(x^3 y^2)^2 = x^6 y^4$

   54. $\left(-\frac{2}{3}\right)^0 = 1$          55. $(3x)^0 = 1$, where $x \neq 0$          56. $7(m - n) = 7m - 7n$

## SUPPLEMENTARY PROBLEMS, Contd.

57. $x - y = x + (-y)$    58. $2a(b + c - d) = 2ab + 2ac - 2ad$
59. $|5| = 5$    60. $|-6| = 6$
61. $-(r - s) = -r + s$    62. $2x + (3y - z) = 2x + 3y - z$

G. Define the following.

63. Rational number    64. Irrational number    65. Real number

H. Calculator Problems. With your instructor's approval, use a calculator to evaluate the following problems.

66. $2.75 + (6.92)(7.81)$
67. $(8.91)(26.7) - (87.1)(23.2)$
68. $(6.2)(.043) + (8.1)(.65) - (72.1)(13.6)$
69. $(8.61)(2.98)(6.04) - (.0954)(19.63)$
70. $8.0962(19.005 + 2.693)$
71. $2.61[(.58)(.49) - (.62)(.73)]$
72. $8.6 - [9.2 + 4.6(.85 - .73) + 1.2]$
73. $(2.658)^5$
74. $(-3.63)^{10}$
75. $(5.013 + 2.914)^3$
76. $(3.052)(6.905)^2 - (1.069)(6.905)^2 + 5.638$

☐ Solutions to Study Exercises    **(10A)**

### Study Exercise One (Frame 10)

A.  1. True    2. True    3. True    4. False
    5. True    6. True    7. False    8. True

B.  9. $\dfrac{1}{4}$    10. $\dfrac{1}{-3}$    11. $\dfrac{1}{1}$ or 1    12. $\dfrac{1}{-1}$ or $-1$

    13. Does not exist.    14. $\dfrac{\frac{1}{3}}{\frac{-}{5}}$

☐    ### Study Exercise Two (Frame 15)    **(15A)**

1. 0.5    2. 0.8    3. $0.\overline{14}$    4. $1.\overline{571428}$    5. $-0.\overline{2}$    6. 0.007

☐    ### Study Exercise Three (Frame 20)    **(20A)**

1. Rational    2. Rational    3. Rational    4. Irrational    5. Rational
6. Rational    7. Irrational    8. Rational    9. Rational    10. Rational

☐    ### Study Exercise Four (Frame 28)    **(28A)**

A.  1. True    2. True

B.  3. Addition Prop. of Equality    4. **apm**    5. **dpma**
    6. **mult. ident.**    7. **mult. inv.**

C.  8. Definition of exponents    9. Addition property of exponents
    10. Distributive property of exponents    11. **dpms**
    12. Extension of distributive properties    13. Removing grouping symbols preceded by minus sign

# Basic Properties of
# Fractional Expressions

## ☐ Objectives **(1)**

By the end of this unit you should be able to define the following properties of fractions:

- the definition of a fraction.
- the equality test for fractions.
- the Fundamental Principle of Fractions (cancellation property).

You will understand the three signs of a fraction.

You will be able to convert a fraction to a basic quotient or a basic product.

By using the equality test, you will be able to tell if two fractions are equal, as well as solve simple equations where the left and right members are fractions.

You will be able to use the Fundamental Principle of Fractions to expand fractions to higher terms and to reduce fractions to lowest terms.

## ☐ The Fraction Symbol **(2)**

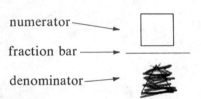

numerator
fraction bar
denominator

**Examples:**

1. $\dfrac{2}{3}$      2. $\dfrac{a}{b}$      3. $\dfrac{m}{m+2}$      4. $\dfrac{5x+3}{x-7}$

*Remember:* The denominator of a fraction must never represent zero.

## ☐ Meanings of a Fraction **(3)**

A fraction can be written as a *basic quotient* or as a *basic product*.

**Example 1:** Basic quotient: $\dfrac{3}{5} = 3 \div 5$      **Example 2:** Basic product: $\dfrac{3}{5} = 3 \cdot \dfrac{1}{5}$

Definition of a fraction: $\dfrac{a}{b} = a \div b$, or $a \cdot \dfrac{1}{b}$, where $b \neq 0$.

## ☐ The Fraction Bar **(4)**

The fraction bar is considered to be an automatic grouping symbol.

**Example 1:** $\dfrac{x+3}{x+5} = (x+3) \div (x+5)$      **Example 2:** $\dfrac{x+3}{x+5} = (x+3) \cdot \dfrac{1}{x+5}$

## ☐ Converting Fractions to Basic Quotients and Basic Products **(5)**

**Example 1:** Convert $\dfrac{2}{x+1}$ to a basic quotient.

**Solution:** $\dfrac{2}{x+1} = 2 \div (x+1)$

144

**Example 2:** Convert $\dfrac{3r^2 - 8}{r + 1}$ to a basic product.

**Solution:** $\dfrac{3r^2 - 8}{r + 1} = (3r^2 - 8) \cdot \dfrac{1}{r + 1}$

☐ **Converting Basic Quotients and Basic Products to Fractional Form** **(6)**

**Example 1:** Convert $(2m + 1) \div (5m - 7)$ to a fraction.

**Solution:** $(2m + 1) \div (5m - 7) = \dfrac{2m + 1}{5m - 7}$

**Example 2:** Convert $(2x^2 - x + 1) \cdot \dfrac{1}{x + 4}$ to a fraction.

**Solution:** $(2x^2 - x + 1) \cdot \dfrac{1}{x + 4} = \dfrac{2x^2 - x + 1}{x + 4}$

☐ **Basic Properties of Fractions** **(7)**

1. The denominator of a fraction can never be zero.

**Example:** $\dfrac{x + 5}{0}$ does not represent a number.

2. If the denominator of a fraction is 1, then the fraction is equal to the numerator.

**Example:** $\dfrac{5m + n}{1} = 5m + n$

3. If the numerator of a fraction is zero and the denominator is not zero, then the fraction is equal to zero.

**Example:** $\dfrac{0}{3x} = 0$, where $x \neq 0$.

4. If the numerator and denominator of a fraction are equal but not zero, then the fraction is equal to one.

**Example:** $\dfrac{4a}{4a} = 1$, where $a \neq 0$.

☐ *Study Exercise One* **(8)**

A. Indicate the numerator and the denominator for each of the following fractions.

     1. $\dfrac{8}{7}$          2. $\dfrac{0}{5}$          3. $\dfrac{x + 2}{x + 3}$

B. Convert each of these fractions to a basic quotient and a basic product.

     4. $\dfrac{x}{y}$          5. $\dfrac{m + 2}{3}$          6. $\dfrac{a - 5}{2a + 7}$

C. Convert each of the following quotients or products to fractional form.

     7. $(-6) \div 5$          8. $2 \div (x + y)$          9. $(2x + 1) \cdot \dfrac{1}{3x - 5}$

D. Simplify these fractions according to the "Basic Properties" listed in Frame 7.

     10. $\dfrac{3a}{1}$          11. $\dfrac{2m}{2m}$, where $m \neq 0$          12. $\dfrac{x + 4}{1}$

     13. $\dfrac{0}{y + 3}$, where $y + 3 \neq 0$

## ☐ The Three Signs of a Fraction (9)

The minus or plus signs of a fraction may appear in any of three positions: in front of the numerator, the denominator, or the fraction bar.

$$\frac{-a}{b} = \frac{a}{-b} = -\frac{a}{b}$$

## ☐ Examples Involving the Three Signs of a Fraction (10)

**Example 1:** $\dfrac{-2}{3} = \dfrac{2}{-3}$  **Example 2:** $\dfrac{1}{-2} = -\dfrac{1}{2}$

**Example 3:** $\dfrac{2x}{-3} = \dfrac{-2x}{3}$  **Example 4:** $\dfrac{-5}{8} \neq \dfrac{-5}{-8}$

**Example 5:** $\dfrac{2m}{3n} = \dfrac{-2m}{-3n}$  **Example 6:** $\dfrac{2m}{3n} \neq -\dfrac{-2m}{-3n}$

## ☐ *Study Exercise Two* (11)

True or False

1. $\dfrac{-3}{4} = \dfrac{3}{-4}$  2. $\dfrac{-3}{4} = -\dfrac{3}{4}$  3. $\dfrac{-3}{4} = \dfrac{-3}{-4}$

4. $\dfrac{2m}{-n} = -\dfrac{2m}{n}$  5. $\dfrac{5x}{2y} = -\dfrac{-5x}{-2y}$

## ☐ Cross Products of Two Fractions (12)

1. You know that $\dfrac{1}{2} = \dfrac{5}{10}$. Observe that the cross products are equal.

$$\frac{1}{2} = \frac{5}{10}$$

cross products

$$1 \cdot 10 = 2 \cdot 5$$

2. You know that $\dfrac{1}{2} \neq \dfrac{3}{4}$. Observe that the cross products are not equal.

$$\frac{1}{2} \neq \frac{3}{4}$$

cross products

$$1 \cdot 4 \neq 2 \cdot 3$$

## ☐ The Equality Test for Fractions (13)

Two fractions are said to be *equal* or *equivalent* provided their cross products are equal. In symbols, this definition states the following:

$b \cdot c = a \cdot d.$

$$\frac{a}{b} = \frac{c}{d} \quad \text{if and only if } a \cdot d = b \cdot c$$

We assume, of course, that $b$ and $d$ do not represent zero.

## ☐ Examples of the Equality Test (14)

**Example 1:** $\dfrac{2}{3} = \dfrac{6}{9}$ because $2 \cdot 9 = 3 \cdot 6$.  **Example 2:** $\dfrac{2}{5} \neq \dfrac{1}{3}$ because $2 \cdot 3 \neq 5 \cdot 1$.

**Example 3:** $\dfrac{2x}{y} = \dfrac{6x}{3y}$ because $(2x)(3y) = (y)(6x)$. **Example 4:** $\dfrac{2a}{b} \neq \dfrac{a}{2b}$ because $(2a)(2b) \neq (b)(a)$.

☐ **Study Exercise Three** (15)

Use the equality test to determine which of the following are correct. (Answer true or false).

1. $\dfrac{3}{5} = \dfrac{6}{10}$

2. $\dfrac{8}{3} = \dfrac{3}{8}$

3. $\dfrac{30}{37} = \dfrac{31}{38}$

4. $\dfrac{3m}{2n} = \dfrac{6m}{4n}$

5. $\dfrac{3x}{2y} = \dfrac{2x}{3y}$

6. $\dfrac{ax}{bx} = \dfrac{a}{b}$

7. $\dfrac{-3}{-4} = \dfrac{3}{4}$

8. $\dfrac{-2}{3} = \dfrac{2}{-3}$

9. $\dfrac{-2}{3} = \dfrac{2}{3}$

☐ **Using the Equality Test to Solve Equations** (16)

The equality test can be used to solve equations when both the left and the right members are fractions.

**Example 1:** Solve $\dfrac{x}{5} = \dfrac{12}{20}$.

    **Solution:** Use the equality test to set the cross products equal.

    line (a)    $\dfrac{x}{5} = \dfrac{12}{20}$

    line (b)   $x \cdot 20 = 5 \cdot 12$

    line (c)    $20x = 60$

    line (d)    $\dfrac{20x}{20} = \dfrac{60}{20}$

    line (e)      $x = 3$

The solution is 3.

☐ **Example 2:** Solve $\dfrac{2y}{5} = \dfrac{7}{3}$. (17)

    **Solution:** Set the cross products equal.

    line (a)   $\dfrac{2y}{5} = \dfrac{7}{3}$

    line (b)   $6y = 35$

    line (c)    $y = \dfrac{35}{6}$

    The solution is $\dfrac{35}{6}$.

☐ **Study Exercise Four** (18)

Use the equality test to solve the following equations.

1. $\dfrac{x}{3} = \dfrac{6}{9}$      2. $\dfrac{y}{7} = \dfrac{-6}{42}$      3. $\dfrac{12}{x} = \dfrac{6}{5}$      4. $\dfrac{3y}{2} = \dfrac{4}{5}$      5. $\dfrac{m+2}{5} = \dfrac{2}{3}$

☐ **The Fundamental Principle of Fractions (Cancellation Property)** (19)

The numerator and denominator of a fraction may be multiplied or divided by the same nonzero number.

$$\frac{a}{b} = \frac{a \cdot n}{b \cdot n} \quad \text{or} \quad \frac{a}{b} = \frac{a \div n}{b \div n} \quad \text{where } n \neq 0$$

☐ Proof of the Fundamental Principle (20)

Use the equality test for fractions to check the cross products.

*line (a)*  $\dfrac{a}{b} = \dfrac{a \cdot n}{b \cdot n}$ because $a \cdot b \cdot n = b \cdot a \cdot n$.

*line (b)*  $\dfrac{a}{b} = \dfrac{a \div n}{b \div n}$ because $a \cdot b \div n = b \cdot a \div n$.

☐ Examples Using the Fundamental Principle (21)

**Example 1:**  $\dfrac{1}{2} = \dfrac{1 \cdot 5}{2 \cdot 5}$ or $\dfrac{5}{10}$     **Example 2:**  $\dfrac{x}{y} = \dfrac{x \cdot 2}{y \cdot 2}$ or $\dfrac{2x}{2y}$

**Example 3:**  $\dfrac{8}{20} = \dfrac{8 \div 4}{20 \div 4}$ or $\dfrac{2}{5}$     **Example 4:**  $\dfrac{4x}{6y} = \dfrac{4x \div 2}{6y \div 2} = \dfrac{2x}{3y}$

☐                           *Study Exercise Five* (22)

A.  Multiply the numerator and the denominator of each of the following fractions by 3.

   1.  $\dfrac{1}{2}$          2.  $\dfrac{4}{5}$          3.  $\dfrac{7}{2}$          4.  $\dfrac{2x}{3y}$

B.  Divide the numerator and the denominator of each of the following fractions by 2.

   5.  $\dfrac{2}{4}$          6.  $\dfrac{6}{2}$          7.  $\dfrac{2x}{8}$          8.  $\dfrac{2a}{10b}$

☐ Expanding Fractions to Higher Terms (23)

When application of the Fundamental Principle results in a fraction having a larger numerator and denominator, we say the fraction has been expanded to *higher terms*.

**Example:**  Expand $\dfrac{3}{5}$ so that its denominator becomes 20.

  **Solution:**  Multiply numerator and denominator by 4.

$$\frac{3}{5} = \frac{3 \cdot 4}{5 \cdot 4} = \frac{12}{20}$$

☐ More Examples (24)

**Example 1:**  Expand $\dfrac{2}{3}$ so that its denominator becomes 12.

  **Solution:**  $\dfrac{2}{3} = \dfrac{2 \cdot 4}{3 \cdot 4} = \dfrac{8}{12}$

**Example 2:**  Expand $\dfrac{5}{7a}$ so that its denominator becomes $21a$

  **Solution:**  $\dfrac{5}{7a} = \dfrac{5 \cdot 3}{(7a) \cdot 3} = \dfrac{15}{21a}$

**Example 3:**  Expand $\dfrac{2x}{5y}$ so that its denominator becomes $15y^2$.

  **Solution:**  $\dfrac{2x}{5y} = \dfrac{(2x) \cdot (3y)}{(5y) \cdot (3y)} = \dfrac{6xy}{15y^2}$

**Example 4:** Expand $\dfrac{3b}{2a^2}$ so that its denominator becomes $4a^2b^2$.

**Solution:** $\dfrac{3b}{2a^2} = \dfrac{(3b)(2b^2)}{(2a^2)(2b^2)} = \dfrac{6b^3}{4a^2b^2}$

□                         *Study Exercise Six*                  **(25)**

A.   Expand the following fractions as directed.

1.   Expand $\dfrac{2}{7}$ so that its denominator becomes 21.

2.   Expand $\dfrac{9}{2}$ so that its denominator becomes 12.

3.   Expand $\dfrac{5}{3x}$ so that its denominator becomes $12x$.

4.   Expand $\dfrac{7}{2m}$ so that its denominator becomes $6m^2$.

5.   Expand $\dfrac{2a}{5b^2}$ so that its denominator becomes $25a^2b^3$.

□   **Reducing to Lowest Terms**                                        **(26)**

When application of the Fundamental Principle results in a fraction having no common factors in the numerator and denominator, we say the fraction has been reduced to *lowest terms*.

**Example:**   Reduce $\dfrac{4}{8}$ to lowest terms.

   **Solution:**

     *Step (1):*   4 is the largest factor common to both the numerator and the denominator because $\dfrac{4}{8} = \dfrac{1 \cdot 4}{2 \cdot 4}$.

     *Step (2):*   Divide numerator and denominator by the largest common factor, namely, 4.

$$\dfrac{4}{8} = \dfrac{4 \div 4}{8 \div 4} = \dfrac{1}{2}$$

*In mathematics, all answers involving fractions should be reduced to lowest terms.*

□   **More Examples**                                                   **(27)**

**Example 1:**   Reduce $\dfrac{24}{30}$ to lowest terms.

   **Solution:**

     *Step (1):*   6 is the largest factor common to both the numerator and the denominator because $\dfrac{24}{30} = \dfrac{4 \cdot 6}{5 \cdot 6}$.

     *Step (2):*   Divide numerator and denominator by 6.

$$\dfrac{24}{30} = \dfrac{24 \div 6}{30 \div 6} = \dfrac{4}{5}$$

**Example 2:** Reduce $\dfrac{2a}{3a^2}$ to lowest terms.

**Solution:**

*Step (1):* $a$ is the largest factor common to both the numerator and the denominator because
$$\frac{2a}{3a^2} = \frac{2 \cdot a}{(3a) \cdot a}.$$

*Step (2):* Divide numerator and denominator by $a$.

$$\frac{2a}{3a^2} = \frac{2a \div a}{3a^2 \div a} = \frac{2}{3a}$$

**Example 3:** Reduce $\dfrac{2mn}{4m^2n}$ to lowest terms.

**Solution:**

*Step (1):* $2mn$ is the largest factor common to both the numerator and the denominator because
$$\frac{2mn}{4m^2n} = \frac{1 \cdot (2mn)}{2m \cdot (2mn)}.$$

*Step (2):* Divide numerator and denominator by $2mn$.

$$\frac{2mn}{4m^2n} = \frac{2mn \div (2mn)}{4m^2n \div (2mn)} = \frac{1}{2m}$$

□                            *Study Exercise Seven*                          **(28)**

Reduce each of the following to lowest terms.

1. $\dfrac{3}{6}$           2. $\dfrac{15}{20}$           3. $\dfrac{18}{24}$           4. $\dfrac{5x}{6x^2}$           5. $\dfrac{6ab}{9a^2b}$

## □ Reducing to Lowest Terms by Cancellation                    **(29)**

When reducing fractions to lowest terms, apply the Fundamental Principle by canceling out the common factors.

**Example:** Reduce $\dfrac{24}{30}$ to lowest terms.

**Solution:**

*Step (1):* 6 is the largest factor common to both numerator and denominator because $\dfrac{24}{30} = \dfrac{4 \cdot 6}{5 \cdot 6}$.

*Step (2):* Cancel the common factors.

$$\frac{24}{30} = \frac{4 \cdot \cancel{6}}{5 \cdot \cancel{6}} = \frac{4}{5}$$

## □ More Examples                                             **(30)**

**Example 1:** Reduce $\dfrac{2a}{3a^2}$ to lowest terms.

**Solution:**

*Step (1):* $a$ is the largest factor common to both the numerator and the denominator because
$$\frac{2a}{3a^2} = \frac{2 \cdot a}{(3a) \cdot a}.$$

*Step (2):* Cancel the common factors.
$$\frac{2a}{3a^2} = \frac{2 \cdot \cancel{a}}{(3a) \cdot \cancel{a}} = \frac{2}{3a}$$

**Example 2:** Reduce $\dfrac{2mn}{4m^2n}$ to lowest terms.

**Solution:**

*Step (1):* $2mn$ is the largest factor common to both numerator and denominator because
$$\dfrac{2mn}{4m^2n} = \dfrac{1 \cdot (2mn)}{2m \cdot (2mn)}.$$

*Step (2):* Cancel the common factors.
$$\dfrac{2mn}{4m^2n} = \dfrac{1 \cdot (\cancel{2mn})}{2m \cdot (\cancel{2mn})} = \dfrac{1}{2m}$$

**Example 3:** Reduce $\dfrac{5(a+3)}{6(a+3)}$.

**Solution:**

*Step (1):* $a+3$ is the largest factor common to both the numerator and the denominator.

*Step (2):* Cancel the common factor.
$$\dfrac{5(\cancel{a+3})}{6(\cancel{a+3})} = \dfrac{5}{6}$$

## ☐ Incorrect Examples of Cancellation (31)

**Example 1:** Reduce $\dfrac{2 \cdot a}{a+b}$ to lowest terms.

**Incorrect Solution:** $\dfrac{2 \cdot \cancel{a}}{\cancel{a}+b} \neq \dfrac{2}{b}$

**Example 2:** Reduce $\dfrac{5(a+b)}{a+c}$ to lowest terms.

**Incorrect Solution:** $\dfrac{5(\cancel{a}+b)}{\cancel{a}+c} \neq \dfrac{5b}{c}$

## ☐ Summary of Cancellation (32)

*Remember,* cancellation is simply a shortcut for dividing numerator and denominator by the same number. Therefore, you may cancel only under the following two conditions:

1. *Both the numerator and the denominator must be basic products.*
2. *The numbers canceled must be factors.*

## ☐ Study Exercise Eight (33)

A. Cancellation has been performed in each of the following examples. Indicate whether or not it has been done correctly.

1. $\dfrac{6}{8} = \dfrac{3 \cdot \cancel{2}}{4 \cdot \cancel{2}} = \dfrac{3}{4}$
2. $\dfrac{\cancel{a}+3}{5\cancel{a}} = \dfrac{3}{5}$
3. $\dfrac{\cancel{m}+3}{\cancel{m}+7} = \dfrac{3}{7}$
4. $\dfrac{2(\cancel{m+3})}{5(\cancel{m+3})} = \dfrac{2}{5}$

B. Reduce each of the following to lowest terms by cancellation.

5. $\dfrac{10}{25}$
6. $\dfrac{8}{24}$
7. $\dfrac{7a}{14b}$
8. $\dfrac{-7a}{9a}$
9. $\dfrac{3m}{-5m^2}$
10. $\dfrac{12bc}{15b^2c}$
11. $\dfrac{6(x+5)}{7(x+5)}$
12. $\dfrac{2y(a-4)}{a-4}$

## □ Reducing Fractions Containing Basic Sums or Differences (34)

As we have seen earlier, fractions may be reduced by cancellation only if the following two conditions hold:

1.  Both the numerator and the denominator must be basic products.
2.  The numbers or expressions which are canceled must be factors.

Therefore, to reduce fractions whose numerators or denominators are basic sums or differences, we must factor by "undistributing" the common element.

**Example:** Reduce $\dfrac{2x + 2y}{3x + 3y}$ to lowest terms.

**Solution:**

*Step (1):* Factor the numerator and the denominator.
$$\frac{2x + 2y}{3x + 3y} = \frac{2(x + y)}{3(x + y)}$$

*Step (2):* Cancel the common factors.
$$\frac{2\cancel{(x + y)}}{3\cancel{(x + y)}} = \frac{2}{3}$$

Therefore, $\dfrac{2x + 2y}{3x + 3y} = \dfrac{2}{3}$.

## □ More Examples (35)

**Example 1:** Reduce $\dfrac{3a + 3b}{3}$.

**Solution:**

*Step (1):* Factor the numerator.
$$\frac{3a + 3b}{3} = \frac{3(a + b)}{3}$$

*Step (2):* Cancel the common factors.
$$\frac{\cancel{3} \cdot (a + b)}{\cancel{3}} = \frac{a + b}{1} \text{ or } a + b$$

Therefore, $\dfrac{3a + 3b}{3} = a + b$.

## □ Example 2: Reduce $\dfrac{2m^2 + 4}{6m}$. (36)

**Solution:**

*Step (1):* Factor the numerator and denominator.
$$\frac{2m^2 + 4}{6m} = \frac{2 \cdot (m^2 + 2)}{2 \cdot 3m}$$

*Step (2):* Cancel the common factors.
$$\frac{\cancel{2} \cdot (m^2 + 2)}{\cancel{2} \cdot 3m} = \frac{m^2 + 2}{3m}$$

Therefore, $\dfrac{2m^2 + 4}{6m} = \dfrac{m^2 + 2}{3m}$.

☐ **Example 3:** Reduce $\dfrac{x-2}{6x-12}$        **(37)**

**Solution:**

*Step (1):* Factor the numerator and denominator.

$$\frac{x-2}{6x-12} = \frac{(x-2)}{6(x-2)}$$

*Step (2):* Cancel the common factors.

$$\frac{(\cancel{x-2})}{6(\cancel{x-2})} = \frac{1}{6}$$

Therefore, $\dfrac{x-2}{6x-12} = \dfrac{1}{6}$.

☐                      *Study Exercise Nine*              **(38)**

Reduce the following to lowest terms.

1. $\dfrac{3a+3b}{5a+5b}$      2. $\dfrac{5x+10y}{5}$      3. $\dfrac{5y^2-15}{10y}$

4. $\dfrac{m+3}{7m+21}$      5. $\dfrac{2a^2-4a}{2a(a-2)}$      6. $\dfrac{3x-6}{3x+6}$

## REVIEW EXERCISES

A. State the following properties.

   1. Definition of the fraction $\dfrac{a}{b}$

   2. The equality test for two fractions
   3. The Fundamental Principle of Fractions (cancellation property)

B. Indicate the numerator and the denominator for each of these fractions.

   4. $\dfrac{2x}{y}$               5. $\dfrac{a+3}{-5a}$

C. Convert each of these fractions to a basic quotient and a basic product.

   6. $\dfrac{2x+3}{7}$            7. $\dfrac{m+2}{m-3}$

D. Convert each of the following to fractional form.

   8. $2x \div (x+1)$         9. $(2x-1) \cdot \dfrac{1}{5}$

E. Simplify these fractions according to the "Basic Properties" listed in Frame 7.

   10. $\dfrac{5x}{1}$              11. $\dfrac{2y}{2y}$, where $2y \neq 0$

   12. $\dfrac{0}{a-5}$, where $a-5 \neq 0$         13. $\dfrac{2m-3}{1}$

F. True or False

   14. $\dfrac{-7}{8} = \dfrac{-7}{-8}$     15. $\dfrac{3y}{-2} = \dfrac{-3y}{2}$     16. $\dfrac{-m}{-n} = \dfrac{m}{n}$     17. $\dfrac{2a}{b} = -\dfrac{2a}{b}$

## REVIEW EXERCISES, Contd.

G. Use the equality test to determine which of the following are correct. (Answer true or false.)

18. $\dfrac{3}{4} = \dfrac{9}{16}$ 
19. $\dfrac{-5}{3} = \dfrac{10}{-6}$ 
20. $\dfrac{2x}{y} = \dfrac{x}{2y}$ 
21. $\dfrac{21}{29} = \dfrac{22}{30}$

H. Use the equality test to solve the following equations.

22. $\dfrac{x}{4} = \dfrac{6}{8}$ 
23. $\dfrac{2y}{3} = \dfrac{-5}{8}$ 
24. $\dfrac{5}{x} = \dfrac{3}{7}$ 
25. $\dfrac{x+1}{4} = \dfrac{1}{2}$

I. Expand the following fractions as directed.

26. Expand $\dfrac{3}{5}$ so that its denominator becomes 15.

27. Expand $\dfrac{2}{7a}$ so that its denominator becomes $14a^2$.

28. Expand $\dfrac{3x}{4y^2}$ so that its denominator becomes $12x^2y^3$.

J. Cancellation has been performed in each of these examples. Indicate whether it has been done correctly. (Answer yes or no.)

29. $\dfrac{8}{12} = \dfrac{2 \cdot \cancel{4}}{3 \cdot \cancel{4}} = \dfrac{2}{3}$ 
30. $\dfrac{\cancel{m} + 2}{3\cancel{m}} = \dfrac{2}{3}$ 
31. $\dfrac{\cancel{a} - 7}{\cancel{a} + 2} = \dfrac{-7}{2}$ 
32. $\dfrac{5(\cancel{x-3})}{7(\cancel{x-3})} = \dfrac{5}{7}$

K. Reduce each of the following fractions to lowest terms. You may use cancellation.

33. $\dfrac{6}{15}$ 
34. $\dfrac{5}{20}$ 
35. $\dfrac{2m}{4}$ 
36. $\dfrac{6a}{12a}$

37. $\dfrac{-2a}{3a^2}$ 
38. $\dfrac{6m^2}{2m}$ 
39. $\dfrac{8ab}{10a^2b}$ 
40. $\dfrac{5s^3}{25s^2t}$

41. $\dfrac{2(a+b)}{-3(a+b)}$ 
42. $\dfrac{3x(x-2)}{x-2}$ 
43. $\dfrac{2x+2y}{7x+7y}$ 
44. $\dfrac{3a+6}{2a+4}$

45. $\dfrac{5y+10}{5y}$ 
46. $\dfrac{m-3}{4m-12}$ 
47. $\dfrac{3a^2-9a}{3a(a-3)}$ 
48. $\dfrac{2y+2}{y+1}$

## Solutions to Review Exercises

A. 1. See Frame 3. 
2. See Frame 13. 
3. See Frame 19.

B. 4. Numerator is $2x$; denominator is $y$. 
5. Numerator is $(a+3)$; denominator is $-5a$.

C. 6. $\dfrac{2x+3}{7} = (2x+3) \div 7$, or $(2x+3) \cdot \dfrac{1}{7}$ 
7. $\dfrac{m+2}{m-3} = (m+2) \div (m-3)$, or $(m+2) \cdot \dfrac{1}{m-3}$

D. 8. $\dfrac{2x}{x+1}$ 
9. $\dfrac{2x-1}{5}$

E. 10. $5x$ 
11. 1 
12. 0 
13. $2m-3$

F. 14. False 
15. True 
16. True 
17. False

G. 18. False; $3 \cdot 16 \neq 4 \cdot 9$ 
19. True; $(-5)(-6) = (3)(10)$ 
20. False; $(2x)(2y) \neq yx$ 
21. False; $21 \cdot 30 \neq 29 \cdot 22$

H. 22. $\dfrac{x}{4} = \dfrac{6}{8}$ 
$8x = 24$ 
$x = 3$ 
Solution is 3

23. $\dfrac{2y}{3} = \dfrac{-5}{8}$ 
$16y = -15$ 
$y = \dfrac{-15}{16}$ 
Solution is $\dfrac{-15}{16}$

24. $\dfrac{5}{x} = \dfrac{3}{7}$ 
$3x = 35$ 
$x = \dfrac{35}{3}$ 
Solution is $\dfrac{35}{3}$

25. $\dfrac{x+1}{4} = \dfrac{1}{2}$ 
$2(x+1) = 4$ 
$2x + 2 = 4$ 
$2x = 2$ 
$x = 1$ 
Solution is 1

## Solutions to Review Exercises, Contd.

I.   26. $\dfrac{3}{5} = \dfrac{3 \cdot 3}{5 \cdot 3}$
      $= \dfrac{9}{15}$

27. $\dfrac{2}{7a} = \dfrac{2 \cdot (2a)}{7a \cdot (2a)}$
      $= \dfrac{4a}{14a^2}$

28. $\dfrac{3x}{4y^2} = \dfrac{3x \cdot (3x^2y)}{4y^2 \cdot (3x^2y)}$
      $= \dfrac{9x^3y}{12x^2y^3}$

J.   29. Yes          30. No          31. No          32. Yes

K.   33. $\dfrac{6}{15} = \dfrac{2 \cdot \cancel{3}}{5 \cdot \cancel{3}}$
      $= \dfrac{2}{5}$

34. $\dfrac{5}{20} = \dfrac{1 \cdot \cancel{5}}{4 \cdot \cancel{5}}$
      $= \dfrac{1}{4}$

35. $\dfrac{2m}{4} = \dfrac{\cancel{2} \cdot m}{\cancel{2} \cdot 2}$
      $= \dfrac{m}{2}$

36. $\dfrac{6a}{12a} = \dfrac{1 \cdot \cancel{6a}}{2 \cdot \cancel{6a}}$
      $= \dfrac{1}{2}$

37. $\dfrac{-2a}{3a^2} = \dfrac{-2 \cdot \cancel{a}}{3 \cdot a \cdot \cancel{a}}$
      $= \dfrac{-2}{3a}$

38. $\dfrac{6m^2}{2m} = \dfrac{3 \cdot \cancel{2m} \cdot m}{1 \cdot \cancel{2m}}$
      $= 3m$

39. $\dfrac{8ab}{10a^2b} = \dfrac{\cancel{2} \cdot 4 \cdot \cancel{a} \cdot \cancel{b}}{\cancel{2} \cdot 5 \cdot \cancel{a} \cdot a \cdot \cancel{b}}$
      $= \dfrac{4}{5a}$

40. $\dfrac{5s^3}{25s^2t} = \dfrac{\cancel{5} \cdot \cancel{s^2} \cdot s}{\cancel{5} \cdot 5 \cdot \cancel{s^2} \cdot t}$
      $= \dfrac{s}{5t}$

41. $\dfrac{2(a + b)}{-3(a + b)} = \dfrac{2 \cdot \cancel{(a + b)}}{-3 \cdot \cancel{(a + b)}}$
      $= \dfrac{2}{-3}$ or $-\dfrac{2}{3}$

42. $\dfrac{3x(x - 2)}{x - 2} = \dfrac{3x \cdot \cancel{(x - 2)}}{\cancel{(x - 2)}}$
      $= 3x$

43. $\dfrac{2x + 2y}{7x + 7y} = \dfrac{2\cancel{(x + y)}}{7\cancel{(x + y)}}$
      $= \dfrac{2}{7}$

44. $\dfrac{3a + 6}{2a + 4} = \dfrac{3 \cdot \cancel{(a + 2)}}{2 \cdot \cancel{(a + 2)}}$
      $= \dfrac{3}{2}$

45. $\dfrac{5y + 10}{5y} = \dfrac{\cancel{5} \cdot (y + 2)}{\cancel{5} \cdot y}$
      $= \dfrac{y + 2}{y}$

46. $\dfrac{m - 3}{4m - 12} = \dfrac{\cancel{(m - 3)}}{4 \cdot \cancel{(m - 3)}}$
      $= \dfrac{1}{4}$

47. $\dfrac{3a^2 - 9a}{3a(a - 3)} = \dfrac{\cancel{3a} \cdot \cancel{(a - 3)}}{\cancel{3a} \cdot \cancel{(a - 3)}}$
      $= 1$

48. $\dfrac{2y + 2}{y + 1} = \dfrac{2 \cdot \cancel{(y + 1)}}{\cancel{(y + 1)}}$
      $= 2$

## SUPPLEMENTARY PROBLEMS

A.   Indicate the numerator and the denominator for each of these fractions.

   1. $\dfrac{3a}{5b}$          2. $\dfrac{x + 5}{x - 6}$          3. $\dfrac{2a - 7}{-3a}$

B.   Convert each of these fractions to a basic quotient and a basic product.

   4. $\dfrac{x + 7}{3}$          5. $\dfrac{2a}{a - 4}$          6. $\dfrac{2x - 5}{3x + 4}$

C.   Convert each of the following to fractional form.

   7. $3y \div (y + 4)$          8. $(m - 3) \div (m + 5)$

   9. $(2x + 1) \cdot \dfrac{1}{7}$          10. $(3x^2 + 4) \cdot \dfrac{1}{x + 7}$

## SUPPLEMENTARY PROBLEMS, Contd.

D. Simplify these fractions according to the "Basic Properties" listed in Frame 7.

11. $\dfrac{a}{1}$

12. $\dfrac{0}{x+3}$, where $x + 3 \neq 0$

13. $\dfrac{a+4}{a+4}$, where $a + 4 \neq 0$

14. $\dfrac{7m-2}{1}$

E. True or False

15. $\dfrac{-8}{9} = -\dfrac{8}{9}$

16. $\dfrac{-8}{9} = \dfrac{8}{-9}$

17. $\dfrac{-2a}{5b} = \dfrac{2a}{5b}$

18. $\dfrac{7x}{5y} = \dfrac{-7x}{-5y}$

F. Use the equality test to determine which of the following are correct. (Answer true or false.)

19. $\dfrac{5}{8} = \dfrac{15}{24}$

20. $\dfrac{-3}{7} = \dfrac{6}{-14}$

21. $\dfrac{36}{41} = \dfrac{37}{42}$

22. $\dfrac{3m}{7n} = \dfrac{7m}{3n}$

G. Use the equality test to solve the following equations.

23. $\dfrac{x}{2} = \dfrac{6}{4}$

24. $\dfrac{3y}{5} = \dfrac{1}{4}$

25. $\dfrac{6}{x} = \dfrac{3}{2}$

26. $\dfrac{2m}{3} = \dfrac{-3}{5}$

27. $\dfrac{x+3}{5} = \dfrac{1}{10}$

28. $\dfrac{3y-2}{3} = \dfrac{5}{4}$

H. Expand the following fractions as directed.

29. Expand $\dfrac{5}{6}$ so that its denominator becomes 24.

30. Expand $\dfrac{3}{5b}$ so that its denominator becomes $10b^2$.

31. Expand $\dfrac{4m}{3n}$ so that its denominator becomes $6mn^2$.

32. Expand $\dfrac{2xy^2}{7a^2b^3}$ so that its denominator becomes $21a^3b^5$.

I. Cancellation has been performed in each of these examples. Indicate whether it has been done correctly.

33. $\dfrac{9}{15} = \dfrac{3 \cdot \cancel{3}}{5 \cdot \cancel{3}} = \dfrac{3}{5}$

34. $\dfrac{6}{7} = \dfrac{4 + \cancel{2}}{5 + \cancel{2}} = \dfrac{4}{5}$

35. $\dfrac{a + \cancel{5}}{\cancel{5}} = a$

36. $\dfrac{2 \cdot \cancel{(a+1)}}{3 \cdot \cancel{(a+1)}} = \dfrac{2}{3}$

37. $\dfrac{\cancel{m}}{3\cancel{m}} = \dfrac{0}{3}$

38. $\dfrac{\cancel{m}}{3\cancel{m}} = \dfrac{1}{3}$

39. $\dfrac{\cancel{y} + 8}{\cancel{y} + 3} = \dfrac{8}{3}$

J. Reduce each of the following fractions to lowest terms. You may use cancellation.

40. $\dfrac{3}{6}$

41. $\dfrac{12}{15}$

42. $\dfrac{9}{6}$

43. $\dfrac{-14}{21}$

44. $\dfrac{7x}{x}$

45. $\dfrac{5x}{2x}$

46. $\dfrac{3n}{2n}$

47. $\dfrac{-3a^2}{2a}$

48. $\dfrac{12xy}{9x^2y}$

49. $\dfrac{6x^3}{36x^2y}$

50. $\dfrac{3(m+n)}{-7(m+n)}$

51. $\dfrac{2y(y+3)}{y+3}$

52. $\dfrac{7m-7n}{7m+7n}$

53. $\dfrac{7m-7n}{14m-14n}$

54. $\dfrac{3x-3y}{5x-5y}$

55. $\dfrac{5y-10}{2y-4}$

56. $\dfrac{6x+12}{6x}$

57. $\dfrac{xy+xz}{x}$

58. $\dfrac{4a^2-8a}{2a(2a-4)}$

59. $\dfrac{3b+3}{b+1}$

60. $\dfrac{xy^2-x^2y}{3xy}$

## SUPPLEMENTARY PROBLEMS, Contd.

 **K.** Calculator Problems. With your instructor's approval, use a calculator to evaluate the following expressions.

61. $\dfrac{26.9}{38.5}$

62. $\dfrac{(82.621)(101.85)}{456.93}$

63. $\dfrac{9.72 + 8.04}{2.15}$

64. $\dfrac{(.021)(.054)}{(.621)(.095)}$

65. $\dfrac{(18.092)^2}{(3.614)^3}$

66. $\dfrac{(19.01)^2 + (7.52)^3}{(6.71)^3 - (12.63)^2}$

67. $\dfrac{(15.851)^2(3.941)^3}{(2.68)^2(.973)^4}$

68. Solve $\dfrac{(2.65)x}{3.95} = \dfrac{8.21}{10.4}$

69. Solve $\dfrac{3.58(x + 2.09)}{6.82} = \dfrac{9.76}{2.17}$

---

☐ **Solutions to Study Exercises** **(8A)**

### Study Exercise One (Frame 8)

**A.** 1. Numerator is 8; denominator is 7.
2. Numerator is 0; denominator is 5.
3. Numerator is $(x + 2)$; denominator is $(x + 3)$.

**B.** 4. $\dfrac{x}{y} = x \div y$, or $x \cdot \dfrac{1}{y}$

5. $\dfrac{m + 2}{3} = (m + 2) \div 3$, or $(m + 2) \cdot \dfrac{1}{3}$

6. $\dfrac{a - 5}{2a + 7} = (a - 5) \div (2a + 7)$, or $(a - 5) \cdot \dfrac{1}{2a + 7}$

**C.** 7. $\dfrac{-6}{5}$

8. $\dfrac{2}{x + y}$

9. $\dfrac{2x + 1}{3x - 5}$

**D.** 10. $3a$   11. 1   12. $x + 4$   13. 0

---

☐ ### Study Exercise Two (Frame 11) **(11A)**

1. True   2. True   3. False   4. True   5. False

---

☐ ### Study Exercise Three (Frame 15) **(15A)**

1. True; $3 \cdot 10 = 5 \cdot 6$
2. False; $8 \cdot 8 \neq 3 \cdot 3$
3. False; $(30)(38) \neq (37)(31)$
4. True; $(3m)(4n) = (2n)(6m)$
5. False; $(3x)(3y) \neq (2y)(2x)$
6. True; $a \times b = b \times a$
7. True; $(-3)(4) = (-4)(3)$
8. True; $(-2)(-3) = (3)(2)$
9. False; $(-2)(3) \neq (3)(2)$

---

☐ ### Study Exercise Four (Frame 18) **(18A)**

1. $\dfrac{x}{3} = \dfrac{6}{9}$
   $9x = 18$
   $x = 2$
   Solution is 2

2. $\dfrac{y}{7} = \dfrac{-6}{42}$
   $42y = -42$
   $y = -1$
   Solution is $-1$

3. $\dfrac{12}{x} = \dfrac{6}{5}$
   $60 = 6x$
   $10 = x$
   Solution is 10

4. $\dfrac{3y}{2} = \dfrac{4}{5}$
   $15y = 8$
   $y = \dfrac{8}{15}$
   Solution is $\dfrac{8}{15}$

5. $\dfrac{m + 2}{5} = \dfrac{2}{3}$
   $3(m + 2) = 10$
   $3m + 6 = 10$
   $3m = 4$
   $m = \dfrac{4}{3}$
   Solution is $\dfrac{4}{3}$

## Solutions to Study Exercises, Contd.

### Study Exercise Five (Frame 22)        (22A)

A. 1. $\dfrac{1\cdot 3}{2\cdot 3}=\dfrac{3}{6}$      2. $\dfrac{4\cdot 3}{5\cdot 3}=\dfrac{12}{15}$      3. $\dfrac{7\cdot 3}{2\cdot 3}=\dfrac{21}{6}$      4. $\dfrac{(2x)\cdot 3}{(3y)\cdot 3}=\dfrac{6x}{9y}$

B. 5. $\dfrac{2\div 2}{4\div 2}=\dfrac{1}{2}$      6. $\dfrac{6\div 2}{2\div 2}=\dfrac{3}{1}$ or $3$      7. $\dfrac{(2x)\div 2}{8\div 2}=\dfrac{x}{4}$      8. $\dfrac{(2a)\div 2}{(10b)\div 2}=\dfrac{a}{5b}$

### Study Exercise Six (Frame 25)        (25A)

A. 1. $\dfrac{2\cdot 3}{7\cdot 3}=\dfrac{6}{21}$      2. $\dfrac{9\cdot 6}{2\cdot 6}=\dfrac{54}{12}$      3. $\dfrac{5\cdot 4}{(3x)\cdot 4}=\dfrac{20}{12x}$

4. $\dfrac{7\cdot (3m)}{(2m)(3m)}=\dfrac{21m}{6m^2}$      5. $\dfrac{(2a)\cdot (5a^2b)}{(5b^2)\cdot (5a^2b)}=\cdot\dfrac{10a^3b}{25a^2b^3}$

### Study Exercise Seven (Frame 28)        (28A)

1. $\dfrac{3\div 3}{6\div 3}=\dfrac{1}{2}$    2. $\dfrac{15\div 5}{20\div 5}=\dfrac{3}{4}$    3. $\dfrac{18\div 6}{24\div 6}=\dfrac{3}{4}$    4. $\dfrac{(5x)\div x}{(6x^2)\div x}=\dfrac{5}{6x}$    5. $\dfrac{(6ab)\div (3ab)}{(9a^2b)\div (3ab)}=\dfrac{2}{3a}$

### Study Exercise Eight (Frame 33)        (33A)

A. 1. Correct
2. Incorrect; the numerator is not a basic product.
3. Incorrect; the numerator and denominator are not basic products.
4. Correct

B. 5. $\dfrac{10}{25}=\dfrac{2\cdot\cancel{5}}{5\cdot\cancel{5}}=\dfrac{2}{5}$      6. $\dfrac{8}{24}=\dfrac{1\cdot\cancel{8}}{3\cdot\cancel{8}}=\dfrac{1}{3}$      7. $\dfrac{7a}{14b}=\dfrac{\cancel{7}\cdot a}{\cancel{7}\cdot 2\cdot b}=\dfrac{a}{2b}$

8. $\dfrac{-7a}{9a}=\dfrac{-7\cdot\cancel{a}}{9\cdot\cancel{a}}=\dfrac{-7}{9}$      9. $\dfrac{3m}{-5m^2}=\dfrac{3\cdot\cancel{m}}{-5\cdot m\cdot\cancel{m}}=\dfrac{3}{-5m}$      10. $\dfrac{12bc}{15b^2c}=\dfrac{\cancel{3}\cdot 4\cdot\cancel{b}\cdot\cancel{c}}{\cancel{3}\cdot 5\cdot b\cdot\cancel{b}\cdot\cancel{c}}=\dfrac{4}{5b}$

11. $\dfrac{6(x+5)}{7(x+5)}=\dfrac{6\cdot\cancel{(x+5)}}{7\cdot\cancel{(x+5)}}=\dfrac{6}{7}$      12. $\dfrac{2y(a-4)}{a-4}=\dfrac{2y\cdot\cancel{(a-4)}}{\cancel{(a-4)}}=\dfrac{2y}{1}$ or $2y$

### Study Exercise Nine (Frame 38)        (38A)

1. $\dfrac{3a+3b}{5a+5b}=\dfrac{3\cdot\cancel{(a+b)}}{5\cdot\cancel{(a+b)}}=\dfrac{3}{5}$      2. $\dfrac{5x+10y}{5}=\dfrac{\cancel{5}\cdot (x+2y)}{\cancel{5}}=\dfrac{x+2y}{1}$ or $x+2y$

3. $\dfrac{5y^2-15}{10y}=\dfrac{\cancel{5}\cdot (y^2-3)}{\cancel{5}\cdot 2y}=\dfrac{y^2-3}{2y}$      4. $\dfrac{m+3}{7m+21}=\dfrac{(m+3)}{7\cdot (m+3)}=\dfrac{1}{7}$

5. $\dfrac{2a^2-4a}{2a(a-2)}=\dfrac{2a(a-2)}{2a(a-2)}=1$      6. $\dfrac{3x-6}{3x+6}=\dfrac{\cancel{3}\cdot (x-2)}{\cancel{3}\cdot (x+2)}=\dfrac{x-2}{x+2}$

# Multiplication and Division of Fractional Expressions

## ☐ Objectives                (1)

By the end of this unit, you should be able to:

- multiply numbers in fractional form.
- divide numbers in fractional form.
- use the Fundamental Principle of Fractions to cancel like factors before multiplying, as an aid to simplifying multiplication of fractions.

## ☐ Multiplication of Numbers in Fractional Form      (2)

**Case 1:** Multiplication of $\frac{1}{a} \cdot \frac{1}{b}$, where $a, b \neq 0$

**Example:** $\frac{1}{2} \cdot \frac{1}{3}$

**Case 2:** Multiplication of $\frac{a}{b} \cdot \frac{c}{d}$, where $b, d \neq 0$

**Example:** $\frac{3}{4} \cdot \frac{5}{7}$

## ☐ Case 1: $\frac{1}{2} \cdot \frac{1}{3}$               (3)

1. $\frac{1}{2} \cdot \frac{1}{3} = \frac{1}{2} \cdot \frac{1}{3} \cdot 1$     [**mult. ident.**]

2. $= \frac{1}{2} \cdot \frac{1}{3} \cdot \left[ (2 \cdot 3) \cdot \frac{1}{2 \cdot 3} \right]$     [**mult. inv.**]

3. $= \left( \frac{1}{2} \cdot 2 \right) \cdot \left( \frac{1}{3} \cdot 3 \right) \cdot \frac{1}{2 \cdot 3}$     [**cpm, apm**]

4. $= 1 \cdot 1 \cdot \frac{1}{2 \cdot 3}$     [**mult. inv.**]

5. $\frac{1}{2} \cdot \frac{1}{3} = \frac{1}{2 \cdot 3}$     [**mult. ident.**]

Therefore, $\frac{1}{2} \cdot \frac{1}{3} = \frac{1}{2 \cdot 3}$ or $\frac{1}{6}$.

## ☐ In general, it appears that:              (4)

$$\frac{1}{a} \cdot \frac{1}{b} = \frac{1}{a \cdot b} \quad \text{where } a, b \neq 0$$

## ☐ Proof                      (5)

1. $\frac{1}{a} \cdot \frac{1}{b} = \frac{1}{a} \cdot \frac{1}{b} \cdot 1$     [**mult. ident.**]

2. $= \frac{1}{a} \cdot \frac{1}{b} \cdot \left[ (ab) \cdot \frac{1}{ab} \right]$     [**mult. inv.**]

3. $= \left( \frac{1}{a} \cdot a \right) \cdot \left( \frac{1}{b} \cdot b \right) \cdot \frac{1}{ab}$     [**cpm, apm**]

4. $= 1 \cdot 1 \cdot \frac{1}{ab}$     [**mult. inv.**]

5. $\frac{1}{a} \cdot \frac{1}{b} = \frac{1}{ab}$     [**mult. ident.**]          Therefore, $\frac{1}{a} \cdot \frac{1}{b} = \frac{1}{ab}$, where $a, b \neq 0$.

☐ **Examples:** **(6)**

1. $\dfrac{1}{4}\cdot\dfrac{1}{5} = \dfrac{1}{4\cdot 5}$ or $\dfrac{1}{20}$

2. $\dfrac{1}{-2}\cdot\dfrac{1}{3}\cdot\dfrac{1}{-5} = \dfrac{1}{(-2)(3)(-5)}$ or $\dfrac{1}{30}$

3. $\dfrac{1}{a}\cdot\dfrac{1}{a} = \dfrac{1}{a\cdot a}$ or $\dfrac{1}{a^2}$

4. $\dfrac{1}{4}\cdot\dfrac{1}{m+n} = \dfrac{1}{4(m+n)}$ or $\dfrac{1}{4m+4n}$

☐ **Study Exercise One** **(7)**

Using the property, $\dfrac{1}{a}\cdot\dfrac{1}{b} = \dfrac{1}{ab}$, multiply the following.

1. $\dfrac{1}{7}\cdot\dfrac{1}{8}$

2. $\dfrac{1}{-5}\cdot\dfrac{1}{2}\cdot\dfrac{1}{-3}$

3. $\dfrac{1}{x}\cdot\dfrac{1}{x}$, where $x \neq 0$

4. $\dfrac{1}{3}\cdot\dfrac{1}{a+b}$, where $a+b \neq 0$

5. Change the fraction $\dfrac{1}{2x}$ to a basic product by reversing the above property.

☐ **Case 2:** $\dfrac{3}{4}\cdot\dfrac{5}{7}$ **(8)**

1. $\dfrac{3}{4}\cdot\dfrac{5}{7} = \left(3\cdot\dfrac{1}{4}\right)\cdot\left(5\cdot\dfrac{1}{7}\right)$    [Definition of a fraction]

2. $= (3\cdot 5)\cdot\left(\dfrac{1}{4}\cdot\dfrac{1}{7}\right)$    [**cpm, apm**]

3. $= (3\cdot 5)\cdot\dfrac{1}{4\cdot 7}$    $\left[\dfrac{1}{a}\cdot\dfrac{1}{b} = \dfrac{1}{ab}\right]$

4. $\dfrac{3}{4}\cdot\dfrac{5}{7} = \dfrac{3\cdot 5}{4\cdot 7}$    [Definition of a fraction]

Therefore, $\dfrac{3}{4}\cdot\dfrac{5}{7} = \dfrac{3\cdot 5}{4\cdot 7}$ or $\dfrac{15}{28}$.

☐ In general, it appears that: **(9)**

$$\dfrac{a}{b}\cdot\dfrac{c}{d} = \dfrac{a\cdot c}{b\cdot d} \quad \text{where } b, d \neq 0$$

When multiplying fractions, multiply the numerators and multiply the denominators.

☐ **Proof** **(10)**

1. $\dfrac{a}{b}\cdot\dfrac{c}{d} = \left(a\cdot\dfrac{1}{b}\right)\cdot\left(c\cdot\dfrac{1}{d}\right)$    [Definition of a fraction]

2. $= (a\cdot c)\cdot\left(\dfrac{1}{b}\cdot\dfrac{1}{d}\right)$    [**cpm, apm**]

3. $= (a\cdot c)\cdot\dfrac{1}{bd}$    $\left[\dfrac{1}{b}\cdot\dfrac{1}{d} = \dfrac{1}{bd}\right]$

4. $\dfrac{a}{b}\cdot\dfrac{c}{d} = \dfrac{ac}{bd}$    [Definition of a fraction]

Therefore, $\dfrac{a}{b}\cdot\dfrac{c}{d} = \dfrac{ac}{bd}$, where $b, d \neq 0$.

## □ Examples

(11)

**Example 1:** Multiply $\dfrac{3x}{5y}\cdot\dfrac{2x}{7y}$.

**Solution:** $\dfrac{3x}{5y}\cdot\dfrac{2x}{7y}=\dfrac{(3x)\cdot(2x)}{(5y)\cdot(7y)}=\dfrac{6x^2}{35y^2}$

**Example 2:** Multiply $\dfrac{2a}{5b^2}\cdot\dfrac{3a^2}{b^3c}$.

**Solution:** $\dfrac{2a}{5b^2}\cdot\dfrac{3a^2}{b^3c}=\dfrac{(2a)\cdot(3a^2)}{(5b^2)\cdot(b^3c)}=\dfrac{6a^3}{5b^5c}$

**Example 3:** Multiply $\dfrac{2}{x}\cdot\dfrac{a+3}{a+5}$.

**Solution:** $\dfrac{2}{x}\cdot\dfrac{a+3}{a+5}=\dfrac{2\cdot(a+3)}{x\cdot(a+5)}$

## □ Study Exercise Two

(12)

Using the property, $\dfrac{a}{b}\cdot\dfrac{c}{d}=\dfrac{ac}{bd}$, multiply the following.

1. $\dfrac{2}{5}\cdot\dfrac{7}{-9}$

2. $\dfrac{2x}{3}\cdot\dfrac{5x^3}{a}$, where $a\neq0$

3. $\dfrac{5}{a+b}\cdot\dfrac{x-y}{6}$, where $a+b\neq0$

4. $\dfrac{2a}{a+1}\cdot b$, where $a+1\neq0$

5. Change $\dfrac{2x}{3y}$ to a basic product by reversing the above property.

## □ Multiplying and Reducing the Answer to Lowest Terms

(13)

Method (1): Multiplying before canceling

**Example:** Multiply $\dfrac{4}{5}\cdot\dfrac{7}{6}$.

**Solution:**

*Step (1):* Multiply the fractions.
$$\dfrac{4}{5}\cdot\dfrac{7}{6}=\dfrac{28}{30}$$

*Step (2):* Reduce the answer.
$$\dfrac{28}{30}=\dfrac{14\cdot\cancel{2}}{15\cdot\cancel{2}}=\dfrac{14}{15}$$

Method (2): Canceling before multiplying (preferred)

**Example:** Multiply $\dfrac{4}{5}\cdot\dfrac{7}{6}$.

**Solution:**

*Step (1):* Write each fraction in factored form and cancel.
$$\dfrac{4}{5}\cdot\dfrac{7}{6}=\dfrac{\cancel{2}\cdot2}{5}\cdot\dfrac{7}{\cancel{2}\cdot3}$$

*Step (2):* Multiply the remaining factors.
$$\dfrac{4}{5}\cdot\dfrac{7}{6}=\dfrac{\cancel{2}\cdot2}{5}\cdot\dfrac{7}{\cancel{2}\cdot3}=\dfrac{14}{15}$$

☐ **More Examples** (14)

**Example 1:** Multiply and reduce $\frac{2}{5} \cdot \frac{15}{4}$.

**Solution:** $\frac{2}{5} \cdot \frac{15}{4} = \frac{1 \cdot \cancel{2}}{1 \cdot \cancel{5}} \cdot \frac{\cancel{5} \cdot 3}{\cancel{2} \cdot 2} = \frac{3}{2}$

**Example 2:** Multiply and reduce $\frac{5a}{9} \cdot \frac{6}{7a}$.

**Solution:** $\frac{5a}{9} \cdot \frac{6}{7a} = \frac{5 \cdot \cancel{a}}{\cancel{3} \cdot 3} \cdot \frac{\cancel{3} \cdot 2}{7 \cdot \cancel{a}} = \frac{10}{21}$

**Example 3:** Multiply and reduce $\frac{2m^2}{3n^2} \cdot \frac{n^3}{6m}$.

**Solution:** $\frac{2m^2}{3n^2} \cdot \frac{n^3}{6m} = \frac{\cancel{2} \cdot \cancel{m} \cdot m}{3 \cdot \cancel{n^2}} \cdot \frac{\cancel{n^2} \cdot n}{\cancel{2} \cdot 3 \cdot \cancel{m}} = \frac{mn}{9}$

**Example 4:** Multiply and reduce $\frac{2(a + 3)}{b} \cdot \frac{b^2}{3(a + 3)}$.

**Solution:** $\frac{2 \cdot \cancel{(a + 3)}}{1 \cdot \cancel{b}} \cdot \frac{\cancel{b} \cdot b}{3 \cdot \cancel{(a + 3)}} = \frac{2b}{3}$

☐ **Study Exercise Three** (15)

Multiply and reduce each of the following. Assume the denominators are not zero.

1. $8 \cdot \frac{5}{8}$

2. $\frac{6}{14} \cdot \frac{21}{2}$

3. $\frac{5m}{2} \cdot \frac{6}{7m}$

4. $\frac{3a^2}{b^2} \cdot \frac{5b}{6a^3}$

5. $\frac{a}{3(b + 2)} \cdot \frac{4(b + 2)}{2a^3}$

☐ **Multiplying Fractions Containing Basic Sums or Differences** (16)

*Remember,* the Fundamental Principle can be used to reduce fractions by cancellation only if the following two conditions hold.

1. Both the numerators and the denominators must be basic products.
2. The numbers or expressions which are canceled must be factors.

Therefore, to use cancellation when multiplying fractions containing basic sums or differences, we must factor the numerators and denominators.

**Example:** Multiply and reduce $\frac{2a + 2b}{5} \cdot \frac{a}{3a + 3b}$.

*Step (1):* Factor numerators and denominators.
$$\frac{2a + 2b}{5} \cdot \frac{a}{3a + 3b} = \frac{2 \cdot (a + b)}{5} \cdot \frac{a}{3 \cdot (a + b)}$$

*Step (2):* Cancel like factors; then multiply.
$$\frac{2 \cdot \cancel{(a + b)}}{5} \cdot \frac{a}{3 \cdot \cancel{(a + b)}} = \frac{2a}{15}$$

Therefore, $\frac{2a + 2b}{5} \cdot \frac{a}{3a + 3b} = \frac{2a}{15}$.

□ **More Examples**                                                                          **(17)**

**Example 1:**  Multiply and reduce $\dfrac{3m+6}{4} \cdot \dfrac{2m}{m+2}$.

   *Step (1):*  Factor numerators and denominators.
$$\frac{3m+6}{4} \cdot \frac{2m}{m+2} = \frac{3 \cdot (m+2)}{2 \cdot 2} \cdot \frac{2 \cdot m}{(m+2)}$$

   *Step (2):*  Cancel like factors; then multiply.
$$\frac{3 \cdot (\cancel{m+2})}{2 \cdot \cancel{2}} = \frac{\cancel{2} \cdot m}{(\cancel{m+2})} = \frac{3m}{2}$$

   Therefore, $\dfrac{3m+6}{4} \cdot \dfrac{2m}{m+2} = \dfrac{3m}{2}$.

□ **Example 2:**  Multiply and reduce $\dfrac{2b}{2a-4b} \cdot \dfrac{3a-6b}{3b^3}$.                **(18)**

   *Step (1):*  Factor numerators and denominators.
$$\frac{2b}{2a-4b} \cdot \frac{3a-6b}{3b^3} = \frac{2 \cdot b}{2 \cdot (a-2b)} \cdot \frac{3 \cdot (a-2b)}{3 \cdot b \cdot b^2}$$

   *Step (2):*  Cancel like factors; then multiply.
$$\frac{\cancel{2} \cdot \cancel{b}}{\cancel{2} \cdot (\cancel{a-2b})} \cdot \frac{\cancel{3} \cdot (\cancel{a-2b})}{\cancel{3} \cdot \cancel{b} \cdot b^2} = \frac{1}{b^2}$$

   Therefore, $\dfrac{2b}{2a-4b} \cdot \dfrac{3a-6b}{3b^3} = \dfrac{1}{b^2}$.

□                                    *Study Exercise Four*                                    **(19)**

   Multiply and reduce the following. Assume the denominators are not zero.

1. $\dfrac{3x+3y}{x} \cdot \dfrac{5}{4x+4y}$     2. $\dfrac{3a}{a-2} \cdot \dfrac{2a-4}{9}$     3. $\dfrac{m}{m+6} \cdot \dfrac{2m+12}{2m}$     4. $\dfrac{x^2-xy}{3x^3} \cdot \dfrac{xy}{x-y}$

□ **Division of Numbers in Fractional Form**                                                  **(20)**

   **Example:**  $\dfrac{2}{3} \div \dfrac{5}{7}$

1. $\dfrac{2}{3} \div \dfrac{5}{7} = \dfrac{\dfrac{2}{3}}{\dfrac{5}{7}}$     [Definition of a fraction]

2. $\qquad = \dfrac{\dfrac{2}{3} \cdot \dfrac{7}{5}}{\dfrac{5}{7} \cdot \dfrac{7}{5}}$     [Fundamental Principle]

3. $\qquad = \dfrac{\dfrac{2}{3} \cdot \dfrac{7}{5}}{1}$     [Mult. of fractions]

4. $\dfrac{2}{3} \div \dfrac{5}{7} = \dfrac{2}{3} \cdot \dfrac{7}{5}$     $\left[\dfrac{x}{1} = x\right]$

   Therefore, $\dfrac{2}{3} \div \dfrac{5}{7} = \dfrac{2}{3} \cdot \dfrac{7}{5}$ or $\dfrac{14}{15}$.

☐ **Review of Multiplicative Inverses** **(21)**

$\frac{5}{7}$ and $\frac{7}{5}$ are multiplicative inverses, because $\frac{5}{7} \cdot \frac{7}{5} = 1$.

☐ **Quotient to a Product** **(22)**

$$\frac{2}{3} \div \frac{5}{7} = \frac{2}{3} \cdot \frac{7}{5}$$

multiplicative inverses

To find the quotient of two fractions, multiply by the *multiplicative inverse* of the divisor. This method is sometimes stated as "Invert the divisor and multiply."

☐ Division is related to multiplication in the same way that subtraction is related to addition. **(23)**

Subtraction: $(+2) - (+7) = (+2) + (-7)$

Add the additive inverse.

Division: $\frac{2}{3} \div \frac{5}{7} = \frac{2}{3} \cdot \frac{7}{5}$

Multiply by the multiplicative inverse.

☐ In general, it appears that: **(24)**

$$\frac{a}{b} \div \frac{c}{d} = \frac{a}{b} \cdot \frac{d}{c} \quad \text{where } b, c, d \neq 0$$

Multiply by the multiplicative inverse of the divisor.

☐ **Proof** **(25)**

1. $\dfrac{a}{b} \div \dfrac{c}{d} = \dfrac{\frac{a}{b}}{\frac{c}{d}}$    [Definition of a fraction]

2. $\qquad = \dfrac{\frac{a}{b} \cdot \frac{d}{c}}{\frac{c}{d} \cdot \frac{d}{c}}$    [Fundamental Principle]

3. $\qquad = \dfrac{\frac{a}{b} \cdot \frac{d}{c}}{1}$    [Mult. of fractions]

4. $\dfrac{a}{b} \div \dfrac{c}{d} = \dfrac{a}{b} \cdot \dfrac{d}{c}$    $\left[ \dfrac{x}{1} = x \right]$

This proof shows that to divide fractions, we invert the divisor and multiply.

☐ **Examples Using the Division Property** (26)

**Example 1:** $\dfrac{2}{x} \div \dfrac{4}{xy}$

**Solution:**

$line\ (a)\quad \dfrac{2}{x} \div \dfrac{4}{xy} = \dfrac{2}{x} \cdot \dfrac{xy}{4}$

$line\ (b)\qquad\qquad = \dfrac{2}{\cancel{x}} \cdot \dfrac{\cancel{x}y}{2 \cdot 2}$

$line\ (c)\qquad\qquad = \dfrac{y}{2}$

☐ **Example 2:** $\dfrac{2x^2}{3y^4} \div \dfrac{6x}{7y^5}$ (27)

**Solution:**

$line\ (a)\quad \dfrac{2x^2}{3y^4} \div \dfrac{6x}{7y^5} = \dfrac{2x^2}{3y^4} \cdot \dfrac{7y^5}{6x}$

$line\ (b)\qquad\qquad = \dfrac{2 \cdot \cancel{x} \cdot x}{3 \cdot \cancel{y^4}} \cdot \dfrac{7 \cdot y \cdot \cancel{y^4}}{2 \cdot 3 \cdot \cancel{x}}$

$line\ (c)\qquad\qquad = \dfrac{7xy}{9}$

☐ **Example 3:** $\dfrac{5a + 10b}{3a^2} \div \dfrac{2a + 4b}{a}$ (28)

**Solution:**

$line\ (a)\quad \dfrac{5a + 10b}{3a^2} \div \dfrac{2a + 4b}{a} = \dfrac{5a + 10b}{3a^2} \cdot \dfrac{a}{2a + 4b}$

$line\ (b)\qquad\qquad\qquad = \dfrac{5 \cdot (a + 2b)}{3 \cdot a \cdot a} \cdot \dfrac{a}{2 \cdot (a + 2b)}$

$line\ (c)\qquad\qquad\qquad = \dfrac{5 \cdot \cancel{(a + 2b)}}{3 \cdot a \cdot \cancel{a}} \cdot \dfrac{\cancel{a}}{2 \cdot \cancel{(a + 2b)}}$

$line\ (d)\qquad\qquad\qquad = \dfrac{5}{6a}$

☐ **A Complex Fraction** (29)

**Example 4:** $\dfrac{\dfrac{6a}{b^2}}{\dfrac{2a^3}{b^3}}$ ⟵ [Means division]

**Solution:**

$line\ (a)\quad \dfrac{\dfrac{6a}{b^2}}{\dfrac{2a^3}{b^3}} = \dfrac{6a}{b^2} \div \dfrac{2a^3}{b^3}$

$line\ (b)\qquad\qquad = \dfrac{6a}{b^2} \cdot \dfrac{b^3}{2a^3}$

$line\ (c)\qquad\qquad = \dfrac{2 \cdot 3 \cdot \cancel{a}}{\cancel{b^2}} \cdot \dfrac{\cancel{b^2} \cdot b}{2 \cdot \cancel{a} \cdot a^2}$

$line\ (d)\qquad\qquad = \dfrac{3b}{a^2}$

☐ *Study Exercise Five* **(30)**

Divide the following and put the answers in reduced form.

1.  $\dfrac{-2}{5} \div \dfrac{4}{25}$

2.  $\dfrac{\frac{-2}{5}}{\frac{4}{25}}$

3.  $\dfrac{10x^2}{3y} \div \dfrac{9y^2}{6xy}$

4.  $\dfrac{3a}{5b} \div \dfrac{6a^3}{25b}$

5.  $1 \div \dfrac{a}{b}$

6.  $\dfrac{1}{\frac{a}{b}}$

7.  $\dfrac{2x + 2y}{3x^2} \div \dfrac{6x + 6y}{x}$

## REVIEW EXERCISES

A.  Fill in the blanks.

   1.  When multiplying two fractions, multiply the _____ and multiply the _____.
   2.  When dividing two fractions, multiply by the _____ _____ of the _____.

   3.  $\dfrac{\frac{2x}{3}}{\frac{1}{5}}$ is an example of a _____ fraction.

B.  Multiply the following and put the answers in reduced form. Use cancellation first, where possible. Assume that the denominators do not represent zero.

   4.  $\dfrac{1}{2} \cdot \dfrac{1}{3}$

   5.  $\dfrac{1}{-5} \cdot \dfrac{1}{-7} \cdot \dfrac{1}{2}$

   6.  $\dfrac{3}{4} \cdot \dfrac{6}{7}$

   7.  $\dfrac{3m}{2n} \cdot \dfrac{5n^2}{9m^2}$

   8.  $\dfrac{2a}{3b} \cdot \dfrac{9b^2}{4a^2}$

   9.  $\dfrac{4(a + b)}{5} \cdot \dfrac{10a}{2(a + b)}$

   10. $\dfrac{3(x + y)^2}{7x} \cdot \dfrac{4}{6(x + y)^3}$

   11. $\left(\dfrac{2x}{-3}\right)^2$

   12. $\dfrac{3m + 3n}{6m} \cdot \dfrac{2m}{5m + 5n}$

   13. $\dfrac{2a - 6b}{5b^2} \cdot \dfrac{10b^4}{3a - 9b}$

C.  Divide the following and put the answer in reduced form.

   14. $\dfrac{3}{5} \div \dfrac{7}{2}$

   15. $1 \div \dfrac{2}{3}$

   16. $\dfrac{-2}{3} \div \dfrac{-4}{5}$

   17. $\dfrac{3a^2}{b} \div \dfrac{2a}{b^3}$

   18. $\dfrac{3m^2n}{2a^2} \div \dfrac{15m^4n^2}{6a^3}$

   19. $\dfrac{3x - 3y}{2x} \div \dfrac{x - y}{2}$

   20. $\dfrac{2ab - 2a}{2} \div \dfrac{b - 1}{3a^2}$

   21. $\dfrac{2m + 2n}{5n} \div \dfrac{3m + 3n}{15n^2}$

   22. $\dfrac{\frac{2}{3}}{\frac{5}{7}}$

   23. $\dfrac{\frac{a}{b}}{\frac{c}{d}}$

   24. $\dfrac{\frac{2x}{y}}{\frac{y^2}{x}}$

   25. $\dfrac{1}{\frac{3x}{y}}$

## Solutions to Review Exercises

A.  1. numerators; denominators     2. multiplicative inverse; divisor     3. complex

B.  4. $\dfrac{1}{2} \cdot \dfrac{1}{3} = \dfrac{1}{6}$

   5. $\dfrac{1}{-5} \cdot \dfrac{1}{-7} \cdot \dfrac{1}{2} = \dfrac{1}{70}$

## Solutions to Review Exercises, Contd.

6. $\dfrac{3}{4} \cdot \dfrac{-6}{7} = \dfrac{3}{2 \cdot 2} \cdot \dfrac{\cancel{2} \cdot (-3)}{7} = \dfrac{-9}{14}$

7. $\dfrac{3m}{2n} \cdot \dfrac{5n^2}{9m^2} = \dfrac{\cancel{3} \cdot \cancel{m}}{2 \cdot \cancel{n}} \cdot \dfrac{5 \cdot \cancel{n} \cdot n}{\cancel{3} \cdot 3 \cdot \cancel{m} \cdot m} = \dfrac{5n}{6m}$

8. $\dfrac{2a}{3b} \cdot \dfrac{9b^2}{4a^2} = \dfrac{\cancel{2} \cdot \cancel{a} \cdot \cancel{3} \cdot 3 \cdot \cancel{b} \cdot b}{\cancel{3} \cdot \cancel{b} \cdot \cancel{2} \cdot 2 \cdot \cancel{a} \cdot a} = \dfrac{3b}{2a}$

9. $\dfrac{4(a + b)}{5} \cdot \dfrac{10a}{2(a + b)} = \dfrac{\cancel{2} \cdot 2 \cdot \cancel{(a + b)}}{\cancel{5}} \cdot \dfrac{2 \cdot \cancel{5} \cdot a}{\cancel{2} \cdot \cancel{(a + b)}} = 4a$

10. $\dfrac{3(x + y)^2}{7x} \cdot \dfrac{4}{6(x + y)^3} = \dfrac{\cancel{3} \cdot \cancel{(x + y)^2}}{7x} \cdot \dfrac{\cancel{2} \cdot 2}{\cancel{2} \cdot \cancel{3} \cdot \cancel{(x + y)^2}(x + y)}$

$= \dfrac{2}{7x(x + y)}$ or $\dfrac{2}{7x^2 + 7xy}$

11. $\left(\dfrac{2x}{-3}\right)^2 = \dfrac{2x}{-3} \cdot \dfrac{2x}{-3} = \dfrac{4x^2}{9}$

12. $\dfrac{3m + 3n}{6m} \cdot \dfrac{2m}{5m + 5n} = \dfrac{\cancel{3} \cdot \cancel{(m + n)}}{\cancel{2} \cdot \cancel{3} \cdot \cancel{m}} \cdot \dfrac{\cancel{2} \cdot \cancel{m}}{5 \cdot \cancel{(m + n)}}$

$= \dfrac{1}{5}$

13. $\dfrac{2a - 6b}{5b^2} \cdot \dfrac{10b^4}{3a - 9b} = \dfrac{2 \cdot \cancel{(a - 3b)}}{\cancel{5} \cdot \cancel{b^2}} \cdot \dfrac{\cancel{5} \cdot 2 \cdot \cancel{b^2} \cdot b^2}{3 \cdot \cancel{(a - 3b)}}$

$= \dfrac{4b^2}{3}$

C. 14. $\dfrac{3}{5} \div \dfrac{7}{2} = \dfrac{3}{5} \cdot \dfrac{2}{7} = \dfrac{6}{35}$

15. $1 \div \dfrac{2}{3} = \dfrac{1}{1} \cdot \dfrac{3}{2} = \dfrac{3}{2}$

16. $\dfrac{-2}{3} \div \dfrac{-4}{5} = \dfrac{-2}{3} \cdot \dfrac{5}{-4} = \dfrac{(\cancel{-2})}{3} \cdot \dfrac{5}{(\cancel{-2}) \cdot (2)} = \dfrac{5}{6}$

17. $\dfrac{3a^2}{b} \div \dfrac{2a}{b^3} = \dfrac{3a^2}{b} \cdot \dfrac{b^3}{2a} = \dfrac{3 \cdot \cancel{a} \cdot a \cdot \cancel{b} \cdot b^2}{\cancel{b}} \cdot \dfrac{}{2 \cdot \cancel{a}} = \dfrac{3ab^2}{2}$

18. $\dfrac{3m^2n}{2a^2} \div \dfrac{15m^4n^2}{6a^3} = \dfrac{3m^2n}{2a^2} \cdot \dfrac{6a^3}{15m^4n^2}$

$= \dfrac{\cancel{3} \cdot m^2 \cdot \cancel{n}}{\cancel{2} \cdot \cancel{a^2}} \cdot \dfrac{\cancel{2} \cdot 3 \cdot \cancel{a^2} \cdot a}{\cancel{3} \cdot 5 \cdot \cancel{m^2} \cdot m^2 \cdot \cancel{n} \cdot n}$

$= \dfrac{3a}{5m^2n}$

19. $\dfrac{3x - 3y}{2x} \div \dfrac{x - y}{2} = \dfrac{3 \cdot (x - y)}{2x} \cdot \dfrac{2}{x - y}$

$= \dfrac{3 \cdot \cancel{(x - y)}}{\cancel{2} \cdot x} \cdot \dfrac{\cancel{2}}{\cancel{(x - y)}}$

$= \dfrac{3}{x}$

20. $\dfrac{2ab - 2a}{2} \div \dfrac{b - 1}{3a^2} = \dfrac{2a(b - 1)}{2} \cdot \dfrac{3a^2}{b - 1}$

$= \dfrac{\cancel{2} \cdot a \cdot \cancel{(b - 1)}}{\cancel{2}} \cdot \dfrac{3a^2}{\cancel{(b - 1)}}$

$= 3a^3$

21. $\dfrac{2m + 2n}{5n} \div \dfrac{3m + 3n}{15n^2} = \dfrac{2m + 2n}{5n} \cdot \dfrac{15n^2}{3m + 3n}$

$= \dfrac{2 \cdot \cancel{(m + n)}}{\cancel{5} \cdot \cancel{n}} \cdot \dfrac{\cancel{3} \cdot \cancel{5} \cdot \cancel{n} \cdot n}{\cancel{3} \cdot \cancel{(m + n)}}$

$= 2n$

22. $\dfrac{\frac{2}{3}}{\frac{5}{7}} = \dfrac{2}{3} \div \dfrac{5}{7} = \dfrac{2}{3} \cdot \dfrac{7}{5} = \dfrac{14}{15}$

23. $\dfrac{\frac{a}{b}}{\frac{c}{d}} = \dfrac{a}{b} \div \dfrac{c}{d} = \dfrac{a}{b} \cdot \dfrac{d}{c} = \dfrac{ad}{bc}$

## Solutions to Review Exercises, Contd.

24. $\dfrac{\dfrac{2x}{y}}{\dfrac{y^2}{x}} = \dfrac{2x}{y} \div \dfrac{y^2}{x} = \dfrac{2x}{y} \cdot \dfrac{x}{y^2} = \dfrac{2x^2}{y^3}$

25. $\dfrac{\dfrac{1}{3x}}{y} = 1 \div \dfrac{3x}{y} = \dfrac{1}{1} \cdot \dfrac{y}{3x} = \dfrac{y}{3x}$

## SUPPLEMENTARY PROBLEMS

A. Multiply the following and put the answers in reduced form. Use cancellation first, where possible. Assume the denominators do not represent zero.

1. $\dfrac{1}{3} \cdot \dfrac{1}{5}$

2. $\dfrac{1}{5} \cdot \dfrac{1}{-6}$

3. $\dfrac{1}{2} \cdot \dfrac{1}{-3} \cdot \dfrac{1}{-4}$

4. $\dfrac{1}{2x} \cdot \dfrac{1}{3x}$

5. $\dfrac{1}{4a} \cdot \dfrac{1}{2ab} \cdot \dfrac{1}{b^3}$

6. $\left(\dfrac{2}{3}\right)^2$

7. $\dfrac{2}{3} \cdot \dfrac{11}{3}$

8. $\dfrac{2}{3} \cdot \dfrac{4}{7} \cdot \dfrac{2}{9}$

9. $\dfrac{3}{7} \cdot \dfrac{21}{15}$

10. $\dfrac{2}{3} \cdot \dfrac{6}{5} \cdot \dfrac{15}{4}$

11. $\dfrac{2x}{y} \cdot \dfrac{3x^2}{y^2}$

12. $\dfrac{5m}{2n^2} \cdot \dfrac{3m^2}{4n^3}$

13. $\dfrac{2a^2b}{c} \cdot \dfrac{3ab^3}{c^3}$

14. $\dfrac{2}{a+b} \cdot \dfrac{c-d}{3}$

15. $\dfrac{a^2}{bc} \cdot \dfrac{b^3}{ac} \cdot \dfrac{c^2}{ab^2}$

16. $\dfrac{2a}{3} \cdot \dfrac{5}{a^2}$

17. $\dfrac{3x^2y}{2a^2} \cdot \dfrac{a}{12xy}$

18. $\dfrac{4x^2y}{16x^3} \cdot \dfrac{4x}{3y^2}$

19. $\dfrac{a(x+y)}{x^2} \cdot \dfrac{xa+xb}{bx+by}$

20. $\dfrac{3a-3b}{4} \cdot \dfrac{20}{5a-5b}$

21. $\dfrac{2m^2+4}{m} \cdot \dfrac{3m^3}{4m^2+16}$

22. $\dfrac{3x+12}{3x-12} \cdot \dfrac{2x-8}{6x+24}$

23. $\dfrac{x+3}{4y} \cdot \dfrac{8y^2}{2(x+3)}$

24. $\dfrac{3a}{a-2} \cdot \dfrac{2a-4}{9}$

25. $\dfrac{3x+3y}{x} \cdot \dfrac{5}{4x+4y}$

26. $\dfrac{x^2-xy}{3x^3} \cdot \dfrac{xy}{x-y}$

27. $\dfrac{m}{m+6} \cdot \dfrac{2m+12}{2m}$

28. $\dfrac{3m+3n}{6m} \cdot \dfrac{2m}{5m+5n}$

29. $\dfrac{2a-6b}{5b^2} \cdot \dfrac{10b^4}{3a-9b}$

30. $\dfrac{a}{3(b+2)} \cdot \dfrac{4(b+2)}{2a^3}$

31. $\dfrac{2a+2b}{3} \cdot \dfrac{12}{(a+b)^2}$

32. $\dfrac{3y+6}{15y-30} \cdot \dfrac{9y-18}{6y+12}$

B. Divide the following and put the answers in reduced form.

33. $\dfrac{1}{2} \div \dfrac{1}{3}$

34. $\dfrac{2}{5} \div \dfrac{4}{7}$

35. $\dfrac{3}{8} \div \dfrac{1}{2}$

36. $\dfrac{6}{5} \div \dfrac{2}{15}$

37. $1 \div \dfrac{1}{3}$

38. $1 \div \dfrac{2}{5}$

39. $\dfrac{ab^2}{c} \div \dfrac{b^2}{c^2}$

40. $\dfrac{2x}{3y} \div \dfrac{6x^2}{y}$

41. $\dfrac{2m^3n}{3} \div \dfrac{9m}{n}$

42. $\dfrac{10a^2}{3b} \div \dfrac{9b^2}{6ab}$

43. $\dfrac{12x^2}{3y} \div \dfrac{9y^2}{4xy}$

44. $1 \div \dfrac{m}{m+n}$

45. $\dfrac{3x+3y}{4x^2} \div \dfrac{5x+5y}{x}$

46. $\dfrac{4a^2+8ab}{2a} \div \dfrac{6a^2+12ab}{6a^2}$

47. $\dfrac{2ab-2a}{2} \div \dfrac{b-1}{3a^2}$

48. $\dfrac{2x+6y}{x^2} \div \dfrac{x+3y}{x^4}$

49. $\dfrac{2m+n}{rs} \div \dfrac{6m+3n}{r^2}$

50. $\dfrac{2m+2n}{5n} \div \dfrac{3m+3n}{15n^2}$

## SUPPLEMENTARY PROBLEMS, Contd.

51. $\dfrac{\dfrac{3}{5}}{\dfrac{2}{7}}$    52. $\dfrac{\dfrac{x}{y}}{\dfrac{z}{w}}$    53. $\dfrac{\dfrac{3a}{b}}{\dfrac{2a^2}{3b}}$    54. $\dfrac{\dfrac{1}{2x}}{y}$

55. $\dfrac{\dfrac{m+n}{rs}}{\dfrac{3m+3n}{r^2}}$    56. $\dfrac{\dfrac{2x+6y}{x^2}}{\dfrac{x+3y}{x^4}}$

C.  Answer the following.

57.  What is the similarity between subtraction and division in terms of the primary operations of addition and multiplication?

58.  In this division problem, $\dfrac{4x^2}{3y} \div \dfrac{4a}{6y^2}$, why are these restrictions assumed?

(a)  $y \neq 0$                          (b)  $a \neq 0$

59.  What must $x$ represent, if $\dfrac{x}{y} = 0$? What numbers could $y$ represent?

□ **Solutions to Study Exercises**                                                    (7A)

### Study Exercise One (Frame 7)

1. $\dfrac{1}{7} \cdot \dfrac{1}{8} = \dfrac{1}{7 \cdot 8}$ or $\dfrac{1}{56}$    2. $\dfrac{1}{-5} \cdot \dfrac{1}{2} \cdot \dfrac{1}{-3} = \dfrac{1}{(-5)(2)(-3)}$ or $\dfrac{1}{30}$    3. $\dfrac{1}{x} \cdot \dfrac{1}{x} = \dfrac{1}{x \cdot x}$ or $\dfrac{1}{x^2}$

4. $\dfrac{1}{3} \cdot \dfrac{1}{a+b} = \dfrac{1}{3(a+b)}$ or $\dfrac{1}{3a+3b}$    5. $\dfrac{1}{2x} = \dfrac{1}{2} \cdot \dfrac{1}{x}$

□                              ### Study Exercise Two (Frame 12)                              (12A)

1. $\dfrac{2}{5} \cdot \dfrac{7}{-9} = \dfrac{2 \cdot 7}{5 \cdot (-9)} = \dfrac{14}{-45}$    2. $\dfrac{2x}{3} \cdot \dfrac{5x^3}{a} = \dfrac{(2x)(5x^3)}{3a} = \dfrac{10x^4}{3a}$

3. $\dfrac{5}{a+b} \cdot \dfrac{x-y}{6} = \dfrac{5(x-y)}{6(a+b)}$ or $\dfrac{5x-5y}{6a+6b}$    4. $\dfrac{2a}{a+1} \cdot b = \dfrac{2a}{a+1} \cdot \dfrac{b}{1} = \dfrac{2ab}{(a+1) \cdot 1}$ or $\dfrac{2ab}{a+1}$

5. $\dfrac{2x}{3y} = \dfrac{2}{3} \cdot \dfrac{x}{y}$

□                              ### Study Exercise Three (Frame 15)                              (15A)

1. $8 \cdot \dfrac{5}{8} = \dfrac{\cancel{8}}{1} \cdot \dfrac{5}{\cancel{8}} = \dfrac{5}{1}$ or $5$    2. $\dfrac{6}{14} \cdot \dfrac{21}{2} = \dfrac{\cancel{2} \cdot 3}{\cancel{2} \cdot \cancel{7}} \cdot \dfrac{\cancel{7} \cdot 3}{2} = \dfrac{9}{2}$

3. $\dfrac{5m}{2} \cdot \dfrac{6}{7m} = \dfrac{5 \cdot \cancel{m}}{\cancel{2}} \cdot \dfrac{\cancel{2} \cdot 3}{7 \cdot \cancel{m}} = \dfrac{15}{7}$    4. $\dfrac{3a^2}{b^2} \cdot \dfrac{5b}{6a^3} = \dfrac{\cancel{3} \cdot \cancel{a^2}}{b \cdot \cancel{b}} \cdot \dfrac{5 \cdot \cancel{b}}{2 \cdot \cancel{3} \cdot a \cdot \cancel{a^2}} = \dfrac{5}{2ab}$

5. $\dfrac{a}{3(b+2)} \cdot \dfrac{4(b+2)}{2a^3} = \dfrac{\cancel{a}}{3 \cdot \cancel{(b+2)}} \cdot \dfrac{\cancel{2} \cdot 2 \cdot \cancel{(b+2)}}{\cancel{2} \cdot \cancel{a} \cdot a^2} = \dfrac{2}{3a^2}$

□                              ### Study Exercise Four (Frame 19)                              (19A)

1. $\dfrac{3x+3y}{x} \cdot \dfrac{5}{4x+4y} = \dfrac{3 \cdot \cancel{(x+y)}}{x} \cdot \dfrac{5}{4 \cdot \cancel{(x+y)}} = \dfrac{15}{4x}$    2. $\dfrac{3a}{a-2} \cdot \dfrac{2a-4}{9} = \dfrac{\cancel{3} \cdot a}{\cancel{(a-2)}} \cdot \dfrac{2 \cdot \cancel{(a-2)}}{\cancel{3} \cdot 3} = \dfrac{2a}{3}$

3. $\dfrac{m}{m+6} \cdot \dfrac{2m+12}{2m} = \dfrac{\cancel{m}}{\cancel{(m+6)}} \cdot \dfrac{2 \cdot \cancel{(m+6)}}{2 \cdot \cancel{m}} = 1$    4. $\dfrac{x^2-xy}{3x^3} \cdot \dfrac{xy}{x-y} = \dfrac{\cancel{x} \cdot \cancel{(x-y)}}{3 \cdot \cancel{x} \cdot x \cdot x} \cdot \dfrac{\cancel{x} \cdot y}{\cancel{(x-y)}} = \dfrac{y}{3x}$

## Solutions to Study Exercises, Contd.

□          *Study Exercise Five (Frame 30)*          **(30A)**

1. $\dfrac{-2}{5} \div \dfrac{4}{25} = \dfrac{-2}{5} \cdot \dfrac{25}{4} = \dfrac{(-2)}{\cancel{5}} \cdot \dfrac{\cancel{5} \cdot 5}{(-2)(-2)} = \dfrac{5}{-2}$

2. $\dfrac{\dfrac{-2}{5}}{\dfrac{4}{25}} = \dfrac{-2}{5} \div \dfrac{4}{25} = \dfrac{5}{-2}$    [Same as problem 1]

3. $\dfrac{10x^2}{3y} \div \dfrac{9y^2}{6xy} = \dfrac{10x^2}{3y} \cdot \dfrac{6xy}{9y^2}$

           $= \dfrac{10x^2}{3y} \cdot \dfrac{\cancel{3} \cdot 2 \cdot x \cdot \cancel{y}}{\cancel{3} \cdot 3 \cdot y \cdot \cancel{y}}$

           $= \dfrac{20x^3}{9y^2}$

4. $\dfrac{3a}{5b} \div \dfrac{6a^3}{25b} = \dfrac{3a}{5b} \cdot \dfrac{25b}{6a^3}$

           $= \dfrac{\cancel{3} \cdot \cancel{a}}{\cancel{5} \cdot \cancel{b}} \cdot \dfrac{\cancel{5} \cdot 5 \cdot \cancel{b}}{\cancel{3} \cdot 2 \cdot \cancel{a} \cdot a^2}$

           $= \dfrac{5}{2a^2}$

5. $1 \div \dfrac{a}{b} = \dfrac{1}{1} \cdot \dfrac{b}{a} = \dfrac{b}{a}$

6. $\dfrac{1}{\dfrac{a}{b}} = 1 \div \dfrac{a}{b} = \dfrac{b}{a}$    [Same as problem 5]

7. $\dfrac{2x + 2y}{3x^2} \div \dfrac{6x + 6y}{x} = \dfrac{2x + 2y}{3x^2} \cdot \dfrac{x}{6x + 6y}$

           $= \dfrac{\cancel{2} \cdot \cancel{(x + y)}}{3 \cdot x \cdot \cancel{x}} \cdot \dfrac{\cancel{x}}{\cancel{2} \cdot 3 \cdot \cancel{(x + y)}}$

           $= \dfrac{1}{9x}$

# Addition and Subtraction of Fractional Expressions

□ **Objectives**                                                                                      **(1)**

By the end of this unit you should be able to:

- classify natural numbers as either prime or composite.
- give the prime factorization of a number.
- find the lowest common denominator of a group of fractions.
- perform addition and subtraction of fractions.

□ **The Natural Numbers**                                                                              **(2)**

The *natural numbers* are all of the whole numbers except zero. They are sometimes called *counting numbers*.

1, 2, 3, 4, 5, 6, 7, 8, 9, 10, 11, 12,...

□ **Prime Numbers**                                                                                    **(3)**

A *prime number* is any natural number which is evenly divisible only by itself and 1.

*Remember*, "evenly divisible" means that the remainder is zero. The number 1 is not considered a prime number.

**Examples:**

1. 2 is a prime number.
2. 3 is a prime number.
3. 4 is not a prime number because 4 is evenly divisible by 2.
4. 13 is a prime number.
5. 15 is not a prime number because 15 is evenly divisible by 3 and 5.

□ **The Prime Numbers Less Than 30**                                                                   **(4)**

2, 3, 5, 7, 11, 13, 17, 19, 23, 29

(*These should be memorized.*)

□ **Composite Numbers**                                                                                **(5)**

A *composite number* is any natural number which is evenly divisible by numbers other than 1 or itself. No number is both prime and composite.

**Examples:**

1. 6 is composite because it is evenly divisible by 2 and 3.
2. 21 is composite because it is evenly divisible by 3 and 7.
3. 26 is composite because it is evenly divisible by 2 and 13.

□                                         *Study Exercise One*                                         **(6)**

Classify each of the following as either prime or composite.

1. 2        2. 5        3. 10        4. 20        5. 25        6. 29        7. 100        8. 132

□ **Prime Factorization**                                                                              **(7)**

Every composite number can be written as a product of prime factors.

$$15 = 3 \cdot 5$$

composite        prime factors

## ☐ The Prime Factorization of 30 (8)

*line (a)*   2 | 30
*line (b)*   3 | 15
*line (c)*      5
$$30 = 2 \cdot 3 \cdot 5$$

## ☐ The Prime Factorization of 12 (9)

*line (a)*   2 | 12
*line (b)*   2 | 6
*line (c)*      3
$$12 = 2 \cdot 2 \cdot 3$$

Exponential form:   $12 = 2^2 \cdot 3^1$

## ☐ The Prime Factorization of 525 (10)

*line (a)*   3 | 525
*line (b)*   5 | 175
*line (c)*   5 | 35
*line (d)*      7
$$525 = 3 \cdot 5 \cdot 5 \cdot 7$$

Exponential form:   $525 = 3^1 \cdot 5^2 \cdot 7^1$

## ☐ *Study Exercise Two* (11)

Use the preceding method to give the prime factorization for each of the following. Put your answers in exponential form.

1.  15          2.  14          3.  24          4.  92          5.  108          6.  180

## ☐ Lowest Common Denominator (LCD) (12)

The *lowest common denominator* (**LCD**) of a group of fractions is the smallest number which each denominator will divide into evenly.

**Example 1:**   The **LCD** of $\frac{1}{4}$ and $\frac{1}{6}$ is 12.          **Example 2:**   The **LCD** of $\frac{2}{3}$, $\frac{1}{2}$, and $\frac{5}{6}$ is 6.

**Example 3:**   The **LCD** of $\frac{3}{4a}$ and $\frac{5}{6a}$ is 12$a$.

## ☐ Finding the Lowest Common Denominator (13)

**Example 1:**   Find the **LCD** of $\frac{3}{8}$ and $\frac{1}{6}$.

**Solution:**

*Step (1):*   Write each denominator in prime factored exponential form.
$$8 = 2^3$$
$$6 = 2^1 \cdot 3^1$$

*Step (2):*   Write each number which is used as a base, but write it only once. Neglect repetitions.
$$2 \cdot 3$$

*Step (3):*   From Step (1), find the largest exponent used on each base.
$$\textbf{LCD} = 2^3 \cdot 3^1$$

*Step (4):*   Evaluate the exponential expression.
$$\textbf{LCD} = 8 \cdot 3, \text{ or } 24$$

☐ **Example 2:** Find the **LCD** of $\frac{5}{12}$, $\frac{7}{45}$, and $\frac{5}{18}$. **(14)**

**Solution:**

*Step (1):* Write each denominator in prime factored exponential form.

$12 = 2^2 \cdot 3^1$

$45 = 3^2 \cdot 5^1$

$18 = 2^1 \cdot 3^2$

*Step (2):* Write each number which is used as a base, but write it only once. Neglect repetitions.

$2 \cdot 3 \cdot 5$

*Step (3):* From Step (1), find the largest exponent used on each base.

**LCD** $= 2^2 \cdot 3^2 \cdot 5^1$

*Step (4):* Evaluate the exponential expression.

**LCD** $= 4 \cdot 9 \cdot 5$, or $180$

☐ **Example 3:** Find the **LCD** of $\frac{3}{10a^3b}$ and $\frac{7}{8ab^2}$. **(15)**

**Solution:**

*Step (1):* Write each denominator in prime factored exponential form.

$10a^3b = 2^1 \cdot 5^1 \cdot a^3 \cdot b^1$

$8ab^2 = 2^3 \cdot a^1 \cdot b^2$

*Step (2):* Write each number which is used as a base, but write it only once. Neglect repetitions.

$2 \cdot 5 \cdot a \cdot b$

*Step (3):* From Step (1), find the largest exponent used on each base.

**LCD** $= 2^3 \cdot 5^1 \cdot a^3 \cdot b^2$

*Step (4):* Evaluate the exponential expression.

**LCD** $= 40a^3b^2$

☐                            *Study Exercise Three*                            **(16)**

Find the **LCD** for each of the following groups of fractions.

1. $\frac{5}{12}$ and $\frac{7}{18}$
2. $\frac{17}{40}$, $\frac{7}{20}$, and $\frac{5}{28}$
3. $\frac{5}{12x^2}$ and $\frac{7}{10xy}$
4. $\frac{5}{6a^2b}$, $\frac{7}{10ab^3}$, and $\frac{4}{15a^2}$

☐ **Addition of Fractional Expressions Having the Same Denominators** **(17)**

**Example:** $\frac{2}{7} + \frac{3}{7}$

**Solution:**

*line (a)* $\quad \frac{2}{7} + \frac{3}{7} = 2 \cdot \frac{1}{7} + 3 \cdot \frac{1}{7}$ [Definition of fractions]

*line (b)* $\qquad\qquad = \frac{1}{7} \cdot 2 + \frac{1}{7} \cdot 3$ [**cpm**]

*line (c)* $\qquad\qquad = \frac{1}{7} \cdot (2 + 3)$ [**dpma**]

*line (d)* $\qquad\qquad = \frac{1}{7} \cdot 5$ [addition]

*line (e)* $\qquad\qquad = 5 \cdot \frac{1}{7}$ [**cpm**]

*line (f)* $\qquad\qquad = \frac{5}{7}$ [Definition of a fraction]

Therefore, $\frac{2}{7} + \frac{3}{7} = \frac{5}{7}$.

**(18)**

Since $\frac{2}{7} + \frac{3}{7} = \frac{5}{7}$, it appears that when fractions having the same denominator are added, the numerators may be added, and their sum placed over the common denominator. In general:

$$\frac{a}{c} + \frac{b}{c} = \frac{a + b}{c} \quad \text{where } c \neq 0$$

**Proof:**

line (a)  $\frac{a}{c} + \frac{b}{c} = a \cdot \frac{1}{c} + b \cdot \frac{1}{c}$  [Definition of fractions]

line (b)  $= \frac{1}{c} \cdot a + \frac{1}{c} \cdot b$  [cpm]

line (c)  $= \frac{1}{c} \cdot (a + b)$  [dpma]

line (d)  $= (a + b) \cdot \frac{1}{c}$  [cpm]

line (e)  $= \frac{a + b}{c}$  [Definition of a fraction]

Therefore, $\frac{a}{c} + \frac{b}{c} = \frac{a + b}{c}$, where $c \neq 0$

**Examples:**

**(19)**

1. $\frac{4}{11} + \frac{3}{11} = \frac{4 + 3}{11}$ or $\frac{7}{11}$

2. $\frac{x}{3} + \frac{y}{3} = \frac{x + y}{3}$

3. $\frac{3x}{y} + \frac{2x}{y} = \frac{3x + 2x}{y}$ or $\frac{5x}{y}$

4. $\frac{2x^2 + x - 3}{(x + y)^2} + \frac{3x^2 + 2x - 5}{(x + y)^2} = \frac{(2x^2 + x - 3) + (3x^2 + 2x - 5)}{(x + y)^2}$

$= \frac{5x^2 + 3x - 8}{(x + y)^2}$

**Study Exercise Four**

**(20)**

Add the following fractions. Assume the denominators do not represent zero.

1. $\frac{5}{17} + \frac{9}{17}$

2. $\frac{1}{8} + \frac{3}{8} + \frac{1}{8}$

3. $\frac{5}{x} + \frac{7}{x}$

4. $\frac{5a}{3b} + \frac{2a}{3b}$

5. $\frac{4x^2 + 3x - 1}{a - b} + \frac{3x^2 - 5x + 7}{a - b}$

## Subtraction of Fractional Expressions Having the Same Denominators  **(21)**

Since subtraction is related to addition, fractional expressions having the same denominators may be subtracted by subtracting the numerators and placing this difference over the common denominator. In general:

$$\frac{a}{c} - \frac{b}{c} = \frac{a - b}{c} \quad \text{where } c \neq 0$$

**Proof:**

line (a)  $\frac{a}{c} - \frac{b}{c} = \frac{a}{c} + \left(-\frac{b}{c}\right)$  [Definition of subtraction]

line (b)  $= \frac{a}{c} + \frac{-b}{c}$  [Three signs of a fraction]

line (c)  $= \frac{a + (-b)}{c}$  [Addition of fractions]

line (d)  $= \frac{a - b}{c}$  [Definition of subtraction]

Therefore, $\frac{a}{c} - \frac{b}{c} = \frac{a - b}{c}$, where $c \neq 0$

□ **Examples:**  (22)

1. $\dfrac{4}{5} - \dfrac{3}{5} = \dfrac{4-3}{5}$ or $\dfrac{1}{5}$

2. $\dfrac{3a}{b} - \dfrac{7a}{b} = \dfrac{3a-7a}{b}$ or $\dfrac{-4a}{b}$

3. $\dfrac{2x+3}{2y^2} - \dfrac{5x-4}{2y^2} = \dfrac{(2x+3)-(5x-4)}{2y^2}$

$\qquad\qquad = \dfrac{2x+3-5x+4}{2y^2}$

$\qquad\qquad = \dfrac{-3x+7}{2y^2}$

□  *Study Exercise Five*  (23)

Subtract the following fractions. Assume that the denominators do not represent zero.

1. $\dfrac{5}{7} - \dfrac{2}{7}$
2. $\dfrac{1}{11} - \dfrac{5}{11} - \dfrac{2}{11}$
3. $\dfrac{5x}{y} - \dfrac{7x}{y}$
4. $\dfrac{2m-5}{3n} - \dfrac{6m-4}{3n}$

■ **Addition and Subtraction of Fractions with Unlike Denominators**  (24)

*Step (1):* Find the lowest common denominator (**LCD**).
*Step (2):* Expand each fraction so it has the **LCD.**
*Step (3):* Combine the fractions and reduce, if possible.

□ **Example 1:**  Add $\dfrac{3}{8} + \dfrac{1}{6}$.  (25)

**Solution:**

*Step (1):* Find the **LCD.** The **LCD** of $\dfrac{3}{8}$ and $\dfrac{1}{6}$ is 24. (See Frame 13.)

*Step (2):* Expand each fraction so it has the **LCD.**

*line (a)* $\quad \dfrac{3}{8} + \dfrac{1}{6} = \dfrac{3\cdot3}{8\cdot3} + \dfrac{1\cdot4}{6\cdot4}$

*line (b)* $\qquad\qquad = \dfrac{9}{24} + \dfrac{4}{24}$

*Step (3):* Combine the fractions and reduce, if possible.

*line (c)* $\quad \dfrac{9}{24} + \dfrac{4}{24} = \dfrac{9+4}{24}$

*line (d)* $\qquad\qquad = \dfrac{13}{24}$

Therefore, $\dfrac{3}{8} + \dfrac{1}{6} = \dfrac{13}{24}$.

□ **Example 2:**  Combine $\dfrac{5}{12} + \dfrac{7}{45} - \dfrac{5}{18}$.  (26)

**Solution:**

*Step (1):* Find the **LCD.** The **LCD** of $\dfrac{5}{12}, \dfrac{7}{45}$, and $\dfrac{5}{18}$ is 180. (See Frame 14.)

*Step (2):* Expand each fraction so it has the **LCD.**

*line (a)* $\quad \dfrac{5}{12} + \dfrac{7}{45} - \dfrac{5}{18} = \dfrac{5\cdot15}{12\cdot15} + \dfrac{7\cdot4}{45\cdot4} - \dfrac{5\cdot10}{18\cdot10}$

*line (b)* $\qquad\qquad\qquad = \dfrac{75}{180} + \dfrac{28}{180} - \dfrac{50}{180}$

*Step (3):* Combine the fractions and reduce, if possible.

*line (c)* $\dfrac{75}{180} + \dfrac{28}{180} - \dfrac{50}{180} = \dfrac{75 + 28 - 50}{180}$

*line (d)* $= \dfrac{53}{180}$

Therefore, $\dfrac{5}{12} + \dfrac{7}{45} - \dfrac{5}{18} = \dfrac{53}{180}$.

☐ **Example 3:** Combine $\dfrac{7}{x} + \dfrac{5}{x^2}$.  **(27)**

**Solution:**

*Step (1):* Find the **LCD.** The **LCD** of $\dfrac{7}{x}$ and $\dfrac{5}{x^2}$ is $x^2$.

*Step (2):* Expand each fraction so it has the **LCD.**

*line (a)* $\dfrac{7}{x} + \dfrac{5}{x^2} = \dfrac{7 \cdot x}{x \cdot x} + \dfrac{5}{x^2}$

*line (b)* $= \dfrac{7x}{x^2} + \dfrac{5}{x^2}$

*Step (3):* Combine the fractions and reduce, if possible.

*line (c)* $\dfrac{7x}{x^2} + \dfrac{5}{x^2} = \dfrac{7x + 5}{x^2}$

Therefore, $\dfrac{7}{x} + \dfrac{5}{x^2} = \dfrac{7x + 5}{x^2}$.

☐ **Example 4:** Combine $\dfrac{3}{10a^3b} + \dfrac{7}{8ab^2}$.  **(28)**

**Solution:**

*Step (1):* Find the **LCD.** The **LCD** of $\dfrac{3}{10a^3b}$ and $\dfrac{7}{8ab^2}$ is $40a^3b^2$. (See Frame 15.)

*Step (2):* Expand each fraction so it has the **LCD.**

*line (a)* $\dfrac{3}{10a^3b} + \dfrac{7}{8ab^2} = \dfrac{3 \cdot (4b)}{10a^3b \cdot (4b)} + \dfrac{7 \cdot (5a^2)}{8ab^2 \cdot (5a^2)}$

*line (b)* $= \dfrac{12b}{40a^3b^2} + \dfrac{35a^2}{40a^3b^2}$

*Step (3):* Combine the fractions and reduce, if possible.

*line (c)* $\dfrac{12b}{40a^3b^2} + \dfrac{35a^2}{40a^3b^2} = \dfrac{12b + 35a^2}{40a^3b^2}$

Therefore, $\dfrac{3}{10a^3b} + \dfrac{7}{8ab^2} = \dfrac{12b + 35a^2}{40a^3b^2}$.

☐ **Example 5:** Combine $\dfrac{1}{a^2} - \dfrac{2}{ab} + \dfrac{1}{b^2}$.  **(29)**

**Solution:**

*Step (1):* Find the **LCD.** The **LCD** of $\dfrac{1}{a^2}, \dfrac{2}{ab}$, and $\dfrac{1}{b^2}$ is $a^2b^2$.

*Step (2):* Expand each fraction so it has the **LCD.**

*line (a)* $\dfrac{1}{a^2} - \dfrac{2}{ab} + \dfrac{1}{b^2} = \dfrac{1 \cdot (b^2)}{a^2 \cdot (b^2)} - \dfrac{2 \cdot (ab)}{(ab) \cdot (ab)} + \dfrac{1 \cdot (a^2)}{b^2 \cdot (a^2)}$

*line (b)* $= \dfrac{b^2}{a^2b^2} - \dfrac{2ab}{a^2b^2} + \dfrac{a^2}{a^2b^2}$

*Step (3):* Combine the fractions and reduce, if possible.

*line (c)* $\dfrac{b^2}{a^2b^2} - \dfrac{2ab}{a^2b^2} + \dfrac{a^2}{a^2b^2} = \dfrac{b^2 - 2ab + a^2}{a^2b^2}$

Therefore, $\dfrac{1}{a^2} - \dfrac{2}{ab} + \dfrac{1}{b^2} = \dfrac{b^2 - 2ab + a^2}{a^2b^2}$.

☐ **Example 6:** Combine $\dfrac{7}{5x} - \dfrac{1+x}{10x^2}$. **(30)**

**Solution:**

*Step (1):* Find the **LCD**. The **LCD** of $\dfrac{7}{5x}$ and $\dfrac{1+x}{10x^2}$ is $10x^2$.

*Step (2):* Expand each fraction so it has the **LCD**.

*line (a)* $\dfrac{7}{5x} - \dfrac{1+x}{10x^2} = \dfrac{7\cdot(2x)}{(5x)\cdot(2x)} - \dfrac{1+x}{10x^2}$

*line (b)* $= \dfrac{14x}{10x^2} - \dfrac{1+x}{10x^2}$

*Step (3):* Combine the fractions and reduce, if possible.

*line (c)* $\dfrac{14x}{10x^2} - \dfrac{1+x}{10x^2} = \dfrac{14x - (1+x)}{10x^2}$

*line (d)* $= \dfrac{14x - 1 - x}{10x^2}$

*line (e)* $= \dfrac{13x - 1}{10x^2}$

Therefore, $\dfrac{7}{5x} - \dfrac{1+x}{10x^2} = \dfrac{13x - 1}{10x^2}$.

☐ **Example 7:** Combine $\dfrac{5}{a+b} - \dfrac{2}{a-b}$. **(31)**

**Solution:**

*Step (1):* Find the **LCD**. The **LCD** of $\dfrac{5}{(a+b)}$ and $\dfrac{2}{(a-b)}$ is $(a+b)(a-b)$.

*Step (2):* Expand each fraction so it has the **LCD**.

*line (a)* $\dfrac{5}{a+b} - \dfrac{2}{a-b} = \dfrac{5\cdot(a-b)}{(a+b)\cdot(a-b)} - \dfrac{2\cdot(a+b)}{(a-b)\cdot(a+b)}$

*line (b)* $= \dfrac{5a - 5b}{(a+b)(a-b)} - \dfrac{2a + 2b}{(a+b)(a-b)}$

*Step (3):* Combine the fractions and reduce, if possible.

*line (c)* $\dfrac{5a - 5b}{(a+b)(a-b)} - \dfrac{2a + 2b}{(a+b)(a-b)} = \dfrac{(5a - 5b) - (2a + 2b)}{(a+b)(a-b)}$

*line (d)* $= \dfrac{5a - 5b - 2a - 2b}{(a+b)(a-b)}$

*line (e)* $= \dfrac{3a - 7b}{(a+b)(a-b)}$

Therefore, $\dfrac{5}{a+b} - \dfrac{2}{a-b} = \dfrac{3a - 7b}{(a+b)(a-b)}$.

☐ ***Study Exercise Six*** **(32)**

Combine the following fractions. Assume that the denominators do not represent zero.

1. $\dfrac{3}{4} + \dfrac{1}{3} - \dfrac{1}{12}$  2. $\dfrac{2}{a} + \dfrac{3}{a^2}$  3. $\dfrac{5}{y} + \dfrac{3}{x}$  4. $\dfrac{c}{d} + 1$

5. $\dfrac{3a}{2b^2} + \dfrac{3}{4b}$     6. $\dfrac{5}{6mn^2} - \dfrac{3}{4m^2n}$     7. $\dfrac{5}{7x} - \dfrac{1+x}{14x^2}$     8. $\dfrac{7}{x+2} - \dfrac{3}{x-5}$

☐ **Mixed Numerals**                                      **(33)**

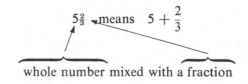

$$5\tfrac{2}{3} \text{ means } 5 + \tfrac{2}{3}$$

whole number mixed with a fraction

☐ 1. To convert a mixed numeral to the fractional form, perform addition.         **(34)**

**Example:** $5\tfrac{2}{3}$

*line (a)*   $5\tfrac{2}{3} = 5 + \dfrac{2}{3}$

*line (b)*       $= \dfrac{5}{1} + \dfrac{2}{3}$

*line (c)*       $= \dfrac{15}{3} + \dfrac{2}{3}$

*line (d)*       $= \dfrac{17}{3}$

2. To convert a fraction where the numerator is greater than the denominator to a mixed numeral, divide the numerator by the denominator and place the remainder over the denominator.

**Example:** $\dfrac{13}{5}$

*line (a)*   $13 \div 5 = 2$ and remainder of 3.

*line (b)*       $= 2 + \dfrac{3}{5}$

*line (c)*       $= 2\tfrac{3}{5}$

☐                              *Study Exercise Seven*                       **(35)**

A. Convert the following mixed numerals to fractional form:

   1. $6\tfrac{5}{8}$                             2.  $-7\tfrac{1}{2}$  *Hint:*  $-7\tfrac{1}{2}$ means $-(7\tfrac{1}{2})$

B. Convert the following fractions to mixed numeral form:

   3. $\dfrac{19}{2}$                             4.  $-\dfrac{23}{3}$

## REVIEW EXERCISES

A. Define the following.

   1. Prime number         2. Composite number         3. Lowest common denominator

B. Classify each of the following natural numbers as being prime or composite.

   4. 7         5. 15         6. 24         7. 29         8. 93         9. 37

C. Give the prime factorization for each of the following. Put your answers in exponential form.

   10. 12         11. 8         12. 36         13. 360

Unit 14

## REVIEW EXERCISES, Contd.

D. Find the **LCD** for each of the following groups of fractions.

14. $\dfrac{5}{12}, \dfrac{11}{36},$ and $\dfrac{3}{10}$

15. $\dfrac{a}{2xy}, \dfrac{6}{3x^2y},$ and $\dfrac{c}{6x^2y^3}$

16. $\dfrac{3}{m+n}$ and $\dfrac{2}{m-n}$

17. $\dfrac{x}{y}$ and $\dfrac{3}{y+1}$

E. Using addition or subtraction, combine the following fractions. Assume that the denominators do not represent zero.

18. $\dfrac{2}{9} + \dfrac{3}{9}$

19. $\dfrac{2}{7} - \dfrac{4}{7}$

20. $\dfrac{5}{18} + \dfrac{1}{3} - \dfrac{1}{2} + \dfrac{2}{9}$

21. $\dfrac{x}{y} + \dfrac{3x}{y}$

22. $\dfrac{2m}{m+n} + \dfrac{6m}{m+n} - \dfrac{3m}{m+n}$

23. $\dfrac{5x}{3y} - \dfrac{2x+1}{3y}$

24. $\dfrac{1}{2} + \dfrac{5}{8}$

25. $\dfrac{2}{3} + \dfrac{3}{8} - \dfrac{1}{2}$

26. $\dfrac{3}{m} + \dfrac{4}{m^2}$

27. $1 + \dfrac{x}{y}$

28. $\dfrac{5a}{3b^2} + \dfrac{3}{6b}$

29. $\dfrac{7}{3x} - \dfrac{1-x}{6x^2}$

30. $\dfrac{x}{x+2} - \dfrac{2x}{x+3}$

31. $\dfrac{3}{m^2} - \dfrac{2}{mn} + \dfrac{5}{n^2}$

F. Convert the following mixed numerals to fractional form.

32. $7\frac{3}{8}$

33. $-5\frac{1}{5}$

G. Convert the following fractions to mixed numeral form.

34. $\dfrac{3}{2}$

35. $-\dfrac{8}{3}$

## Solutions to Review Exercises

A. 1. See Frame 3.    2. See Frame 5.    3. See Frame 12.

B. 4. Prime   5. Composite   6. Composite   7. Prime   8. Composite   9. Prime

C. 10. $12 = 2^2 \cdot 3^1$    11. $8 = 2^3$    12. $36 = 2^2 \cdot 3^2$    13. $360 = 2^3 \cdot 3^2 \cdot 5^1$

D. 14. $12 = 2^2 \cdot 3^1$
$36 = 2^2 \cdot 3^2$
$10 = 2^1 \cdot 5^1$
$\mathbf{LCD} = 2^2 \cdot 3^2 \cdot 5^1$
$\mathbf{LCD} = 180$

15. $2xy = 2^1 \cdot x^1 \cdot y^1$
$3x^2y = 3^1 \cdot x^2 \cdot y^1$
$6x^2y^3 = 2^1 \cdot 3^1 \cdot x^2 \cdot y^3$
$\mathbf{LCD} = 2^1 \cdot 3^1 \cdot x^2 \cdot y^3$
$\mathbf{LCD} = 6x^2y^3$

16. $m + n = (m + n)^1$
$m - n = (m - n)^1$
$\mathbf{LCD} = (m + n)^1 \cdot (m - n)^1$
$\mathbf{LCD} = (m + n)(m - n)$

17. $y = y^1$
$y + 1 = (y + 1)^1$
$\mathbf{LCD} = y^1 \cdot (y + 1)^1$
$\mathbf{LCD} = y(y + 1)$

E. 18. $\dfrac{2}{9} + \dfrac{3}{9} = \dfrac{5}{9}$

19. $\dfrac{2}{7} - \dfrac{4}{7} = \dfrac{-2}{7}$

20. $\dfrac{5}{18} + \dfrac{1}{3} - \dfrac{1}{2} + \dfrac{2}{9} = \dfrac{5}{18} + \dfrac{1 \cdot 6}{3 \cdot 6} - \dfrac{1 \cdot 9}{2 \cdot 9} + \dfrac{2 \cdot 2}{9 \cdot 2}$
$= \dfrac{5}{18} + \dfrac{6}{18} - \dfrac{9}{18} + \dfrac{4}{18}$
$= \dfrac{6}{18}$ or $\dfrac{1}{3}$

21. $\dfrac{x}{y} + \dfrac{3x}{y} = \dfrac{x + 3x}{y}$ or $\dfrac{4x}{y}$

## Solutions to Review Exercises, Contd.

22. $\dfrac{2m}{m+n} + \dfrac{6m}{m+n} - \dfrac{3m}{m+n} = \dfrac{2m+6m-3m}{m+n}$ or $\dfrac{5m}{m+n}$

23. $\dfrac{5x}{3y} - \dfrac{2x+1}{3y} = \dfrac{5x-(2x+1)}{3y}$

$= \dfrac{5x-2x-1}{3y}$

$= \dfrac{3x-1}{3y}$

24. $\dfrac{1}{2} + \dfrac{5}{8} = \dfrac{1\cdot 4}{2\cdot 4} + \dfrac{5}{8}$

$= \dfrac{4}{8} + \dfrac{5}{8}$

$= \dfrac{9}{8}$

25. $\dfrac{2}{3} + \dfrac{3}{8} - \dfrac{1}{2} = \dfrac{2\cdot 8}{3\cdot 8} + \dfrac{3\cdot 3}{8\cdot 3} - \dfrac{1\cdot 12}{2\cdot 12}$

$= \dfrac{16}{24} + \dfrac{9}{24} - \dfrac{12}{24}$

$= \dfrac{13}{24}$

26. $\dfrac{3}{m} + \dfrac{4}{m^2} = \dfrac{3\cdot m}{m\cdot m} + \dfrac{4}{m^2}$

$= \dfrac{3m}{m^2} + \dfrac{4}{m^2}$

$= \dfrac{3m+4}{m^2}$

27. $1 + \dfrac{x}{y} = \dfrac{1}{1} + \dfrac{x}{y}$

$= \dfrac{1\cdot y}{1\cdot y} + \dfrac{x}{y}$

$= \dfrac{y}{y} + \dfrac{x}{y}$

$= \dfrac{y+x}{y}$

28. $\dfrac{5a}{3b^2} + \dfrac{3}{6b} = \dfrac{5a\cdot 2}{3b^2\cdot 2} + \dfrac{3\cdot b}{6b\cdot b}$

$= \dfrac{10a}{6b^2} + \dfrac{3b}{6b^2}$

$= \dfrac{10a + 3b}{6b^2}$

29. $\dfrac{7}{3x} - \dfrac{1-x}{6x^2} = \dfrac{7\cdot(2x)}{3x\cdot(2x)} - \dfrac{1-x}{6x^2}$

$= \dfrac{14x}{6x^2} - \dfrac{1-x}{6x^2}$

$= \dfrac{14x-(1-x)}{6x^2}$

$= \dfrac{14x-1+x}{6x^2}$

$= \dfrac{15x-1}{6x^2}$

30. $\dfrac{x}{x+2} - \dfrac{2x}{x+3} = \dfrac{x\cdot(x+3)}{(x+2)\cdot(x+3)} - \dfrac{2x\cdot(x+2)}{(x+3)(x+2)}$

$= \dfrac{x^2+3x}{(x+2)(x+3)} - \dfrac{2x^2+4x}{(x+2)(x+3)}$

$= \dfrac{(x^2+3x)-(2x^2+4x)}{(x+2)(x+3)}$

$= \dfrac{x^2+3x-2x^2-4x}{(x+2)(x+3)}$

$= \dfrac{-x^2-x}{(x+2)(x+3)}$

31. $\dfrac{3}{m^2} - \dfrac{2}{mn} + \dfrac{5}{n^2} = \dfrac{3\cdot n^2}{m^2\cdot n^2} - \dfrac{2\cdot(mn)}{(mn)\cdot(mn)} + \dfrac{5\cdot m^2}{n^2\cdot m^2}$

$= \dfrac{3n^2}{m^2n^2} - \dfrac{2mn}{m^2n^2} + \dfrac{5m^2}{m^2n^2}$

$= \dfrac{3n^2-2mn+5m^2}{m^2n^2}$

F. 32. $7\frac{3}{8} = \dfrac{59}{8}$

33. $-5\frac{1}{5} = -(5\frac{1}{5}) = -\dfrac{26}{5}$

G. 34. $\dfrac{3}{2} = 1\frac{1}{2}$

35. $-\dfrac{8}{3} = -(2\frac{2}{3}) = -2\frac{2}{3}$

## SUPPLEMENTARY PROBLEMS

A. Classify each of the following numbers as prime or composite.

   1. 2     2. 10     3. 13     4. 19     5. 27     6. 42     7. 93     8. 144

B. Give the prime factorization for each of the following. Put your answers in exponential form.

   9. 4     10. 9     11. 15     12. 28     13. 40     14. 108     15. 240     16. 720

## SUPPLEMENTARY PROBLEMS, Contd.

C. Find the **LCD** for each of the following groups of fractions.

17. $\dfrac{5}{18}, \dfrac{3}{20},$ and $\dfrac{7}{24}$

18. $\dfrac{2}{10a^2}, \dfrac{3}{a^2b},$ and $\dfrac{7}{5ab^2}$

19. $\dfrac{5}{12}, \dfrac{7}{36},$ and $\dfrac{3}{5}$

20. $\dfrac{a}{2xy^2}$ and $\dfrac{b}{3x^2y}$

21. $\dfrac{5}{x+3}$ and $\dfrac{1}{x-2}$

22. $\dfrac{x}{2xy}$ and $\dfrac{5}{15y^3}$

23. $\dfrac{a}{b+1}$ and $\dfrac{c}{b}$

24. $\dfrac{3}{xy^2}$ and $\dfrac{5}{x^2(y+1)}$

D. Using addition or subtraction, combine the following fractions. Assume that the denominators do not represent zero.

25. $\dfrac{2}{9} + \dfrac{5}{9}$

26. $\dfrac{6}{11} - \dfrac{8}{11}$

27. $\dfrac{1}{7} - \dfrac{6}{7} + \dfrac{2}{7}$

28. $\dfrac{m}{n} + \dfrac{3m}{n}$

29. $\dfrac{2m}{n} - \dfrac{7m}{n}$

30. $\dfrac{2}{a+b} + \dfrac{5}{a+b} - \dfrac{3}{a+b}$

31. $\dfrac{3a}{2b} - \dfrac{a+7}{2b}$

32. $\dfrac{3a}{2b} + \dfrac{a+7}{2b}$

33. $\dfrac{3}{4} + \dfrac{5}{8}$

34. $\dfrac{3}{5} - \dfrac{7}{20} + \dfrac{1}{2}$

35. $\dfrac{4}{a} + \dfrac{3}{b}$

36. $\dfrac{2}{mn} + \dfrac{2}{n}$

37. $\dfrac{r+2}{3} + \dfrac{r-3}{9}$

38. $\dfrac{x-2}{6} - \dfrac{x+1}{3}$

39. $\dfrac{2a-b}{2} - \dfrac{a+b}{3}$

40. $\dfrac{3}{x+y} + \dfrac{1}{x-y}$

41. $\dfrac{7}{2a} - \dfrac{4+a}{4a^2}$

42. $\dfrac{3}{y} - \dfrac{2}{x+y}$

43. $4 + \dfrac{x}{y}$

44. $m + \dfrac{n}{m}$

45. $\dfrac{2}{5a} - \dfrac{3-a}{10a^2}$

46. $\dfrac{3}{x^2} + \dfrac{2}{xy} - \dfrac{5}{y^2}$

47. $\dfrac{5}{m+n} + \dfrac{2}{(m+n)^2}$

48. $\dfrac{x}{2(x-2)} + \dfrac{2x-1}{x-2}$

49. $\dfrac{3a}{a-b} + \dfrac{2b}{a+b}$

50. $\dfrac{4r-3}{8} - \dfrac{3r+1}{6} + \dfrac{r+2}{2}$

51. $\dfrac{3x+y}{3} + \dfrac{x+2y}{6} - \dfrac{x+y}{2}$

E. Convert the following mixed numerals to fractional form.

52. $8\frac{2}{3}$

53. $-10\frac{1}{2}$

54. $13\frac{5}{9}$

55. $1\frac{9}{10}$

56. $-3\frac{4}{5}$

57. $12\frac{1}{8}$

F. Convert the following fractions to mixed numeral form.

58. $\dfrac{10}{3}$

59. $-\dfrac{23}{8}$

60. $\dfrac{13}{2}$

61. $\dfrac{15}{4}$

62. $-\dfrac{13}{3}$

63. $\dfrac{83}{5}$

## ☐ Solutions to Study Exercises (6A)

### Study Exercise One (Frame 6)

1. Prime     2. Prime     3. Composite     4. Composite
5. Composite   6. Prime     7. Composite    8. Composite

## ☐ Study Exercise Two (Frame 11) (11A)

1. $3\,\lfloor\,15$     *Answer:* $15 = 3^1 \cdot 5^1$
      $5$

2. $2\,\lfloor\,14$    *Answer:* $14 = 2^1 \cdot 7^1$
      $7$

3. $2\,\lfloor\,24$    *Answer:* $24 = 2^3 \cdot 3^1$
      $2\,\lfloor\,12$
      $2\,\lfloor\,6$
      $3$

4. $2\,\lfloor\,92$    *Answer:* $92 = 2^2 \cdot 23^1$
      $2\,\lfloor\,46$
      $23$

5. $2\,\lfloor\,108$    *Answer:* $108 = 2^2 \cdot 3^3$
      $2\,\lfloor\,54$
      $3\,\lfloor\,27$
      $3\,\lfloor\,9$
      $3$

6. $2\,\lfloor\,180$    *Answer:* $180 = 2^2 \cdot 3^2 \cdot 5^1$
      $2\,\lfloor\,90$
      $3\,\lfloor\,45$
      $3\,\lfloor\,15$
      $5$

## ☐ Study Exercise Three (Frame 16) (16A)

1. *Step (1):* $12 = 2^2 \cdot 3^1$, $18 = 2^1 \cdot 3^2$
   *Step (2):* $2 \cdot 3$
   *Step (3):* **LCD** $= 2^2 \cdot 3^2$
   *Step (4):* **LCD** $= 36$

2. *Step (1):* $40 = 2^3 \cdot 5^1$, $20 = 2^2 \cdot 5^1$, $28 = 2^2 \cdot 7^1$
   *Step (2):* $2 \cdot 5 \cdot 7$
   *Step (3):* **LCD** $= 2^3 \cdot 5^1 \cdot 7^1$
   *Step (4):* **LCD** $= 280$

3. *Step (1):* $12x^2 = 2^2 \cdot 3^1 \cdot x^2$, $10xy = 2^1 \cdot 5^1 \cdot x^1 \cdot y^1$
   *Step (2):* $2 \cdot 3 \cdot 5 \cdot x \cdot y$
   *Step (3):* **LCD** $= 2^2 \cdot 3^1 \cdot 5^1 \cdot x^2 \cdot y^1$
   *Step (4):* **LCD** $= 60x^2y$

4. *Step (1):* $6a^2b = 2^1 \cdot 3^1 \cdot a^2 \cdot b^1$, $10ab^3 = 2^1 \cdot 5^1 \cdot a^1 \cdot b^3$
            $15a^2 = 3^1 \cdot 5^1 \cdot a^2$
   *Step (2):* $2 \cdot 3 \cdot 5 \cdot a \cdot b$
   *Step (3):* **LCD** $= 2^1 \cdot 3^1 \cdot 5^1 \cdot a^2 \cdot b^3$
   *Step (4):* **LCD** $= 30a^2b^3$

## ☐ Study Exercise Four (Frame 20) (20A)

1. $\dfrac{5}{17} + \dfrac{9}{17} = \dfrac{5+9}{17}$ or $\dfrac{14}{17}$

2. $\dfrac{1}{8} + \dfrac{3}{8} + \dfrac{1}{8} = \dfrac{1+3+1}{8}$ or $\dfrac{5}{8}$

3. $\dfrac{5}{x} + \dfrac{7}{x} = \dfrac{5+7}{x}$ or $\dfrac{12}{x}$

4. $\dfrac{5a}{3b} + \dfrac{2a}{3b} = \dfrac{5a+2a}{3b}$ or $\dfrac{7a}{3b}$

5. $\dfrac{4x^2 + 3x - 1}{a - b} + \dfrac{3x^2 - 5x + 7}{a - b} = \dfrac{(4x^2 + 3x - 1) + (3x^2 - 5x + 7)}{a - b}$

              $= \dfrac{7x^2 - 2x + 6}{a - b}$

## ☐ Study Exercise Five (Frame 23) (23A)

1. $\dfrac{5}{7} - \dfrac{2}{7} = \dfrac{5-2}{7}$ or $\dfrac{3}{7}$

2. $\dfrac{1}{11} - \dfrac{5}{11} - \dfrac{2}{11} = \dfrac{1-5-2}{11}$ or $\dfrac{-6}{11}$

3. $\dfrac{5x}{y} - \dfrac{7x}{y} = \dfrac{5x - 7x}{y}$ or $\dfrac{-2x}{y}$

4. $\dfrac{2m - 5}{3n} - \dfrac{6m - 4}{3n} = \dfrac{(2m - 5) - (6m - 4)}{3n}$

            $= \dfrac{2m - 5 - 6m + 4}{3n}$

            $= \dfrac{-4m - 1}{3n}$

## Solutions to Study Exercises, Contd.

1. $\dfrac{3}{4} + \dfrac{1}{3} - \dfrac{1}{12} = \dfrac{3 \cdot 3}{4 \cdot 3} + \dfrac{1 \cdot 4}{3 \cdot 4} - \dfrac{1}{12}$

$$= \dfrac{9}{12} + \dfrac{4}{12} - \dfrac{1}{12}$$

$$= \dfrac{12}{12} \text{ or } 1$$

2. $\dfrac{2}{a} + \dfrac{3}{a^2} = \dfrac{2 \cdot a}{a \cdot a} + \dfrac{3}{a^2}$

$$= \dfrac{2a}{a^2} + \dfrac{3}{a^2}$$

$$= \dfrac{2a + 3}{a^2}$$

3. $\dfrac{5}{y} + \dfrac{3}{x} = \dfrac{5 \cdot x}{y \cdot x} + \dfrac{3 \cdot y}{x \cdot y}$

$$= \dfrac{5x}{xy} + \dfrac{3y}{xy}$$

$$= \dfrac{5x + 3y}{xy}$$

4. $\dfrac{c}{d} + 1 = \dfrac{c}{d} + \dfrac{1}{1}$

$$= \dfrac{c}{d} + \dfrac{1 \cdot d}{1 \cdot d}$$

$$= \dfrac{c}{d} + \dfrac{d}{d}$$

$$= \dfrac{c + d}{d}$$

5. $\dfrac{3a}{2b^2} + \dfrac{3}{4b} = \dfrac{3a \cdot 2}{2b^2 \cdot 2} + \dfrac{3 \cdot b}{4b \cdot b}$

$$= \dfrac{6a}{4b^2} + \dfrac{3b}{4b^2}$$

$$= \dfrac{6a + 3b}{4b^2}$$

6. $\dfrac{5}{6mn^2} - \dfrac{3}{4m^2n} = \dfrac{5 \cdot (2m)}{6mn^2 \cdot (2m)} - \dfrac{3 \cdot (3n)}{4m^2n \cdot (3n)}$

$$= \dfrac{10m}{12m^2n^2} - \dfrac{9n}{12m^2n^2}$$

$$= \dfrac{10m - 9n}{12m^2n^2}$$

7. $\dfrac{5}{7x} - \dfrac{1 + x}{14x^2} = \dfrac{5 \cdot (2x)}{7x \cdot (2x)} - \dfrac{1 + x}{14x^2}$

$$= \dfrac{10x}{14x^2} - \dfrac{1 + x}{14x^2}$$

$$= \dfrac{10x - (1 + x)}{14x^2}$$

$$= \dfrac{10x - 1 - x}{14x^2}$$

$$= \dfrac{9x - 1}{14x^2}$$

8. $\dfrac{7}{x + 2} - \dfrac{3}{x - 5} = \dfrac{7 \cdot (x - 5)}{(x + 2) \cdot (x - 5)} - \dfrac{3 \cdot (x + 2)}{(x - 5) \cdot (x + 2)}$

$$= \dfrac{7x - 35}{(x + 2)(x - 5)} - \dfrac{3x + 6}{(x + 2)(x - 5)}$$

$$= \dfrac{(7x - 35) - (3x + 6)}{(x + 2)(x - 5)}$$

$$= \dfrac{7x - 35 - 3x - 6}{(x + 2)(x - 5)}$$

$$= \dfrac{4x - 41}{(x + 2)(x - 5)}$$

A. 1. $6\frac{5}{8} = \dfrac{53}{8}$

2. $-7\frac{1}{2} = -(7\frac{1}{2}) = -\dfrac{15}{2}$

B. 3. $\dfrac{19}{2} = 9\frac{1}{2}$

4. $-\dfrac{23}{3} = -(7\frac{2}{3}) = -7\frac{2}{3}$

## Module 3 Review Problems

A. Classify each of these numbers as being either rational or irrational.

1. $\frac{2}{3}$
2. $0.\overline{56}$
3. $0.202002000200002\ldots$
4. $1.29$
5. $\pi$
6. $0$
7. $-3$

B. True or False

8. A real number is any number which can be written as a decimal.
9. No number is both rational and irrational.
10. The set of real numbers is the union of the rationals with the irrationals.
11. The integers are a subset of the rationals.
12. The multiplicative inverse of 10 is $\frac{1}{10}$.
13. The multiplicative inverse of 0 is $\frac{1}{0}$.

C. Use the operation of division to write each of these rational numbers as a decimal. (Do not round off.)

14. $\frac{3}{5}$
15. $\frac{6}{7}$

D. Each of the following equations illustrates one of the properties of real numbers. Name the property which each illustrates. (**You may use abbreviations.**)

16. $a \cdot \frac{1}{a} = 1$, where $a \neq 0$
17. $x^2 + 7x = 7x + x^2$
18. $a(b + c) = ab + ac$
19. $m + (-m) = 0$
20. $(2x + y) \cdot 0 = 0$
21. $x = 1 \cdot x$
22. $(ab)c = c(ab)$
23. If $x$ and $y$ represent real numbers, then $x \cdot y$ represents a real number.

E. Convert these fractions to basic products and basic quotients.

24. $\frac{x}{y}$
25. $\frac{x + 5}{x + 7}$

F. Simplify these fractional expressions.

26. $\frac{a}{1}$
27. $\frac{5x}{5x}$, where $x \neq 0$
28. $\frac{0}{a + 3}$, where $a + 3 \neq 0$

G. True or False

29. $\frac{-5}{8} = \frac{5}{-8}$
30. $\frac{3a}{5b} = \frac{-3a}{-5b}$
31. $\frac{7m}{n} = -\frac{7m}{n}$

H. Expand these fractions as directed.

32. $\frac{3}{5y}$, so that its denominator becomes $15y^2$.
33. $\frac{2a}{3bc^2}$, so that its denominator becomes $6b^2c^3$.

I. Reduce these fractions to lowest terms.

34. $\frac{3x}{6x^2}$
35. $\frac{10a^2b^3}{15a^3b^5}$
36. $\frac{3(b + 2)}{5a(b + 2)}$
37. $\frac{2x + 6}{5x + 15}$
38. $\frac{3m(n - 2)}{n - 2}$

## Module 3 Review Problems, Contd.

### Units 11–14

J.  Multiply or divide the following fractions and put the answers in reduced form.

39. $\dfrac{15}{21} \cdot \dfrac{7}{3}$

40. $\dfrac{2m}{n} \cdot \dfrac{5n^2}{m^2}$

41. $\dfrac{3x}{7} \cdot \dfrac{5}{x^2}$

42. $\dfrac{3a^2b}{2x^2} \cdot \dfrac{x}{9ab}$

43. $\dfrac{5a - 5b}{3} \cdot \dfrac{6}{7a - 7b}$

44. $\dfrac{4}{7} \div \dfrac{2}{5}$

45. $1 \div \dfrac{4}{7}$

46. $\dfrac{xy^2}{z} \div \dfrac{y^2}{z^2}$

47. $\dfrac{3m + 3n}{4m^2} \div \dfrac{5m + 5n}{m}$

48. $\dfrac{\dfrac{5x}{y}}{\dfrac{7x^2}{2y}}$

K.  Classify the following natural numbers as being either prime or composite.

49.  10

50.  13

51.  27

L.  Give the prime factorization for each of these numbers. Put your answers in exponential form.

52.  24

53.  108

M.  Combine these fractions by addition or subtraction. Be sure your answers are in reduced form.

54. $\dfrac{1}{5} + \dfrac{3}{5} - \dfrac{2}{5}$

55. $\dfrac{3}{a} + \dfrac{7}{a}$

56. $\dfrac{2x}{5} - \dfrac{6x}{5}$

57. $\dfrac{5}{12} + \dfrac{7}{18}$

58. $\dfrac{3}{x} + \dfrac{5}{x^2}$

59. $\dfrac{3}{10x^3y} + \dfrac{7}{8x^2y^2}$

60. $\dfrac{3}{2x} - \dfrac{x + 2}{4x^2}$

61. $\dfrac{x + 3}{6} - \dfrac{x + 1}{2}$

62. $a + \dfrac{b}{c}$

63. $\dfrac{1}{x} + \dfrac{1}{y}$

N.  Do as directed.

64.  Convert $-2\frac{5}{8}$ to fractional form.

65.  Convert $\dfrac{17}{3}$ to a mixed numeral.

## Answers to Module 3 Review Problems

A.  1. Rational    2. Rational    3. Irrational    4. Rational
     5. Irrational    6. Rational    7. Rational

B.  8. True    9. True    10. True    11. True    12. True    13. False

C.  14. 0.6      15. $0.\overline{857142}$

D.  16. mult. inv.    17. cpa    18. dpma    19. add. inv.
     20. mult. by zero    21. mult. ident.    22. cpm    23. clpm

E.  24. $x \cdot \dfrac{1}{y}$ and $x \div y$      25. $(x + 5) \cdot \dfrac{1}{x + 7}$ and $(x + 5) \div (x + 7)$

F.  26. $a$      27. 1      28. 0

G.  29. True      30. True      31. False

H.  32. $\dfrac{9y}{15y^2}$      33. $\dfrac{4abc}{6b^2c^3}$

I.  34. $\dfrac{1}{2x}$    35. $\dfrac{2}{3ab^2}$    36. $\dfrac{3}{5a}$    37. $\dfrac{2}{5}$    38. $3m$

## Answers to Module 3 Review Problems, Contd.

**Units 11–14**

J.    39. $\dfrac{5}{3}$      40. $\dfrac{10n}{m}$      41. $\dfrac{15}{7x}$      42. $\dfrac{a}{6x}$      43. $\dfrac{10}{7}$

     44. $\dfrac{10}{7}$      45. $\dfrac{7}{4}$      46. $xz$      47. $\dfrac{3}{20m}$      48. $\dfrac{10}{7x}$

K.    49. Composite      50. Prime      51. Composite

L.    52. $2^3 \cdot 3$      53. $2^2 \cdot 3^3$

M.    54. $\dfrac{2}{5}$      55. $\dfrac{10}{a}$      56. $\dfrac{-4x}{5}$      57. $\dfrac{29}{36}$      58. $\dfrac{3x + 5}{x^2}$

     59. $\dfrac{12y + 35x}{40x^3 y^2}$      60. $\dfrac{5x - 2}{4x^2}$      61. $\dfrac{-x}{3}$      62. $\dfrac{ac + b}{c}$      63. $\dfrac{y + x}{xy}$

N.    64. $-\dfrac{21}{8}$      65. $5\frac{2}{3}$

# Operations with Polynomial and Rational Expressions

# Multiplication and Division of Polynomial Expressions

☐ **Objectives**  (1)

By the end of this unit you should be able to:

- recognize and evaluate polynomial expressions.
- classify polynomial expressions as monomials, binomials, or trinomials.
- perform the following types of multiplication:
  - (a) monomial times a monomial.
  - (b) monomial times any polynomial.
  - (c) any polynomial times any polynomial.
- perform multiplication by the following shortcuts:
  - (a) FOIL.
  - (b) sum times a difference.
  - (c) binomial squared.
- perform the following types of division:
  - (a) monomial divided by a monomial.
  - (b) polynomial divided by a monomial.

☐ **Terms**  (2)

In an expression, the quantities which are added or subtracted are called terms.

$$3x^2 - 5x + 7$$

terms

☐ **Polynomial**  (3)

A <u>polynomial</u> is an expression consisting of one or more terms where each term is a product of a number and a variable raised to a whole number power. Each term must fit the pattern $ax^n$ where $a$ represents any real number and $n$ represents any whole number.

☐ **Illustrations of Polynomials**  (4)

**Example 1:** $5x^3$                    **Example 2:** $3y^2 - 5y + 2$

**Example 3:** $6$                      **Example 4:** $0$

☐ **Expressions Which Are Not Polynomials**  (5)

**Example 1:** $\dfrac{3}{x^2}$          **Example 2:** $2y^3 + \dfrac{1}{y^2}$

**Example 3:** $\dfrac{x^2 + 5}{x - 1}$

☐ **Polynomials of Several Variabes**  (6)

Each term must still be a product where the variables are raised to whole number powers.

**Example 1:** $3x^2 + 2y^3$              **Example 2:** $5x^3y^2 - 2x^2y^3$
**Example 3:** $3a + 2b - 4c$

194

## ☐ Polynomial Notation (7)

Polynomials can be symbolized by an uppercase letter together with the variable, such as $P(x)$ (read "P of $x$").

**Example 1:** $P(x) = 2x^3 - x + 4$ **Example 2:** $P(y) = 4y^4 - 3y^2 + 2$

## ☐ Evaluating Polynomials (8)

In polynomial notation the variable may be replaced by a number. The polynomial would then be evaluated for that value of the variable. $P(1)$ would represent the value of the polynomial when $x = 1$.

**Example:** If $P(x) = 2x^3 - x + 4$, find $P(1)$.

   **Solution:** Let $x = 1$ and evaluate.
   *line (a):* $P(x) = 2x^3 - x + 4$
   *line (b):* $P(1) = 2(1)^3 - (1) + 4$
   *line (c):* $P(1) = 2 - 1 + 4$
   *line (d):* $P(1) = 5$

## ☐ Special Types of Polynomials (9)

A monomial is any polynomial consisting of one term.

**Example 1:** 5 **Example 2:** $3x$

**Example 3:** $-2a^2b^3c$ **Example 4:** $\dfrac{x^2}{10}$

A binomial is any polynomial consisting of two terms.

**Example 5:** $2a + 3b$ **Example 6:** $3x - 5$

A trinomial is any polynomial consisting of three terms.

**Example 7:** $3x^2 + 4x - 5$ **Example 8:** $5a^2 - 2ab + b^2$

## ☐ Study Exercise One (10)

A. Indicate which of the following are polynomials.

   1. $5x^2 - \dfrac{3}{x}$ 2. $x^2 - 3x + 4$
   3. $6r^2 - 2s^3$ 4. $3a^2b^3 - 5ab + 2$
   5. $-2$ 6. $\dfrac{1}{x}$

B. If $P(x) = 2x^3 - 3x^2 + x - 5$, find each of the following.

   7. $P(0)$ 8. $P(3)$
   9. $P(-2)$ 10. $P(-3)$

C. Classify each of these polynomials as being either monomial, binomial, or trinomial.

   11. $a^2 - b^2$ 12. $2x^2$ 13. $5x^2 - 4x - 1$
   14. $\dfrac{3x^2}{10}$ 15. $y$ 16. $x + 2$

## ☐ Review of the Properties of Exponents (11)

1. The Zero Power Property

**Example:** $x^0 = 1$, where $x \neq 0$

2. The Addition Property of Exponents

**Example:** $x^5 \cdot x^4 = x^9$

3. The Subtraction Property of Exponents

**Example:** $\dfrac{a^7}{a^2} = a^5$

4. The Power to a Power Property

**Example:** $(y^4)^3 = y^{12}$

5. The Distributive Property of Exponents

**Example:** $(2a^2b^3c)^3 = 2^3a^6b^9c^3$ or $8a^6b^9c^3$

## ☐ Multiplying a Monomial Times a Monomial (12)

To multiply a monomial times a monomial, multiply the numerical coefficients and add the exponents which appear on identical bases.

☐ **Example 1:** Multiply $-3(4a)$. (13)

Multiply.

**Solution:** $-3(4a) = -12a$

**Example 2:** Multiply $(-5x^2)(-3x^4)$.

Multiply.

**Solution:** $(-5x^2)(-3x^4) = 15x^6$

Add exponents.

**Example 3:** Multiply $(-2a^2b^3)(6ab^2c)$.

Multiply.

**Solution:** $(-2a^2b^3)(6ab^2c) = -12a^3b^5c$

Add exponents.

**Example 4:** Multiply $(5x^2y^3)(-3x^2yz)(-2xy^2z^3)$.

**Solution:** $(5x^2y^3)(-3x^2yz)(-2xy^2z^3) = 30x^5y^6z^4$

## ☐ *Study Exercise Two* (14)

Multiply the following.

1. $-4(5x)$   2. $(-3a^2)(-2a^5)$   3. $(5x^2y)(-2xy^2)$
4. $(-2ab^2c)(-3ab)(4a^2c^2)$   5. $(xy^2)(x^2y)(3y^2z)$

## ☐ Multiplying a Monomial Times any Polynomial (15)

*Remember*, the Distributive Property of Multiplication with Respect to Addition and Subtraction states that *the multiplier of a sum or a difference must be shared over each term.*

$$a(b + c) = ab + ac$$

☐ **Example 1:** Multiply $3(2x - 4)$. **(16)**

    **Solution:** $3(2x - 4) = (3)(2x) - (3)(4)$

                              $= 6x - 12$

**Example 2:** Multiply $-2a(3a^2 - 4b^2)$.

    **Solution:** $-2a(3a^2 - 4b^2) = (-2a)(3a^2) - (-2a)(4b^2)$

                                $= -6a^3 + 8ab^2$

**Example 3:** Multiply $-3x(2x^2 - 3y^2)$.

    **Solution:** $-3x(2x^2 - 3y^2) = -6x^3 + 9xy^2$

**Example 4:** Multiply $-2xy(3x + 4y - 5)$.

    **Solution:** $-2xy(3x + 4y - 5) = -6x^2y - 8xy^2 + 10xy$

☐                                  *Study Exercise Three*                         **(17)**

Multiply the following.

1.  $2(x - 3)$                    2.  $-5(a - 6)$              3.  $2x(3x^2 - 5y^2)$
4.  $3a^2(4a^2b - 3ab + 2)$      5.  $-5x^2y(3x^2 - y^2 + 2x)$

☐ **Vertical Multiplication**                                           **(18)**

    **Example 1:** Multiply $3x(2x^2 - 5x + 2)$.

    **Solution:** Arrange in a vertical format and multiply the monomial times each term of the trinomial.

$$\begin{array}{r} 2x^2 - 5x + 2 \\ 3x \\ \hline 6x^3 - 15x^2 + 6x \end{array}$$

☐ **Example 2:** Multiply $(x + 2)(3x^2 - 5x + 4)$.                    **(19)**

    **Solution:** Arrange each in a vertical format and multiply each term of the binomial times each term of the trinomial.

$$3x^2 - 5x + 4$$
$$x + 2$$

line (a)  $3x^3 - 5x^2 + 4x$
line (b)           $6x^2 - 10x + 8$
line (c)  $3x^3 + x^2 - 6x + 8$

☐ **Example 3:** Multiply $(2x^2 - 5x - 2)(3x^2 + 2x - 4)$.              **(20)**

    **Solution:** Arrange in a vertical format and multiply each term of one polynomial by each term of the other polynomial.

$$3x^2 + 2x - 4$$
$$2x^2 - 5x - 2$$

line (a)  $6x^4 + 4x^3 - 8x^2$
line (b)          $- 15x^3 - 10x^2 + 20x$
line (c)                 $- 6x^2 - 4x + 8$
line (d)  $6x^4 - 11x^3 - 24x^2 + 16x + 8$

Multiply each of the following by arranging in a vertical format.

1.  $5x(2x^2 - 3x + 2)$      2. $(x + 4)(5x^2 - 3x + 2)$
3.  $(2m - 3)(3m^2 - 5m + 2)$      4. $(3a^2 - 4a - 5)(2a^2 + a - 3)$

## Special Products (22)

We will develop shortcuts for three special types of multiplication problems.

1.  Product of two binomials

**Example:** $(2x + 3)(3x + 2)$

2.  Product of a sum times a difference

**Example:** $(2x + 5)(2x - 5)$

3.  Binomial squared

**Example:** $(3x - 4)^2$

## Product of Two Binomials (23)

Multiply $(a + b)(c + d)$.

$$
\begin{array}{r}
c + d \\
a + b \\
\hline
ac + ad \\
+ bc + bd \\
\hline
ac + ad + bc + bd
\end{array}
$$

Therefore, $(a + b)(c + d) = ac + ad + bc + bd$.

## The FOIL Shortcut (24)

$$(a + b)(c + d) = ac + ad + bc + bd$$

|  | First | Outer | Inner | Last |
|---|---|---|---|---|
|  | F | O | I | L |

## Examples Using the FOIL Shortcut (25)

**Example 1:** Multiply $(x + 3)(x + 1)$.

   **Solution:**

*line (a)*   $(x + 3)(x + 1) = \underbrace{x \cdot x}_{F} + \underbrace{x \cdot 1}_{O} + \underbrace{3 \cdot x}_{I} + \underbrace{3 \cdot 1}_{L}$

*line (b)*         $= x^2 + \underbrace{x + 3x} + 3$

*line (c)*         $= x^2 + \quad 4x \quad + 3$

**Example 2:** Multiply $(2x + 5)(3x + 4)$.

   **Solution:**

*line (a)*   $(2x + 5)(3x + 4) = \underbrace{2x \cdot 3x}_{F} + \underbrace{2x \cdot 4}_{O} + \underbrace{5 \cdot 3x}_{I} + \underbrace{5 \cdot 4}_{L}$

*line (b)*         $= 6x^2 + \underbrace{8x + 15x} + 20$

*line (c)*         $= 6x^2 + \quad 23x \quad + 20$

**Example 3:** Multiply $(2a + 5)(3a - 2)$.

**Solution:**

*line (a)* $\quad (2a + 5)(3a - 2) = \underbrace{2a \cdot 3a}_{} - \underbrace{2a \cdot 2}_{} + \underbrace{5 \cdot 3a}_{} - \underbrace{5 \cdot 2}_{}$

$$\qquad\qquad\qquad\quad\ \ \, \text{F} \qquad\ \ \text{O} \qquad\ \ \ \text{I} \qquad\ \ \ \text{L}$$

*line (b)* $\qquad\qquad\qquad = 6a^2 \ - \ \underbrace{4a \ + \ 15a}_{} \ - \ 10$

*line (c)* $\qquad\qquad\qquad = 6a^2 \ + \qquad 11a \qquad - \ 10$

☐ **Study Exercise Five** (26)

Multiply the following according to the FOIL shortcut.

1. $(x + 2)(x + 3)$       2. $(a - 4)(a + 5)$       3. $(m - 2)(m - 3)$
4. $(2x - 3)(x - 7)$      5. $(3a + 5)(2a + 1)$      6. $(x + 3)(x - 3)$

☐ **Recognizing a "Sum Times a Difference"** (27)

$$(x + 3) \cdot (x - 3)$$
$$\qquad\uparrow \qquad\quad \uparrow$$
$$\text{sum} \quad \text{difference}$$

The two binomials are identical except for their signs of operation.

**Examples:**

1. $(x + 7)(x - 7)$      2. $(3a + 4)(3a - 4)$      3. $(x - 1)(x + 1)$      4. $(2m - 3)(2m + 3)$

☐ **Multiplying a "Sum Times a Difference" by FOIL** (28)

**Example:** Multiply $(x + 3)(x - 3)$.

**Solution:**

$$\qquad\qquad\qquad\quad \text{F} \qquad \text{O} \qquad \text{I} \qquad \text{L}$$

*line (a)* $\quad (x + 3)(x - 3) = x \cdot x - 3 \cdot x + 3 \cdot x - 3 \cdot 3$
*line (b)* $\qquad\qquad\qquad = x^2 - \underbrace{3x + 3x}_{} - 9$

*line (c)* $\qquad\qquad\qquad = x^2 - \qquad 0 \qquad - 9$
*line (d)* $\qquad\qquad\qquad = x^2 - 9$

In a "sum times a difference," the outer and inner products produce zero. The result, $x^2 - 9$, is said to be a *difference of two squares*.

☐ **The "Sum Times a Difference" Shortcut** (29)

$$(x + 3) \cdot (x - 3) = x \cdot x - 3 \cdot 3 \quad \text{or} \quad x^2 - 9$$

In a "sum times a difference," multiply the first terms and the last terms. This will produce a "difference of two squares."

**Examples:**

1. $(x + 7)(x - 7) = x^2 - 49$         2. $(3a + 4)(3a - 4) = 9a^2 - 16$
3. $(x - 1)(x + 1) = x^2 - 1$          4. $(2m - 3)(2m + 3) = 4m^2 - 9$

☐ **Study Exercise Six** (30)

Multiply the following by using the "sum times a difference" shortcut.

1. $(x + 2)(x - 2)$       2. $(m + 1)(m - 1)$       3. $(3a + 5)(3a - 5)$
4. $(5x - y)(5x + y)$      5. $(2m - 3n)(2m + 3n)$      6. $(2x^2 - y)(2x^2 + y)$

☐ **Squaring a Binomial** **(31)**

$$\underbrace{(x + 5)^2}$$
binomial   squared

☐ **Squaring a Binomial by FOIL** **(32)**

**Example:** Multiply $(x + 5)^2$.

**Solution:**

*line (a)*   $(x + 5)^2 = (x + 5) \cdot (x + 5)$

$$\quad\quad\quad\quad\quad F \quad O \quad I \quad L$$

*line (b)*   $\quad\quad = x \cdot x + \underline{5 \cdot x + 5 \cdot x} + 5 \cdot 5$

The outer and inner products are the same.

*line (c)*   $\quad\quad = x^2 + 2 \cdot (5x) + 25$

*line (d)*   $\quad\quad = x^2 + 10x + 25$

Therefore, $(x + 5)^2 = x^2 + 10x + 25$.

☐ **The "Binomial Squared" Shortcut** **(33)**

first term    second term

$$(x + 4)^2 \quad = \quad x^2 \quad + \quad 2 \cdot (4x) \quad + \quad 4^2$$

Square the first term.

Double the product of the first and second terms.

Square the second term.

**Examples:**

1.  $(x + 3)^2 = x^2 + 2(3x) + 3^2$ or $x^2 + 6x + 9$
2.  $(x + 5)^2 = x^2 + 10x + 25$
3.  $(x - 5)^2 = x^2 - 10x + 25$
4.  $(2m + 3)^2 = 4m^2 + 12m + 9$

☐ *Study Exercise Seven* **(34)**

Multiply the following using the "binomial squared" shortcut.

1.  $(x + 6)^2$
2.  $(x - 6)^2$
3.  $(2m + 1)^2$
4.  $(2m - 1)^2$
5.  $(3x + 2y)^2$
6.  $(x + 1)^2$

☐ **Dividing a Monomial by a Monomial** **(35)**

To divide a monomial by a monomial, divide the numerical coefficients and subtract the exponents which appear on identical bases.

**Example 1:** Divide $(-10x^5) \div (2x^3)$.

**Solution:**   $(-10x^5) \div (2x^3) = -5x^2$

Subtract exponents.

**Example 2:** Divide $\dfrac{24a^2b^3}{-3ab}$.

**Solution:**   $\dfrac{24a^2b^3}{-3ab} = -8ab^2$

**Example 3:** Divide $\dfrac{-15x^3y^4z^2}{-5xy^2}$.

Solution: $\dfrac{-15x^3y^4z^2}{-5xy^2} = 3x^2y^2z^2$

☐                             *Study Exercise Eight*                 **(36)**

Divide the following.

1. $(-12a^7) \div (2a^3)$       2. $\dfrac{27x^5y^6}{3x^2y^2}$       3. $\dfrac{-14a^3b^5c}{-2ab^2c}$       4. $\dfrac{-42m^3n^5r}{7m^3nr}$

☐ **Dividing a Polynomial by a Monomial**                                  **(37)**

To divide a polynomial by a monomial, divide the monomial into each term of the polynomial.

**Example 1:** $(4x^2 + 6x) \div (2x)$

Divide.

Solution: $(4x^2 + 6x) \div (2x) = 2x + 3$

Divide.

**Example 2:** $\dfrac{10a^2b^3 - 15ab^2}{5ab}$

Solution: $\dfrac{10a^2b^3 - 15ab^2}{5ab} = 2ab^2 - 3b$

**Example 3:** $\dfrac{12x^3 - 6x^2 + 3x}{3x}$

Solution: $\dfrac{12x^3 - 6x^2 + 3x}{3x} = 4x^2 - 2x + 1$

☐                             *Study Exercise Nine*                 **(38)**

Divide the following

1. $(9a^2 + 6a) \div (-3a)$       2. $\dfrac{12x^2y^3 - 8xy^2}{4xy}$       3. $\dfrac{15a^3 + 10a^2 - 5a}{5a}$

## REVIEW EXERCISES

A.   Which of the following expressions are polynomials?

    1. $3x^2 - x + 2$       2. $2y^3 + \dfrac{3}{y^2}$

    3. $6x$                4. $5$

B.   If $P(x) = x^3 - 3x^2 + x - 5$, find the following values.

    5. $P(0)$            6. $P(-2)$          7. $P(1)$

C.   Classify each of the following polynomials as monomial, binomial, or trinomial.

    8. $x$              9. $3a$           10. $2x^2 + 3x - 5$      11. $2x + 3$

D.   Multiply the following.

    12. $(-2a)(-3a)$       13. $(3x^2y)(-4xy^2)$       14. $-3x(4x^2 - 5)$       15. $2ab(-3a^2 - 4b + 2)$

## REVIEW EXERCISES. Contd.

E. Multiply the following using vertical multiplication.

16. $(x + 3)(2x^2 - 7x + 3)$            17. $(2x^2 - 5x + 3)(3x^2 + x - 1)$

F. Multiply the following using the FOIL shortcut.

18. $(x + 2)(x + 1)$        19. $(m + 2)(m + 3)$       20. $(a - 4)(a + 2)$
21. $(2x + 3)(3x - 4)$       22. $(5x - 2y)(3x + y)$

G. Multiply the following using the "sum times a difference" shortcut.

23. $(a + 6)(a - 6)$                   24. $(m + 1)(m - 1)$
25. $(2x + 7)(2x - 7)$              26. $(5a - 3b)(5a + 3b)$

H. Multiply the following using the "binomial squared" shortcut.

27. $(x + 3)^2$       28. $(x - 3)^2$         29. $(2x - 5)^2$        30. $(3a - 4b)^2$

I. Divide the following.

31. $\dfrac{-26a^2b^3}{13ab}$         32. $\dfrac{-4x^3 + 2x}{2x}$         33. $\dfrac{20x^2y^3 - 10xy^2 + 5xy}{5xy}$

## Solutions to Review Exercises

A.   1. Polynomial                                 2. Not a polynomial
     3. Polynomial                                 4. Polynomial

B.   5. $P(0) = 0^3 - 3(0)^2 + 0 - 5 = -5$
     6. $P(-2) = (-2)^3 - 3(-2)^2 + (-2) - 5 = -27$
     7. $P(1) = 1^3 - 3(1)^2 + 1 - 5 = -6$

C.   8. Monomial      9. Monomial      10. Trinomial      11. Binomial

D.   12. $6a^2$      13. $-12x^3y^3$      14. $-12x^3 + 15x$      15. $-6a^3b - 8ab^2 + 4ab$

E.   16. 
$$
\begin{array}{r}
2x^2 - 7x + 3 \\
x + 3 \\
\hline
2x^3 - 7x^2 + 3x \\
+\ 6x^2 - 21x + 9 \\
\hline
2x^3 - x^2 - 18x + 9
\end{array}
$$

     17.
$$
\begin{array}{r}
3x^2 + x - 1 \\
2x^2 - 5x + 3 \\
\hline
6x^4 + 2x^3 - 2x^2 \\
-\ 15x^3 - 5x^2 + 5x \\
9x^2 + 3x - 3 \\
\hline
6x^4 - 13x^3 + 2x^2 + 8x - 3
\end{array}
$$

F.   18. $x^2 + 3x + 2$     19. $m^2 + 5m + 6$     20. $a^2 - 2a - 8$     21. $6x^2 + x - 12$
     22. $15x^2 - xy - 2y^2$

G.   23. $a^2 - 36$     24. $m^2 - 1$     25. $4x^2 - 49$     26. $25a^2 - 9b^2$

H.   27. $x^2 + 6x + 9$     28. $x^2 - 6x + 9$     29. $4x^2 - 20x + 25$     30. $9a^2 - 24ab + 16b^2$

I.   31. $-2ab^2$           32. $-2x^2 + 1$          33. $4xy^2 - 2y + 1$

## SUPPLEMENTARY PROBLEMS

A. Which of the following expressions are polynomials?

1. $\dfrac{10}{x^3}$           2. $5x^2 + 1$           3. $x$

4. $6xy^2 - 2x^2y$       5. $4a^2 - 2 + \dfrac{4}{a}$       6. $\dfrac{x + 2}{3x - 4}$

B. If $P(x) = 2x^4 - 3x^3 + x^2 - 2x + 4$, find the following values.

7. $P(0)$         8. $P(1)$         9. $P(-1)$         10. $P(3)$

## SUPPLEMENTARY PROBLEMS, Contd.

C. Multiply the following.

11. $(-5x)(-7x)$
12. $(-3a^2)(2a^3)$
13. $(-4x^2y)(-3xy^2)$
14. $(2m^2n)(-6mn)(3mn^3)$
15. $(-4x^2y^3)(-2xyz)(-3y^3z^2)$
16. $2(x-5)$
17. $-3a(7a^2-5)$
18. $-2mn(4m^2n - 5m + 2n)$
19. $3x^2y(-2xy + 3x^2 - 4y^2)$

D. Multiply vertically.

20. $(x+2)(x^2 - 5x + 1)$
21. $(a-3)(2a^2 + 7a - 5)$
22. $(2x+1)(x^2 - x + 2)$
23. $(m^2 + 2m + 1)(m^2 - 3m - 2)$
24. $(2x^2 - 3x + 5)(3x^2 + 4x - 1)$

E. Multiply, using any shortcut which applies.

25. $(a+3)(a+2)$
26. $(a+4)(a-2)$
27. $(2x+3)(3x-2)$
28. $(x-3)(3x-2)$
29. $(2x+1)(x+3)$
30. $(m+4)(m-4)$
31. $(a+3)^2$
32. $(2x-3)(2x+3)$
33. $(2x-5)(2x-5)$
34. $(x+y)(x-y)$
35. $(5x+2)(4x-3)$
36. $(2m^2 - 3n^2)(2m^2 + 3n^2)$
37. $(2a^3 + 5b^2)(2a^3 - 5b^2)$
38. $(3m^2 + 2n^3)^2$
39. $(3x-2)(x+5)$
40. $(2a+1)(3a-4)$
41. $(x+4)(x-5)$
42. $(x+5)(x-5)$
43. $(2x+5)(3x-2)$
44. $(2x+5)(2x-5)$
45. $(x+6)^2$
46. $(x-6)^2$
47. $(3x+4)^2$
48. $(x+y+3)(x+y-3)$
49. $(2x^2 + y^2)(2x^2 - y^2)$
50. $(4x-7)(2x-1)$
51. $\left(a + \dfrac{2}{3}\right)\left(a - \dfrac{2}{3}\right)$
52. $(2a^2 - 3b^3)^2$
53. $(x-y)^2$
54. $(x-y)(x-y)$
55. $(2-x)(3-2x)$
56. $(x^2 - 4)^2$
57. $(a^2 + b^2)(a^2 - b^2)$
58. $(4-x)^2$
59. $(-x-3)(-x+2)$
60. $(2-x)(2+x)$
61. $(2m-3)(4m^2 + 6m + 9)$
62. $(3a+4)(2a^2 - a + 3)$

F. Divide the following.

63. $(-4a^2) \div a$
64. $(-4a^2) \div 2$
65. $\dfrac{-9x^2}{3}$
66. $\dfrac{-9x^2}{3x}$
67. $\dfrac{10xy^3}{-10xy^3}$
68. $\dfrac{-20a^3b^2}{-10ab^2}$
69. $\dfrac{15x^5y^7z^3}{-3x^2y^4z}$
70. $(-18m^2n + 9mn) \div (3n)$
71. $\dfrac{-18m^2n + 9mn}{3mn}$
72. $\dfrac{20x^3y^2 - 15xy^3}{-5xy^2}$
73. $\dfrac{18x^5y^3 - 24x^3y^2 + 12x^2y^3}{-6x^2y}$
74. $\dfrac{-12m + 4}{-4}$
75. $\dfrac{2m + 2n}{2}$
76. $\dfrac{6x^3 - x^2 + x}{x}$

G. Calculator Problems. With your instructor's approval, use a calculator to evaluate the following.
   If $P(x) = 3x^5 - 2x^4 + 4x^3 - 7x^2 + 6x - 7$, find the following:

77. $P(3.215)$
78. $P(-2.674)$
79. $P(0.521)$
80. $P(1.06)$

☐ Solutions to Study Exercises  (10A)

## Study Exercise One (Frame 10)

A.  1.  Not a polynomial
    3.  Polynomial
    5.  Polynomial

    2.  Polynomial
    4.  Polynomial
    6.  Not a polynomial

B.  7.  $P(0) = 2(0)^3 - 3(0)^2 + 0 - 5 = -5$
    8.  $P(3) = 2(3)^3 - 3(3)^2 + 3 - 5 = 25$
    9.  $P(-2) = 2(-2)^3 - 3(-2)^2 + (-2) - 5 = -35$
    10.  $P(-3) = 2(-3)^3 - 3(-3)^2 + (-3) - 5 = -89$

C.  11.  Binomial
    14.  Monomial

    12.  Monomial
    15.  Monomial

    13.  Trinomial
    16.  Binomial

☐  ## Study Exercise Two (Frame 14)  (14A)

1. $-20x$    2. $6a^7$    3. $-10x^3y^3$    4. $24a^4b^3c^3$    5. $3x^3y^5z$

☐  ## Study Exercise Three (Frame 17)  (17A)

1. $2x - 6$    2. $-5a + 30$    3. $6x^3 - 10xy^2$
4. $12a^4b - 9a^3b + 6a^2$    5. $-15x^4y + 5x^2y^3 - 10x^3y$

☐  ## Study Exercise Four (Frame 21)  (21A)

1.
$$
\begin{array}{r}
2x^2 - 3x + 2 \\
5x \\
\hline
10x^3 - 15x^2 + 10x
\end{array}
$$

2.
$$
\begin{array}{r}
5x^2 - 3x + 2 \\
x + 4 \\
\hline
5x^3 - 3x^2 + 2x \\
20x^2 - 12x + 8 \\
\hline
5x^3 + 17x^2 - 10x + 8
\end{array}
$$

3.
$$
\begin{array}{r}
3m^2 - 5m + 2 \\
2m - 3 \\
\hline
6m^3 - 10m^2 + 4m \\
- 9m^2 + 15m - 6 \\
\hline
6m^3 - 19m^2 + 19m - 6
\end{array}
$$

4.
$$
\begin{array}{r}
2a^2 + a - 3 \\
3a^2 - 4a - 5 \\
\hline
6a^4 + 3a^3 - 9a^2 \\
- 8a^3 - 4a^2 + 12a \\
- 10a^2 - 5a + 15 \\
\hline
6a^4 - 5a^3 - 23a^2 + 7a + 15
\end{array}
$$

☐  ## Study Exercise Five (Frame 26)  (26A)

1. $x^2 + 5x + 6$    2. $a^2 + a - 20$    3. $m^2 - 5m + 6$
4. $2x^2 - 17x + 21$    5. $6a^2 + 13a + 5$    6. $x^2 + 0x - 9$ or $x^2 - 9$

☐  ## Study Exercise Six (Frame 30)  (30A)

1. $x^2 - 4$    2. $m^2 - 1$    3. $9a^2 - 25$    4. $25x^2 - y^2$    5. $4m^2 - 9n^2$    6. $4x^4 - y^2$

☐  ## Study Exercise Seven (Frame 34)  (34A)

1. $x^2 + 12x + 36$    2. $x^2 - 12x + 36$    3. $4m^2 + 4m + 1$
4. $4m^2 - 4m + 1$    5. $9x^2 + 12xy + 4y^2$    6. $x^2 + 2x + 1$

☐  ## Study Exercise Eight (Frame 36)  (36A)

1. $-6a^4$    2. $9x^3y^4$    3. $7a^2b^3c^0$ or $7a^2b^3$    4. $-6m^0n^4r^0$ or $-6n^4$

☐  ## Study Exercise Nine (Frame 38)  (38A)

1. $-3a - 2$    2. $3xy^2 - 2y$    3. $3a^2 + 2a - 1$

# Factoring Polynomial Expressions

## ☐ Objectives (1)

By the end of this unit you should be able to:

- find the largest common monomial factor of a polynomial.
- factor the largest common monomial from a polynomial.
- recognize a "difference of two squares" and factor it into a "sum times a difference."
- factor trinomials into a product of binomials by reversing the FOIL shortcut.

## ☐ Factoring (2)

To *factor* an expression means to write it as a *basic product*.

|  | Expression | Factored Form |
|--------|------------|----------------|
| line (a) | $3a + 3b$ | $3 \cdot (a + b)$ |
| line (b) | $x^2 - 4$ | $(x + 2) \cdot (x - 2)$ |
| line (c) | $x^2 + 5x + 6$ | $(x + 2) \cdot (x + 3)$ |

## ☐ Common Monomial Factors (3)

A *common monomial factor of a polynomial* is a monomial which is a factor of each term of the polynomial.

**Example 1:** 3 is the common monomial factor of $3a + 3b$.

**Example 2:** 2 and $x$ are the common monomial factors of $4x^2 - 6x$.

**Example 3:** $x$ and $y^2$ are the common monomial factors of $2x^2y^2 + 3xy^3 + 4xy^2$.

## ☐ Largest Common Monomial Factor (4)

The *largest common monomial factor* is the product of all the common monomial factors.

**Example 1:** 3 is the largest common monomial factor of $3a + 3b$.

**Example 2:** $2x$ is the largest common monomial factor of $4x^2 - 6x$.

**Example 3:** $xy^2$ is the largest common monomial factor of $2x^2y^2 + 3xy^3 + 4xy^2$.

## ☐ Study Exercise One (5)

Find the largest common monomial factor for each of the following.

1. $5x + 5y$
2. $10xy + 5xz$
3. $4x^3 + 6x^2 - 8x$
4. $9a^3b^2 - 6a^2b^3 + 3a^2b^2$

## ☐ Review of the Distributive Properties (6)

1. **dpma:** $a \cdot b + a \cdot c = a \cdot (b + c)$

   The common monomial factor is undistributed.

2. **dpms:** $a \cdot b - a \cdot c = a \cdot (b - c)$

   The common monomial factor is undistributed.

**Example:** $5x + 5y = 5(x + y)$

## ☐ Common Monomial Factoring (7)

*Step (1):* Find the largest common monomial factor.
*Step (2):* Write the expression so that the largest common monomial factor is seen in each term.
*Step (3):* Remove the largest common monomial factor by undistributing it from each term.

☐ **Example 1:** Factor $10xy + 5xz$. **(8)**

   **Solution:**

   *Step (1):* The largest common monomial factor is $5x$.
   *Step (2):* Write the expression so that $5x$ appears in each term.
   $$10xy + 5xz = (5x) \cdot 2y + (5x) \cdot z$$
   *Step (3):* Undistribute $5x$ from each term.
   $$(5x) \cdot 2y + (5x) \cdot z = 5x(2y + z)$$

   Therefore, $10xy + 5xz = 5x(2y + z)$.

☐ **Checking the Answer to a Factoring Problem** **(9)**

To check a factoring problem, multiply out the answer according to the distributive properties. The result should be the original expression.

**Example:** $10xy + 5xz = 5x(2y + z)$

   *Check:* $5x(2y + z) = 10xy + 5xz$

☐ **Example 2:** Factor $4x^3 + 6x^2 - 8x$. **(10)**

   **Solution:**

   *Step (1):* The largest common factor is $2x$.
   *Step (2):* Write the expression so that $2x$ appears in each term.
   $$4x^3 + 6x^2 - 8x = (2x) \cdot 2x^2 + (2x) \cdot 3x - (2x) \cdot 4$$
   *Step (3):* Undistribute $2x$ from each term.
   $$(2x) \cdot 2x^2 + (2x) \cdot 3x - (2x) \cdot 4 = 2x(2x^2 + 3x - 4)$$

   Therefore, $4x^3 + 6x^2 - 8x = 2x(2x^2 + 3x - 4)$.

☐ **Example 3:** Factor $9a^3b^2 - 6a^2b^3 + 3a^2b^2$. **(11)**

   **Solution:**

   *Step (1):* The largest common factor is $3a^2b^2$.
   *Step (2):* Write the expression so that $3a^2b^2$ appears in each term.
   $$9a^3b^2 - 6a^2b^3 + 3a^2b^2 = (3a^2b^2) \cdot 3a - (3a^2b^2) \cdot 2b + (3a^2b^2) \cdot 1$$
   *Step (3):* Undistribute $3a^2b^2$ from each term.
   $$(3a^2b^2) \cdot 3a - (3a^2b^2) \cdot 2b + (3a^2b^2) \cdot 1 = 3a^2b^2(3a - 2b + 1)$$

   Therefore, $9a^3b^2 - 6a^2b^3 + 3a^2b^2 = 3a^2b^2(3a - 2b + 1)$

☐ *Study Exercise Two* **(12)**

Factor each of the following completely.

1. $7a + 7b$
2. $3x + 9$
3. $5x^2 + 2x$
4. $25m^2n - 10mn^3 + 5mn$
5. $9a^2b^3c^4 - 6a^2bc^3 + 12a^3b^3c^2$

☐ **Recognizing a Difference of Two Squares** **(13)**

*Remember,* a "sum times a difference" produces a "difference of two squares."

**Example:** $\underbrace{(a + b) \cdot (a - b)}_{\text{sum times a difference}} = \underbrace{a^2 - b^2}_{\text{difference of two squares}}$

207

☐ A "difference of two squares" will fit the pattern $a^2 - b^2$. **(14)**

    **Example 1:** $x^2 - 9 = x^2 - 3^2$              **Example 2:** $4m^2 - 25 = (2m)^2 - 5^2$

    **Example 3:** $9x^2 - 16y^2 = (3x)^2 - (4y)^2$     **Example 4:** $m^6 - n^6 = (m^3)^2 - (n^3)^2$

☐                                *Study Exercise Three* **(15)**

Which of the following expressions could be classified as a "difference of two squares"? Answer yes or no.

1. $x^2 - 25$                   2. $x^2 + 25$                   3. $a^2 - 1$

4. $m^3 - n^3$                 5. $4a^2b^4 - 25x^2y^2$         6. $x^4 - y^4$

☐ **Factoring a Difference of Two Squares** **(16)**

A "sum times a difference" produces a "difference of two squares."

**Example:** $(x + 5)(x - 5) = x^2 - 5^2$
$$= x^2 - 25$$

Consequently, a "difference of two squares" must factor into a "sum times a difference."

**Example:** $x^2 - 25 = x^2 - 5^2$
$$= (x + 5)(x - 5)$$

☐ **More Examples** **(17)**

    **Example 1:** Factor $9x^2 - 4$.

      **Solution:**

        *line (a)*   $9x^2 - 4 = (3x)^2 - 2^2$
        *line (b)*        $= (3x + 2)(3x - 2)$

    **Example 2:** Factor $a^2 - 1$.

      **Solution:**

        *line (a)*   $a^2 - 1 = a^2 - 1^2$
        *line (b)*      $= (a + 1)(a - 1)$

    **Example 3:** Factor $4m^2 - 25n^2$.

      **Solution:**

        *line (a)*   $4m^2 - 25n^2 = (2m)^2 - (5n)^2$
        *line (b)*          $= (2m + 5n)(2m - 5n)$

    **Example 4:** Factor $x^4 - y^4$.

      **Solution:**

        *line (a)*   $x^4 - y^4 = (x^2)^2 - (y^2)^2$
        *line (b)*      $= (x^2 + y^2) \cdot (x^2 - y^2)$
        *line (c)*      $= (x^2 + y^2)\overbrace{(x + y)(x - y)}$

    The completely factored form of $x^4 - y^4$ is $(x^2 + y^2)(x + y)(x - y)$.

☐ **A Special Case** **(18)**

    **Example:** Factor $3x^2 - 27$.

      **Solution:** First factor the largest common monomial; then factor into a "sum times a difference."

        *line (a)*   $3x^2 - 27 = 3 \cdot (x^2 - 9)$
        *line (b)*        $= 3\overbrace{(x + 3)(x - 3)}$

    The completely factored form of $3x^2 - 27$ is $3(x + 3)(x - 3)$.

*Study Exercise Four* **(19)**

Each of the following is a "difference of two squares." Factor each completely.

1. $x^2 - 36$      2. $16m^2 - 9n^2$      3. $b^2 - 1$
4. $9y^2 - 1$      5. $16a^4 - b^4$      6. $5x^2 - 20$

☐ **Factoring Trinomials by Reversing the FOIL Shortcut** **(20)**

**Example 1:** Factor $x^2 + 5x + 6$.

  **Solution:**

  *Step (1):* $x^2 + 5x + 6$ was produced from a product of two binomials. Therefore, we may write:

$$( \ + \ )\cdot( \ + \ )$$

  *Step (2):* The term $x^2$ came from the product of the first terms of the binomials, namely, $x\cdot x$. Therefore, we may write:

$$(x + \ )(x + \ )$$

  *Step (3):* The term 6 came from the product of the last terms of the two binomials. The choices for factors of 6 are:

$$2\cdot 3$$
$$(-2)\cdot(-3)$$
$$1\cdot 6$$
$$(-1)\cdot(-6)$$

  *Step (4):* Put these choices in as last terms of the two binomials; then check the sum of the outer and inner products to determine the correct choice:

$$(x + 2)(x + 3) \ \longleftarrow$$

☐ **Review of Example 1** **(21)**

  **Example 1:** Factor $x^2 + 5x + 6$.

  **Solution:**

  *Step (1):* $x^2 + 5x + 6 = ( \ + \ )\cdot( \ + \ )$
  *Step (2):* $x^2 + 5x + 6 = (x + \ )\cdot(x + \ )$
  *Step (3):* Factors giving the last term of 6 are: $2\cdot 3$, $(-2)\cdot(-3)$, $1\cdot 6$, and $(-1)\cdot(-6)$.
  *Step (4):* $x^2 + 5x + 6 = (x + 2)\cdot(x + 3)$

  *Check:* The sum of the outer and inner products must produce $5x$.

$$3x$$
$$(x + 2)\cdot(x + 3)$$
$$2x$$
$$3x + 2x = 5x$$

☐ **Example 2:** Factor $x^2 + 7x + 12$. **(22)**

  **Solution:**

  *Step (1):* $x^2 + 7x + 12 = ( \ + \ )( \ + \ )$
  *Step (2):* $x^2 + 7x + 12 = (x + \ )(x + \ )$
  *Step (3):* Factors giving the last term of 12 are: $3\cdot 4$, $(-3)\cdot(-4)$, $2\cdot 6$, $(-2)\cdot(-6)$, $1\cdot 12$, and $(-1)\cdot(-12)$.
  *Step (4):* $x^2 + 7x + 12 = (x + 3)(x + 4)$

*Check:* The sum of the outer and inner products must produce $7x$.

$$4x$$

$$(x + 3)\cdot(x + 4)$$

$$3x$$

$$4x + 3x = 7x$$

☐ **Example 3:** Factor $2x^2 + 7x + 6$. **(23)**

    **Solution:**

      *Step (1):* $2x^2 + 7x + 6 = (\quad + \quad)(\quad + \quad)$
      *Step (2):* $2x^2 + 7x + 6 = (2x + \quad)(x + \quad)$
      *Step (3):* Factors giving the last term of 6 are: $3\cdot2$, $(-3)\cdot(-2)$, $6\cdot1$, and $(-6)\cdot(-1)$.
      *Step (4):* $2x^2 + 7x + 6 = (2x + 3)(x + 2)$

*Check:* The sum of the outer and inner products must produce $7x$.

$$4x$$

$$(2x + 3)\cdot(x + 2)$$

$$3x$$

$$4x + 3x = 7x$$

☐ **Example 4:** Factor $x^2 + 3x - 10$. **(24)**

    **Solution:**

      *Step (1):* $x^2 + 3x - 10 = (\quad)\cdot(\quad)$
      *Step (2):* $x^2 + 3x - 10 = (x\quad)\cdot(x\quad)$
      *Step (3):* Factors giving the last term of $-10$ are: $(+5)\cdot(-2)$, $(-5)\cdot(+2)$, $(+10)\cdot(-1)$, and $(-10)\cdot(+1)$.
      *Step (4):* $x^2 + 3x - 10 = (x + 5)\cdot(x - 2)$

*Check:* The sum of the outer and inner products must produce $+3x$.

$$-2x$$

$$(x + 5)\cdot(x - 2)$$

$$+5x$$

$$-2x + 5x = +3x$$

☐ **Example 5:** Factor $15m^2 + 7m - 2$. **(25)**

    **Solution:**

      *Step (1):* $15m^2 + 7m - 2 = (\quad)(\quad)$
      *Step (2):* $15m^2 + 7m - 2 = (5m\quad)(3m\quad)$
      *Step (3):* Factors giving the last term of $-2$ are: $(-1)\cdot(+2)$ and $(+1)\cdot(-2)$.
      *Step (4):* $15m^2 + 7m - 2 = (5m - 1)(3m + 2)$

*Check:* The sum of the outer and inner products must produce $+7m$.

$$10m$$

$$(5m - 1)\cdot(3m + 2)$$

$$-3m$$

$$10m - 3m = 7m$$

☐ **Example 6:** Factor $3a^2 - 11a + 10$. (26)

   **Solution:**

   *Step (1):* $3a^2 - 11a + 10 = ($    $)($    $)$
   *Step (2):* $3a^2 - 11a + 10 = (3a$   $)(a$   $)$
   *Step (3):* Factors giving the last term of $+10$ are: $(+5) \cdot (+2)$, $(-5) \cdot (-2)$, $(+10) \cdot (+1)$, and $(-10) \cdot (-1)$.
   *Step (4):* $3a^2 - 11a + 10 = (3a - 5)(a - 2)$

   *Check:* The sum of the outer and inner products must produce $-11a$.

$$\overset{\displaystyle -6a}{\overbrace{\phantom{(3a-5)\cdot(a-2)}}}$$
$$(3a - 5) \cdot (a - 2)$$
$$\underset{\displaystyle -5a}{\underbrace{\phantom{(3a-5)\cdot(a-2)}}}$$
$$-6a - 5a = -11a$$

☐ **The Pattern of Signs When Factoring Trinomials** (27)

   **Case (1):** $x^2 + 6x + 8 = (x + 4)(x + 2)$
   $$\underbrace{A + B + C}_{\text{all signs } plus} = \underbrace{(\ +\ )(\ +\ )}_{\text{all signs } plus}$$

   **Case (2):** $x^2 - 6x + 8 = (x - 4)(x - 2)$
   $$\underbrace{A - B + C}_{\substack{\text{middle term} \\ \textit{minus} \\ \text{last term } plus}} = \underbrace{(\ -\ )(\ -\ )}_{\text{both signs } minus}$$

   **Case (3):** $x^2 + 2x - 8 = (x + 4)(x - 2)$
            or
      $x^2 - 2x - 8 = (x + 2)(x - 4)$
   $$\underbrace{A \pm B - C}_{\text{last term } minus} = \underbrace{(\ +\ )(\ -\ )}_{\substack{\text{one term } plus \\ \text{one term } minus}}$$

☐ **More Examples** (28)

   **Example 1:** $x^2 + 5x + 6 = (\ +\ )(\ +\ )$
   **Example 2:** $x^2 - 5x + 6 = (\ -\ )(\ -\ )$
   **Example 3:** $x^2 + x - 6 = (\ +\ )(\ -\ )$ or $(\ -\ )(\ +\ )$
   **Example 4:** $x^2 - x - 6 = (\ +\ )(\ -\ )$ or $(\ -\ )(\ +\ )$

☐                    *Study Exercise Five* (29)

Factor each of the following trinomials.

| | | |
|---|---|---|
| 1. $x^2 + 5x + 6$ | 2. $x^2 - 5x + 6$ | 3. $m^2 - 6m + 8$ |
| 4. $m^2 - 2m - 8$ | 5. $a^2 + 6a + 9$ | 6. $a^2 - 6a + 9$ |
| 7. $2a^2 + 5a + 3$ | 8. $2a^2 - a - 3$ | 9. $2a^2 - 5a + 3$ |
| 10. $6x^2 + 5x - 6$ | 11. $10x^2 - 19x - 15$ | |

☐ **Special Cases of Factoring Trinomials**    **(30)**

**Example 1:**  Factor $x^2 + 2x + 3$.

   **Solution:**  The only possible factors are $(x + 3)(x + 1)$.

$$1x$$

$$\textit{Check:} \quad (x + 3)(x + 1)$$

$$3x$$

$$1x + 3x = 4x$$

The choices do not give $2x$. Therefore, this trinomial cannot be factored.

☐ **Example 2:**  Factor $2m^2 - 4m - 30$.    **(31)**

   **Solution:**  First factor the largest common monomial. Then factor as a trinomial.

   *line (a)*  $2m^2 - 4m - 30 = 2(m^2 - 2m - 15)$

   *line (b)*  $\qquad\qquad\qquad = 2(m - 5)(m + 3)$

The completely factored form of $2m^2 - 4m - 30$ is $2(m - 5)(m + 3)$.

☐ **Example 3:**  Factor $6x^3 - 3x^2 - 9x$.    **(32)**

   **Solution:**  First factor the largest common monomial. Then factor as a trinomial.

   *line (a)*  $6x^3 - 3x^2 - 9x = 3x(2x^2 - x - 3)$

   *line (b)*  $\qquad\qquad\qquad = 3x(2x - 3)(x + 1)$

The completely factored form of $6x^3 - 3x^2 - 9x$ is $3x(2x - 3)(x + 1)$.

☐                       *Study Exercise Six*    **(33)**

If possible, factor each of the following completely.

1.  $x^2 + x + 1$            2.  $2x^2 + 10x + 12$          3.  $6x^3 - 3x^2 - 63x$
4.  $2x^4 - 7x^3 - 15x^2$       5.  $2x^3 - x^2 + 3x$

## REVIEW EXERCISES

A.  Factor the largest common monomial from each of the following.

   1.  $2m + 2n$               2.  $3ab + 3ac$            3.  $3a^2 - 6a$
   4.  $5x^2 - 5x$              5.  $3x^3y^2 - 6x^2y^3 + 9x^2y^2$

B.  Factor completely each of the following "differences of two squares."

   6.  $x^2 - y^2$               7.  $m^2 - 4$              8.  $25x^4 - 9y^2$
   9.  $27m^2 - 12$          10.  $9a^2 - 4b^2$        11.  $m^4 - n^4$

C.  Factor completely each of the following trinomials by using the reverse of FOIL.

   12.  $x^2 + 5x + 6$         13.  $x^2 - 5x - 6$        14.  $x^2 - 5x + 6$
   15.  $x^2 + x - 6$          16.  $2m^2 - 14m + 12$     17.  $6a^2 + 5a - 6$
   18.  $6a^2 + a - 1$         19.  $12x^2 - x - 6$      20.  $-2x^2 + 5x - 3$
   21.  $5x - 3 - 2x^2$       22.  $a^2 + 6a + 9$       23.  $a^2 - 6a + 9$
   24.  $8x^2 - 10xy - 3y^2$     25.  $9x^2 + 12xy + 4y^2$    26.  $18a^3 + 33a^2 - 30a$

## Solutions to Review Exercises

A. 1. $2(m + n)$
   4. $5x(x - 1)$

2. $3a(b + c)$
5. $3x^2y^2(x - 2y + 3)$

3. $3a(a - 2)$

B. 6. $(x + y)(x - y)$
   9. $3(3m + 2)(3m - 2)$

7. $(m + 2)(m - 2)$
10. $(3a + 2b)(3a - 2b)$

8. $(5x^2 + 3y)(5x^2 - 3y)$
11. $(m^2 + n^2)(m + n)(m - n)$

C. 12. $(x + 3)(x + 2)$
   14. $(x - 3)(x - 2)$
   16. $2(m - 6)(m - 1)$
   18. $(3a - 1)(2a + 1)$
   20. $(-2x + 3)(x - 1)$ or $(2x - 3)(-x + 1)$
   22. $(a + 3)(a + 3)$ or $(a + 3)^2$
   24. $(4x + y)(2x - 3y)$
   26. $3a(3a - 2)(2a + 5)$

13. $(x - 6)(x + 1)$
15. $(x + 3)(x - 2)$
17. $(3a - 2)(2a + 3)$
19. $(4x - 3)(3x + 2)$
21. $(-2x + 3)(x - 1)$ or $(2x - 3)(-x + 1)$
23. $(a - 3)(a - 3)$ or $(a - 3)^2$
25. $(3x + 2y)(3x + 2y)$ or $(3x + 2y)^2$

## SUPPLEMENTARY PROBLEMS

Factor completely each of the following:

1. $15y - 5x^2y^2$
2. $4x^2y^2 - 49$
3. $15a^3b^2c - 10a^2bc^3 + 5abc$
4. $y^2 - 25$
5. $x^2 + 4xy + 4y^2$
6. $x^2 - 6x + 9$
7. $a^2 + 3a - 4$
8. $3m^2 - 5mn + 2n^2$
9. $3a^2 - 27$
10. $x^2 - 2x + 1$
11. $3x^2 + 7x + 4$
12. $5m^2 - 9m + 4$
13. $6a^2 - 13a + 6$
14. $3m^2 - m - 4$
15. $5x^2 - 3x - 2$
16. $4a^2 + 9a + 5$
17. $2a^2 + 5ab - 3b^2$
18. $9m^2 - 3mn - 2n^2$
19. $3x^2 + 7xy + 2y^2$
20. $16x^2 - 25y^2$
21. $2x^2 + 10x + 12$
22. $4x^2 - 12xy - 72y^2$
23. $3m^3 - 3m$
24. $x^4 - y^6$
25. $6m^3n^2 - 21m^2n + 9m$
26. $9ab^2 + 6b$
27. $xy + xz - xw$
28. $x^2 + 9x + 30$
29. $2ab - 4a^2b^2 - 8a^3b^3$
30. $25m^2 + 20mn + 4n^2$
31. $9r^2 - 42rs + 49s^2$
32. $18x^3 - 8xy^2$
33. $3r^3s^2 + 6r^2s^2 + 3rs^2$
34. $9x^2 - 4$
35. $9x^2 + 4$
36. $16m^4 - 81n^4$
37. $7hm - 7h$
38. $\pi R^2 + \pi r^2$
39. $10x^3 + 20x^2 - 55x$
40. $5RS - 10RT$
41. $y^5 + y^4$
42. $81 - c^2d^2$
43. $9x^2 - 1600$
44. $R^2S^2 - 121$
45. $m^6 - 25n^{10}$
46. $3a^2 - 3$
47. $\pi R^3 - 25\pi R$
48. $x^2 + 14xy + 24y^2$
49. $m^2 + 19m + 48$
50. $h^2 - 27h + 50$
51. $c^2 - 17cd + 30d^2$
52. $3b^2 + 24b + 45$
53. $2y^3 - 6y^2 - 8y$
54. $3a^4 + 21a^3 + 30a^2$
55. $3m - 3m^{13}$

☐ Solutions to Study Exercises                                               **(5A)**

### Study Exercise One (Frame 5)

1. $5$
2. $5x$
3. $2x$
4. $3a^2b^2$

☐                                 ### Study Exercise Two (Frame 12)                         **(12A)**

1. $7(a + b)$
2. $3(x + 3)$
3. $x(5x + 2)$
4. $5mn(5m - 2n^2 + 1)$
5. $3a^2bc^2(3b^2c^2 - 2c + 4ab^2)$

☐                                 ### Study Exercise Three (Frame 15)                   **(15A)**

1. Yes; $x^2 - 5^2$
2. No
3. Yes; $a^2 - 1^2$
4. No
5. Yes; $(2ab^2)^2 - (5xy)^2$
6. Yes; $(x^2)^2 - (y^2)^2$

Solutions to Study Exercises, Contd.

☐ ### *Study Exercise Four* (Frame 19)      **(19A)**

1. $(x + 6)(x - 6)$ or $(x - 6)(x + 6)$    2. $(4m + 3n)(4m - 3n)$    3. $(b + 1)(b - 1)$
4. $(3y + 1)(3y - 1)$    5. $(4a^2 + b^2)(2a + b)(2a - b)$    6. $5(x + 2)(x - 2)$

☐ ### *Study Exercise Five* (Frame 29)      **(29A)**

1. $(x + 3)(x + 2)$ or $(x + 2)(x + 3)$    2. $(x - 3)(x - 2)$    3. $(m - 4)(m - 2)$
4. $(m - 4)(m + 2)$    5. $(a + 3)(a + 3)$ or $(a + 3)^2$    6. $(a - 3)(a - 3)$ or $(a - 3)^2$
7. $(2a + 3)(a + 1)$    8. $(2a - 3)(a + 1)$    9. $(2a - 3)(a - 1)$
10. $(3x - 2)(2x + 3)$    11. $(5x + 3)(2x - 5)$

☐ ### *Study Exercise Six* (Frame 33)      **(33A)**

1. Not factorable      2. $2(x + 3)(x + 2)$ or $2(x + 2)(x + 3)$
3. $3x(2x - 7)(x + 3)$      4. $x^2(2x + 3)(x - 5)$
5. $x(2x^2 - x + 3)$

# Solving Equations—
# First Degree and Quadratic

## ☐ Objectives (1)

By the end of this unit you should be able to:

- determine whether an equation is first degree or quadratic.
- solve first degree equations.
- solve quadratic equations by factoring.
- solve word problems using first degree and quadratic equations.

## ☐ Review of the Properties of Equivalent Equations (2)

1. **The Addition Property:** The same number or expression may be added to both sides of an equation, and the resulting equation is equivalent to the original.

   **Example:** Original equation: $x + 3 = 7$
   Add $-3$ to each side. $x + 3 + (-3) = 7 + (-3)$
   The equation becomes $x = 4$

2. **The Subtraction Property:** The same number or expression may be subtracted from both sides of an equation, and the resulting equation is equivalent to the original.

   **Example:** Original equation: $x + 7 = 9$
   Subtract 7 from both sides. $x + 7 - 7 = 9 - 7$
   The equation becomes $x = 2$

3. **The Multiplication Property:** The same number or expression, other than zero, may be multiplied times both sides of an equation, and the resulting equation is equivalent to the original.

   **Example:** Original equation: $-x = -3$
   Multiply both sides by $-1$. $(-1)(-x) = (-1)(-3)$
   The equation becomes $x = 3$

4. **The Division Property:** The same number or expression, other than zero, may be divided into each side of an equation, and the resulting equation is equivalent to the original.

   **Example:** Original equation: $5x = -15$
   Divide each side by 5. $\dfrac{5x}{5} = \dfrac{-15}{5}$
   The equation becomes $x = -3$

## ☐ First Degree Equations (3)

A *first degree equation* in one unknown is any equation which can be made to fit the following form:

$$ax + b = c \quad \text{where } a, b, c \text{ are constants}$$

First degree equations have a highest exponent of 1.

*Note:* First degree equations may also be called *linear* equations.

## ☐ Examples of First Degree Equations (4)

**Example 1:** $3x + 1 = 10$ is first degree.
$$3x + 1 = 10$$
$$\downarrow \quad \downarrow \quad \downarrow$$
$$ax + b = c$$

**Example 2:** $5x = 15$ is first degree.
$$5x + 0 = 15$$
$$\downarrow \quad \downarrow \quad \downarrow$$
$$ax + b = c$$

**Example 3:** $5x + 2 - 3x = x - 5$ is first degree.

$$1 \cdot x + 2 = -5$$
$$\downarrow \quad\quad \downarrow \quad\quad \downarrow$$
$$ax + b = c$$

☐ Equations Which Are Not First Degree **(5)**

**Example 1:** $x^3 = 8$ is not first degree because the highest exponent is 3.

**Example 2:** $2x^2 - x - 3 = 0$ is not first degree because the highest exponent is 2.

☐ Quadratic Equations **(6)**

A *quadratic equation* in one unknown is any equation which can be made to fit the following pattern:

$$ax^2 + bx + c = 0 \quad \text{where } a, b, c \text{ are constants} \quad \text{and} \quad a \neq 0$$

Quadratic equations have a highest exponent of 2.

☐ Examples of Quadratic Equations **(7)**

**Example 1:** $3x^2 + 5x + 2 = 0$ is quadratic.

$$3x^2 + 5x + 2 = 0$$
$$\downarrow \quad \downarrow \quad \downarrow$$
$$ax^2 + bx + c = 0$$

**Example 2:** $x^2 = 9$ is quadratic.

$$1 \cdot x^2 + 0 \cdot x + (-9) = 0$$
$$\downarrow \quad\quad \downarrow \quad\quad \downarrow$$
$$ax^2 + bx + c = 0$$

**Example 3:** $2x - 3x^2 = -4$ is quadratic.

$$-3x^2 + 2x + 4 = 0$$
$$\downarrow \quad \downarrow \quad \downarrow$$
$$ax^2 + bx + c = 0$$

☐ Equations Which Are Not Quadratic **(8)**

**Example 1:** $4x^3 + 3x^2 + 5x + 6 = 0$ is not quadratic because the highest exponent is 3.

**Example 2:** $3x^2 + 4x - 5 = 3x^2$ is not quadratic because it can be written as $4x - 5 = 0$.

☐ *Study Exercise One* **(9)**

Classify each of the following equations as either first degree or quadratic.

1. $5x + 3 = 8$
2. $2x = -12$
3. $x^2 - 5x + 6 = 0$
4. $4x^2 - 3x + 6 = 4x^2$
5. $x^2 - 3x = 0$
6. $2(x + 2) = 12$
7. $x^2 - 25 = 0$

☐ Solving First Degree Equations **(10)**

*Step (1):* Combine like terms.

*Step (2):* Obtain a form where the terms containing a variable are on one side of the equal sign and the numbers are on the other side.

*Step (3):* Use the division property of equivalent equations to obtain an equation of the form $x = a$.

☐ **Example 1:** Solve $5x + x + 3 = 3x - 9$. **(11)**

**Solution:**

*Step (1):* Combine like terms.

$$5x + x + 3 = 3x - 9$$
$$6x + 3 = 3x - 9$$

*Step (2):* Obtain an equation with variables on one side and numbers on the other.
line (a)  $6x + 3 = 3x - 9$
line (b)  $6x - 3x = -9 - 3$
line (c)  $3x = -12$
*Step (3):* Obtain an equation of the form $x = a$.
line (d)  $3x = -12$
line (e)  $\dfrac{3x}{3} = \dfrac{-12}{3}$
line (f)  $x = -4$

The solution is $-4$.

## ☐ Checking the Solution  (12)

*Remember,* a solution may be checked by replacing it for the variable in the original equation.

$$\text{Original equation:} \quad 5x + x + 3 = 3x - 9$$

$$\text{Solution:} \quad -4$$

$$\text{Check:} \quad \underbrace{5(-4) + (-4) + 3}_{-21} = \underbrace{3(-4) - 9}_{-21}$$

## ☐ Example 2:  Solve $2(3x - 7) = 3(4x + 2) + 10$.  (13)

**Solution:**

*Step (1):* Multiply and combine like terms.
line (a)  $2(3x - 7) = 3(4x + 2) + 10$
line (b)  $6x - 14 = 12x + 6 + 10$
line (c)  $6x - 14 = 12x + 16$
*Step (2):* Obtain an equation with variables on one side and numbers on the other.
line (d)  $6x - 14 = 12x + 16$
line (e)  $6x - 12x = 16 + 14$
line (f)  $-6x = 30$
*Step (3):* Obtain an equation of the form $x = a$.
line (g)  $-6x = 30$
line (h)  $\dfrac{-6x}{-6} = \dfrac{30}{-6}$
line (i)  $x = -5$

The solution is $-5$.

## ☐ Example 3:  Solve $3(2 + x) = 9 - 2x$.  (14)

**Solution:**

*Step (1):* Multiply and combine like terms.
line (a)  $3(2 + x) = 9 - 2x$
line (b)  $6 + 3x = 9 - 2x$
*Step (2):* Obtain an equation with variables on one side and numbers on the other.
line (c)  $6 + 3x = 9 - 2x$
line (d)  $3x + 2x = 9 - 6$
line (e)  $5x = 3$
*Step (3):* Obtain an equation of the form $x = a$.
line (f)  $5x = 3$
line (g)  $\dfrac{5x}{5} = \dfrac{3}{5}$

*line (h)*    $x = \dfrac{3}{5}$

The solution is $\dfrac{3}{5}$.

## ☐ Two Special Cases of First Degree Equations                                    **(15)**

**Case (1):**   Solve $3(x + 2) = 3x + 5$.

*Step (1):*   Multiply and combine like terms.
$$3(x + 2) = 3x + 5$$
$$3x + 6 = 3x + 5$$

*Step (2):*   Obtain an equation with variables on one side and numbers on the other.
$$3x + 6 = 3x + 5$$
$$3x - 3x = 5 - 6$$
$$0 = -1 \qquad \text{(False equation)}$$

This equation has no solutions.

**Case (2):**   Solve $3(x + 2) = 3x + 6$.

*Step (1):*   Multiply and combine like terms.
$$3(x + 2) = 3x + 6$$
$$3x + 6 = 3x + 6$$

*Step (2):*   Obtain an equation with variables on one side and numbers on the other.
$$3x + 6 = 3x + 6$$
$$3x - 3x = 6 - 6$$
$$0 = 0 \qquad \text{(True equation)}$$

This equation is true for all values of $x$ and is therefore an identity. Every real number is a solution.

## ☐                                *Study Exercise Two*                              **(16)**

Solve each of the following first degree equations, and check your solutions.

1.  $x + 5 = 0$
2.  $2x + 14 = 2$
3.  $4x - 9x + 22 = 3(x + 10)$
4.  $4(y - 9) = 10(2 - y)$
5.  $3m + 5 - m = 2(m - 1)$
6.  $7 - m = 3m + 7 - 4m$
7.  $5(2 + x) = 2(x + 6)$

## ☐ Solving Quadratic Equations by Factoring                                        **(17)**

**Property:**   If $a \cdot b = 0$, then either $a = 0$ or $b = 0$.

**Example:**   Suppose $(x - 4) \cdot (x + 3) = 0$. Then either $x - 4 = 0$ or $x + 3 = 0$.

$$\underset{a}{\uparrow} \quad \cdot \quad \underset{b}{\uparrow} \quad = 0 \qquad\qquad \underset{a}{\uparrow} \quad = 0 \qquad \underset{b}{\uparrow} \quad = 0$$

## ☐ To solve a quadratic equation:                                                  **(18)**

*Step (1):*   Put the equation in the form $ax^2 + bx + c = 0$.
*Step (2):*   Factor the left member.
*Step (3):*   Set each factor containing a variable equal to zero.
*Step (4):*   Solve the resulting first degree equations.

## ☐ Example 1:   Solve $x^2 + 7x = -12$.                                            **(19)**

**Solution:**

*Step (1):*   Put the equation in the form $ax^2 + bx + c = 0$.
*line (a)*   $x^2 + 7x = -12$
*line (b)*   $x^2 + 7x + 12 = 0$

*Step (2):* Factor the left member.
  *line (c)* $(x + 4)(x + 3) = 0$
*Step (3):* Set each factor containing a variable equal to zero.
  *line (d)* $x + 4 = 0$ or $x + 3 = 0$
*Step (4):* Solve the resulting first degree equations.
  *line (e)* $x + 4 = 0 \qquad x = -4$
  *line (f)* $x + 3 = 0 \qquad x = -3$

The solutions are $-4$ and $-3$.

☐ **Checking the Solutions** **(20)**

The solutions of a quadratic equation may be checked by substituting them, one at a time, into the original equation.

**Original equation:** $x^2 + 7x = -12$

$\qquad$ **Solutions:** $-4$ and $-3$

$\quad$ **Check for $-4$:** $(-4)^2 + 7(-4) = -12$
$\qquad\qquad\qquad \underbrace{16 \quad - \quad 28}\ \ = -12$
$\qquad\qquad\qquad\qquad -12 \qquad = -12$

$\quad$ **Check for $-3$:** $(-3)^2 + 7(-3) = -12$
$\qquad\qquad\qquad \underbrace{9 \quad - \quad 21}\ \ = -12$
$\qquad\qquad\qquad\qquad -12 \qquad = -12$

☐ **Example 2:** Solve $x^2 - 10 = 3x$. **(21)**

$\quad$ **Solution:**

$\quad$ *Step (1):* Put the equation in the form $ax^2 + bx + c = 0$.
$\qquad$ *line (a)* $x^2 - 10 = 3x$
$\qquad$ *line (b)* $x^2 - 3x - 10 = 0$
$\quad$ *Step (2):* Factor the left member.
$\qquad$ *line (c)* $(x - 5)(x + 2) = 0$
$\quad$ *Step (3):* Set each factor containing a variable equal to zero.
$\qquad$ *line (d)* $x - 5 = 0$, or $x + 2 = 0$
$\quad$ *Step (4):* Solve the resulting first degree equations.
$\qquad$ *line (e)* $x - 5 = 0 \qquad x = 5$
$\qquad$ *line (f)* $x + 2 = 0 \qquad x = -2$

$\quad$ The solutions are $5$ and $-2$.

☐ **Example 3:** Solve $3x^2 + x = 2$. **(22)**

$\quad$ **Solution:**

$\quad$ *Step (1):* Put the equation in the form $ax^2 + bx + c = 0$.
$\qquad$ *line (a)* $3x^2 + x = 2$
$\qquad$ *line (b)* $3x^2 + x - 2 = 0$
$\quad$ *Step (2):* Factor the left member.
$\qquad$ *line (c)* $(3x - 2)(x + 1) = 0$
$\quad$ *Step (3):* Set each factor containing a variable equal to zero.
$\qquad$ *line (d)* $3x - 2 = 0$, or $x + 1 = 0$
$\quad$ *Step (4):* Solve the resulting first degree equations.
$\qquad$ *line (e)* $3x - 2 = 0 \qquad 3x = 2 \qquad x = \dfrac{2}{3}$
$\qquad$ *line (f)* $x + 1 = 0 \qquad x = -1$

$\quad$ The solutions are $\dfrac{2}{3}$ and $-1$.

☐ **Example 4:** Solve $x^2 + 2x = 0$. **(23)**

   **Solution:**

      *Step (1):*   $x^2 + 2x = 0$ is in the form $ax^2 + bx + c = 0$.

      *Step (2):*   Factor the left member.

        *line (a)*   $x(x + 2) = 0$

      *Step (3):*   Set each factor containing a variable equal to zero.

        *line (b)*   $x = 0$, or $x + 2 = 0$

      *Step (4):*   Solve the resulting first degree equations.

        *line (c)*   $x = 0$

        *line (d)*   $x + 2 = 0$      $x = -2$

   The solutions are 0 and $-2$.

☐                             *Study Exercise Three*                        **(24)**

Solve the resulting quadratic equations by factoring.

1.   $x^2 - 5x - 6 = 0$          2.   $m^2 - 2m = 8$          3.   $x^2 - 3x = 0$
4.   $2m^2 - m = 3$            5.   $r^2 - 9 = 0$             6.   $2x^2 - x = 0$
7.   $x^2 + 9 = 6x$

☐ **Using Equations to Solve Word Problems**                                   **(25)**

*Step (1):*   Let some letter represent one of the unknowns.

*Step (2):*   If possible, draw a picture and describe the other unknowns with variable **expressions using the** same letter.

*Step (3):*   Relate the variable expressions in terms of an equation using the information given in the problem.

*Step (4):*   Solve the equation.

*Step (5):*   Interpret the solution in terms of the original problem.

☐                                                                            **(26)**

**Example 1:**   A 10-ft board is cut in two pieces. One piece is 2 ft longer than the other. How long is each piece?

   **Solution:**

      *Step (1):*   Let $x$ represent the shorter piece.

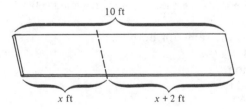

      *Step (2):*   $x + 2$ represents the longer piece.

      *Step (3):*   The sum is 10 ft.

            $x + (x + 2) = 10$

      *Step (4):*   Solve the equation.

$$x + (x + 2) = 10$$
$$2x + 2 = 10$$
$$2x = 8$$
$$x = 4$$

      *Step (5):*   If $x = 4$, then $x + 2 = 6$. The shorter piece is 4 ft, and the longer piece is 6 ft.

□ **(27)**

**Example 2:** Water tank A has a capacity of 75 gal more than tank B. Water tank C has a capacity three times that of tank B. Together the tanks have a capacity of 1075 gal. Find the capacity of each tank.

**Solution:**

*Step (1):* Let $x$ represent the capacity of tank B.

A
$(x + 75)$ gal

B
$x$ gal

C
$3x$ gal

*Step (2):* $x + 75$ represents the capacity of tank A. $3x$ represents the capacity of tank C.

*Step (3):* The sum is 1075 gal.
$$x + (x + 75) + 3x = 1075$$

*Step (4):* Solve the equation.
$$x + (x + 75) + 3x = 1075$$
$$5x + 75 = 1075$$
$$5x = 1000$$
$$x = 200$$

*Step (5):* If $x = 200$, then $x + 75 = 275$ and $3x = 600$. The capacity of tank B is 200 gal. The capacity of tank A is 275 gal. The capacity of tank C is 600 gal.

□ **(28)**

**Example 3:** A man made a trip at an average speed of 50 miles per hour. A second man made the same trip in one hour less time at an average speed of 60 miles per hour. What was the distance of the trip?

**Solution:** Use the formula $d = rt$. Distance equals rate multiplied by time.

*Step (1):* Let $t$ represent the time necessary for the first man to make the trip. $t - 1$ would then represent the time necessary for the second man to make the same trip.

```
1st man: rate = 50 mph
         time = t
         dist. = 50t
●━━━━━━━━━━━━━━━●  ←── trip
2nd man: rate = 60 mph
         time = t − 1
         dist. = 60(t − 1)
```

*Step (2):* $50t$ represents the distance the first man traveled. $60(t - 1)$ represents the distance traveled by the second man.

*Step (3):* The distance was the same for both men.
$$50t = 60(t - 1)$$

*Step (4):* Solve the equation.
$$50t = 60(t - 1)$$
$$50t = 60t - 60$$
$$-10t = -60$$
$$t = 6$$

*Step (5):* If $t = 6$, then $50t = 300$. Therefore, the trip was 300 miles.

□ **(29)**

**Example 4:** A positive number subtracted from the square of the number produces 6. Find the number.

**Solution:**

*Step (1):* Let $x$ represent the positive number.

*Step (2):* $x^2$ represents the square of the number.

*Step (3):* The difference is 6.

$x^2 - x = 6$

*Step (4):* Solve the equation.

*line (a)* $x^2 - x = 6$

*line (b)* $x^2 - x - 6 = 0$

*line (c)* $(x - 3)(x + 2) = 0$

*line (d)* $x - 3 = 0$, or $x + 2 = 0$

*line (e)* $x = 3$, or $x = -2$

*Step (5):* Since $x$ must represent a positive number, the only solution to the problem is 3.

☐ **(30)**

**Example 5:** The length of a rectangle is 4 feet more than the width. The area of the rectangle is 12 square feet. Find the length and the width.

**Solution:**

*Step (1):* Let $w$ represent the width of the rectangle.

| $w$ ft | Area = 12 ft² |
|---|---|

$(w + 4)$ ft

*Step (2):* $w + 4$ represents the length.

*Step (3):* The product of the width and the length gives the area.

$w(w + 4) = 12$

*Step (4):* Solve the equation.

$w(w + 4) = 12$

$w^2 + 4w = 12$

$w^2 + 4w - 12 = 0$

$(w + 6)(w - 2) = 0$

$w + 6 = 0$, or $w - 2 = 0$

$w = -6$, or $w = 2$

*Step (5):* The width must be positive. Therefore, the only solution is a width of 2 feet and a length of 6 feet.

☐ *Study Exercise Four* **(31)**

Solve the following problems.

1. A 100-ft rope is cut into two pieces. One piece is 16 ft longer than the other. How long is each piece?

2. Oil tank A has a capacity twice that of tank B. Tank C has a capacity of 100 gal more than tank B. Together the tanks have a capacity of 3700 gal. Find the capacity of each tank.

3. A jet airliner made a trip at an average speed of 400 miles per hour. A second jet airliner made the same trip in two hours less time at an average speed of 600 miles per hour. What was the distance of the trip?

4. Six times a positive number when added to the square of the number will produce 16. Find the number.

5. The length of a rectangle is 10 feet more than the width. The area of the rectangle is 24 square feet. Find the length and the width.

## REVIEW EXERCISES

A. Classify each of the following equations as either first degree or quadratic.

1. $x - 3 = 4$ 
2. $x^2 = 9$ 
3. $2x^2 - 3x = 5$
4. $3x^2 + 4x = 3x^2 - 16$ 
5. $3(x - 2) = 4(x + 7)$

## REVIEW EXERCISES, Contd.

B.  Solve the following first degree equations.

6.  $x - 6 = 0$

7.  $3m + 4 = -8$

8.  $2(a - 5) = 5(a + 1)$

9.  $2(y + 3) = 2y + 6$

10.  $5x - 4 + x = 3(2x - 1)$

C.  Solve the following quadratic equations.

11.  $x^2 - 2x = 3$

12.  $m^2 - 9m + 14 = 0$

13.  $x^2 - 5x = 0$

14.  $a^2 - 16 = 0$

15.  $x^2 = 25$

16.  $2y^2 - 9y = 0$

17.  $5x^2 - 20 = 0$

18.  $m^2 + 4m + 4 = 0$

D.  The following group contains both first degree and quadratic equations. Solve each.

19.  $a + 2 = 1$

20.  $3x + 2 - x = x$

21.  $x^2 + 2x = 15$

22.  $3m^2 = 9m$

23.  $4(2x - 3) = 2x + 6$

24.  $x(x + 2) = 3$

25.  $3r^2 = 6 - 7r$

E.  Solve the following problems.

26.  An 84-ft rope is cut into three pieces. The second piece is twice the length of the first. The third piece is 4 ft longer than the first. Find the length of each piece.

27.  A man traveled to and from a city over the same route. His average speed to the city was 60 miles per hour. His return trip took 1 hour longer at an average speed of 45 miles per hour. What was the distance of the trip (one way)?

28.  Three times a negative number added to the square of the number produces 10. Find the number.

## Solutions to Review Exercises

A.  1.  First degree   2.  Quadratic   3.  Quadratic   4.  First degree   5.  First degree

B.  6.  $x - 6 = 0$
$x = 6$
The solution is 6.

7.  $3m + 4 = -8$
$3m = -12$
$m = -4$
The solution is $-4$.

8.  $2(a - 5) = 5(a + 1)$
$2a - 10 = 5a + 5$
$-3a = 15$
$a = -5$
The solution is $-5$.

9.  $2(y + 3) = 2y + 6$
$2y + 6 = 2y + 6$
$0 = 0$
The equation is true for all values of $x$ and is therefore an identity.

10.  $5x - 4 + x = 3(2x - 1)$
$6x - 4 = 6x - 3$
$-4 = -3$
The equation has no solutions.

C.  11.  $x^2 - 2x = 3$
$x^2 - 2x - 3 = 0$
$(x - 3)(x + 1) = 0$
$x = 3$ or $x = -1$
The solutions are 3 and $-1$.

12.  $m^2 - 9m + 14 = 0$
$(m - 7)(m - 2) = 0$
$m = 7$ or $m = 2$
The solutions are 7 and 2.

13.  $x^2 - 5x = 0$
$x(x - 5) = 0$
$x = 0$ or $x = 5$
The solutions are 0 and 5.

14.  $a^2 - 16 = 0$
$(a + 4)(a - 4) = 0$
$a = -4$ or $a = 4$
The solutions are $-4$ and 4.

15.  $x^2 = 25$
$x^2 - 25 = 0$
$(x + 5)(x - 5) = 0$
$x = -5$ or $x = 5$
The solutions are $-5$ and 5.

16.  $2y^2 - 9y = 0$
$y(2y - 9) = 0$
$y = 0$ or $y = \dfrac{9}{2}$
The solutions are 0 and $\dfrac{9}{2}$.

## Solutions to Review Exercises, Contd.

17. $5x^2 - 20 = 0$
    $5(x^2 - 4) = 0$
    $5(x + 2)(x - 2) = 0$
    $x = -2$ or $x = 2$
    The solutions are $-2$ and $2$.

18. $m^2 + 4m + 4 = 0$
    $(m + 2)(m + 2) = 0$
    $m = -2$
    The solution is $-2$.

D. 19. $a + 2 = 1$
    $a = -1$
    The solution is $-1$.

20. $3x + 2 - x = x$
    $2x + 2 = x$
    $x = -2$
    The solution is $-2$.

21. $x^2 + 2x = 15$
    $x^2 + 2x - 15 = 0$
    $(x + 5)(x - 3) = 0$
    $x = -5$ or $x = 3$
    The solutions are $-5$ and $3$.

22. $3m^2 = 9m$
    $3m^2 - 9m = 0$
    $3m(m - 3) = 0$
    $m = 0$ or $m = 3$
    The solutions are $0$ and $3$.

23. $4(2x - 3) = 2x + 6$
    $8x - 12 = 2x + 6$
    $6x = 18$
    $x = 3$
    The solution is $3$.

24. $x(x + 2) = 3$
    $x^2 + 2x = 3$
    $x^2 + 2x - 3 = 0$
    $(x + 3)(x - 1) = 0$
    $x = -3$ or $x = 1$
    The solutions are $-3$ and $1$.

25. $3r^2 = 6 - 7r$
    $3r^2 + 7r - 6 = 0$
    $(3r - 2)(r + 3) = 0$
    $r = \dfrac{2}{3}$ or $r = -3$
    The solutions are $\dfrac{2}{3}$ and $-3$.

E. 26. $x + 2x + x + 4 = 84$
    $4x + 4 = 84$
    $4x = 80$
    $x = 20$
    First piece is 20 ft, second is 40 ft, and third is 24 ft.

27. $60t = 45(t + 1)$
    $60t = 45t + 45$
    $15t = 45$
    $t = 3$
    The distance $60t$ is $60 \cdot 3$ or 180 miles

28. $x^2 + 3x = 10$
    $x^2 + 3x - 10 = 0$
    $(x + 5)(x - 2) = 0$
    $x = -5$ or $x = 2$
    The number is negative; therefore, $-5$ is the only solution.

## SUPPLEMENTARY PROBLEMS

A. Solve the following first degree equations.

1. $x - 7 = 0$
2. $m + 2 = 0$
3. $3m = 21$
4. $5a - 15 = 0$
5. $6t + 2 = -4$
6. $3(t + 1) = 0$
7. $5(m - 4) = 5$
8. $6y + 3(y + 1) = y - 2(y - 3) + 7$
9. $3(2x - 5) = 2(5x + 1) - 1$
10. $5 - 2a = 13$
11. $2y + 14 = 5y + 2$
12. $3(1 - 2x) = x - 4$
13. $3(m - 1) + m = 2(m - 1) - 3$
14. $2(x + 4) = 2x - 1$
15. $3(x - 1) = 3x - 3$

B. Solve the following quadratic equations.

16. $x^2 - 4 = 0$
17. $3x^2 = 27$
18. $m^2 = 1$
19. $m^2 = 2m$
20. $5a^2 + 2a = 0$
21. $x^2 - 2x + 1 = 0$
22. $m^2 + m = 2$
23. $p^2 = p + 12$
24. $a^2 - 2a - 15 = 0$
25. $3x^2 = 6 - 3x$
26. $5x^2 + 13x - 6 = 0$
27. $2m^2 = 1 - m$
28. $72 = n^2 + 14n$
29. $2x^2 - 25x + 72 = 0$
30. $n^2 = 21 - 4n$

## SUPPLEMENTARY PROBLEMS, Contd.

C.  Solve the following problems.

31.  The sum of a certain number and 25 is equal to six times the number. What is the number?

32.  A certain number is four times another. Their sum is 135. Find the numbers.

33.  An 8-ft board is cut into two pieces. One piece is 2 ft longer than the other. Find the length of each piece.

34.  A 16-ft board is cut into three pieces. The second piece is twice as long as the first. The third piece is 4 ft longer than the first. Find the length of each piece.

35.  The length of a rectangle is 6 ft greater than its width. The perimeter is 44 ft. Find the length and width.

36.  The length of a rectangle is 4 ft more than its width. If the perimeter is 56 ft, find the dimensions.

37.  When each side of a square is increased by 3 inches, the area is increased by 51 square inches. Find the length of each side of the new square.

38.  Two test rockets are fired over a 5600-mile range. One rocket travels twice the speed of the other. The faster rocket covers the distance in two hours less time than the slower. Find the speed of each rocket.

39.  Two planes leave a certain airport in opposite directions. The speed of one plane averages 60 miles per hour faster than that of the other. At the end of 5 hours, the planes are 1550 miles apart. Find the rate of the slower plane.

40.  Two planes start from the same airport at the same time, one flying north, the other, south. The ground speed of the first plane is 200 miles per hour less than the ground speed of the other plane. After two hours they are 1680 miles apart. What is the speed of each plane?

41.  The sum of three currents coming together at a point in the circuit is zero. If the second current is three times the first, and if the third is 10 more than the first, find the respective currents in amperes.

42.  A negative number subtracted from the square of the same number produces 6. Find the number.

43.  Three times a positive number added to the square of the same number produces 10. Find the number.

44.  The length of a rectangle is 2 feet more than the width. The area of the rectangle is 15 square feet. Find the length and the width.

45.  The formula $s = 16t^2$ gives the distance an object falls due to gravity. $s$ is distance in feet and $t$ is time in seconds. How long will it take for an object to fall 64 feet?

☐ Solutions to Study Exercises                                                    (9A)

### Study Exercise One (Frame 9)

1.  First degree
2.  First degree
3.  Quadratic
4.  First degree
5.  Quadratic
6.  First degree
7.  Quadratic

☐                              Study Exercise Two (Frame 16)                      (16A)

1.  $x + 5 = 0$
    $x = -5$
    The solution is $-5$.

2.  $2x + 14 = 2$
    $2x = -12$
    $x = -6$
    The solution is $-6$.

3.  $4x - 9x + 22 = 3(x + 10)$
    $-5x + 22 = 3x + 30$
    $-5x - 3x = 30 - 22$
    $-8x = 8$
    $x = -1$
    The solution is $-1$.

4.  $4(y - 9) = 10(2 - y)$
    $4y - 36 = 20 - 10y$
    $4y + 10y = 20 + 36$
    $14y = 56$
    $y = 4$
    The solution is 4.

## Solutions to Study Exercises, Contd.

5. $3m + 5 - m = 2(m - 1)$
   $2m + 5 = 2m - 2$
   $2m - 2m = -2 - 5$
   $0 = -7$

   The equation has no solutions.

6. $7 - m = 3m + 7 - 4m$
   $7 - m = -m + 7$
   $-m + m = 7 - 7$
   $0 = 0$

   The equation is true for all values of $m$ and is therefore an identity. Every number is a solution.

7. $5(2 + x) = 2(x + 6)$
   $10 + 5x = 2x + 12$
   $5x - 2x = 12 - 10$
   $3x = 2$

   $x = \dfrac{2}{3}$

   The solution is $\dfrac{2}{3}$.

☐                    *Study Exercise Three (Frame 24)*                    **(24A)**

1. $x^2 - 5x - 6 = 0$
   $(x - 6)(x + 1) = 0$
   $x - 6 = 0$  or  $x + 1 = 0$
   $x = 6$  or  $x = -1$
   The solutions are 6 and $-1$.

2. $m^2 - 2m = 8$
   $m^2 - 2m - 8 = 0$
   $(m - 4)(m + 2) = 0$
   $m - 4 = 0$  or  $m + 2 = 0$
   $m = 4$  or  $m = -2$
   The solutions are 4 and $-2$.

3. $x^2 - 3x = 0$
   $x(x - 3) = 0$
   $x = 0$  or  $x - 3 = 0$
   $x = 0$  or  $x = 3$
   The solutions are 0 and 3.

4. $2m^2 - m = 3$
   $2m^2 - m - 3 = 0$
   $(2m - 3)(m + 1) = 0$
   $2m - 3 = 0$  or  $m + 1 = 0$

   $m = \dfrac{3}{2}$  or  $m = -1$

   The solutions are $\dfrac{3}{2}$ and $-1$.

5. $r^2 - 9 = 0$
   $(r + 3)(r - 3) = 0$
   $r + 3 = 0$  or  $r - 3 = 0$
   $r = -3$  or  $r = 3$
   The solutions are $-3$ and 3.

6. $2x^2 - x = 0$
   $x(2x - 1) = 0$
   $x = 0$  or  $2x - 1 = 0$

   $x = 0$  or  $x = \dfrac{1}{2}$

   The solutions are 0 and $\dfrac{1}{2}$.

7. $x^2 + 9 = 6x$
   $x^2 - 6x + 9 = 0$
   $(x - 3)(x - 3) = 0$
   $x - 3 = 0$  or  $x - 3 = 0$
   $x = 3$
   The solution is 3.

☐                    *Study Exercise Four (Frame 31)*                    **(31A)**

1. Let $x$ represent the shorter piece. $x + 16$ represents the longer piece. The sum is 100 ft.

   $x + (x + 16) = 100$
   $2x + 16 = 100$
   $2x = 84$
   $x = 42$

   The shorter piece is 42 ft, and the longer piece is 58 ft.

2. Let $x$ represent the capacity of tank B. $2x$ represents the capacity of tank A. $x + 100$ represents the capacity of tank C. The sum is 3700.

   $x + 2x + (x + 100) = 3700$
   $4x + 100 = 3700$
   $4x = 3600$
   $x = 900$

   The capacity of tank B is 900 gal. The capacity of tank A is 1800 gal. The capacity of tank C is 1000 gal.

## Solutions to Study Exercises, Contd.

3. Let $t$ represent the time of the first jet. $t - 2$ represents the time of the second jet. $400t$ represents the distance traveled by the first jet. $600(t - 2)$ represents the distance traveled by the second jet. The distances traveled by each jet are the same.

$$400t = 600(t - 2)$$
$$400t = 600t - 1200$$
$$-200t = -1200$$
$$t = 6$$

The distance is $400t$, or $(400)(6)$, or 2400 miles.

4. Let $x$ represent the positive number. $6x$ represents six times the positive number. $x^2$ represents the square of the number. The sum is 16.

$$x^2 + 6x = 16$$
$$x^2 + 6x - 16 = 0$$
$$(x + 8)(x - 2) = 0$$
$$x = -8 \quad \text{and} \quad x = 2$$

Since $x$ represents a positive number, the only solution is 2.

5. Let $w$ represent the width. $w + 10$ represents the length. $w(w + 10)$ represents the area. The area is 24.

$$w(w + 10) = 24$$
$$w^2 + 10w = 24$$
$$w^2 + 10w - 24 = 0$$
$$(w + 12)(w - 2) = 0$$
$$w = -12 \quad \text{and} \quad w = 2$$

The width must be positive; therefore, the width is 2 feet and the length is 12 feet.

# Rational Expressions—
# Expansion, Reduction,
# Multiplication and Division

## ☐ Objectives (1)

By the end of this unit you should be able to:

- expand rational expressions to higher terms.
- reduce rational expressions to lowest terms, using previously learned factoring techniques.
- raise a rational expression to a power.
- multiply and divide rational expressions, using previously learned multiplication and factoring techniques.

## ☐ Rational Expressions (2)

A quotient of two polynomials is a rational expression.

**Example 1:** $\dfrac{x+5}{x-2}$ is a rational expression.

**Example 2:** $\dfrac{y^2+3y+1}{y^2-9}$ is a rational expression.

**Example 3:** $\dfrac{5x}{2}$ is a rational expression.

## ☐ Domain of a Rational Expression (3)

The domain of a rational expression is the set of all real numbers for which the expression is defined. The denominator of a rational expression can never represent zero.

**Example 1:** The domain of $\dfrac{x+5}{x-2}$ consists of all real numbers except 2.

**Example 2:** The domain of $\dfrac{y^2+3y+1}{y^2-9}$ consists of all real numbers except 3 and $-3$.

**Example 3:** The domain of $\dfrac{5x}{2}$ consists of all real numbers.

## ☐ Review of the Basic Properties of Fractions (4)

1.  The denominator of a fraction can never be zero.

**Example:** $\dfrac{x+5}{0}$ is not a number.

2.  If the denominator of a fraction is 1, then the fraction is equal to the numerator.

**Example:** $\dfrac{5m+n}{1} = 5m+n$

3.  If the numerator of a fraction is zero and the denominator is not zero, then the fraction is equal to zero.

**Example:** $\dfrac{0}{x^2+5x+6} = 0$

4.  If the numerator and denominator of a fraction are equal, but not zero, then the fraction is equal to one.

**Example:** $\dfrac{3m+2}{3m+2} = 1$, where $m \neq -\dfrac{2}{3}$.

5.  The numerator and denominator of a fraction may be multiplied or divided by the same nonzero number (Fundamental Principle of Fractions).

**Examples:** $\dfrac{a}{b} = \dfrac{a \cdot n}{b \cdot n}$, or $\dfrac{a}{b} = \dfrac{a \div n}{b \div n}$, where $n \neq 0$.

☐ **Expanding Rational Expressions to Higher Terms** **(5)**

The Fundamental Principle of Fractions allows us to expand a rational expression to higher terms by multiplying the numerator and denominator by the same nonzero number.

**Example:** Expand $\frac{3a}{4bc}$ so that its denominator becomes $12b^2c^3$.

   **Solution:** Multiply numerator and denominator by $3bc^2$.

$$\frac{3a}{4bc} = \frac{3a(3bc^2)}{4bc(3bc^2)} = \frac{9abc^2}{12b^2c^3}$$

☐ **More Examples** **(6)**

**Example 1:** Expand $\frac{2x}{5}$ so that its denominator becomes $5x + 5y$.

   **Solution:** Factor $5x + 5y$.

   *line (a)*   $5x + 5y = 5(x + y)$

   *line (b)*   Multiply numerator and denominator by $x + y$.

   *line (c)*   $\frac{2x}{5} = \frac{2x(x + y)}{5(x + y)}$, or $\frac{2x^2 + 2xy}{5x + 5y}$

☐ **Example 2:** Expand $\frac{m - 3}{m + 2}$ so that its denominator becomes $m^2 - 4$. **(7)**

   **Solution:** Factor $m^2 - 4$.

   *line (a)*   $m^2 - 4 = (m + 2)(m - 2)$

   *line (b)*   Multiply numerator and denominator by $m - 2$.

   *line (c)*   $\frac{m - 3}{m + 2} = \frac{(m - 3)(m - 2)}{(m + 2)(m - 2)}$ or $\frac{m^2 - 5m + 6}{m^2 - 4}$

☐ **Example 3:** Expand $\frac{x + 1}{x - 5}$ so that its denominator becomes $2x^2 - 7x - 15$. **(8)**

   **Solution:** Factor $2x^2 - 7x - 15$.

   *line (a)*   $2x^2 - 7x - 15 = (x - 5)(2x + 3)$

   *line (b)*   Multiply numerator and denominator by $2x + 3$.

   *line (c)*   $\frac{x + 1}{x - 5} = \frac{(x + 1)(2x + 3)}{(x - 5)(2x + 3)}$ or $\frac{2x^2 + 5x + 3}{2x^2 - 7x - 15}$

☐                           *Study Exercise One* **(9)**

A.    Give the domain for each of the following rational expressions.

    1.   $\frac{x - 2}{x - 7}$             2.   $\frac{4y}{7}$             3.   $\frac{3}{8x}$             4.   $\frac{7m^2 + 2m - 3}{m^2 - 4}$

B.    Expand the following rational expressions as indicated. Assume that the denominators do not represent zero.

    5.   Expand $\frac{3r}{7st}$ so that its denominator becomes $21s^2t^4$.

    6.   Expand $\frac{3m}{7}$ so that its denominator becomes $7m + 7n$.

    7.   Expand $\frac{x - 4}{x + 3}$ so that its denominator becomes $x^2 - 9$.

    8.   Expand $\frac{2m - 1}{m - 2}$ so that its denominator becomes $3m^2 - 7m + 2$.

☐ **Reducing to Lowest Terms** **(10)**

The Fundamental Principle of Fractions allows us to reduce a rational expression to lowest terms by canceling out the common factors.

**Example:** Reduce $\dfrac{6m}{9m^2n}$.

**Solution:** $\dfrac{6m}{9m^2n} = \dfrac{2 \cdot \cancel{3} \cdot \cancel{m}}{3 \cdot \cancel{3} \cdot \cancel{m} \cdot m \cdot n} = \dfrac{2}{3mn}$

☐ **More Examples** **(11)**

**Example 1:** Reduce $\dfrac{3x - 3y}{3x + 3y}$.

**Solution:**

*Step (1):* Factor the numerator and denominator.
$$\frac{3x - 3y}{3x + 3y} = \frac{3(x - y)}{3(x + y)}$$

*Step (2):* Cancel the identical factors.
$$\frac{\cancel{3}(x - y)}{\cancel{3}(x + y)} = \frac{x - y}{x + y}$$

Therefore, $\dfrac{3x - 3y}{3x + 3y} = \dfrac{x - y}{x + y}$.

☐ **Example 2:** Reduce $\dfrac{8a^2 + 4ab}{24a^2 - 8ab}$. **(12)**

**Solution:**

*Step (1):* $\dfrac{8a^2 + 4ab}{24a^2 - 8ab} = \dfrac{4a(2a + b)}{8a(3a - b)}$

*Step (2):* $= \dfrac{\cancel{4} \cdot \cancel{a} \cdot (2a + b)}{2 \cdot \cancel{4} \cdot \cancel{a} \cdot (3a - b)}$

Therefore, $\dfrac{8a^2 + 4ab}{24a^2 - 8ab} = \dfrac{2a + b}{2(3a - b)}$, or $\dfrac{2a + b}{6a - 2b}$.

☐ **Example 3:** Reduce $\dfrac{4m^2 - 9}{(2m + 3)^2}$. **(13)**

**Solution:**

*Step (1):* $\dfrac{4m^2 - 9}{(2m + 3)^2} = \dfrac{(2m + 3)(2m - 3)}{(2m + 3)(2m + 3)}$

*Step (2):* $= \dfrac{\cancel{(2m + 3)}(2m - 3)}{\cancel{(2m + 3)}(2m + 3)}$

Therefore, $\dfrac{4m^2 - 9}{(2m + 3)^2} = \dfrac{2m - 3}{2m + 3}$.

☐ **Example 4:** Reduce $\dfrac{x^2 - 6x - 7}{x^2 - 10x + 21}$. **(14)**

**Solution:**

*Step (1):* $\dfrac{x^2 - 6x - 7}{x^2 - 10x + 21} = \dfrac{(x - 7)(x + 1)}{(x - 7)(x - 3)}$

*Step (2):*  $= \dfrac{(\cancel{x - 7})(x + 1)}{(\cancel{x - 7})(x - 3)}$

Therefore, $\dfrac{x^2 - 6x - 7}{x^2 - 10x + 21} = \dfrac{x + 1}{x - 3}.$

□                                    *Study Exercise Two*                                    **(15)**

Reduce each of the following to lowest terms. Assume that the denominators do not represent zero.

1. $\dfrac{2a + 2b}{2a - 2b}$          2. $\dfrac{ax + ay}{bx + by}$          3. $\dfrac{9a^2 - 4}{(3a - 2)^2}$

4. $\dfrac{m^2 - m - 20}{m^2 + 7m + 12}$          5. $\dfrac{6x^2 - 11x - 10}{9x^2 - 4}$

□ **Numbers Which Are Opposites**                                    **(16)**

*Opposites* are numbers which differ only in sign.

**Example 1:**  $-3$ and $3$ are opposites.

**Example 2:**  $-15$ and $+15$ are opposites.

**Example 3:**  $-x$ and $x$ are opposites.

□ **A Pattern Which Gives Opposites**                                    **(17)**

The binomials $a - b$ and $b - a$ will produce opposites.

**Example 1:**  Let $a = 5$ and $b = 3$:

$$\begin{array}{cccc} a & - & b & \qquad b & - & a \\ \downarrow & & \downarrow & \qquad \downarrow & & \downarrow \\ 5 & - & 3 & \qquad 3 & - & 5 \\ & \downarrow & & \qquad & \downarrow & \\ & 2 & & \qquad & -2 & \end{array}$$

**Example 2:**  Let $a = -4$ and $b = -7$:

$$\begin{array}{cccc} a & - & b & \qquad b & - & a \\ \downarrow & & \downarrow & \qquad \downarrow & & \downarrow \\ (-4) & - & (-7) & \qquad (-7) & - & (-4) \\ & \downarrow & & \qquad & \downarrow & \\ & +3 & & \qquad & -3 & \end{array}$$

□                                    *Study Exercise Three*                                    **(18)**

Remembering that the patterns $a - b$ and $b - a$ produce opposites, decide which of the following pairs represent opposites. Answer yes or no.

1. $x - y$ and $y - x$          2. $3m - n$ and $n - 3m$          3. $5a + b$ and $5a - b$
4. $r^2 - t^2$ and $t^2 - r^2$          5. $2x - b$ and $-2x - b$

□ **Reducing Rational Expressions Having Factors Which Are Opposites**                                    **(19)**

Opposites, when divided or canceled, produce negative one $(-1)$.

**Example 1:**  $\dfrac{-5}{5} = -1$          **Example 2:**  $\dfrac{-x}{x} = -1$          **Example 3:**  $\dfrac{a - b}{b - a} = -1$

□ **More Examples**                                    **(20)**

**Example 1:**  Reduce $\dfrac{ax - ay}{by - bx}.$

**Solution:**

*Step (1):* Factor the numerator and denominator.

$$\frac{ax - ay}{by - bx} = \frac{a(x - y)}{b(y - x)}$$

*Step (2):* Cancel, remembering that opposites will produce $-1$.

$$\frac{a(x - y)}{b(y - x)} = \frac{a \cdot (-1)}{b}, \text{ or } \frac{-a}{b}$$

Therefore, $\dfrac{ax - ay}{by - bx} = \dfrac{-a}{b}, \text{ or } \dfrac{a}{-b}$.

☐ **Example 2:** Reduce $\dfrac{9 - 4x^2}{2x^2 - x - 3}$. **(21)**

**Solution:**

*Step (1):* Factor the numerator and denominator.

$$\frac{9 - 4x^2}{2x^2 - x - 3} = \frac{(3 + 2x)(3 - 2x)}{(x + 1)(2x - 3)}$$

*Step (2):* Cancel, remembering that opposites will produce $-1$.

$$\frac{(3 + 2x)(3 - 2x)}{(x + 1)(2x - 3)} = \frac{(3 + 2x)(-1)}{x + 1}, \text{ or } \frac{-3 - 2x}{x + 1}$$

Therefore, $\dfrac{9 - 4x^2}{2x^2 - x - 3} = \dfrac{-3 - 2x}{x + 1}$.

☐ ### Study Exercise Four **(22)**

Reduce each of the following to lowest terms. Assume that the denominators do not represent zero.

1. $\dfrac{3a - 3b}{4b - 4a}$      2. $\dfrac{3a - 3b}{4a - 4b}$      3. $\dfrac{2 - x}{x^2 - 4}$      4. $\dfrac{25 - 9m^2}{3m^2 + m - 10}$

☐ ### Review of Multiplying Fractions **(23)**

The product of two fractions is found by multiplying the numerators and denominators.

$$\frac{a}{b} \cdot \frac{c}{d} = \frac{a \cdot c}{b \cdot d} \quad \text{where } b, d \neq 0$$

**Example 1:** $\dfrac{2}{3} \cdot \dfrac{5a^2}{7b^2} = \dfrac{(2)(5a^2)}{(3)(7b^2)} = \dfrac{10a^2}{21b^2}$       **Example 2:** $\dfrac{5a}{b} \cdot \dfrac{3c^2}{2d} = \dfrac{(5a)(3c^2)}{(b)(2d)} = \dfrac{15ac^2}{2bd}$

**Example 3:** $\dfrac{m + 2}{m + 3} \cdot \dfrac{m - 2}{m - 5} = \dfrac{(m + 2)(m - 2)}{(m + 3)(m - 5)}, \text{ or } \dfrac{m^2 - 4}{m^2 - 2m - 15}$

☐ ### Raising a Rational Expression to a Power **(24)**

To raise a rational expression to a power, raise both the numerator and the denominator to the power.

$$\left(\frac{a}{b}\right)^n = \frac{a^n}{b^n} \quad \text{where } b \neq 0$$

**Example 1:** $\left(\dfrac{3}{4}\right)^3 = \dfrac{3^3}{4^3} = \dfrac{27}{64}$       **Example 2:** $\left(\dfrac{2x^3}{3y}\right)^4 = \dfrac{(2x^3)^4}{(3y)^4} = \dfrac{2^4 \cdot x^{12}}{3^4 \cdot y^4} = \dfrac{16x^{12}}{81y^4}$

**Example 3:** $\left(\dfrac{m - 3}{2m + 5}\right)^2 = \dfrac{(m - 3)^2}{(2m + 5)^2} = \dfrac{m^2 - 6m + 9}{4m^2 + 20m + 25}$

A.  Multiply the following. Assume that the denominators do not represent zero.

1.  $\dfrac{3}{4} \cdot \dfrac{5x^3}{7y^2}$
2.  $\dfrac{3x}{y^2} \cdot \dfrac{4w^2}{7z}$
3.  $\dfrac{2x+3}{3x-1} \cdot \dfrac{2x-3}{2x+1}$

B.  Raise the following to the indicated power.

4.  $\left(\dfrac{-2}{5}\right)^3$
5.  $\left(\dfrac{3a^2}{2b}\right)^4$
6.  $\left(\dfrac{3x+2}{x-1}\right)^2$

## Multiplying Rational Expressions Where Numerators and Denominators Share Common Factors **(26)**

*Step (1):*  Factor numerators and denominators.
*Step (2):*  Cancel like factors, then multiply numerators and denominators.

**Example 1:**  $\dfrac{4a^3}{3b} \cdot \dfrac{5b^2}{2a^2}$                                                    **(27)**

**Solution:**

*Step (1):*  Factor numerators and denominators.
$$\frac{4a^3}{3b} \cdot \frac{5b^2}{2a^2} = \frac{2\cdot 2\cdot a\cdot a^2}{3\cdot b} \cdot \frac{5\cdot b\cdot b}{2\cdot a^2}$$

*Step (2):*  Cancel like factors; then multiply.
$$\frac{2\cdot 2\cdot a\cdot a^2}{3\cdot b} \cdot \frac{5\cdot b\cdot b}{2\cdot a^2} = \frac{10ab}{3}$$

Therefore, $\dfrac{4a^3}{3b} \cdot \dfrac{5b^2}{2a^2} = \dfrac{10ab}{3}$.

**Example 2:**  $\dfrac{3x+3y}{10x^2} \cdot \dfrac{15x}{2x+2y}$                                              **(28)**

**Solution:**

*Step (1):*  Factor numerators and denominators.
$$\frac{3x+3y}{10x^2} \cdot \frac{15x}{2x+2y} = \frac{3\cdot(x+y)}{5\cdot 2\cdot x\cdot x} \cdot \frac{5\cdot 3\cdot x}{2\cdot(x+y)}$$

*Step (2):*  Cancel like factors; then multiply.
$$\frac{3\cdot(x+y)}{5\cdot 2\cdot x\cdot x} \cdot \frac{5\cdot 3\cdot x}{2\cdot(x+y)} = \frac{9}{4x}$$

Therefore, $\dfrac{3x+3y}{10x^2} \cdot \dfrac{15x}{2x+2y} = \dfrac{9}{4x}$.

**Example 3:**  $\dfrac{a^2-4}{a^2-2a-15} \cdot \dfrac{a^2-9}{a^2-5a+6}$                                  **(29)**

**Solution:**

*Step (1):*  Factor numerators and denominators.
$$\frac{a^2-4}{a^2-2a-15} \cdot \frac{a^2-9}{a^2-5a+6} = \frac{(a+2)\cdot(a-2)}{(a-5)\cdot(a+3)} \cdot \frac{(a+3)\cdot(a-3)}{(a-2)\cdot(a-3)}$$

*Step (2):*  Cancel like factors; then multiply.
$$\frac{(a+2)\cdot(a-2)}{(a-5)\cdot(a+3)} \cdot \frac{(a+3)\cdot(a-3)}{(a-2)\cdot(a-3)} = \frac{a+2}{a-5}$$

Therefore, $\dfrac{a^2-4}{a^2-2a-15} \cdot \dfrac{a^2-9}{a^2-5a+6} = \dfrac{a+2}{a-5}$.

☐ **Example 4:** $\dfrac{3m^2 - 3m}{m^2 - m - 6} \cdot \dfrac{m + 2}{3 - 3m}$  **(30)**

**Solution:**

*Step (1):* Factor numerators and denominators.

$$\frac{3m^2 - 3m}{m^2 - m - 6} \cdot \frac{m + 2}{3 - 3m} = \frac{3 \cdot m \cdot (m - 1)}{(m - 3) \cdot (m + 2)} \cdot \frac{(m + 2)}{3 \cdot (1 - m)}$$

*Step (2):* Cancel like factors; then multiply.

$$\frac{\cancel{3} \cdot m \cdot \cancel{(m - 1)}}{(m - 3) \cdot \cancel{(m + 2)}} \cdot \frac{\cancel{(m + 2)}}{\cancel{3} \cdot (1 - m)} = \frac{-m}{m - 3}$$

Therefore, $\dfrac{3m^2 - 3m}{m^2 - m - 6} \cdot \dfrac{m + 2}{3 - 3m} = \dfrac{-m}{m - 3}$.

☐ **Example 5:** $\dfrac{2x^2 - 5x - 3}{x^2 - 3x - 4} \cdot \dfrac{x^2 - 2x - 8}{2x^2 + 11x + 5}$  **(31)**

**Solution:**

*Step (1):* Factor numerators and denominators.

$$\frac{2x^2 - 5x - 3}{x^2 - 3x - 4} \cdot \frac{x^2 - 2x - 8}{2x^2 + 11x + 5} = \frac{(2x + 1) \cdot (x - 3)}{(x + 1) \cdot (x - 4)} \cdot \frac{(x + 2) \cdot (x - 4)}{(2x + 1) \cdot (x + 5)}$$

*Step (2):* Cancel like factors; then multiply.

$$\frac{\cancel{(2x + 1)} \cdot (x - 3)}{(x + 1) \cdot \cancel{(x - 4)}} \cdot \frac{(x + 2) \cdot \cancel{(x - 4)}}{\cancel{(2x + 1)} \cdot (x + 5)} = \frac{(x - 3)(x + 2)}{(x + 1)(x + 5)}$$

The result may be left in factored form.

Therefore, $\dfrac{2x^2 - 5x - 3}{x^2 - 3x - 4} \cdot \dfrac{x^2 - 2x - 8}{2x^2 + 11x + 5} = \dfrac{(x - 3)(x + 2)}{(x + 1)(x + 5)}$.

☐ ### Study Exercise Six  **(32)**

Multiply the following. The results may be left in factored form. Assume that the denominators do not represent zero.

1. $\dfrac{6m^3}{5n^2} \cdot \dfrac{7n}{12m^2}$

2. $\dfrac{5a + 5b}{8a^2} \cdot \dfrac{4a}{3a + 3b}$

3. $\dfrac{m^2 - 9}{m^2 + 8m + 15} \cdot \dfrac{m^2 - 25}{m^2 - m - 6}$

4. $\dfrac{5a^2 - 10a}{a^2 + 4a + 3} \cdot \dfrac{a + 3}{20 - 10a}$

5. $\dfrac{3x^2 + 10x - 8}{x^2 - 7x + 10} \cdot \dfrac{x^2 + x - 6}{3x^2 + x - 2}$

☐ ### Division of Rational Expressions  **(33)**

When dividing two fractions, multiply by the reciprocal of the divisor. Then follow the steps for multiplication.

$$\frac{a}{b} \div \frac{c}{d} = \frac{a}{b} \cdot \frac{d}{c} \quad \text{where } b, c, d \neq 0$$

☐ **Example 1:** $\dfrac{2a + 4}{3b} \div \dfrac{a + 2}{5b^2}$  **(34)**

**Solution:** Multiply by the reciprocal of the divisor, obtaining:

$$\frac{2a + 4}{3b} \cdot \frac{5b^2}{a + 2}$$

*Step (1):* Factor numerators and denominators.

$$\frac{2a + 4}{3b} \cdot \frac{5b^2}{a + 2} = \frac{2 \cdot (a + 2)}{3 \cdot b} \cdot \frac{5 \cdot b \cdot b}{(a + 2)}$$

*Step (2):* Cancel like factors; then multiply.

$$\frac{2 \cdot \cancel{(a+2)}}{3 \cdot \cancel{b}} \cdot \frac{5 \cdot b \cdot \cancel{b}}{\cancel{(a+2)}} = \frac{10b}{3}$$

Therefore, $\dfrac{2a+4}{3b} \div \dfrac{a+2}{5b^2} = \dfrac{10b}{3}$.

□ **Example 2:** $\dfrac{4a^2 - 9}{3a} \div (2a + 3)$ **(35)**

**Solution:** Multiply by the reciprocal of the divisor, obtaining:

$$\frac{4a^2 - 9}{3a} \cdot \frac{1}{2a + 3}$$

*Step (1):* Factor numerators and denominators.

$$\frac{4a^2 - 9}{3a} \cdot \frac{1}{2a + 3} = \frac{(2a + 3) \cdot (2a - 3)}{3a} \cdot \frac{1}{(2a + 3)}$$

*Step (2):* Cancel like factors; then multiply.

$$\frac{\cancel{(2a+3)} \cdot (2a - 3)}{3a} \cdot \frac{1}{\cancel{(2a+3)}} = \frac{2a - 3}{3a}$$

Therefore, $\dfrac{4a^2 - 9}{3a} \div (2a + 3) = \dfrac{2a - 3}{3a}$.

□ **Example 3:** $\dfrac{2x^2 + 3x - 2}{2x^2 - 11x + 5} \div \dfrac{x^2 - x - 6}{x^2 - 8x + 15}$ **(36)**

**Solution:** Multiply by the reciprocal of the divisor, obtaining:

$$\frac{2x^2 + 3x - 2}{2x^2 - 11x + 5} \cdot \frac{x^2 - 8x + 15}{x^2 - x - 6}$$

*Step (1):* Factor numerators and denominators.

$$\frac{2x^2 + 3x - 2}{2x^2 - 11x + 5} \cdot \frac{x^2 - 8x + 15}{x^2 - x - 6} = \frac{(2x - 1) \cdot (x + 2)}{(2x - 1) \cdot (x - 5)} \cdot \frac{(x - 5) \cdot (x - 3)}{(x + 2) \cdot (x - 3)}$$

*Step (2):* Cancel like factors; then multiply.

$$\frac{\cancel{(2x-1)} \cdot \cancel{(x+2)}}{\cancel{(2x-1)} \cdot \cancel{(x-5)}} \cdot \frac{\cancel{(x-5)} \cdot \cancel{(x-3)}}{\cancel{(x+2)} \cdot \cancel{(x-3)}} = 1$$

Therefore, $\dfrac{2x^2 + 3x - 2}{2x^2 - 11x + 5} \div \dfrac{x^2 - x - 6}{x^2 - 8x + 15} = 1$.

□ *Study Exercise Seven* **(37)**

Divide the following. Assume that the denominators and divisors are not zero.

1. $\dfrac{3m - 6}{5n^2} \div \dfrac{m - 2}{10n}$

2. $\dfrac{9x^2 - 1}{4x} \div (3x + 1)$

3. $\dfrac{3m^2 + m - 2}{m^2 + 2m - 8} \div \dfrac{3m^2 + 4m - 4}{m^2 + m - 12}$

4. $\dfrac{9x^2 - 16}{3x^2 + 2x - 8} \div \dfrac{3x^2 - 5x - 12}{x^2 - x - 6}$

## REVIEW EXERCISES

A. Give the domain for each of the following rational expressions.

1. $\dfrac{2}{m}$

2. $\dfrac{x + 8}{x - 7}$

3. $\dfrac{3x + 4}{2x - 6}$

4. $\dfrac{2y^2 - 3y + 1}{y^2 - 16}$

## REVIEW EXERCISES, Contd.

**B.** By remembering that $a - b$ and $b - a$ represent opposites, decide which of the following pairs represent opposites. Answer yes or no.

5. $x - y$ and $y - x$          6. $2a + b$ and $2a - b$

7. $2a - b$ and $b - 2a$         8. $x^2 - y^2$ and $y^2 - x^2$

**C.** Expand the following fractions as indicated. Assume that the denominators do not represent zero.

9. Expand $\dfrac{3a}{4bc}$ so that its denominator becomes $20b^3c^2$.

10. Expand $\dfrac{m + 2}{m - 3}$ so that its denominator becomes $m^2 - 9$.

11. Expand $\dfrac{2x + 1}{x + 3}$ so that its denominator becomes $x^2 + 5x + 6$.

**D.** Reduce each of the following to lowest terms. Assume that the denominators do not represent zero.

12. $\dfrac{5m^2n}{15m}$    13. $\dfrac{3a - 6b}{4a - 8b}$    14. $\dfrac{3a - 6b}{8b - 4a}$    15. $\dfrac{10m^2 + 5mn}{10m^2 - 30mn}$

16. $\dfrac{x^2 + 4x + 3}{x^2 + 5x + 6}$    17. $\dfrac{3 - m}{m^2 - 9}$    18. $\dfrac{a^2 - 9b^2}{3ab - 9b^2}$    19. $\dfrac{2x^2 + 9x + 4}{2x^2 - 5x - 3}$

**E.** Raise the following to the indicated power. Assume that the denominators do not represent zero.

20. $\left(\dfrac{-2}{3}\right)^2$    21. $\left(\dfrac{-2}{3}\right)^3$    22. $\left(\dfrac{-5x^2}{y^4}\right)^3$    23. $\left(\dfrac{x + 1}{x + 2}\right)^2$

**F.** Multiply or divide as indicated. Assume that the denominators and divisors do not represent zero.

24. $\dfrac{4}{9} \cdot \dfrac{3m}{7}$                     25. $\dfrac{8a}{15} \cdot \dfrac{5}{a^2}$

26. $\dfrac{5x^2}{3} \div \dfrac{x}{6}$                 27. $\dfrac{a - 3}{15} \cdot \dfrac{5a + 10}{3a - 9}$

28. $\dfrac{x^2 - 5x + 4}{x^2 - x - 6} \div \dfrac{x^2 + 2x - 3}{x^2 - 4}$    29. $\dfrac{m^2 - m - 2}{2m^2 + m - 10} \cdot \dfrac{12m^2 + 16m - 35}{6m^2 - m - 7}$

30. $\dfrac{x^2 - 1}{14x} \div \dfrac{3x + 3}{35x^2}$        31. $\dfrac{3a^2 - 13a - 10}{4a^2 - 4} \div \dfrac{a^2 - 6a + 5}{4a + 4}$

32. $\dfrac{5x^2 - 10x}{x^2 - 3x - 4} \cdot \dfrac{x + 1}{6 - 3x}$     33. $\dfrac{9m^2 - 4}{2a} \div (6m - 4)$

34. $\dfrac{2y^2 - y - 3}{3y^2 + y - 2} \div \dfrac{2y^2 - 5y + 3}{3y^2 - 5y + 2}$    35. $\dfrac{a^2 - b^2}{2a^2 - 5ab + 2b^2} \cdot \dfrac{2a^2 - 7ab + 3b^2}{a^2 + 2ab + b^2}$

## Solutions to Review Exercises

**A.** 1. All real numbers except 0.        2. All real numbers except 7.

     3. All real numbers except 3.        4. All real numbers except 4 and $-4$.

**B.** 5. Yes        6. No           7. Yes          8. Yes

**C.** 9. $\dfrac{3a}{4bc} = \dfrac{3a(5b^2c)}{4bc(5b^2c)} = \dfrac{15ab^2c}{20b^3c^2}$

10. $\dfrac{m + 2}{m - 3} = \dfrac{(m + 2)(m + 3)}{(m - 3)(m + 3)} = \dfrac{m^2 + 5m + 6}{m^2 - 9}$

11. $\dfrac{2x + 1}{x + 3} = \dfrac{(2x + 1)(x + 2)}{(x + 3)(x + 2)} = \dfrac{2x^2 + 5x + 2}{x^2 + 5x + 6}$

**D.** 12. $\dfrac{5m^2n}{15m} = \dfrac{\cancel{5} \cdot \cancel{m} \cdot m \cdot n}{\cancel{5} \cdot 3 \cdot \cancel{m}} = \dfrac{mn}{3}$     13. $\dfrac{3a - 6b}{4a - 8b} = \dfrac{3 \cdot \cancel{(a - 2b)}}{4 \cdot \cancel{(a - 2b)}} = \dfrac{3}{4}$

238

## Solutions to Review Exercises, Contd.

14. $\dfrac{3a - 6b}{8b - 4a} = \dfrac{3 \cdot (a - 2b)}{4 \cdot (2b - a)} = \dfrac{3 \cdot (-1)}{4} = \dfrac{-3}{4}$

15. $\dfrac{10m^2 + 5mn}{10m^2 - 30mn} = \dfrac{5 \cdot m \cdot (2m + n)}{5 \cdot 2 \cdot m \cdot (m - 3n)} = \dfrac{2m + n}{2(m - 3n)}$, or $\dfrac{2m + n}{2m - 6n}$

16. $\dfrac{x^2 + 4x + 3}{x^2 + 5x + 6} = \dfrac{(x + 3)(x + 1)}{(x + 3)(x + 2)} = \dfrac{x + 1}{x + 2}$

17. $\dfrac{3 - m}{m^2 - 9} = \dfrac{(3 - m)}{(m + 3)(m - 3)} = \dfrac{-1}{m + 3}$

18. $\dfrac{a^2 - 9b^2}{3ab - 9b^2} = \dfrac{(a + 3b)(a - 3b)}{3 \cdot b \cdot (a - 3b)} = \dfrac{a + 3b}{3b}$

19. $\dfrac{2x^2 + 9x + 4}{2x^2 - 5x - 3} = \dfrac{(2x + 1) \cdot (x + 4)}{(2x + 1) \cdot (x - 3)} = \dfrac{x + 4}{x - 3}$

E.  20. $\left(\dfrac{-2}{3}\right)^2 = \dfrac{(-2)^2}{3^2} = \dfrac{4}{9}$

21. $\left(\dfrac{-2}{3}\right)^3 = \dfrac{(-2)^3}{3^3} = \dfrac{-8}{27}$

22. $\left(\dfrac{-5x^2}{y^4}\right)^3 = \dfrac{(-5x^2)^3}{(y^4)^3} = \dfrac{-125x^6}{y^{12}}$

23. $\left(\dfrac{x + 1}{x + 2}\right)^2 = \dfrac{(x + 1)^2}{(x + 2)^2}$, or $\dfrac{x^2 + 2x + 1}{x^2 + 4x + 4}$

F.  24. $\dfrac{4}{9} \cdot \dfrac{3m}{7} = \dfrac{4}{3 \cdot 3} \cdot \dfrac{3 \cdot m}{7} = \dfrac{4m}{21}$

25. $\dfrac{8a}{15} \cdot \dfrac{5}{a^2} = \dfrac{8 \cdot a}{3 \cdot 5} \cdot \dfrac{5}{a \cdot a} = \dfrac{8}{3a}$

26. $\dfrac{5x^2}{3} \div \dfrac{x}{6} = \dfrac{5x^2}{3} \cdot \dfrac{6}{x} = \dfrac{5 \cdot x \cdot x \cdot 3 \cdot 2}{3} \cdot \dfrac{1}{x} = 10x$

27. $\dfrac{a - 3}{15} \cdot \dfrac{5a + 10}{3a - 9} = \dfrac{(a - 3)}{3 \cdot 5} \cdot \dfrac{5 \cdot (a + 2)}{3 \cdot (a - 3)} = \dfrac{a + 2}{9}$

28. $\dfrac{x^2 - 5x + 4}{x^2 - x - 6} \div \dfrac{x^2 + 2x - 3}{x^2 - 4} = \dfrac{(x - 4) \cdot (x - 1)}{(x - 3) \cdot (x + 2)} \cdot \dfrac{(x + 2) \cdot (x - 2)}{(x + 3) \cdot (x - 1)}$

$= \dfrac{(x - 4) \cdot (x - 2)}{(x - 3) \cdot (x + 3)}$, or $\dfrac{x^2 - 6x + 8}{x^2 - 9}$

29. $\dfrac{m^2 - m - 2}{2m^2 + m - 10} \cdot \dfrac{12m^2 + 16m - 35}{6m^2 - m - 7} = \dfrac{(m - 2) \cdot (m + 1)}{(2m + 5) \cdot (m - 2)} \cdot \dfrac{(6m - 7) \cdot (2m + 5)}{(6m - 7) \cdot (m + 1)}$

$= 1$

30. $\dfrac{x^2 - 1}{14x} \div \dfrac{3x + 3}{35x^2} = \dfrac{(x + 1) \cdot (x - 1)}{7 \cdot 2 \cdot x} \cdot \dfrac{7 \cdot 5 \cdot x \cdot x}{3 \cdot (x + 1)}$

$= \dfrac{5x(x - 1)}{6}$, or $\dfrac{5x^2 - 5x}{6}$

31. $\dfrac{3a^2 - 13a - 10}{4a^2 - 4} \div \dfrac{a^2 - 6a + 5}{4a + 4} = \dfrac{(3a + 2) \cdot (a - 5)}{4(a + 1) \cdot (a - 1)} \cdot \dfrac{4(a + 1)}{(a - 5) \cdot (a - 1)}$

$= \dfrac{3a + 2}{(a - 1)(a - 1)}$ or $\dfrac{3a + 2}{(a - 1)^2}$

canceled opposites

32. $\dfrac{5x^2 - 10x}{x^2 - 3x - 4} \cdot \dfrac{x + 1}{6 - 3x} = \dfrac{5 \cdot x \cdot (x - 2)}{(x - 4) \cdot (x + 1)} \cdot \dfrac{(x + 1)}{3 \cdot (2 - x)}$

$= \dfrac{-5x}{3(x - 4)}$, or $\dfrac{-5x}{3x - 12}$

33. $\dfrac{9m^2 - 4}{2a} \div (6m - 4) = \dfrac{9m^2 - 4}{2a} \cdot \dfrac{1}{6m - 4}$

$= \dfrac{(3m + 2)(3m - 2)}{2a} \cdot \dfrac{1}{2 \cdot (3m - 2)}$

$= \dfrac{3m + 2}{4a}$

34. $\dfrac{2y^2 - y - 3}{3y^2 + y - 2} \div \dfrac{2y^2 - 5y + 3}{3y^2 - 5y + 2} = \dfrac{(2y - 3) \cdot (y + 1)}{(3y - 2) \cdot (y + 1)} \cdot \dfrac{(3y - 2) \cdot (y - 1)}{(2y - 3) \cdot (y - 1)} = 1$

## Solutions to Review Exercises, Contd.

35. $\dfrac{a^2 - b^2}{2a^2 - 5ab + 2b^2} \cdot \dfrac{2a^2 - 7ab + 3b^2}{a^2 + 2ab + b^2} = \dfrac{(a + b) \cdot (a - b)}{(2a - b) \cdot (a - 2b)} \cdot \dfrac{(2a - b) \cdot (a - 3b)}{(a + b) \cdot (a + b)}$

$\qquad\qquad = \dfrac{(a - b)(a - 3b)}{(a - 2b)(a + b)}, \text{ or } \dfrac{a^2 - 4ab + 3b^2}{a^2 - ab - 2b^2}$

## SUPPLEMENTARY PROBLEMS

A. Give the domain for each of the following rational expressions.

1. $\dfrac{8x}{5}$      2. $\dfrac{3}{y}$      3. $\dfrac{2x^2 - 4x + 1}{x + 3}$      4. $\dfrac{m^2 - 25}{m^2 - 36}$

B. Expand the following fractions as indicated. Assume that the denominators do not represent zero.

5. Expand $\dfrac{2x}{3yz}$ so that its denominator becomes $12y^3z^2$.

6. Expand $\dfrac{a - 5}{a - 6}$ so that its denominator becomes $a^2 - 36$.

7. Expand $\dfrac{3m + 2}{2m + 1}$ so that its denominator becomes $6m^2 - m - 2$.

C. Reduce each of the following to lowest terms. Assume that the denominators do not represent zero.

8. $\dfrac{8mn}{12mn^2}$      9. $\dfrac{12a^2b^3}{24a^3b}$      10. $\dfrac{12abc^2}{21abc^3}$

11. $\dfrac{ab - ac}{ab + ac}$      12. $\dfrac{5x - 10y}{7x - 14y}$      13. $\dfrac{5x - 10y}{14y - 7x}$

14. $\dfrac{3b - 2a}{4a^2 - 9b^2}$      15. $\dfrac{x^2 - 1}{x^2 - 2x + 1}$      16. $\dfrac{x^2 + 3x - 4}{x^2 + 5x + 4}$

17. $\dfrac{a^2 - 4a + 4}{a^2 - 5a + 6}$      18. $\dfrac{a^2 - 1}{a^2 - 3a + 2}$      19. $\dfrac{x^2 - 8x + 7}{x^2 - 10x + 21}$

20. $\dfrac{m^2 - 3m}{m^2 - 2m - 3}$      21. $\dfrac{x^2 - 4xy + 4y^2}{x^2 - 4y^2}$      22. $\dfrac{(3 - a)(2a - 1)(a - 4)}{(a - 2)(4 - a)(a - 3)}$

D. Raise the following to the indicated power. Assume that the denominators do not represent zero.

23. $\left(-\dfrac{1}{2}\right)^5$      24. $\left(-\dfrac{1}{2}\right)^4$      25. $\left(\dfrac{-2a}{3}\right)^4$

26. $\left(\dfrac{-2a}{3}\right)^5$      27. $\left(\dfrac{3a^2b}{2c^3}\right)^3$      28. $\left(\dfrac{2x - 3}{x + 3}\right)^2$

E. Multiply or divide as indicated. Assume that the denominators and divisors do not represent zero.

29. $\dfrac{5y^2}{27x^2} \div \dfrac{25y}{3x}$      30. $\dfrac{3a^2b}{4ac^2} \cdot \dfrac{5a^3b^2}{6ab}$

31. $\dfrac{10xy^3}{9x^2y^2} \cdot \dfrac{72x^3y^4}{40}$      32. $\dfrac{m - 5n}{m + n} \div \dfrac{m - 5n}{3m + 3n}$

33. $\dfrac{3y - 9}{5y + 10} \cdot \dfrac{15}{y - 3}$      34. $\dfrac{2a}{15a - 30} \cdot \dfrac{5a - 10}{3a^2}$

35. $\dfrac{m^2 - n^2}{27} \cdot \dfrac{3}{m + n}$      36. $\dfrac{4x^2 - 9y^2}{x^2 - 1} \cdot \dfrac{x - 1}{6x - 9y}$

37. $\dfrac{x^2y^2 + y^2}{x^2y - xy^2} \div \dfrac{4x^2 + 4}{2xy^2 - 2x^2y}$      38. $\dfrac{r - 3}{r + 4} \div \dfrac{r^2 - 9}{r^2 - 16}$

39. $\dfrac{x^2 + 4x + 3}{x^2 + x - 6} \cdot \dfrac{x^2 - 2x}{x^2 + 3x + 2}$      40. $\dfrac{2x - 4y}{8x + 24y} \cdot \dfrac{2x + 6y}{4x - 8y}$

## SUPPLEMENTARY PROBLEMS, Contd.

41. $\dfrac{x^2 + 9x + 14}{x^2 + 4x - 21} \cdot \dfrac{x^2 + 2x - 35}{x^2 - 3x - 10}$

42. $\dfrac{3y + 3}{10y + 5} \div \dfrac{y^2 + y}{2y + 1}$

43. $\dfrac{x^2 - 6x + 5}{x^2 + 8x + 7} \cdot \dfrac{x^2 + 3x + 2}{x^2 - 3x - 10}$

44. $\dfrac{a^2 + 3a}{a^2 - 3a - 4} \div \dfrac{a^2 + 2a - 3}{a^2 - 5a + 4}$

45. $\dfrac{x^2 - 2x - 3}{x^2 + 3x + 2} \div \dfrac{x^2 - 4}{x^2 - 5x + 6}$

46. $\dfrac{2}{m + 3} \cdot \dfrac{m + 3}{m} \div \dfrac{4m^2}{m^2 + 3m}$

47. $\dfrac{x - 4}{9 - x^2} \div \dfrac{2x - 8}{x + 1} \cdot \dfrac{2x^2}{2x + 6}$

48. $\dfrac{4m^2 + 12m + 9}{2 - 6m} \cdot \dfrac{9m^2 - 1}{4m^2 - 9} \cdot \dfrac{4m - 6}{6m^2 + 11m + 3}$

 **F.** Calculator Problems. With your instructor's approval, use a calculator to evaluate the following rational expressions. Let $x = 2.615$, $y = 6.021$, and $z = -3.654$.

49. $\dfrac{3x^2 - 4x - 1}{2x^2 + x - 5}$

50. $\dfrac{3y^2 - 8}{7y^2 + 1}$

51. $\dfrac{z^2 - 4z + 3}{5z^2 + 2z - 7}$

52. $\dfrac{3x^2y + 2y^2z}{5xz^3 + 3yz^2}$

☐ **Solutions to Study Exercises** **(9A)**

### Study Exercise One (Frame 9)

**A.** 1. All real numbers except 7.
2. All real numbers.
3. All real numbers except 0.
4. All real numbers except 2 and −2.

**B.** 5. $\dfrac{3r}{7st} = \dfrac{3r \cdot (3st^3)}{7st \cdot (3st^3)} = \dfrac{9rst^3}{21s^2t^4}$

6. $\dfrac{3m}{7} = \dfrac{3m \cdot (m + n)}{7 \cdot (m + n)} = \dfrac{3m^2 + 3mn}{7m + 7n}$

7. $\dfrac{x - 4}{x + 3} = \dfrac{(x - 4) \cdot (x - 3)}{(x + 3) \cdot (x - 3)} = \dfrac{x^2 - 7x + 12}{x^2 - 9}$

8. $\dfrac{2m - 1}{m - 2} = \dfrac{(2m - 1) \cdot (3m - 1)}{(m - 2) \cdot (3m - 1)} = \dfrac{6m^2 - 5m + 1}{3m^2 - 7m + 2}$

### Study Exercise Two (Frame 15) **(15A)**

1. $\dfrac{2a + 2b}{2a - 2b} = \dfrac{\cancel{2} \cdot (a + b)}{\cancel{2} \cdot (a - b)} = \dfrac{a + b}{a - b}$

2. $\dfrac{ax + ay}{bx + by} = \dfrac{a \cdot \cancel{(x + y)}}{b \cdot \cancel{(x + y)}} = \dfrac{a}{b}$

3. $\dfrac{9a^2 - 4}{(3a - 2)^2} = \dfrac{(3a + 2) \cdot \cancel{(3a - 2)}}{(3a - 2) \cdot \cancel{(3a - 2)}} = \dfrac{3a + 2}{3a - 2}$

4. $\dfrac{m^2 - m - 20}{m^2 + 7m + 12} = \dfrac{(m - 5) \cdot \cancel{(m + 4)}}{\cancel{(m + 4)} \cdot (m + 3)} = \dfrac{m - 5}{m + 3}$

5. $\dfrac{6x^2 - 11x - 10}{9x^2 - 4} = \dfrac{\cancel{(3x + 2)} \cdot (2x - 5)}{\cancel{(3x + 2)} \cdot (3x - 2)} = \dfrac{2x - 5}{3x - 2}$

### Study Exercise Three (Frame 18) **(18A)**

1. Yes      2. Yes      3. No      4. Yes      5. No

### Study Exercise Four (Frame 22) **(22A)**

1. $\dfrac{3a - 3b}{4b - 4a} = \dfrac{3 \cdot \cancel{(a - b)}}{4 \cdot \cancel{(b - a)}} = \dfrac{3 \cdot (-1)}{4} = \dfrac{-3}{4}$

2. $\dfrac{3a - 3b}{4a - 4b} = \dfrac{3 \cdot \cancel{(a - b)}}{4 \cdot \cancel{(a - b)}} = \dfrac{3}{4}$

3. $\dfrac{2 - x}{x^2 - 4} = \dfrac{\cancel{(2 - x)}}{(x + 2) \cdot \cancel{(x - 2)}} = \dfrac{-1}{x + 2}$

4. $\dfrac{25 - 9m^2}{3m^2 + m - 10} = \dfrac{(5 + 3m) \cdot \cancel{(5 - 3m)}}{\cancel{(3m - 5)} \cdot (m + 2)} = \dfrac{(5 + 3m) \cdot (-1)}{m + 2} = \dfrac{-5 - 3m}{m + 2}$

### Study Exercise Five (Frame 25) **(25A)**

**A.** 1. $\dfrac{3}{4} \cdot \dfrac{5x^3}{7y^2} = \dfrac{(3)(5x^3)}{(4)(7y^2)} = \dfrac{15x^3}{28y^2}$

2. $\dfrac{3x}{y^2} \cdot \dfrac{4w^2}{7z} = \dfrac{(3x)(4w^2)}{(y^2)(7z)} = \dfrac{12xw^2}{7y^2z}$

## Solutions to Study Exercises, Contd.

3. $\dfrac{2x+3}{3x-1} \cdot \dfrac{2x-3}{2x+1} = \dfrac{(2x+3)(2x-3)}{(3x-1)(2x+1)}$, or $\dfrac{4x^2-9}{6x^2+x-1}$

B. 4. $\left(\dfrac{-2}{5}\right)^3 = \dfrac{(-2)^3}{5^3} = \dfrac{-8}{125}$

5. $\left(\dfrac{3a^2}{2b}\right)^4 = \dfrac{(3a^2)^4}{(2b)^4} = \dfrac{81a^8}{16b^4}$

6. $\left(\dfrac{3x+2}{x-1}\right)^2 = \dfrac{(3x+2)^2}{(x-1)^2}$, or $\dfrac{9x^2+12x+4}{x^2-2x+1}$

☐ ### *Study Exercise Six (Frame 32)* (32A)

1. $\dfrac{6m^3}{5n^2} \cdot \dfrac{7n}{12m^2} = \dfrac{\cancel{6} \cdot m \cdot \cancel{m^2}}{5 \cdot n \cdot \cancel{n}} \cdot \dfrac{7 \cdot \cancel{n}}{\cancel{6} \cdot 2 \cdot \cancel{m^2}} = \dfrac{7m}{10n}$

2. $\dfrac{5a+5b}{8a^2} \cdot \dfrac{4a}{3a+3b} = \dfrac{5 \cdot \cancel{(a+b)}}{2 \cdot \cancel{4} \cdot a \cdot \cancel{a}} \cdot \dfrac{\cancel{4} \cdot \cancel{a}}{3 \cdot \cancel{(a+b)}} = \dfrac{5}{6a}$

3. $\dfrac{m^2-9}{m^2+8m+15} \cdot \dfrac{m^2-25}{m^2-m-6} = \dfrac{\cancel{(m+3)} \cdot (m-3)}{\cancel{(m+5)} \cdot \cancel{(m+3)}} \cdot \dfrac{\cancel{(m+5)} \cdot (m-5)}{(m-3) \cdot (m+2)}$

$= \dfrac{m-5}{m+2}$

canceled opposites

4. $\dfrac{5a^2-10a}{a^2+4a+3} \cdot \dfrac{a+3}{20-10a} = \dfrac{\cancel{5} \cdot a \cdot (a-2)}{\cancel{(a+3)} \cdot (a+1)} \cdot \dfrac{\cancel{(a+3)}}{\cancel{5} \cdot 2 \cdot (2-a)}$

$= \dfrac{-a}{2(a+1)}$, or $\dfrac{-a}{2a+2}$

5. $\dfrac{3x^2+10x-8}{x^2-7x+10} \cdot \dfrac{x^2+x-6}{3x^2+x-2} = \dfrac{\cancel{(3x-2)} \cdot (x+4)}{(x-5) \cdot \cancel{(x-2)}} \cdot \dfrac{\cancel{(x-2)} \cdot (x+3)}{\cancel{(3x-2)} \cdot (x+1)}$

$= \dfrac{(x+4)(x+3)}{(x-5)(x+1)}$, or $\dfrac{x^2+7x+12}{x^2-4x-5}$

☐ ### *Study Exercise Seven (Frame 37)* (37A)

1. $\dfrac{3m-6}{5n^2} \div \dfrac{m-2}{10n} = \dfrac{3m-6}{5n^2} \cdot \dfrac{10n}{m-2}$

$= \dfrac{3 \cdot \cancel{(m-2)}}{\cancel{5} \cdot \cancel{n} \cdot n} \cdot \dfrac{\cancel{5} \cdot 2 \cdot \cancel{n}}{\cancel{(m-2)}}$

$= \dfrac{6}{n}$

2. $\dfrac{9x^2-1}{4x} \div (3x+1) = \dfrac{9x^2-1}{4x} \cdot \dfrac{1}{3x+1}$

$= \dfrac{\cancel{(3x+1)} \cdot (3x-1)}{4x} \cdot \dfrac{1}{\cancel{(3x+1)}}$

$= \dfrac{3x-1}{4x}$

3. $\dfrac{3m^2+m-2}{m^2+2m-8} \div \dfrac{3m^2+4m-4}{m^2+m-12} = \dfrac{3m^2+m-2}{m^2+2m-8} \cdot \dfrac{m^2+m-12}{3m^2+4m-4}$

$= \dfrac{\cancel{(3m-2)} \cdot (m+1)}{\cancel{(m+4)} \cdot (m-2)} \cdot \dfrac{\cancel{(m+4)} \cdot (m-3)}{\cancel{(3m-2)} \cdot (m+2)}$

$= \dfrac{(m+1)(m-3)}{(m-2)(m+2)}$ or $\dfrac{m^2-2m-3}{m^2-4}$

4. $\dfrac{9x^2-16}{3x^2+2x-8} \div \dfrac{3x^2-5x-12}{x^2-x-6} = \dfrac{9x^2-16}{3x^2+2x-8} \cdot \dfrac{x^2-x-6}{3x^2-5x-12}$

$= \dfrac{\cancel{(3x+4)} \cdot \cancel{(3x-4)}}{\cancel{(3x-4)} \cdot \cancel{(x+2)}} \cdot \dfrac{\cancel{(x-3)} \cdot \cancel{(x+2)}}{\cancel{(3x+4)} \cdot \cancel{(x-3)}}$

$= 1$

UNIT

19

# Rational Expressions—
# Addition, Subtraction, and
# Simplifying Complex Fractions

□ **Objectives** **(1)**

By the end of this unit you should be able to:

- find the lowest common denominator (LCD) of a group of rational expressions.
- combine rational expressions using addition and subtraction.
- recognize a complex fraction.
- simplify a complex fraction to lowest terms.

□ **Review of the Lowest Common Denominator (LCD)** **(2)**

The *lowest common denominator* (**LCD**) of a group of fractions is the smallest number which each denominator will divide into evenly.

**Example 1:** The LCD of $\frac{1}{6}$ and $\frac{1}{8}$ is 24.      **Example 2:** The LCD of $\frac{5}{4x}$ and $\frac{7}{2x^2}$ is $4x^2$.

□ **Review of Method Used to Find the Lowest Common Denominator** **(3)**

**Example 1:** Find the LCD of $\frac{3}{8a^2}$ and $\frac{5}{6a^3}$.

**Solution:**

*Step (1):* Write each denominator in prime factored exponential form.
$$8a^2 = 2^3 \cdot a^2$$
$$6a^3 = 2^1 \cdot 3^1 \cdot a^3$$

*Step (2):* Write each number which is used as a base, but write it only once. Neglect repetitions.
$$2 \cdot 3 \cdot a$$

*Step (3):* From Step (1), find the largest exponent used on each base.
$$\text{LCD} = 2^3 \cdot 3^1 \cdot a^3$$

*Step (4):* Evaluate the exponential expression.
$$\text{LCD} = 24a^3$$

□ **Example 2:** Find the LCD of $\frac{2}{6x-6}$ and $\frac{3}{4x-4}$. **(4)**

**Solution:**

*Step (1):* Write each denominator in prime factored exponential form.
$$6x - 6 = 2 \cdot 3 \cdot (x - 1)$$
$$4x - 4 = 2^2 \cdot (x - 1)$$

*Step (2):* Write each number which is used as a base, but write it only once. Neglect repetitions.
$$2 \cdot 3 \cdot (x - 1)$$

*Step (3):* From Step (1), find the largest exponent used on each base.
$$\text{LCD} = 2^2 \cdot 3 \cdot (x - 1)$$

*Step (4):* Evaluate the exponential expressions. Binomial factors, however, are usually left in factored form.
$$\text{LCD} = 12(x - 1)$$

□ **Example 3:** Find the LCD of $\frac{5}{x^2 + 2x + 1}$ and $\frac{7}{x^2 + 4x + 3}$. **(5)**

**Solution:**

*Step (1):* Write each denominator in prime factored exponential form.
$$x^2 + 2x + 1 = (x + 1)^2$$
$$x^2 + 4x + 3 = (x + 1) \cdot (x + 3)$$

*Step (2):* Write each number which is used as a base, but write it only once. Neglect repetitions.

$(x + 1) \cdot (x + 3)$

*Step (3):* From Step (1), find the largest exponent used on each base.

LCD $= (x + 1)^2(x + 3)$

*Step (4):* Evaluate the exponential expressions. Binomial factors, however, are usually left in factored form.

LCD $= (x + 1)^2(x + 3)$

☐ **Example 4:** Find the LCD of $\dfrac{m}{m^2 - 9}$ and $\dfrac{7}{15 - 5m}$. **(6)**

**Solution:**

*Step (1):* Write each denominator in prime factored exponential form.

$m^2 - 9 = (m + 3) \cdot (m - 3)$

$15 - 5m = 5 \cdot (3 - m)$

Notice that $(m - 3)$ and $(3 - m)$ are opposites.

*Step (2):* Write each number which is used as a base, but write it only once. Neglect repetitions.

$5 \cdot (m + 3) \cdot (m - 3)$

Notice that $(m - 3)$ and $(3 - m)$ are considered as repetitions and, therefore, only one is written down.

*Step (3):* From Step (1), find the largest exponent used on each base.

LCD $= 5(m + 3)(m - 3)$

*Step (4):* Evaluate the exponential expressions. Binomial factors, however, are usually left in factored form.

LCD $= 5(m + 3)(m - 3)$

☐                  *Study Exercise One* **(7)**

Find the LCD for each of the following groups of fractions. Assume that the denominators do not represent zero.

1. $\dfrac{7}{18a^2b}$ and $\dfrac{5}{12ab^2}$ 
         2. $\dfrac{5}{20m - 40}$ and $\dfrac{3}{24m - 48}$

3. $\dfrac{2x}{x^2 - 6x + 9}$ and $\dfrac{3x}{x^2 - x - 6}$ 
         4. $\dfrac{a}{4a^2 - 25}$ and $\dfrac{3a}{10 - 4a}$

5. $\dfrac{y}{y + 2}, \dfrac{y - 1}{y + 1}$ and $\dfrac{2y - 3}{y^2 + 3y + 2}$ 
         6. $\dfrac{a}{a + 3}$ and $\dfrac{4}{a - 2}$

☐ **Addition of Rational Expressions** **(8)**

*Step (1):* Write all denominators in factored form.

*Step (2):* Find the LCD and expand all fractions to that denominator.

*Step (3):* Combine the fractions by adding the numerators and placing this sum over the LCD.

*Step (4):* If possible, reduce the resulting fraction to lowest terms.

☐ **Example 1:** $\dfrac{2}{3x - 3} + \dfrac{1}{x - 1}$ **(9)**

**Solution:**

*Step (1):* Factor the denominators.

*line (a)* $\dfrac{2}{3x - 3} + \dfrac{1}{x - 1} = \dfrac{2}{3(x - 1)} + \dfrac{1}{(x - 1)}$

*Step (2):* Expand the fractions to the LCD of $3(x - 1)$.

*line (b)* $= \dfrac{2}{3(x - 1)} + \dfrac{3 \cdot 1}{3 \cdot (x - 1)}$

245

*Step (3):* Combine the fractions.

*line (c)*
$$= \frac{5}{3(x - 1)}$$

*Step (4):* The resulting fraction cannot be reduced. Therefore, the answer is:

$$\frac{5}{3(x - 1)}, \text{ or } \frac{5}{3x - 3}.$$

☐ **Example 2:** $\dfrac{3x}{x^2 + x - 6} + \dfrac{5}{x - 2}$ **(10)**

**Solution:**

*Step (1):* Factor the denominators.

*line (a)* $\dfrac{3x}{x^2 + x - 6} + \dfrac{5}{x - 2} = \dfrac{3x}{(x - 2)(x + 3)} + \dfrac{5}{(x - 2)}$

*Step (2):* Expand the fractions to the LCD of $(x - 2)(x + 3)$.

*line (b)*
$$= \frac{3x}{(x - 2)(x + 3)} + \frac{5(x + 3)}{(x - 2)(x + 3)}$$

*Step (3):* Combine the fractions.

*line (c)*
$$= \frac{3x + 5(x + 3)}{(x - 2)(x + 3)}$$

*line (d)*
$$= \frac{3x + 5x + 15}{(x - 2)(x + 3)}$$

*line (e)*
$$= \frac{8x + 15}{(x - 2)(x + 3)}$$

*Step (4):* The resulting fraction cannot be reduced. Therefore, the answer is:

$$\frac{8x + 15}{(x - 2)(x + 3)}, \text{ or } \frac{8x + 15}{x^2 + x - 6}.$$

☐ **Example 3:** $\dfrac{3}{2 - a} + \dfrac{a - 1}{a^2 - 4}$ **(11)**

**Solution:**

*Step (1):* Factor the denominators.

*line (a)* $\dfrac{3}{2 - a} + \dfrac{a - 1}{a^2 - 4} = \dfrac{3}{(2 - a)} + \dfrac{a - 1}{(a - 2)(a + 2)}$

*line (b)*
$$= \frac{-1 \cdot 3}{-1 \cdot (2 - a)} + \frac{a - 1}{(a - 2)(a + 2)}$$

*line (c)*
$$= \frac{-3}{a - 2} + \frac{a - 1}{(a - 2)(a + 2)}$$

*Step (2):* Expand the fractions to the LCD of $(a - 2)(a + 2)$.

*line (d)*
$$= \frac{-3(a + 2)}{(a - 2)(a + 2)} + \frac{a - 1}{(a - 2)(a + 2)}$$

*Step (3):* Combine the fractions.

*line (e)*
$$= \frac{-3(a + 2) + a - 1}{(a - 2)(a + 2)}$$

*line (f)*
$$= \frac{-3a - 6 + a - 1}{(a - 2)(a + 2)}$$

*line (g)*
$$= \frac{-2a - 7}{(a - 2)(a + 2)}$$

*Step (4):* The resulting fraction cannot be reduced. Therefore, the answer is:
$$\frac{-2a - 7}{(a - 2)(a + 2)}, \text{ or } \frac{-2a - 7}{a^2 - 4}.$$

☐ **Example 4:** $\dfrac{-8}{x^2 - 4} + \dfrac{x}{x + 2}$      **(12)**

**Solution:**

*Step (1):* Factor the denominators.

*line (a)*    $\dfrac{-8}{x^2 - 4} + \dfrac{x}{x + 2} = \dfrac{-8}{(x + 2)(x - 2)} + \dfrac{x}{(x + 2)}$

*Step (2):* Expand each fraction to the LCD of $(x + 2)(x - 2)$.

*line (b)*    $= \dfrac{-8}{(x + 2)(x - 2)} + \dfrac{x(x - 2)}{(x + 2)(x - 2)}$

*Step (3):* Combine the fractions.

*line (c)*    $= \dfrac{-8 + x(x - 2)}{(x + 2)(x - 2)}$

*line (d)*    $= \dfrac{-8 + x^2 - 2x}{(x + 2)(x - 2)}$

*Step (4):* Reduce the result to lowest terms.

*line (e)*    $= \dfrac{x^2 - 2x - 8}{(x + 2)(x - 2)}$

*line (f)*    $= \dfrac{\cancel{(x + 2)}(x - 4)}{\cancel{(x + 2)}(x - 2)}$

Therefore, the answer is $\dfrac{x - 4}{x - 2}$.

☐                       *Study Exercise Two*                      **(13)**

Add the following rational expressions. Assume that the denominators do not represent zero.

1.   $\dfrac{7}{18a^2 b} + \dfrac{5}{12ab^2}$          2.   $\dfrac{5}{2m - 2} + \dfrac{1}{m - 1}$

3.   $\dfrac{2m}{m^2 + 2m - 15} + \dfrac{3}{m + 5}$      4.   $\dfrac{2}{3 - x} + \dfrac{x - 2}{x^2 - 9}$

5.   $\dfrac{-18}{a^2 - 9} + \dfrac{a}{a + 3}$         6.   $\dfrac{x + 3}{2x^2 - x - 6} + \dfrac{2x + 1}{2x^2 + x - 3}$

☐ **Subtraction of Rational Expressions**                   **(14)**

*Step (1):* Write all denominators in factored form.
*Step (2):* Find the LCD and expand all fractions to that denominator.
*Step (3):* Combine the fractions by subtracting the numerators and placing this difference over the LCD.
*Step (4):* If possible, reduce the resulting fraction to lowest terms.

☐ **Example 1:** $\dfrac{7}{5a - 5} - \dfrac{2}{a - 1}$          **(15)**

**Solution:**

*Step (1):* Factor the denominators.

*line (a)*    $\dfrac{7}{5a - 5} - \dfrac{2}{a - 1} = \dfrac{7}{5(a - 1)} - \dfrac{2}{(a - 1)}$

*Step (2):* Expand the fractions to the LCD of $5(a-1)$.

line (b)
$$= \frac{7}{5(a-1)} - \frac{5 \cdot 2}{5(a-1)}$$

*Step (3):* Combine the fractions.

line (c)
$$= \frac{7-10}{5(a-1)}$$

line (d)
$$= \frac{-3}{5(a-1)}$$

*Step (4):* The resulting fraction cannot be reduced. Therefore, the answer is:

$$\frac{-3}{5(a-1)}, \text{ or } \frac{-3}{5a-5}.$$

□ **Example 2:** $\dfrac{2x^2}{x^2-9} - \dfrac{x-1}{x+3}$  (16)

**Solution:**

*Step (1):* Factor the denominators.

line (a) $\dfrac{2x^2}{x^2-9} - \dfrac{x-1}{x+3} = \dfrac{2x^2}{(x+3)(x-3)} - \dfrac{x-1}{(x+3)}$

*Step (2):* Expand the fractions to the LCD of $(x+3)(x-3)$.

line (b)
$$= \frac{2x^2}{(x+3)(x-3)} - \frac{(x-1)(x-3)}{(x+3)(x-3)}$$

*Step (3):* Combine the fractions.

line (c)
$$= \frac{2x^2 - [(x-1)(x-3)]}{(x+3)(x-3)}$$

line (d)
$$= \frac{2x^2 - [x^2 - 4x + 3]}{(x+3)(x-3)}$$

line (e)
$$= \frac{2x^2 - x^2 + 4x - 3}{(x+3)(x-3)}$$

line (f)
$$= \frac{x^2 + 4x - 3}{(x+3)(x-3)}$$

*Step (4):* The resulting fraction cannot be reduced. Therefore, the answer is:

$$\frac{x^2 + 4x - 3}{(x+3)(x-3)}, \text{ or } \frac{x^2 + 4x - 3}{x^2 - 9}.$$

□ **Example 3:** $\dfrac{3m-1}{2m^2 - 5m - 3} - \dfrac{m+1}{2m^2 + 5m + 2}$  (17)

**Solution:**

*Step (1):* Factor the denominators.

line (a) $\dfrac{3m-1}{2m^2 - 5m - 3} - \dfrac{m+1}{2m^2 + 5m + 2} = \dfrac{3m-1}{(2m+1)(m-3)} - \dfrac{m+1}{(2m+1)(m+2)}$

*Step (2):* Expand each fraction to the LCD of $(2m+1)(m-3)(m+2)$.

line (b)
$$= \frac{(3m-1)(m+2)}{(2m+1)(m-3)(m+2)} - \frac{(m+1)(m-3)}{(2m+1)(m+2)(m-3)}$$

*Step (3):* Combine the fractions.

line (c)
$$= \frac{(3m-1)(m+2) - [(m+1)(m-3)]}{(2m+1)(m-3)(m+2)}$$

line (d)
$$= \frac{3m^2 + 5m - 2 - [m^2 - 2m - 3]}{(2m+1)(m-3)(m+2)}$$

*line (e)*
$$= \frac{3m^2 + 5m - 2 - m^2 + 2m + 3}{(2m + 1)(m - 3)(m + 2)}$$

*line (f)*
$$= \frac{2m^2 + 7m + 1}{(2m + 1)(m - 3)(m + 2)}$$

*Step (4):* The resulting fraction cannot be reduced. Therefore, the answer is:

$$\frac{2m^2 + 7m + 1}{(2m + 1)(m - 3)(m + 2)}.$$

☐ **Study Exercise Three** **(18)**

Subtract the following rational expressions. Assume that the denominators do not represent zero.

1. $\dfrac{2}{10xy^2} - \dfrac{3}{5x^2y}$      2. $\dfrac{4}{3a - 12} - \dfrac{2}{a - 4}$

3. $\dfrac{3m}{m^2 - m - 6} - \dfrac{4}{m + 2}$      4. $\dfrac{2a + 1}{3a^2 + 5a + 2} - \dfrac{a - 3}{3a^2 - 4a - 4}$

☐ **Complex Fractions** **(19)**

A *complex fraction* is any fraction which contains at least one fraction in its numerator or denominator.

**Example 1:** $\dfrac{\frac{7}{2}}{3}$      **Example 2:** $\dfrac{m + \frac{2}{3}}{5}$      **Example 3:** $\dfrac{\frac{3}{a}}{\frac{1}{2a} - \frac{3}{a^2}}$

☐ **Simplifying Complex Fractions** **(20)**

To *simplify* a complex fraction means to write it as a common fraction reduced to lowest terms. This is accomplished by first finding the LCD of all denominators and multiplying the main numerator and denominator by the LCD.

**Example:** Simplify $\dfrac{\frac{2}{3}}{\frac{1}{5}}$.

**Solution:**

*Step (1):* Find the LCD of $\frac{2}{3}$ and $\frac{1}{5}$, which is 15.

*Step (2):* Multiply numerator and denominator by 15.

*line (a)*
$$\frac{\frac{2}{3}}{\frac{1}{5}} = \frac{\frac{2}{3} \cdot \frac{15}{1}}{\frac{1}{5} \cdot \frac{15}{1}}$$

*line (b)*
$$= \frac{\frac{2}{\cancel{3}} \cdot \frac{\cancel{3} \cdot 5}{1}}{\frac{1}{\cancel{5}} \cdot \frac{3 \cdot \cancel{5}}{1}}$$

*line (c)*
$$= \frac{10}{3}$$

*Step (3):* The resulting fraction cannot be reduced. Therefore, $\dfrac{\frac{2}{3}}{\frac{1}{5}} = \dfrac{10}{3}$.

☐ **More Examples**

## 21

**Example 1:** Simplify $\dfrac{a + \frac{2}{3}}{5}$.

**Solution:**

*Step (1):* The LCD of $\frac{2}{3}$ is 3.

*Step (2):* Multiply numerator and denominator by 3.

*line (a)* $\quad \dfrac{a + \frac{2}{3}}{5} = \dfrac{\left(a + \frac{2}{3}\right) \cdot \frac{3}{1}}{5 \cdot \frac{3}{1}}$

*line (b)* $\quad\quad = \dfrac{3a + \frac{2}{3} \cdot \frac{3}{1}}{5 \cdot \frac{3}{1}}$

*line (c)* $\quad\quad = \dfrac{3a + \frac{2}{\cancel{3}} \cdot \frac{\cancel{3}}{1}}{5 \cdot \frac{3}{1}}$

*line (d)* $\quad\quad = \dfrac{3a + 2}{15}$

*Step (3):* The resulting fraction cannot be reduced. Therefore, $\dfrac{a + \frac{2}{3}}{5} = \dfrac{3a + 2}{15}$.

☐

**Example 2:** Simplify $\dfrac{\frac{2}{m}}{\frac{1}{m} - \frac{1}{m^2}}$.

**Solution:**

*Step (1):* The LCD of $\frac{2}{m}$, $\frac{1}{m}$, and $\frac{1}{m^2}$ is $m^2$.

*Step (2):* Multiply numerator and denominator by $m^2$.

*line (a)* $\quad \dfrac{\frac{2}{m}}{\frac{1}{m} - \frac{1}{m^2}} = \dfrac{\frac{2}{m} \cdot \frac{m^2}{1}}{\left(\frac{1}{m} - \frac{1}{m^2}\right) \cdot \frac{m^2}{1}}$

*line (b)* $\quad\quad = \dfrac{\frac{2}{m} \cdot \frac{m^2}{1}}{\frac{1}{m} \cdot \frac{m^2}{1} - \frac{1}{m^2} \cdot \frac{m^2}{1}}$

*line (c)* $\quad\quad = \dfrac{\frac{2}{\cancel{m}} \cdot \frac{\cancel{m} \cdot m}{1}}{\frac{1}{\cancel{m}} \cdot \frac{\cancel{m} \cdot m}{1} - \frac{1}{\cancel{m^2}} \cdot \frac{\cancel{m^2}}{1}}$

*line (d)* $\quad\quad = \dfrac{2m}{m - 1}$

*Step (3):* The resulting fraction cannot be reduced. Therefore, $\dfrac{\frac{2}{m}}{\frac{1}{m} - \frac{1}{m^2}} = \dfrac{2m}{m - 1}$.

(23)

**Example 3:** Simplify $\dfrac{a - \frac{4}{a}}{1 + \frac{2}{a}}$.

**Solution:**

*Step (1):* The LCD of $\dfrac{4}{a}$ and $\dfrac{2}{a}$ is $a$.

*Step (2):* Multiply numerator and denominator by $a$.

line (a) $\quad \dfrac{a - \frac{4}{a}}{1 + \frac{2}{a}} = \dfrac{\left(a - \frac{4}{a}\right)\cdot\frac{a}{1}}{\left(1 + \frac{2}{a}\right)\cdot\frac{a}{1}}$

line (b) $\quad = \dfrac{a\cdot\frac{a}{1} - \frac{4}{a}\cdot\frac{a}{1}}{1\cdot\frac{a}{1} + \frac{2}{a}\cdot\frac{a}{1}}$

line (c) $\quad = \dfrac{a^2 - \frac{4}{a}\cdot\frac{a}{1}}{a + \frac{2}{a}\cdot\frac{a}{1}}$

line (d) $\quad = \dfrac{a^2 - 4}{a + 2}$

*Step (3):* Reduce the result to lowest terms.

$= \dfrac{(a + 2)(a - 2)}{(a + 2)}$

Therefore, $\dfrac{a - \frac{4}{a}}{1 + \frac{2}{a}} = a - 2$.

### Study Exercise Four (24)

Simplify the following complex fractions. Assume that the denominators do not represent zero.

1. $\dfrac{\frac{3}{4}}{\frac{5}{7}}$

2. $\dfrac{2m + \frac{1}{2}}{3}$

3. $\dfrac{a - \frac{1}{3}}{\frac{1}{a} - 3}$

4. $\dfrac{\frac{a}{2} + \frac{b}{3}}{\frac{a}{b} + 5}$

5. $\dfrac{\frac{3}{n}}{\frac{1}{2n} - \frac{2}{n^2}}$

### REVIEW EXERCISES

A. Find the LCD for each of the following groups of rational expressions.

1. $\dfrac{5}{12xy^2}$ and $\dfrac{8}{15x^2y}$

2. $\dfrac{7}{5a - 15}$ and $\dfrac{5}{3a - 9}$

3. $\dfrac{4m}{m^2 - 3m - 10}$ and $\dfrac{2m}{m^2 + 3m + 2}$

4. $\dfrac{3x}{x^2 + 6x + 9}$, $\dfrac{5x}{x^2 + 2x - 3}$ and $\dfrac{x}{x - 1}$

B. Combine the following by addition or subtraction.

5. $\dfrac{5}{3a^2b} + \dfrac{1}{6ab}$

6. $\dfrac{1}{6mn^2} - \dfrac{5}{3m^3n}$

## REVIEW EXERCISES, Contd.

7. $\dfrac{2}{a^2b} - \dfrac{3}{ab} + \dfrac{1}{ab^2}$

8. $\dfrac{7}{4x - 8} + \dfrac{1}{2x - 4}$

9. $\dfrac{2a}{2a^2 - 3a - 5} + \dfrac{3a}{2a^2 - a - 10}$

10. $\dfrac{5}{4 - x} + \dfrac{x - 3}{x^2 - 16}$

11. $\dfrac{m}{m + 2} - \dfrac{8}{m^2 - 4}$

12. $\dfrac{2x - 3}{3x^2 + 10x + 8} - \dfrac{x + 1}{3x^2 - 5x - 12}$

13. $\dfrac{2x - 3}{x^2 + 3x + 2} - \dfrac{x - 1}{x + 1} + \dfrac{x}{x + 2}$

C. Simplify the following complex fractions.

14. $\dfrac{\frac{3}{4}}{\frac{1}{2}}$

15. $\dfrac{\frac{2a}{b}}{\frac{c}{}}$

16. $\dfrac{3x + \frac{1}{3}}{5}$

17. $\dfrac{x + \frac{1}{2}}{\frac{1}{x} - 2}$

18. $\dfrac{a + \frac{a}{b}}{b + \frac{b}{a}}$

## Solutions to Review Exercises

A.  1.  $60x^2y^2$  2.  $15(a - 3)$  3.  $(m - 5)(m + 2)(m + 1)$  4.  $(x + 3)^2(x - 1)$

B.  5.  $\dfrac{5}{3a^2b} + \dfrac{1}{6ab} = \dfrac{5 \cdot 2}{(3a^2b) \cdot (2)} + \dfrac{1 \cdot a}{(6ab) \cdot (a)}$

$= \dfrac{10}{6a^2b} + \dfrac{a}{6a^2b}$

$= \dfrac{10 + a}{6a^2b}$

6.  $\dfrac{1}{6mn^2} - \dfrac{5}{3m^3n} = \dfrac{1 \cdot m^2}{(6mn^2)(m^2)} - \dfrac{5 \cdot (2n)}{(3m^3n)(2n)}$

$= \dfrac{m^2}{6m^3n^2} - \dfrac{10n}{6m^3n^2}$

$= \dfrac{m^2 - 10n}{6m^3n^2}$

7.  $\dfrac{2}{a^2b} - \dfrac{3}{ab} + \dfrac{1}{ab^2} = \dfrac{2 \cdot b}{a^2b \cdot b} - \dfrac{3 \cdot ab}{(ab)(ab)} + \dfrac{1 \cdot a}{ab^2 \cdot a}$

$= \dfrac{2b}{a^2b^2} - \dfrac{3ab}{a^2b^2} + \dfrac{a}{a^2b^2}$

$= \dfrac{2b - 3ab + a}{a^2b^2}$

8.  $\dfrac{7}{4x - 8} + \dfrac{1}{2x - 4} = \dfrac{7}{4(x - 2)} + \dfrac{1}{2(x - 2)}$

$= \dfrac{7}{4(x - 2)} + \dfrac{2 \cdot 1}{2 \cdot 2(x - 2)}$

$= \dfrac{7}{4(x - 2)} + \dfrac{2}{4(x - 2)}$

$= \dfrac{9}{4(x - 2)}, \text{ or } \dfrac{9}{4x - 8}$

9.  $\dfrac{2a}{2a^2 - 3a - 5} + \dfrac{3a}{2a^2 - a - 10} = \dfrac{2a}{(2a - 5)(a + 1)} + \dfrac{3a}{(2a - 5)(a + 2)}$

$= \dfrac{2a(a + 2)}{(2a - 5)(a + 1)(a + 2)} + \dfrac{3a(a + 1)}{(2a - 5)(a + 2)(a + 1)}$

$= \dfrac{2a(a + 2) + 3a(a + 1)}{(2a - 5)(a + 1)(a + 2)}$

$= \dfrac{2a^2 + 4a + 3a^2 + 3a}{(2a - 5)(a + 1)(a + 2)}$

$= \dfrac{5a^2 + 7a}{(2a - 5)(a + 1)(a + 2)}$

10.  $\dfrac{5}{4 - x} + \dfrac{x - 3}{x^2 - 16} = \dfrac{5}{4 - x} + \dfrac{x - 3}{(x + 4)(x - 4)}$

$= \dfrac{-1 \cdot 5}{-1 \cdot (4 - x)} + \dfrac{x - 3}{(x + 4)(x - 4)}$

$= \dfrac{-5}{x - 4} + \dfrac{x - 3}{(x + 4)(x - 4)}$

## Solutions to Review Exercises, Contd.

$$= \frac{-5(x+4)}{(x-4)(x+4)} + \frac{x-3}{(x+4)(x-4)}$$

$$= \frac{-5x-20+x-3}{(x-4)(x+4)}$$

$$= \frac{-4x-23}{(x-4)(x+4)} \text{ or } \frac{-4x-23}{x^2-16}$$

11. $\dfrac{m}{m+2} - \dfrac{8}{m^2-4} = \dfrac{m}{m+2} - \dfrac{8}{(m+2)(m-2)}$

$$= \frac{m(m-2)}{(m+2)(m-2)} - \frac{8}{(m+2)(m-2)}$$

$$= \frac{m(m-2)-8}{(m+2)(m-2)}$$

$$= \frac{m^2-2m-8}{(m+2)(m-2)}$$

$$= \frac{\cancel{(m+2)}(m-4)}{\cancel{(m+2)}(m-2)}$$

$$= \frac{m \quad 4}{m-2}$$

12. $\dfrac{2x-3}{3x^2+10x+8} - \dfrac{x+1}{3x^2-5x-12} = \dfrac{2x-3}{(3x+4)(x+2)} - \dfrac{x+1}{(3x+4)(x-3)}$

$$= \frac{(2x-3)(x-3)}{(3x+4)(x+2)(x-3)} - \frac{(x+1)(x+2)}{(3x+4)(x-3)(x+2)}$$

$$= \frac{(2x-3)(x-3) - [(x+1)(x+2)]}{(3x+4)(x+2)(x-3)}$$

$$= \frac{2x^2-9x+9 - [x^2+3x+2]}{(3x+4)(x+2)(x-3)}$$

$$= \frac{2x^2-9x+9 - x^2-3x-2}{(3x+4)(x+2)(x-3)}$$

$$= \frac{x^2-12x+7}{(3x+4)(x+2)(x-3)}$$

13. $\dfrac{2x-3}{x^2+3x+2} - \dfrac{x-1}{x+1} + \dfrac{x}{x+2} = \dfrac{2x-3}{(x+2)(x+1)} - \dfrac{x-1}{(x+1)} + \dfrac{x}{(x+2)}$

$$= \frac{2x-3}{(x+2)(x+1)} - \frac{(x-1)(x+2)}{(x+1)(x+2)} + \frac{x(x+1)}{(x+2)(x+1)}$$

$$= \frac{2x-3 - [(x-1)(x+2)] + x(x+1)}{(x+2)(x+1)}$$

$$= \frac{2x-3 - [x^2+x-2] + x^2+x}{(x+2)(x+1)}$$

$$= \frac{2x-3 - x^2-x+2+x^2+x}{(x+2)(x+1)}$$

$$= \frac{2x-1}{(x+2)(x+1)}, \text{ or } \frac{2x-1}{x^2+3x+2}$$

C. 14. $\dfrac{\dfrac{3}{4}}{\dfrac{1}{2}} = \dfrac{\dfrac{3}{4}\cdot\dfrac{4}{1}}{\dfrac{1}{2}\cdot\dfrac{4}{1}} = \dfrac{3}{2}$

15. $\dfrac{\dfrac{2a}{b}}{\dfrac{c}{b}} = \dfrac{\dfrac{2a}{\cancel{b}}\cdot\dfrac{\cancel{b}}{1}}{\dfrac{c}{b}\cdot\dfrac{b}{1}} = \dfrac{2a}{cb}$

16. $\dfrac{3x+\dfrac{1}{3}}{5} = \dfrac{\left(3x+\dfrac{1}{3}\right)\cdot\dfrac{3}{1}}{5 \cdot \dfrac{3}{1}} = \dfrac{9x+1}{15}$

17. $\dfrac{x+\dfrac{1}{2}}{\dfrac{1}{x}-2} = \dfrac{\left(x+\dfrac{1}{2}\right)\cdot\dfrac{2x}{1}}{\left(\dfrac{1}{x}-2\right)\cdot\dfrac{2x}{1}} = \dfrac{2x^2+x}{2-4x} \text{ or } \dfrac{x(2x+1)}{2(1-2x)}$

## Solutions to Review Exercises, Contd.

18. $\dfrac{a + \dfrac{a}{b}}{b + \dfrac{b}{a}} = \dfrac{\left(a + \dfrac{a}{b}\right)\cdot\dfrac{ab}{1}}{\left(b + \dfrac{b}{a}\right)\cdot\dfrac{ab}{1}} = \dfrac{a^2b + a^2}{ab^2 + b^2}, \text{ or } \dfrac{a^2(b + 1)}{b^2(a + 1)}$

## □ SUPPLEMENTARY PROBLEMS

A.  Combine the following by addition or subtraction.

1. $\dfrac{2}{9m} + \dfrac{3}{12m}$

2. $\dfrac{5}{2x} + \dfrac{1}{3x} - \dfrac{4}{3}$

3. $\dfrac{1}{x^2} + \dfrac{2}{xy} - \dfrac{1}{y^2}$

4. $\dfrac{2}{x^2y} - \dfrac{3}{2xy} - \dfrac{1}{3x^2}$

5. $\dfrac{3}{a^2b} + \dfrac{5}{b} - \dfrac{2}{a}$

6. $\dfrac{2}{a + 1} - \dfrac{3}{a^2 - 1} + \dfrac{6}{(a + 1)^2}$

7. $\dfrac{2}{3x + 3} - \dfrac{1}{x + 1}$

8. $\dfrac{1 - y}{2 - y} - \dfrac{2}{y + 2} + \dfrac{1}{y - 2}$

9. $\dfrac{a - b}{a^2 + ab - 2b^2} - \dfrac{a + b}{3a + 6b}$

10. $\dfrac{2x - 3}{x^2 + 3x + 2} - \dfrac{x - 1}{x + 1} + \dfrac{x}{x + 2}$

11. $\dfrac{7}{a^2 - 3a - 10} + \dfrac{5}{a^2 - a - 6}$

12. $\dfrac{3x + 4}{3x^2 + x - 4} - \dfrac{3x + 7}{3x^2 - 5x + 2}$

13. $\dfrac{1}{m^2 + 2m + 1} - \dfrac{1}{m^2 - 1}$

14. $\dfrac{2x + y}{x^2 + 4xy + 3y^2} - \dfrac{x - 2y}{x^2 + 2xy + y^2}$

15. $\dfrac{5x}{x + y} + \dfrac{7}{2x + 2y}$

16. $\dfrac{5x}{x^2 - x - 6} - \dfrac{7x - 2}{x^2 - 3x - 10}$

17. $\dfrac{2}{m + n} - \dfrac{1}{m - n} + \dfrac{m - 1}{m^2 - n^2}$

18. $\dfrac{a + 1}{a^2 - 9} + \dfrac{1}{3a + 2} + \dfrac{2a}{3a^2 + 11a + 6}$

19. $\dfrac{t}{t^2 - 9} + \dfrac{1}{t^2 + 4t - 21}$

20. $\dfrac{2}{x^2 - 5x + 6} + \dfrac{1}{x^2 - 4}$

21. $\dfrac{2a}{a^2 - 2a - 15} + \dfrac{3a}{a^2 + 2a - 3}$

22. $\dfrac{1}{x^2 - 4x + 4} - \dfrac{1}{x^2 - 4}$

23. $\dfrac{t + 7}{t^2 + 5t + 6} + \dfrac{t - 1}{t^2 + 3t + 2}$

24. $\dfrac{y + 3}{y^2 - y - 2} - \dfrac{y - 1}{y^2 + 2y + 1}$

25. $\dfrac{m - 3}{2m^2 - 3m - 2} + \dfrac{m - 2}{2m^2 - 5m - 3}$ .

26. $\dfrac{a + 1}{a^2 + a - 2} + \dfrac{a + 3}{a^2 - 4a + 3}$

27. $\dfrac{y}{y^2 - 9} - \dfrac{1}{y^2 + 4y - 21}$

28. $\dfrac{3}{x^2 - 9} + \dfrac{2}{x^2 - x - 6}$

29. $\dfrac{m - n}{m^2 + 4mn + 3n^2} + \dfrac{m + 3n}{m^2 + 2mn + n^2}$

30. $\dfrac{6t + 18}{8t^2 + 6t - 5} + \dfrac{2}{1 - 2t} + \dfrac{3}{4t + 5}$

31. $\dfrac{3}{y - 1} - \dfrac{y - 1}{y^2 + 2y + 1} - \dfrac{y + 1}{y^2 - 1}$

32. $\dfrac{5}{3 - 2x} + \dfrac{10x + 24}{6x^2 - 5x - 6} + \dfrac{4}{3x + 2}$

33. $\dfrac{\dfrac{2}{x} + \dfrac{1}{2x}}{\dfrac{2}{x}}$

34. $\dfrac{2 - \dfrac{1}{n}}{4 - \dfrac{1}{n^2}}$

35. $\dfrac{a - \dfrac{1}{a}}{a + \dfrac{1}{a}}$

## Supplementary Problems, Contd.

36. $\dfrac{m + \dfrac{m}{n}}{1 + \dfrac{1}{n}}$

37. $\dfrac{3 - \dfrac{r}{t}}{3 - \dfrac{t}{r}}$

38. $\dfrac{\dfrac{a - b}{b}}{\dfrac{1}{a} - \dfrac{1}{b}}$

39. $\dfrac{x + \dfrac{2}{x}}{\dfrac{x^2 + 2}{2}}$

40. $\dfrac{b - \dfrac{1}{b}}{\dfrac{1}{b} + 1}$

41. $\dfrac{m + \dfrac{1}{n}}{\dfrac{1}{m} + n}$

42. $\dfrac{a - \dfrac{1}{3}}{\dfrac{1}{a} - 3}$

43. $\dfrac{\dfrac{a}{2} + \dfrac{b}{3}}{\dfrac{a}{b} + 5}$

44. $\dfrac{3x + \dfrac{1}{3}}{\dfrac{1}{5}}$

45. $\dfrac{x + \dfrac{1}{2}}{\dfrac{1}{x} + 2}$

46. $\dfrac{\dfrac{a}{b} + 1}{\dfrac{a}{b} - 1}$

47. $\dfrac{\dfrac{1}{3} - \dfrac{1}{x}}{\dfrac{1}{3} + \dfrac{1}{x}}$

48. $\dfrac{\dfrac{2}{a} + \dfrac{3}{2a}}{5 + \dfrac{1}{a}}$

49. $\dfrac{\dfrac{1}{2} - \dfrac{a}{3b}}{\dfrac{2}{a} - \dfrac{4}{3b}}$

50. $\dfrac{\dfrac{1}{x} - \dfrac{1}{xy}}{\dfrac{1}{xy} - \dfrac{1}{y}}$

51. $\dfrac{m + 2}{1 - \dfrac{4}{m^2}}$

52. $\dfrac{2x - \dfrac{1}{3}}{3x + \dfrac{1}{6}}$

53. $\dfrac{x - 2 + \dfrac{3}{x - 6}}{x - 1 + \dfrac{6}{x - 6}}$

54. $\dfrac{\dfrac{4}{a^2 - b^2}}{\dfrac{1}{a - b}}$

55. $\dfrac{\dfrac{1}{x + 2}}{\dfrac{1}{x - 2}}$

56. $\dfrac{\dfrac{1}{a + 3}}{\dfrac{1}{2a + 1}}$

57. $\dfrac{\dfrac{4}{y^2 - 9}}{\dfrac{1}{y + 3} - \dfrac{1}{y - 3}}$

58. $2 + \dfrac{n}{1 - \dfrac{2}{n + 3}}$

59. $\dfrac{\dfrac{1}{a}}{1 + \dfrac{1}{1 + \dfrac{1}{a}}}$

60. $\dfrac{\dfrac{x - 1}{x + 1} + \dfrac{x + 1}{x - 1}}{\dfrac{x + 1}{x - 1} - \dfrac{x - 1}{x + 1}}$

## □ Solutions to Study Exercises

### *Study Exercise One (Frame 7)*

1. $18a^2b = 2 \cdot 3^2 \cdot a^2 \cdot b$
$12ab^2 = 2^2 \cdot 3 \cdot a \cdot b^2$
LCD $= 2^2 \cdot 3^2 \cdot a^2 \cdot b^2$, or $36a^2b^2$

2. $20m - 40 = 2^2 \cdot 5 \cdot (m - 2)$
$24m - 48 = 2^3 \cdot 3 \cdot (m - 2)$
LCD $= 2^3 \cdot 3 \cdot 5 \cdot (m - 2)$, or $120(m - 2)$

3. $x^2 - 6x + 9 = (x - 3)^2$
$x^2 - x - 6 = (x - 3)(x + 2)$
LCD $= (x - 3)^2(x + 2)$

4. $4a^2 - 25 = (2a + 5)(2a - 5)$
$10 - 4a = 2(5 - 2a)$
LCD $= 2 \cdot (2a + 5)(2a - 5)$
Remember, $5 - 2a$ and $2a - 5$ are opposites.

## Solutions to Study Exercises, Contd.

5.  $y + 2 = (y + 2)$
    $y + 1 = (y + 1)$
    $y^2 + 3y + 2 = (y + 2)(y + 1)$
    $\text{LCD} = (y + 2)(y + 1)$

6.  $a + 3 = (a + 3)$
    $a - 2 = (a - 2)$
    $\text{LCD} = (a + 3)(a - 2)$

□        *Study Exercise Two (Frame 13)*        **(13A)**

1.  $\dfrac{7}{18a^2b} + \dfrac{5}{12ab^2} = \dfrac{7 \cdot (2b)}{(18a^2b) \cdot (2b)} + \dfrac{5 \cdot (3a)}{(12ab^2) \cdot (3a)}$

    $\qquad = \dfrac{14b}{36a^2b^2} + \dfrac{15a}{36a^2b^2}$

    $\qquad = \dfrac{14b + 15a}{36a^2b^2}$

2.  $\dfrac{5}{2m - 2} + \dfrac{1}{m - 1} = \dfrac{5}{2(m - 1)} + \dfrac{1}{(m - 1)}$

    $\qquad = \dfrac{5}{2(m - 1)} + \dfrac{2 \cdot 1}{2(m - 1)}$

    $\qquad = \dfrac{7}{2(m - 1)}, \text{ or } \dfrac{7}{2m - 2}$

3.  $\dfrac{2m}{m^2 + 2m - 15} + \dfrac{3}{m + 5} = \dfrac{2m}{(m + 5)(m - 3)} + \dfrac{3}{(m + 5)}$

    $\qquad = \dfrac{2m}{(m + 5)(m - 3)} + \dfrac{3(m - 3)}{(m + 5)(m - 3)}$

    $\qquad = \dfrac{2m + 3(m - 3)}{(m + 5)(m - 3)}$

    $\qquad = \dfrac{2m + 3m - 9}{(m + 5)(m - 3)}$

    $\qquad = \dfrac{5m - 9}{(m + 5)(m - 3)}, \text{ or } \dfrac{5m - 9}{m^2 + 2m - 15}$

4.  $\dfrac{2}{3 - x} + \dfrac{x - 2}{x^2 - 9} = \dfrac{2}{(3 - x)} + \dfrac{x - 2}{(x + 3)(x - 3)}$

    $\qquad = \dfrac{-1 \cdot 2}{-1 \cdot (3 - x)} + \dfrac{x - 2}{(x + 3)(x - 3)}$

    $\qquad = \dfrac{-2}{x - 3} + \dfrac{x - 2}{(x + 3)(x - 3)}$

    $\qquad = \dfrac{-2(x + 3)}{(x - 3)(x + 3)} + \dfrac{x - 2}{(x + 3)(x - 3)}$

    $\qquad = \dfrac{-2(x + 3) + x - 2}{(x + 3)(x - 3)}$

    $\qquad = \dfrac{-2x - 6 + x - 2}{(x + 3)(x - 3)}$

    $\qquad = \dfrac{-x - 8}{(x + 3)(x - 3)}, \text{ or } \dfrac{-x - 8}{x^2 - 9}$

5.  $\dfrac{-18}{a^2 - 9} + \dfrac{a}{a + 3} = \dfrac{-18}{(a + 3)(a - 3)} + \dfrac{a}{(a + 3)}$

    $\qquad = \dfrac{-18}{(a + 3)(a - 3)} + \dfrac{a(a - 3)}{(a + 3)(a - 3)}$

    $\qquad = \dfrac{-18 + a(a - 3)}{(a + 3)(a - 3)}$

    $\qquad = \dfrac{-18 + a^2 - 3a}{(a + 3)(a - 3)}$

    $\qquad = \dfrac{a^2 - 3a - 18}{(a + 3)(a - 3)}$

    $\qquad = \dfrac{\cancel{(a + 3)}(a - 6)}{\cancel{(a + 3)}(a - 3)}$

    $\qquad = \dfrac{a - 6}{a - 3}$

6.  $\dfrac{x + 3}{2x^2 - x - 6} + \dfrac{2x + 1}{2x^2 + x - 3} = \dfrac{x + 3}{(2x + 3)(x - 2)} + \dfrac{2x + 1}{(2x + 3)(x - 1)}$

    $\qquad = \dfrac{(x + 3)(x - 1)}{(2x + 3)(x - 2)(x - 1)} + \dfrac{(2x + 1)(x - 2)}{(2x + 3)(x - 1)(x - 2)}$

    $\qquad = \dfrac{(x + 3)(x - 1) + (2x + 1)(x - 2)}{(2x + 3)(x - 2)(x - 1)}$

    $\qquad = \dfrac{x^2 + 2x - 3 + 2x^2 - 3x - 2}{(2x + 3)(x - 2)(x - 1)}$

    $\qquad = \dfrac{3x^2 - x - 5}{(2x + 3)(x - 2)(x - 1)}$

## Solutions to Study Exercises, Contd.

☐            *Study Exercise Three (Frame 18)*       **(18A)**

1. $\dfrac{2}{10xy^2} - \dfrac{3}{5x^2y} = \dfrac{2 \cdot (x)}{(10xy^2) \cdot (x)} - \dfrac{3 \cdot (2y)}{(5x^2y) \cdot (2y)}$

$\qquad = \dfrac{2x}{10x^2y^2} - \dfrac{6y}{10x^2y^2}$

$\qquad = \dfrac{2x - 6y}{10x^2y^2}$

$\qquad = \dfrac{\cancel{2}(x - 3y)}{\cancel{2} \cdot 5x^2y^2}$

$\qquad = \dfrac{x - 3y}{5x^2y^2}$

2. $\dfrac{4}{3a - 12} - \dfrac{2}{a - 4} = \dfrac{4}{3(a - 4)} - \dfrac{2}{(a - 4)}$

$\qquad = \dfrac{4}{3(a - 4)} - \dfrac{3 \cdot 2}{3(a - 4)}$

$\qquad = \dfrac{4 - 3 \cdot 2}{3(a - 4)}$

$\qquad = \dfrac{-2}{3(a - 4)}, \text{ or } \dfrac{-2}{3a - 12}$

3. $\dfrac{3m}{m^2 - m - 6} - \dfrac{4}{m + 2} = \dfrac{3m}{(m + 2)(m - 3)} - \dfrac{4}{(m + 2)}$

$\qquad = \dfrac{3m}{(m + 2)(m - 3)} - \dfrac{4(m - 3)}{(m + 2)(m - 3)}$

$\qquad = \dfrac{3m - [4(m - 3)]}{(m + 2)(m - 3)}$

$\qquad = \dfrac{3m - [4m - 12]}{(m + 2)(m - 3)}$

$\qquad = \dfrac{3m - 4m + 12}{(m + 2)(m - 3)}$

$\qquad = \dfrac{-m + 12}{(m + 2)(m - 3)}, \text{ or } \dfrac{12 - m}{m^2 - m - 6}$

4. $\dfrac{2a + 1}{3a^2 + 5a + 2} - \dfrac{a - 3}{3a^2 - 4a - 4} = \dfrac{2a + 1}{(3a + 2)(a + 1)} - \dfrac{a - 3}{(3a + 2)(a - 2)}$

$\qquad = \dfrac{(2a + 1)(a - 2)}{(3a + 2)(a + 1)(a - 2)} - \dfrac{(a - 3)(a + 1)}{(3a + 2)(a - 2)(a + 1)}$

$\qquad = \dfrac{(2a + 1)(a - 2) - [(a - 3)(a + 1)]}{(3a + 2)(a + 1)(a - 2)}$

$\qquad = \dfrac{2a^2 - 3a - 2 - [a^2 - 2a - 3]}{(3a + 2)(a + 1)(a - 2)}$

$\qquad = \dfrac{2a^2 - 3a - 2 - a^2 + 2a + 3}{(3a + 2)(a + 1)(a - 2)}$

$\qquad = \dfrac{a^2 - a + 1}{(3a + 2)(a + 1)(a - 2)}$

☐            *Study Exercise Four (Frame 24)*       **(24A)**

1. $\dfrac{\frac{3}{4}}{\frac{5}{7}} = \dfrac{\frac{3}{4} \cdot \frac{28}{1}}{\frac{5}{7} \cdot \frac{28}{1}} = \dfrac{\frac{3}{\cancel{4}} \cdot \frac{7 \cdot \cancel{4}}{1}}{\frac{5}{\cancel{7}} \cdot \frac{\cancel{7} \cdot 4}{1}} = \dfrac{21}{20}$

2. $\dfrac{2m + \frac{1}{2}}{3} = \dfrac{\left(2m + \frac{1}{2}\right) \cdot \frac{2}{1}}{3 \cdot \frac{2}{1}} = \dfrac{2m \cdot \frac{2}{1} + \frac{1}{2} \cdot \frac{\cancel{2}}{1}}{6} = \dfrac{4m + 1}{6}$

3. $\dfrac{a - \frac{1}{3}}{\frac{1}{a} - 3} = \dfrac{\left(a - \frac{1}{3}\right) \cdot \frac{3a}{1}}{\left(\frac{1}{a} - 3\right) \cdot \frac{3a}{1}} = \dfrac{a \cdot \frac{3a}{1} - \frac{1}{\cancel{3}} \cdot \frac{\cancel{3}a}{1}}{\frac{1}{\cancel{a}} \cdot \frac{3\cancel{a}}{1} - 3 \cdot \frac{3a}{1}}$

$\qquad = \dfrac{3a^2 - a}{3 - 9a}$

$\qquad = \dfrac{a(3a - 1)}{3(1 - 3a)} \left.\rule{0pt}{16pt}\right\}$ canceled opposites

$\qquad = \dfrac{-a}{3}$

## Solutions to Study Exercises, Contd.

4.
$$\frac{\dfrac{a}{2}+\dfrac{b}{3}}{\dfrac{a}{b}+5}=\frac{\left(\dfrac{a}{2}+\dfrac{b}{3}\right)\cdot\dfrac{6b}{1}}{\left(\dfrac{a}{b}+5\right)\cdot\dfrac{6b}{1}}$$

$$=\frac{\dfrac{a}{\cancel{2}}\cdot\dfrac{\cancel{6}b}{1}+\dfrac{b}{\cancel{3}}\cdot\dfrac{\cancel{6}b}{1}}{\dfrac{a}{\cancel{b}}\cdot\dfrac{6\cancel{b}}{1}+5\cdot\dfrac{6b}{1}}$$

$$=\frac{3ab+2b^2}{6a+30b},\text{ or }\frac{b(3a+2b)}{6(a+5b)}$$

5.
$$\frac{\dfrac{3}{n}}{\dfrac{1}{2n}-\dfrac{2}{n^2}}=\frac{\dfrac{3}{n}\cdot 2n^2}{\left(\dfrac{1}{2n}-\dfrac{2}{n^2}\right)\cdot 2n^2}$$

$$=\frac{\dfrac{3}{n}\cdot 2n^2}{\dfrac{1}{2n}\cdot 2n^2-\dfrac{2}{n^2}\cdot 2n^2}$$

$$=\frac{\dfrac{3}{\cancel{n}}\cdot 2n\cdot\cancel{n}}{\dfrac{1}{\cancel{2}\cancel{n}}\cdot\cancel{2}\cdot\cancel{n}\cdot n-\dfrac{2}{\cancel{n^2}}\cdot 2\cancel{n^2}}$$

$$=\frac{6n}{n-4}$$

# Solving Equations — Fractional and Absolute Value

## ☐ Objectives                                                        (1)

By the end of this unit you should be able to:

- classify equations as first degree, quadratic, fractional, or absolute value.
- solve fractional equations and absolute value equations.
- recognize extraneous solutions for fractional equations.
- solve equations for a specified symbol.
- use fractional equations to solve word problems.

## ☐ Types of Equations                                                 (2)

1.  A *first degree* or *linear equation* in one unknown is any equation which can be made to fit this pattern:

$$ax + b = c \quad \text{where } a, b, \text{ and } c \text{ are constants}$$

The variable has a highest exponent of 1.

**Example:** $3x + 5 = 17$ is a first degree equation.

2.  A *quadratic equation* in one unknown is any equation which can be made to fit this pattern:

$$ax^2 + bx + c = 0 \quad \text{where } a, b, \text{ and } c \text{ are constants} \quad \text{and} \quad a \neq 0$$

The variable has a highest exponent of 2.

**Example:** $3x^2 - 14x - 5 = 0$ is a quadratic equation.

3.  A *fractional equation* in one unknown is any equation which contains a fraction.

**Example:** $\dfrac{x}{2} + 7 = \dfrac{5x}{3}$

4.  An *absolute value equation* in one unknown is any equation where a variable or a variable expression is contained within absolute value symbols.

**Example:** $|2x - 3| = 5$

## ☐ Review of Solving First Degree Equations                                (3)

**Example:** Solve $3(2x - 1) + 2x = 4(x - 3)$.

  **Solution:**

    *Step (1):*   Multiply and combine like terms.
      *line (a)*   $3(2x - 1) + 2x = 4(x - 3)$
      *line (b)*   $6x - 3 + 2x = 4x - 12$
      *line (c)*   $8x - 3 = 4x - 12$

    *Step (2):*   Obtain a form where the terms containing a variable are on one side and the numbers are on the other side.
      *line (d)*   $8x - 3 = 4x - 12$
      *line (e)*   $8x - 4x = -12 + 3$
      *line (f)*   $4x = -9$

    *Step (3):*   Use the division property to obtain an equation of the form $x = a$.
      *line (g)*   $4x = -9$
      *line (h)*   $x = \dfrac{-9}{4}$

The solution is $-\dfrac{9}{4}$.

*Remember*, a solution may be checked by replacing it for the variable in the original equation.

☐ **Review of Solving Quadratic Equations by Factoring** **(4)**

**Example:** Solve $2x^2 - x = 6$.

**Solution:**

*Step (1):* Place the equation in the form $ax^2 + bx + c = 0$ by obtaining all terms on one side.
line (a) $2x^2 - x = 6$
line (b) $2x^2 - x - 6 = 0$

*Step (2):* Factor the left side.
line (c) $(2x + 3)(x - 2) = 0$

*Step (3):* Set each factor containing a variable equal to zero.
line (d) $2x + 3 = 0$, or $x - 2 = 0$

*Step (4):* Solve the resulting first degree equations.
line (e) $2x + 3 = 0$, $2x = -3$, $x = -\dfrac{3}{2}$

line (f) $x - 2 = 0$, $x = 2$

The solutions are $-\dfrac{3}{2}$ and 2.

*Remember*, the solutions may be checked by replacing them, one at a time, for the variable in the original equation.

☐ *Study Exercise One* **(5)**

Solve the following equations.

1. $5x + 3 = 18$
2. $x^2 + x = 12$
3. $2m^2 - 3m = 0$
4. $2(3x - 1) = 5x - (x + 2)$
5. $3x^2 + 5x = 12$

☐ **Solving Fractional Equations** **(6)**

To solve a fractional equation:

*Step (1):* Find the lowest common denominator (LCD).
*Step (2):* Multiply both sides of the equation by the LCD.
*Step (3):* Classify the resulting equation as first degree or quadratic and solve accordingly.

☐ **Example 1:** Solve $\dfrac{x}{6} = \dfrac{3}{4}$. **(7)**

**Solution:**

*Step (1):* The LCD of $\dfrac{x}{6}$ and $\dfrac{3}{4}$ is 12.

*Step (2):* Multiply both sides of the equation by the LCD.
line (a) $\dfrac{x}{6} = \dfrac{3}{4}$

line (b) $12 \cdot \dfrac{x}{6} = 12 \cdot \dfrac{3}{4}$

line (c) $2x = 9$

*Step (3):* Classify the resulting equation and solve accordingly.
line (d) $2x = 9$ is first degree.

line (e) $x = \dfrac{9}{2}$

The solution is $\dfrac{9}{2}$.

□ **Checking the Solution** (8)

The solution may be checked by substituting it for the variable in the original equation.

Original equation: $\dfrac{x}{6} = \dfrac{3}{4}$

*line (a)* $\quad \dfrac{\frac{9}{2}}{6} = \dfrac{3}{4}$

*line (b)* $\quad \dfrac{\frac{9 \cdot \cancel{2}}{\cancel{2} \cdot 1}}{6 \cdot \frac{\cancel{2}}{1}} = \dfrac{3}{4}$

*line (c)* $\quad \dfrac{9}{12} = \dfrac{3}{4} \qquad$ (True)

□ **Example 2:** Solve $\dfrac{5x}{3} = \dfrac{x}{2} - 7$. (9)

**Solution:**

*Step (1):* The LCD of $\dfrac{5x}{3}$ and $\dfrac{x}{2}$ is 6.

*Step (2):* Multiply both sides of the equation by the LCD.

*line (a)* $\quad \dfrac{5x}{3} = \dfrac{x}{2} - 7$

*line (b)* $\quad 6 \cdot \dfrac{5x}{3} = 6 \cdot \left( \dfrac{x}{2} - 7 \right)$

*line (c)* $\quad 6 \cdot \dfrac{5x}{3} = 6 \cdot \dfrac{x}{2} - 6 \cdot 7$

*line (d)* $\quad 10x \ = \ 3x \ - \ 42$

*Step (3):* Classify the resulting equation and solve accordingly.
*line (e)* $\quad 10x = 3x - 42$ is first degree.
*line (f)* $\quad 10x - 3x = -42$
*line (g)* $\quad 7x = -42$
*line (h)* $\quad x = -6$.

The solution is $-6$. You should check this solution.

□ **Example 3:** Solve $m - 7 = \dfrac{21}{m-3}$. (10)

**Solution:**

*Step (1):* The LCD is $m - 3$.

*Step (2):* Multiply both sides of the equation by the LCD.

*line (a)* $\quad m - 7 = \dfrac{21}{m-3}$

*line (b)* $\quad (m-3) \cdot (m-7) = (m-3) \cdot \dfrac{21}{m-3}$

*line (c)* $\quad (m-3) \cdot (m-7) = \qquad 21$
*line (d)* $\quad m^2 - 10m + 21 = 21$

*Step (3):* Classify the resulting equation and solve accordingly.
*line (e)* $m^2 - 10m + 21 = 21$ is quadratic.
*line (f)* $m^2 - 10m = 0$
*line (g)* $m(m - 10) = 0$
*line (h)* $m = 0$, or $m - 10 = 0$
*line (i)* $m = 0$, or $m = 10$

The solutions are 0 and 10. You should check them both.

□                          *Study Exercise Two*                           **(11)**

Solve the following fractional equations and check the solutions.

1. $\dfrac{x}{10} = \dfrac{5}{6}$      2. $\dfrac{4m}{5} = \dfrac{m}{2} - 3$      3. $\dfrac{25}{3x} + \dfrac{1}{3} = \dfrac{10}{x}$      4. $m + 5 = \dfrac{15}{m + 3}$

□ **Extraneous Solutions**                                                               **(12)**

A solution which fails to check in the original equation is said to be an *extraneous solution*. Whenever both sides of a fractional equation are multiplied by an LCD which contains a variable, there is danger of producing an extraneous solution.

□ **Example 1:**   Solve $\dfrac{2}{m - 2} + \dfrac{3}{m} = \dfrac{4}{m^2 - 2m}$.                             **(13)**

**Solution:**

*Step (1):* Factor the denominators and find the LCD.
*line (a)*   $\dfrac{2}{(m - 2)} + \dfrac{3}{m} = \dfrac{4}{m(m - 2)}$
*line (b)*   The LCD is $m(m - 2)$.

*Step (2):* Multiply both sides of the equation by the LCD.
*line (c)*   $m(m - 2) \cdot \left[ \dfrac{2}{(m - 2)} + \dfrac{3}{m} \right] = m(m - 2) \cdot \dfrac{4}{m(m - 2)}$
*line (d)*   $\dfrac{m(m - 2) \cdot 2}{(m - 2)} + \dfrac{m(m - 2) \cdot 3}{m} = \dfrac{m(m - 2) \cdot 4}{m(m - 2)}$
*line (e)*   $\dfrac{m(m-2) \cdot 2}{(m-2)} + \dfrac{m(m - 2) \cdot 3}{m} = \dfrac{m(m-2) \cdot 4}{m(m-2)}$
*line (f)*     $2m \quad + \quad (m - 2) \cdot 3 \quad = \quad 4$

*Step (3):* Classify the resulting equation and solve accordingly.
*line (g)*   $2m + (m - 2) \cdot 3 = 4$ is first degree.
*line (h)*   $2m + 3m - 6 = 4$
*line (i)*   $5m = 10$
*line (j)*   $m = 2$

*Step (4):* The LCD contained a variable; therefore, we must check the solution.
*line (k)*   $\dfrac{2}{m - 2} + \dfrac{3}{m} = \dfrac{4}{m^2 - 2m}$     (Original equation)
*line (l)*   $\dfrac{2}{2 - 2} + \dfrac{3}{2} = \dfrac{4}{2^2 - 2 \cdot 2}$
*line (m)*   $\dfrac{2}{0} + \dfrac{3}{2} = \dfrac{4}{0}$

Since division by zero is not possible, 2 is an extraneous solution. Therefore, the original equation has no solutions.

□ **Example 2:** Solve $\dfrac{3x}{4x^2 - 9} = \dfrac{3}{2x - 3}$. **(14)**

**Solution:**

*Step (1):* Factor the denominators and find the LCD.

line (a) $\dfrac{3x}{(2x + 3)(2x - 3)} = \dfrac{3}{(2x - 3)}$

line (b) The LCD is $(2x + 3)(2x - 3)$.

*Step (2):* Multiply both sides of the equation by the LCD.

line (c) $(2x + 3)(2x - 3) \cdot \dfrac{3x}{(2x + 3)(2x - 3)} = (2x + 3)(2x - 3) \cdot \dfrac{3}{(2x - 3)}$

line (d) $\cancel{(2x + 3)}\cancel{(2x - 3)} \cdot \dfrac{3x}{\cancel{(2x + 3)}\cancel{(2x - 3)}} = (2x + 3)\cancel{(2x - 3)} \cdot \dfrac{3}{\cancel{(2x - 3)}}$

line (e) $3x = (2x + 3) \cdot 3$

*Step (3):* Classify the resulting equation and solve accordingly.

line (f) $3x = (2x + 3) \cdot 3$ is first degree.

line (g) $3x = 6x + 9$

line (h) $-3x = 9$

line (i) $x = -3$

*Step (4):* The LCD contained a variable; therefore, we must check the solution.

line (j) $\dfrac{3x}{4x^2 - 9} = \dfrac{3}{2x - 3}$ (Original equation)

line (k) $\dfrac{3(-3)}{4(-3)^2 - 9} = \dfrac{3}{2(-3) - 3}$

line (l) $\dfrac{-9}{27} = \dfrac{3}{-9}$

line (m) $\dfrac{-1}{3} = \dfrac{1}{-3}$ (True)

The solution checks. No extraneous solutions were introduced. The solution is $-3$.

□ **Example 3:** Solve $\dfrac{2n}{n + 2} - \dfrac{n - 1}{n + 3} = \dfrac{7n + 17}{n^2 + 5n + 6}$. **(15)**

**Solution:**

*Step (1):* Factor the denominators and find the LCD.

line (a) $\dfrac{2n}{(n + 2)} - \dfrac{n - 1}{(n + 3)} = \dfrac{7n + 17}{(n + 2)(n + 3)}$

line (b) The LCD is $(n + 2)(n + 3)$.

*Step (2):* Multiply both sides of the equation by the LCD.

line (c) $(n + 2)(n + 3) \cdot \left[\dfrac{2n}{n + 2} - \dfrac{n - 1}{n + 3}\right] = (n + 2)(n + 3) \cdot \dfrac{7n + 17}{(n + 2)(n + 3)}$

line (d) $(n + 3) \cdot 2n - (n + 2)(n - 1) = 7n + 17$

line (e) $2n^2 + 6n - [n^2 + n - 2] = 7n + 17$

line (f) $2n^2 + 6n - n^2 - n + 2 = 7n + 17$

line (g) $n^2 + 5n + 2 = 7n + 17$

*Step (3):* Classify the resulting equation and solve accordingly.

line (h) $n^2 + 5n + 2 = 7n + 17$ is quadratic.

line (i) $n^2 - 2n - 15 = 0$

line (j) $(n - 5)(n + 3) = 0$

line (k) $n = 5$ or $n = -3$

*Step (4):* The LCD contained a variable; therefore, we must check the solution.

*line (l)* $\dfrac{2n}{n+2} - \dfrac{n-1}{n+3} = \dfrac{7n+17}{n^2+5n+6}$   (Original equation)

Notice that $-3$ will make the last two denominators zero. Since division by zero is not possible, $-3$ is an extraneous solution. The only solution to the original equation is 5.

☐ **Study Exercise Three** **(16)**

Solve the following fractional equations. Indicate any extraneous solutions.

1. $\dfrac{3}{x-3} - \dfrac{5}{x} = \dfrac{9}{x^2-3x}$   2. $\dfrac{2}{m+3} = \dfrac{5m}{m^2+4m+3}$   3. $\dfrac{x+2}{x-2} - \dfrac{3x}{x-1} = \dfrac{6x-8}{x^2-3x+2}$

☐ **Solving Absolute Value Equations** **(17)**

$$|x| = 3$$

$+3$  or  $-3$

If $|x| = 3$, then $x = 3$, or $x = -3$.

☐ In general: **(18)**

If $|x| = a$, where $a \geq 0$, then $x = a$, or $x = -a$.

☐ **Example 1:** Solve $|y + 4| = 7$. **(19)**

**Solution:**

*line (a)* If $|y + 4| = 7$, then $y + 4 = 7$, or $y + 4 = -7$.
*line (b)* Solve the two first degree equations.
*line (c)* $y = 3$, or $y = -11$.

The solutions are 3 and $-11$.

☐ **Checking the Solution** **(20)**

Solutions to absolute value equations may be checked by substituting them *one at a time* for the variable in the original equation.

Original equation: $|y + 4| = 7$. Solutions are 3 and $-11$.

**Check 1:** $|3 + 4| = 7$      **Check 2:** $|-11 + 4| = 7$
$|7| = 7$             $|-7| = 7$
$7 = 7$  [True]       $7 = 7$  [True]

☐ **Example 2:** Solve $|3x - 7| = 2$. **(21)**

**Solution:**

*line (a)* If $|3x - 7| = 2$, then $3x - 7 = 2$, or $3x - 7 = -2$.
*line (b)* Solve the two first degree equations.
*line (c)* $x = 3$, or $x = \dfrac{5}{3}$.

The solutions are 3 and $\dfrac{5}{3}$.

☐ **Example 3:** Solve $|3x - 7| = -8$. **(22)**

**Solution:**

*line (a)* Absolute value can never represent a negative number. **The equation has no solutions.**

□

Solve the following absolute value equations:

1. $|x| = 5$        2. $|y + 9| = 20$        3. $|4m - 7| = 13$        4. $|3x + 1| = -9$

## □ Solving Equations for a Specified Symbol       **(24)**

Equations having more than one variable or having constants represented by letters may be solved for a specified symbol.

□ **Example 1:** Given $d = rt$, solve for $r$.       **(25)**

**Solution:**

line (a)   $d = rt$

line (b)   $\dfrac{d}{t} = \dfrac{rt}{t}$

line (c)   $\dfrac{d}{t} = r$, or $r = \dfrac{d}{t}$, where $t \neq 0$.

□ **Example 2:** Given $b = \dfrac{1}{a}$, solve for $a$.       **(26)**

**Solution:**

line (a)   $b = \dfrac{1}{a}$

line (b)   The LCD is $a$.

line (c)   $a \cdot b = a \cdot \dfrac{1}{a}$

line (d)   $a \cdot b = 1$

line (e)   $\dfrac{a \cdot b}{b} = \dfrac{1}{b}$

line (f)   $a = \dfrac{1}{b}$ where $b \neq 0$.

□ **Example 3:** Given $ac + bc = ab$, solve for $a$.       **(27)**

**Solution:**

line (a)   $ac + bc = ab$

line (b)   $ac - ab = -bc$

line (c)   $a(c - b) = -bc$

line (d)   $\dfrac{a(c - b)}{c - b} = \dfrac{-bc}{c - b}$

line (e)   $a = \dfrac{-bc}{c - b}$, or $a = \dfrac{bc}{b - c}$, where $c - b \neq 0$.

□ **Example 4:** Given $\dfrac{1}{p} + \dfrac{1}{q} = \dfrac{1}{f}$, solve for $f$.       **(28)**

**Solution:**

line (a)   $\dfrac{1}{p} + \dfrac{1}{q} = \dfrac{1}{f}$

line (b)   The LCD is $pqf$.

line (c)   $pqf \cdot \left[ \dfrac{1}{p} + \dfrac{1}{q} \right] = pqf \cdot \dfrac{1}{f}$

line (d) $\quad pqf \cdot \dfrac{1}{p} + pqf \cdot \dfrac{1}{q} = pqf \cdot \dfrac{1}{f}$

$\qquad\qquad \downarrow \qquad\quad \downarrow \qquad\quad \downarrow$

line (e) $\qquad qf \ + \ pf \ = \ pq$

line (f) $\quad f(q + p) = pq$

line (g) $\quad \dfrac{f(q + p)}{q + p} = \dfrac{pq}{q + p}$

line (h) $\quad f = \dfrac{pq}{q + p}$ where $q + p \neq 0$.

### Study Exercise Five (29)

Solve the following equations for the specified symbol.

1. $f = ma$, for $a$.
2. $a = \dfrac{b}{x}$, for $x$.
3. $xy + k = xw$, for $x$.
4. $\dfrac{1}{a} + \dfrac{1}{b} = \dfrac{1}{c}$, for $a$.

## Solving Word Problems Using Fractional Equations (30)

*Step (1):* Let some letter represent one of the unknowns.

*Step (2):* Describe the other unknowns with variable expressions using the same letter.

*Step (3):* Form an equation using the information given in the problem.

*Step (4):* Solve the equation.

*Step (5):* Interpret the solution in terms of the original problem.

(31)

**Example 1:** The difference between two numbers is 3. If five times the smaller number is divided by the larger, the quotient is 4. Find the numbers.

**Solution:**

*Step (1):* Let $x$ represent the smaller number.

*Step (2):* $x + 3$ represents the larger number and $5x$ represents five times the smaller number.

*Step (3):* The quotient is 4.

$$\frac{5x}{x + 3} = 4$$

*Step (4):* Solve the equation.

line (a) $\quad \dfrac{5x}{x + 3} = 4$

line (b) $\quad (x + 3) \cdot \dfrac{5x}{(x + 3)} = (x + 3) \cdot 4$

line (c) $\quad 5x = 4x + 12$

line (d) $\quad x = 12$

*Step (5):* The smaller number is 12. The larger number, $x + 3$, is 15.

(32)

**Example 2:** Two electric resistances are 20 ohms and 30 ohms, respectively. How much must each resistance be increased so that their ratio is $\dfrac{5}{6}$? Assume that each resistance is increased the same amount.

**Solution:**

*Step (1):* Let $x$ represent the amount of increase.

*Step (2):*   $20 + x$ represents the numerator and $30 + x$ represents the denominator.

*Step (3):*   The ratio must equal $\frac{5}{6}$.

$$\frac{20 + x}{30 + x} = \frac{5}{6}$$

*Step (4):*   Solve the equation.

*line (a)*   $6 \cdot \cancel{(30 + x)} \cdot \dfrac{20 + x}{\cancel{(30 + x)}} = \cancel{6} \cdot (30 + x) \cdot \dfrac{5}{\cancel{6}}$

*line (b)*   $6 \cdot (20 + x) = (30 + x) \cdot 5$

*line (c)*   $120 + 6x = 150 + 5x$

*line (d)*   $x = 30$

*Step (5):*   Each resistance must be increased by 30 ohms.

□ **(33)**

**Example 3:**   How many pints of a 20% salt solution should be added to 30 pints of a 50% solution in order to obtain a 40% salt solution?

**Solution:**   $\boxed{\begin{array}{c}\text{Pure salt in} \\ \text{50\% solution}\end{array}} + \boxed{\begin{array}{c}\text{Pure salt in} \\ \text{20\% solution}\end{array}} \Rightarrow \boxed{\begin{array}{c}\text{Pure salt in} \\ \text{40\% solution}\end{array}}$

*Step (1):*   Let $x$ represent the number of pints of the 20% solution.

            30 pints                $x$ pints         $(30 + x)$ pints

*Step (2):*   $\boxed{\begin{array}{c}\text{Pure salt in} \\ \text{50\% solution}\end{array}} + \boxed{\begin{array}{c}\text{Pure salt in} \\ \text{20\% solution}\end{array}} \Rightarrow \boxed{\begin{array}{c}\text{Pure salt in} \\ \text{40\% solution}\end{array}}$

            50%(30)          20%($x$)        40%(30 + $x$)

*Step (3):*   The amount of salt in the 50% solution plus the amount of salt in the 20% solution must equal the amount of salt in the 40% solution.

$$50\%(30) + 20\%(x) = 40\%(30 + x)$$

*Step (4):*   Solve the equation.

*line (a)*   $0.5(30) + 0.2(x) = 0.4(30 + x)$

*line (b)*   $5(30) + 2x = 4(30 + x)$

*line (c)*   $150 + 2x = 120 + 4x$

*line (d)*   $-2x = -30$

*line (e)*   $x = 15$

*Step (5):*   15 pints of the 20% solution must be added.

□ **(34)**

**Example 4:**   How many ounces of an alloy containing 40% aluminum must be melted with an alloy containing 70% aluminum in order to obtain 20 ounces of an alloy containing 45% aluminum?

**Solution:**   $\boxed{\begin{array}{c}\text{Pure aluminum} \\ \text{in 40\% alloy}\end{array}} + \boxed{\begin{array}{c}\text{Pure aluminum} \\ \text{in 70\% alloy}\end{array}} \Rightarrow \boxed{\begin{array}{c}\text{Pure aluminum} \\ \text{in 45\% alloy}\end{array}}$

*Step (1):*   Let $x$ represent the number of ounces of the 40% alloy. $20 - x$ will then represent the number of ounces of the 70% alloy.

           $x$ ounces        $(20 - x)$ ounces      20 ounces

*Step (2):*   $\boxed{\begin{array}{c}\text{Pure aluminum} \\ \text{in 40\% alloy}\end{array}} + \boxed{\begin{array}{c}\text{Pure aluminum} \\ \text{in 70\% alloy}\end{array}} \Rightarrow \boxed{\begin{array}{c}\text{Pure aluminum} \\ \text{in 45\% alloy}\end{array}}$

            40%($x$)         70%(20 − $x$)       45%(20)

*Step (3):* $40\%(x) + 70\%(20 - x) = 45\%(20)$

*Step (4):* Solve the equation.
 *line (a)* $0.40(x) + 0.70(20 - x) = 0.45(20)$
 *line (b)* $40x + 70(20 - x) = 45(20)$
 *line (c)* $40x + 1400 - 70x = 900$
 *line (d)* $-30x = -500$
 *line (e)* $x = \dfrac{50}{3}$, or $16\frac{2}{3}$

*Step (5):* $16\frac{2}{3}$ ounces of the 40% alloy must be melted.

☐ *Study Exercise Six*      **(35)**

1. The sum of two numbers is 18. If the smaller number is divided by the larger, the quotient is $\dfrac{4}{5}$. Find the numbers.

2. Two electric resistances are 2.0 ohms and 3.0 ohms, respectively. How much must each resistance be increased so that the ratio is $\dfrac{3}{4}$? Assume that each resistance is increased by the same amount.

3. How many pounds of an alloy containing 10% titanium must be melted with an alloy of 25% titanium in order to obtain 40 pounds of an alloy containing 15% titanium?

## REVIEW EXERCISES

A. Solve the following equations.

  1. $3x + 2 = -19$                     2. $5(x + 5) = 3(x - 1) + 2$

  3. $2x^2 - 3x = 0$                      4. $x^2 - 9 = 0$

  5. $2x^2 + 5x = 3$                     6. $\dfrac{x}{7} = \dfrac{2}{3}$

  7. $\dfrac{3m}{5} = \dfrac{1}{2}$                     8. $\dfrac{3x}{2} = \dfrac{x}{4} + 2$

  9. $\dfrac{y}{5} - \dfrac{y}{2} = 9$                10. $\dfrac{2m}{3} - \dfrac{2m + 5}{6} = \dfrac{1}{2}$

11. $\dfrac{2}{5x} + \dfrac{3}{10} = \dfrac{1}{2}$            12. $m + 2 = \dfrac{6}{m + 3}$

13. $\dfrac{5}{x - 5} - \dfrac{2}{x} = \dfrac{25}{x^2 - 5x}$     14. $\dfrac{x + 3}{x - 4} - \dfrac{4}{x + 5} = \dfrac{2x^2 + 3x + 19}{x^2 + x - 20}$

15. $|x| = 4$                       16. $|y - 3| = 2$

17. $|2m + 1| = 5$              18. $|3a - 1| = -6$

B. Solve the following equations for the specified symbol.

19. $pr = c$, for $p$               20. $e = mc^2$, for $m$

21. $\dfrac{1}{R} = \dfrac{1}{R_1} + \dfrac{1}{R_2}$, for $R$     22. $p = 2s + 2w$, for $w$

23. $\dfrac{1}{a} + \dfrac{1}{b} = 1$, for $a$

C. Solve the following word problems.

24. The difference between two numbers is 6. If three times the smaller number is divided by the larger the quotient is 4. Find the numbers.

25. How many liters of a 30% acid solution should be added to 20 liters of a 60% solution in order to obtain a 50% acid solution?

## Solutions to Review Exercises

A. 1. $3x + 2 = -19$
$3x = -21$
$x = -7$
The solution is $-7$.

2. $5(x + 5) = 3(x - 1) + 2$
$5x + 25 = 3x - 3 + 2$
$2x = -26$
$x = -13$
The solution is $-13$.

3. $2x^2 - 3x = 0$
$x(2x - 3) = 0$
$x = 0$ or $2x - 3 = 0$
$x = 0$, or $x = \dfrac{3}{2}$

The solutions are 0 and $\dfrac{3}{2}$.

4. $x^2 - 9 = 0$
$(x + 3)(x - 3) = 0$
$x + 3 = 0$, or $x - 3 = 0$
$x = -3$, or $x = 3$
The solutions are $-3$ and 3.

5. $2x^2 + 5x = 3$
$2x^2 + 5x - 3 = 0$
$(2x - 1)(x + 3) = 0$
$2x - 1 = 0$, or $x + 3 = 0$
$x = \dfrac{1}{2}$, or $x = -3$

The solutions are $\dfrac{1}{2}$ and $-3$.

6. $\dfrac{x}{7} = \dfrac{2}{3}$

$21 \cdot \dfrac{x}{7} = 21 \cdot \dfrac{2}{3}$

$3x = 14$

$x = \dfrac{14}{3}$

The solution is $\dfrac{14}{3}$.

7. $\dfrac{3m}{5} = \dfrac{1}{2}$

$10 \cdot \dfrac{3m}{5} = 10 \cdot \dfrac{1}{2}$

$6m = 5$

$m = \dfrac{5}{6}$

The solution is $\dfrac{5}{6}$.

8. $\dfrac{3x}{2} = \dfrac{x}{4} + 2$

$4 \cdot \dfrac{3x}{2} = 4 \cdot \left[ \dfrac{x}{4} + 2 \right]$

$4 \cdot \dfrac{3x}{2} = 4 \cdot \dfrac{x}{4} + 4 \cdot 2$

$6x = x + 8$

$5x = 8$

$x = \dfrac{8}{5}$

The solution is $\dfrac{8}{5}$.

9. $\dfrac{y}{5} - \dfrac{y}{2} = 9$

$10 \cdot \left[ \dfrac{y}{5} - \dfrac{y}{2} \right] = 10 \cdot 9$

$10 \cdot \dfrac{y}{5} - 10 \cdot \dfrac{y}{2} = 90$

$2y - 5y = 90$
$-3y = 90$
$y = -30$
The solution is $-30$.

10. $\dfrac{2m}{3} - \dfrac{2m + 5}{6} = \dfrac{1}{2}$

$6 \cdot \left[ \dfrac{2m}{3} - \dfrac{2m + 5}{6} \right] = 6 \cdot \dfrac{1}{2}$

$6 \cdot \dfrac{2m}{3} - 6 \cdot \dfrac{2m + 5}{6} = 6 \cdot \dfrac{1}{2}$

$4m - (2m + 5) = 3$
$4m - 2m - 5 = 3$
$2m = 8$
$m = 4$
The solution is 4.

11. $\dfrac{2}{5x} + \dfrac{3}{10} = \dfrac{1}{2}$

$10x \cdot \left[ \dfrac{2}{5x} + \dfrac{3}{10} \right] = 10x \cdot \dfrac{1}{2}$

$10x \cdot \dfrac{2}{5x} + 10x \cdot \dfrac{3}{10} = 10x \cdot \dfrac{1}{2}$

$4 + 3x = 5x$
$4 = 2x$
$2 = x$, or $x = 2$
The solution is 2.

12. $m + 2 = \dfrac{6}{m + 3}$

$(m + 3) \cdot (m + 2) = (m + 3) \cdot \dfrac{6}{m + 3}$

$(m + 3)(m + 2) = 6$
$m^2 + 5m + 6 = 6$
$m^2 + 5m = 0$
$m(m + 5) = 0$
$m = 0$, or $m = -5$
The solutions are 0 and $-5$.

## Solutions to Review Exercises, Contd.

13. $\dfrac{5}{x-5} - \dfrac{2}{x} = \dfrac{25}{x^2-5x}$

$\dfrac{5}{x-5} - \dfrac{2}{x} = \dfrac{25}{x(x-5)}$

$x(x-5) \cdot \left[\dfrac{5}{x-5} - \dfrac{2}{x}\right] = x(x-5) \cdot \dfrac{25}{x(x-5)}$

$5x - 2(x-5) = 25$

$5x - 2x + 10 = 25$

$3x = 15$

$x = 5$

5 is an extraneous solution. The original equation has no solutions.

14. $\dfrac{x+3}{x-4} - \dfrac{4}{x+5} = \dfrac{2x^2+3x+19}{x^2+x-20}$

$\dfrac{x+3}{x-4} - \dfrac{4}{x+5} = \dfrac{2x^2+3x+19}{(x-4)(x+5)}$

$(x-4)(x+5) \cdot \left[\dfrac{x+3}{x-4} - \dfrac{4}{x+5}\right] = (x-4)(x+5) \cdot \dfrac{2x^2+3x+19}{(x-4)(x+5)}$

$(x+5)(x+3) - 4(x-4) = 2x^2 + 3x + 19$

$x^2 + 8x + 15 - 4x + 16 = 2x^2 + 3x + 19$

$-x^2 + x + 12 = 0$

$x^2 - x - 12 = 0$ (Each side is multiplied by $-1$.)

$(x-4)(x+3) = 0$

$x = 4$, or $x = -3$

4 is an extraneous solution. Therefore, the only solution is $-3$.

15. $|x| = 4$

$x = 4$, or $x = -4$

The solutions are 4 and $-4$.

16. $|y - 3| = 2$

$y - 3 = 2$, or $y - 3 = -2$

$y = 5$, or $y = 1$

The solutions are 5 and 1.

17. $|2m + 1| = 5$

$2m + 1 = 5$, or $2m + 1 = -5$

$2m = 4$, or $2m = -6$

$m = 2$, or $m = -3$

The solutions are 2 and $-3$.

18. $|3a - 1| = -6$

An absolute value cannot equal a negative number. The equation has no solutions.

B. 19. $pr = c$

$\dfrac{pr}{r} = \dfrac{c}{r}$

$p = \dfrac{c}{r}$ where $r \neq 0$

20. $e = mc^2$

$\dfrac{e}{c^2} = \dfrac{mc^2}{c^2}$

$\dfrac{e}{c^2} = m$, or $m = \dfrac{e}{c^2}$, where $c \neq 0$

21. $\dfrac{1}{R} = \dfrac{1}{R_1} + \dfrac{1}{R_2}$ ($R$, $R_1$, and $R_2$ represent different numbers.)

$RR_1R_2 \cdot \dfrac{1}{R} = RR_1R_2 \cdot \left[\dfrac{1}{R_1} + \dfrac{1}{R_2}\right]$

$\cancel{R}R_1R_2 \cdot \dfrac{1}{\cancel{R}} = R\cancel{R_1}R_2 \cdot \dfrac{1}{\cancel{R_1}} + RR_1\cancel{R_2} \cdot \dfrac{1}{\cancel{R_2}}$

$R_1R_2 = RR_2 + RR_1$

$R_1R_2 = R(R_2 + R_1)$

$\dfrac{R_1R_2}{R_2 + R_1} = R$, or $R = \dfrac{R_1R_2}{R_2 + R_1}$, where $R_2 + R_1 \neq 0$

## Solutions to Review Exercises, Contd.

22. $p = 2s + 2w$
$p - 2s = 2w$

$\dfrac{p - 2s}{2} = w$, or $w = \dfrac{p - 2s}{2}$

23. $\dfrac{1}{a} + \dfrac{1}{b} = 1$

$ab \cdot \left[ \dfrac{1}{a} + \dfrac{1}{b} \right] = ab \cdot 1$

$ab \cdot \dfrac{1}{a} + ab \cdot \dfrac{1}{b} = ab \cdot 1$

$b + a = ab$

$b = ab - a$

$b = a(b - 1)$

$\dfrac{b}{b - 1} = a$, or $a = \dfrac{b}{b - 1}$, where $b - 1 \neq 0$

C. 24. Let $x$ represent the smaller number. Then $3x$ represents three times the smaller and $x + 6$ represents the larger number.

$$\dfrac{3x}{x + 6} = 4$$

$$(x + 6) \cdot \dfrac{3x}{(x + 6)} = (x + 6) \cdot 4$$

$$3x = (x + 6) \cdot 4$$

$$3x = 4x + 24$$

$$-24 = x$$

The smaller number is $-24$. The larger number is $-24 + 6$, or $-18$.

25. Let $x$ represent the number of liters to be added of the 30% solution.

| $x$ liters | | 20 liters | | $(x + 20)$ liters |
|---|---|---|---|---|
| Pure acid in 30% solution | $+$ | Pure acid in 60% solution | $\Rightarrow$ | Pure acid in 50% solution |
| 30%$(x)$ | | 60%$(20)$ | | 50%$(x + 20)$ |

$30\%(x) + 60\%(20) = 50\%(x + 20)$
$0.30(x) + 0.60(20) = 0.50(x + 20)$
$3x + 6(20) = 5(x + 20)$
$3x + 120 = 5x + 100$
$-2x = -20$
$x = 10$

Ten liters of the 30% solution must be added.

## SUPPLEMENTARY PROBLEMS

A. Solve the following equations.

1. $2m - 1 = 4$
2. $5x + 3(x - 1) = 2(x + 3)$
3. $x^2 - 3x = 0$
4. $4x^2 - 25 = 0$
5. $x^2 + 3x = 10$
6. $6m^2 + 7m - 3 = 0$
7. $\dfrac{x}{3} = \dfrac{1}{2}$
8. $\dfrac{2m}{3} = \dfrac{1}{6}$
9. $\dfrac{m}{2} - m = -3$
10. $\dfrac{x - 5}{6} = \dfrac{x}{2} - 4$
11. $\dfrac{2m - 3}{6} - \dfrac{5}{18} = \dfrac{2}{9}$
12. $\dfrac{7}{2} + \dfrac{2}{x} = 4$
13. $y + 2 = \dfrac{10}{y + 5}$
14. $\dfrac{r}{5} - 7 = \dfrac{r}{3} - r$
15. $\dfrac{2 + x}{4} - \dfrac{5 - 6x}{3} = x$
16. $\dfrac{1}{2y - 2} - \dfrac{1}{1 - y} = \dfrac{3}{y + 2}$

## SUPPLEMENTARY PROBLEMS, Contd.

17. $\dfrac{5}{x-3} = \dfrac{x+2}{x-3} + 3$

18. $2m + \dfrac{1}{2} = \dfrac{1}{4}$

19. $\dfrac{x^2+3}{x^2+x-12} = \dfrac{2x-2}{x-3} - \dfrac{x+1}{x+4}$

20. $\dfrac{7}{x} + 3 = \dfrac{10}{x^2}$

21. $\dfrac{m-3}{m-2} = \dfrac{2}{3}$

22. $\dfrac{12}{x-2} = 4$

23. $\dfrac{2}{3y} + 4 = \dfrac{6}{y}$

24. $\dfrac{3}{2x-7} = 1$

25. $\dfrac{x^2+3}{x^2+x-12} = \dfrac{2x-2}{x-3} - \dfrac{x+1}{x+4}$

26. $\dfrac{1}{2y-8} + \dfrac{2}{y-4} = 5$

27. $\dfrac{m-3}{m-2} + \dfrac{m+4}{m^2+m-6} = \dfrac{m+2}{m+3}$

28. $\dfrac{7}{2y-1} - \dfrac{5y}{2y^2-3y+1} = \dfrac{2}{4y-2}$

29. $\dfrac{1}{x^2-3x+2} + \dfrac{1}{x^2-5x+6} = \dfrac{-1}{x^2-4x+3}$

30. $\dfrac{x}{x^2-3x+2} + \dfrac{x}{x^2-5x+6} = \dfrac{-x}{x^2-4x+3}$

31. $\dfrac{t+3}{t+2} + \dfrac{t+1}{t-2} = \dfrac{2}{t^2-4}$

32. $\dfrac{7}{2y-1} - \dfrac{5y}{2y^2-3y+1} = \dfrac{3}{4y-2}$

33. $|x| = 6$

34. $|y+3| = 2$

35. $|2y+5| = -3$

36. $|3x-2| = 6$

B. Solve the following equations for the specified symbol.

37. $s = \dfrac{1}{2}at^2$, for $a$

38. $s = \dfrac{a}{1-r}$, for $r$

39. $A = \dfrac{h(b+c)}{2}$, for $b$

40. $w = I^2R$, for $R$

41. $\dfrac{1}{p} + \dfrac{1}{q} = \dfrac{1}{f}$, for $q$

42. $C = \dfrac{5}{9}(F - 32)$, for $F$

43. $F = \dfrac{mv^2}{gr}$, for $m$

44. $F = \dfrac{mv^2}{gr}$, for $r$

45. $S = \dfrac{rl-a}{r-l}$, for $r$

46. $T = \dfrac{E}{R+r}$, for $R$

47. $T = \dfrac{12(D-d)}{l}$, for $D$

48. $s = at - \dfrac{1}{2}gt^2$, for $a$

C. Solve the following word problems.

49. The sum of two numbers is 18. If the smaller number is divided by the larger, the quotient is ⅘. Find the numbers.

50. If ⅔ of a certain number is subtracted from twice the number, the result is 20. Find the number.

51. Find two consecutive integers such that the sum of ½ the first and ⅖ of the next is 22.

52. The denominator of a certain fraction is 6 more than the numerator, and the fraction is equivalent to ⅝. Find the numerator.

53. The denominator of a certain fraction is 8 more than the numerator, and the fraction is equivalent to ⅔. Find the denominator.

54. The numerator of a fraction is 5 less than the denominator. If the numerator is decreased by 2 and the denominator is increased by 3, the value of the new fraction is ⅓. Find the original fraction.

## SUPPLEMENTARY PROBLEMS, Contd.

55. Two electric resistances are 2 ohms ($\Omega$) and 3 $\Omega$, respectively. How much must each resistance be increased so that the ratio is ¾? Assume that each resistance is increased by the same amount.
56. The width of a rectangular plate is ⅔ of its length. If the perimeter is 8 in., find its dimensions.
57. A 20-qt solution of acid and water is 30% acid. How many quarts of pure acid must be added so that the solution will be 65% acid?
58. How many quarts of an 80% salt solution must be added to 15 qt of a 12% solution to make a 30% salt solution?
59. How many pounds of an alloy containing 10% titanium must be melted with an alloy of 25% titanium in order to obtain 40 lb of an alloy containing 15% titanium?
60. How many pounds of walnuts at 49¢ per pound should a grocer mix with 20 lb of pecans at 58¢ a pound to give a mixture worth 54¢ a pound?
61. A man has an amount of money in savings at 5% and another investment at 6% simple interest. The amount invested at 6% is $2,000 more than that invested at 5%. The total annual interest is $395.00. How much money is invested at each rate?
62. Two investments produce an annual income of $910. $5,600 more is invested at 8% than at 6%. How much is invested at each interest rate?
63. Two investments produce an annual income of $3,090; $13,000 more is invested at 9% than at 7%. How much is invested at each interest rate?

☐ **Solutions to Study Exercises**                                                  **(5A)**

### Study Exercise One (Frame 5)

1. $5x + 3 = 18$
   $5x = 15$
   $x = 3$
   The solution is 3.

2. $x^2 + x = 12$
   $x^2 + x - 12 = 0$
   $(x + 4)(x - 3) = 0$
   $x + 4 = 0$, or $x - 3 = 0$
   $x = -4$, or $x = 3$
   The solutions are $-4$ and 3.

3. $2m^2 - 3m = 0$
   $m(2m - 3) = 0$
   $m = 0$, or $2m - 3 = 0$
   $m = 0$, or $m = \dfrac{3}{2}$
   The solutions are 0 and $\dfrac{3}{2}$.

4. $2(3x - 1) = 5x - (x + 2)$
   $6x - 2 = 5x - x - 2$
   $6x - 2 = 4x - 2$
   $2x = 0$
   $x = 0$
   The solution is 0.

5. $3x^2 + \cdot 5x = 12$
   $3x^2 + 5x - 12 = 0$
   $(3x - 4)(x + 3) = 0$
   $3x - 4 = 0$, or $x + 3 = 0$
   $x = \dfrac{4}{3}$, or $x = -3$
   The solutions are $\dfrac{4}{3}$ and $-3$.

## Solutions to Study Exercises, Contd.

1. $\dfrac{x}{10} = \dfrac{5}{6}$

$30 \cdot \dfrac{x}{10} = 30 \cdot \dfrac{5}{6}$

$3x = 25$

$x = \dfrac{25}{3}$

The solution is $\dfrac{25}{3}$.

2. $\dfrac{4m}{5} = \dfrac{m}{2} - 3$

$10 \cdot \dfrac{4m}{5} = 10 \cdot \left[ \dfrac{m}{2} - 3 \right]$

$10 \cdot \dfrac{4m}{5} = 10 \cdot \dfrac{m}{2} - 10 \cdot 3$

$8m = 5m - 30$

$3m = -30$

$m = -10$

The solution is $-10$.

3. $\dfrac{25}{3x} + \dfrac{1}{3} = \dfrac{10}{x}$

$3x \cdot \left[ \dfrac{25}{3x} + \dfrac{1}{3} \right] = 3x \cdot \dfrac{10}{x}$

$3x \cdot \dfrac{25}{3x} + 3x \cdot \dfrac{1}{3} = 3x \cdot \dfrac{10}{x}$

$25 + x = 30$

$x = 5$

The solution is 5.

4. $m + 5 = \dfrac{15}{m + 3}$

$(m + 3) \cdot (m + 5) = (m + 3) \cdot \dfrac{15}{(m + 3)}$

$(m + 3) \cdot (m + 5) = 15$

$m^2 + 8m + 15 = 15$

$m^2 + 8m = 0$

$m(m + 8) = 0$

$m = 0, \text{ or } m = -8$

The solutions are 0 and $-8$.

1. $\dfrac{3}{x - 3} - \dfrac{5}{x} = \dfrac{9}{x^2 - 3x}$

$\dfrac{3}{x - 3} - \dfrac{5}{x} = \dfrac{9}{x(x - 3)}$

$x(x - 3) \cdot \left[ \dfrac{3}{x - 3} - \dfrac{5}{x} \right] = x(x - 3) \cdot \dfrac{9}{x(x - 3)}$

$x(x - 3) \cdot \dfrac{3}{x - 3} - x(x - 3) \cdot \dfrac{5}{x} = x(x - 3) \cdot \dfrac{9}{x(x - 3)}$

$3x - (x - 3) \cdot 5 = 9$

$3x - [5x - 15] = 9$

$3x - 5x + 15 = 9$

$-2x = -6$

$x = 3$

3 is an extraneous solution. The equation has no solutions.

2. $\dfrac{2}{m + 3} = \dfrac{5m}{m^2 + 4m + 3}$

$\dfrac{2}{m + 3} = \dfrac{5m}{(m + 3)(m + 1)}$

$(m + 3)(m + 1) \cdot \dfrac{2}{(m + 3)} = (m + 3)(m + 1) \cdot \dfrac{5m}{(m + 3)(m + 1)}$

$(m + 1) \cdot 2 = 5m$

$2m + 2 = 5m$

$2 = 3m$

$\dfrac{2}{3} = m, \text{ or } m = \dfrac{2}{3}$

There are no extraneous solutions. The solution is $\dfrac{2}{3}$.

## Solutions to Study Exercises, Contd.

3. $\dfrac{x+2}{x-2} - \dfrac{3x}{x-1} = \dfrac{6x-8}{x^2-3x+2}$

$\dfrac{x+2}{x-2} - \dfrac{3x}{x-1} = \dfrac{6x-8}{(x-2)(x-1)}$

$(x-2)(x-1) \cdot \left[ \dfrac{x+2}{x-2} - \dfrac{3x}{x-1} \right] = (x-2)(x-1) \cdot \dfrac{6x-8}{(x-2)(x-1)}$

$(x-1)(x+2) - (x-2)\cdot 3x = 6x-8$

$x^2 + x - 2 - [3x^2 - 6x] = 6x - 8$

$x^2 + x - 2 - 3x^2 + 6x = 6x - 8$

$-2x^2 + x + 6 = 0$

$2x^2 - x - 6 = 0 \qquad$ (Both sides are multiplied by $-1$.)

$(2x+3)(x-2) = 0$

$2x + 3 = 0$, or $x - 2 = 0$

$x = -\dfrac{3}{2}$, or $x = 2$

2 is an extraneous solution. The only solution is $-\dfrac{3}{2}$.

---

□ ### *Study Exercise Four (Frame 23)* (23A)

1. $|x| = 5$
   $x = 5$, or $x = -5$
   The solutions are 5 and $-5$.

2. $|y + 9| = 20$
   $y + 9 = 20$, or $y + 9 = -20$
   $y = 11$, or $y = -29$
   The solutions are 11 and $-29$.

3. $|4m - 7| = 13$
   $4m - 7 = 13$, or $4m - 7 = -13$
   $4m = 20$, or $4m = -6$
   $m = 5$, or $m = \dfrac{-3}{2}$

   The solutions are 5 and $-\dfrac{3}{2}$.

4. $|3x + 1| = -9$. Absolute value can never represent a negative number. There are no solutions.

---

□ ### *Study Exercise Five (Frame 29)* (29A)

1. $f = ma$
   $\dfrac{f}{m} = \dfrac{ma}{m}$
   $\dfrac{f}{m} = a$, or $a = \dfrac{f}{m}$, where $m \neq 0$

2. $a = \dfrac{b}{x}$
   $x \cdot a = x \cdot \dfrac{b}{x}$
   $x \cdot a = b$
   $x = \dfrac{b}{a}$, where $a \neq 0$

3. $xy + k = xw$
   $xy - xw = -k$
   $x(y - w) = -k$
   $x = \dfrac{-k}{y-w}$, or $x = \dfrac{k}{w-y}$, where $y - w \neq 0$

4. $\dfrac{1}{a} + \dfrac{1}{b} = \dfrac{1}{c}$
   $abc \cdot \left[ \dfrac{1}{a} + \dfrac{1}{b} \right] = abc \cdot \dfrac{1}{c}$
   $abc \cdot \dfrac{1}{a} + abc \cdot \dfrac{1}{b} = abc \cdot \dfrac{1}{c}$
   $bc + ac = ab$
   $ac - ab = -bc$
   $a(c - b) = -bc$
   $a = \dfrac{-bc}{c-b}$, or $a = \dfrac{bc}{b-c}$, where $c - b \neq 0$

## Solutions to Study Exercises, Contd.

*Study Exercise Six (Frame 35)*                                                    (35A)

1. Let $x$ represent the smaller number; then $18 - x$ represents the larger.

$$\frac{x}{18 - x} = \frac{4}{5}$$

$$5(18 - x) \cdot \frac{x}{18 - x} = 5(18 - x) \cdot \frac{4}{5}$$

$$5x = (18 - x) \cdot 4$$
$$5x = 72 - 4x$$
$$9x = 72$$
$$x = 8$$

The smaller number is 8 and the larger number is $18 - 8$, or 10.

2. Let $x$ represent the amount of increase on both resistances.

$$\frac{2 + x}{3 + x} = \frac{3}{4}$$

$$4(3 + x) \cdot \frac{2 + x}{3 + x} = 4(3 + x) \cdot \frac{3}{4}$$

$$4 \cdot (2 + x) = (3 + x) \cdot 3$$
$$8 + 4x = 9 + 3x$$
$$x = 1$$

Each resistance must be increased by 1.0 ohm.

3. Let $x$ represent the number of pounds to be added of the 10% alloy; then $40 - x$ represents the number of pounds of the 25% alloy.

| $x$ pounds | | $(40 - x)$ pounds | | 40 pounds |
|---|---|---|---|---|
| Pure titanium in 10% alloy | $+$ | Pure titanium in 25% alloy | $\Rightarrow$ | Pure titanium in 15% alloy |
| $10\%(x)$ | | $25\%(40 - x)$ | | $15\%(40)$ |

$$10\%(x) + 25\%(40 - x) = 15\%(40)$$
$$0.10(x) + 0.25(40 - x) = 0.15(40)$$
$$10x + 25(40 - x) = 15(40)$$
$$10x + 1000 - 25x = 600$$
$$-15x = -400$$
$$x = \frac{400}{15}, \text{ or } \frac{80}{3}, \text{ or } 26\frac{2}{3}$$

$26\frac{2}{3}$ pounds of the 10% alloy must be added.

# Solving Inequalities

☐ **Objectives** **(1)**

By the end of this unit, you should be able to solve first degree and fractional inequalities and describe the solutions by using set notation and the standard number line.

☐ **Review of the "Greater Than" and "Less Than" Symbols** **(2)**

| > or < |
|:---:|
| (points to the symbol representing the smaller number) |

| $5 > -6$ | $-10 < -5$ |
|:---:|:---:|
| 5 is greater than $-6$ | $-10$ is less than $-5$ |
| or | or |
| $-6$ is less than 5 | $-5$ is greater than $-10$ |

☐ "Greater than" means "names a point to the right of . . ." on the standard real number line. **(3)**

"Less than" means "names a point to the left of . . ." on the standard real number line.

☐ **Example 1:** $5 > -6$ **(4)**

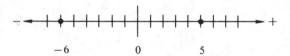

The point named by 5 is to the right of the point named by $-6$.

**Example 2:** $-10 < -5$

The point named by $-10$ is to the left of the point named by $-5$.

☐ An inequality must have: **(5)**

1. a greater than or a less than symbol.
2. a left and a right member which both represent a number.

☐ **(6)**

**Example 1:** An inequality: $3x + 5 > 7$ **Example 2:** *Not* an inequality: $3x \div 0 > 5x$

☐ Inequalities may be classified as true, false, or open. **(7)**

**Examples:**

1. $3 > 2$  True   2. $5 < -8$  False   3. $2x > 6$  Open

☐ **Solving an Inequality** **(8)**

To "solve an inequality" means to find every element in the variable's replacement set which will make the inequality true.

□ **Example:** Solve $2x > 6$. **(9)**

By inspection, we see that every real number greater than 3 will make the inequality true.

*line (a)* $2(3.1) > 6$   True
*line (b)* $2(4) > 6$   True
*line (c)* $2(10) > 6$   True
*line (d)* $2(1000) > 6$   True

□ **Two Methods of Finding the Solutions** **(10)**

1. Solution set notation:

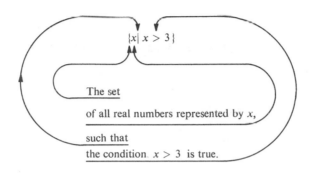

2. Illustrating on the real number line:

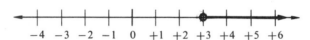

The *open circle* denotes that 3 is not in the solution set.

□ *Study Exercise One* **(11)**

Solve the following inequalities by inspection. Give the solutions by both methods.

1. $2x > 8$            2. $3x < 6$

□ **Properties of Inequalities** **(12)**

Three properties or axioms of inequalities will be assumed. Each will be stated and followed by a number line illustration.

□ **The Addition–Subtraction Property of Inequalities** **(13)**

The same real number can be added to both members or subtracted from both members of an inequality and the result is equivalent to the original inequality.

$$\text{If } a < b, \text{ then } a + c < b + c \text{ and } a - c < b - c$$

The addition–subtraction property holds true for all inequality symbols, $<$, $\leq$, $>$, and $\geq$.

**Example 1:** If $-5 < 2$ then $-5 + 3 < 2 + 3$.

**Example 2:** If $8 > 1$ then $8 - 2 > 1 - 2$.

☐ **Number Line Illustration** **(14)**

**Example:** $-5 < 2$

    **Solution:**

      *line (a)*

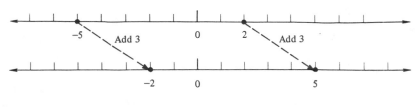

    *line (b)*

$$-5 + 3 < 2 + 3 \quad \text{or} \quad -2 < 5$$

☐ **The Multiplication–Division Property of Inequalities (Positive Numbers)** **(15)**

The same positive real number may be multiplied times both members or divided into both members of an inequality and the result is equivalent to the original inequality.

$$\text{If } a < b \text{ and } c \text{ is positive, then } ac < bc \text{ and } \frac{a}{c} < \frac{b}{c}$$

This property holds true for all inequality symbols.

**Example 1:** If $-3 < 1$, then $-3 \cdot 2 < 1 \cdot 2$.

**Example 2:** If $8 > -4$, then $\dfrac{8}{2} > \dfrac{-4}{2}$

☐ **Number Line Illustration** **(16)**

**Example:** $-3 < 1$

    **Solution:**

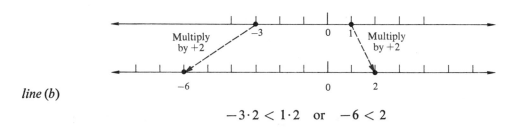

    *line (b)*

$$-3 \cdot 2 < 1 \cdot 2 \quad \text{or} \quad -6 < 2$$

☐ **The Multiplication–Division Property of Inequalities (Negative Numbers)** **(17)**

The same negative real number may be multiplied times both members or divided into both members of an inequality and the result is equivalent to the original inequality, providing the inequality symbol is reversed.

$$\text{If } a < b \text{ and } c \text{ is negative, then } ac > bc \text{ and } \frac{a}{c} > \frac{b}{c}$$

**Example 1:** If $-1 < 3$, then $(-1)(-2) > 3(-2)$.

**Example 2:** If $10 > -6$, then $\dfrac{10}{-2} < \dfrac{-6}{-2}$.

☐ Number Line Illustration  **(18)**

**Example:** $-1 < 3$

   **Solution:**

     *line (a)*

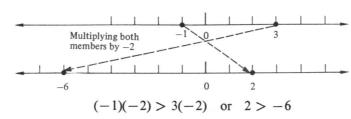

     *line (b)*

$$(-1)(-2) > 3(-2) \quad \text{or} \quad 2 > -6$$

(Notice that the inequality symbol has been reversed from the original.)

☐ First Degree and Fractional Inequalities in One Unknown  **(19)**

  1.  A *first degree inequality* in one unknown is any inequality that has an equivalent form which fits the pattern:

$$mx + b > c \quad \text{or} \quad mx + b < c$$

    where $m$, $b$, $c$ are constants and $x$ represents the variable.

  2.  A *fractional inequality* in one unknown is any inequality which contains at least one fraction.

☐ **First Degree:**  $\begin{array}{ccc} 2x & + \ 3 & > \ 9 \\ \uparrow & \uparrow & \uparrow \\ mx & + \ b & > \ c \end{array}$  **(20)**

**Fractional:**  $\dfrac{2x}{3} - \dfrac{5}{2} > \dfrac{3x}{2} + \dfrac{5}{6}$

(Contains at least one fraction)

☐ Solving Inequalities  **(21)**

First degree and fractional inequalities are solved in the same manner as first degree and fractional equations, *except that the inequality symbol must be reversed when each member is multiplied or divided by a negative number.*

☐ **Example 1:**  $2x + 3 > 9$  **(22)**

   **Solution:**

     *line (a)*  $2x + 3 + (-3) > 9 + (-3)$
     *line (b)*        $2x + 0 > 6$
     *line (c)*          $2x > 6$
     *line (d)*          $\dfrac{2x}{2} > \dfrac{6}{2}$
     *line (e)*          $x > 3$
     *line (f)*  Solution set is $\{x|x > 3\}$, or

     *line (g)*

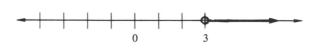

□ **Example 2:** $-2x + 3 > 9$           **(23)**

    **Solution:**

*line (a)*    $-2x + 3 + (-3) > 9 + (-3)$

*line (b)*          $-2x + 0 > 6$

*line (c)*            $-2x > 6$

*line (d)*          $\dfrac{-2x}{-2} < \dfrac{6}{-2}$       (Inequality symbol reversed)

*line (e)*            $x < -3$

*line (f)*   Solution set is $\{x \mid x < -3\}$, or

*line (g)*

□ **Example 3:** $\dfrac{2x}{3} - \dfrac{5}{2} > \dfrac{3x}{2} + \dfrac{5}{6}$          **(24)**

    **Solution:**

*line (a)*   Obtain the **LCD**, which is 6.

*line (b)*        $6 \cdot \left( \dfrac{2x}{3} - \dfrac{5}{2} \right) > 6 \cdot \left( \dfrac{3x}{2} + \dfrac{5}{6} \right)$

*line (c)*        $\dfrac{6(2x)}{3} - \dfrac{6 \cdot 5}{2} > \dfrac{6(3x)}{2} + \dfrac{6 \cdot 5}{6}$

*line (d)*         $4x - 15 > 9x + 5$

*line (e)*   $4x - 15 + (-9x) > 9x + 5 + (-9x)$

*line (f)*         $-5x - 15 > 5$

*line (g)*      $-5x - 15 + 15 > 5 + 15$

*line (h)*          $-5x > 20$

*line (i)*         $\dfrac{-5x}{-5} < \dfrac{20}{-5}$      (Inequality symbol reversed)

*line (j)*           $x < -4$

*line (k)*   Solution set is $\{x \mid x < -4\}$, or

*line (l)*

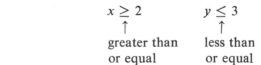

□ **Special Symbols**          **(25)**

               $x \geq 2$           $y \leq 3$

                 ↑             ↑

          greater than    less than

           or equal       or equal

*line (a)*

*line (b)*

☐ **Example:** Solve $5x - 3 \geq 7x - 8$. **(26)**

**Solution:**

line (a)   $5x - 3 + (-7x) \geq 7x - 8 + (-7x)$
line (b)   $-2x - 3 \geq -8$
line (c)   $-2x - 3 + 3 \geq -8 + 3$
line (d)   $-2x \geq -5$
line (e)   $\dfrac{-2x}{-2} \leq \dfrac{-5}{-2}$    (Inequality symbol reversed)

line (f)   $x \leq \dfrac{5}{2}$

line (g)   Solution set is $\left\{ x \mid x \leq \dfrac{5}{2} \right\}$, or

line (h)

$$\begin{array}{ccccccc} & -1 & 0 & 1 & 2 & \frac{5}{2} & 3 \end{array}$$

☐ **Two Special Cases of Solving Inequalities** **(27)**

**Example 1:**   $2(3x - 1) > 6x + 3$

**Solution:**

line (a)   $6x - 2 > 6x + 3$
line (b)   $6x - 2 + (-6x) > 6x + 3 + (-6x)$
line (c)   $-2 > 3$
line (d)   This inequality is false. It has no solutions. The solution set is empty, Ø.

**Example 2:**   $2(3x - 1) > 6x - 5$

**Solution:**

line (a)   $6x - 2 > 6x - 5$
line (b)   $6x - 2 + (-6x) > 6x - 5 + (-6x)$
line (c)   $-2 > -5$
line (d)   This inequality is true. Hence the solution set is all reals or $\{ x \mid x \text{ is any real number} \}$.

☐ *Study Exercise Two* **(28)**

Solve the following inequalities. Give the solutions by using set notation and by illustrating on the real number line.

1.  $2(x + 3) > 9$
2.  $-3(x - 1) \geq 9$
3.  $4(y + 1) < 4y + 3$
4.  $4(y + 1) < 4y + 7$
5.  $\dfrac{a}{3} + \dfrac{1}{6} < \dfrac{a}{6} + \dfrac{2}{3}$
6.  $3(2x + 1) \geq 3$

**REVIEW EXERCISES**

A.  Write, in words, the meaning of the following notation: $\{ x \mid x > 3 \}$.

B.  Give the three properties of inequalities and a specific example for each.

C.  Explain what it means to "solve an inequality."

D.  Solve the following inequalities. Give the solutions by using set notation and by illustrating on the real number line.

1.  $3x < -6$
2.  $3x > 6$
3.  $4(2x - 1) > 8x + 3$
4.  $3x + 5 > -10$

## REVIEW EXERCISES, Contd.

5. $-3x + 5 > -10$

6. $4x + 3 \leq 6x - 6$

7. $\frac{x}{3} > \frac{x}{4}$

8. $\frac{3x}{2} + \frac{1}{3} < \frac{5x}{6} - \frac{2}{3}$

9. $\frac{x + 3}{5} - \frac{x + 2}{2} \geq \frac{x - 5}{10}$

10. $6x + 7 \leq 6x + 9$

## Solutions to Review Exercises

A.  See Frame 10.

B.  See Frames 13, 15, and 17.

C.  See Frame 8.

D.  1.  $\{x \mid x < -2\}$

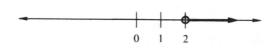

2.  $\{x \mid x > 2\}$

3.  $\emptyset$, the empty set

4.  $\{x \mid x > -5\}$

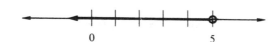

5.  $\{x \mid x < 5\}$

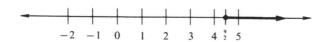

6.  $\left\{x \mid x \geq \frac{9}{2}\right\}$

7.  $\{x \mid x > 0\}$

8.  $\left\{x \mid x < -\frac{3}{2}\right\}$

286

## Solutions to Review Exercises, Contd.

9. $\left\{x \mid x \le \frac{1}{4}\right\}$

10. $\{x \mid x$ is any real number$\}$. This would represent the entire number line.

## SUPPLEMENTARY PROBLEMS

A. Classify each of the following inequalities as true, false, or open:

  1. $5 > 2$  2. $3 < -7$  3. $3x > 6$  4. $-5x < 0$

B. Solve the following inequalities, giving the solutions on the real number line:

  5. $2x > 6$
  7. $-2x + 3 \ge 9$
  9. $\frac{x}{2} + 3 \le \frac{5x}{3}$

  6. $2x + 3 > -5$
  8. $2x + 5 - 6x > 2 + 3x - 8$

C. Solve the following inequalities, giving the solutions in solution set notation:

  10. $2x < 6$
  12. $4m \le 8$
  14. $-3t > -9$
  16. $2n < 5$
  18. $2(x + 3) > 9$
  20. $2y + 13 > -5$
  22. $3n + 15 > -10$
  24. $5x - 6 \le 2 - x$
  26. $5m + 19 > 3m - 6 - (3 + 2m)$
  28. $4(x - 6) + 3 \le 2(x - 5) + 3x$
  30. $4x + 3 \le 6x - 16$
  32. $\frac{3x}{2} + \frac{1}{3} < \frac{5x}{6}$
  34. $4(2y - 1) > 8y + 3$
  36. $4x + 3 \le 6x - 6(x - 2)$
  38. $6(x - 2) < 6x - 12$
  40. $3(2y + 4) \ge 2(y - 1)$
  42. $-2(n - 1) \le 2$
  44. $5(x + 2) \le 5x + 10$
  46. $2(x + 3) \ge x + 3(x - 1)$
  48. $-x < 0$

  11. $5y > -15$
  13. $-3t < 9$
  15. $-8x \ge 16$
  17. $-2n < 5$
  19. $-3(m - 1) \ge 9$
  21. $-2x + 13 \ge 9$
  23. $-3n + 15 > -10$
  25. $10t - 3 - t > t - 20 - 23$
  27. $5y + 3 \ge 2y + 12$
  29. $8m + 12 \le 8 + 6m$
  31. $\frac{x}{5} > \frac{x}{6}$
  33. $\frac{a}{3} + \frac{1}{6} < \frac{a}{6} + \frac{2}{3}$
  35. $6x + 7 \le 6x + 9$
  37. $\frac{7y}{6} + \frac{1}{2} \le \frac{5y}{3} + \frac{3}{4}$
  39. $2y + 3 > 5y - 6$
  41. $4m - 3 < 2m + 7$
  43. $\frac{3m}{2} \ge \frac{5}{3}$
  45. $2b - 7 \le 8$
  47. $-x \ge 2$
  49. $\frac{3m}{5} + \frac{1}{10} < \frac{m}{5} - \frac{3}{10}$

## SUPPLEMENTARY PROBLEMS, Contd.

50. $-3(x + 1) \geqq -x - 2(x - 2)$

51. $\frac{y}{3} + 1 < 2$

52. $\frac{t}{4} + 2 > 4$

53. $\frac{5x - 7}{3} \leq 1$

54. $\frac{3m - 2}{2} \geqq \frac{2m + 1}{5}$

55. $\frac{3x + 1}{2} < \frac{2x + 1}{5}$

56. $6 - \frac{5y}{3} \leq \frac{y}{2} - 7$

57. $3(2x + 1) + 6x < 5(x + 3) + 4x$

58. $5t < 7t$

59. $\frac{t}{2} + \frac{3}{4} \geqq \frac{1}{2} - t$

D. True or False

60. "Greater than" means "names a point to the left of" on the standard real number line.
61. $7x < 4x \div 0$ is an inequality.

62. $2 \cdot \frac{3}{7} > 1$

63. For all real numbers, $a$, $b$, $c$, if $a > b$, then $a + c > b + c$.
64. For all real numbers, $a$, $b$, $c$, if $a > b$, then $a \cdot c > b \cdot c$.
65. $2x^2 + 3x > 9$ is a first degree inequality.

□ Solutions to Study Exercises                                              (11A)

### *Study Exercise One (Frame 11)*

1. $\{x \mid x > 4\}$

2. $\{x \mid x < 2\}$

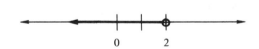

□                          *Study Exercise Two (Frame 28)*               (28A)

1. $2(x + 3) > 9$
   $2x + 6 > 9$
   $2x > 3$
   $x > \frac{3}{2}$
   $\{x \mid x > \frac{3}{2}\}$

## Solutions to Study Exercises, Contd.

2. $-3(x - 1) \geq 9$
$-3x + 3 \geq 9$
$-3x \geq 6$
$x \leq -2$
$\{x \mid x \leq -2\}$

3. $4(y + 1) < 4y + 3$
$4y + 4 < 4y + 3$
$4 < 3$
$\emptyset$

4. $4(y + 1) < 4y + 7$
$4y + 4 < 4y + 7$
$4 < 7$
$\{y \mid y \text{ is any real number}\}$

5. $\dfrac{a}{3} + \dfrac{1}{6} < \dfrac{a}{6} + \dfrac{2}{3}$

$6\left[\dfrac{a}{3} + \dfrac{1}{6}\right] < 6\left[\dfrac{a}{6} + \dfrac{2}{3}\right]$

$2a + 1 < a + 4$
$a < 3$
$\{a \mid a < 3\}$

6. $3(2x + 1) \geq 3$
$6x + 3 \geq 3$
$6x \geq 0$
$x \geq 0$
$\{x \mid x \geq 0\}$

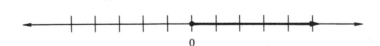

A. Indicate which of these are polynomials.

   1. $5x$                2. $\dfrac{x-5}{2x+3}$           3. $y^2 - 2y + 1$

B. If $P(x) = 3x^2 - x - 4$ find each of the following:

   4. $P(0)$      5. $P(3)$      6. $P(-3)$      7. $P\left(\dfrac{4}{3}\right)$

C. Indicate the domain for each of these rational expressions.

   8. $\dfrac{5}{x}$          9. $\dfrac{x+4}{x-5}$        10. $\dfrac{x^2 + 3x + 2}{x^2 - 9}$

D. Classify each of these expressions as a monomial, binomial, or trinomial.

   11. $x^2 + 5x + 6$     12. $\dfrac{2a}{b}$       13. $3m - 5$       14. $2(a + 3b)$

E. Multiply the following vertically.

   15. $x^2 + 2x - 3$                16. $3a^2 - 2a + 4$
            $x + 2$                           $3a - 4$

F. Multiply the following using any shortcut which applies.

   17. $(-3a^2b)(2ab^3c)$     18. $2x^2(3xy^2 + 2x^2y - 3y)$     19. $(x + 2)(x + 1)$
   20. $(x - 3)(x + 2)$       21. $(2x - 3)(x + 2)$         22. $(3a - 4)(2a - 3)$
   23. $(2x + 3)(2x - 3)$     24. $(3m + 5n)(3m - 5n)$     25. $(x + 3)^2$
   26. $(x - 3)^2$         27. $(2a - 3b)^2$

G. Factor each of these expressions completely.

   28. $3a - 6$           29. $2x^2 - 4x$          30. $15m^2n - 10mn^2 + 5mn$
   31. $x^2 - 9$          32. $4a^2 - 25$        33. $9m^2 - 1$
   34. $a^2 + 3a - 10$     35. $x^2 - 2x - 8$      36. $2m^2 - 5m + 3$
   37. $6a^3 - 3a^2 - 63a$

H. Solve the following equations.

   38. $x + 6 = 0$         39. $3m + 2 = 7$        40. $2(x + 1) = 2x + 3$
   41. $2(x + 1) = 2x + 2$    42. $3a + 5 = 2(a - 1) - a$    43. $x^2 + 3x + 2 = 0$
   44. $x^2 - 2x = 8$       45. $2y^2 - 3y = 0$
   46. $\dfrac{x}{5} = \dfrac{2}{3}$         47. $\dfrac{4x}{5} + 3 = \dfrac{x}{2}$

## Module 4 Review Problems, Contd.

Units 15–21

48. $y + 2 = \dfrac{6}{y + 3}$

49. $\dfrac{3}{4m} + \dfrac{1}{8} = \dfrac{1}{2}$

50. $\dfrac{9}{m^2 - 3m} + \dfrac{5}{m} = \dfrac{3}{m - 3}$

51. $\dfrac{2x^2 + 3x + 19}{x^2 + x - 20} + \dfrac{4}{x + 5} = \dfrac{x + 3}{x - 4}$

I. Solve the following formulas for the indicated symbol.

52. $a = \dfrac{1}{x}$, for $x$

53. $ab + ac = d$, for $a$

54. $\dfrac{1}{p} + \dfrac{1}{q} = \dfrac{1}{f}$, for $p$

J. Solve the following inequalities. Give the solutions in set notation.

55. $3x - 5 < 10$

56. $2x + 3 > 4x - 1$

57. $\dfrac{3m}{2} + \dfrac{1}{3} \geq \dfrac{5}{6}$

58. $2x + 3 < 2(x + 1)$

59. $2x + 3 > 2(x + 1)$

K. Reduce these fractions to lowest terms.

60. $\dfrac{8m^3n^2}{20m^4n^2}$

61. $\dfrac{2m - 8n}{5m - 20n}$

62. $\dfrac{x^2 + 3x - 4}{2x^2 - 5x + 3}$

L. Multiply or divide as indicated.

63. $\dfrac{10m}{9n^2} \cdot \dfrac{3n^3}{5m^2}$

64. $\dfrac{4x^2 - 9}{x^2 + x - 2} \cdot \dfrac{x^2 - 2x + 1}{2x^2 - x - 3}$

65. $\dfrac{a^2 + a - 6}{a^2 - a - 12} \div \dfrac{a^2 - 9}{a^2 - 16}$

66. $\dfrac{m + \dfrac{1}{3}}{\dfrac{1}{m} - 3}$

M. Add or subtract as indicated.

67. $\dfrac{5}{4m - 12} + \dfrac{1}{2m - 6}$

68. $\dfrac{8}{n^2 - 4} - \dfrac{n}{n + 2}$

69. $\dfrac{3x - 1}{x^2 + 5x + 6} - \dfrac{x + 1}{x + 2} + \dfrac{x}{x + 3}$

N. Solve these applied problems. Give the equation as well as the solutions.

70. The width of a rectangular plate is $\dfrac{3}{4}$ of its length. If the perimeter is 42 inches, find its dimensions.

71. How many milliliters of a 30% acid solution should be added to 50 milliliters of a 60% solution in order to obtain a 50% acid solution.

## Answers to Module 4 Review Problems

A. 1. Polynomial      2. Not a polynomial      3. Polynomial

B. 4. $P(0) = -4$      5. $P(3) = 20$      6. $P(-3) = 26$      7. $P(\frac{4}{3}) = 0$

C. 8. All real numbers except 0.      9. All real numbers except 5.
  10. All real numbers except 3 and $-3$.

D. 11. Trinomial      12. Monomial      13. Binomial      14. Monomial

E. 15. $x^3 + 4x^2 + x - 6$      16. $9a^3 - 18a^2 + 20a - 16$

F. 17. $-6a^3b^4c$      18. $6x^3y^2 + 4x^4y - 6x^2y$      19. $x^2 + 3x + 2$      20. $x^2 - x - 6$
  21. $2x^2 + x - 6$      22. $6a^2 - 17a + 12$      23. $4x^2 - 9$      24. $9m^2 - 25n^2$
  25. $x^2 + 6x + 9$      26. $x^2 - 6x + 9$      27. $4a^2 - 12ab + 9b^2$

## Answers to Module 4 Review Problems, Contd.

Units 15–21

G. 28. $3(a - 2)$     29. $2x(x - 2)$     30. $5mn(3m - 2n + 1)$     31. $(x + 3)(x - 3)$
   32. $(2a + 5)(2a - 5)$     33. $(3m + 1)(3m - 1)$     34. $(a + 5)(a - 2)$     35. $(x - 4)(x + 2)$
   36. $(2m - 3)(m - 1)$     37. $3a(2a - 7)(a + 3)$

H. 38  $-6$     39. $\dfrac{5}{3}$     40. No solutions     41. All real numbers

   42. $-\dfrac{7}{2}$     43. $-1, -2$     44. $4, -2$     45. $0, \dfrac{3}{2}$

   46. $\dfrac{10}{3}$     47. $-10$     48. $0, -5$     49. $2$

   50. No solutions     51. $-3$

I. 52. $x = \dfrac{1}{a}$, where $a \neq 0$     53. $a = \dfrac{d}{b + c}$, where $b + c \neq 0$     54. $p = \dfrac{qf}{q - f}$, where $q - f \neq 0$

J. 55. $\{x \mid x < 5\}$     56. $\{x \mid x < 2\}$     57. $\left\{ m \mid m \geq \dfrac{1}{3} \right\}$

   58. $\varnothing$     59. $\{x \mid x \text{ is any real number}\}$

K. 60. $\dfrac{2}{5m}$     61. $\dfrac{2}{5}$     62. $\dfrac{x + 4}{2x - 3}$

L. 63. $\dfrac{2n}{3m}$     64. $\dfrac{(2x + 3)(x - 1)}{(x + 2)(x + 1)}$, or $\dfrac{2x^2 + x - 3}{x^2 + 3x + 2}$

   65. $\dfrac{(a - 2)(a + 4)}{(a + 3)(a - 3)}$, or $\dfrac{a^2 + 2a - 8}{a^2 - 9}$     66. $\dfrac{3m^2 + m}{3 - 9m}$

M. 67. $\dfrac{7}{4(m - 3)}$     68. $\dfrac{-n + 4}{n - 2}$

   69. $\dfrac{x - 4}{(x + 2)(x + 3)}$

N. 70. $\dfrac{3}{4} \cdot l + l = 21$; width is 9 inches and length is 12 inches.

   71. $(.3)x + (.6)(50) = .5(x + 50)$; 25 milliliters of the 30% solution needs to be added.

# Exponents and Radicals

# Negative Exponents and Scientific Notation

☐ Objectives **(1)**

By the end of this unit you should be able to:

- explain the meaning of negative exponents.
- change negative exponents to positive exponents.
- change numbers from scientific notation to ordinary notation.
- change numbers from ordinary notation to scientific notation.
- use scientific notation in performing calculations.

☐ Review of the Properties of Exponents **(2)**

1. *The Zero Power Property*

$$a^0 = 1 \quad \text{where } a \neq 0$$

**Example:** $3^0 = 1$

2. *The Addition Property of Exponents*

$$a^m \cdot a^n = a^{m+n}$$

**Example:** $x^4 \cdot x^5 = x^9$

3. *The Subtraction Property of Exponents*

$$a^m \div a^n = a^{m-n} \quad \text{or} \quad \frac{a^m}{a^n} = a^{m-n}$$
$$\text{where } a \neq 0$$

**Example:** $\dfrac{x^6}{x^2} = x^4$

4. *The Power to a Power Property of Exponents*

$$(a^m)^n = a^{mn}$$

**Example:** $(y^2)^3 = y^6$

5. *The Distributive Property of Exponents*

$$(a^m \cdot b^n)^x = a^{m \cdot x} \cdot b^{n \cdot x} \quad \text{or} \quad \left(\frac{a^m}{b^n}\right)^x = \frac{a^{m \cdot x}}{b^{n \cdot x}}$$
$$\text{where } b \neq 0$$

**Example:** $(x^2 y^4)^3 = x^6 y^{12}$

☐ *Study Exercise One* **(3)**

A. Simplify each of the following and name the property of exponents which is used.

1. $\dfrac{m^7}{m^2}$  2. $5x^0$, where $x \neq 0$  3. $(5x)^0$, where $x \neq 0$

4. $(m^5)^2$  5. $(2x^2)^3$  6. $\left(\dfrac{3m^4}{2n^2}\right)^3$

B. True or False

7. $4^2 = 8$  8. $(x+y)^2 = x^2 + y^2$  9. $(xy)^2 = x^2 y^2$  10. $(3a)^2 = 9a^2$

☐ The Meaning of $x^{-n}$ **(4)**

line (a) $\quad x^n \cdot x^{-n} = x^{n+(-n)}$, where $x \neq 0$

296

*line (b)* $\qquad = x^0$
*line (c)* $\qquad = 1$

Since $x^n \cdot x^{-n} = 1$, then $x^{-n}$ must be the multiplicative inverse of $x^n$. In other words, $x^{-n} = \frac{1}{x^n}$, where $x \neq 0$. This pattern will change a negative exponent to a positive exponent.

☐ **Examples of Negative Exponents** (5)

1. $a^{-n} = \frac{1}{a^n}$
2. $x^{-2} = \frac{1}{x^2}$
3. $3^{-2} = \frac{1}{3^2}$
4. $(2m)^{-3} = \frac{1}{(2m)^3}$, or $\frac{1}{8m^3}$
5. $2m^{-3} = 2 \cdot \frac{1}{m^3}$, or $\frac{2}{m^3}$

☐ *Study Exercise Two* (6)

Using the pattern $x^{-n} = \frac{1}{x^n}$, where $x \neq 0$, change the following to positive exponents.

1. $m^{-3}$    2. $n^{-1}$    3. $5^{-2}$    4. $(3x)^{-2}$    5. $3x^{-2}$

☐ **Evaluating Expressions Containing Negative Exponents** (7)

1. $5^{-2} = \frac{1}{5^2} = \frac{1}{25}$
2. $3^{-1} = \frac{1}{3^1} = \frac{1}{3}$
3. $10^{-1} = \frac{1}{10^1} = \frac{1}{10}$, or $0.1$
4. $10^{-3} = \frac{1}{10^3} = \frac{1}{1000}$, or $0.001$
5. $\left(\frac{2}{3}\right)^{-2} = \frac{1}{\left(\frac{2}{3}\right)^2} = \frac{1}{\frac{4}{9}} = \frac{9}{4}$

☐ *Study Exercise Three* (8)

Evaluate each of the following.

1. $2^{-3}$    2. $5^{-1}$    3. $10^{-2}$    4. $10^{-5}$    5. $\left(\frac{1}{2}\right)^{-1}$    6. $\left(\frac{3}{5}\right)^{-2}$

☐ **Simplifying Exponential Expressions** (9)

An exponential expression is said to be *simplified* when all negative exponents have been converted to positive exponents and when the fraction, if any, is in lowest terms. We will simplify two types of exponential expressions:

1. exponential expressions where the numerator and the denominator are products or single terms.

**Example:** $\frac{5a^{-4}}{2}$

2. exponential expressions where the numerator or the denominator is a sum or a difference.

**Example:** $x^{-2} + y^{-2}$

☐ **Simplifying Exponential Expressions Where the Numerator and the Denominator Are Products or Single Terms** (10)

**Example 1:** Simplify $\frac{5a^{-4}}{2}$, where $a \neq 0$.

**Solution:** Multiply numerator and denominator by $a^4$.

*line (a)* $\frac{5a^{-4}}{2} = \frac{5a^{-4} \cdot a^4}{2 \cdot a^4}$

line (b)    $= \dfrac{5a^0}{2a^4}$

line (c)    $= \dfrac{5 \cdot 1}{2a^4}$

line (d)    $= \dfrac{5}{2a^4}$

Therefore, $\dfrac{5a^{-4}}{2} = \dfrac{5}{2a^4}$. The net effect is to transfer the factor $a^{-4}$ across the fraction bar and change the sign of its exponent.

☐ **Example 2:** Simplify $\dfrac{n^{-2}}{3m}$, where $m, n \neq 0$.    **(11)**

   **Solution:** Multiply numerator and denominator by $n^2$.

line (a)    $\dfrac{n^{-2}}{3m} = \dfrac{n^{-2} \cdot n^2}{3m \cdot n^2}$

line (b)    $= \dfrac{n^0}{3mn^2}$

line (c)    $= \dfrac{1}{3mn^2}$

Therefore, $\dfrac{n^{-2}}{3m} = \dfrac{1}{3mn^2}$. The net effect is to transfer the factor $n^{-2}$ across the fraction bar and change the sign of its exponent.

## ☐ A Shortcut    **(12)**

If the numerator and the denominator are products or single terms, the factors having negative exponents may be transferred across the fraction bar, provided the negative exponent is changed to a positive exponent.

## ☐ Examples Using the Shortcut    **(13)**

**Example 1:** Simplify $\dfrac{2x^{-3}}{5}$, where $x \neq 0$.

   **Solution:** Transfer $x^{-3}$ across the fraction bar.

line (a)    $\dfrac{2x^{-3}}{5} = \dfrac{2}{5x^3}$

☐ **Example 2:** Simplify $\dfrac{b^{-5}}{4a}$, where $a, b \neq 0$.    **(14)**

   **Solution:** Transfer $b^{-5}$ across the fraction bar.

line (a)    $\dfrac{b^{-5}}{4a} = \dfrac{1}{4ab^5}$

If a single term is transferred, a factor of 1 must be left behind.

☐ **Example 3:** Simplify $\dfrac{3a^{-2}b^{-3}}{2c^{-4}d^2}$, where $a, b, c, d \neq 0$.    **(15)**

   **Solution:** Transfer $a^{-2}$, $b^{-3}$, and $c^{-4}$ across the fraction bar.

line (a)    $\dfrac{3a^{-2}b^{-3}}{2c^{-4}d^2} = \dfrac{3c^4}{2a^2b^3d^2}$

□                                 *Study Exercise Four*                           **(16)**

Simplify the following. You may use the shortcut. Assume that the variables do not represent zero.

1. $\dfrac{3m^{-4}}{2}$        2. $\dfrac{y^{-2}}{5x}$        3. $\dfrac{2a}{b^{-3}}$        4. $\dfrac{3x^{-1}}{2y^{-1}}$

5. $\dfrac{7x^{-3}y^{-5}}{5z^{-2}w^3}$        6. $(5x)^{-2}$        7. $5x^{-2}$

□ **Simplifying Exponential Expressions Where the Numerator or the Denominator Is a Sum or a Difference**        **(17)**

**Example 1:**   Simplify $x^{-2} + y^{-2}$, where $x, y \neq 0$.

    **Solution:**   Remember $x^{-2} = \dfrac{1}{x^2}$ and $y^{-2} = \dfrac{1}{y^2}$.

    *line (a)*   $x^{-2} + y^{-2} = \dfrac{1}{x^2} + \dfrac{1}{y^2}$

    *line (b)*            $= \dfrac{1 \cdot y^2}{x^2 \cdot y^2} + \dfrac{1 \cdot x^2}{y^2 \cdot x^2}$

    *line (c)*            $= \dfrac{y^2}{x^2 y^2} + \dfrac{x^2}{x^2 y^2}$

    *line (d)*            $= \dfrac{y^2 + x^2}{x^2 y^2}$

□ **Example 2:**   Simplify $\dfrac{a^{-3} - b^{-3}}{2}$, where $a, b \neq 0$.        **(18)**

    **Solution:**   Remember $a^{-3} = \dfrac{1}{a^3}$ and $b^{-3} = \dfrac{1}{b^3}$.

    *line (a)*    $\dfrac{a^{-3} - b^{-3}}{2} = \dfrac{\dfrac{1}{a^3} - \dfrac{1}{b^3}}{2}$

    *line (b)*           $= \dfrac{\left(\dfrac{1}{a^3} - \dfrac{1}{b^3}\right) \cdot a^3 b^3}{2 \cdot a^3 b^3}$

    *line (c)*           $= \dfrac{\dfrac{1}{a^3} \cdot a^3 b^3 - \dfrac{1}{b^3} \cdot a^3 b^3}{2a^3 b^3}$

    *line (d)*           $= \dfrac{b^3 - a^3}{2a^3 b^3}$

□                                 *Study Exercise Five*                           **(19)**

Simplify the following. Assume that the variables do not represent zero.

1. $m^{-1} + n^{-1}$        2. $\dfrac{m^{-2} - n^{-2}}{5}$        3. $\dfrac{2}{x^{-2} + 1}$

□ **Operating with Negative Exponents**        **(20)**

Negative exponents obey the properties of exponents listed on Frame 2.

**Example 1:**   Simplify $(3x^{-4})(2x^6)$, where $x \neq 0$.

    **Solution:**   Use the Addition Property of Exponents.

    *line (a)*   $(3x^{-4})(2x^6) = 6x^{-4+6}$
    *line (b)*             $= 6x^2$

□ **Example 2:** Simplify $\frac{8x^{-2}}{2x^{-5}}$, where $x \neq 0$. **(21)**

**Solution:** Use the Subtraction Property of Exponents.

line (a) $\quad \frac{8x^{-2}}{2x^{-5}} = 4x^{(-2)-(-5)}$

line (b) $\quad\quad\quad = 4x^{(-2)+(+5)}$

line (c) $\quad\quad\quad = 4x^3$

□ **Example 3:** Simplify $(2a^{-2}b^4)^3$, where $a, b \neq 0$. **(22)**

**Solution:** Use the Distributive Property of Exponents.

line (a) $\quad (2a^{-2}b^4)^3 = 2^3a^{-6}b^{12}$

line (b) $\quad\quad\quad = 8a^{-6}b^{12}$

line (c) $\quad\quad\quad = \frac{8b^{12}}{a^6}$

□ **Example 4:** Simplify $\frac{(3m^{-3}n)^2(-2mn^{-1})^3}{(6m^{-2}n^3p^2)^2}$, where $m, n, p \neq 0$. **(23)**

**Solution:**

line (a) $\quad \frac{(3m^{-3}n)^2(-2mn^{-1})^3}{(6m^{-2}n^3p^2)^2} = \frac{(9m^{-6}n^2)(-8m^3n^{-3})}{36m^{-4}n^6p^4}$

line (b) $\quad\quad\quad = \frac{-72m^{-3}n^{-1}}{36m^{-4}n^6p^4}$

line (c) $\quad\quad\quad = \frac{-2m^1n^{-7}}{p^4}$

line (d) $\quad\quad\quad = \frac{-2m}{p^4n^7}$

□ **Study Exercise Six** **(24)**

Simplify the following using the properties listed on Frame 2. (No final answers should have negative exponents.) Assume that the variables do not represent zero.

1. $(2a^{-5})(7a^8)$

2. $\frac{15m^{-7}}{3m^{-2}}$

3. $(3x^2y^{-1})^2(-2x^{-3}y^2)^3$

4. $\frac{(2a^{-2}b^{-1}c^3)^2(-3a^2b^{-3})^3}{(3a^3b^{-2}c)^2}$

□ **Scientific Notation** **(25)**

Some numbers are extremely large or small and involve an excessive number of zeros. A convenient method of writing these numbers is known as *scientific notation*.

**Example 1:** The speed of light is about 30,000,000,000 cm/sec. Written in scientific notation, this becomes $3 \times 10^{10}$ cm/sec.

**Example 2:** The wavelength of red light is about 0.000076 cm. Written in scientific notation, this becomes $7.6 \times 10^{-5}$ cm.

□ **(26)**

A number is written in scientific notation when it is expressed as the product of a number between 1 and 10, and a power of ten.

$$30{,}000{,}000{,}000 \text{ cm/sec} = 3 \times 10^{10} \text{ cm/sec}$$

number between 1 and 10 $\quad$ power of 10

## ☐ Powers of Ten (27)

| Positive Powers of 10 | Negative Powers of 10 |
|---|---|
| $10^1 = 10$ | $10^{-1} = \dfrac{1}{10} = 0.1$ |
| $10^2 = 100$ | $10^{-2} = \dfrac{1}{100} = 0.01$ |
| $10^3 = 1000$ | $10^{-3} = \dfrac{1}{1000} = 0.001$ |
| $10^4 = 10{,}000$ | $10^{-4} = \dfrac{1}{10{,}000} = 0.0001$ |

*Remember,* $10^0 = 1$

## ☐ More Examples of Scientific Notation (28)

**Example 1:** $5 \times 10^2$ means $5 \times 100$ or 500.

**Example 2:** $2 \times 10^{-3}$ means $2 \times 0.001$ or 0.002.

**Example 3:** $1.64 \times 10^4$ means $1.64 \times 10{,}000$ or 16,400.

**Example 4:** $8.03 \times 10^{-1}$ means $8.03 \times 0.1$ or 0.803.

**Example 5:** $5.39 \times 10^0$ means $5.39 \times 1$ or 5.39.

*Remember,* in scientific notation, numbers which are less than 1 will have negative exponents.

## ☐ Changing from Scientific Notation to Ordinary Notation (29)

**Example 1:** $2.39 \times 10^3$

   **Solution:** The exponent 3 tells us to move the decimal point 3 places to the right.
   $2.39 \times 10^3 = 2390.$

   3 places

**Example 2:** $5.91 \times 10^{-2}$

   **Solution:** The exponent $-2$ tells us to move the decimal point 2 places to the left.
   $5.91 \times 10^{-2} = 0.0591$

   2 places

**Example 3:** $9.03 \times 10^5$

   **Solution:** The exponent 5 tells us to move the decimal point 5 places to the right.
   $9.03 \times 10^5 = 903{,}000.$

   5 places

**Example 4:** $1.34 \times 10^{-6}$

   **Solution:** The exponent $-6$ tells us to move the decimal point 6 places to the left.
   $1.34 \times 10^{-6} = 0.00000134$

   6 places

## ☐ Study Exercise Seven (30)

Change each of the following from scientific to ordinary notation.

1. $5.91 \times 10^2$   2. $6.04 \times 10^{-2}$   3. $1.10 \times 10^6$   4. $9.60 \times 10^{-4}$   5. $4.87 \times 10^0$

## ☐ Changing to Scientific Notation (31)

When a number is changed to scientific notation, the exponent will be negative if the original number is less than 1.

**Example 1:** 0.000316

  **Solution:** Move the decimal point 4 places. The number is less than 1.

  $0.000316 = 3.16 \times 10^{-4}$

  4 places

**Example 2:** 4380

  **Solution:** Move the decimal point 3 places. The number is more than 1.

  $4380 = 4.38 \times 10^{3}$

  3 places

**Example 3:** 805,000

  **Solution:** Move the decimal point 5 places. The number is more than 1.

  $805,000 = 8.05 \times 10^{5}$

  5 places

**Example 4:** 0.0120

  **Solution:** Move the decimal point 2 places. The number is less than 1.

  $0.0120 = 1.20 \times 10^{-2}$

  2 places

## ☐ Study Exercise Eight (32)

Change each of the following to scientific notation.

1. 364          2. 5,300,000          3. 0.000402          4. 0.560          5. 2.91

## ☐ Using Scientific Notation to Perform Calculations (33)

**Example 1:** Evaluate $\dfrac{6000}{0.03}$.

  **Solution:** Convert to scientific notation and use the properties of exponents.

  *line (a)* $\quad \dfrac{6000}{0.03} = \dfrac{6 \times 10^{3}}{3 \times 10^{-2}}$

  *line (b)* $\quad\quad\quad = \dfrac{2 \times 10^{3}}{10^{-2}}$

  *line (c)* $\quad\quad\quad = 2 \times 10^{3-(-2)}$

  *line (d)* $\quad\quad\quad = 2 \times 10^{5}$, or 200,000

## ☐ Example 2: Evaluate $\dfrac{(200)(0.006)}{3000}$. (34)

  **Solution:** Convert to scientific notation and use the properties of exponents.

  *line (a)* $\quad \dfrac{(200)(0.006)}{3000} = \dfrac{(2 \times 10^{2})(6 \times 10^{-3})}{3 \times 10^{3}}$

  *line (b)* $\quad\quad\quad\quad = \dfrac{12 \times 10^{-1}}{3 \times 10^{3}}$

302

line (c)         $= 4 \times 10^{-1-3}$
line (d)         $= 4 \times 10^{-4}$, or $0.0004$

## Study Exercise Nine (35)

A. Use scientific notation to perform the following calculations.

1. $\dfrac{(0.08)(2000)}{0.0004}$      2. $\dfrac{(0.006)(0.8)}{(0.04)(20)}$      3. $\dfrac{(0.006)(80)}{(0.02)(0.3)}$      4. $\dfrac{8000}{(20)(0.1)}$

## REVIEW EXERCISES

A. Using the pattern $x^{-n} = \dfrac{1}{x^n}$, where $x \neq 0$, change the following negative exponents to positive exponents.

1. $n^{-2}$      2. $y^{-1}$      3. $(2m)^{-3}$      4. $2m^{-3}$

B. Evaluate each of the following.

5. $2^{-4}$    6. $3^{-1}$    7. $10^{-1}$    8. $10^{-3}$    9. $\left(\dfrac{3}{5}\right)^{-2}$

C. Simplify each of the following. Assume that the variables do not represent zero.

10. $\dfrac{2x^{-3}}{5}$      11. $\dfrac{m^{-4}}{7n^2}$      12. $\dfrac{4a^{-2}}{5b^{-2}}$

13. $\dfrac{3x^{-2}y^4}{5z^2w^{-3}}$      14. $a^{-2} + b^{-2}$      15. $\dfrac{1}{m^{-1} + 1}$

D. Simplify the following using the properties of exponents listed on Frame 2. (No final answers should have negative exponents.) Assume that the variables do not represent zero.

16. $(3x^{-2})(5x^6)$      17. $\dfrac{20m^{-4}}{5m^{-2}}$      18. $\dfrac{(4a^{-2}b^{-3}c^4)^2(-2a^4bc^{-2})^3}{(2ab^{-1}c^2)^2}$

E. Change each of the following to ordinary notation.

19. $6.03 \times 10^4$            20. $8.90 \times 10^{-5}$

F. Change each of the following to scientific notation.

21. $0.00000103$            22. $651,000,000$

G. Evaluate the following by using scientific notation.

23. $\dfrac{(4000)(600)}{80}$            24. $\dfrac{(0.06)(0.009)}{(0.3)(0.02)}$

## Solutions to Review Exercises

A. 1. $n^{-2} = \dfrac{1}{n^2}$    2. $y^{-1} = \dfrac{1}{y}$    3. $(2m)^{-3} = \dfrac{1}{(2m)^3}$, or $\dfrac{1}{8m^3}$    4. $2m^{-3} = 2 \cdot \dfrac{1}{m^3}$, or $\dfrac{2}{m^3}$

B. 5. $2^{-4} = \dfrac{1}{2^4} = \dfrac{1}{16}$    6. $3^{-1} = \dfrac{1}{3}$    7. $10^{-1} = \dfrac{1}{10}$

     8. $10^{-3} = \dfrac{1}{10^3} = \dfrac{1}{1000}$, or $0.001$    9. $\left(\dfrac{3}{5}\right)^{-2} = \dfrac{3^{-2}}{5^{-2}} = \dfrac{5^2}{3^2} = \dfrac{25}{9}$

C. 10. $\dfrac{2x^{-3}}{5} = \dfrac{2}{5x^3}$      11. $\dfrac{m^{-4}}{7n^2} = \dfrac{1}{7n^2m^4}$

     12. $\dfrac{4a^{-2}}{5b^{-2}} = \dfrac{4b^2}{5a^2}$      13. $\dfrac{3x^{-2}y^4}{5z^2w^{-3}} = \dfrac{3y^4w^3}{5z^2x^2}$

## Solutions to Review Exercises, Contd.

14. $a^{-2} + b^{-2} = \dfrac{1}{a^2} + \dfrac{1}{b^2} = \dfrac{b^2 + a^2}{a^2 b^2}$

15. $\dfrac{1}{m^{-1} + 1} = \dfrac{1}{\dfrac{1}{m} + 1} = \dfrac{m}{1 + m}$

D. 16. $(3x^{-2})(5x^6) = 15x^4$

17. $\dfrac{20m^{-4}}{5m^{-2}} = 4m^{-2} = \dfrac{4}{m^2}$

18. $\dfrac{(4a^{-2}b^{-3}c^4)^2(-2a^4bc^{-2})^3}{(2ab^{-1}c^2)^2} = \dfrac{(16a^{-4}b^{-6}c^8)(-8a^{12}b^3c^{-6})}{4a^2b^{-2}c^4}$

$= \dfrac{-128a^8b^{-3}c^2}{4a^2b^{-2}c^4}$

$= -32a^6b^{-1}c^{-2}$

$= \dfrac{-32a^6}{bc^2}$

E. 19. $6.03 \times 10^4 = 60{,}300$

20. $8.90 \times 10^{-5} = 0.0000890$

F. 21. $0.00000103 = 1.03 \times 10^{-6}$

22. $651{,}000{,}000 = 6.51 \times 10^8$

G. 23. $\dfrac{(4000)(600)}{80} = \dfrac{(4 \times 10^3)(6 \times 10^2)}{8 \times 10^1}$

$= \dfrac{24 \times 10^5}{8 \times 10^1}$

$= 3 \times 10^4$, or $30{,}000$

24. $\dfrac{(0.06)(0.009)}{(0.3)(0.02)} = \dfrac{(6 \times 10^{-2})(9 \times 10^{-3})}{(3 \times 10^{-1})(2 \times 10^{-2})}$

$= \dfrac{54 \times 10^{-5}}{6 \times 10^{-3}}$

$= 9 \times 10^{-2}$, or $0.09$

## SUPPLEMENTARY PROBLEMS

A. Evaluate the following.

1. $3^{-3}$
2. $2^{-1}$
3. $2^{-5}$
4. $10^0$

5. $10^{-1}$
6. $10^{-5}$
7. $\left(\dfrac{3}{4}\right)^{-2}$
8. $\left(\dfrac{1}{10}\right)^{-1}$

B. Simplify the following. Assume that the variables do not represent zero.

9. $\dfrac{x^{-2}}{3y}$
10. $\dfrac{x^{-1}}{y^{-1}}$
11. $\dfrac{n^2}{3m^{-5}}$
12. $\dfrac{3a^{-4}}{5b^{-3}}$

13. $\dfrac{a^{-2}b^{-3}}{c^{-4}}$
14. $\dfrac{2m^{-2}n^3}{3p^{-4}q}$
15. $a^{-1} + b^{-1}$
16. $\dfrac{3}{x^{-2} + y^{-2}}$

17. $\dfrac{m^{-3} - n^{-3}}{4}$
18. $\left(\dfrac{a^{-3}}{b^{-4}}\right)^{-2}$
19. $3(x + y)^{-2}$
20. $\dfrac{2a^{-3}}{a^{-3} + 1}$

C. Simplify the following using the properties of exponents listed on Frame 2. (No final answers should have negative exponents.) Assume that the variables do not represent zero.

21. $m^{-3} \cdot m^{-4}$
22. $\dfrac{a^{-5}}{a^{-2}}$
23. $(x^{-2})^3$
24. $(2a^{-3})(3a^{-1})$

25. $\dfrac{15x^2}{3x^{-5}}$
26. $\dfrac{24m^{-2}n^3}{8m^{-3}n^5}$
27. $\dfrac{(3a^{-2}b^2c)^3 \cdot (2ab^3c^{-4})^2}{(-a^{-2}b^3c^{-1})^3}$

D. Change the following from scientific to ordinary notation.

28. $5.06 \times 10^{-4}$
29. $1.21 \times 10^{-1}$
30. $3.80 \times 10^0$

31. $4.65 \times 10^3$
32. $1.05 \times 10^7$

E. Change the following to scientific notation.

33. $0.00203$
34. $0.158$
35. $63.9$

36. $805$
37. $9{,}120{,}000$
38. $2340$

## SUPPLEMENTARY PROBLEMS, Contd.

F.  Use scientific notation to perform the following calculations.

39. $\dfrac{(40)(6000)}{800}$    40. $\dfrac{(0.006)(0.9)}{(200)(0.003)}$    41. $\dfrac{(0.05)(20)}{50}$    42. $\dfrac{(300)(40)(0.8)}{(200)(30)}$

G.  Calculator Problems. With your instructor's approval, use a calculator to evaluate the following expressions.

43. $(8.41)^{-1}$    44. $(0.264)^{-2}$    45. $(1.29)^{-3}$

46. $(56.4)^{-4}$    47. $(3.2)^{-2}(4.8)^{-3}$    48. $\dfrac{(3.05)^{-4}}{(8.09)^{-2}}$

49. $(10.9)^{-2} + (8.3)^{-3}$    50. $(2.64)(.0513)^{-3} - (4.33)^{-1}$

□  Solutions to Study Exercises    (3A)

### Study Exercise One (Frame 3)

A.  1. $\dfrac{m^7}{m^2} = m^5$    (Subtraction Property of Exponents)

2. $5x^0 = 5 \cdot 1 = 5$    (Zero Power Property)
3. $(5x)^0 = 1$    (Zero Power Property)
4. $(m^5)^2 = m^{10}$    (Power to a Power Property)
5. $(2x^2)^3 = 8x^6$    (Distributive Property of Exponents)
6. $\left(\dfrac{3m^4}{2n^2}\right)^3 = \dfrac{27m^{12}}{8n^6}$    (Distributive Property of Exponents)

B.  7. False; $4^2 = 16$.
8. False; an exponent may not be shared over a sum or difference.
9. True    10. True

### Study Exercise Two (Frame 6)    (6A)

1. $m^{-3} = \dfrac{1}{m^3}$    2. $n^{-1} = \dfrac{1}{n^1}$, or $\dfrac{1}{n}$    3. $5^{-2} = \dfrac{1}{5^2}$, or $\dfrac{1}{25}$

4. $(3x)^{-2} = \dfrac{1}{(3x)^2}$, or $\dfrac{1}{9x^2}$    5. $3x^{-2} = 3 \cdot \dfrac{1}{x^2}$, or $\dfrac{3}{x^2}$

### Study Exercise Three (Frame 8)    (8A)

1. $2^{-3} = \dfrac{1}{2^3} = \dfrac{1}{8}$    2. $5^{-1} = \dfrac{1}{5^1} = \dfrac{1}{5}$    3. $10^{-2} = \dfrac{1}{10^2} = \dfrac{1}{100}$, or $0.01$

4. $10^{-5} = \dfrac{1}{10^5} = \dfrac{1}{100,000}$, or $0.00001$    5. $\left(\dfrac{1}{2}\right)^{-1} = \dfrac{1}{\frac{1}{2}} = 2$    6. $\left(\dfrac{3}{5}\right)^{-2} = \dfrac{1}{\left(\frac{3}{5}\right)^2} = \dfrac{1}{\frac{9}{25}} = \dfrac{25}{9}$

### Study Exercise Four (Frame 16)    (16A)

1. $\dfrac{3m^{-4}}{2} = \dfrac{3}{2m^4}$    2. $\dfrac{y^{-2}}{5x} = \dfrac{1}{5xy^2}$    3. $\dfrac{2a}{b^{-3}} = \dfrac{2ab^3}{1}$, or $2ab^3$    4. $\dfrac{3x^{-1}}{2y^{-1}} = \dfrac{3y^1}{2x^1}$, or $\dfrac{3y}{2x}$

5. $\dfrac{7x^{-3}y^{-5}}{5z^{-2}w^3} = \dfrac{7z^2}{5w^3x^3y^5}$    6. $(5x)^{-2} = \dfrac{1}{(5x)^2}$, or $\dfrac{1}{25x^2}$    7. $5x^{-2} = 5 \cdot \dfrac{1}{x^2}$, or $\dfrac{5}{x^2}$

## Solutions to Study Exercises, Contd.

☐                 *Study Exercise Five (Frame 19)*             **(19A)**

1. 
$$m^{-1} + n^{-1} = \frac{1}{m} + \frac{1}{n}$$
$$= \frac{1 \cdot n}{m \cdot n} + \frac{1 \cdot m}{n \cdot m}$$
$$= \frac{n}{mn} + \frac{m}{mn}$$
$$= \frac{n + m}{mn}$$

2. 
$$\frac{m^{-2} - n^{-2}}{5} = \frac{\frac{1}{m^2} - \frac{1}{n^2}}{5}$$
$$= \frac{\left(\frac{1}{m^2} - \frac{1}{n^2}\right) \cdot m^2 n^2}{5 \cdot m^2 n^2}$$
$$= \frac{\frac{1}{m^2} \cdot m^2 n^2 - \frac{1}{n^2} \cdot m^2 n^2}{5 \cdot m^2 n^2}$$
$$= \frac{n^2 - m^2}{5m^2 n^2}$$

3. 
$$\frac{2}{x^{-2} + 1} = \frac{2}{\frac{1}{x^2} + 1}$$
$$= \frac{2 \cdot x^2}{\left(\frac{1}{x^2} + 1\right) \cdot x^2}$$
$$= \frac{2x^2}{\frac{1}{x^2} \cdot x^2 + 1 \cdot x^2}$$
$$= \frac{2x^2}{1 + x^2}$$

☐                 *Study Exercise Six (Frame 24)*             **(24A)**

1. $(2a^{-5})(7a^8) = 14a^3$

2. 
$$\frac{15m^{-7}}{3m^{-2}} = 5m^{(-7)-(-2)}$$
$$= 5m^{(-7)+(+2)}$$
$$= 5m^{-5}$$
$$= \frac{5}{m^5}$$

3. 
$$(3x^2y^{-1})^2(-2x^{-3}y^2)^3 = (9x^4y^{-2})(-8x^{-9}y^6)$$
$$= -72x^{-5}y^4$$
$$= \frac{-72y^4}{x^5}$$

4. 
$$\frac{(2a^{-2}b^{-1}c^3)^2(-3a^2b^{-3})^3}{(3a^3b^{-2}c)^2} = \frac{(4a^{-4}b^{-2}c^6)(-27a^6b^{-9})}{9a^6b^{-4}c^2}$$
$$= \frac{-108a^2b^{-11}c^6}{9a^6b^{-4}c^2}$$
$$= -12a^{-4}b^{-7}c^4$$
$$= \frac{-12c^4}{a^4b^7}$$

☐                 *Study Exercise Seven (Frame 30)*             **(30A)**

1. $5.91 \times 10^2 = 591$      2. $6.04 \times 10^{-2} = 0.0604$      3. $1.10 \times 10^6 = 1,100,000$

4. $9.60 \times 10^{-4} = 0.000960$      5. $4.87 \times 10^0 = 4.87$

☐                 *Study Exercise Eight (Frame 32)*             **(32A)**

1. $364 = 3.64 \times 10^2$      2. $5,300,000 = 5.3 \times 10^6$      3. $0.000402 = 4.02 \times 10^{-4}$

4. $0.560 = 5.60 \times 10^{-1}$      5. $2.91 = 2.91 \times 10^0$

☐                 *Study Exercise Nine (Frame 35)*             **(35A)**

A. 1. 
$$\frac{(0.08)(2000)}{0.0004} = \frac{(8 \times 10^{-2})(2 \times 10^3)}{4 \times 10^{-4}}$$
$$= \frac{16 \times 10^1}{4 \times 10^{-4}}$$
$$= 4 \times 10^5, \text{ or } 400,000$$

2. 
$$\frac{(0.006)(0.8)}{(0.04)(20)} = \frac{(6 \times 10^{-3})(8 \times 10^{-1})}{(4 \times 10^{-2})(2 \times 10^1)}$$
$$= \frac{48 \times 10^{-4}}{8 \times 10^{-1}}$$
$$= 6 \times 10^{-3}, \text{ or } 0.006$$

## Solutions to Study Exercises, Contd.

3. $\dfrac{(0.006)(80)}{(0.02)(0.3)} = \dfrac{(6 \times 10^{-3})(8 \times 10^{1})}{(2 \times 10^{-2})(3 \times 10^{-1})}$

$= \dfrac{48 \times 10^{-2}}{6 \times 10^{-3}}$

$= 8 \times 10^{1}$, or 80

4. $\dfrac{8000}{(20)(0.1)} = \dfrac{8 \times 10^{3}}{(2 \times 10^{1})(1 \times 10^{-1})}$

$= \dfrac{8 \times 10^{3}}{2 \times 10^{0}}$

$= 4 \times 10^{3}$, or 4000

# Introduction to Radicals and Rational Exponents

## ☐ Objectives                                                                    (1)

By the end of this unit you should be able to:

- state the meaning of square root, cube root, and fourth root.
- state the meaning of "principal" roots.
- state the meaning of rational exponents of the form $1/n$ and $m/n$.
- convert rational exponents to radical form and radicals to exponential form.
- evaluate certain numbers raised to a rational power.

## ☐ Square Root                                                                   (2)

A *square root* of a number is one of its two equal factors.

## ☐ Examples:                                                                     (3)

1.  A square root of 4 is $+2$ because $4 = (+2)(+2)$. Another square root of 4 is $-2$ because $4 = (-2)(-2)$.
2.  A square root of 36 is $+6$ because $36 = (+6)(+6)$. Another square root of 36 is $-6$ because $36 = (-6)(-6)$.
3.  0 is the only square root of 0 because $0 = 0 \cdot 0$, and these are the only two equal factors whose product is zero.
4.  $-25$ has no square root in the set of real numbers because no two equal factors produce a negative product.

## ☐ Properties of Square Roots                                                    (4)

1.  Each positive real number has two real square roots.
2.  Zero has only one real square root.
3.  Each negative real number has no real square roots.

## ☐                                *Study Exercise One*                            (5)

Find all of the square roots for each of the following.

1. 0     2. 1     3. 49     4. 100     5. 169     6. $-81$

7. $\dfrac{1}{4}$     8. $\dfrac{4}{9}$     9. $3^2$     10. $(-3)^2$     11. $-3^2$     12. $x^2$

13. $\dfrac{a^2}{b^2}$, where $b \neq 0$

## ☐ We need a symbol to indicate "square root." This symbol should have a *unique* meaning.   (6)

## ☐ Principal Square Root                                                         (7)

The *principal square root* of a number is the nonnegative square root.

**Example 1:**   The principal square root of 9 is $+3$.

**Example 2:**   The principal square root of 0 is 0.

## ☐                                *Study Exercise Two*                            (8)

Give the principal square root for each of the following.

1. 0     2. 1     3. 49     4. 100     5. 169     6. $-81$

7. $\dfrac{1}{4}$     8. $\dfrac{4}{9}$     9. $3^2$     10. $(-3)^2$     11. $-3^2$

☐ The symbol for principal square root, $\sqrt{\ }$, is called a *radical sign*. **(9)**

**Example 1:** The principal square root of 4 is symbolized as $\sqrt{4}$, where $\sqrt{4} = +2$.

**Example 2:** The principal square root of 144 is symbolized as $\sqrt{144}$, where $\sqrt{144} = +12$.

**Example 3:** $-\sqrt{9}$ means the opposite or additive inverse of the principal square root of 9. Hence, $-\sqrt{9} = -3$.

☐ **The Principal Square Root of $x^2$** **(10)**

The principal square root of $x^2$ is symbolized as $\sqrt{x^2}$.

1. $\sqrt{x^2} = x$, where $x \geq 0$

2. $\sqrt{x^2} = -x$, where $x < 0$

positive number

In general, $\sqrt{x^2} = |x|$, where $x$ is any real number.

☐ **Study Exercise Three** **(11)**

Simplify each of the following.

**Example:** $\sqrt{49} = 7$

1. $\sqrt{25}$
2. $\sqrt{-25}$
3. $-\sqrt{25}$
4. $\sqrt{\dfrac{25}{16}}$

5. $\sqrt{13^2}$
6. $\sqrt{(-13)^2}$
7. $\sqrt{y^2}$
8. $\sqrt{(a+b)^2}$

9. $\sqrt{\left(\dfrac{a}{b}\right)^2}$
10. $\sqrt{b^2}$, where $b < 0$

☐ **1/2 Used as an Exponent** **(12)**

**Example:** $9^{1/2} = ?$

Assume that the previous properties of exponents hold true.

1. $a^m \cdot a^n = a^{m+n}$
2. $(a^m)^n = a^{mn}$
3. $(a^m \cdot b^n)^x = a^{mx} \cdot b^{nx}$

4. $a^0 = 1$, where $a \neq 0$
5. $a^{-n} = \dfrac{1}{a^n}$, where $a \neq 0$
6. $\dfrac{a^m}{a^n} = a^{m-n}$, where $a \neq 0$

☐ $9^{1/2} \cdot 9^{1/2} = 9^{1/2+1/2}$, or $9^1$, or 9. **(13)**

Therefore, $9 = 9^{1/2} \cdot 9^{1/2}$

Two equal factors of 9, one of which is a square root of 9.

Then $9^{1/2}$ is a square root of 9. Hence, $9^{1/2}$ represents either $+3$ or $-3$, but which one?

☐ Define $9^{1/2} = \sqrt{9}$. **(14)**

principal square root

So $9^{1/2} = +3$.

☐ **Definition** **(15)**

$x^{1/2} = \sqrt{x}$ where $x \geq 0$

*Remember:* principal square root

☐ Cube Root (16)

A *cube root* of a number is one of its three equal factors.

☐ **Examples:** (17)

1. The cube root of 8 is 2, because $8 = 2 \cdot 2 \cdot 2$.
2. The cube root of $-8$ is $-2$, because $-8 = (-2)(-2)(-2)$.
3. The cube root of 27 is 3, because $27 = 3 \cdot 3 \cdot 3$.

☐ Properties of Cube Roots (18)

1. Every real number has exactly one real cube root.
2. The cube root of a positive real number is a positive real number.
3. The cube root of zero is zero.
4. The cube root of a negative real number is a negative real number.

☐ *Study Exercise Four* (19)

Find the cube root for each of the following:

| | | | | |
|---|---|---|---|---|
| 1. 1 | 2. $-1$ | 3. 0 | 4. 64 | 5. $-64$ |
| 6. 1000 | 7. $-1000$ | 8. $\dfrac{1}{8}$ | 9. $-\dfrac{1}{8}$ | 10. $\dfrac{8}{125}$ |
| 11. $x^3$ | 12. $(-x)^3$ | 13. $x^6$ | 14. $a^{-12}$, where $a \neq 0$ | |

☐ The symbol for cube root is $\sqrt[3]{\phantom{x}}$. (20)

**Example:** $\text{index} \longrightarrow \sqrt[3]{8} = 2$

radicand

radical sign

☐ (21)

There is no need for a principal cube root because every real number has exactly one real cube root.

☐ *Study Exercise Five* (22)

Simplify each of the following.

| | | | | |
|---|---|---|---|---|
| 1. $\sqrt[3]{1}$ | 2. $\sqrt[3]{-1}$ | 3. $\sqrt[3]{0}$ | 4. $\sqrt[3]{64}$ | 5. $\sqrt[3]{-64}$ |
| 6. $\sqrt[3]{1000}$ | 7. $\sqrt[3]{-1000}$ | 8. $\sqrt[3]{\dfrac{1}{8}}$ | 9. $\sqrt[3]{-\dfrac{1}{8}}$ | 10. $\sqrt[3]{\dfrac{8}{125}}$ |
| 11. $\sqrt[3]{x^3}$ | 12. $\sqrt[3]{(-x)^3}$ | 13. $\sqrt[3]{x^6}$ | 14. $\sqrt[3]{a^{-12}}$, where $a \neq 0$ | |

☐ 1/3 Used as an Exponent (23)

**Example:** $8^{1/3} = ?$

☐ **Example:** $8^{1/3} \cdot 8^{1/3} \cdot 8^{1/3} = 8^{1/3 + 1/3 + 1/3}$, or $8^1$, or 8. (24)

$8^{1/3}$ is one of the three equal factors of 8. Therefore, we define $8^{1/3} = \sqrt[3]{8}$, or 2.

☐ Definition (25)

$x^{1/3} = \sqrt[3]{x}$, where $x$ is any real number.

Simplify each of the following.

**Example:**   $125^{1/3} = \sqrt[3]{125} = 5$

1.  $1^{1/3}$          2.  $(-1)^{1/3}$          3.  $0^{1/3}$          4.  $64^{1/3}$          5.  $(-64)^{1/3}$

6.  $1000^{1/3}$     7.  $(-1000)^{1/3}$     8.  $\left(\dfrac{1}{8}\right)^{1/3}$     9.  $\left(-\dfrac{1}{8}\right)^{1/3}$     10.  $\left(\dfrac{8}{125}\right)^{1/3}$

11.  $(x^3)^{1/3}$     12.  $[(-x)^3]^{1/3}$     13.  $(x^6)^{1/3}$     14.  $(a^{-12})^{1/3}$, where $a \neq 0$

## □ Fourth Root                                                        (27)

A *fourth root* of a number is one of its four equal factors.

## □ Examples:                                                         (28)

1.  A fourth root of 16 is $+2$, because $16 = (+2)(+2)(+2)(+2)$.
    A fourth root of 16 is also $-2$, because $16 = (-2)(-2)(-2)(-2)$.
2.  A fourth root of 81 is $+3$, because $81 = (+3)(+3)(+3)(+3)$.
    A fourth root of 81 is also $-3$, because $81 = (-3)(-3)(-3)(-3)$.

## □ Properties of Fourth Roots                                         (29)

1.  Fourth roots behave similarly to square roots.
2.  Each positive real number has two real fourth roots.
3.  Each negative real number has no real fourth roots.

## □ The symbol for principal fourth root is $\sqrt[4]{\phantom{x}}$.         (30)

**Example:**   $\sqrt[4]{16} = +2$

*Principal fourth root is never negative.*

Simplify each of the following.

**Example:**   $\sqrt[4]{625} = 5$

1.  $\sqrt[4]{0}$          2.  $\sqrt[4]{1}$          3.  $\sqrt[4]{-1}$          4.  $-\sqrt[4]{1}$

5.  $\sqrt[4]{\dfrac{1}{16}}$     6.  $\sqrt[4]{\dfrac{81}{16}}$     7.  $\sqrt[4]{256}$     8.  $\sqrt[4]{x^4}$

## □ 1/4 Used as an Exponent                                            (32)

**Example:**   $16^{1/4} = ?$

## □ Example:   $16^{1/4} \cdot 16^{1/4} \cdot 16^{1/4} \cdot 16^{1/4} = 16^{1/4+1/4+1/4+1/4}$, or 16.   (33)

$16^{1/4}$ is a fourth root of 16. We define it to be the principal fourth root. So $16^{1/4} = \sqrt[4]{16}$, or 2.

## □ Definition                                                         (34)

$x^{1/4} = \sqrt[4]{x}$   where $x \geq 0$

*Remember:* principal fourth root

Simplify the following.

**Example:** $625^{1/4} = \sqrt[4]{625} = 5$

1. $0^{1/4}$       2. $1^{1/4}$      3. $(-1)^{1/4}$      4. $-1^{1/4}$

5. $\left(\dfrac{1}{16}\right)^{1/4}$      6. $\left(\dfrac{81}{16}\right)^{1/4}$      7. $256^{1/4}$      8. $(x^4)^{1/4}$

## □ Summary (36)

Definition:

$$\sqrt[n]{x} = x^{1/n} \quad \text{where}$$

1. $x \geq 0$ for $n$, an even natural number.
2. $x$ is any real number, $n$ an odd natural number, and $n \neq 1$.

This table summarizes the different roots.

| Square Roots | Cube Roots | Fourth Roots | $n$th Roots* |
|---|---|---|---|
| $\sqrt{x}$ | $\sqrt[3]{x}$ | $\sqrt[4]{x}$ | $\sqrt[n]{x}$ |
| $x^{1/2}$ | $x^{1/3}$ | $x^{1/4}$ | $x^{1/n}$ |
| principal | not needed | principal | even — principal<br>odd — not needed |

*where $n$ is a natural number and $n \geq 2$

## □ Rational Exponents of the Form $m/n$ (37)

We now develop rational exponents of the form $m/n$, where $m$ and $n$ are integers and $n \geq 2$. This will allow us to give meaning to expressions such as $8^{2/3}$ and $x^{3/5}$.

Using the definition in frame 36 that $x^{1/n} = \sqrt[n]{x}$, we formulate the following definition:

$$x^{m/n} = (x^m)^{1/n} \quad \text{or} \quad (x^{1/n})^m$$
$$= \sqrt[n]{x^m} \quad \text{or} \quad (\sqrt[n]{x})^m$$

This definition holds true providing $\sqrt[n]{x}$ exists.

## □ Meaning of the Definition (38)

This definition lets us convert back and forth between exponential and radical form.

$$\overset{\text{power}}{\underset{\text{root}}{x^{m/n}}} = \overset{\text{root}}{\underset{\text{power}}{\sqrt[n]{x^m}}} = \overset{\text{root}}{\underset{\text{power}}{(\sqrt[n]{x})^m}}$$

## □ Converting Exponents to Radicals (39)

**Example 1:** Convert $x^{2/3}$ to radical form.

**Solution:** The power is 2 and the root is 3.

$$x^{2/3} = \sqrt[3]{x^2} \text{ or } (\sqrt[3]{x})^2$$

**Example 2:**   Convert $(x + y)^{3/4}$ to radical form.

**Solution:**   The power is 3 and the root is 4.

$$(x + y)^{3/4} = \sqrt[4]{(x + y)^3} \text{ or } (\sqrt[4]{x + y})^3, \text{ where } x + y \geqq 0$$

**Example 3:**   Convert $a^{-3/5}$ to radical form.

**Solution:**   Remember, a negative exponent means "one over."

$$a^{-3/5} = \frac{1}{a^{3/5}}$$

$$= \frac{1}{\sqrt[3]{a^5}} \quad \text{or} \quad \frac{1}{(\sqrt[3]{a})^5} \text{ , where } a \neq 0.$$

## □ Converting Radicals to Exponents                                    **(40)**

**Example 1:**   Convert $\sqrt[5]{y^4}$ to exponential form.

**Solution:**   The power is 4 and the root is 5.

$$\sqrt[5]{y^4} = y^{4/5}$$

**Example 2:**   Convert $(\sqrt[4]{2a - b})^5$ to exponential form.

**Solution:**   The power is 5 and the root is 4.

$$(\sqrt[4]{2a - b})^5 = (2a - b)^{5/4}, \text{ where } 2a - b \geqq 0.$$

**Example 3:**   Convert $\dfrac{2}{\sqrt[5]{x}}$ to a form involving a negative exponent.

**Solution:**   Change to a rational exponent by using the definition, $x^{1/n} = \sqrt[n]{x}.$

$$\frac{2}{\sqrt[5]{x}} = \frac{2}{x^{1/5}}$$

$$= 2x^{-1/5}, \text{ where } x \neq 0.$$

## □ Evaluating Exponential Expressions                                    **(41)**

The definition of rational exponents can also be used to evaluate certain exponential expressions.

**Example 1:**   Evaluate $8^{2/3}$

**Solution:**   There are two methods of evaluation.

$$\textit{Method (a):} \quad 8^{2/3} = \sqrt[3]{8^2} = \sqrt[3]{64} = 4$$
$$\textit{Method (b):} \quad 8^{2/3} = (\sqrt[3]{8})^2 = (2)^2 = 4$$

Either method is correct. However, it is usually easier to apply the root first and the power second, as shown in method (b).

## □ More Illustrations                                    **(42)**

**Example 1:**   Evaluate $16^{3/4}$

**Solution:**   $16^{3/4} = (\sqrt[4]{16})^3 = 2^3 = 8$

**Example 2:** Evaluate $(-32)^{3/5}$

**Solution:**   $(-32)^{3/5} = (\sqrt[5]{-32})^3 = (-2)^3 = -8$

**Example 3:** Evaluate $(-16)^{3/4}$

**Solution:** There is no answer since the root is even and the base is negative.

**Example 4:** Evaluate $16^{-3/2}$

**Solution:** $16^{-3/2} = \dfrac{1}{16^{3/2}} = \dfrac{1}{(\sqrt{16})^3} = \dfrac{1}{4^3} = \dfrac{1}{64}$

□            *Study Exercise Nine*            **(43)**

A. Convert each of the following to radical form. List any necessary restrictions on the variables.

    1. $a^{1/2}$       2. $(3x)^{1/3}$       3. $3x^{1/3}$       4. $5m^{3/4}$       5. $(x+y)^{-2/3}$

B. Convert each of the following to exponential form. List any necessary restrictions on the variables.

    6. $\sqrt[7]{5x}$       7. $5\sqrt[7]{x}$       8. $2\sqrt[3]{x^2}$       9. $\dfrac{3}{\sqrt[5]{y^2}}$

C. Evaluate each of these expressions.

    10. $36^{1/2}$       11. $36^{-1/2}$       12. $(-36)^{1/2}$       13. $1^{2/3}$

    14. $0^{4/5}$       15. $100^{3/2}$       16. $(-64)^{2/3}$       17. $\left(\dfrac{4}{9}\right)^{3/2}$

## REVIEW EXERCISES

A. Tell what is meant by:

    1. Square root       2. Cube root       3. Fourth root
    4. Principal square root       5. An exponent of $1/2$       6. An exponent of $1/5$
    7. An exponent of $-1/4$       8. An exponent of $2/3$       9. An exponent of $-3/5$

B. Simplify the following as far as possible.

    10. $\sqrt{16}$       11. $8^{1/3}$       12. $\sqrt[3]{-8}$

    13. $32^{1/5}$       14. $27^{-1/3}$       15. $-\sqrt[4]{256}$

    16. $\left(\dfrac{25}{9}\right)^{1/2}$       17. $100^{-1/2}$       18. $\sqrt{a^2}$ where $a < 0$

    19. $\sqrt{a^2}$ where $a \geq 0$       20. $\sqrt[3]{y^3}$       21. $\sqrt[4]{(x+y)^4}$

    22. $16^{3/4}$       23. $16^{-3/4}$       24. $(-16)^{3/4}$

    25. $25^{3/2}$       26. $25^{-3/2}$       27. $\left(\dfrac{8}{27}\right)^{2/3}$

    28. $\left(\dfrac{9}{100}\right)^{-3/2}$       29. $-16^{5/4}$       30. $1000^{2/3}$

C. Convert each of the following to radical form. List any necessary restrictions on the variables.

    31. $(a+b)^{1/3}$       32. $5y^{-2/3}$       33. $(2x+y)^{3/4}$

D. Convert each of the following to exponential form. List any necessary restrictions on the variables.

    34. $\sqrt[5]{4x}$       35. $(\sqrt{3y})^3$       36. $\dfrac{4}{5\sqrt[3]{x^2}}$

## Solutions to Review Exercises

A.    1. See frame 2                         2. See frame 16
       3. See frame 27                      4. See frame 7
       5. Principal square root         6. Fifth root
       7. One over the principal fourth root.

## Solutions to Review Exercises, Contd.

8. The square of a cube root. Or, the cube root of a square.
9. One over the cube of a fifth root. Or, one over the fifth root of a cube.

B. 10. $\sqrt{16} = 4$

11. $8^{1/3} = \sqrt[3]{8}$
   $= 2$

12. $\sqrt[3]{-8} = -2$

13. $32^{1/5} = \sqrt[5]{32}$
   $= 2$

14. $27^{-1/3} = \dfrac{1}{27^{1/3}}$

   $= \dfrac{1}{\sqrt[3]{27}}$

   $= \dfrac{1}{3}$

15. $-\sqrt[4]{256} = -4$

16. $\left(\dfrac{25}{9}\right)^{1/2} = \sqrt{\dfrac{25}{9}}$

   $= \dfrac{5}{3}$

17. $100^{-1/2} = \dfrac{1}{100^{1/2}}$

   $= \dfrac{1}{\sqrt{100}}$

   $= \dfrac{1}{10}$

18. $\sqrt{a^2} = -a$, where $a < 0$

19. $\sqrt{a^2} = a$, where $a \geqslant 0$

20. $\sqrt[3]{y^3} = y$

21. $\sqrt[4]{(x+y)^4} = |x+y|$

22. $16^{3/4} = (\sqrt[4]{16})^3$
   $= 2^3$
   $= 8$

23. $16^{-3/4} = \dfrac{1}{16^{3/4}}$

   $= \dfrac{1}{8}$

24. $(-16)^{3/4} =$ no answer, since $\sqrt[4]{-16}$ fails to exist

25. $25^{3/2} = (\sqrt{25})^3$
   $= 5^3$
   $= 125$

26. $25^{-3/2} = \dfrac{1}{25^{3/2}}$

   $= \dfrac{1}{125}$

27. $\left(\dfrac{8}{27}\right)^{2/3} = \left(\sqrt[3]{\dfrac{8}{27}}\right)^2$

   $= \left(\dfrac{2}{3}\right)^2$

   $= \dfrac{4}{9}$

28. $\left(\dfrac{9}{100}\right)^{-3/2} = \dfrac{1}{\left(\dfrac{9}{100}\right)^{3/2}}$

   $= \dfrac{1}{\left(\dfrac{3}{10}\right)^3}$

   $= \dfrac{1}{\dfrac{27}{1000}}$

   $= \dfrac{1000}{27}$

29. $-16^{5/4} = -(\sqrt[4]{16})^5$
   $= -(2)^5$
   $= -32$

30. $1000^{2/3} = (\sqrt[3]{1000})^2$
   $= 10^2$
   $= 100$

C. 31. $(a+b)^{1/3} = \sqrt[3]{a+b}$

32. $5y^{-2/3} = \dfrac{5}{\sqrt[3]{y^2}}$ or $\dfrac{5}{(\sqrt[3]{y})^2}$, where $y \neq 0$

33. $(2x+y)^{3/4} = (\sqrt[4]{2x+y})^3$ or $\sqrt[4]{(2x+y)^3}$, where $2x+y \geqslant 0$

D. 34. $\sqrt[5]{4x} = (4x)^{1/5}$

35. $(\sqrt{3y})^3 = (3y)^{3/2}$, where $y \geqslant 0$

36. $\dfrac{4}{5\sqrt[3]{x^2}} = \dfrac{4}{5x^{2/3}}$ or $\dfrac{4x^{-2/3}}{5}$, where $x \neq 0$

## SUPPLEMENTARY PROBLEMS

A.  1.  Why do we need principal square roots but do not need principal cube roots?

B.  True or False

2.  3 is a square root of 9.       3.  $-3$ is a square root of 9.

4.  $-3$ is the principal square root of 9.       5.  $\sqrt{9} = -3$

6.  $9^{1/2} = 3$       7.  For every real number, $\sqrt{a^2} = a$.

8.  If $x < 0$, then $\sqrt[3]{x} < 0$.       9.  If $x < 0$, then $\sqrt[4]{x^4} = -x$.

10.  For every real number, $x$ and $y$, $\sqrt{x^2 + y^2} = x + y$.

11.  $\sqrt{3^2 + 4^2} = 3 + 4$

C.  Simplify each of the following as far as possible:

12.  $49^{1/2}$       13.  $-49^{1/2}$       14.  $(-49)^{1/2}$

15.  $\left(\dfrac{1}{8}\right)^{1/3}$       16.  $\sqrt{64}$       17.  $\sqrt[4]{81}$

18.  $\sqrt[5]{\dfrac{1}{32}}$       19.  $16^{-1/2}$       20.  $\left(\dfrac{1}{64}\right)^{-1/3}$

21.  $\sqrt[5]{m^5}$       22.  $\sqrt[3]{(2x + 3y)^3}$       23.  $\sqrt{k^2}$

24.  $\sqrt{4x^2}$       25.  $\sqrt[4]{16m^4}$, where $m < 0$       26.  $16^{3/2}$

27.  $-16^{3/2}$       28.  $(-16)^{3/2}$

29.  $16^{-3/2}$       30.  $0^{5/6}$

31.  $1^{4/5}$       32.  $(-64)^{2/3}$

33.  $(-27)^{2/3}$       34.  $(-27)^{-2/3}$

35.  $(-1)^{3/5}$       36.  $100^{1/2}$

37.  $100^{3/2}$       38.  $1000^{1/3}$

39.  $1000^{2/3}$       40.  $1000^{-2/3}$

41.  $4^{-3/2}$       42.  $32^{4/5}$

43.  $(-32)^{4/5}$       44.  $(-32)^{-4/5}$

45.  $(-8)^{5/3}$       46.  $81^{-3/4}$

47.  $\left(\dfrac{4}{9}\right)^{3/2}$       48.  $\left(-\dfrac{8}{27}\right)^{-2/3}$

49.  $\left(\dfrac{16}{81}\right)^{3/4}$       50.  $\left(\dfrac{27}{64}\right)^{2/3}$

D.  Convert each of the following to radical form. List any necessary restrictions on the variables.

51.  $7(m + n)^{1/2}$       52.  $7(m + n)^{-1/2}$       53.  $2x^{3/5} \cdot y^{1/8}$

54.  $2x^{2/3} + 5y^{1/2}$       55.  $a^{1/2} - b^{1/2}$       56.  $[(5x)^{1/2}]^{1/3}$

E.  Convert the following to exponential form. List any necessary restrictions on the variables.

57.  $\sqrt{k}$       58.  $\sqrt[5]{\dfrac{a}{b}}$       59.  $11\sqrt{x + y}$

60.  $5\sqrt[3]{a^2} - 3\sqrt{b}$       61.  $\sqrt[m]{a} - \sqrt[3]{b}$       62.  $13(\sqrt[4]{mn})^3$

F.  Calculator Problems. With your instructor's approval, use a calculator to evaluate the following expressions.

63.  $\sqrt{2.34}$       64.  $\sqrt{\dfrac{82.6}{31.5}}$       65.  $\sqrt{91.6 + 17.4}$

66.  $(8.23)^{1/3}$       67.  $(78.4)^{1/5}$       68.  $\sqrt[4]{1295}$

69.  $(23.5)^{4/5}$       70.  $(63.4)^{-2/3}$       71.  $3.65^{2/5} + 18.4^{3/4}$

72.  $(3.65)^3\sqrt{19.8}$       73.  $(\sqrt[3]{18.04})^2$       74.  $(\sqrt{0.569})^3$

☐ **Solutions to Study Exercises** **(5A)**

### Study Exercise One (Frame 5)

1. 0
2. 1, $-1$
3. 7, $-7$
4. 10, $-10$
5. $+13, -13$

6. none
7. $\frac{1}{2}, -\frac{1}{2}$
8. $\frac{2}{3}, -\frac{2}{3}$
9. 3, $-3$
10. 3, $-3$

11. none
12. $x, -x$
13. $\frac{a}{b}, -\frac{a}{b}$

☐ ### Study Exercise Two (Frame 8) **(8A)**

1. 0
2. 1
3. 7
4. 10
5. 13
6. none

7. $\frac{1}{2}$
8. $\frac{2}{3}$
9. 3
10. 3
11. none

☐ ### Study Exercise Three (Frame 11) **(11A)**

1. 5
2. none
3. $-5$
4. $\frac{5}{4}$
5. 13

6. 13
7. $|y|$
8. $|a + b|$
9. $\left|\frac{a}{b}\right|$
10. $-b$

☐ ### Study Exercise Four (Frame 19) **(19A)**

1. 1
2. $-1$
3. 0
4. 4
5. $-4$
6. 10

7. $-10$
8. $\frac{1}{2}$
9. $-\frac{1}{2}$
10. $\frac{2}{5}$
11. $x$
12. $-x$

13. $x^2$, because $x^2 \cdot x^2 \cdot x^2 = x^6$

14. $a^{-4}$, or $\frac{1}{a^4}$, because $a^{-4} \cdot a^{-4} \cdot a^{-4} = a^{-12}$

☐ ### Study Exercise Five (Frame 22) **(22A)**

Same as solutions to Study Exercise Four on Frame 19A.

☐ ### Study Exercise Six (Frame 26) **(26A)**

Same as solutions to Study Exercise Four on Frame 19A.

☐ ### Study Exercise Seven (Frame 31) **(31A)**

1. 0
2. 1
3. none
4. $-1$
5. $\frac{1}{2}$
6. $\frac{3}{2}$
7. 4

8. $|x|$; the absolute value symbol must be included to guarantee that the answer is not negative.

☐ ### Study Exercise Eight (Frame 35) **(35A)**

Same as solutions to Study Exercise Seven on Frame 31A.

☐ ### Study Exercise Nine (Frame 43) **(43A)**

A.
1. $a^{1/2} = \sqrt{a}$, where $a \geqslant 0$
2. $(3x)^{1/3} = \sqrt[3]{3x}$
3. $3x^{1/3} = 3\sqrt[3]{x}$
4. $5m^{3/4} = 5\sqrt[4]{m^3}$ or $5(\sqrt[4]{m})^3$, where $m \geqslant 0$
5. $(x + y)^{-2/3} = \dfrac{1}{\sqrt[3]{(x + y)^2}}$ or $\dfrac{1}{(\sqrt[3]{x + y})^2}$, where $x + y \neq 0$.

## Solutions to Study Exercises, Contd.

B.  6. $\sqrt[7]{5x} = (5x)^{1/7}$

   8. $2\sqrt[3]{x^2} = 2x^{2/3}$

7. $5\sqrt[7]{x} = 5x^{1/7}$

9. $\dfrac{3}{\sqrt[5]{y^2}} = \dfrac{3}{y^{2/5}}$ or $3y^{-2/5}$, where $y \neq 0$.

C. 10. $36^{1/2} = \sqrt{36}$
      $= 6$

11. $36^{-1/2} = \dfrac{1}{36^{1/2}}$
      $= \dfrac{1}{6}$

12. $(-36)^{1/2} = \sqrt{-36}$
      $= $ no answer

13. $1^{2/3} = (\sqrt[3]{1})^2$
      $= 1^2$
      $= 1$

14. $0^{4/5} = (\sqrt[5]{0})^4$
      $= 0^4$
      $= 0$

15. $100^{3/2} = (\sqrt{100})^3$
      $= 10^3$
      $= 1000$

16. $(-64)^{2/3} = (\sqrt[3]{-64})^2$
      $= (-4)^2$
      $= 16$

17. $\left(\dfrac{4}{9}\right)^{3/2} = \left(\sqrt{\dfrac{4}{9}}\right)^3$
      $= \left(\dfrac{2}{3}\right)^3$
      $= \dfrac{8}{27}$

# Operations with
# Radical Expressions

## ☐ Objectives  (1)

By the end of this unit you should be able to:

- simplify radicals by using the Basic Property of Radicals.
- evaluate radicals with use of a table.
- add and subtract radicals.
- multiply radicals.
- rationalize denominators of fractions containing radicals.

## ☐ Tables of Selected Perfect Squares and Perfect Cubes  (2)

| Perfect Squares | Principal Square Root | Perfect Cubes | Cube Root |
|---|---|---|---|
| 0 | 0 | −216 | −6 |
| 1 | 1 | −125 | −5 |
| 4 | 2 | −64 | −4 |
| 9 | 3 | −27 | −3 |
| 16 | 4 | −8 | −2 |
| 25 | 5 | −1 | −1 |
| 36 | 6 | 0 | 0 |
| 49 | 7 | 1 | 1 |
| 64 | 8 | 8 | 2 |
| 81 | 9 | 27 | 3 |
| 100 | 10 | 64 | 4 |
| 121 | 11 | 125 | 5 |
| 144 | 12 | 216 | 6 |

## ☐ The Basic Property of Radicals  (3)

*The radical of a product is equal to the product of the radicals.*

$$\sqrt[n]{a \cdot b} = \sqrt[n]{a} \cdot \sqrt[n]{b} \quad \text{where} \begin{cases} 1. & n \text{ is even and } a, b \geq 0 \\ 2. & n \text{ is odd and } a, b \text{ any real} \end{cases}$$

This property is true because of the properties of exponents.

*line (a)* $\quad \sqrt[n]{a \cdot b} = (a \cdot b)^{1/n}$
*line (b)* $\quad\quad\quad = a^{1/n} \cdot b^{1/n}$
*line (c)* $\quad\quad\quad = \sqrt[n]{a} \cdot \sqrt[n]{b}$

## ☐ Using the Basic Property of Radicals  (4)

**Example 1:** Simplify $\sqrt{4 \cdot 5}$.

**Solution:** Convert to a product of radicals.

*line (a)* $\quad \sqrt{4 \cdot 5} = \sqrt{4} \cdot \sqrt{5}$
*line (b)* $\quad\quad\quad\quad \downarrow$
$\quad\quad\quad = 2 \cdot \sqrt{5}$

**Example 2:** Simplify $\sqrt[3]{8 \cdot 3}$.

**Solution:** Convert to a product of radicals.

*line (a)* $\quad \sqrt[3]{8 \cdot 3} = \sqrt[3]{8} \cdot \sqrt[3]{3}$
$\quad\quad\quad\quad\quad \downarrow$
*line (b)* $\quad\quad\quad 2 \cdot \sqrt[3]{3}$

(5)

□ **Study Exercise One**

Use the Basic Property of Radicals to simplify the following.

1. $\sqrt{16 \cdot 3}$      2. $\sqrt[3]{27 \cdot 2}$      3. $\sqrt[3]{-8 \cdot 5}$      4. $\sqrt[5]{4x^5}$

## □ Simplifying Radicals    (6)

**Example 1:** Simplify $\sqrt{18}$.

**Solution:** Factor the radicand 18 into two factors, one of which is the largest possible perfect square; then use the Basic Property of Radicals.

*Step (1):* $\sqrt{18} = \sqrt{9 \cdot 2}$
*Step (2):* $= \sqrt{9} \cdot \sqrt{2}$
*Step (3):* $= 3 \cdot \sqrt{2}$

□ **Example 2:** Simplify $\sqrt[3]{54}$.    (7)

**Solution:** Factor the radicand 54 into two factors, one of which is the largest possible perfect cube; then use the Basic Property of Radicals.

*Step (1):* $\sqrt[3]{54} = \sqrt[3]{27 \cdot 2}$
*Step (2):* $= \sqrt[3]{27} \cdot \sqrt[3]{2}$
*Step (3):* $= 3 \cdot \sqrt[3]{2}$

□ **Example 3:** Simplify $3\sqrt[3]{-40}$.    (8)

**Solution:** Factor the radicand $-40$ into two factors, one of which is the largest possible perfect cube; then use the Basic Property of Radicals.

*Step (1):* $3\sqrt[3]{-40} = 3 \cdot \sqrt[3]{-8 \cdot 5}$
*Step (2):* $= 3 \cdot \sqrt[3]{-8} \cdot \sqrt[3]{5}$
*Step (3):* $= 3 \cdot (-2) \cdot \sqrt[3]{5}$
*Step (4):* $= -6 \cdot \sqrt[3]{5}$

□ **Example 4:** Simplify $\sqrt{98a^3b}$, where $a \geq 0$ and $b \geq 0$.    (9)

**Solution:** Factor the radicand into perfect squares; then use the Basic Property of Radicals.

*Step (1):* $\sqrt{98a^3b} = \sqrt{49 \cdot 2 \cdot a^2 \cdot a \cdot b}$
*Step (2):* $= \sqrt{49 \cdot a^2 \cdot 2 \cdot a \cdot b}$
*Step (3):* $= \sqrt{49a^2} \cdot \sqrt{2ab}$
*Step (4):* $= 7a \sqrt{2ab}$

□ **Study Exercise Two**    (10)

Simplify the following radicals.

1. $\sqrt{12}$    2. $3\sqrt{72}$    3. $\sqrt[3]{-24}$    4. $3\sqrt[3]{128}$    5. $\sqrt{75m^3n}$

## □ Evaluating Square Roots and Cube Roots with the Table    (11)

**Example 1:** Evaluate $\sqrt{7}$.

**Solution:** Turn to the table on page 514; find 7 and its corresponding square root.

$\sqrt{7} \approx 2.646$    (Approximately equal to.)

**Example 2:** Evaluate $\sqrt[3]{71}$.

    **Solution:** Turn to the table on page 514; find 71 and its corresponding cube root.

$$\sqrt[3]{71} \approx 4.141 \quad \text{(Approximately equal to.)}$$

## ☐ Evaluating Additional Square Roots and Cube Roots (12)

**Example 1:** Evaluate $\sqrt{200}$.

    **Solution:** Simplify the radical; then refer to the table.

*line (a)* $\quad \sqrt{200} = \sqrt{100 \cdot 2}$

*line (b)* $\qquad\quad = \sqrt{100} \cdot \sqrt{2}$

*line (c)* $\qquad\quad = 10 \cdot \sqrt{2}$

$\qquad\qquad\qquad\quad \downarrow$

*line (d)* $\qquad\quad \approx 10(1.414)$

*line (e)* $\qquad\quad \approx 14.14$

## ☐ **Example 2:** Evaluate $\sqrt[3]{-128}$. (13)

    **Solution:** Simplify the radical; then refer to the table.

*line (a)* $\quad \sqrt[3]{-128} = \sqrt[3]{-64 \cdot 2}$

*line (b)* $\qquad\qquad = \sqrt[3]{-64} \cdot \sqrt[3]{2}$

*line (c)* $\qquad\qquad = \quad -4 \cdot \sqrt[3]{2}$

$\qquad\qquad\qquad\qquad\quad \downarrow$

*line (d)* $\qquad\qquad \approx \quad -4(1.260)$

*line (e)* $\qquad\qquad \approx -5.040$

## ☐                         *Study Exercise Three* (14)

Use the Table of Square Roots and Cube Roots to evaluate the following.

1. $\sqrt{79}$        2. $\sqrt[3]{47}$        3. $\sqrt{300}$        4. $\sqrt{175}$        5. $\sqrt[3]{-250}$

## ☐ Addition and Subtraction of Radicals (15)

Expressions having identical radicals may be added or subtracted by combining the coefficients of the radicals.

**Example 1:** $3\sqrt{7} + 9\sqrt{7} = 12\sqrt{7}$

**Example 2:** $9\sqrt[3]{2x} - 4\sqrt[3]{2x} = 5\sqrt[3]{2x}$

**Example 3:** $2\sqrt[3]{6} + 8\sqrt[4]{6}$ cannot be combined.

**Example 4:** $6\sqrt{7} + 3\sqrt{5}$ cannot be combined.

## ☐ More Examples of Combining Radicals (16)

**Example 1:** Combine $2\sqrt[3]{4} + 5\sqrt[3]{11} - 5\sqrt[3]{4} + 2\sqrt[3]{11}$.

    **Solution:** Combine only the terms having identical radicals.

$$2\sqrt[3]{4} + 5\sqrt[3]{11} - 5\sqrt[3]{4} + 2\sqrt[3]{11} = -3\sqrt[3]{4} + 7\sqrt[3]{11}$$

☐ **Example 2:** Combine $2\sqrt{75} + 5\sqrt{27}$. **(17)**

   **Solution:** Simplify each radical.

   *line (a)* $2 \cdot \sqrt{75} + 5 \cdot \sqrt{27}$
   *line (b)* $2 \cdot \sqrt{25 \cdot 3} + 5 \cdot \sqrt{9 \cdot 3}$
   $\qquad\qquad \downarrow \qquad\qquad \downarrow$
   *line (c)* $2 \cdot \quad 5 \cdot \sqrt{3} + 5 \cdot 3 \cdot \sqrt{3}$
   *line (d)* $10\sqrt{3} + 15\sqrt{3}$
   *line (e)* $25\sqrt{3}$

☐ **Example 3:** Combine $3\sqrt[3]{16} - 5\sqrt[3]{54}$. **(18)**

   **Solution:** Simplify each radical.

   *line (a)* $3 \cdot \sqrt[3]{16} - 5\sqrt[3]{54}$
   *line (b)* $3 \cdot \sqrt[3]{8 \cdot 2} - 5 \cdot \sqrt[3]{27 \cdot 2}$
   $\qquad\qquad \downarrow \qquad\qquad \downarrow$
   *line (c)* $3 \cdot \quad 2 \cdot \sqrt[3]{2} - 5 \cdot 3 \cdot \sqrt[3]{2}$
   *line (d)* $6\sqrt[3]{2} - 15\sqrt[3]{2}$
   *line (e)* $-9\sqrt[3]{2}$

☐ **Example 4:** Combine $3\sqrt{24} + \sqrt{6} - 2\sqrt{27} + 5\sqrt{12}$. **(19)**

   **Solution:** Simplify each radical.

   *line (a)* $3\sqrt{24} + \sqrt{6} - 2\sqrt{27} + 5\sqrt{12}$
   *line (b)* $3 \cdot \sqrt{4 \cdot 6} + \sqrt{6} - 2 \cdot \sqrt{9 \cdot 3} + 5 \cdot \sqrt{4 \cdot 3}$
   $\qquad\qquad \downarrow \qquad\qquad\qquad \downarrow \qquad\qquad \downarrow$
   *line (c)* $3 \cdot \quad 2 \cdot \sqrt{6} + \sqrt{6} - 2 \cdot 3 \cdot \sqrt{3} + 5 \cdot 2 \cdot \sqrt{3}$
   *line (d)* $6\sqrt{6} + \sqrt{6} - 6\sqrt{3} + 10\sqrt{3}$
   *line (e)* $7\sqrt{6} + 4\sqrt{3}$

☐ *Study Exercise Four* **(20)**

Combine each of the following.

1. $4\sqrt{5} + 3\sqrt{5}$
2. $12\sqrt[3]{3a^2} - 5\sqrt[3]{3a^2}$
3. $3\sqrt{5} + 6\sqrt{7} - \sqrt{5} + 2\sqrt{7}$
4. $3\sqrt{8} + 7\sqrt{50}$
5. $4\sqrt{18} - 7\sqrt{98} + 5\sqrt[3]{16} - \sqrt[3]{54}$

☐ **Multiplication of Radicals** **(21)**

The Basic Property of Radicals allows us to multiply radicals.

$$\sqrt[n]{a} \cdot \sqrt[n]{b} = \sqrt[n]{ab}$$

Radicals may be multiplied by taking the product of the radicands, provided the radicals are of the same order.

**Example 1:** $\sqrt[3]{5} \cdot \sqrt[3]{7} = \sqrt[3]{35}$

**Example 2:** $\sqrt{6} \cdot \sqrt{5} = \sqrt{30}$

**Example 3:** $\sqrt[3]{5} \cdot \sqrt{3}$ cannot be multiplied.

## ☐ More Examples of Multiplication (22)

**Example 1:** Multiply $(2\sqrt{5})(3\sqrt{7})$.

**Solution:** Multiply the coefficients and multiply the radicals.

*line (a)* $(2\sqrt{5})(3\sqrt{7}) = 2\cdot 3\sqrt{5\cdot 7}$

*line (b)* $\qquad = 6\sqrt{35}$

## ☐ Example 2: Multiply $(4\sqrt[5]{2a^2})(7\sqrt[5]{3a})$. (23)

**Solution:** Multiply the coefficients and multiply the radicals.

*line (a)* $(4\sqrt[5]{2a^2})(7\sqrt[5]{3a}) = 4\cdot 7\sqrt[5]{(2a^2)(3a)}$

*line (b)* $\qquad = 28\sqrt[5]{6a^3}$

## ☐ Example 3: Multiply $\sqrt{2}(\sqrt{5} + 2\sqrt{7})$. (24)

**Solution:** Multiply $\sqrt{2}$ times each term of the sum.

*line (a)* $\sqrt{2}(\sqrt{5} + 2\sqrt{7}) = \sqrt{2}\cdot\sqrt{5} + \sqrt{2}\cdot 2\sqrt{7}$

*line (b)* $\qquad = \sqrt{10} + 2\sqrt{14}$

## ☐ Example 4: Multiply $(5 + \sqrt{3})(5 - \sqrt{3})$. (25)

**Solution:** Use the "sum times a difference" shortcut.

*line (a)* $(5 + \sqrt{3})(5 - \sqrt{3}) = 5\cdot 5 - \sqrt{3}\cdot\sqrt{3}$

*line (b)* $\qquad = 25 - \sqrt{9}$

*line (c)* $\qquad = 25 - 3$

*line (d)* $\qquad = 22$

## ☐ Example 5: Multiply $(5 + \sqrt{3})(3 + 2\sqrt{3})$. (26)

**Solution:** Use the **FOIL** shortcut.

$$\text{F}\qquad\text{O}\qquad\text{I}\qquad\text{L}$$

*line (a)* $(5 + \sqrt{3})(3 + 2\sqrt{3}) = 5\cdot 3 + 5\cdot 2\sqrt{3} + 3\sqrt{3} + \sqrt{3}\cdot 2\sqrt{3}$

*line (b)* $\qquad = 15 + 10\sqrt{3} + 3\sqrt{3} + \underline{2\sqrt{9}}$

*line (c)* $\qquad = 15 + \underline{10\sqrt{3} + 3\sqrt{3}} + 2\cdot 3$

*line (d)* $\qquad = 15 + \qquad 13\sqrt{3} \quad + \; 6$

*line (e)* $\qquad = 21 + 13\sqrt{3}$

## ☐ Study Exercise Five (27)

Multiply each of the following.

1. $\sqrt{5}\cdot\sqrt{6}$

2. $(2\sqrt[3]{a})(5\sqrt[3]{6a})$

3. $\sqrt{3}(\sqrt{2} - 4\sqrt{5})$

4. $(3 + \sqrt{2})(3 - \sqrt{2})$

5. $(2 + \sqrt{5})(3 + 4\sqrt{5})$

## ☐ Evaluating a Quotient Containing a Radical (28)

Suppose you wanted to evaluate $\dfrac{2}{\sqrt{3}}$. You would look up the $\sqrt{3}$ in the table and find 1.732. Then you could divide 2 by 1.732.

$$
\begin{array}{r}
1.154 \\
1.732_x)\overline{2.000_x000} \\
1\ 732 \\
\hline
268\ 0 \\
173\ 2 \\
\hline
94\ 80 \\
86\ 60 \\
\hline
8\ 200 \\
6\ 928 \\
\hline
\end{array}
$$

Therefore, $\dfrac{2}{\sqrt{3}}$ when evaluated becomes 1.154.

## ☐ An Easier Method (29)

The expression $\dfrac{2}{\sqrt{3}}$ can be evaluated more easily if the denominator is converted to a whole number before performing the division. This process is called *rationalizing the denominator.*

**Solution:** Multiply numerator and denominator by $\sqrt{3}$.

line (a) $\quad \dfrac{2}{\sqrt{3}} = \dfrac{2 \cdot \sqrt{3}}{\sqrt{3} \cdot \sqrt{3}}$

line (b) $\qquad = \dfrac{2\sqrt{3}}{\sqrt{9}}$

line (c) $\qquad = \dfrac{2\sqrt{3}}{3}$

line (d) $\qquad \approx \dfrac{2(1.732)}{3}$

line (e) $\qquad \approx \dfrac{3.464}{3}$

Perform the division:
$$
\begin{array}{r}
1.154 \\
3)\overline{3.464} \\
3 \\
\hline
4 \\
3 \\
\hline
16 \\
15 \\
\hline
14 \\
12 \\
\hline
\end{array}
$$

Notice that we obtained the same answer as in Frame 28. However, this division was much easier because the denominator of the original expression had been rationalized.

## ☐ Rationalizing the Denominator (30)

To rationalize the denominator of a fraction containing a radical:

*Step (1):* Find a number to multiply times the denominator which will produce a perfect $n$ power.

*Step (2):* Multiply the numerator and the denominator by this number. The resulting fraction will be rationalized (no radical in the denominator).

## ☐ **Example 1:** Rationalize the denominator of $\dfrac{2\sqrt{3}}{3\sqrt{5}}$. (31)

327

**Solution:**

*Step (1):* Multiplying the denominator by $\sqrt{5}$ will produce a factor of $\sqrt{25}$ or 5.

*Step (2):* Multiply numerator and denominator by $\sqrt{5}$.

*line (a)* $\dfrac{2\sqrt{3}}{3\sqrt{5}} = \dfrac{2\sqrt{3}\cdot\sqrt{5}}{3\sqrt{5}\cdot\sqrt{5}}$

*line (b)* $\phantom{\dfrac{2\sqrt{3}}{3\sqrt{5}}} = \dfrac{2\sqrt{15}}{3\sqrt{25}}$

*line (c)* $\phantom{\dfrac{2\sqrt{3}}{3\sqrt{5}}} = \dfrac{2\sqrt{15}}{3\cdot 5}$

*line (d)* $\phantom{\dfrac{2\sqrt{3}}{3\sqrt{5}}} = \dfrac{2\sqrt{15}}{15}$

☐ **Example 2:** Rationalize the denominator of $\sqrt{\dfrac{2}{3}}$. **(32)**

**Solution:** $\sqrt{\dfrac{2}{3}}$ means $\dfrac{\sqrt{2}}{\sqrt{3}}$.

*Step (1):* Multiplying the denominator by $\sqrt{3}$ will produce $\sqrt{9}$ or 3.

*Step (2):* Multiply numerator and denominator by $\sqrt{3}$.

*line (a)* $\dfrac{\sqrt{2}}{\sqrt{3}} = \dfrac{\sqrt{2}\cdot\sqrt{3}}{\sqrt{3}\cdot\sqrt{3}}$

*line (b)* $\phantom{\dfrac{\sqrt{2}}{\sqrt{3}}} = \dfrac{\sqrt{6}}{\sqrt{9}}$

*line (c)* $\phantom{\dfrac{\sqrt{2}}{\sqrt{3}}} = \dfrac{\sqrt{6}}{3}$

☐ **Example 3:** Rationalize the denominator of $\dfrac{5\sqrt[3]{7}}{6\sqrt[3]{2}}$. **(33)**

**Solution:**

*Step (1):* Multiplying the denominator by $\sqrt[3]{4}$ will produce a factor of $\sqrt[3]{8}$ or 2.

*Step (2):* Multiply numerator and denominator by $\sqrt[3]{4}$.

*line (a)* $\dfrac{5\sqrt[3]{7}}{6\sqrt[3]{2}} = \dfrac{5\sqrt[3]{7}\cdot\sqrt[3]{4}}{6\sqrt[3]{2}\cdot\sqrt[3]{4}}$

*line (b)* $\phantom{\dfrac{5\sqrt[3]{7}}{6\sqrt[3]{2}}} = \dfrac{5\sqrt[3]{28}}{6\sqrt[3]{8}}$

*line (c)* $\phantom{\dfrac{5\sqrt[3]{7}}{6\sqrt[3]{2}}} = \dfrac{5\sqrt[3]{28}}{6\cdot 2}$

*line (d)* $\phantom{\dfrac{5\sqrt[3]{7}}{6\sqrt[3]{2}}} = \dfrac{5\sqrt[3]{28}}{12}$

☐ <center>*Study Exercise Six*</center> **(34)**

A. Rationalize the denominators. Do not evaluate.

1. $\dfrac{2}{\sqrt{5}}$
2. $\dfrac{2\sqrt{3}}{3\sqrt{7}}$
3. $\dfrac{5}{2\sqrt[3]{2}}$
4. $\dfrac{\sqrt[3]{4}}{3\sqrt[3]{x^2}}$

B. Rationalize the denominators, then evaluate.

5. $\dfrac{5}{\sqrt{3}}$
6. $\dfrac{1}{\sqrt[3]{4}}$

☐ Rationalizing Binomial Denominators Containing Square Roots **(35)**

**Example 1:** Rationalize the denominator of $\dfrac{5}{\sqrt{6} + \sqrt{2}}$.

**Solution:** Remember that a "sum times a difference" produces a "difference of two squares."

*Step (1):* Multiplying the denominator by $\sqrt{6} - \sqrt{2}$ will produce a "sum times a difference."

*Step (2):* Multiply numerator and denominator by $\sqrt{6} - \sqrt{2}$.

*line (a)* $\quad \dfrac{5}{\sqrt{6} + \sqrt{2}} = \dfrac{5 \cdot (\sqrt{6} - \sqrt{2})}{(\sqrt{6} + \sqrt{2})(\sqrt{6} - \sqrt{2})}$

*line (b)* $\quad = \dfrac{5 \cdot (\sqrt{6} - \sqrt{2})}{\sqrt{6} \cdot \sqrt{6} - \sqrt{2} \cdot \sqrt{2}}$

*line (c)* $\quad = \dfrac{5 \cdot (\sqrt{6} - \sqrt{2})}{\sqrt{36} - \sqrt{4}}$

*line (d)* $\quad = \dfrac{5 \cdot (\sqrt{6} - \sqrt{2})}{6 - 2}$

*line (e)* $\quad = \dfrac{5 \cdot (\sqrt{6} - \sqrt{2})}{4}$, or $\dfrac{5\sqrt{6} - 5\sqrt{2}}{4}$

☐ **Example 2:** Rationalize the denominator of $\dfrac{\sqrt{5} - \sqrt{3}}{2\sqrt{5} - \sqrt{3}}$. **(36)**

**Solution:**

*Step (1):* Multiplying the denominator by $2\sqrt{5} + \sqrt{3}$ will produce a "sum times a difference."

*Step (2):* Multiply numerator and denominator by $2\sqrt{5} + \sqrt{3}$.

*line (a)* $\quad \dfrac{\sqrt{5} - \sqrt{3}}{2\sqrt{5} - \sqrt{3}} = \dfrac{(\sqrt{5} - \sqrt{3})(2\sqrt{5} + \sqrt{3})}{(2\sqrt{5} - \sqrt{3})(2\sqrt{5} + \sqrt{3})}$

*line (b)* $\quad = \dfrac{(\sqrt{5} - \sqrt{3})(2\sqrt{5} + \sqrt{3})}{2\sqrt{5} \cdot 2\sqrt{5} - \sqrt{3} \cdot \sqrt{3}}$

*line (c)* $\quad = \dfrac{(\sqrt{5} - \sqrt{3})(2\sqrt{5} + \sqrt{3})}{20 - 3}$

*line (d)* $\quad = \dfrac{(\sqrt{5} - \sqrt{3})(2\sqrt{5} + \sqrt{3})}{17}$

$$\qquad\quad \text{F} \qquad\quad \text{O} \qquad\quad \text{I} \qquad\quad \text{L}$$

*line (e)* $\quad = \dfrac{\sqrt{5} \cdot 2\sqrt{5} + \sqrt{5} \cdot \sqrt{3} - \sqrt{3} \cdot 2\sqrt{5} - \sqrt{3} \cdot \sqrt{3}}{17}$

*line (f)* $\quad = \dfrac{10 + \sqrt{15} - 2\sqrt{15} - 3}{17}$

*line (g)* $\quad = \dfrac{7 - \sqrt{15}}{17}$

☐ *Study Exercise Seven* **(37)**

Rationalize the denominators.

1. $\dfrac{3}{\sqrt{7} + \sqrt{3}}$
2. $\dfrac{\sqrt{2} + \sqrt{3}}{3\sqrt{2} - 2\sqrt{3}}$

# REVIEW EXERCISES

**A.** Simplify each of the following as far as possible.

1. $\sqrt{8}$      2. $\sqrt[3]{-54}$      3. $3\sqrt{48}$

4. $2\sqrt[3]{40}$      5. $7x\sqrt[3]{-32x^7}$

**B.** Combine the following by addition or subtraction.

6. $5\sqrt{7} - 8\sqrt{7}$      7. $3\sqrt[3]{16} - \sqrt[3]{54} + \sqrt{2} + \sqrt{8}$

8. $2\sqrt{8x} + 5\sqrt{27y} - 3\sqrt{32x} - \sqrt{48y}$

**C.** Multiply the following.

9. $(3\sqrt{5x})(6\sqrt{7y})$      10. $\sqrt{3}(2\sqrt{5} - 3\sqrt{11})$

11. $(\sqrt{2} - 3\sqrt{5})(4\sqrt{2} + \sqrt{5})$      12. $(\sqrt{2} + 3\sqrt{5})(\sqrt{2} - 3\sqrt{5})$

13. $(2\sqrt{m} + 5\sqrt{n})(\sqrt{m} - 3\sqrt{n})$

**D.** Rationalize the denominators. Do not evaluate.

14. $\dfrac{3}{\sqrt{5}}$      15. $\dfrac{3}{\sqrt[3]{4}}$      16. $\sqrt{\dfrac{5}{6}}$

17. $\dfrac{\sqrt{x}}{3\sqrt{y}}$      18. $\dfrac{3}{\sqrt{7} + \sqrt{5}}$      19. $\dfrac{2\sqrt{3} + \sqrt{5}}{\sqrt{3} - 3\sqrt{5}}$

**E.** Rationalize the denominators, then evaluate.

20. $\dfrac{1}{\sqrt{2}}$      21. $\dfrac{2}{\sqrt[3]{4}}$

## Solutions to Review Exercises

**A.**
1. $\sqrt{8} = \sqrt{4 \cdot 2} = 2\sqrt{2}$      2. $\sqrt[3]{-54} = \sqrt[3]{-27 \cdot 2} = -3\sqrt[3]{2}$

3. $3\sqrt{48} = 3\sqrt{16 \cdot 3} = 12\sqrt{3}$      4. $2\sqrt[3]{40} = 2\sqrt[3]{8 \cdot 5} = 4\sqrt[3]{5}$

5. $7x\sqrt[3]{-32x^7} = 7x\sqrt[3]{-8 \cdot 4 \cdot x^6 \cdot x} = -14x^3\sqrt[3]{4x}$

**B.**
6. $5\sqrt{7} - 8\sqrt{7} = -3\sqrt{7}$

7. $3\sqrt[3]{16} - \sqrt[3]{54} + \sqrt{2} + \sqrt{8} = 3\sqrt[3]{8 \cdot 2} - \sqrt[3]{27 \cdot 2} + \sqrt{2} + \sqrt{4 \cdot 2}$
$$= 6\sqrt[3]{2} - 3\sqrt[3]{2} + \sqrt{2} + 2\sqrt{2}$$
$$= 3\sqrt[3]{2} + 3\sqrt{2}$$

8. $2\sqrt{8x} + 5\sqrt{27y} - 3\sqrt{32x} - \sqrt{48y} = 2\sqrt{4 \cdot 2x} + 5\sqrt{9 \cdot 3y} - 3\sqrt{16 \cdot 2x} - \sqrt{16 \cdot 3y}$
$$= 4\sqrt{2x} + 15\sqrt{3y} - 12\sqrt{2x} - 4\sqrt{3y}$$
$$= -8\sqrt{2x} + 11\sqrt{3y}$$

**C.**
9. $(3\sqrt{5x})(6\sqrt{7y}) = 18\sqrt{35xy}$

10. $\sqrt{3}(2\sqrt{5} - 3\sqrt{11}) = 2\sqrt{15} - 3\sqrt{33}$

$$\qquad\qquad\qquad\quad \mathbf{F}\qquad \mathbf{O}\qquad \mathbf{I}\qquad \mathbf{L}$$

11. $(\sqrt{2} - 3\sqrt{5})(4\sqrt{2} + \sqrt{5}) = \sqrt{2} \cdot 4\sqrt{2} + \sqrt{2} \cdot \sqrt{5} - 3\sqrt{5} \cdot 4\sqrt{2} - 3\sqrt{5} \cdot \sqrt{5}$
$$= \quad 8 \quad + \quad \sqrt{10} \quad - \quad 12\sqrt{10} \quad - \quad 15$$
$$= -7 - 11\sqrt{10}$$

12. $(\sqrt{2} + 3\sqrt{5})(\sqrt{2} - 3\sqrt{5}) = \sqrt{4} - 9\sqrt{25}$
$$= 2 - 45$$
$$= -43$$

13. $(2\sqrt{m} + 5\sqrt{n})(\sqrt{m} - 3\sqrt{n}) = 2\sqrt{m} \cdot \sqrt{m} - 2\sqrt{m} \cdot 3\sqrt{n} + 5\sqrt{n} \cdot \sqrt{m} - 5\sqrt{n} \cdot 3\sqrt{n}$
$$= 2m - 6\sqrt{mn} + 5\sqrt{mn} - 15n$$
$$= 2m - \sqrt{mn} - 15n$$

## Solutions to Review Exercises, Contd.

D.  14. $\dfrac{3}{\sqrt{5}} = \dfrac{3 \cdot \sqrt{5}}{\sqrt{5} \cdot \sqrt{5}} = \dfrac{3 \cdot \sqrt{5}}{5}$

15. $\dfrac{3}{\sqrt[3]{4}} = \dfrac{3 \cdot \sqrt[3]{2}}{\sqrt[3]{4} \cdot \sqrt[3]{2}} = \dfrac{3\sqrt[3]{2}}{2}$

16. $\sqrt{\dfrac{5}{6}} = \dfrac{\sqrt{5}}{\sqrt{6}} = \dfrac{\sqrt{5} \cdot \sqrt{6}}{\sqrt{6} \cdot \sqrt{6}} = \dfrac{\sqrt{30}}{6}$

17. $\dfrac{\sqrt{x}}{3\sqrt{y}} = \dfrac{\sqrt{x} \cdot \sqrt{y}}{3\sqrt{y} \cdot \sqrt{y}} = \dfrac{\sqrt{xy}}{3y}$

18. $\dfrac{3}{\sqrt{7} + \sqrt{5}} = \dfrac{3 \cdot (\sqrt{7} - \sqrt{5})}{(\sqrt{7} + \sqrt{5}) \cdot (\sqrt{7} - \sqrt{5})}$

$= \dfrac{3\sqrt{7} - 3\sqrt{5}}{\sqrt{49} - \sqrt{25}}$

$= \dfrac{3\sqrt{7} - 3\sqrt{5}}{7 - 5}$

$= \dfrac{3\sqrt{7} - 3\sqrt{5}}{2}$

19. $\dfrac{2\sqrt{3} + \sqrt{5}}{\sqrt{3} - 3\sqrt{5}} = \dfrac{(2\sqrt{3} + \sqrt{5}) \cdot (\sqrt{3} + 3\sqrt{5})}{(\sqrt{3} - 3\sqrt{5}) \cdot (\sqrt{3} + 3\sqrt{5})}$

$\qquad\qquad\qquad$ **F** $\qquad$ **O** $\qquad$ **I** $\qquad$ **L**

$= \dfrac{2\sqrt{3} \cdot \sqrt{3} + 2\sqrt{3} \cdot 3\sqrt{5} + \sqrt{5} \cdot \sqrt{3} + \sqrt{5} \cdot 3\sqrt{5}}{\sqrt{9} - 9\sqrt{25}}$

$= \dfrac{6 + 6\sqrt{15} + \sqrt{15} + 15}{3 - 45}$

$= \dfrac{21 + 7\sqrt{15}}{-42} = \dfrac{7(3 + \sqrt{15})}{-6 \cdot 7}$, or $\dfrac{3 + \sqrt{15}}{-6}$

E.  20. $\dfrac{1}{\sqrt{2}} = \dfrac{1 \cdot \sqrt{2}}{\sqrt{2} \cdot \sqrt{2}}$

$= \dfrac{\sqrt{2}}{2}$

$\approx \dfrac{1.414}{2}$

$\approx 0.707$

21. $\dfrac{2}{\sqrt[3]{4}} = \dfrac{2 \cdot \sqrt[3]{2}}{\sqrt[3]{4} \cdot \sqrt[3]{2}}$

$= \dfrac{2\sqrt[3]{2}}{\sqrt[3]{8}}$

$= \dfrac{2\sqrt[3]{2}}{2}$

$= \sqrt[3]{2}$

$\approx 1.260$

## SUPPLEMENTARY PROBLEMS

A.  Simplify each of the following as far as possible.

1. $\sqrt{8}$
2. $3\sqrt{8}$
3. $\sqrt{18}$
4. $\sqrt{150}$
5. $\sqrt{18x^3}$
6. $\sqrt{m^3 n^2}$
7. $\sqrt{12a^5}$
8. $\sqrt[3]{8}$
9. $\sqrt[3]{-8}$
10. $3\sqrt[3]{54}$
11. $\sqrt[3]{m^4 n^3}$
12. $2\sqrt[3]{-8xy^4}$

B.  Combine the following by addition or subtraction.

13. $3\sqrt{2} + 5\sqrt{2}$
14. $5\sqrt{3} - 6\sqrt{3}$
15. $7\sqrt[3]{5} - 9\sqrt[3]{5}$
16. $4\sqrt{3} + 7\sqrt{27}$
17. $3\sqrt{27} - \sqrt{75}$
18. $5\sqrt[3]{54} + 2\sqrt[3]{128}$
19. $6\sqrt[3]{2x} + 3\sqrt[3]{16x}$
20. $2\sqrt{8} + 3\sqrt{18} - \sqrt{32}$
21. $5\sqrt{12} - \sqrt{27} + 2\sqrt{48}$
22. $3\sqrt{24} - \sqrt{128} + 3\sqrt{6} - 2\sqrt{54}$
23. $4\sqrt{8} - 2\sqrt{12} + \sqrt{50} + 3\sqrt{75}$
24. $\sqrt{8x} - \sqrt{32x^3} + \sqrt{2x}$
25. $5\sqrt{3x} + 7\sqrt{3x} - 8\sqrt{2x} + 10\sqrt{2x}$
26. $2\sqrt{50a} + 3\sqrt{32a} - 3\sqrt{2a}$
27. $2\sqrt{16x^3} - 5\sqrt{8x^2} + 7\sqrt{64x^3} + 12\sqrt{32x^2}$
28. $2\sqrt[3]{5ab} - 3\sqrt[5]{ab} + 6\sqrt[3]{5ab} + 7\sqrt[5]{ab}$

C.  Multiply the following.

29. $\sqrt{6} \cdot \sqrt{7}$
30. $\sqrt{5} \cdot \sqrt{2}$
31. $\sqrt{x} \cdot \sqrt{y}$
32. $\sqrt{x} \cdot \sqrt{xy^2}$
33. $(2\sqrt{5})(6\sqrt{3})$
34. $(5x\sqrt{11})(2x\sqrt{3})$
35. $\sqrt[3]{3} \cdot \sqrt[3]{2}$
36. $(5\sqrt[3]{7})(2\sqrt[3]{2})$
37. $(3\sqrt[5]{16})(4\sqrt[5]{2})$
38. $(2\sqrt[3]{3x})(4\sqrt[3]{2x})(-3\sqrt[3]{x})$
39. $\sqrt{3} \cdot (x + \sqrt{2})$
40. $2\sqrt{3x}(3\sqrt{4y} - 5\sqrt{3z})$
41. $(\sqrt{2} - \sqrt{3})(\sqrt{2} + \sqrt{3})$
42. $(\sqrt{x} + 2)(\sqrt{x} - 2)$

## SUPPLEMENTARY PROBLEMS, Contd.

43. $(5\sqrt{a} + 3\sqrt{b})(5\sqrt{a} - 3\sqrt{b})$

44. $(\sqrt{3} + \sqrt{2})^2$

45. $(2\sqrt{5} - 3\sqrt{2})^2$

46. $(\sqrt{2} + \sqrt{5})(\sqrt{2} + 3\sqrt{5})$

47. $(5\sqrt{7} - 2\sqrt{3})(2\sqrt{7} + 4\sqrt{3})$

**D.** Rationalize the denominators. Do not evaluate.

48. $\dfrac{3}{\sqrt{3}}$

49. $\sqrt{\dfrac{1}{3}}$

50. $\sqrt{\dfrac{3}{2}}$

51. $\dfrac{3}{\sqrt{2}}$

52. $\dfrac{\sqrt{a}}{\sqrt{b}}$

53. $\dfrac{5\sqrt{3}}{7\sqrt{5}}$

54. $\dfrac{-4}{\sqrt[3]{4}}$

55. $\dfrac{-2\sqrt[3]{2}}{3\sqrt[3]{25}}$

56. $\dfrac{3}{2\sqrt{5x}}$

57. $\dfrac{2\sqrt[3]{x}}{3\sqrt[3]{2}}$

58. $\dfrac{2}{\sqrt{5} - \sqrt{7}}$

59. $\dfrac{2\sqrt{7}}{3\sqrt{2} - 5\sqrt{7}}$

60. $\dfrac{2\sqrt{5x} - 3\sqrt{7y}}{5\sqrt{5x} - 2\sqrt{7y}}$

**E.** Rationalize the denominators; then evaluate.

61. $\dfrac{7}{\sqrt{2}}$

62. $\dfrac{1}{\sqrt{3}}$

63. $\dfrac{1}{\sqrt[3]{4}}$

64. $\dfrac{3}{\sqrt{5} + \sqrt{6}}$

**F.** Calculator Problems. With your instructor's approval, use a calculator to evaluate the following expressions.

65. $\sqrt{287}$

66. $\sqrt[3]{476}$

67. $(3.85)\sqrt{22.97}$

68. $\sqrt{79} + \sqrt{56}$

69. $\sqrt{79 + 56}$

70. $(15.67)\sqrt[4]{364}$

71. $\sqrt{\dfrac{23}{41}}$

72. $(7\sqrt{2} + 3)^2$

73. $\dfrac{5\sqrt{8} - 3\sqrt{5}}{\sqrt{7}}$

74. $\dfrac{7\sqrt[3]{21} + 3\sqrt[8]{5}}{\sqrt[3]{2}}$

75. $(1 - \sqrt{2})(2 + \sqrt{2})$

□ **Solutions to Study Exercises** **(5A)**

### Study Exercise One (Frame 5)

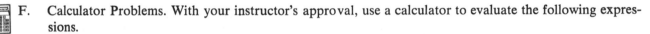

1. $\sqrt{16 \cdot 3} = \sqrt{16} \cdot \sqrt{3} = 4 \cdot \sqrt{3}$

2. $\sqrt[3]{27 \cdot 2} = \sqrt[3]{27} \cdot \sqrt[3]{2} = 3 \cdot \sqrt[3]{2}$

3. $\sqrt[3]{-8 \cdot 5} = \sqrt[3]{-8} \cdot \sqrt[3]{5} = -2 \cdot \sqrt[3]{5}$

4. $\sqrt[5]{4x^5} = \sqrt[5]{4} \cdot \sqrt[5]{x^5} = \sqrt[5]{4} \cdot x$, or $x \cdot \sqrt[5]{4}$

□ **Study Exercise Two (Frame 10)** **(10A)**

1. $\sqrt{12} = \sqrt{4 \cdot 3} = \sqrt{4} \cdot \sqrt{3} = 2\sqrt{3}$

2. $3\sqrt{72} = 3\sqrt{36 \cdot 2} = 3 \cdot \sqrt{36} \cdot \sqrt{2} = 3 \cdot 6 \cdot \sqrt{2} = 18\sqrt{2}$

3. $\sqrt[3]{-24} = \sqrt[3]{-8 \cdot 3} = \sqrt[3]{-8} \cdot \sqrt[3]{3} = -2\sqrt[3]{3}$

4. $3\sqrt[3]{128} = 3\sqrt[3]{64 \cdot 2} = 3\sqrt[3]{64} \cdot \sqrt[3]{2} = 3 \cdot 4 \cdot \sqrt[3]{2} = 12\sqrt[3]{2}$

5. $\sqrt{75m^3n} = \sqrt{25 \cdot 3 \cdot m^2 \cdot m \cdot n} = 5m\sqrt{3mn}$

□ **Study Exercise Three (Frame 14)** **(14A)**

1. $\sqrt{79} \approx 8.888$

2. $\sqrt[3]{47} \approx 3.609$

3. $\sqrt{300} = 10\sqrt{3} \approx 10(1.732) = 17.32$

4. $\sqrt{175} = 5\sqrt{7} \approx 5(2.646) = 13.23$

5. $\sqrt[3]{-250} = -5\sqrt[3]{2} \approx -5(1.260) = -6.3000$

## Solutions to Study Exercises, Contd.

☐             *Study Exercise Four (Frame 20)*          **(20A)**

1. $4\sqrt{5} + 3\sqrt{5} = 7\sqrt{5}$

2. $12\sqrt[3]{3a^2} - 5\sqrt[3]{3a^2} = 7\sqrt[3]{3a^2}$

3. $3\sqrt{5} + 6\sqrt{7} - \sqrt{5} + 2\sqrt{7} = 2\sqrt{5} + 8\sqrt{7}$

4. $\begin{aligned}3\sqrt{8} + 7\sqrt{50} &= 3\sqrt{4\cdot 2} + 7\sqrt{25\cdot 2}\\ &= 3\cdot\sqrt{4}\cdot\sqrt{2} + 7\cdot\sqrt{25}\cdot\sqrt{2}\\ &= 3\cdot 2\cdot\sqrt{2} + 7\cdot 5\cdot\sqrt{2}\\ &= 6\sqrt{2} + 35\sqrt{2}\\ &= 41\sqrt{2}\end{aligned}$

5. $\begin{aligned}4\sqrt{18} - 7\sqrt{98} + 5\sqrt[3]{16} - \sqrt[3]{54} &= 4\sqrt{9\cdot 2} - 7\sqrt{49\cdot 2} + 5\sqrt[3]{8\cdot 2} - \sqrt[3]{27\cdot 2}\\ &= 4\cdot\sqrt{9}\cdot\sqrt{2} - 7\cdot\sqrt{49}\cdot\sqrt{2} + 5\cdot\sqrt[3]{8}\cdot\sqrt[3]{2} - \sqrt[3]{27}\cdot\sqrt[3]{2}\\ &= 4\cdot 3\cdot\sqrt{2} - 7\cdot 7\cdot\sqrt{2} + 5\cdot 2\cdot\sqrt[3]{2} - 3\cdot\sqrt[3]{2}\\ &= 12\sqrt{2} - 49\sqrt{2} + 10\sqrt[3]{2} - 3\sqrt[3]{2}\\ &= -37\sqrt{2} + 7\sqrt[3]{2}\end{aligned}$

☐             *Study Exercise Five (Frame 27)*          **(27A)**

1. $\sqrt{5}\cdot\sqrt{6} = \sqrt{30}$

2. $(2\sqrt[3]{a})(5\sqrt[3]{6a}) = 10\sqrt[3]{6a^2}$

3. $\sqrt{3}(\sqrt{2} - 4\sqrt{5}) = \sqrt{6} - 4\sqrt{15}$

4. $\begin{aligned}(3 + \sqrt{2})(3 - \sqrt{2}) &= 3\cdot 3 - \sqrt{2}\cdot\sqrt{2}\\ &= 9 - \sqrt{4}\\ &= 9 - 2\\ &= 7\end{aligned}$

                         **F**       **O**       **I**       **L**

5. $\begin{aligned}(2 + \sqrt{5})(3 + 4\sqrt{5}) &= 2\cdot 3 + 2\cdot 4\sqrt{5} + 3\cdot\sqrt{5} + \sqrt{5}\cdot 4\cdot\sqrt{5}\\ &= 6 + 8\sqrt{5} + 3\sqrt{5} + 4\sqrt{25}\\ &= 6 + 8\sqrt{5} + 3\sqrt{5} + 4\cdot 5\\ &= 6 + 11\sqrt{5} + 20\\ &= 26 + 11\sqrt{5}\end{aligned}$

☐             *Study Exercise Six (Frame 34)*          **(34A)**

A.  1. $\dfrac{2}{\sqrt{5}} = \dfrac{2\cdot\sqrt{5}}{\sqrt{5}\cdot\sqrt{5}} = \dfrac{2\sqrt{5}}{\sqrt{25}} = \dfrac{2\sqrt{5}}{5}$

2. $\dfrac{2\sqrt{3}}{3\sqrt{7}} = \dfrac{2\sqrt{3}\cdot\sqrt{7}}{3\sqrt{7}\cdot\sqrt{7}} = \dfrac{2\sqrt{21}}{3\sqrt{49}} = \dfrac{2\sqrt{21}}{3\cdot 7} = \dfrac{2\sqrt{21}}{21}$

3. $\dfrac{5}{2\sqrt[3]{2}} = \dfrac{5\cdot\sqrt[3]{4}}{2\sqrt[3]{2}\cdot\sqrt[3]{4}} = \dfrac{5\sqrt[3]{4}}{2\sqrt[3]{8}} = \dfrac{5\sqrt[3]{4}}{2\cdot 2} = \dfrac{5\sqrt[3]{4}}{4}$

4. $\dfrac{\sqrt[3]{4}}{3\sqrt[3]{x^2}} = \dfrac{\sqrt[3]{4}\cdot\sqrt[3]{x}}{3\sqrt[3]{x^2}\cdot\sqrt[3]{x}} = \dfrac{\sqrt[3]{4x}}{3\sqrt[3]{x^3}} = \dfrac{\sqrt[3]{4x}}{3x}$

B.  5. $\dfrac{5}{\sqrt{3}} = \dfrac{5\cdot\sqrt{3}}{\sqrt{3}\cdot\sqrt{3}} = \dfrac{5\sqrt{3}}{3} \approx \dfrac{5(1.732)}{3} = 2.887$

6. $\dfrac{1}{\sqrt[3]{4}} = \dfrac{1\cdot\sqrt[3]{2}}{\sqrt[3]{4}\cdot\sqrt[3]{2}} = \dfrac{\sqrt[3]{2}}{2} = \dfrac{1.260}{2} = 0.630$

☐             *Study Exercise Seven (Frame 37)*          **(37A)**

1. $\begin{aligned}\dfrac{3}{\sqrt{7} + \sqrt{3}} &= \dfrac{3\cdot(\sqrt{7} - \sqrt{3})}{(\sqrt{7} + \sqrt{3})(\sqrt{7} - \sqrt{3})}\\[2mm] &= \dfrac{3(\sqrt{7} - \sqrt{3})}{\sqrt{49} - \sqrt{9}}\\[2mm] &= \dfrac{3(\sqrt{7} - \sqrt{3})}{7 - 3}\\[2mm] &= \dfrac{3(\sqrt{7} - \sqrt{3})}{4} \quad\text{or}\quad \dfrac{3\sqrt{7} - 3\sqrt{3}}{4}\end{aligned}$

2. $\dfrac{\sqrt{2} + \sqrt{3}}{3\sqrt{2} - 2\sqrt{3}} = \dfrac{(\sqrt{2} + \sqrt{3})\cdot(3\sqrt{2} + 2\sqrt{3})}{(3\sqrt{2} - 2\sqrt{3})\cdot(3\sqrt{2} + 2\sqrt{3})}$

                                        **F**       **O**       **I**       **L**

$\begin{aligned}&= \dfrac{\sqrt{2}\cdot 3\sqrt{2} + \sqrt{2}\cdot 2\sqrt{3} + \sqrt{3}\cdot 3\sqrt{2} + \sqrt{3}\cdot 2\sqrt{3}}{9\sqrt{4} - 4\sqrt{9}}\\[2mm] &= \dfrac{6 + 2\sqrt{6} + 3\sqrt{6} + 6}{9\cdot 2 - 4\cdot 3}\\[2mm] &= \dfrac{12 + 5\sqrt{6}}{6}\end{aligned}$

# Using the Quadratic Formula and Solving Radical Equations

## ☐ Objectives (1)

By the end of this unit you should be able to:

- state the quadratic formula from memory.
- use the quadratic formula to find all the real solutions of quadratic equations.
- solve radical equations.

## ☐ Quadratic Equations and Radical Equations in One Unknown (2)

In this unit we will be concerned with solving two types of equations: *quadratic* equations and *radical* equations.

1.  A *quadratic* equation in one unknown is any equation which can be put into the form:

$$ax^2 + bx + c = 0 \quad \text{where } a, b, c \text{ are constants} \quad \text{and} \quad a \neq 0$$

The highest exponent is 2.

**Example:** $3x^2 + 5x - 2 = 0$ is quadratic.

2.  A *radical* equation in one unknown is any equation which contains a radical.

**Example:** $\sqrt{2x - 3} = 1$ is a radical equation.

## ☐ Review of Solving Quadratic Equations by Factoring (3)

**Example:** Solve $2x^2 + x = 6$ by factoring.

**Solution:**

*Step (1):* Place the equation in the form $ax^2 + bx + c = 0$ by obtaining all terms on one side.
line (a)  $2x^2 + x = 6$
line (b)  $2x^2 + x - 6 = 0$

*Step (2):* Factor the left side.
line (c)  $(2x - 3)(x + 2) = 0$

*Step (3):* Set each factor containing a variable equal to zero.
line (d)  $2x - 3 = 0$, or $x + 2 = 0$

*Step (4):* Solve the resulting first degree equations.

line (e)  $2x - 3 = 0, 2x = 3, x = \dfrac{3}{2}$

line (f)  $x + 2 = 0, x = -2$

The solutions are $\dfrac{3}{2}$ and $-2$.

## ☐ Study Exercise One (4)

Solve each of the following quadratic equations by factoring.

1.  $x^2 - 3x - 10 = 0$
2.  $3x^2 - x = 2$
3.  $2x^2 - 5x = 0$
4.  $x^2 - 4x + 2 = 0$

## ☐ The Quadratic Formula (5)

Many quadratic equations such as $x^2 - 4x + 2 = 0$ cannot be solved by factoring. In order to solve all quadratic equations we use the quadratic formula. For quadratic equations in the form $ax^2 + bx + c = 0$:

$$x = \frac{-b \pm \sqrt{b^2 - 4ac}}{2a}, \text{ where } a \neq 0.$$

**Memorize!**

☐ **Recognizing the Values of a, b, and c** **(6)**

**Example 1:** Given the equation $2x^2 + 3x = 6$, specify the values of $a$, $b$, and $c$.

**Solution:** Write the equation with all terms on one side of the equal sign.

line (a) $2x^2 + 3x = 6$
line (b) $2x^2 + 3x - 6 = 0$

line (c) $ax^2 + bx + c = 0$
line (d) $a = 2, b = 3, c = -6$

☐ **Example 2:** Given the equation $x^2 - 3x = 7$, specify the values of $a$, $b$, and $c$. **(7)**

**Solution:** Write the equation with all terms on one side of the equal sign.

line (a) $x^2 - 3x = 7$
line (b) $x^2 - 3x - 7 = 0$
line (c) $1x^2 - 3x - 7 = 0$

line (d) $ax^2 + bx + c = 0$
line (e) $a = 1, b = -3, c = -7$

☐ **Example 3:** Given the equation $4x^2 + 5 = 0$, specify the values of $a$, $b$, and $c$. **(8)**

**Solution:** Replace the missing term with $0 \cdot x$.

line (a) $4x^2 + 5 = 0$
line (b) $4x^2 + 0x + 5 = 0$
          ↑      ↑      ↑
line (c) $ax^2 + bx + c = 0$
line (d) $a = 4, b = 0, c = 5$

☐ **Study Exercise Two** **(9)**

Specify the values of $a$, $b$, and $c$ for each of the following equations.

1. $3x^2 + 4x = 7$      2. $x^2 - 5x + 2 = 0$
3. $2x^2 + 3 = x$       4. $3x^2 - x = 0$

☐ **Using the Quadratic Formula** **(10)**

$$x = \frac{-b \pm \sqrt{b^2 - 4ac}}{2a}, \text{ where } a \neq 0.$$

**Example 1:** Solve $x^2 + 5x + 6 = 0$.

**Solution:** Determine the values of $a$, $b$, and $c$; then substitute these values into the formula.

*Step (1):* $1x^2 + 5x + 6 = 0; a = 1, b = 5, c = 6$
*Step (2):* Substitute these values into the formula and simplify.

line (a) $x = \dfrac{-b \pm \sqrt{b^2 - 4ac}}{2a}$

line (b) $= \dfrac{-5 \pm \sqrt{25 - 4 \cdot 1 \cdot 6}}{2 \cdot 1}$

line (c) $= \dfrac{-5 \pm \sqrt{25 - 24}}{2}$

line (d) $= \dfrac{-5 \pm \sqrt{1}}{2}$

337

line (e) $\quad = \dfrac{-5 \pm 1}{2}$

line (f) $\quad \pm$ means to add the two numbers; then subtract the two numbers.

line (g) $\quad x = \dfrac{-5 + 1}{2}, \quad x = \dfrac{-5 - 1}{2}$

$\qquad\qquad\quad \downarrow \qquad\qquad\quad \downarrow$

line (h) $\quad x = \dfrac{-4}{2} \qquad\quad x = \dfrac{-6}{2}$

$\qquad\qquad\quad \downarrow \qquad\qquad\quad \downarrow$

line (i) $\quad x = -2 \qquad\quad x = -3$

Therefore, the solutions are $-2$ and $-3$.

☐ **Example 2:** Solve $3x^2 + x = 2$. $\hfill$ **(11)**

$\quad$ **Solution:** Determine the values of $a$, $b$, and $c$; then substitute these values into the formula.

$\quad$ *Step (1):* $\quad 3x^2 + x - 2 = 0; a = 3, b = 1, c = -2$

$\quad$ *Step (2):* $\quad$ Substitute these values into the formula and simplify.

line (a) $\quad x = \dfrac{-b \pm \sqrt{b^2 - 4ac}}{2a}$

line (b) $\quad = \dfrac{-1 \pm \sqrt{1 - 4 \cdot 3 \cdot (-2)}}{2 \cdot 3}$

line (c) $\quad = \dfrac{-1 \pm \sqrt{1 + 24}}{6}$

line (d) $\quad = \dfrac{-1 \pm \sqrt{25}}{6}$

line (e) $\quad = \dfrac{-1 \pm 5}{6}$

line (f) $\quad$ Add and subtract to obtain the solutions.

line (g) $\quad x = \dfrac{-1 + 5}{6}, \quad x = \dfrac{-1 - 5}{6}$

$\qquad\qquad\quad \downarrow \qquad\qquad\quad \downarrow$

line (h) $\quad x = \dfrac{4}{6} \qquad\qquad x = \dfrac{-6}{6}$

$\qquad\qquad\quad \downarrow \qquad\qquad\quad \downarrow$

line (i) $\quad x = \dfrac{2}{3} \qquad\qquad x = -1$

Therefore, the solutions are $\dfrac{2}{3}$ and $-1$.

☐ **Example 3:** Solve $x^2 - 4x + 2 = 0$ (cannot be factored). $\hfill$ **(12)**

$\quad$ **Solution:**

$\quad$ *Step (1):* $\quad 1x^2 - 4x + 2 = 0; a = 1, b = -4, c = 2$

$\quad$ *Step (2):* $\quad$ Substitute these values into the formula and simplify.

line (a) $\quad x = \dfrac{-b \pm \sqrt{b^2 - 4ac}}{2a}$

line (b) $\quad = \dfrac{4 \pm \sqrt{16 - 4 \cdot 1 \cdot 2}}{2 \cdot 1}$

line (c) $\quad = \dfrac{4 \pm \sqrt{16 - 8}}{2}$

line (d) $\quad = \dfrac{4 \pm \sqrt{8}}{2}$

$$\text{line } (e) \quad = \frac{4 \pm \sqrt{4 \cdot 2}}{2}$$

$$\text{line } (f) \quad = \frac{4 \pm 2\sqrt{2}}{2}$$

$$\text{line } (g) \quad = \frac{\cancel{2}(2 \pm 1 \cdot \sqrt{2})}{\cancel{2}}$$

$$\text{line } (h) \quad = 2 \pm \sqrt{2}$$

Therefore, the solutions are $2 + \sqrt{2}$ and $2 - \sqrt{2}$. These are exact solutions. On many occasions you will want to approximate these solutions with decimals.

☐ **Converting Radical Solutions to Decimals** (13)

According to the square root table:

$$\sqrt{2} \approx 1.414$$
$$\uparrow$$

"approximately equal to"

line (a) $2 + \sqrt{2} \approx 2 + 1.414$, or 3.414
line (b) $2 - \sqrt{2} \approx 2 - 1.414$, or 0.586

The approximate solutions are 3.414 and 0.586.

☐ **Example 4:** Solve $2x^2 + x + 3 = 0$ [a special case]. (14)

    **Solution:**

line (a) $a = 2, b = 1, c = 3$

line (b) $x = \dfrac{-1 \pm \sqrt{1 - 4 \cdot 2 \cdot 3}}{2 \cdot 2}$

line (c) $= \dfrac{-1 \pm \sqrt{1 - 24}}{4}$

line (d) $= \dfrac{-1 \pm \sqrt{-23}}{4}$

The principal square root of a negative number does not exist in the set of real numbers. Therefore, $x = \dfrac{-1 \pm \sqrt{-23}}{4}$ is telling you that the original equation has no solutions in the set of real numbers.

☐                             *Study Exercise Three* (15)

Solve the following quadratic equations by using the quadratic formula.

1. $x^2 + 7x + 12 = 0$          2. $6x^2 - x - 2 = 0$          3. $3x^2 - 4x = 0$
4. $x^2 - 4x + 1 = 0$ (Give the radical solutions and the decimal solutions.)
5. $3x^2 + 2x + 5 = 0$

☐ **Solving Radical Equations** (16)

*Remember,* a radical equation is any equation which contains a radical.

**Example:** $\sqrt{2x - 3} - 1 = 0$

Radical equations may be solved by following these steps:

   *Step (1):*   Isolate the term containing the radical on one side of the equation.
   *Step (2):*   Square each side of the equation.
   *Step (3):*   Solve for the unknown.
   *Step (4):*   Check all answers in the original equation.

☐ **Example 1:** Solve $\sqrt{2x-3} - 1 = 0$. (17)

  **Solution:**

  *Step (1):*  Isolate the radical.

  line (a)  $\sqrt{2x-3} - 1 = 0$

  line (b)  $\sqrt{2x-3} = 1$

  *Step (2):*  Square each side.

  line (c)  $(\sqrt{2x-3})^2 = (1)^2$

  line (d)  $2x - 3 = 1$

  *Step (3):*  Solve for the unknown.

  line (e)  $2x = 4$

  line (f)  $x = 2$

  *Step (4):*  Check for extraneous solutions.

$$\sqrt{2x-3} - 1 = 0$$
$$\sqrt{2(2)-3} - 1 = 0$$
$$\sqrt{1} - 1 = 0$$
$$1 - 1 = 0$$

There are no extraneous solutions; therefore, the solution is 2.

☐ **Example 2:** Solve $x = 5 + \sqrt{x-3}$. (18)

  **Solution:**

  *Step (1):*  Isolate the radical.

  line (a)  $x = 5 + \sqrt{x-3}$

  line (b)  $x - 5 = \sqrt{x-3}$

  *Step (2):*  Square each side.

  line (c)  $(x-5)^2 = (\sqrt{x-3})^2$

  line (d)  $x^2 - 10x + 25 = x - 3$

  *Step (3):*  Solve for the unknown.

  line (e)  $x^2 - 11x + 28 = 0$

  line (f)  $(x-7)(x-4) = 0$

  line (g)  $x = 7$, or $x = 4$

  *Step (4):*  Check for extraneous solutions.

| | |
|---|---|
| $x = 5 + \sqrt{x-3}$ | $x = 5 + \sqrt{x-3}$ |
| $7 = 5 + \sqrt{7-3}$ | $4 = 5 + \sqrt{4-3}$ |
| $7 = 5 + \sqrt{4}$ | $4 = 5 + \sqrt{1}$ |
| $7 = 5 + 2$ | $4 = 5 + 1$ |
| $7 = 7$ | $4 \neq 6$ |

Since 4 does not check, it is an extraneous solution. Thus, the only solution is 7.

☐                               *Study Exercise Four* (19)

Solve each of the following radical equations.

1.  $\sqrt{5x} = 10$      2.  $\sqrt{7x+5} = 3$      3.  $\sqrt{3m+4} - 5 = 0$      4.  $y = 3 + \sqrt{y-1}$

## REVIEW EXERCISES

A. Solve the following quadratic equations by factoring.

1. $x^2 - 5x + 6 = 0$      2. $2m^2 + 3m = 2$      3. $x^2 - 9 = 0$
4. $2t^2 = 5t$      5. $3a^2 = 8a + 3$

B. Solve the following quadratic equations by the formula. If the solutions contain radicals, then also give the decimal approximations.

6. $x^2 + 3x - 10 = 0$      7. $2x^2 + x = 6$      8. $x^2 - 3x + 1 = 0$
9. $2x^2 + 4x + 3 = 0$      10. $3x^2 + 2x + 5 = 0$

C. Solve the following radical equations.

11. $\sqrt{3x} = 6$      12. $\sqrt{x + 3} = 4$      13. $\sqrt{2x - 5} = 3$
14. $\sqrt{2x - 7} + 8 = 11$      15. $\sqrt{x - 3} = x - 5$

D. Solve the following problems by using a quadratic equation.

16. A rectangle whose length is 4 inches more than its width has an area of 45 square inches. Find the length and the width.

17. If a square machine part is changed to a rectangular part by decreasing one dimension of the square by 3.0 mm, the area becomes 21.0 mm². Find the dimensions of the square machine part·

## Solutions to Review Exercises

A. 1. $x^2 - 5x + 6 = 0$
$(x - 3)(x - 2) = 0$
$x - 3 = 0$, or $x - 2 = 0$
$x = 3$, or $x = 2$
The solutions are 3 and 2.

2. $2m^2 + 3m = 2$
$2m^2 + 3m - 2 = 0$
$(2m - 1)(m + 2) = 0$
$2m - 1 = 0$, or $m + 2 = 0$
$m = \dfrac{1}{2}$, or $m = -2$
The solutions are $\dfrac{1}{2}$ and $-2$.

3. $x^2 - 9 = 0$
$(x + 3)(x - 3) = 0$
$x + 3 = 0$, or $x - 3 = 0$
$x = -3$, or $x = 3$
The solutions are $-3$ and 3.

4. $2t^2 = 5t$
$2t^2 - 5t = 0$
$t(2t - 5) = 0$
$t = 0$, or $2t - 5 = 0$
$t = 0$, or $t = \dfrac{5}{2}$
The solutions are 0 and $\dfrac{5}{2}$.

5. $3a^2 = 8a + 3$
$3a^2 - 8a - 3 = 0$
$(3a + 1)(a - 3) = 0$
$3a + 1 = 0$, or $a - 3 = 0$
$a = -\dfrac{1}{3}$, or $a = 3$
The solutions are $-\dfrac{1}{3}$ and 3.

B. 6. $x^2 + 3x - 10 = 0$
$x = \dfrac{-3 \pm \sqrt{9 - 4 \cdot 1 \cdot (-10)}}{2 \cdot 1}$
$= \dfrac{-3 \pm \sqrt{49}}{2}$
$= \dfrac{-3 \pm 7}{2}$
$x = 2$, or $x = -5$
The solutions are 2 and $-5$.

7. $2x^2 + x - 6 = 0$
$x = \dfrac{-1 \pm \sqrt{1 - 4 \cdot 2 \cdot (-6)}}{2 \cdot 2}$
$= \dfrac{-1 \pm \sqrt{49}}{4}$
$= \dfrac{-1 \pm 7}{4}$
$x = \dfrac{3}{2}$, or $x = -2$

The solutions are $\dfrac{3}{2}$ and $-2$.

8. $x^2 - 3x + 1 = 0$
$x = \dfrac{3 \pm \sqrt{9 - 4 \cdot 1 \cdot 1}}{2 \cdot 1}$
$= \dfrac{3 \pm \sqrt{5}}{2}$
$x \approx 2.618$, or $x \approx 0.382$

## Solutions to Review Exercises, Contd.

9. $2x^2 + 4x + 3 = 0$

$$x = \frac{-4 \pm \sqrt{16 - 4 \cdot 2 \cdot 3}}{2 \cdot 2}$$

$$= \frac{-4 \pm \sqrt{-8}}{4}$$

No real solutions.

10. $3x^2 + 2x + 5 = 0$

$$x = \frac{-2 \pm \sqrt{4 - 4 \cdot 3 \cdot 5}}{2 \cdot 3}$$

$$= \frac{-2 \pm \sqrt{-56}}{6}$$

No real solutions.

C. 11. $\sqrt{3x} = 6$
$3x = 36$
$x = 12$
The solution is 12.

12. $\sqrt{x + 3} = 4$
$x + 3 = 16$
$x = 13$
The solution is 13.

13. $\sqrt{2x - 5} = 3$
$2x - 5 = 9$
$2x = 14$
$x = 7$
The solution is 7.

14. $\sqrt{2x - 7} + 8 = 11$
$\sqrt{2x - 7} = 3$
$2x - 7 = 9$
$2x = 16$
$x = 8$
The solution is 8.

15. $\sqrt{x - 3} = x - 5$
$x - 3 = x^2 - 10x + 25$
$0 = x^2 - 11x + 28$
$0 = (x - 7)(x - 4)$
$x = 7$, or $x = 4$, but 4 is extraneous. Therefore, the only solution is 7.

D. 16. Let $x$ represent the width; then $x + 4$ represents the length. Since the area is 45, we can write:
$x \cdot (x + 4) = 45$
$x^2 + 4x = 45$
$x^2 + 4x - 45 = 0$
$(x + 9)(x - 5) = 0$
$x = -9$, or $x = 5$. The width is 5 inches and the length is 9 inches. The value $-9$ is not pertinent to the problem.

17. Let $x$ represent the length of one side of the square; then $x - 3$ represents one side of the rectangle. Since the area of the rectangle is 21.0 mm$^2$, we can write:
$x \cdot (x - 3) = 21$
$x^2 - 3x = 21$
$x^2 - 3x - 21 = 0$

$$x = \frac{3 \pm \sqrt{9 - 4 \cdot 1 \cdot (-21)}}{2 \cdot 1}$$

$$= \frac{3 \pm \sqrt{93}}{2}$$

$$\approx \frac{3 \pm 9.644}{2}$$

$x \approx 6.322$, or $x \approx -3.322$. Each side of the square measures 6.322 inches. $-3.322$ is not pertinent to the problem.

## SUPPLEMENTARY PROBLEMS

A. Solve the following quadratic equations by factoring.

1. $x^2 - 2x = 8$
2. $m^2 - 25 = 0$
3. $a^2 = 9$
4. $x^2 + x = 0$
5. $3x^2 = 7x$
6. $4m^2 - 9 = 0$
7. $x^2 + 9 = -6x$
8. $10m^2 + 29m = 21$
9. $3r^2 - 4 = 4r$
10. $9n^2 + 30n + 25 = 0$

B. Solve the following equations by the quadratic formula. If the solutions contain radicals, then also give the decimal approximations.

11. $x^2 - 4x + 3 = 0$
12. $3x^2 + 4x - 5 = 0$
13. $5m^2 - 4m = 33$
14. $x^2 - 2x - 10 = 0$
15. $2r^2 = 2r + 3$
16. $x^2 - 4x + 1 = 0$
17. $2x^2 - 3x + 4 = 0$
18. $6m^2 + m = 2$
19. $3x^2 - 5x = 10$
20. $x^2 - x + 1 = 0$

## SUPPLEMENTARY PROBLEMS, Contd.

C.  Solve the following radical equations.

21. $\sqrt{2x} = 4$      22. $\sqrt{3x} = 2$      23. $\sqrt{m+2} = 3$

24. $\sqrt{3n-5} = 3$      25. $\sqrt{4x+1} + 3 = 8$      26. $m = 5 + \sqrt{m-3}$

27. $t - 3 = \sqrt{t-1}$      28. $\sqrt{4x-11} = x - 2$

D.  Solve the following problems by using a quadratic equation.

29. If two positive numbers differ by 3 and their product is 54, find the numbers.
30. A certain number plus four times its reciprocal is $8\frac{1}{2}$. Find the number.
31. The base of a triangle is 4 ft less than its height. The area of the triangle is 48 ft². Find the length of the base.
32. The area of a border around a picture 10 inches long and 8 inches wide is one-half the area of the picture. What are the outside dimensions of the border?

E.  Given the quadratic formula $x = \dfrac{-b \pm \sqrt{b^2 - 4ac}}{2a}$, $b^2 - 4ac$ is called the *discriminant*. What can be said about the real solutions of a quadratic equation when:

33. $b^2 < 4ac$, i.e., the discriminant represents a negative number.
34. $b^2 = 4ac$, i.e., the discriminant represents zero.
35. $b^2 > 4ac$, i.e., the discriminant represents a positive number.

F.  The following are difficult equations. Solve each for only the exact solutions. You may use either factoring or the quadratic formula.

36. $2x^2 = 2x + 3$      37. $-x^2 + 5x - 7 = 0$

38. $4y = 2y^2 + 21$      39. $(2x - 3)(3x - 1) = 5$

40. $(3y - 5)(7y + 1) = (2y + 7)(6y - 1)$      41. $2x^2 + \frac{2}{3}x - 1 = 0$

42. $3z^2 + 2 = \frac{1}{3}z$      43. $\dfrac{3x+1}{2x-1} = \dfrac{2x}{x-2}$

44. $\dfrac{m+1}{m} - \dfrac{13}{6} = \dfrac{-m}{m+1}$      45. $\dfrac{t+3}{t-1} = \dfrac{t^2 - t + 3}{t^2 - 4t + 5}$

46. $(x - 8)(2x - 3) = 34$      47. $2 + \dfrac{5}{x} = \dfrac{12}{x^2}$

G.  Calculator Problems. With your instructor's approval, use a calculator together with the quadratic formula to solve the following quadratic equations. Give the answers in decimal form.

48. $3x^2 + 4x - 8 = 0$      49. $-7x^2 + 5x + 11 = 0$

50. $2.3x^2 - 4.2x - 1.9 = 0$      51. $6.5x^2 - 3.7x - 5.4 = 0$

52. $13.7x^2 + 7.2x - 6.3 = 0$      53. $-4.2x^2 + 3.9x - 5.2 = 0$

□ **Solutions to Study Exercises**          **(4A)**

### Study Exercise One (Frame 4)

1. $x^2 - 3x - 10 = 0$
   $(x - 5)(x + 2) = 0$
   $x - 5 = 0$, or $x + 2 = 0$
   $x = 5$, or $x = -2$

   The solutions are 5 and $-2$

2. $3x^2 - x = 2$
   $3x^2 - x - 2 = 0$
   $(3x + 2)(x - 1) = 0$
   $3x + 2 = 0$, or $x - 1 = 0$
   $x = -\frac{2}{3}$, or $x = 1$

   The solutions are $-\frac{2}{3}$ and 1

3. $2x^2 - 5x = 0$
   $x(2x - 5) = 0$
   $x = 0$, or $2x - 5 = 0$
   $x = 0$, or $x = \frac{5}{2}$

   The solutions are 0 and $\frac{5}{2}$

## Solutions to Study Exercises, Contd.

4. $x^2 - 4x + 2 = 0$ (cannot be factored). Therefore, we will develop, in the next few frames, a method of solving any quadratic equation. This method will not depend upon factoring.

☐ <center>*Study Exercise Two (Frame 9)*</center> **(9A)**

1. $3x^2 + 4x = 7$
   $3x^2 + 4x - 7 = 0$
   $a = 3, b = 4, c = -7$

2. $x^2 - 5x + 2 = 0$
   $1x^2 - 5x + 2 = 0$
   $a = 1, b = -5, c = 2$

3. $2x^2 + 3 = x$
   $2x^2 - 1x + 3 = 0$
   $a = 2, b = -1, c = 3$

4. $3x^2 - x = 0$
   $3x^2 - 1x + 0 = 0$
   $a = 3, b = -1, c = 0$

☐ <center>*Study Exercise Three (Frame 15)*</center> **(15A)**

1. $1x^2 + 7x + 12 = 0; a = 1, b = 7, c = 12$

$$x = \frac{-7 \pm \sqrt{49 - 4 \cdot 1 \cdot 12}}{2 \cdot 1}$$

$$= \frac{-7 \pm \sqrt{49 - 48}}{2}$$

$$= \frac{-7 \pm \sqrt{1}}{2}$$

$$= \frac{-7 \pm 1}{2}$$

$x = -3$, or $x = -4$
The solutions are $-3$ and $-4$.

2. $6x^2 - 1x - 2 = 0; a = 6, b = -1, c = -2$

$$x = \frac{1 \pm \sqrt{1 - 4 \cdot 6 \cdot (-2)}}{2 \cdot 6}$$

$$= \frac{1 \pm \sqrt{1 + 48}}{12}$$

$$= \frac{1 \pm \sqrt{49}}{12}$$

$$= \frac{1 \pm 7}{12}$$

$x = \dfrac{2}{3}$, or $x = -\dfrac{1}{2}$

The solutions are $\dfrac{2}{3}$ and $-\dfrac{1}{2}$.

3. $3x^2 - 4x + 0 = 0; a = 3, b = -4, c = 0$

$$x = \frac{4 \pm \sqrt{16 - 4 \cdot 3 \cdot 0}}{2 \cdot 3}$$

$$= \frac{4 \pm \sqrt{16 - 0}}{6}$$

$$= \frac{4 \pm \sqrt{16}}{6}$$

$$= \frac{4 \pm 4}{6}$$

$x = \dfrac{4}{3}$, or $x = 0$

The solutions are $\dfrac{4}{3}$ and 0.

4. $1x^2 - 4x + 1 = 0; a = 1, b = -4, c = 1$

$$x = \frac{4 \pm \sqrt{16 - 4 \cdot 1 \cdot 1}}{2 \cdot 1}$$

$$= \frac{4 \pm \sqrt{16 - 4}}{2}$$

$$= \frac{4 \pm \sqrt{12}}{2}$$

$$= \frac{4 \pm 2\sqrt{3}}{2}$$

$x = 2 \pm \sqrt{3}$     (Radical solutions)
$\approx 2 \pm 1.732$
$x \approx 3.732$, or $x \approx 0.268$     (Decimal solutions)

5. $3x^2 + 2x + 5 = 0; a = 3, b = 2, c = 5$

$$x = \frac{-2 \pm \sqrt{4 - 4 \cdot 3 \cdot 5}}{6}$$

$$= \frac{-2 \pm \sqrt{4 - 60}}{6}$$

$$= \frac{-2 \pm \sqrt{-56}}{6}$$

This equation has no solutions in the set of real numbers.

## Solutions to Study Exercises, Contd.

☐                  *Study Exercise Four (Frame 19)*           **(19A)**

1. $\sqrt{5x} = 10$
$(\sqrt{5x})^2 = (10)^2$
$5x = 100$
$x = 20$
The solution is 20.

2. $\sqrt{7x + 5} = 3$
$(\sqrt{7x + 5})^2 = (3)^2$
$7x + 5 = 9$
$7x = 4$
$x = \dfrac{4}{7}$

The solution is $\dfrac{4}{7}$.

3. $\sqrt{3m + 4} - 5 = 0$
$\sqrt{3m + 4} = 5$
$(\sqrt{3m + 4})^2 = (5)^2$
$3m + 4 = 25$
$3m = 21$
$m = 7$
The solution is 7.

4. $y = 3 + \sqrt{y - 1}$
$y - 3 = \sqrt{y - 1}$
$(y - 3)^2 = (\sqrt{y - 1})^2$
$y^2 - 6y + 9 = y - 1$
$y^2 - 7y + 10 = 0$
$(y - 5)(y - 2) = 0$

$y = 5$, or $y = 2$. 2 is an extraneous solution since it will not check in the original equation. Therefore, the only solution is 5.

## Module 5 Review Problems

Units 22–25

A. Simplify each of these expressions completely (evaluate).

1. $3^{-2}$  2. $10^{-1}$  3. $\left(\frac{2}{3}\right)^{-2}$  4. $\sqrt{16}$  5. $-\sqrt{16}$

6. $4^{1/2}$  7. $8^{2/3}$  8. $9^{-3/2}$  9. $(-27)^{-1/3}$  10. $\left(\frac{4}{49}\right)^{1/2}$

B. Simplify by converting negative exponents to positive exponents.

11. $\dfrac{3x^{-2}}{5y^{-3}}$  12. $\dfrac{2a^2b^{-3}c^{-1}}{7d^{-3}e^4}$  13. $\dfrac{5}{x^{-2}+y^{-2}}$

C. Using the properties of exponents, simplify. The final answer should not contain negative exponents.

14. $(3a^{-5})(2a^8)$  15. $\dfrac{12x^3y^{-2}}{4x^5y^{-1}}$  16. $\dfrac{(-3a^2b^{-3})(2ab^4)}{(3a^2b^{-1})^2}$

D. Convert these expressions to scientific notation.

17. 26,700  18. 0.00000703

E. Convert these expressions to ordinary notation.

19. $5.13 \times 10^6$  20. $9.11 \times 10^{-4}$

F. Simplify as far as possible. Do not evaluate.

21. $2\sqrt{75}$  22. $5\sqrt[3]{54}$

G. Combine, using addition or subtraction.

23. $3\sqrt{2} - 5\sqrt{2}$  24. $2\sqrt[3]{7} + 3\sqrt{5} - 4\sqrt[3]{7} - 2\sqrt{5}$  25. $5\sqrt[3]{16} - 2\sqrt[3]{54} + 3\sqrt{2} - \sqrt{8}$

H. Multiply the following.

26. $(3\sqrt{5})(2\sqrt{3})$  27. $3\sqrt[3]{2}(2\sqrt[3]{7} - 4\sqrt[3]{3})$

28. $(2\sqrt{3} + \sqrt{5})(2\sqrt{3} - \sqrt{5})$  29. $(3\sqrt{2} + 1)(4\sqrt{2} - 3)$

I. Rationalize the denominators. Do not evaluate.

30. $\dfrac{2}{\sqrt{7}}$  31. $\dfrac{3\sqrt{2}}{5\sqrt{3}}$  32. $\dfrac{2}{3\sqrt[3]{2}}$  33. $\sqrt{\dfrac{1}{2}}$  34. $\dfrac{4}{3\sqrt{2} + \sqrt{3}}$

J. Solve the following quadratic equations by factoring.

35. $2x^2 + 3x = 20$  36. $x^2 - 5x = 0$

K. Solve the following quadratic equations by using the quadratic formula. If the answers involve a radical, give the approximate solutions as well as the exact solutions.

37. $x^2 - 3x - 4 = 0$  38. $x^2 - 3x + 1 = 0$

39. $2y^2 + 4y + 3 = 0$  40. $m^2 - 4m + 2 = 0$

## Module 5 Review Problems, Contd.

Units 22–25

L.  Solve the following radical equations.

41.  $\sqrt{2y} = 4$          42.  $\sqrt{2x - 5} = 1$          43.  $\sqrt{2m - 3} = m - 3$

M.  Solve the following applied problems. Give the equation as well as the solutions.

44.  Two positive numbers differ by 4, and their product is 117. Find the numbers.

45   A rectangle whose length is 3 inches more than its width has an area of 40 square inches. Find the length and the width.

## Answers to Module 5 Review Problems

A.  1.  $\dfrac{1}{9}$          2.  $\dfrac{1}{10}$          3.  $\dfrac{9}{4}$          4.  4          5.  $-4$

6.  2          7.  4          8.  $\dfrac{1}{27}$          9.  $-\dfrac{1}{3}$          10.  $\dfrac{2}{7}$

B.  11.  $\dfrac{3y^3}{5x^2}$          12.  $\dfrac{2a^2d^3}{7b^3ce^4}$          13.  $\dfrac{5x^2y^2}{y^2 + x^2}$

C.  14.  $6a^3$          15.  $\dfrac{3}{x^2y}$          16.  $\dfrac{-2b^3}{3a}$

D.  17.  $2.67 \times 10^4$          18.  $7.03 \times 10^{-6}$

E.  19.  5,130,000          20.  0.000911

F.  21.  $10\sqrt{3}$          22.  $15\sqrt[3]{2}$

G.  23.  $-2\sqrt{2}$          24.  $-2\sqrt[3]{7} + \sqrt{5}$          25.  $4\sqrt[3]{2} + \sqrt{2}$

H.  26.  $6\sqrt{15}$          27.  $6\sqrt[3]{14} - 12\sqrt[3]{6}$          28.  7          29.  $21 - 5\sqrt{2}$

I.  30.  $\dfrac{2\sqrt{7}}{7}$          31.  $\dfrac{\sqrt{6}}{5}$          32.  $\dfrac{\sqrt[3]{4}}{3}$

33.  $\dfrac{\sqrt{2}}{2}$          34.  $\dfrac{4(3\sqrt{2} - \sqrt{3})}{15}$ or $\dfrac{12\sqrt{2} - 4\sqrt{3}}{15}$

J.  35.  $\dfrac{5}{2}, -4$          36.  0, 5

K.  37.  $-1, 4$          38.  $\dfrac{3 \pm \sqrt{5}}{2}$ ; 2.618, 0.382

39.  No solutions          40.  $2 \pm \sqrt{2}$; 3.414, 0.586

L.  41.  8          42.  3          43.  6

M.  44.  $x(x - 4) = 117$; the numbers are 13 and 9.

45.  $w(w + 3) = 40$; the length is 8 inches and the width is 5 inches.

MODULE

# 6

# Introduction to Graphing

# The Rectangular Coordinate System

## ☐ Objectives **(1)**

By the end of this unit you should be able to:

- construct a Table of Values for an equation of two variables.
- determine the independent and dependent variables for an equation of two variables.
- name points by using ordered pairs.
- graph equations of two variables with use of a Table of Values.
- obtain data by analyzing graphs.

## ☐ Equations of Two Variables **(2)**

Each of the following is an equation of two variables.

**Example 1:** $y = 2x$

**Example 2:** $y = x^2 + 5x + 6$

**Example 3:** $A = \pi r^2$, where $\pi \approx 3.14$

## ☐ Analyzing Equations of Two Variables **(3)**

**Example 1:** Given $y = 2x$, find $y$ when $x = 3$, $x = 0$, and $x = -2$.

**Solution:** Substitute each of the values of $x$ into the equation $y = 2x$.

*line (a)* When $x = 3$, $y = 2 \cdot 3$, or 6.
*line (b)* When $x = 0$, $y = 2 \cdot 0$, or 0.
*line (c)* When $x = -2$, $y = 2 \cdot (-2)$, or $-4$.

*line (d)* Table of Values:

| $x$ | 3 | 0 | $-2$ |
|-----|---|---|------|
| $y$ | 6 | 0 | $-4$ |

## ☐ Example 2: Given $y = x^2 + 5x + 6$, find $y$ when $x = -2$, $x = -1$, $x = 0$, and $x = 3$. **(4)**

**Solution:** Substitute each of the values of $x$ into the equation $y = x^2 + 5x + 6$.

*line (a)* When $x = -2$, $y = (-2)^2 + 5(-2) + 6$
$$y = 4 - 10 + 6$$
$$y = 0$$
*line (b)* When $x = -1$, $y = (-1)^2 + 5(-1) + 6$
$$y = 1 - 5 + 6$$
$$y = 2$$
*line (c)* When $x = 0$, $y = 0^2 + 5(0) + 6$
$$y = 0 + 0 + 6$$
$$y = 6$$
*line (d)* When $x = 3$, $y = 3^2 + 5(3) + 6$
$$y = 9 + 15 + 6$$
$$y = 30$$

*line (e)* Table of Values:

| $x$ | $-2$ | $-1$ | 0 | 3 |
|-----|------|------|---|----|
| $y$ | 0 | 2 | 6 | 30 |

## ☐ Example 3: Given $A = \pi r^2$, find $A$ when $r = 1$, $r = 3$, and $r = 5$. **(5)**

**Solution:** Substitute each of the values of $r$ into the equation $A = \pi r^2$, where $\pi \approx 3.14$.

*line (a)*   When $r = 1$, $A = (3.14)(1)^2$
$A = (3.14)(1)$
$A = (3.14)(1)$
$A = 3.14$
*line (b)*   When $r = 3$, $A = (3.14)(3)^2$
$A = (3.14)(9)$
$A = 28.26$
*line (c)*   When $r = 5$, $A = (3.14)(5)^2$
$A = (3.14)(25)$
$A = 78.5$

*line (d)*   Table of Values:

| $r$ | 1 | 3 | 5 |
|---|---|---|---|
| $A$ | 3.14 | 28.26 | 78.5 |

## ☐ Independent and Dependent Variables (6)

In the equation $A = \pi r^2$, the area $A$ depends upon the radius $r$. Therefore, $A$ is the *dependent variable* and $r$ is the *independent variable*.

## ☐ More Examples (7)

**Example 1:**   In the equation $y = 2x$, $x$ is the independent variable and $y$ is the dependent variable.

**Example 2:**   In the equation $y = x^2 + 5x + 6$, $x$ is the independent variable and $y$ is the dependent variable.

**Example 3:**   In the equation $s = 16t^2$, $t$ is the independent variable and $s$ is the dependent variable.

## ☐ *Study Exercise One* (8)

A.   Give a Table of Values illustrating each of the following.

1.   Given $y = 5x$, find $y$ when $x = -2$, $x = 0$, $x = 1$, and $x = 3$.
2.   Given $y = x^2 - 6x + 8$, find $y$ when $x = -2$, $x = 0$, and $x = 3$.

B.   Given the following equations, name the independent variable and the dependent variable.

3.   $y = 3x + 2$        4.   $F = \dfrac{9}{5}C + 32$        5.   $C = \pi d$        6.   $y = 2x^2 + 3x - 5$

C.   Complete the following tables.

7.   $y = 2x + 1$

| $x$ | $-3$ | $-2$ | $-1$ | 0 | 1 | 2 | 3 |
|---|---|---|---|---|---|---|---|
| $y$ | $-5$ | | | | | | |

8.   $y = 3x^2 + 2$

| $x$ | $-4$ | $-3$ | $-2$ | $-1$ | 0 | 1 | 2 | 3 | 4 |
|---|---|---|---|---|---|---|---|---|---|
| $y$ | 50 | | | | | | | | |

## ☐ Ordered Pairs (9)

A Table of Values can also be written as *ordered pairs* of numbers where the $x$-value (independent variable) is listed first and the $y$-value (dependent variable) is listed second.

**Example:**

Table of Values for $y = 2x$

| $x$ | $-2$ | $-1$ | 0 | 1 | 2 |
|---|---|---|---|---|---|
| $y$ | $-4$ | $-2$ | 0 | 2 | 4 |

$(-2, -4)$   $(-1, -2)$   $(0, 0)$   $(1, 2)$   $(2, 4)$

*Remember*, the ordered pair $(-2, -4)$ means $x = -2$ and $y = -4$.

353

☐ **Terminology** (10)

The two numbers in an ordered pair are called *coordinates*.

The first number or *x*-value is called the *abscissa*.

The second number or *y*-value is called the *ordinate*.

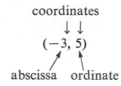

☐ **Set Builder Notation** (11)

Equations of two variables are sometimes described using set notation. The equation $y = 2x$, since it generates ordered pairs, can be written as follows:

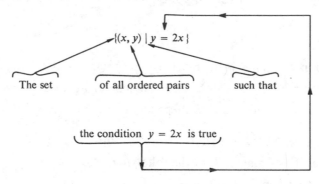

**Example 1:** $y = 2x + 1$ can be written as $\{(x, y) \mid y = 2x + 1\}$.

**Example 2:** $y = x^2 + 1$ can be written as $\{(x, y) \mid y = x^2 + 1\}$.

☐ *Study Exercise Two* (12)

A. The following is a Table of Values for $y = 3x$:

| $x$ | $-3$ | $-2$ | $-1$ | 0 | 1 | 2 |
|---|---|---|---|---|---|---|
| $y$ | $-9$ | $-6$ | $-3$ | 0 | 3 | 6 |

1. Write the corresponding values as ordered pairs.

B. Indicate the abscissa and the ordinate for each of the following ordered pairs.

2. $(-7, 5)$      3. $(0, -2)$      4. $\left(\frac{1}{2}, \frac{2}{3}\right)$

C. Write an ordered pair such that:

5. the abscissa is $-2$ and the ordinate is 5.      6. the abscissa is 5 and the ordinate is $-2$.

7. $x = 2$ and $y = -8$.      8. $x = 0$ and $y = 1$.

D. Write the following equations in set builder notation.

9. $y = 3x - 2$      10. $y = x^2 - 5$

## ☐ Using Ordered Pairs     **(13)**

Ordered pairs are used to denote *points* or *locations* on a plane. A *plane* is a flat level surface having no thickness.

## ☐ Partitioning a Plane     **(14)**

A plane is partitioned by drawing a infinite set of lines, running both vertically and horizontally.

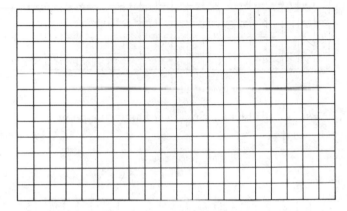

This produces an infinite set of squares. We now need a method of naming the points or locations at the corners of the squares.

## ☐ The Coordinate Axes     **(15)**

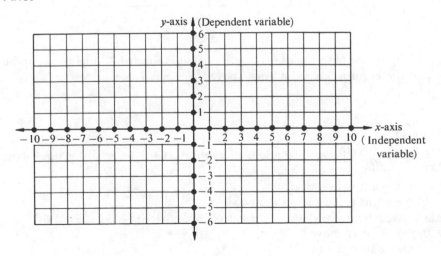

## ☐ Naming a Point with an Ordered Pair　　　　　　　　　　　　　　　　　　**(16)**

We wish to name this point by using an ordered pair.

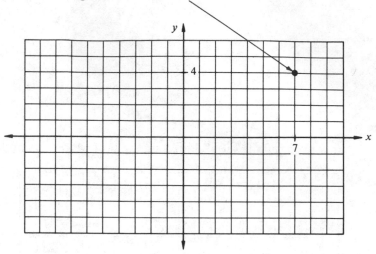

The point is 7 units to the *right* and 4 units *up*. So, (7, 4) names the point.

## ☐ Abscissa and Ordinate　　　　　　　　　　　　　　　　　　　　　　　　**(17)**

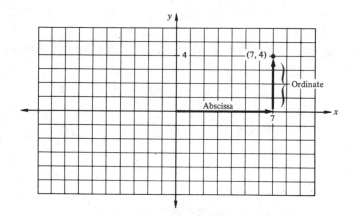

In the ordered pair (7, 4), the abscissa 7 tells that the point is located 7 units to the right of the *y*-axis. The ordinate 4 tells that the point is located 4 units above the *x*-axis.

## ☐ Summary　　　　　　　　　　　　　　　　　　　　　　　　　　　　　**(18)**

In the ordered pair $(x, y)$:

1.　The abscissa $x$ gives the distance the point is located to the right or left of the *y*-axis.
　　(a)　If $x > 0$, the point is to the right.
　　(b)　If $x < 0$, the point is to the left.
　　(c)　If $x = 0$, the point is located on the *y*-axis.
2.　The ordinate $y$ gives the distance the point is located above or below the *x*-axis.
　　(a)　If $y > 0$, the point is above.
　　(b)　If $y < 0$, the point is below.
　　(c)　If $y = 0$, the point is located on the *x*-axis.

☐ **Examples Naming Points in a Plane** **(19)**

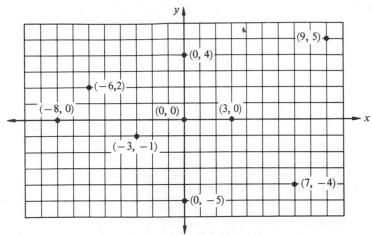

The point named by (0, 0) is called *origin*.

This system of naming points in a plane is called the *Cartesian coordinate system* or the *rectangular coordinate system*.

☐ **The Plane Divided into Quadrants** **(20)**

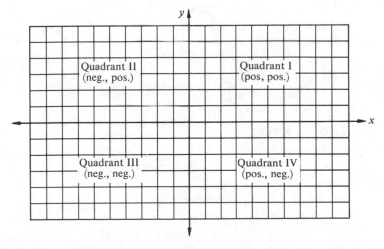

Any point located on the *x*-axis or *y*-axis is not in any quadrant.

□                      *Study Exercise Three*                     **(21)**

A.   Using ordered pairs, name each of the following points:

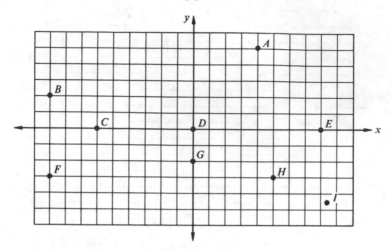

B.   Fill in the blanks to make each statement true.

    1.   The $x$- and $y$-axes intersect at the point named (____, ____), and this point is called the ____.
    2.   Any point located on the $x$-axis has an ordinate of ____.
    3.   Any point located on the $y$-axis has an abscissa of ____.
    4.   The point named by $(-2, -6)$ is located ____ units below the $x$-axis and ____ units to the left of the $y$-axis.

C.   Give the quadrant in which each of the following points is located:

    5.   $(-3, 5)$                 6.   $(-10, +12)$          7.   $\left(\frac{1}{3}, \frac{4}{5}\right)$

    8.   $(-2, -6)$            9.   $(0, 0)$                   10.   $(\sqrt{2}, -\sqrt[3]{5})$
   11.   $(1, 1)$               12.   $(-5, 10)$            13.   $(a, b)$, where $a > 0$, $b < 0$

□ **Graphing Equations of Two Variables**                          **(22)**

*Step (1):*   Make a Table of Values.
*Step (2):*   Plot each of the points.
*Step (3):*   Connect the points with a smooth curve.

☐ **Example 1:** Graph $y = 2x$. **(23)**

**Solution:**

*Step (1):* Make a Table of Values.

| $x$ | $-3$ | $-2$ | $-1$ | $0$ | $1$ | $2$ | $3$ |
|---|---|---|---|---|---|---|---|
| $y$ | $-6$ | $-4$ | $-2$ | $0$ | $2$ | $4$ | $6$ |

*Step (2):* Plot each of the points.

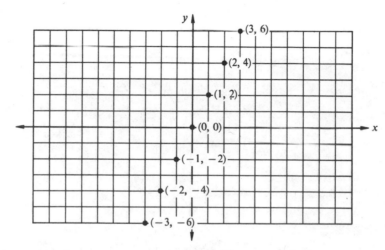

*Step (3):* Connect the points with a smooth line.

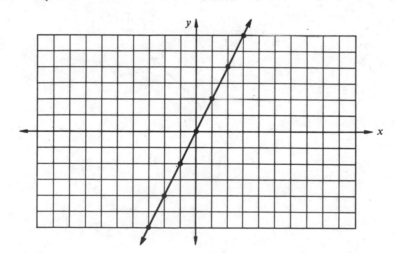

□ **Example 2:** Graph $\{(x, y) \mid y = x + 2\}$. **(24)**

**Solution:**

*Step (1):* Make a Table of Values.

| $x$ | $-4$ | $-3$ | $-2$ | $-1$ | 0 | 1 | 2 |
|---|---|---|---|---|---|---|---|
| $y$ | $-2$ | $-1$ | 0 | 1 | 2 | 3 | 4 |

*Step (2):* Plot each of the points.

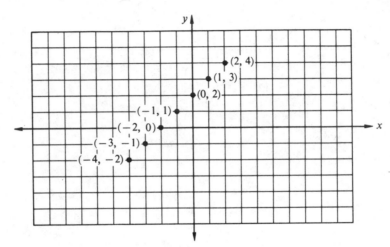

*Step (3):* Connect the points with a smooth line.

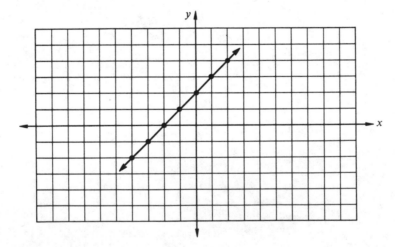

□ **Example 3:**  Graph $\{(x, y) \mid y = |x|\}$. **(25)**

**Solution:**

*Step (1):*  Make a Table of Values.

| $x$ | −5 | −3 | −1 | 0 | 1 | 3 |
|---|---|---|---|---|---|---|
| $y$ | 5 | 3 | 1 | 0 | 1 | 3 |

*Step (2):*  Plot each of the points.

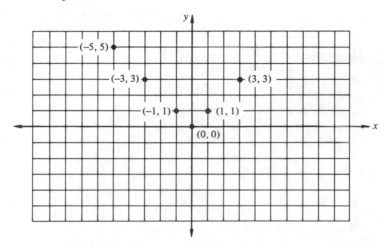

*Step (3):*  Connect the points with a V-shaped curve.

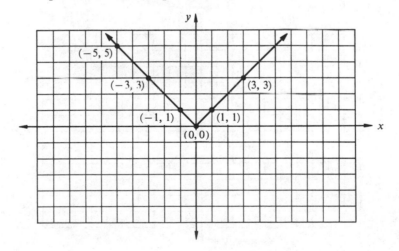

□ **Example 4:**   Graph $\{(x, y) \mid x = |y|\}$.   **(26)**

**Solution:**

*Step (1):*   Make a Table of Values.

| $x$ | 5 | 3 | 1 | 0 | 1 | 3 |
|---|---|---|---|---|---|---|
| $y$ | −5 | −3 | −1 | 0 | 1 | 3 |

Easiest to choose $y$-values first

*Step (2):*   Plot each of the points.

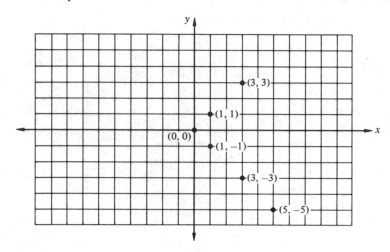

*Step (3):*   Connect the points with a V-shaped curve.

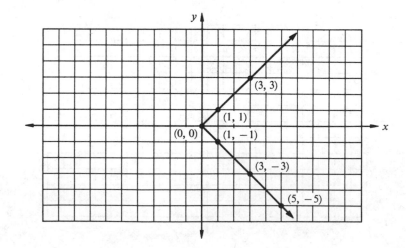

☐ **Example 5:** Graph $\{(x, y) \mid y = x^2\}$. **(27)**

**Solution:**

*Step (1):* Make a Table of Values.

| $x$ | $-3$ | $-2$ | $-1$ | 0 | 1 | 2 | 3 |
|---|---|---|---|---|---|---|---|
| $y$ | 9 | 4 | 1 | 0 | 1 | 4 | 9 |

*Step (2):* Plot each of the points.

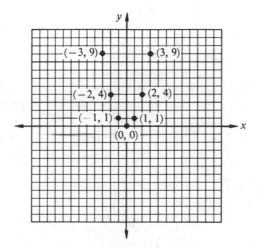

*Step (3):* Connect the points with a smooth curve.

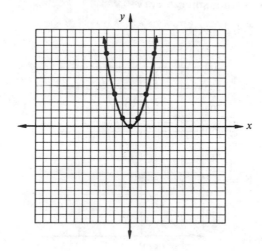

□ **Example 6:** The formula $s = 16t^2$ gives the distance in feet that a dropped object falls in $t$ seconds. **(28)**

**Solution:**

*Step (1):* Make a Table of Values.

| $t$ | 0 | 1 | 2 | 3 | 4 | 5 |
|---|---|---|---|---|---|---|
| $s$ | 0 | 16 | 64 | 144 | 256 | 400 |

*Step (2):* Plot each of the points.

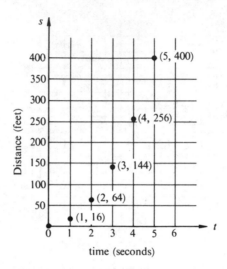

*Step (3):* Connect the points with a smooth curve.

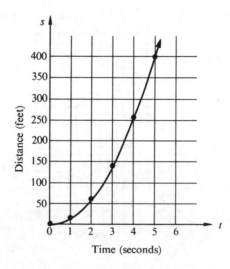

□ *Study Exercise Four* **(29)**

Make a Table of Values and graph each of the following.

1. $y = 3x$        2. $\{(x, y) \mid y = x - 2\}$        3. $\{(x, y) \mid y = x^2 + 1\}$

4. $y = |x - 2|$        5. $\{(x, y) \mid x = |y + 1|\}$

6. $V = \dfrac{100}{P}$. This is a formula which gives the volume in cubic inches that a particular gas occupies at a given pressure $P$ in pounds per square inch.

□ **Obtaining Data from Graphs** **(30)**

    **Example 1:** Given the following graph:
           (a) find $y$ when $x = -3$.
           (b) find $x$ when $y = 3$.

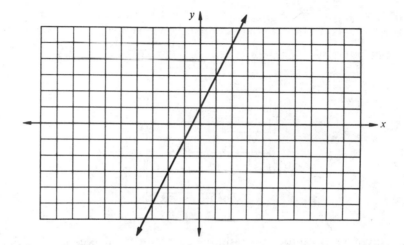

    **Solution:** Locate the values on the graph.

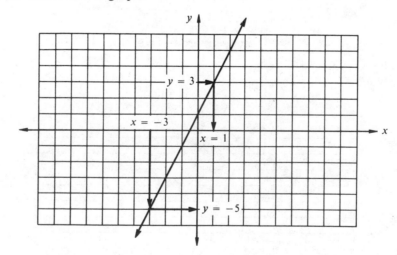

        (a) $y = -5$ when $x = -3$.
        (b) $x = 1$ when $y = 3$.

**(31)**

**Example 2:** The following is a graph of a relationship between voltage and current in a circuit where the resistance is constant. Voltage is measured in *volts* and current is measured in *amperes*.

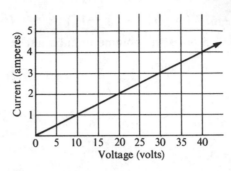

(a) If 20 volts are applied to the circuit, what is the resulting current?

(b) If 3.5 amperes of current are desired, how much voltage must be applied to the circuit?

**Solution:** Locate the values on the graph.

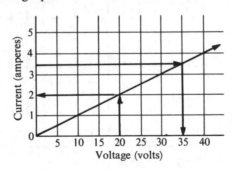

(a) If 20 volts are applied, the resulting current is 2 amperes.

(b) If 3.5 amperes are desired, then 35 volts must be applied.

*Study Exercise Five*

**(32)**

1. Given the following graph:
   (a) find $y$ when $x = -3$.
   (b) find $x$ when $y = -5$.

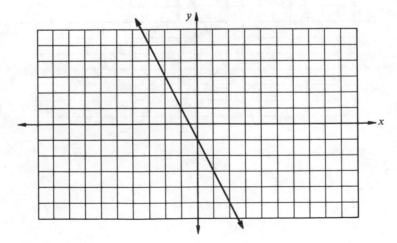

2.  The following is a graph of a relationship between pressure and volume of a gas at a constant temperature. Pressure is measured in pounds per square inch and volume is measured in cubic inches.
    (a)   When a pressure of 50 pounds per square inch is applied, what is the resulting volume?
    (b)   What pressure is necessary to give a volume of 25 cubic inches?

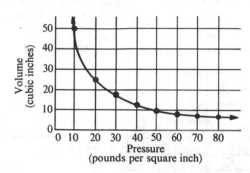

## REVIEW EXERCISES

A.  Given the following equations, name the independent variable and the dependent variable.

1.  $y = 2x - 3$      2.  $y = 3x^2 - 2x + 1$      3.  $C = 2\pi r$

4.  $C = \frac{5}{9}(F - 32)$      5.  $P = \frac{100}{V}$

B.  Complete the following tables.

6.  $y = 3x + 1$

| x | −2 | −1 | 0 | 1 | 2 | 3 |
|---|----|----|---|---|---|---|
| y | −5 |    |   |   |   |   |

7.  $y = |x - 3|$

| x | 0 | 1 | 2 | 3 | 4 | 5 | −1 | −2 |
|---|---|---|---|---|---|---|----|----|
| y |   |   |   |   |   |   |    |    |

8.  $x = |y - 1|$

| x |    |    |    |   |   |   |   |
|---|----|----|----|---|---|---|---|
| y | −3 | −2 | −1 | 0 | 1 | 2 | 3 |

9.  $y = 2x^2 + 1$

| x | −3 | −2 | −1 | 0 | 1 | 2 | 3 |
|---|----|----|----|---|---|---|---|
| y | 19 |    |    |   |   |   |   |

10.  $y = \frac{1}{x}$

| x | −100 | −10 | −5 | −2 | 1 | 3 | 10 | $\frac{1}{10}$ | $\frac{1}{100}$ |
|---|------|-----|----|----|---|---|----|----------------|-----------------|
| y | $-\frac{1}{100}$ |    |    |    |   |   |    |                |                 |

C.  Indicate the abscissa and the ordinate for each of the following ordered pairs.

11.  $(-2, 1)$      12.  $(0, 3)$      13.  $\left(\frac{1}{2}, \frac{3}{5}\right)$

367

## REVIEW EXERCISES, Contd.

D. Write an ordered pair such that:

14. the abscissa is $-1$ and the ordinate is 5.    15. the abscissa is 5 and the ordinate is $-1$.
16. $x = 3$ and $y = -6$.    17. $x = -4$ and $y = 0$
18. Using ordered pairs, name each of the following points.

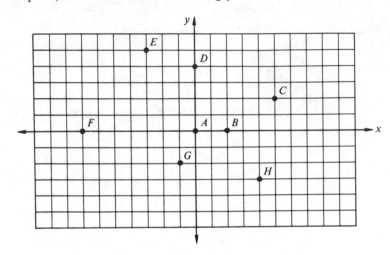

E. Give the quadrant in which each of the following points is located.

19. $(1, 3)$    20. $(-3, 5)$    21. $\left(-\frac{3}{4}, 6\right)$

22. $(-2, -1)$    23. $\left(\frac{2}{3}, -\frac{5}{8}\right)$    24. $(5, 0)$

F. Make a Table of Values and graph each of the following.

25. $y = 2x + 1$    26. $\{(x, y) \mid y = x^2 - 1\}$    27. $y = \frac{12}{x}$    28. $y = |x + 1|$

29. $s = 50t$. This is a formula which gives a relationship between distance $s$ and time $t$ when traveling at a constant speed of 50 miles per hour. $s$ is measured in miles and $t$ is measured in hours.

G. The following is a graph of a relationship between voltage and current in a circuit where the resistance is constant. Voltage is measured in volts and current is measured in amperes.

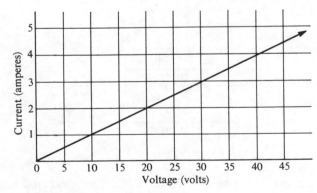

30. If 35 volts are applied to the circuit, what is the resulting current?
31. If 2 amperes of current are desired, how much voltage must be applied to the circuit?

## Solutions to Review Exercises

A. 1. Independent variable is $x$. Dependent variable is $y$.  2. Independent variable is $x$. Dependent variable is $y$.
   3. Independent variable is $r$. Dependent variable is $C$.  4. Independent variable is F. Dependent variable is C.
   5. Independent variable is $V$. Dependent variable is $P$.

B. 6. $y = 3x + 1$

| $x$ | $-2$ | $-1$ | 0 | 1 | 2 | 3 |
|---|---|---|---|---|---|---|
| $y$ | $-5$ | $-2$ | 1 | 4 | 7 | 10 |

7. $y = |x - 3|$

| $x$ | 0 | 1 | 2 | 3 | 4 | 5 | $-1$ | $-2$ |
|---|---|---|---|---|---|---|---|---|
| $y$ | 3 | 2 | 1 | 0 | 1 | 2 | 4 | 5 |

8. $x = |y - 1|$

| $x$ | 4 | 3 | 2 | 1 | 0 | 1 | 2 |
|---|---|---|---|---|---|---|---|
| $y$ | $-3$ | $-2$ | $-1$ | 0 | 1 | 2 | 3 |

9. $y = 2x^2 + 1$

| $x$ | $-3$ | $-2$ | $-1$ | 0 | 1 | 2 | 3 |
|---|---|---|---|---|---|---|---|
| $y$ | 19 | 9 | 3 | 1 | 3 | 9 | 19 |

10. $y = \dfrac{1}{x}$

| $x$ | $-100$ | $-10$ | $-5$ | $-2$ | 1 | 3 | 10 | $\frac{1}{10}$ | $\frac{1}{100}$ |
|---|---|---|---|---|---|---|---|---|---|
| $y$ | $-\frac{1}{100}$ | $-\frac{1}{10}$ | $-\frac{1}{5}$ | $-\frac{1}{2}$ | 1 | $\frac{1}{3}$ | $\frac{1}{10}$ | 10 | 100 |

C. 11. Abscissa is $-2$. Ordinate is 1.  12. Abscissa is 0. Ordinate is 3.  13. Abscissa is $\frac{1}{2}$. Ordinate is $\frac{3}{5}$.

D. 14. $(-1, 5)$  15. $(5, -1)$  16. $(3, -6)$  17. $(-4, 0)$
   18. $A(0, 0)$, $B(2, 0)$, $C(5, 2)$, $D(0, 4)$, $E(-3, 5)$, $F(-7, 0)$, $G(-1, -2)$, $H(4, -3)$

E. 19. I  20. II  21. II
   22. III  23. IV  24. No quadrant

F. 25. $y = 2x + 1$  26. $\{(x, y) \mid y = x^2 - 1\}$

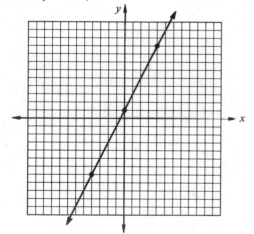

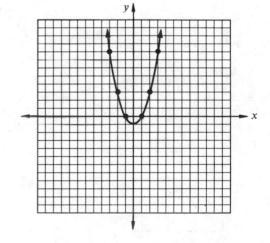

## Solutions to Review Exercises, Contd.

27.  $y = \dfrac{12}{x}$

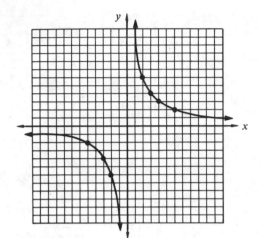

28.  $y = |x + 1|$

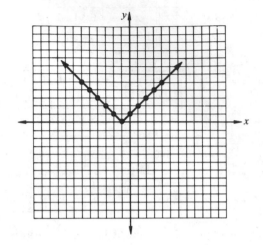

29.  $s = 50t$

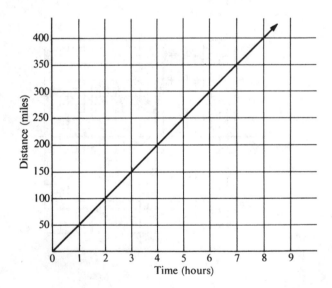

G.  30.  3.5 amperes

31.  20 volts

## SUPPLEMENTARY PROBLEMS

A.  Given the following equations, name the independent variable and the dependent variable.

1.  $y = 3x + 4$          2.  $y = 2x^2 + 5x - 6$          3.  $A = \pi r^2$

4.  $C = \pi d$          5.  $s = 16t^2$          6.  $P = \dfrac{1000}{V}$

7.  $A = s^2$

B.  Complete the following tables.

8.  $y = 2x + 4$

| $x$ | $-3$ | $-2$ | $-1$ | 0 | 1 | 2 | 3 |
|---|---|---|---|---|---|---|---|
| $y$ | | | | | | | |

9.  $y = x^2 - 1$

| $x$ | $-6$ | $-4$ | $-2$ | 0 | 2 | 4 | 6 |
|---|---|---|---|---|---|---|---|
| $y$ | | | | | | | |

10.  $y = \dfrac{10}{x}$

| $x$ | $-10$ | $-5$ | $-1$ | 1 | 5 | 10 | 100 |
|---|---|---|---|---|---|---|---|
| $y$ | | | | | | | |

11.  $y = |x - 4|$

| $x$ | $-2$ | $-1$ | 0 | 1 | 2 | 3 | 4 | 5 | 6 |
|---|---|---|---|---|---|---|---|---|---|
| $y$ | | | | | | | | | |

12.  $s = \dfrac{1}{t^2}$

| $t$ | $-10$ | $-5$ | $-2$ | $-\dfrac{1}{2}$ | $-1$ | 0 | $\dfrac{1}{3}$ | 4 | 10 |
|---|---|---|---|---|---|---|---|---|---|
| $s$ | | | | | | | | | |

C.  Indicate the abscissa and the ordinate for each of the following ordered pairs.

13.  $(-5, 1)$          14.  $(0, 3)$          15.  $(3, 0)$          16.  $\left(-\dfrac{1}{2}, \dfrac{4}{5}\right)$          17.  $(2, 3)$

D.  Write an ordered pair such that:

18.  the abscissa is $-6$ and the ordinate is 3.          19.  the abscissa is 3 and the ordinate is $-6$.

20.  $x = -1$ and $y = 4$          21.  $x = 4$ and $y = -1$

22.  it names a point which is 5 units below the $x$-axis and 3 units to the right of the $y$-axis.

23.  it names the origin.

24.  Using ordered pairs, name each of the following points.

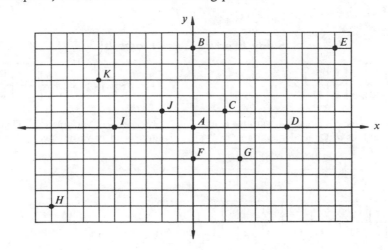

## SUPPLEMENTARY PROBLEMS, Contd.

E. Give the quadrant in which each of the following points is located.

25. $(2, 4)$　　26. $(-3, 5)$　　27. $(1, -6)$　　28. $\left(-\dfrac{1}{2}, -4\right)$　　29. $(0, -6)$

F. Make a Table of Values and graph each of the following.

30. $y = 3x$

31. $y = x + 2$

32. $\{(x, y) \mid y = x^2 + 3\}$

33. $\left\{(x, y) \mid y = -\dfrac{1}{x}\right\}$

34. $y = x$

35. $y = -x$

36. $\{(x, y) \mid y = 3x - 1\}$

37. $\{(x, y) \mid x + y = 6\}$

38. $y = -x^2$

39. $y = x^2 + x - 6$

40. $\{(x, y) \mid y = \mid x - 4 \mid\}$

41. $x = \mid 2y + 3 \mid$

42. $s = 16t^2$. This is a formula which gives the distance in feet that a dropped object will fall in $t$ seconds.

G. The following is a graph of a relationship between pressure and volume of a gas at a constant temperature. Pressure is measured in pounds per square inch and volume is measured in cubic inches.

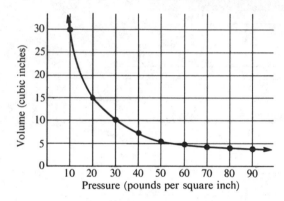

43. When a pressure of 30 pounds per square inch is applied, what is the resulting volume?
44. When a pressure of 40 pounds per square inch is applied, what is the resulting volume?
45. What pressure is necessary to give a volume of 30 cubic inches?
46. What pressure is necessary to give a volume of 5 cubic inches?
47. As the pressure increases, does the volume increase or decrease?
48. As the pressure decreases, does the volume increase or decrease?

□ **Solutions to Study Exercises**　　　　　　　　　　　　　　　　　　　**(8A)**

### Study Exercise One (Frame 8)

A.　1.　$y = 5x$

| $x$ | $-2$ | $0$ | $1$ | $3$ |
|---|---|---|---|---|
| $y$ | $-10$ | $0$ | $5$ | $15$ |

2.　$y = x^2 - 6x + 8$

| $x$ | $-2$ | $0$ | $3$ |
|---|---|---|---|
| $y$ | $24$ | $8$ | $-1$ |

B.　3.　Independent variable is $x$. Dependent variable is $y$.
　　5.　Independent variable is $d$. Dependent variable is $C$.

4.　Independent variable is C. Dependent variable is F.
6.　Independent variable is $x$. Dependent variable is $y$.

C.　7.　$y = 2x + 1$

| $x$ | $-3$ | $-2$ | $-1$ | $0$ | $1$ | $2$ | $3$ |
|---|---|---|---|---|---|---|---|
| $y$ | $-5$ | $-3$ | $-1$ | $1$ | $3$ | $5$ | $7$ |

8.　$y = 3x^2 + 2$

| $x$ | $-4$ | $-3$ | $-2$ | $-1$ | $0$ | $1$ | $2$ | $3$ | $4$ |
|---|---|---|---|---|---|---|---|---|---|
| $y$ | $50$ | $29$ | $14$ | $5$ | $2$ | $5$ | $14$ | $29$ | $50$ |

## Solutions to Study Exercises, Contd.

☐ *Study Exercise Two (Frame 12)* **(12A)**

A. 1. $(-3, -9)$, $(-2, -6)$, $(-1, -3)$, $(0, 0)$, $(1, 3)$, $(2, 6)$

B. 2. Abscissa is $-7$. Ordinate is 5.  3. Abscissa is 0. Ordinate is $-2$.  4. Abscissa is $\frac{1}{2}$. Ordinate is $\frac{2}{3}$.

C. 5. $(-2, 5)$  6. $(5, -2)$  7. $(2, -8)$
   8. $(0, 1)$  9. $\{(x, y) \mid y = 3x - 2\}$  10. $\{(x, y) \mid y = x^2 - 5\}$

☐ *Study Exercise Three (Frame 21)* **(21A)**

A. $A(1, 5)$, $B(-9, 2)$, $C(-6, 0)$, $D(0, 0)$, $E(8, 0)$, $F(-9, -3)$, $G(0, -2)$, $H(5, -3)$, $I$ approximately $\left(\frac{17}{2}, -\frac{9}{2}\right)$

B. 1. $(0, 0)$ origin  2. zero  3. zero
   4. 6 units below the $x$-axis and 2 units to the left of the $y$-axis

C. 5. II  6. II  7. I  8. III  9. no quadrant
   10. IV  11. I  12. II  13. IV

☐ *Study Exercise Four (Frame 29)* **(29A)**

1. $y = 3x$

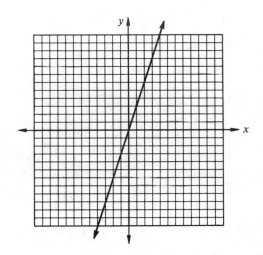

2. $\{(x, y) \mid y = x - 2\}$

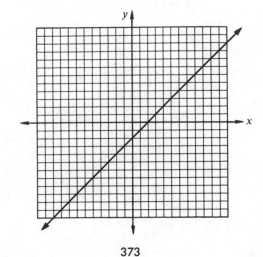

## Solutions to Study Exercises, Contd.

### Study Exercise Four (Frame 29, Contd.)

3. $\{(x, y) \mid y = x^2 + 1\}$

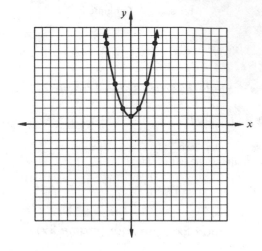

4. $y = |x - 2|$

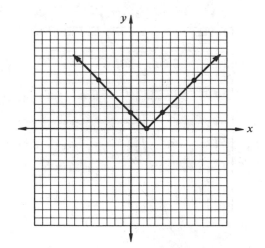

5. $x = |y + 1|$

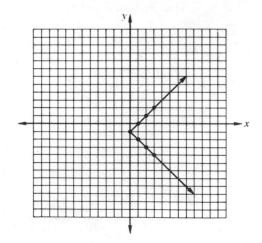

Solutions to Study Exercises, Contd.

## Study Exercise Four (Frame 29, Contd.)

6. $V = \dfrac{100}{P}$

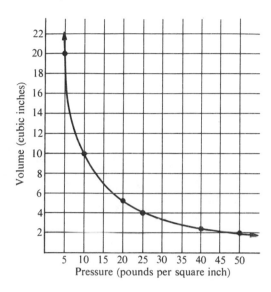

☐

## Study Exercise Five (Frame 32)                                                    (32A)

1. (a) $y = 5$, when $x = -3$
   (b) $x = 2$, when $y = -5$

2. (a) The resulting volume is 10 cubic inches.
   (b) The necessary pressure is 20 pounds per square inch.

# Graphing Linear and Quadratic Equations

## ☐ Objectives (1)

By the end of this unit you should be able to:

- graph linear equations in two variables, obtaining straight lines.
- find the slope of a straight line.
- find the *x*- and *y*-intercepts of a straight line.
- graph quadratic equations in two variables, obtaining U-shaped curves called *parabolas*.

## ☐ Linear Equations (2)

A *linear equation in two variables* is any equation which can be written in the form:

$$y = mx + b \quad \text{where } m \text{ and } b \text{ are constants}$$

The graph of a linear equation is a straight line.

## ☐ Examples of Linear Equations (3)

**Example 1:** $y = 2x + 3$ is a linear equation.

**Example 2:** $x + y = 5$ is a linear equation because it can be written as $y = -x + 5$.

**Example 3:** $3x + 2y = 5$ is a linear equation because it can be written as $y = -\dfrac{3}{2}x + \dfrac{5}{2}$.

## ☐ Graphing Linear Equations (4)

*The graph of a linear equation is a straight line.* Two points are all that are necessary to determine a straight line. However, we will obtain three points in order to have a checkpoint.

To graph a linear equation:

*Step (1):* Make a Table of Values containing at least three points.
*Step (2):* Plot the points and connect them with a straight line.

## ☐ Example 1: Graph $y = x$. (5)

**Solution:**

*Step (1):* Make a Table of Values.

| $x$ | $-3$ | 0 | 4 |
|---|---|---|---|
| $y$ | $-3$ | 0 | 4 |

*Step (2):* Plot the points and connect them with a straight line.

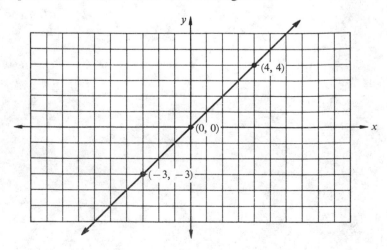

☐ **Example 2:**   Graph $\{(x, y) \mid y = x + 5\}$.                                                    **(6)**

**Solution:**

*Step (1):*   Make a Table of Values.

| $x$ | $-6$ | $-2$ | $0$ |
|---|---|---|---|
| $y$ | $-1$ | $3$ | $5$ |

*Step (2):*   Plot the points and connect them with a straight line.

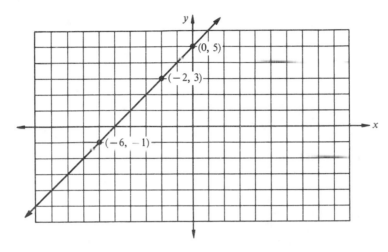

☐ **Example 3:**   Graph $\{(x, y) \mid y = -2x - 1\}$.                                              **(7)**

**Solution:**

*Step (1):*   Make a Table of Values.

| $x$ | $-3$ | $0$ | $2$ |
|---|---|---|---|
| $y$ | $5$ | $-1$ | $-5$ |

*Step (2):*   Plot the points and connect them with a straight line.

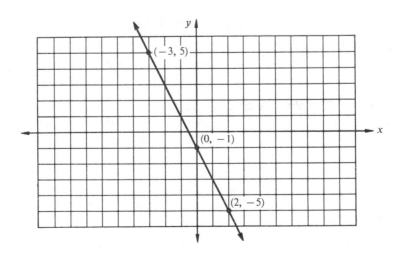

☐ **Example 4:** Graph $3x + 2y = 6$. **(8)**

    **Solution:**

      *Step (1):* Make a Table of Values.

        *line (a)* Let $x = 0$: $3 \cdot 0 + 2y = 6$
                                 $2y = 6$
                                   $y = 3$

        *line (b)* Let $y = 0$: $3x + 2 \cdot 0 = 6$
                                   $3x = 6$
                                   $x = 2$

        *line (c)* Let $x = -2$: $3(-2) + 2y = 6$
                                  $-6 + 2y = 6$
                                      $2y = 12$
                                       $y = 6$

        *line (d)* Table of Values:

| $x$ | 0 | 2 | $-2$ |
|---|---|---|---|
| $y$ | 3 | 0 | 6 |

      *Step (2):* Plot the points and connect them with a straight line.

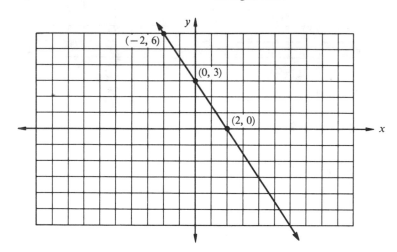

☐                         *Study Exercise One* **(9)**

Graph the following linear equations.

1. $y = -x$        2. $y = x - 2$        3. $y = -2x + 1$        4. $2x - 3y = 6$

☐ **Two Special Cases Where Graphs Are Straight Lines** **(10)**

    **Case 1:** $\{(x, y) \mid y = \text{constant}\}$

    **Example:** $\{(x, y) \mid y = 4\}$

    **Case 2:** $\{(x, y) \mid x = \text{constant}\}$

    **Example:** $\{(x, y) \mid x = 3\}$

☐ **Case One** **(11)**

    Graph $\{(x, y) \mid y = 4\}$.

      *Step (1):* Make a Table of Values.

| $x$ | $-5$ | $-3$ | $-1$ | 0 | 2 | 4 |
|---|---|---|---|---|---|---|
| $y$ | 4 | 4 | 4 | 4 | 4 | 4 |

$y$ always represents 4, no matter what number $x$ represents.

*Step (2):* Plot the points and connect them with a straight line.

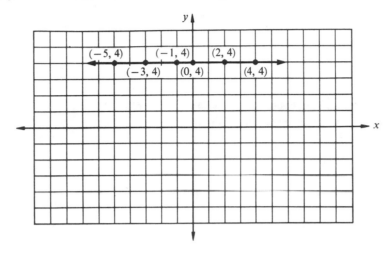

The graph of any equation of the form, $y = c$ where $c$ is a constant, is a horizontal straight line, $c$ units from the $x$-axis.

☐ **Case Two**                                                                                  **(12)**

Graph $\{(x, y) \mid x = 3\}$.

*Step (1):* Make a Table of Values.

| $x$ | 3 | 3 | 3 | 3 | 3 |
|---|---|---|---|---|---|
| $y$ | $-4$ | $-2$ | 0 | 1 | 3 |

$x$ always represents 3, no matter what number $y$ represents.

*Step (2):* Plot the points and connect them with a straight line.

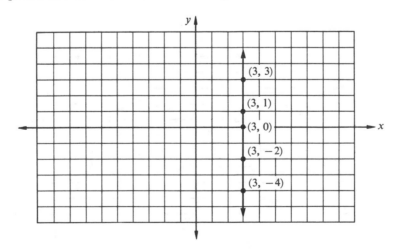

The graph of any equation of the form, $x = c$ where $c$ is a constant, is a vertical straight line, $c$ units from the $y$-axis.

☐                                    *Study Exercise Two*                                    **(13)**

A.  Graph the following.

1.  $\{(x, y) \mid y = -2\}$        2.  $\{(x, y) \mid x = -3\}$            3.  $y = 0$
4.  $x = 0$                              5.  $y = -5$                          6.  $x = -5$

B.  Write an equation which describes:

7.  the $x$-axis.                                    8.  the $y$-axis.
9.  a vertical line 6 units to the left of the $y$-axis.    10.  a horizontal line 1 unit above the $x$-axis.

☐ **The Rise and Run of a Straight Line**                                    **(14)**

Given two points on a straight line:

1.  the directed vertical distance between these two points is called the *rise*.
2.  the directed horizontal distance between these two points is called the *run*.

☐ **Example 1:**  $y = 2x - 4$                                    **(15)**

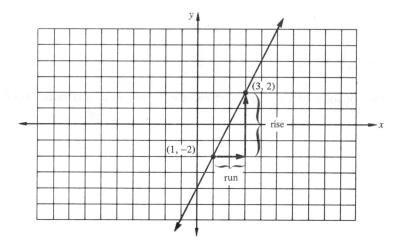

Starting at the point $(1, -2)$ and going to the point $(3, 2)$, we find that the rise is $+4$ and the run is $+2$.

☐ **Example 2:**  $y = -\dfrac{1}{3}x + 1$                                    **(16)**

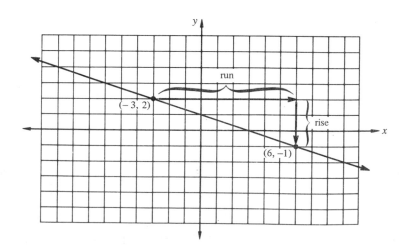

Starting at the point $(-3, 2)$ and going to the point $(6, -1)$, we find that the rise is $-3$ and the run is $+9$.

## □ Slope of a Straight Line (17)

The *slope* of a straight line is a measure of its slant. Slope is found by dividing the rise by the run.

$$\text{slope} = \frac{\text{rise}}{\text{run}}$$

## □ **Example 1:** $y = 2x - 4$ (18)

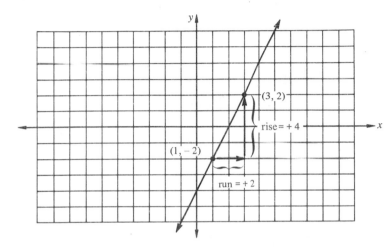

$$\text{slope} = \frac{\text{rise}}{\text{run}}$$
$$\text{slope} = \frac{+4}{+2}$$
$$\text{slope} = 2$$

This means that the straight line rises 2 units for every 1 unit that it goes to the right.

## □ **Example 2:** $y = -\frac{1}{3}x + 1$ (19)

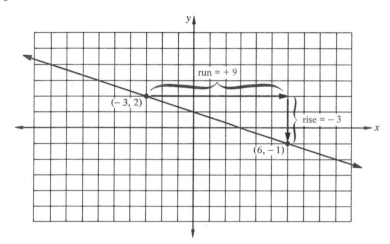

$$\text{slope} = \frac{\text{rise}}{\text{run}}$$
$$\text{slope} = \frac{-3}{+9}$$
$$\text{slope} = -\frac{1}{3}$$

This means that the straight line falls 1 unit for every 3 units that it goes to the right.

## □ Some Facts About Slope (20)

1. Straight lines having a positive slope will slant from lower left to upper right.
2. Straight lines having a negative slope will slant from upper left to lower right.
3. A horizontal straight line has a slope of zero.
4. If the equation of a straight line is in the form $y = mx + b$, then $m$ will equal the slope.

## □ *Study Exercise Three* (21)

A. Find the slopes of the following straight lines using the given points.

   1. $y = -2x - 2$

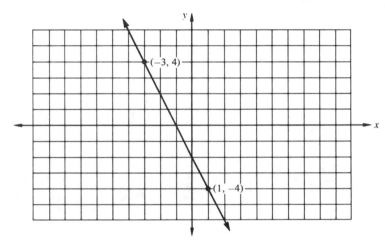

   2. $y = \frac{1}{4}x + 1$

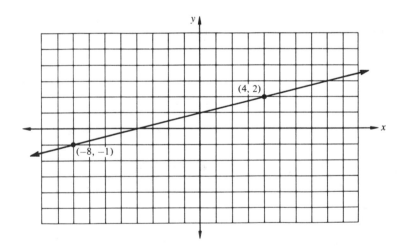

B.   Find the slopes for the following straight lines by locating any two points.

3.   $y = -3x - 6$

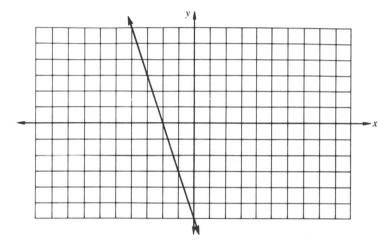

4.   $x - 3y = 0$

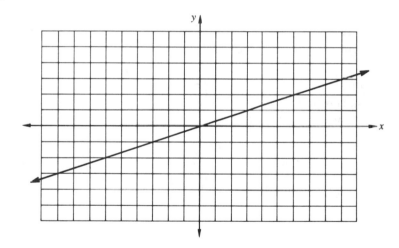

## ☐ X- and Y-Intercepts                                              **(22)**

1. The *x-intercept* is the value of $x$ where the graph crosses the $x$-axis.
2. The *y-intercept* is the value of $y$ where the graph crosses the $y$-axis.

**Example:**  Find the $x$- and $y$-intercepts of $y = 2x + 4$.

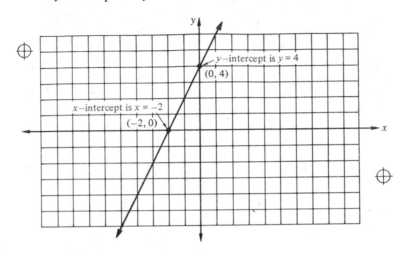

**Solution:**  The $x$-intercept is $x = -2$. The coordinates of the $x$-intercept are $(-2,0)$.
The $y$-intercept is $y = 4$. The coordinates of the $y$-intercept are $(0,4)$.

## ☐ Using Algebra to Find Intercepts                                 **(23)**

1. To find the $x$-intercept, substitute 0 for $y$.
2. To find the $y$-intercept, substitute 0 for $x$.

## ☐ **Example 1:**  Find the $x$- and $y$-intercepts of $y = 2x + 4$.   **(24)**

**Solution:**

*Step (1):*  The $x$-intercept is found by substituting 0 for $y$.

$$y = 2x + 4$$
$$0 = 2x + 4$$
$$-2x = 4$$
$$x = -2$$

*Step (2):*  The $y$-intercept is found by substituting 0 for $x$.

$$y = 2x + 4$$
$$y = 2 \cdot 0 + 4$$
$$y = 0 + 4$$
$$y = 4$$

Therefore, the $x$-intercept is $-2$ and the $y$-intercept is 4.

☐ **Example 2:**   Find the $x$- and $y$-intercepts and use them to graph $2x + 3y = 6$.          **(25)**

**Solution:**

*Step (1):*   The $x$-intercept is found by substituting 0 for $y$.

$$2x + 3y = 6$$
$$2x + 3 \cdot 0 = 6$$
$$2x = 6$$
$$x = 3$$

*Step (2):*   The $y$-intercept is found by substituting 0 for $x$.

$$2x + 3y = 6$$
$$2 \cdot 0 + 3y = 6$$
$$3y = 6$$
$$y = 2$$

*Step (3):*   Plot the $x$- and $y$-intercepts; then draw in the line.

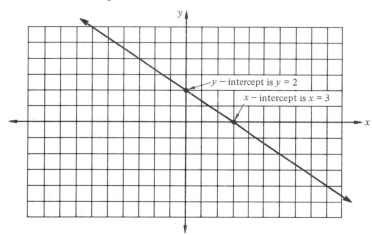

☐                                  *Study Exercise Four*                                  **(26)**

A.   Find the $x$- and $y$-intercepts of the following graphs.

    1.   $5x + 3y = 15$

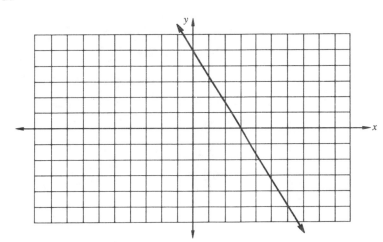

387

2.  $y = -\dfrac{1}{2}x - 2$

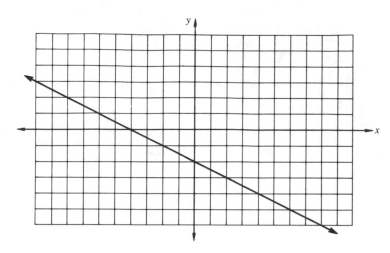

B.  For the following linear equations, give the $x$- and $y$-intercepts; then use these values to graph the equation.

3.  $y = 2x - 4$                4.  $x + 3y = 6$

## □ Quadratic Equations                                                 (27)

A *quadratic equation in two variables* is any equation which can be written in the form:

$$y = ax^2 + bx + c \quad \text{where } a, b, \text{ and } c \text{ are constants} \quad \text{and} \quad a \neq 0$$

The graph of a quadratic equation is a U-shaped curve called a *parabola*.

## □ Examples of Quadratic Equations                                     (28)

1.  $y = x^2$            2.  $x = y^2$            3.  $y = -x^2 + 2$            4.  $y = 2x^2 + 3x - 5$

☐ **Example 1:** Graph $y = x^2$.　　　　　　　　　　　　　　　　　　　　**(29)**

　**Solution:**

　　*Step (1):*　Make a Table of Values

| $x$ | $-3$ | $-2$ | $-1$ | 0 | 1 | 2 | 3 |
|---|---|---|---|---|---|---|---|
| $y$ | 9 | 4 | 1 | 0 | 1 | 4 | 9 |

　　*Step (2):*　Plot the points and connect them with a smooth U-shaped curve.

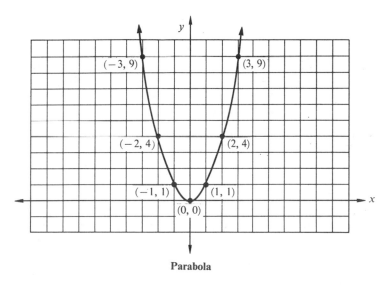

Parabola

☐ **Example 2:** Graph $x = y^2$.　　　　　　　　　　　　　　　　　　　　**(30)**

　**Solution:**

　　*Step (1):*　Make a Table of Values.

| $x$ | 9 | 4 | 1 | 0 | 1 | 4 | 9 |
|---|---|---|---|---|---|---|---|
| $y$ | 3 | 2 | 1 | 0 | $-1$ | $-2$ | $-3$ |

Easiest to select $y$-values first

　　*Step (2):*　Plot the points and connect them with a smooth U-shaped curve.

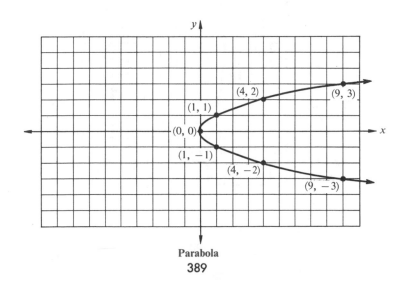

Parabola

389

☐ **Example 3:** Graph $y = -x^2 + 2$. **(31)**

  **Solution:**

  *Step (1):* Make a Table of Values.

| $x$ | $-3$ | $-2$ | $-1$ | 0 | 1 | 2 | 3 |
|---|---|---|---|---|---|---|---|
| $y$ | $-7$ | $-2$ | 1 | 2 | 1 | $-2$ | $-7$ |

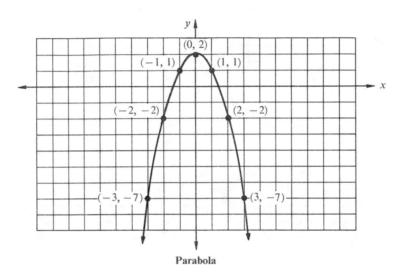

**Parabola**

☐ **Example 4:** Graph $y = 2x^2 + 3x - 5$. **(32)**

  **Solution:**

  *Step (1):* Make a Table of Values.

| $x$ | $-3$ | $-2$ | $-1$ | 0 | 1 | 2 |
|---|---|---|---|---|---|---|
| $y$ | 4 | $-3$ | $-6$ | $-5$ | 0 | 9 |

  *Step (2):* Plot the points and connect them with a smooth U-shaped curve.

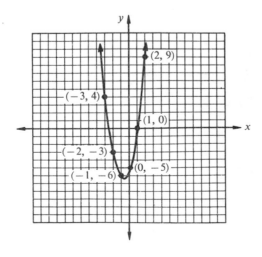

*Study Exercise Five*                                                                 **(33)**

A.   Graph the following quadratic equations.

   1.   $y = x^2 + 1$                                    2.   $y = -x^2$
   3.   $y = x^2 + 2x - 8$                               4.   $x = 2y^2 + y - 6$

B.   Find the $x$- and $y$-intercepts of the following quadratic equations. Remember that the $x$-intercept is found by substituting 0 for $y$, and the $y$-intercept is found by substituting 0 for $x$.

   5.   $y = x^2 - 9$                                     6.   $y = x^2 + x - 6$

## REVIEW EXERCISES

A.   Given $\{(x, y)\,|\,y = 2x^2 + 3x - 5\}$, which of the following ordered pairs belong to this set? Answer yes or no.

   1.   $(0, -5)$        2.   $\left(\dfrac{5}{2}, 0\right)$        3.   $(1, 0)$        4.   $\left(\dfrac{-3}{4}, \dfrac{-49}{8}\right)$        5.   $(9, 2)$

B.   Graph each of the following linear equations by plotting at least three points.

   6.   $y = x + 1$                  7.   $y = 3x - 4$                  8.   $y = -2x + 5$
   9.   $2x + 3y = 12$              10.   $y = -1$                     11.   $x = 5$

C.   Find the $x$- and $y$-intercepts and use these to graph the following linear equations.

   12.   $y = x + 3$                 13.   $x + y = 4$                  14.   $5x + 3y = 15$

D.   Find the slopes of the following straight lines by locating any two points.

   15.   $y = 2x + 2$

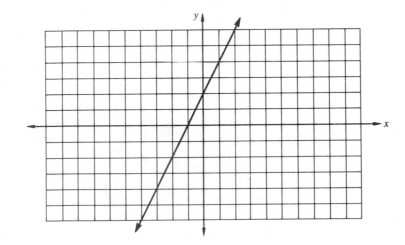

REVIEW EXERCISES, Contd.

16. $x + 2y = -1$

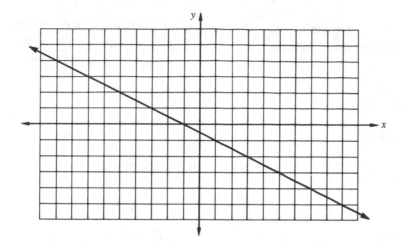

E. Graph the following quadratic equations.

17. $y = x^2 + 3$          18. $y = x^2 - 3$          19. $y = x^2 + 2x - 3$
20. $y = -x^2 - 2x + 3$       21. $x = 2y^2 + 2y + 4$

## Solutions to Review Exercises

A.   1.   Yes, $-5 = 2 \cdot 0^2 + 3 \cdot 0 - 5.$      2.   No, $0 \neq 2 \cdot \left(\dfrac{5}{2}\right)^2 + 3 \cdot \dfrac{5}{2} - 5.$      3.   Yes, $0 = 2 \cdot 1^2 + 3 \cdot 1 - 5.$

    4   Yes, $\dfrac{-49}{8} = 2 \cdot \left(\dfrac{-3}{4}\right)^2 + 3 \cdot \left(\dfrac{-3}{4}\right) - 5.$

    5.   No, $2 \neq 2 \cdot 9^2 + 3 \cdot 9 - 5.$

B.   6.   $y = x + 1$

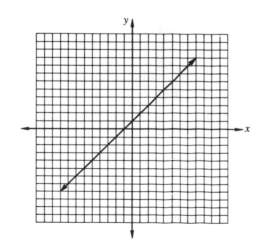

## Solutions to Review Exercises, Contd.

7.   $y = 3x - 4$

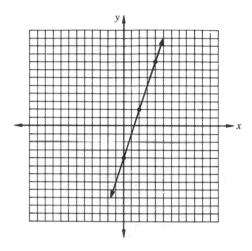

8.   $y = -2x + 5$

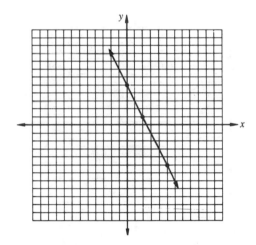

9.   $2x + 3y = 12$

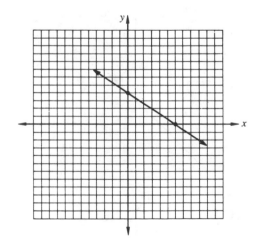

## Solutions to Review Exercises, Contd.

10. $y = -1$

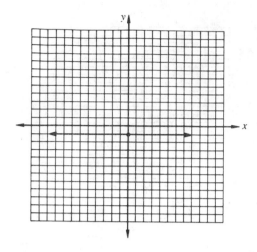

11. $x = 5$

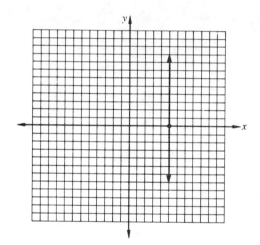

C. 12. $y = x + 3$; $x$-intercept $= -3$, $y$-intercept $= 3$

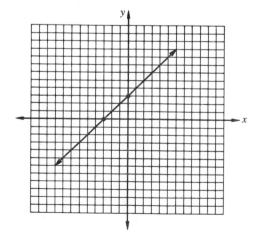

## Solutions to Review Exercises, Contd.

13.  $x + y = 4$; $x$-intercept $= 4$, $y$-intercept $= 4$

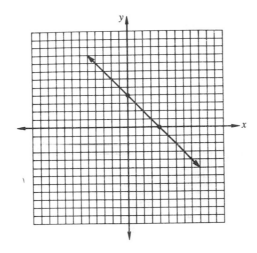

14.  $5x + 3y = 15$; $x$-intercept $= 3$, $y$-intercept $= 5$

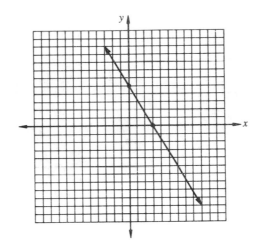

D.  15.  $y = 2x + 2$; slope $= 2$

16.  $x + 2y = -1$; slope $= -\dfrac{1}{2}$

## Solutions to Review Exercises, Contd.

E.   17.   $y = x^2 + 3$

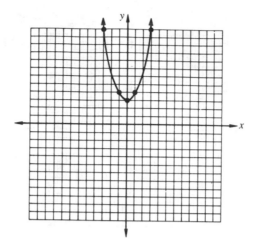

18.   $y = x^2 - 3$

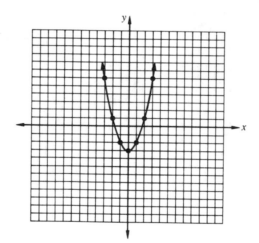

19.   $y = x^2 + 2x - 3$

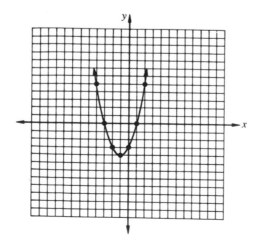

Solutions to Review Exercises, Contd.

20. $y = -x^2 - 2x + 3$

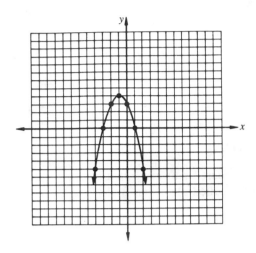

21. $x = -2y^2 + 2y + 4$

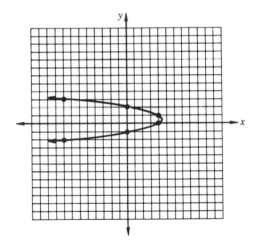

## SUPPLEMENTARY PROBLEMS

A.  Graph each of the following linear equations by plotting at least three points.

| | | |
|---|---|---|
| 1. $y = x$ | 2. $y = -x$ | 3. $y = x + 4$ |
| 4. $y = x - 4$ | 5. $y = 2x + 3$ | 6. $y = -2x + 3$ |
| 7. $x + y = 3$ | 8. $2x + y = 4$ | 9. $2x - 5y = 10$ |
| 10. $x = -4$ | | |

B.  Find the $x$- and $y$-intercepts and use these to graph the following linear equations.

| | | |
|---|---|---|
| 11. $y = x - 2$ | 12. $x + y = 6$ | 13. $3x - 4y = 12$ |

C.  For each of the following linear equations, obtain two points, then use these to find the slope of the graph.

| | |
|---|---|
| 14. $y = 3x - 1$ | 15. $x + y = 1$ |
| 16. $x - 2y = 4$ | 17. $5x + 2y = 10$ |

SUPPLEMENTARY PROBLEMS, Contd.

D.  Graph the following quadratic equations.

18.  $y = x^2$            19.  $y = -x^2$            20.  $x = y^2$
21.  $y = x^2 - 1$        22.  $y = x^2 + 1$         23.  $x = y^2 + 1$
24.  $y = x^2 + 2x - 8$   25.  $x = y^2 + 2y - 8$    26.  $y = 2x^2 + x - 10$

E.  Find the $x$- and $y$-intercepts for the following quadratic equations.

27.  $y = x^2 - 4$                    28.  $y = x^2 + x - 12$
29.  $y = 2x^2 - 9x - 5$             30.  $y = x^2 + x$

F.  Review of Unit 26:   True or False

31.  The two elements of an ordered pair are called *coordinates*.
32.  The point named $(0, 0)$ is called the *origin*.
33.  The equation of the $x$-axis is $x = 0$.
34.  In the ordered pair $\left(-5, \frac{2}{3}\right)$ the abscissa is $\frac{2}{3}$.
35.  The ordered pair $(0, 3)$ belongs to the set $\{(x, y) \mid y = x + 3\}$.
36.  The graph of the equation $y = 2$ is a vertical line.
37.  The ordered pair $(0, 5)$ names a point on the $x$-axis.
38.  The $x$-axis and the $y$-axis intersect at the origin.
39.  For the point named by $(-3, 6)$, the 6 tells us that the point is located 6 units to the right of the $y$-axis.
40.  The point named by $(-5, -6)$ is a quadrant III.

G.  Define the following.

41.  Linear equation in two variables        42.  Quadratic equation in two variables
43.  Abscissa                                 44.  Ordinate
45.  Origin

□ Solutions to Study Exercises                                              **(9A)**

*Study Exercise One (Frame 9)*

1.  $y = -x$                              2.  $y = x - 2$

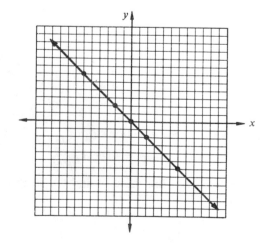
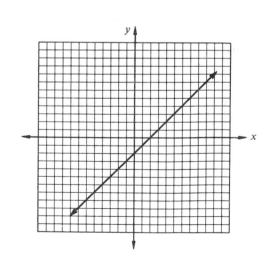

# Solutions to Study Exercises, Contd.

3. $y = -2x + 1$

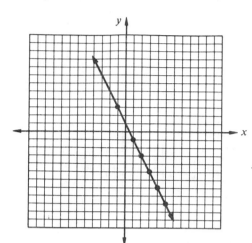

4. $2x - 3y = 6$

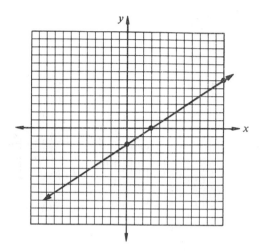

□

*Study Exercise Two (Frame 13)*

**(13A)**

A.  1.  $\{(x, y) \mid y = -2\}$

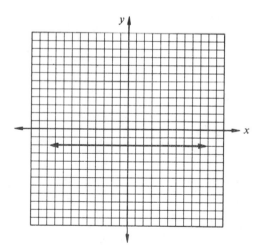

2.  $\{(x, y) \mid x = -3\}$

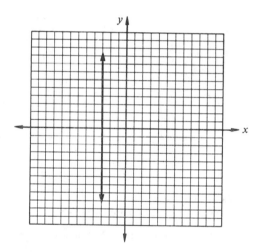

3.  $y = 0$

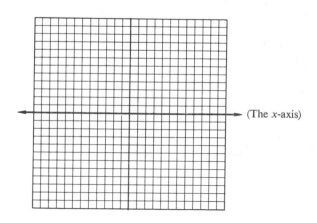

(The $x$-axis)

4.  $x = 0$

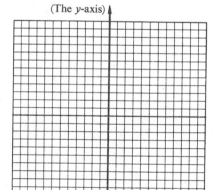

(The $y$-axis)

## Solutions to Study Exercises, Contd.

### Study Exercise Two (Frame 13, Contd.)

5.  $y = -5$                                                6.  $x = -5$

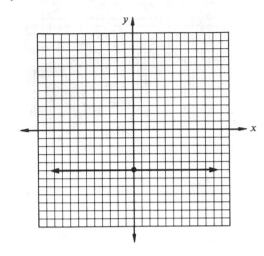                                        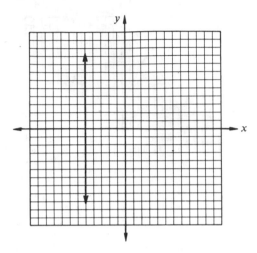

B.   7.  $y = 0$          8.  $x = 0$          9.  $x = -6$          10.  $y = 1$

☐                     ### Study Exercise Three (Frame 21)                  **(21A)**

A.   1.   slope $= \dfrac{\text{rise}}{\text{run}}$          2.   slope $= \dfrac{\text{rise}}{\text{run}}$

$= \dfrac{-8}{4}$                                            $= \dfrac{3}{12}$

$= -2$                                                       $= \dfrac{1}{4}$

B.   3.   slope $= -3$          4.   slope $= \dfrac{1}{3}$

☐                     ### Study Exercise Four (Frame 26)                  **(26A)**

A.   1.   $x$-intercept $= 3$; $y$-intercept $= 5$
     2.   $x$-intercept $= -4$; $y$-intercept $= -2$

B.   3.   $y = 2x - 4$; $x$-intercept $= 2$, $y$-intercept $= -4$

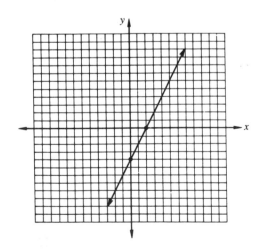

## Solutions to Study Exercises, Contd.

### *Study Exercise Four (Frame 26, Contd.)*

4. $x + 3y = 6$; $x$-intercept $= 6$, $y$-intercept $= 2$

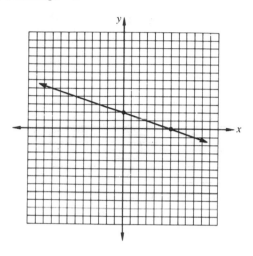

□

### *Study Exercise Five (Frame 33)*

**(33A)**

A. 1. $y = x^2 + 1$

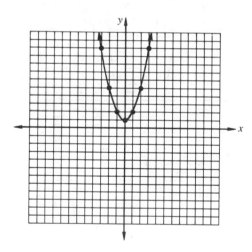

Solutions to Study Exercises, Contd.

## Study Exercise Five (Frame 33, Contd.)

2. $y = -x^2$

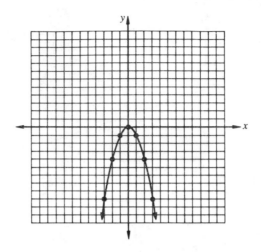

3. $y = x^2 + 2x - 8$

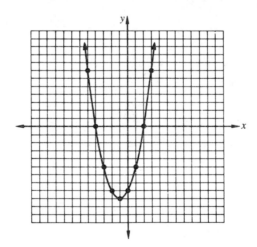

## Solutions to Study Exercises, Contd.

### *Study Exercise Five (Frame 33, Contd.)*

4.  $x = 2y^2 + y - 6$

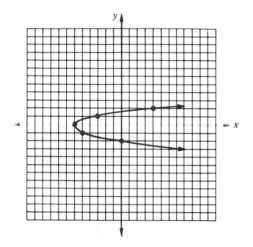

B.  5.  x-intercepts

$y = x^2 - 9$

$0 = x^2 - 9$

$0 = (x + 3)(x - 3)$

$x = -3$  and  $x = 3$

y-intercepts

$y = x^2 - 9$

$y = 0^2 - 9$

$y = 0 - 9$

$y = -9$

6.  x-intercepts

$y = x^2 + x - 6$

$0 = x^2 + x - 6$

$0 = (x + 3)(x - 2)$

$x = -3$  and  $x = 2$

y-intercepts

$y = x^2 + x - 6$

$y = 0^2 + 0 - 6$

$y = 0 + 0 - 6$

$y = -6$

# Solving Systems of
# Linear Equations

## ☐ Objectives **(1)**

By the end of this unit, you should be able to:

- understand the concept of "intersection of sets."
- understand the meaning of a system of linear equations.
- know what it means to solve a system of linear equations.
- solve a system of linear equations by
    (a) graphing.        (b) addition.        (c) substitution.
- classify systems of linear equations as
    (a) consistent.        (b) inconsistent.        (c) dependent.
- use systems of linear equations to solve applied problems.

## ☐ Review of Intersection of Sets **(2)**

The *intersection of two sets*, $A$ and $B$, is the set of elements which are common to both $A$ and $B$.

**Example 1:** If $A = \{e, g, h, k, t\}$ and $B = \{a, e, d, g, m, k\}$ then

$$A \cap B = \{e, g, k\}.$$
$$\uparrow$$
$$\text{intersection}$$

**Example 2:** If $E = \{(2, 3), (1, 2), (-3, 0)\}$ and $F = \{(1, 2), (-3, 0), (-5, 1)\}$, then $E \cap F = \{(1, 2), (-3, 0)\}$.

## ☐ *Study Exercise One* **(3)**

Find the intersection for each of the following:

1. $A = \{m, n, o, p, k\}$ and $B = \{f, m, t, n, o, z\}$
2. $G = \{a, b, c\}$ and $H = \{d, e, f\}$
3. $S = \varnothing$ and $T = \{a, c, e\}$
4. $C = \{(1, 2), (3, -5), (0, 0), (-6, 4)\}$ and
   $D = \{(2, 1), (0, 0), (3, -2), (3, -5), (0, 6)\}$
5. $E = \{(1, 2), (-3, 4), (-6, -7), (0, -1)\}$ and
   $F = \{(0, -1), (-3, 4), (-6, -7), (1, 2)\}$

## ☐ A System of Linear Equations **(4)**

$$x + y = 5$$
$$x - y = 1$$

## ☐ Solving a System of Linear Equations **(5)**

To *solve a system of linear equations* means to find all of the ordered pairs held in common between both sets or simply to find the members of the intersection set.

In set notation, this means to find $\{(x, y) \mid x + y = 5\} \cap \{(x, y) \mid x - y = 1\}$.

## ☐ We shall investigate three methods for solving a system of linear equations. **(6)**

**Method 1:** Graphing       **Method 2:** Addition       **Method 3:** Substitution

☐ Solving Systems of Linear Equations **(7)**
  Method One: Graphing

*Step (1):*  Graph both conditions.
*Step (2):*  Locate the point where the graphs cross
*Step (3):*  The ordered pair which names the point of intersection is the solution of the system.

☐ **Example 1:**  $\{(x, y) \mid x + y = 5\} \cap \{(x, y) \mid x - y = 1\}$. **(8)**

  **Solution:**

  *Step (1):*  Graph both conditions.

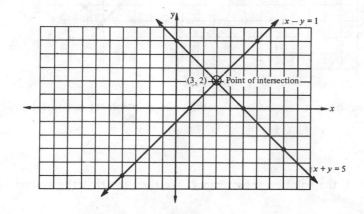

  *Step (2):*  Find the point of intersection. The intersection occurs at the point named by (3, 2).
  *Step (3):*  The ordered pair which names the point of intersection is the solution. The solution set
       is $\{(3, 2)\}$.

  Therefore, $\{(x, y) \mid x + y = 5\} \cap \{(x, y) \mid x - y = 1\} = \{(3, 2)\}$.

☐ Checking the Solution **(9)**

  To check the solution (3, 2), substitute 3 for $x$ and 2 for $y$ in both conditions.

|       Check 1       |       Check 2       |
| :-----------------: | :-----------------: |
| $x + y = 5$         | $x - y = 1$         |
| $3 + 2 = 5$         | $3 - 2 = 1$         |
| True                | True                |

  The solution checks.

☐ Consistent System **(10)**

  When the two lines cross at exactly one point, there is exactly one ordered pair in the solution set. We then
  say that the system of linear equations is *consistent*.

□ **Example 2:**  $\{(x, y) \mid x + y = 3\} \cap \{(x, y) \mid x + y = 5\}$ **(11)**

   **Solution:**

   *Step (1):*  Graph both conditions.

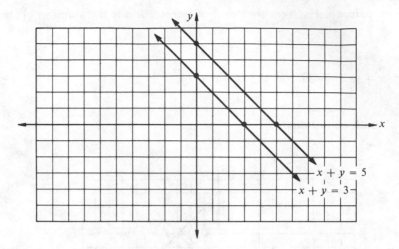

The lines are parallel and do not cross. Consequently, the solution set is empty. Therefore,

$$\{(x, y) \mid x + y = 3\} \cap \{(x, y) \mid x + y = 5\} = \varnothing.$$

□ **Inconsistent System** **(12)**

When two lines are parallel, the solution set is empty. We then say that the system of linear equations is *inconsistent*.

□ **Example 3:**  $\{(x, y) \mid x + y = 3\} \cap \{(x, y) \mid 2x + 2y = 6\}$ **(13)**

   **Solution:**

   *Step (1):*  Graph both conditions.

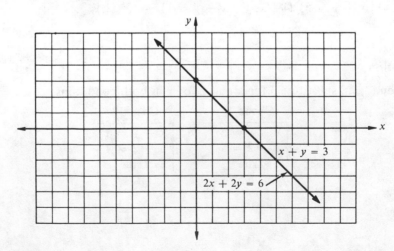

Both conditions have the same graph. The graphs have every point in common. Consequently, the solution set contains every ordered pair in either set. Therefore, $\{(x, y) \mid x + y = 3\} \cap \{(x, y) \mid 2x + 2y = 6\} = \{(x, y) \mid x + y = 3\}$, or $\{(x, y) \mid 2x + 2y = 6\}$.

☐ **Dependent System** **(14)**

When the graph of both conditions is the same line, the solution set is either of the two original sets. The system of linear equations is then said to be *dependent*.

☐ **A Matter of Notation** **(15)**

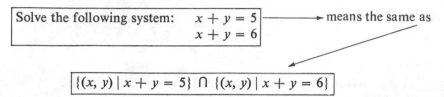

Solve the following system: $x + y = 5$ ⟶ means the same as
$x + y = 6$

$\{(x, y) \mid x + y = 5\} \cap \{(x, y) \mid x + y = 6\}$

☐ *Study Exercise Two* **(16)**

Solve the following systems by graphing. Indicate whether each is consistent, inconsistent, or dependent.

1. $\{(x, y) \mid x + y = 1\} \cap \{(x, y) \mid 2x + y = -1\}$    2. $\{(x, y) \mid 2x + 3y = 2\} \cap \{(x, y) \mid 4x + 6y = 4\}$
3. $x + 2y = 1$                                                  4. $3x + 3y = 5$
   $3x + 6y = 30$                                                   $x + 2y = 5$

☐ **Solving Systems of Linear Equations
Method Two: Addition** **(17)**

Given a system of two linear equations, we shall write two equations equivalent to the originals, such that when these equations are added together, either the terms involving $x$ or the terms involving $y$ will add to zero.

☐ **Example 1:** Solve $2x - y = 3$ **(18)**
$x + y = 3$

**Solution:** Add the two equations and eliminate the $y$-terms.
*Step (1):* Add the two equations.
$2x - y = 3$
$\underline{x + y = 3}$
$3x + 0 = 6$, or $3x = 6$
*Step (2):* Solve the resulting equation.
$3x = 6$
$x = 2$
*Step (3):* To find $y$, substitute 2 for $x$ into either of the two original equations.
$x + y = 3$
$2 + y = 3$
$y = 1$

Since $x = 2$ and $y = 1$, the solution set for the system is $\{(2, 1)\}$.

☐ **Example 2:** $2x + 3y = 11$                           **(19)**
                  $5x - 2y = -20$

    **Solution:** We shall eliminate the $y$-terms.

      *Step (1):*    In order to have the terms involving $y$ add to zero, multiply the first equation by 2 and multiply the second equation by 3.

                     $2 \cdot (2x + 3y) = 2 \cdot 11$, or $4x + 6y = 22$
                     $3 \cdot (5x - 2y) = 3(-20)$, or $15x - 6y = -60$

      *Step (2):*    Add the two equations and solve for $x$.

$$\begin{array}{r} 4x + 6y = \phantom{-}22 \\ 15x - 6y = -60 \\ \hline 19x + \phantom{0}0 = -38 \end{array}, \text{ or } 19x = -38$$

$$x = \frac{-38}{19}$$
$$x = -2$$

      *Step (3):*    Substitute the value of $x$ into either of the two original equations and solve for $y$.

$$2x + 3y = 11$$
$$2(-2) + 3y = 11$$
$$-4 + 3y = 11$$
$$3y = 15$$
$$y = 5$$

Since $x = -2$ and $y = 5$, the solution set for this system is $\{(-2, 5)\}$.

☐ **Example 3:** $3x + 6y = 30$      [**An inconsistent system**]             **(20)**
                 $x + 2y = \phantom{0}1$

    **Solution:** We shall eliminate the $x$-terms.

      *Step (1):*    In order to have the terms involving $x$ add to zero, leave the first equation as is and multiply the second equation by $-3$.
                     $-3(x + 2y) = -3 \cdot 1$, or $-3x - 6y = -3$

      *Step (2):*    Add the two equations.

$$\begin{array}{r} 3x + 6y = \phantom{-}30 \\ -3x - 6y = -3 \\ \hline 0x + 0y = \phantom{-}27 \end{array}, \text{ or } 0 = 27$$

This equation is false. There are no replacements of $x$ or $y$ which will make it true. The solution set is $\varnothing$.

☐ **Example 4:** $2x + 3y = 2$      [**A dependent system**]                **(21)**
                 $4x + 6y = 4$

    **Solution:** We shall eliminate the $x$-terms.

      *Step (1):*    In order to have the terms involving $x$ add to zero, multiply the first equation by $-2$ and leave the second equation as is.
                     $-2(2x + 3y) = -2 \cdot 2$, or $-4x - 6y = -4$

      *Step (2):*    Add the two equations.

$$\begin{array}{r} -4x - 6y = -4 \\ 4x + 6y = \phantom{-}4 \\ \hline 0x + 0y = \phantom{-}0 \end{array}, \text{ or } 0 = 0$$

This equation is true. It tells you that the two equations are equivalent and, consequently, are dependent. Hence, the solution set is $\{(x, y) \mid 2x + 3y = 2\}$, or $\{(x, y) \mid 4x + 6y = 4\}$.

☐                                         *Study Exercise Three*                                    **(22)**

Solve the following systems by the addition method. Classify each as consistent, inconsistent or dependent.

1.  $\{(x, y) \mid 2x - 3y = 1\} \cap \{(x, y) \mid 5x + 2y = -26\}$   2.   $6x - 2y = 7$
                                                                               $-3x + \ y = 5$

3.  $-x + 2y = \ \ 3$                                            4.  $x + y = 5$
    $3x - 6y = -9$                                                   $x - y = 8$


☐ **Solving Systems of Linear Equations**                                                      **(23)**
  **Method Three: Substitution**

Solve one of the equations for either $x$ or $y$; then use the substitution property to replace this value for the corresponding variable in the other equation.


☐ **Example 1:**   Solve $x + 3y = 14$                                                          **(24)**
                         $y = 2x$

 **Solution:**   Substitute $2x$ for $y$ in the first equation.

  *Step (1).*   Substitute into the first equation and solve for $x$.
$$x + 3y = 14$$
$$x + 3(2x) = 14$$
$$x + 6x = 14$$
$$7x = 14$$
$$x = 2$$

  *Step (2):*   To find the corresponding value of $y$, substitute 2 for $x$ in the second equation.
$$y = 2x$$
$$y = 2 \cdot 2$$
$$y = 4$$

Since $x = 2$ and $y = 4$, the solution set for the system is $\{(2, 4)\}$.


☐ **Example 2:**   Solve $2x + 3y = 3$                                                          **(25)**
                         $x + 2y = 4$

 **Solution:**   We shall solve the second equation for $x$ and substitute this value into the first equation.

  *Step (1):*   Solve the second equation for $x$.
$$x + 2y = 4$$
$$x = 4 - 2y$$

  *Step (2):*   Substitute $4 - 2y$ for $x$ in the first equation.
$$2x + 3y = 3$$
$$2(4 - 2y) + 3y = 3$$

  *Step (3):*   Solve for $y$.
$$2(4 - 2y) + 3y = 3$$
$$8 - 4y + 3y = 3$$
$$-y = -5$$
$$y = 5$$

  *Step (4):*   To find the corresponding value of $x$, substitute 5 for $y$ in any of the equations.
$$x = 4 - 2y \quad \text{[From Step (1)]}$$
$$x = 4 - 2(5)$$
$$x = 4 - 10$$
$$x = -6$$

Since $x = -6$ and $y = 5$, the solution set for this system is $\{(-6, 5)\}$.

☐ **Example 3:**  Solve $3x + 6y = 30$    (An inconsistent system)    **(26)**
$x + 2y = 1$

  **Solution:**  We shall solve the second equation for $x$ and substitute this value into the first equation.

  *Step (1):*  Solve the second equation for $x$.
  $x + 2y = 1$
  $x = 1 - 2y$

  *Step (2):*  Substitute $1 - 2y$ for $x$ in the first equation.
  $3x + 6y = 30$
  $3(1 - 2y) + 6y = 30$

  *Step (3):*  Solve for $y$.
  $3(1 - 2y) + 6y = 30$
  $3 - 6y + 6y = 30$
  $3 = 30$    (False)

This result is false. The equations, if graphed, would be parallel. There are no values of $x$ and $y$ that will solve this system. Therefore, the solution set is $\varnothing$.

☐ **Example 4:**  $2x + 4y = 6$    (A dependent system)    **(27)**
$x + 2y = 3$

  **Solution:**  We shall solve the second equation for $x$ and substitute this value into the first equation.

  *Step (1):*  Solve the second equation for $x$.
  $x + 2y = 3$
  $x = 3 - 2y$

  *Step (2):*  Substitute $3 - 2y$ for $x$ in the first equation.
  $2x + 4y = 6$
  $2(3 - 2y) + 4y = 6$

  *Step (3):*  Solve for $y$.
  $2(3 - 2y) + 4y = 6$
  $6 - 4y + 4y = 6$
  $6 = 6$    (True)

This equation is true. The two equations of this system are equivalent. If graphed, they would coincide at every point. The solution set is $\{(x, y) \mid 2x + 4y = 6\}$, or $\{(x, y) \mid x + 2y = 3\}$.

☐                          *Study Exercise Four*                          **(28)**

Solve the following systems by using the substitution method. Classify each system as consistent, inconsistent, or dependent.

1.  $x + y = 8$
   $y = x + 6$

2.  $\{(x, y) \mid x + 5y = 7\} \cap \{(x, y) \mid 3x - 2y = 4\}$

3.  $3x - 15y = 8$
   $x = 5y + 2$

4.  $\{(x, y) \mid 3x - 15y = 6\} \cap \{(x, y) \mid x = 5y + 2\}$

☐ **When to Use the Various Methods**    **(29)**

1.  The graphing method is used when a visual interpretation is desired.
2.  The substitution method is difficult to use unless one of the equations is easily solved for one of its variables. For example, the substitution method works well when one of the numerical coefficients is 1.

$$2x + y = 4$$
$$3x + 4y = 7$$    (Easily solved for $y$)

412

☐ **Examples:** **(30)**

1. $3x + 4y = 2$    (Use the addition method.)    2. $3x - 2y = 5$    (Use the substitution method.)
   $5x - 4y = 1$                                           $x = 3y - 6$

3. $2x + 5y = 1$    (Use the addition method.)
   $3x - 6y = 7$

☐ **Solving Applied Problems** **(31)**

**Example 1:** The sum of two electric voltages is 110 volts. If the larger voltage is tripled and the other is doubled, the sum becomes 290 volts. What are the voltages?

**Solution:** Let $x$ represent the larger voltage and $y$ represent the smaller voltage.

*Step (1):* Set up a system of equations.
$$x + y = 110$$
$$3x + 2y = 290$$

*Step (2):* Solve the system (addition method).
*line (a)*   $-3(x + y) = -3 \cdot 110$, or $-3x - 3y = -330$
*line (b)*   $-3x - 3y = -330$
$$\underline{\phantom{-}3x + 2y = \phantom{-}290}$$
$$-y = -40, \text{ or } y = 40$$
*line (c)*   $x + y = 110$
$$x + 40 = 110$$
$$x = 70$$

The larger voltage is 70 volts and the smaller voltage is 40 volts.

☐ **(32)**

**Example 2:** A man invests $6000. Part of it is invested at 5% and the remainder at 7%. How much is invested at each interest rate if the total annual interest income is $350?

**Solution:** Let $x$ represent the part invested at 5% and let $y$ represent the part invested at 7%.

*Step (1):* Set up a system of equations.
$$x + y = 6000$$
$$0.05x + 0.07y = 350$$

*Step (2):* Solve the system (addition method).
*line (a)*   $-5(x + y) = -5 \cdot (6000)$, or $-5x - 5y = -30000$
*line (b)*   $100 \cdot (0.05x + 0.07y) = 100 \cdot (350)$, or $5x + 7y = 35000$
*line (c)*   $-5x - 5y = -30000$
$$\underline{\phantom{-}5x + 7y = \phantom{-}35000}$$
$$2y = 5000$$
$$y = 2500$$
*line (d)*   $x + y = 6000$
$$x + 2500 = 6000$$
$$x = 3500$$

$3500 is invested at 5% and $2500 is invested at 7%.

☐ (33)

**Example 3:** A rectangular steel plate has a perimeter of 60 cm. Find the dimensions of the plate if the length is 3 cm less than twice its width.

**Solution:** Let $l$ represent the length of the plate and let $w$ represent the width of the plate.

*Step (1):* Set up a system of equations.
$$2l + 2w = 60$$
$$l = 2w - 3$$

*Step (2):* Solve the system (substitution method).

line (a)
$$2l + 2w = 60$$
$$2(2w - 3) + 2w = 60$$
$$4w - 6 + 2w = 60$$
$$6w = 66$$
$$w = 11$$

line (b)
$$l = 2w - 3$$
$$l = 2 \cdot (11) - 3$$
$$l = 19$$

The length of the plate is 19 cm and the width is 11 cm.

☐ *Study Exercise Five* (34)

Solve the following problems.

1. The sum of two voltages is 120 volts. If the larger voltage is tripled and the smaller voltage is quadrupled, the sum becomes 400 volts. What are the voltages?
2. A man invests $4000. Part of it is invested at 6% and the remainder is invested at 8%. How much is invested at each interest rate if the total annual interest is $270?
3. A rectangular steel plate has a perimeter of 28 in. Find the dimensions of the plate if the length is 2 in. less than three times its width.

## REVIEW EXERCISES

A. Find the set representing the intersection of the following.
   1. $\{a, b, c, d, e\} \cap \{c, d, e, f, g, h\}$
   2. $\{a, b, c\} \cap \{d, e\}$
   3. $\{a, b, c, d,\} \cap \{b, a, d, c\}$
   4. $\{(1, 2), (3, -4), (-2, 3)\} \cap \{(0, 0), (2, 1), (3, -4), (6, 8)\}$

B. What is meant by this notation?
   5. $2x + y = -2$
      $x + 2y = 5$

C. What does the graph look like for the following.
   6. A consistent system of two linear equations?
   7. An inconsistent system of two linear equations?
   8. A dependent system of two linear equations?

D. Solve the following systems of linear equations by graphing.
   9. $\{(x, y) \mid 2x + y = -2\} \cap \{(x, y) \mid x + 2y = 5\}$
   10. $y = 2x + 6$
       $y = x + 5$

E. Solve the following system of linear equations by the addition method.
   11. $2x + 3y = 5$
       $3x - 2y = -12$

## REVIEW EXERCISES, Contd.

F.  Solve the following system of linear equations by the substitution method.

12.  $3x - 4y = -5$
     $y = 2x$

G.  Solve the following systems of linear equations, using any method you wish. Classify each as consistent inconsistent, or dependent.

13.  $\{(x, y) \mid 2x + y = 7\} \cap \{(x, y) \mid x - y = 2\}$

14.  $2x + 3y = 1$
     $x + y = 4$

15.  $3x + y = 5$
     $2x + 3y = 9$

16.  $\{(x, y) \mid 3x + 5y = 1\} \cap \{(x, y) \mid 4x + 7y = 2\}$

17.  $2x = 6 - 2y$
     $x + y = 4$

18.  $2x = 6 - 2y$
     $x + y = 3$

H.  Solve the following problems.

19.  The sum of two numbers is 63. If the larger number is doubled and the smaller number is tripled, the difference is 41. Find the numbers.

20.  A man invests \$10,000. Part of it is invested at 5% and the remainder is invested at 6%. How much is invested at each interest rate if the total annual interest is \$540?

21.  A rectangular field has a perimeter of 130 yd. Find the dimensions of the field if the length is 10 yd less than twice its width.

22.  How many milliliters of a mixture containing 70% acid should be added to a mixture containing 20% acid in order to produce 16 milliliters of a mixture containing 50% acid?

## Solutions to Review Exercises

A.  1.  $\{c, d, e\}$      2.  $\varnothing$      3.  $\{a, b, c, d\}$      4.  $\{(3, -4)\}$

B.  5.  To find the ordered pairs in this intersection: $\{(x, y) \mid 2x + y = -2\} \cap \{(x, y) \mid x + 2y = 5\}$

C.  6.  Two straight lines intersecting or crossing at exactly one point.
    7.  Two parallel straight lines. No point of intersection.
    8.  The two sets share the same graph. Hence, they intersect at every point on the line.

D.  9.  $\{(x, y) \mid 2x + y = -2\} \cap \{(x, y) \mid x + 2y = 5\}$

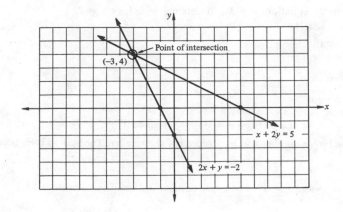

The solution set is $\{(-3, 4)\}$

## Solutions to Review Exercises, Contd.

10. $y = 2x + 6$
    $y = x + 5$

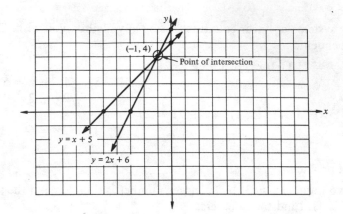

The solution set is $\{(-1, 4)\}$

E. 11. $2(2x + 3y) = 2 \cdot 5$
       $3(3x - 2y) = 3(-12)$
       $4x + 6y = 10$
       $\underline{9x - 6y = -36}$
       $13x \qquad = -26$
       $\qquad x = -2$

Substitute $-2$ for $x$ in either equation.

$2x + 3y = 5$
$2 \cdot (-2) + 3y = 5$
$-4 + 3y = 5$
$3y = 9$
$y = 3$

The solution set is $\{(-2, 3)\}$.

F. 12. Substitute $2x$ for $y$ in the equation, $3x - 4y = -5$, to obtain $3x - 4(2x) = -5$.
       Solve the equation for $x$:

$3x - 4(2x) = -5$
$3x - 8x = -5$
$-5x = -5$
$\quad x = 1$

Substitute 1 for $x$ in the equation, $y = 2x$, to obtain $y = 2 \cdot 1$, or $y = 2$.
The solution set is $\{(1, 2)\}$.

G. 13. $\{(3, 1)\}$     Consistent
   14. $\{(11, -7)\}$     Consistent
   15. $\left\{\left(\dfrac{6}{7}, \dfrac{17}{7}\right)\right\}$     Consistent
   16. $\{(-3, 2)\}$     Consistent
   17. $\varnothing$     Inconsistent
   18. $\{(x, y) \mid 2x = 6 - 2y\}$, or $\{(x, y) \mid x + y = 3\}$     Dependent

H. 19. Let $x$ represent the larger number and let $y$ represent the smaller. The system then becomes:
       $x + y = 63$
       $2x - 3y = 41$

The solution is $x = 46$ and $y = 17$. The larger number is 46 and the smaller is 17.

## Solutions to Review Exercises, Contd.

20. Let $x$ represent the amount invested at 5% and let $y$ represent the amount invested at 6%. The system then becomes:

$$x + y = 10000$$
$$0.05x + 0.06y = 540$$

The solution is $x = 6000$ and $y = 4000$. $6000 is invested at 5% and $4000 is invested at 6%.

21. Let $l$ represent the length of the field and let $w$ represent the width. The system then becomes:

$$2l + 2w = 130$$
$$l = 2w - 10$$

The solution is $l = 40$ and $w = 25$. The length is 40 yd and the width is 25 yd.

22. Let $x$ represent the amount of the 70% solution and let $y$ represent the amount of the 20% solution. The system then becomes:

$$x + y = 16$$
$$0.70x + 0.20y = (0.50)(16)$$

The solution is $x = 9.6$ and $y = 6.4$. Thus, 9.6 milliliters of the 70% solution should be added to 6.4 milliliters of the 20% solution.

## SUPPLEMENTARY PROBLEMS

A. Solve the following systems by graphing.

1. $x + y = 4$
   $x - y = 2$

2. $x + 2y = 3$
   $2x + 4y = 7$

3. $y = 3x - 4$
   $y = 5x - 6$

4. $3x - 2y = 6$
   $6x - 4y = 12$

5. $\{(x, y) \mid 2x + y = 4\} \cap \{(x, y) \mid 4x + 2y = 3\}$

B. Solve the following systems by the addition method.

6. $x + y = 4$
   $x - y = 2$

7. $2x - y = 1$
   $x + y = 11$

8. $m + n = 5$
   $m - 2n = 1$

9. $a + 2b = 3$
   $3a + 6b = 9$

10. $6x + 7y = 0$
    $2x - 3y = 32$

11. $r - 4s = 5$
    $2r - 8s = 7$

12. $\{(x, y) \mid 7x - 8y = 2\} \cap \{(x, y) \mid 5x - 3y = -9\}$

C. Solve the following systems by the substitution method.

13. $x = 1 - 4y$
    $2x - 8y = 1$

14. $m - n = 2$
    $2m + n = 8$

15. $x - 4y = 0$
    $2x = 3y$

16. $a - b = 1$
    $a = b + 5$

17. $r = 2s$
    $2r - 3s = 1$

18. $x + y = 3$
    $y = 2x + 9$

19. $3x + 6y = 9$
    $x + 2y = 3$

20. $\{(x, y) \mid y = 3x - 1\} \cap \{(x, y) \mid 6x - 2y = 1\}$

D. Solve the following systems using any method you wish. Classify each as consistent, inconsistent, or dependent.

21. $x + 3y = 1$
    $2x + 5y = 1$

22. $5m + 3n = 17$
    $m + 3n = 1$

23. $y = 2x - 1$
    $2x + 5y = -23$

24. $2x - 5y = 1$
    $6x - 15y = 3$

25. $2m - 5n = 1$
    $6m - 15n = 1$

26. $3r + 4s = 6$
    $r + s = 2$

27. $a - 2b = 3$
    $4a - 8b = 12$

28. $x = 3 - y$
    $y = 2x + 9$

29. $5x - 2y = 6$
    $3x - 4y = 12$

30. $3x - 2y = 1$
    $2x + 5y = 7$

31. $7m + 3n = 4$
    $9m + 5n = 8$

32. $u = 4 - v$
    $v = -5u$

E. Solve the following problems.

33. The sum of two numbers is 53. If the larger number is doubled and the smaller number is tripled, the sum is 121. Find the numbers.

## SUPPLEMENTARY PROBLEMS, Contd.

34. A board 96 in. long is cut into two pieces so that one piece is 12 in. longer than the other. Find the length of each piece.

35. A man invests $4000. Part of it is invested at 7% and the remainder is invested at 8%. How much is invested at each interest rate if the total annual interest is $295?

36. A rectangular field has a perimeter of 176 yd. Find the dimensions of the field if the length is 4 yd more than twice the width.

37. How many ounces of an alloy containing 10% titanium must be melted with an alloy containing 25% titanium in order to produce 40 ounces of an alloy containing 15% titanium?

38. Two cars make a trip of 168 miles each. The faster car averages 14 miles per hour faster and makes the trip in 1 hour less time than the slower car. Find the average rate of each car.

39. A boat can travel 6 miles downstream in 40 minutes. The return trip requires 1 hour. Find the rate of the boat in still water and the rate of the current.

40. A 20-ft board is cut into two pieces, one of which is 2 ft longer than the other. How long is each piece?

41. How many quarts of a 15% solution of alcohol should be added to 30 quarts of a 50% solution of alcohol to produce a 40% solution?

42. A 54-ft rope is cut into two pieces so that one piece is 20 ft longer than the other. Find the length of each piece.

43. The sum of two numbers is 76. One of the numbers is three times the other. Find the numbers.

44. Find the dimensions of a rectangle of perimeter 126 inches whose length is two and one-half times the width.

45. The voltage across a resistor is equal to the product of the current times the resistance. The sum of two resistances is 20 ohms. When a current of 4 amperes passes through the larger resistor and 6 amperes through the smaller resistor, the sum of the voltages is 90 volts. What is the value of each resistor?

F. Answer the following.

46. What is the graph of a dependent system of linear equations?
47. What is the graph of an inconsistent system of linear equations?
48. What is the graph of a consistent system of linear equations?

G. Find the intersection of the following sets:

49. $\{a, k, t, c, p, o\} \cap \{b, c, k, o, m\}$
50. $\{(2, 3), (4, -5), (0, 0), (5, 1)\} \cap \{(3, 2), (-5, 4), (5, 1)\}$
51. $A \cap \emptyset$, where $A$ represents any set
52. $A \cap A$, where $A$ represents any set

□ Solutions to Study Exercises                    (3A)

### Study Exercise One (Frame 3)

1. $A \cap B = \{m, n, o\}$    2. $G \cap H = \emptyset$    3. $S \cap T = \emptyset$    4. $C \cap D = \{(0, 0), (3, -5)\}$
5. $E \cap F = \{(1, 2), (-3, 4), (-6, -7), (0, -1)\}$, or $E \cap F = E$ or, $E \cap F = F$

## Solutions to Study Exercises, Contd.

1. $\{(x, y) \mid x + y = 1\} \cap \{(x, y) \mid 2x + y = -1\}$

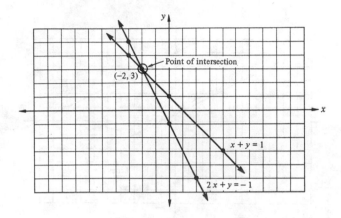

The solution set is $\{(-2, 3)\}$ and the system is consistent.

2. $\{(x, y) \mid 2x + 3y = 2\} \cap \{(x, y) \mid 4x + 6y = 4\}$

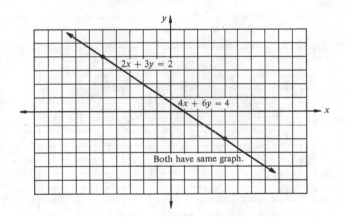

The solution set is $\{(x, y) \mid 2x + 3y = 2\}$, or $\{(x, y) \mid 4x + 6y = 4\}$. The system is dependent.

## Solutions to Study Exercises, Contd.

### Study Exercise Two (Frame 16, Contd.)

3.　$x + 2y = 1$
　　$3x + 6y = 30$

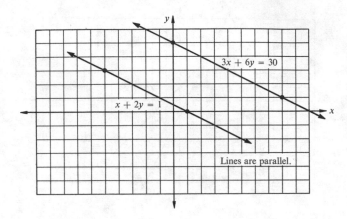

3x + 6y = 30

x + 2y = 1

Lines are parallel.

The solution set is $\varnothing$, and the system is inconsistent.

4.　$3x + 3y = 5$
　　$x + 2y = 5$

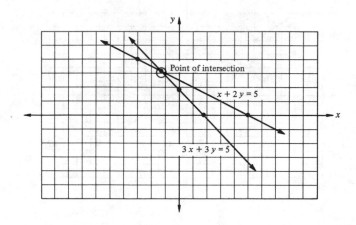

Point of intersection

x + 2y = 5

3x + 3y = 5

$x$ is somewhere between $-1$ and $-2$. $y$ is somewhere between 3 and 4. The graphing method can be inaccurate if $x$ and $y$ do not represent integers in the solution set. Therefore, we will next look at algebraic methods.

☐　　　　　### Study Exercise Three (Frame 22)　　　　　(22A)

1.　$\quad 5(2x - 3y) = 5 \cdot 1$
　$\quad -2(5x + 2y) = -2(-26)$
　$\quad\quad 10x - 15y = \phantom{0}5$
　$\quad\underline{-10x - \phantom{0}4y = 52}$
　$\quad\quad\quad -19y = \overline{57}$
　$\quad\quad\quad\quad\quad y = -3$

If $y = -3$, then $x = -4$. Solution set is $\{(-4, -3)\}$. The system is consistent.

## Solutions to Study Exercises, Contd.

2.    $6x - 2y = 7$
       $2(-3x + y) = 2 \cdot 5$

$$6x - 2y = 7$$
$$\underline{-6x + 2y = 10}$$
$$0 = 17$$

The solution set is $\emptyset$, and the system is inconsistent.

3.    $3(-x + 2y) = 3 \cdot 3$
       $3x - 6y = -9$

$$-3x + 6y = 9$$
$$\underline{3x - 6y = -9}$$
$$0 = 0$$

The system is dependent, and the solution set is $\{(x, y) \mid -x + 2y = 3\}$, or $\{(x, y) \mid 3x - 6y = -9\}$.

4.    $x + y = 5$
      $\underline{x - y = 8}$
      $2x\phantom{- y} = 13$
$$x = \frac{13}{2}$$

If $x = \dfrac{13}{2}$, then $y = -\dfrac{3}{2}$. Solution set is $\left\{ \left( \dfrac{13}{2}, -\dfrac{3}{2} \right) \right\}$, or $\{(6\frac{1}{2}, -1\frac{1}{2})\}$. The system is consistent.

☐                 *Study Exercise Four (Frame 28)*                **(28A)**

1.  Substitute $x + 6$ for $y$ in the first equation, obtaining $x + (x + 6) = 8$.
    Solve for $x$:   $x + (x + 6) = 8$
                     $2x + 6 = 8$
                        $2x = 2$
                          $x = 1$

    Substitute 1 for $x$ in the second equation.

    $y = x + 6$
    $y = 1 + 6$
    $y = 7$

    The solution set is $\{(1, 7)\}$ and the system is consistent.

2.  Solve $x + 5y = 7$ for $x$, obtaining $x = 7 - 5y$. Substitute $7 - 5y$ for $x$ in the second equation:
                $3x - 2y = 4$
            $3(7 - 5y) - 2y = 4$
    Solve for $y$:   $3(7 - 5y) - 2y = 4$
                $21 - 15y - 2y = 4$
                        $-17y = -17$
                        $-17y = -17$
                           $y = 1$

    Substitute 1 for $y$ in the equation, $x = 7 - 5y$, obtaining $x = 7 - 5 \cdot 1$, or $x = 2$. The solution set is $\{(2, 1)\}$ and the system is consistent.

3.  Substitute $5y + 2$ for $x$ in the first equation:
                $3x - 15y = 8$
            $3(5y + 2) - 15y = 8$
    Solve for $y$:   $3(5y + 2) - 15y = 8$
                $15y + 6 - 15y = 8$
                           $6 = 8$

    The equation is false. Therefore, the system is inconsistent and the solution set is $\emptyset$.

## Solutions to Study Exercises, Contd.

4. Substitute $5y + 2$ for $x$ in the first equation:
$$3x - 15y = 6$$
$$3(5y + 2) - 15y = 6$$
Solve for $y$:    $15y + 6 - 15y = 6$
$$6 = 6$$

The equation is true. Therefore, the system is dependent and the solution set is $\{(x, y) \mid 3x - 15y = 6\}$, or $\{(x, y) \mid x = 5y + 2\}$.

□                          *Study Exercise Five (Frame 34)*                          **(34A)**

1. Let $x$ represent the larger voltage and let $y$ represent the smaller voltage. The system then becomes:
$$x + y = 120$$
$$3x + 4y = 400$$
The solution is $x = 80$ and $y = 40$. The larger voltage is 80 volts and the smaller voltage is 40 volts.

2. Let $x$ represent the amount invested at 6% and let $y$ represent the amount invested at 8%. The system then becomes:
$$x + y = 4000$$
$$0.06x + 0.08y = 270$$
The solution is $x = 2500$ and $y = 1500$. $2500 is invested at 6% interest and $1500 is invested at 8% interest.

3. Let $l$ represent the length of the plate and let $w$ represent the width of the plate. The system then becomes:
$$2l + 2w = 28$$
$$l = 3w - 2$$
The solution is $l = 10$ and $w = 4$. The length of the plate is 10 in. and the width of the plate is 4 in.

# Linear Inequalities and
# Systems of Linear Inequalities

## ☐ Objectives **(1)**

By the end of this unit you should be able to:

- graph a linear inequality in two unknowns by graphing its boundary and selecting a test point.
- graph a system of linear inequalities in two unknowns by graphing each inequality and selecting the over-lapping region.

## ☐ Linear Inequalities **(2)**

Linear inequalities in two unknowns are similar to linear equations except the equal sign has been replaced by one of these inequality symbols:

$<$ "less than"
$\leq$ "less than or equal to"
$>$ "greater than"
$\geq$ "greater than or equal to"

## ☐ Examples **(3)**

Each of these is a linear inequality in two unknowns.

1. $x + 2y < 6$
2. $2x + 5y \leq 10$
3. $y > 2x + 3$
4. $y \geq 3x - 4$
5. $\{(x,y) \mid 2x + 4y \leq 1\}$

## ☐ Some Information **(4)**

To graph a linear inequality we will make use of the following information:

1. The graph of a linear equation is a straight line.
2. Every non-vertical straight line divides the coordinate plane into an upper region and a lower region.
3. The straight line itself is called a boundary and is not contained in either region. Thus, it is illustrated by a broken line.

   **Example:** Consider the graph of $x + 2y = 6$.

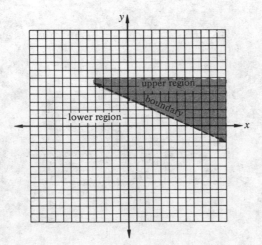

4. As we shall see, the graph of a linear inequality will consist of either the upper region or the lower region, but not both. The boundary line will be part of the graph if the given inequality includes an equal sign, such as $\leq$ or $\geq$. Otherwise, the boundary line is not part of the graph.

☐ **Graphing a Linear Inequality in Two Unknowns** **(5)**

To graph a linear inequality follow these steps:

1. Graph the boundary line. If the boundary is to be included, it is drawn solid; otherwise, it is designated by a broken line.

2. Select a test point from either the upper or lower region. Substitute the coordinates into the original inequality. If the resulting statement is true, then the graph includes that region. But if the statement is false, the graph includes the other region.

☐ **Example 1:** Graph $x + 2y \leqslant 6$ **(6)**

**Solution:**

*Step (1):* Graph the boundary given by the equation $x + 2y = 6$. The original inequality contains an equal sign. Therefore, the graph will include the boundary, drawn as a solid line.

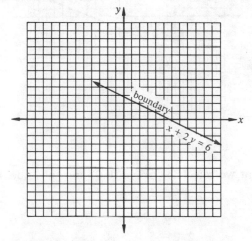

*Step (2):* Select a test point from either region. Do not choose a point on the boundary. The origin $(0, 0)$ is a convenient point located in the lower region. Substitute the coordinates into the original inequality and determine whether the resulting statement is true or false.

$$x + 2y \leqslant 6$$
$$0 + 2 \cdot 0 \leqslant 6$$
$$0 \leqslant 6 \quad [\text{true}]$$

Since the statement is true, the graph includes the lower region containing the test point $(0, 0)$. And, as noted in Step (1), it will also include the boundary. The graph is the shaded region, together with the solid line.

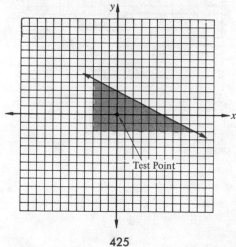

425

☐ **Example 2:**   Graph $2x - 5y > 10$   **(7)**

**Solution:**

*Step (1):*   Graph the boundary given by the equation $2x - 5y = 10$. The original inequality contains no equal sign. Therefore, the graph will not include the boundary, which is drawn as a broken line.

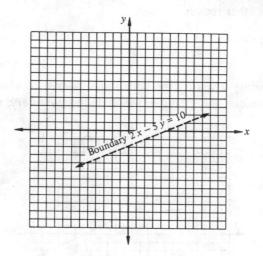

*Step (2):*   For our test point we select the origin (0,0) and substitute the coordinates into the original inequality.

$$2x - 5y > 10$$
$$2 \cdot 0 - 5 \cdot 0 > 10$$
$$0 > 10 \quad \text{[false]}$$

Since the statement is false, the graph of the inequality will not include the upper region, containing the test point (0, 0). Therefore, as illustrated, the graph will contain the lower region, but not the boundary.

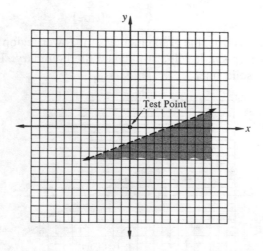

☐ **Example 3:** Graph $\{(x, y) \mid y \geqq 3x\}$ **(8)**

**Solution:**

*Step (1):* Graph the boundary, given by the equation $y = 3x$. Since the original inequality contains an equal sign, the graph will include the boundary. Thus, it is drawn as a solid line.

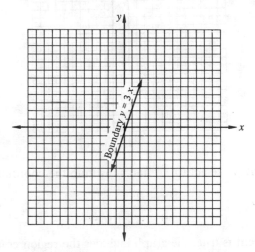

*Step (2):* For the test point we can select any point not on the boundary. Therefore, we cannot choose the point $(0, 0)$, because it lies on the line $y = 3x$. Instead, we arbitrarily select the point $(0, 2)$, lying in the upper region. Substituting 0 for $x$ and 2 for $y$ in the original inequality, we arrive at the following true statement:

$$y \geqq 3x$$
$$2 \geqq 3 \cdot 0$$
$$2 \geqq 0 \quad \text{[true]}$$

Thus, as illustrated by the shaded portion, the graph includes the upper region as well as the boundary.

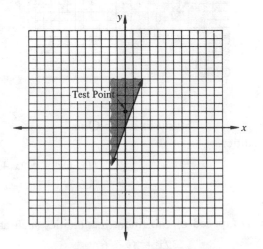

☐ **Example 4:** Graph $x < 2$ **(9)**

**Solution:**

*Step (1):* Graph the boundary given by the equation $x = 2$. This is a *vertical* line dividing the plane into a left region and a right region. Since there is no equal sign in the original inequality, the graph will not include the boundary. Therefore, it is pictured as a broken line.

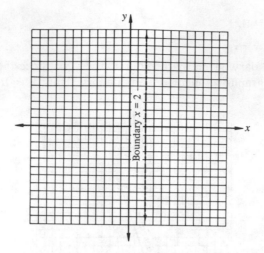

*Step (2):*  For the test point we select (0, 0) and substitute the coordinates into the original inequality.

$$x < 2$$

$$0 < 2 \quad \text{[true]}$$

Since the statement is true, the graph includes the region containing the test point. Thus, the graph includes the region to the left of the boundary.

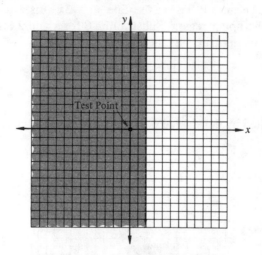

## Study Exercise One     (10)

Graph the following linear inequalities.

1.  $3x - 5y > 15$
2.  $\{(x, y) \mid y \geq 2x + 1\}$
3.  $y < 3$
4.  $\{(x, y) \mid x \leq -3\}$

## Systems of Linear Inequalities     (11)

A system of linear inequalities is composed of two linear inequalities such as:

$$2x + 3y > 6$$

$$3x - 5y > 15$$

It means to find the intersection of the two sets. In set notation it means to find:

$$\{(x, y) \mid 2x + 3y > 6\} \cap \{(x, y) \mid 3x - 5y > 15\}$$

The graph of a system of linear inequalities is the overlapping region.

☐ **Graphing a System of Linear Inequalities in Two Unknowns**                    **(12)**

To graph a system of linear inequalities we follow these steps:

(1)   Graph both inequalities on the same coordinate system.
(2)   Find the overlapping region; it represents the solution of the system.

☐ **Example 1:**   Graph the solution of this system.                              **(13)**

$$2x + 3y > 6$$
$$3x - 5y < 15$$

**Solution:**

*Step (1):*   Graph both inequalities.

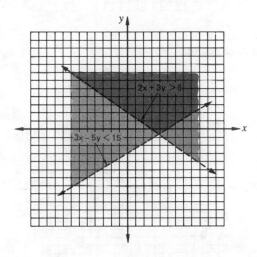

*Step (2):*   Find the overlapping region.

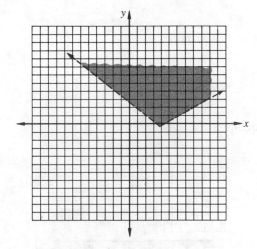

☐ **Example 2:**   Graph the solution of this system.                              **(14)**

$$\{(x, y) \mid 3x - 4y \geq -12\} \cap \{(x, y) \mid x + 3y \geq -3\}$$

**Solution:**

*Step (1):*   Graph both inequalities.

429

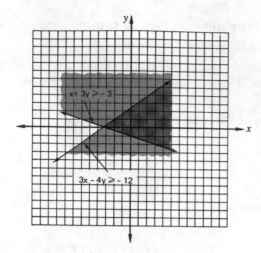

*Step (2):*   Find the overlapping region.

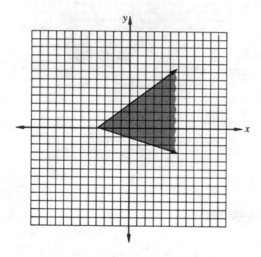

☐ **Example 3:**   Graph the solution of this system.                **(15)**

$$x + 2y \geq 6$$
$$y \leq 3$$

**Solution:**

*Step (1):*   Graph both inequalities.

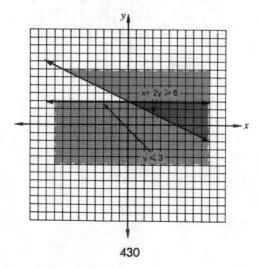

*Step* (2): Find the overlapping region.

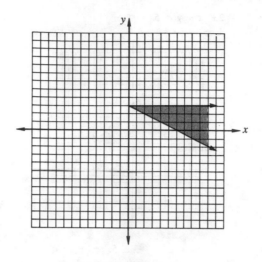

*Study Exercise Two* (16)

Graph the following systems.

1. $x + y \le 6$
   $x - y \le 1$

2. $3x + 2y < 6$
   $2x - y > -2$

3. $\{(x, y) \mid 3x - 5y \ge 15\} \cap \{(x, y) \mid y \ge -1\}$
4. $\{(x, y) \mid x > -2\} \cap \{(x, y) \mid y < 3\}$

## REVIEW EXERCISES

A. Graph the following linear inequalities.

1. $x + y \ge 3$                     2. $x + y < 5$
3. $x - y < 1$                       4. $x - y \le 0$
5. $x + 2y < 6$                      6. $2x - y > 4$
7. $x - 3y \ge 9$                    8. $x + 5y < 10$
9. $3x + 7y < 21$                    10. $3x + 8y < -24$
11. $\{(x, y) \mid y \ge 3x + 2\}$   12. $\{(x, y) \mid y < 3\}$

B. Graph the following systems of linear inequalities.

13. $x + y < 5$                      14. $x + y \ge 4$
    $x - y < 2$                          $x - y \le 1$

15. $2x + 3y \ge 6$                  16. $4x + y \ge 8$
    $3x - y \ge 3$                       $x - 2y \ge -4$

17. $3x + 2y \ge 6$                  18. $x - y \ge -2$
    $x - y \ge 4$                        $x \le y$

19. $x + y \le 4$                    20. $3x + 2y \ge 6$
    $y \le 2x$                           $2x - 5y \ge 10$

21. $\{(x, y) \mid 3x + y > 5\} \cap \{(x, y) \mid 2x - y > 10\}$

22. $\{(x, y) \mid x + y < 8\} \cap \{(x, y) \mid 5x - 2y < 5\}$

23. $\{(x, y) \mid x + y \le 3\} \cap \{(x, y) \mid x \le 2\}$

24. $\{(x, y) \mid x - 5 < 0\} \cap \{(x, y) \mid y > -2\}$

431

## Solutions to Review Exercises

A. 1. $x + y \geqslant 3$

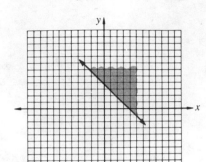

2. $x + y < 5$

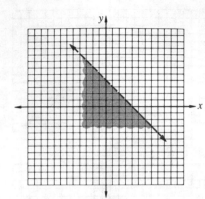

3. $x - y < 1$

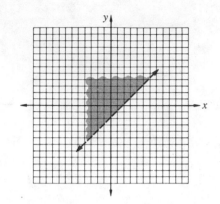

4. $x - y \leqslant 0$

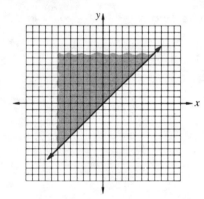

5. $x + 2y < 6$

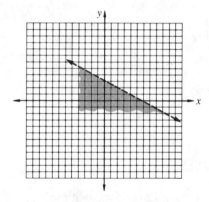

6. $2x - y > 4$

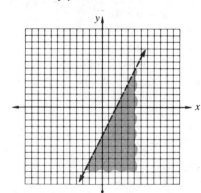

7. $x - 3y \geqslant 9$

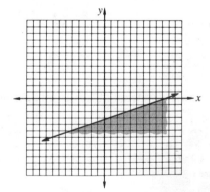

## Solutions to Review Exercises, Contd.

8. $x + 5y < 10$

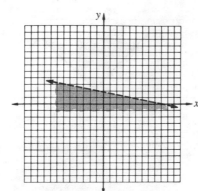

9. $3x + 7y < 21$

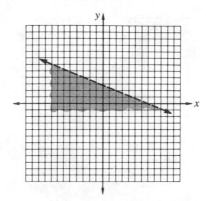

10. $3x + 8y < -24$

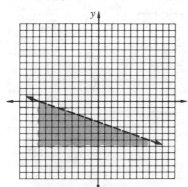

11. $y \geqslant 3x + 2$

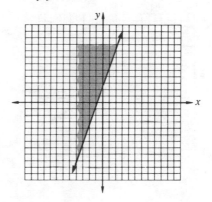

12. $y < 3$

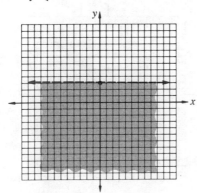

## Solutions to Review Exercises, Contd.

B.

13.

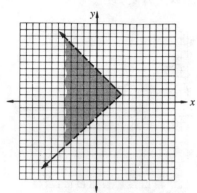

14.

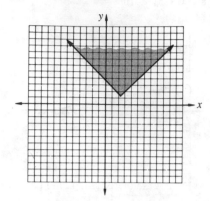

15.

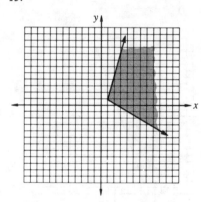

16.

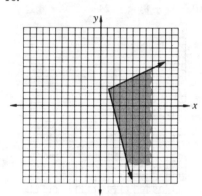

17.

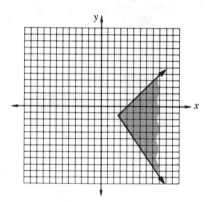

18.

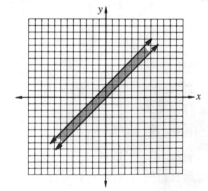

## Solutions to Review Exercises, Contd.

19.

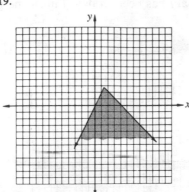

20.

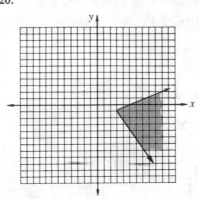

21.

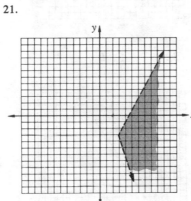

22.

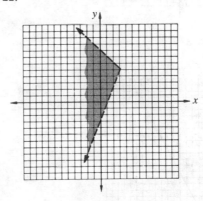

23.

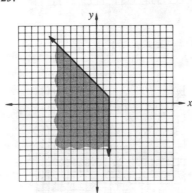

24.

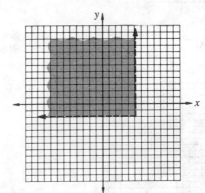

## SUPPLEMENTARY PROBLEMS

A.  In each of the following figures, the required boundary has been drawn. Finish the graph for each inequality by shading the correct region.

1.  $2x + y \geqq 4$

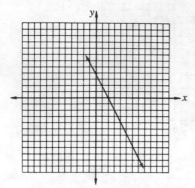

2.  $6y - x < 6$

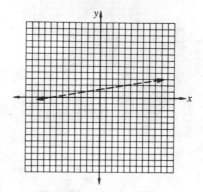

3.  $y \geqq 2x - 4$

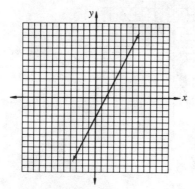

4.  $3x - 2y < -6$

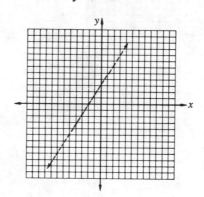

5.  $y + x > 0$

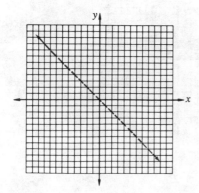

6.  $y \leqq -x - 2$

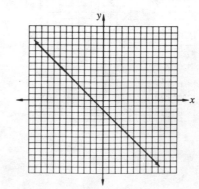

## SUPPLEMENTARY PROBLEMS, Contd.

7.  $x + 2y + 6 > 0$

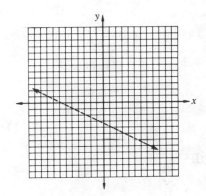

8.  $y > -2$

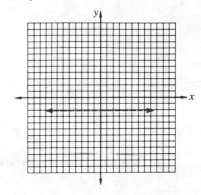

9.  $x + 4 \geqq 0$

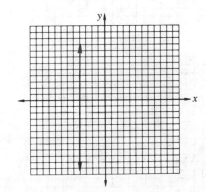

10.  $x < 5$

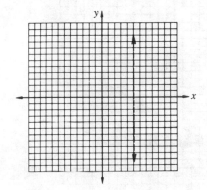

B.  Graph the following linear inequalities.

11.  $x + y \leqq 1$  
13.  $x - y \geqq 4$  
15.  $x - 2y > 6$  
17.  $y - 3x \leqq 6$  
19.  $3x - 4y \leqq 12$  
21.  $3x + 5y < 15$  
23.  $x \leqq 3y$  
25.  $x - 4y < 8$  
27.  $y \geqq \dfrac{1}{2}x + 7$  
29.  $\{(x, y) \mid y + 2 \geqq 0\}$  
31.  $\{(x, y) \mid x - 1 < 0\}$  
32.  $x + y \leqq 6$  
    $x - y \leqq 1$  
34.  $x + 2y < 4$  
    $2x - y < 6$  
36.  $x + y < 4$  
    $2x - y < 2$  
38.  $2x + y > 2$  
    $x + y < 4$

12.  $x + y > 6$  
14.  $x - y > 3$  
16.  $2x + y \leqq 2$  
18.  $y - 4x \geqq 4$  
20.  $4x - 5y \leqq 20$  
22.  $2x - 5y + 10 \geqq 0$  
24.  $x \geqq -2y$  
26.  $y \leqq 2x + 5$  
28.  $\{(x, y) \mid y > \dfrac{2}{3}x + 1\}$  
30.  $\{(x, y) \mid x > -1\}$  
33.  $3x + 2y < 6$  
    $2x - y > -2$  
35.  $2x + y \leqq 2$  
    $x + 3y \geqq 4$  
37.  $x - 2y \geqq 2$  
    $2x + y \geqq 1$  
39.  $x + 3y > 12$  
    $3x - 2y > -6$

SUPPLEMENTARY PROBLEMS, Contd.

40. $2x + 3y \geqq 4$
$3x - 5y \leqq -5$

41. $3x + 3y \geqq 5$
$x + 2y \leqq 5$

42. $x - y \geqq 4$
$y \geqq 2$

43. $\{(x, y) \mid 3x - 5y \geqq 15\} \cap \{(x, y) \mid y \geqq -1\}$

44. $\{(x, y) \mid 5x - 4y > 20\} \cap \{(x, y) \mid y > -2\}$

45. $\{(x, y) \mid x \geqq 0\} \cap \{(x, y) \mid y \geqq 0\}$

46. $\{(x, y) \mid x + 1 > 0\} \cap \{(x, y) \mid y - 3 < 0\}$

☐ Solutions to Study Exercises

**(10A)**

## Study Exercise One (Frame 10)

1. $3x - 5y > 15$

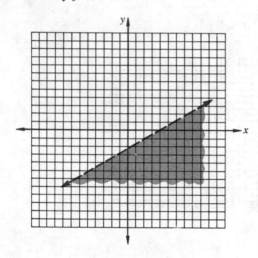

2. $y \geqq 2x + 1$

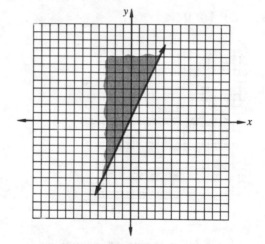

3. $y < 3$

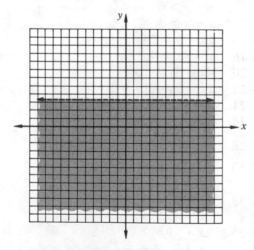

4. $x \leqq -3$

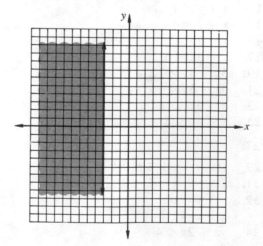

Solutions to Study Exercises, Contd.

☐

1.  $x + y \leqslant 6$
    $x - y \leqslant 1$

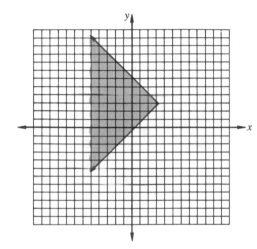

2.  $3x + 2y < 6$
    $2x - y > -2$

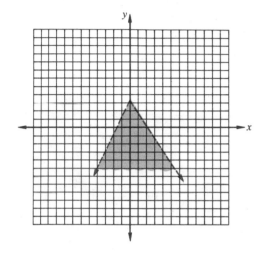

3.  $3x - 5y \geqslant 15$
    $y \geqslant -1$

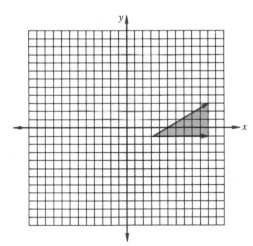

4.  $x > -2$
    $y < 3$

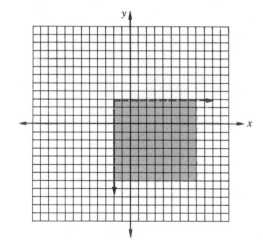

# Introduction to Relations and Functions

☐ **Objectives** (1)

By the end of this unit, you should know the meaning of each of the following terms:

- relation.
- graph of a relation.
- domain of a relation.
- range of a relation.
- function.
- functional notation.

You should be able to graph relations and use the vertical line test to determine which are functions.

You should also be able to determine the domain and the range of a function or a relation by analyzing its graph.

☐ **Relation** (2)

A *relation* is a nonempty set of ordered pairs.

**Examples:** 1. $\{(-5, 2), (3, 0), (3, 4)\}$
2. $\{(x, y) \mid y = 2x - 1\}$
3. $\{(x, y) \mid x = y^2\}$

☐ **Graph of a Relation** (3)

The *graph of a relation* is the set of points corresponding to the ordered pairs which are members of the relation.

☐ **Example 1:** Graph of the relation, $\{(-5, 2), (3, 0), (3, 4)\}$ (4)

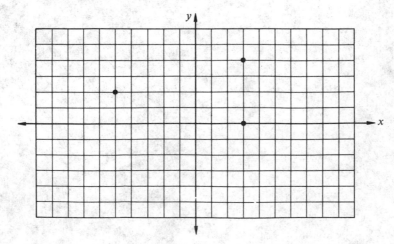

**Example 2:** Graph of the relation, $\{(x, y) \mid y = 2x - 1\}$ **(5)**

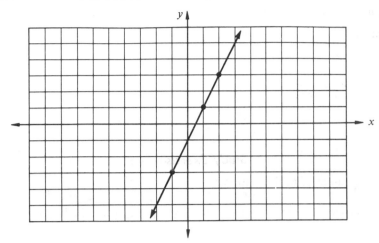

**Example 3:** Graph of the relation, $\{(x, y) \mid x = y^2\}$ **(6)**

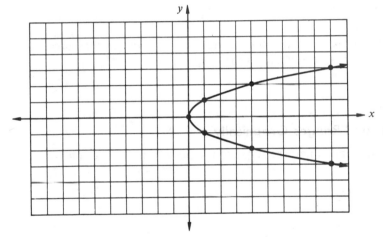

*Study Exercise One* **(7)**

Graph the following relations.

1. $\{(-2, 0), (3, 5), (-2, 1), (0, 4)\}$        2. $\{(x, y) \mid y = 3x + 1\}$
3. $\{(x, y) \mid y = |x - 3|\}$        4. $\{(x, y) \mid x = y^2 - 2\}$

**Domain of a Relation** **(8)**

The *domain of a relation* is the set consisting of the first elements of the ordered pairs.

**Example:** Relation is $\{(-5, 2), (3, 0), (3, 4), (2, -6)\}$.

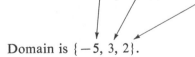

Domain is $\{-5, 3, 2\}$.

443

## □ Range of a Relation (9)

The *range of a relation* is the set consisting of the second elements of the ordered pairs.

**Example:** Relation is $\{(-5, 2), (3, 0), (3, 4), (2, -6)\}$.

Range is $\{2, 0, 4, -6\}$.

## □ *Study Exercise Two* (10)

Find the domain and the range of each relation.

1. $\{(-4, 2), (-2, 0), (1, 1), (5, -3)\}$
2. $\left\{\left(-\frac{1}{2}, 5\right), (\sqrt{2}, 5), (5, 5)\right\}$
3. $\left\{(-3, 0), \left(-3, \frac{1}{2}\right), (-3, 4), (-3, -3)\right\}$

## □ (11)

In a relation consisting of ordered pairs of the form, $(x, y)$, the variable $x$ represents an element of the domain, and the variable $y$ represents an element of the range.

## □ Obtaining Domains and Ranges Graphically (12)

We will now obtain the domain and the range of relations from their graph. The relations which will be used are:

1. $\{(-5, 4), (-1, 2), (3, -3)\}$
2. $\{(x, y) \mid x = y^2\}$

## □ **Example 1:** $\{(-5, 4), (-1, 2), (3, -3)\}$ (13)

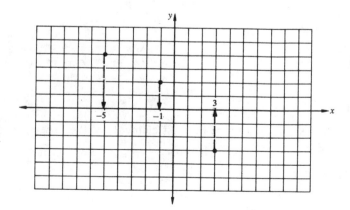

The *domain* is $\{-5, -1, 3\}$

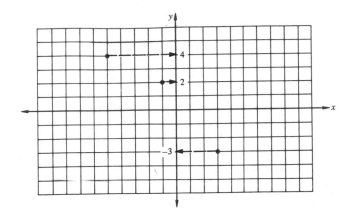

The *range* is $\{4, 2, -3\}$

☐ **Example 2:**   $\{(x, y) \mid x = y^2\}$                                                    **(14)**

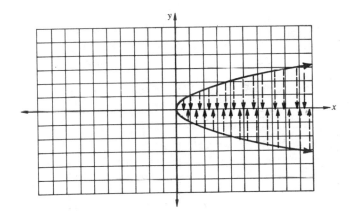

The *domain* is $\{x \mid x \geq 0\}$

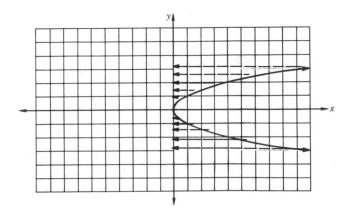

The *range* is $\{y \mid y$ is any real number$\}$

445

☐ *Study Exercise Three*

Find the domain and the range for each of the relations whose graph follows.

1.

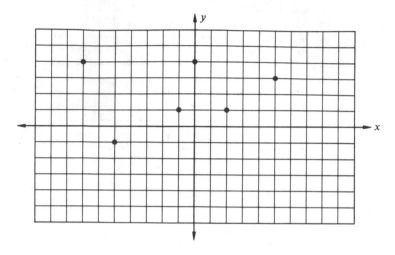

2.

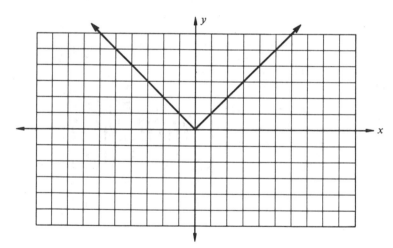

3.

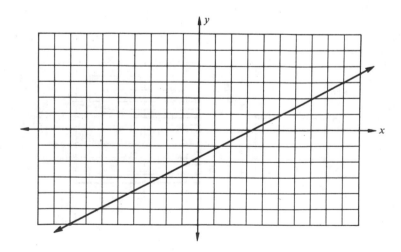

*Study Exercise Three, Contd.*

4.

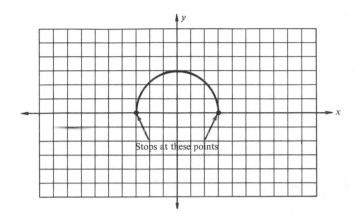

Stops at these points

☐ **Function** **(16)**

A *function* is a relation such that for each first element, there exists one and only one second element.

☐ **Examples:** **(17)**

1. {(−2, 5), (1, 6), (−1, −3)}
   (a) For the first element, −2, there is exactly one second element, 5.
   (b) For the first element, 1, there is exactly one second element, 6.
   (c) For the first element, −1, there is exactly one second element, −3.
2. {(2, 6), (3, 6), (4, 6)}
   (a) For the first element, 2, there is exactly one second element, 6.
   (b) For thc first element, 3, there is exactly one second element, 6.
   (c) For the first element, 4, there is exactly one second element, 6.
3. {(x, y) | y = 2x}
   x is the domain variable representing the set of first elements.
   y is the range variable representing the set of second elements.
   The condition, y = 2x, states that for each first element, x, the second element, y, is 2 times x. Since multiplication produces exactly one result, we can say that for each first element, there is exactly one second element.

☐ **Examples of Relations Which Are Not Functions** **(18)**

1. {(2, 5), (2, 6), (3, 1)}

   For the first element, 2, there are two second elements, 5 and 6. Therefore, this is not a function.

2. {(−1, 5), (−6, −3), (−1, 1), (−1, 0), (2, 4)}

   For the first element, −1, there are three second elements, 5, 1, and 0. Therefore, this is not a function

447

3. $\{(x, y) \mid x = y^2\}$

Let $x = 4$. Then $4 = y^2$.

Hence, $y$ represents 2 or $-2$. Therefore, the ordered pairs, (4, 2) and (4, $-2$), belong to the relation. The relation is not a function since the first element, 4, has two second elements; namely, 2 and $-2$.

☐                 *Study Exercise Four*                  **(19)**

Given the following relations, indicate which are functions. Answer yes or no.

1. $\{(-3, -4), (-2, 1), (0, -5), (-3, 8)\}$      2. $\{(-3, -4), (-2, 1), (0, -5)\}$
3. $\{(3, -1), (3, 0), (3, 1), (3, 2)\}$              4. $\{(-1, 3), (0, 3), (1, 3), (2, 3)\}$
5. $\{(x, y) \mid y = |x|\}$                           6. $\{(x, y) \mid x = |y|\}$

☐ **Recognizing Functions from a Graph**                          **(20)**

For a function to exist, for each domain element $x$, there must exist exactly one corresponding range element $y$.

Graphically, this means that for each domain value $x$, there is exactly one point of the graph.

☐ **Example:**   $\{(x, y) \mid y = |x|\}$                                       **(21)**

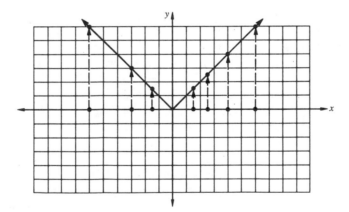

☐                                                           **(22)**

If a relation is not a function, then for at least one $x$ in the domain, *there are two or more different points on the graph*.

☐ **Example:**  $\{(x, y) \mid x = |y|\}$                                                    **(23)**

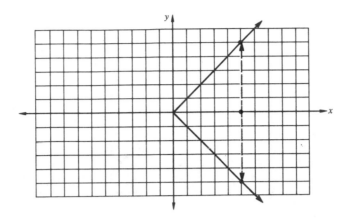

There are two points for the same value of $x$. Hence, the relation is not a function.

☐ **The Vertical Line Test**                                                                **(24)**

Imagine an infinite set of vertical lines passing through a graph. *If any one of the lines intersects the graph more than once, then the relation is not a function.*

☐ **Examples:**                                                                             **(25)**

1.  $\{(x, y) \mid y = |x|\}$

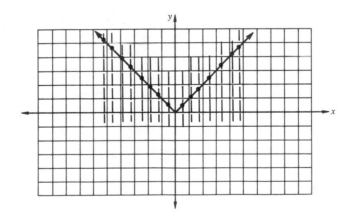

No vertical line intersects the graph in more than one point. Hence, $\{(x, y) \mid y = |x|\}$ is a function.

2.  $\{(x, y) \mid x = |y|\}$

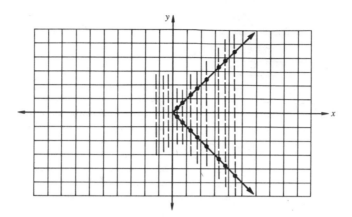

Some vertical lines intersect the graph at more than one point. Hence, $\{(x, y) \mid x = |y|\}$ is not a function.

☐                    *Study Exercise Five*                    **(26)**

Given the following graphs, use the vertical line test to determine which are graphs of functions. Answer yes or no.

1.  $\{(x, y) \mid x = y^2\}$

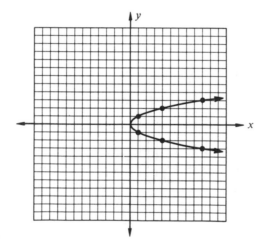

## Study Exercise Five, Contd.

2. $\{(x, y) \mid y = x^2\}$

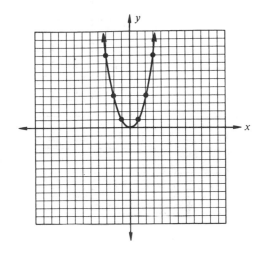

3. $\{(x, y) \mid x - 4y = -4\}$

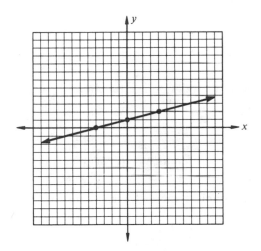

4. $\{(x, y) \mid x^2 + y^2 = 9\}$

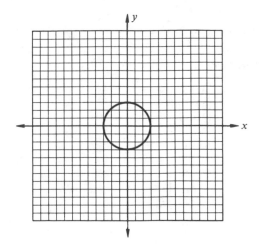

## Study Exercise Five, Cont.

5.  $\{(x, y) \mid y = -\sqrt{9 - x^2}\}$

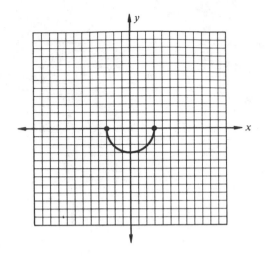

☐ **Functional Notation** (27)

Lowercase letters such as $f$, $g$, and $h$ are used to name functions.

**Examples:**  1.  $f = \{(x, y) \mid y = x + 3\}$
2.  $g = \{(x, y) \mid y = x^2\}$
3.  $h = \{(x, y) \mid y = |x - 4|\}$

☐ $f(x)$ is another way to write $y$, where the relation is a function. (28)

$f(x)$ is read "$f$ of $x$," not "$f$ times $x$."

☐ 1.  $f = \{(x, y) \mid y = x + 3\}$ may also be written as $f = \{(x, f(x)) \mid f(x) = x + 3\}$. (29)
2.  $g = \{(x, y) \mid y = x^2\}$ may also be written as $g = \{(x, g(x)) \mid g(x) = x^2\}$.
3.  $h = \{(x, y) \mid y = |x - 4|\}$ may also be written as $h = \{(x, h(x)) \mid h(x) = |x - 4|\}$.

*Remember*, $f(x)$, $g(x)$, and $h(x)$ are simply symbols for $y$.

☐ (30)

Let $f = \{(x, f(x)) \mid f(x) = x + 3\}$. The symbol $f(2)$ instructs us to go to the function named $f$ and find the $y$-value when $x = 2$. Therefore, $f(2) = 2 + 3$, or 5.

*Remember*, $f(2) = 5$ means that when $x = 2$, $y = 5$.

☐ **Examples Using Functional Notation** (31)

For the following examples, $f = \{(x, f(x)) \mid f(x) = x + 3\}$
$g = \{(x, g(x)) \mid g(x) = x^2\}$
$h = \{(x, h(x)) \mid h(x) = |x - 4|\}$

**Example 1:**  Evaluate $f(3)$.

**Solution:**  $f(x) = x + 3$
$f(3) = 3 + 3$
$f(3) = 6$

**Example 2:**  Evaluate $g(4)$.

**Solution:**  $g(x) = x^2$
$g(4) = 4^2$
$g(4) = 16$

**Example 3:** Evaluate $h(0)$.

**Solution:** $h(x) = |x - 4|$
$h(0) = |0 - 4|$
$h(0) = |-4|$
$h(0) = 4$

**Example 4:** Evaluate $g(2a)$.

**Solution:** $g(x) = x^2$
$g(2a) = (2a)^2$
$g(2a) = 4a^2$

☐ *Study Exercise Six* **(32)**

For the following exercises, $f = \{(x, f(x)) \mid f(x) = x - 2\}$
$g = \{(x, g(x)) \mid g(x) = x^2 + 3\}$
$h = \{(x, h(x)) \mid h(x) = |x + 1|\}$

Evaluate the following.

1. $f(5)$      2. $g(2)$      3. $h(0)$
4. $g(-2)$      5. $f(-3)$      6. $h(-4)$
7. $f(a)$      8. $f(3a)$      9. $g(2a)$

## REVIEW EXERCISES

A. Define each of the following terms.

    1. relation      2. graph of a relation      3. domain of a relation
    4. range of a relation      5. function

B. Graph the following relations and use the vertical line test to determine which are functions.

    6. $\{(x, y) \mid x = y^2 + 3\}$      7. $\{(x, y) \mid y = x^2 + 3\}$
    8. $\{(x, y) \mid y = 2x - 3\}$      9. $\{(x, y) \mid x = |y - 2|\}$
    10. $\{(2, -1), (0, -1), (5, 4)\}$      11. $\{(1, -1), (1, -2), (2, 0), (2, 5)\}$
    12. $\{(x, y) \mid |x| + |y| = 6\}$

C. Find the domain and the range for each of the relations whose graph follows.

    13. $\{(x, y) \mid y = x^2 - 3\}$      14. $\{(x, y) \mid y = -2x - 3\}$

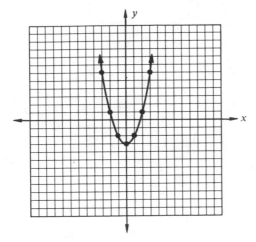 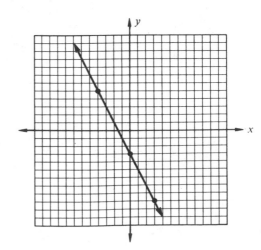

## REVIEW EXERCISES, Contd.

15. $\{(x, y) \mid x^2 + y^2 = 16\}$

16. $\{(3, 2), (1, -3), (-3, 1), (-3, -7)\}$

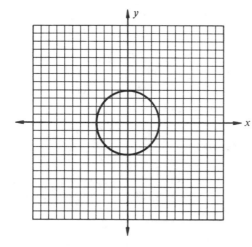

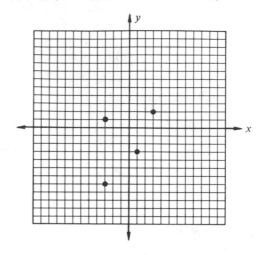

D. Let $f = \{(x, f(x)) \mid f(x) = 3x^2 - 5\}$. Find:

17. $f(3)$      18. $f(0)$      19. $f(-3)$      20. $f(u)$      21. $f(u + 1)$

## Solutions to Review Exercises

A.    1. See Frame 2.      2. See Frame 3.      3. See Frame 8.      4. See Frame 9.      5. See Frame 16.

B.    6. $\{(x, y) \mid x = y^2 + 3\}$. It is not a function.

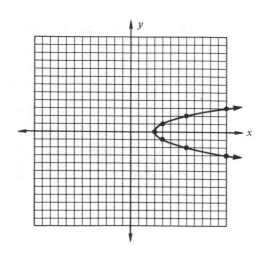

454

## Solutions to Review Exercises, Contd.

7. $\{x, y) \mid y = x^2 + 3\}$. It is a function.

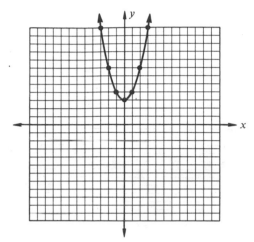

8. $\{(x, y) \mid y = 2x - 3\}$. It is a function.

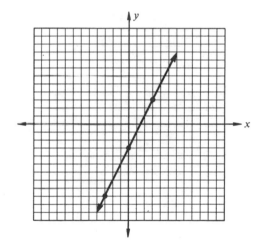

9. $\{(x, y \mid x = |y - 2|\}$. It is not a function.

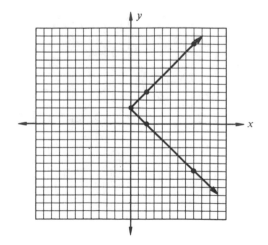

## Solutions to Review Exercises, Contd.

10. $\{(2, -1), (0, -1), (5, 4)\}$. It is a function.

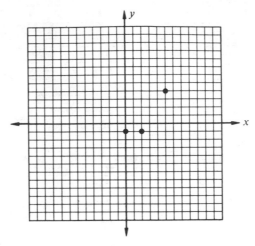

11. $\{(1, -1), (1, -2), (2, 0), (2, 5)\}$. It is not a function.

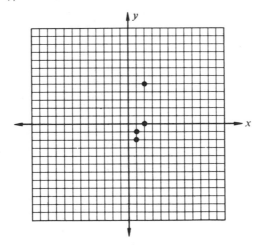

12. $\{(x, y)\,|\,|x| + |y| = 6\}$. It is not a function.

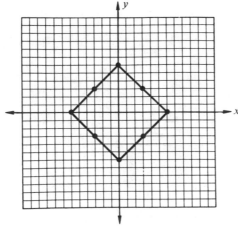

## Solutions to Review Exercises, Contd.

C. 13. Domain is $\{x \mid x$ is any real number$\}$. Range is $\{y \mid y \geq -3\}$.
   14. Domain is $\{x \mid x$ is any real number$\}$. Range is $\{y \mid y$ is any real number$\}$.
   15. Domain is $\{x \mid -4 \leq x \leq 4\}$.

   $x$ represents all real numbers between $-4$ and $4$, including $4$ and $-4$.

   Range is $\{y \mid -4 \leq y \leq 4\}$.

   $y$ represents all real numbers between $-4$ and $4$, including $4$ and $-4$.

   16. Domain is $\{3, 1, -3\}$. Range is $\{2, -3, 1, -7\}$.

D. 17. $f(3) = 3(3)^2 - 5$, or $f(3) - 22$
   18. $f(0) = 3(0)^2 - 5$, or $f(0) = -5$
   19. $f(-3) = 3(-3)^2 - 5$, or $f(-3) = 22$
   20. $f(u) = 3u^2 - 5$
   21. $f(u + 1) = 3(u + 1)^2 - 5$, or $f(u + 1) = 3u^2 + 6u - 2$

## SUPPLEMENTARY PROBLEMS

A. Graph each of the following relations and use the vertical line test to determine which are functions.

   1. $\{(6, -1), (-2, 3), (4, -5), (3, 2), (-2, 2)\}$    2. $\{(-5, 0), (0, -5), (-1, 2), (-3, 2)\}$
   3. $\{(-7, 1), (-3, 5), (4, -3), (-3, -6)\}$    4. $\{(x, y) \mid x + y = 4\}$
   5. $\{(x, y) \mid y = 3\}$    6. $\{(x, y) \mid x = -5\}$
   7. $\{(x, y) \mid x = y^2 - 7\}$    8. $\{(x, y) \mid x = |y + 3|\}$
   9. $\{(x, y) \mid y = |2x - 1|\}$    10. $\{(x, y) \mid y = 2x^2 + 3x - 1\}$
   11. $\{(x, y) \mid |x| + |y| = 10\}$    12. $\{(x, y) \mid y = -3x^2 - x + 2\}$

B. Each of the following is a function. Graph each, and then determine the domain and the range.

   13. $\{(-1, 6), (-2, 6), (0, 0), (5, 0), (4, 5)\}$    14. $\{(x, y) \mid y = 2x\}$
   15. $\{(x, f(x)) \mid f(x) = x - 6\}$    16. $\{(x, g(x)) \mid g(x) = x^2 + 5\}$
   17. $\{(x, h(x)) \mid h(x) = -3x^2 - 1\}$    18. $\left\{(x, s(x)) \mid s(x) = \dfrac{1}{x}\right\}$
   19. $\left\{(x, t(x)) \mid t(x) = \dfrac{1}{x^2}\right\}$

C. Given these functions:

   $f = \{(x, f(x)) \mid f(x) = 2x + 5\}$
   $g = \{(x, g(x)) \mid g(x) = 2x^2 - 5x - 3\}$
   $h = \{(x, h(x)) \mid h(x) = |x + 6|\}$
   evaluate the following.

   20. $f(1)$          21. $g(0)$          22. $h(2)$
   23. $f(2)$          24. $g(-2)$         25. $h(-7)$
   26. $f(-2)$         27. $g(-1)$         28. $h(0)$
   29. $f(a)$          30. $g(a)$          31. $h(a)$
   32. $f(a + 1)$      33. $g(2a)$         34. $h(3a + 1)$

D. 35. Using the definition of a function, explain why the "vertical line test" works.

Solutions to Study Exercises

## Study Exercise One (Frame 7)

1. $\{(-2, 0), (3, 5), (-2, 1), (0, 4)\}$.

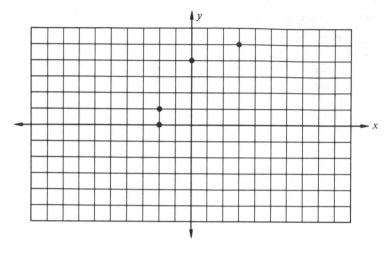

2. $\{(x, y) \mid y = 3x + 1\}$

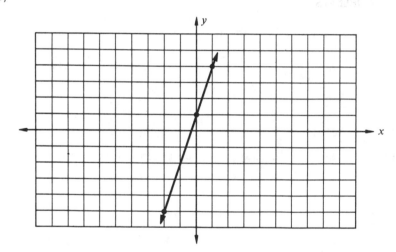

3. $\{(x, y) \mid y = |x - 3|\}$

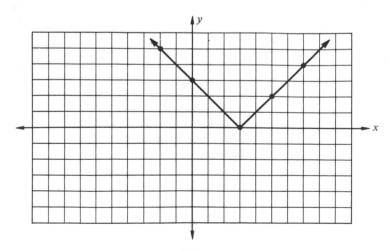

## Solutions to Study Exercises, Contd.

### Study Exercise One (Frame 7, Contd.)

4. $\{(x, y) \mid x = y^2 - 2\}$

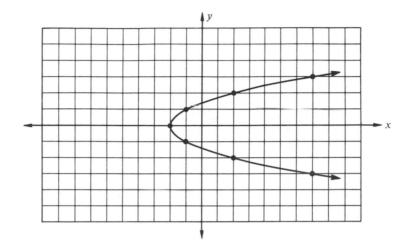

### Study Exercise Two (Frame 10)                    (10A)

1. Domain is $\{-4, -2, 1, 5\}$. Range is $\{2, 0, 1, -3\}$.

2. Domain is $\left\{-\dfrac{1}{2}, \sqrt{2}, 5\right\}$. Range is $\{5\}$.

3. Domain is $\{-3\}$. Range is $\left\{0, \dfrac{1}{2}, 4, -3\right\}$.

### Study Exercise Three (Frame 15)                    (15A)

1. Domain is $\{-7, -5, -1, 0, 2, 5\}$. Range is $\{-1, 1, 3, 4\}$.
2. Domain is $\{x \mid x \text{ is any real number}\}$. Range is $\{y \mid y \geq 0\}$.
3. Domain is $\{x \mid x \text{ is any real number}\}$. Range is $\{y \mid y \text{ is any real number}\}$.
4. Domain is $\{x \mid \underbrace{-3 \leq x \leq 3}\}$.

        $x$ represents all real numbers between $-3$ and $3$, including $-3$ and $3$.

Range is $\{y \mid \underbrace{0 \leq y \leq 3}\}$.

        $y$ represents all real numbers between $0$ and $3$, including $0$ and $3$.

### Study Exercise Four (Frame 19)                    (19A)

1. No, it is not a function because for the first element, $-3$, there are two second elements, $-4$ and $8$.
2. Yes, it is a function, because for each first element there is exactly one second element.
3. No, it is not a function, because for the first element, $3$, there are four second elements, $-1, 0, 1,$ and $2$.
4. Yes, it is a function. The second elements happen to be identical. But for each first element, there is exactly one second element. For example, $-1$ has only one corresponding second element, namely, $3$.
5. Yes, it is a function, because for each number replaced for $x$, there is exactly one absolute value which is the second element $y$.
6. No, it is not a function. Suppose the first element, $x$, represents $3$. Then $y$ could represent $3$ or $-3$.

### Study Exercise Five (Frame 26)                    (26A)

1. No, it is not a function.       2. Yes, it is a function.       3. Yes, it is a function.
4. No, it is not a function.       5. Yes, it is a function.

## Solutions to Study Exercises, Contd.

☐

### Study Exercise Six (Frame 32) (32A)

1. $f(5) = 5 - 2$, or 3
2. $g(2) = 2^2 + 3$, or 7
3. $h(0) = |0 + 1|$, or 1
4. $g(-2) = (-2)^2 + 3$, or 7
5. $f(-3) = -3 - 2$, or $-5$
6. $h(-4) = |-4 + 1|$, or 3
7. $f(a) = a - 2$
8. $f(3a) = 3a - 2$
9. $g(2a) = (2a)^2 + 3$, or $4a^2 + 3$

## Module 6 Review Problems

Units 26–30

A. Complete the following tables.

1. $y = 3x - 2$

| x | −4 | −3 | −2 | 0 | 2 | 5 | 10 |
|---|---|---|---|---|---|---|---|
| y | | | | | | | |

2. $y = 2x^2 - 3x + 1$

| x | −3 | −2 | −1 | 0 | 1 | 2 | 3 | 4 | 5 |
|---|---|---|---|---|---|---|---|---|---|
| y | | | | | | | | | |

3. $y = \dfrac{10}{x}$

| x | −10 | −5 | −2 | −1 | 1 | 2 | 5 | 10 | 20 | 100 |
|---|---|---|---|---|---|---|---|---|---|---|
| y | | | | | | | | | | |

B. Write an ordered pair such that:

4. the abscissa is −5 and the ordinate is 2.

5. $x = \dfrac{3}{4}$ and $y = -3$.

C. Name the quadrant in which the following points are located.

6. (3, 6)          7. (−1, 4)          8. (−2, −3)          9. $\left(2, -\dfrac{1}{2}\right)$

D. The following is a graph of a relationship between voltage and current in a circuit where the resistance is constant. Voltage is measured in volts and current is measured in amperes.

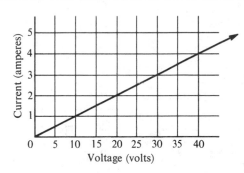

10. If 40 volts are applied to the circuit, what is the resulting current?
11. If 25 volts are applied to the circuit, what is the resulting current?
12. What voltage is necessary to produce a current of 1 ampere?
13. What voltage is necessary to produce a current of 3.5 amperes?

E. Which of the following ordered pairs belong to this set: $\{(x, y) \mid y = x^2 - x\}$?
    14. (−2, 2)                    15. (0, 0)                    16. (−3, 12)

F. Graph the following equations.
    17. $y = 2x - 3$              18. $y = -6$                  19. $x = 5$
    20. $y = -x^2 + 9$           21. $y = x^2 + 2x - 8$

G. Solve the following systems of linear equations using any method you wish. State whether each system is consistent, inconsistent, or dependent.

| 22. $x + y = 7$ | 23. $2x + 5y = 1$ | 24. $3x - 6y = 9$ | 25. $3m - 2n = 8$ |
|---|---|---|---|
| $x - y = 3$ | $x + 2y = -4$ | $x = 2y + 3$ | $6m - 4n = 7$ |

461

## Module 6 Review Problems, Contd.

Units 26–30

H.  Define the following terms.
  26.  function                                      27.  relation
I.  Graph the following relations and use the vertical line test to determine which are functions.
  28.  $\{(x, y) \mid y = -x^2\}$                    29.  $\{(x, y) \mid x = y^2 + 3\}$
  30.  $\{(x, y) \mid y = -2x - 3\}$                 31.  $\{(x, y) \mid x = |y - 2|\}$
J.  Find the domain and the range of the following relations.
  32.  $\{(1, 5), (2, -3), (0, -1), (-4, 5)\}$       33.  $\{(x, y) \mid y = x^2\}$
K.  Given these functions:

$f = \{(x, f(x)) \mid f(x) = x - 5\}$
$g = \{(x, g(x)) \mid g(x) = x^2 + 3x\}$
evaluate the following.

  34.  $f(0)$     35.  $g(-2)$     36.  $f(3)$     37.  $g(1)$     38.  $g(a)$     39.  $f(u + 2)$
L.  Solve the following applied problems using systems of linear equations. Give both the system and the solutions.
  40.  The sum of two numbers is 17 and their difference is 5. Find the two numbers.
  41.  A man invests $6000. Part of it is invested at 7% and the remainder is invested at 5%. How much is invested at each rate if the total annual interest is $384?
M.  Graph the following.
  42.  $\{(x, y) \mid x - y \geq 2\}$                 43.  $\{(x, y) \mid y \leq 3x\} \cap \{(x, y) \mid x + y \geq 5\}$

## Answers to Module 6 Review Problems

A.  1.  $y = 3x - 2$

| $x$ | $-4$ | $-3$ | $-2$ | $0$ | $2$ | $5$ | $10$ |
|---|---|---|---|---|---|---|---|
| $y$ | $-14$ | $-11$ | $-8$ | $-2$ | $4$ | $13$ | $28$ |

  2.  $y = 2x^2 - 3x + 1$

| $x$ | $-3$ | $-2$ | $-1$ | $0$ | $1$ | $2$ | $3$ | $4$ | $5$ |
|---|---|---|---|---|---|---|---|---|---|
| $y$ | $28$ | $15$ | $6$ | $1$ | $0$ | $3$ | $10$ | $21$ | $36$ |

  3.  $y = \dfrac{10}{x}$

| $x$ | $-10$ | $-5$ | $-2$ | $-1$ | $1$ | $2$ | $5$ | $10$ | $20$ | $100$ |
|---|---|---|---|---|---|---|---|---|---|---|
| $y$ | $-1$ | $-2$ | $-5$ | $-10$ | $10$ | $5$ | $2$ | $1$ | $\frac{1}{2}$ | $\frac{1}{10}$ |

B.  4.  $(-5, 2)$                                     5.  $\left(\dfrac{3}{4}, -3\right)$

C.  6.  I             7.  II            8.  III            9.  IV

D.  10.  4 amperes    11.  2.5 amperes  12.  10 volts       13.  35 volts

E.  14.  No           15.  Yes          16.  Yes

# Answers to Module 6 Review Problems, Contd.

Units 26–30

F.  17.  $y = 2x - 3$

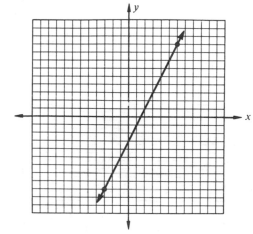

18.  $y = -6$

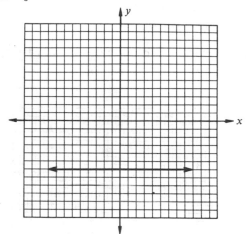

19.  $x = 5$

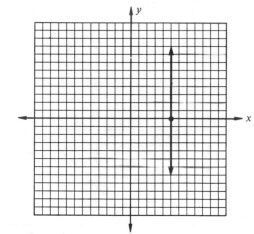

20.  $y = -x^2 + 9$

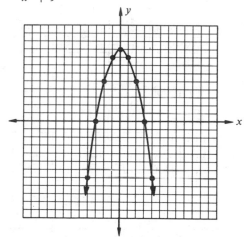

21.  $y = x^2 + 2x - 8$

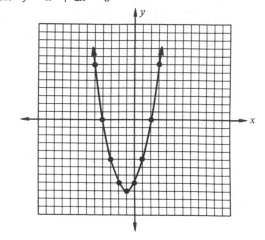

## Answers to Module 6 Review Problems, Contd.

**Units 26–30**

G. 22. {(5, 2)}    Consistent
   24. {(x, y) | x = 2y + 3}    Dependent

23. {(−22, 9)}    Consistent
25. ∅    Inconsistent

H. 26. A *function* is a relation such that for each first element, there exists one and only one second element.
   27. A *relation* is a nonempty set of ordered pairs.

I. 28. It is a function.

29. It is not a function.

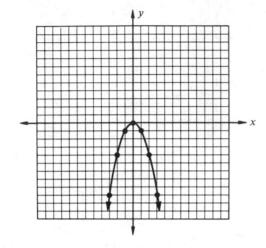

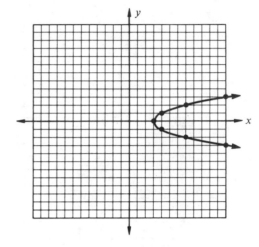

30. It is a function.

31. It is not a function.

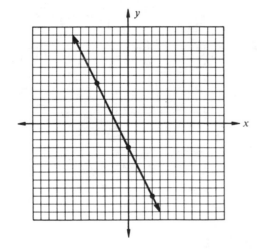

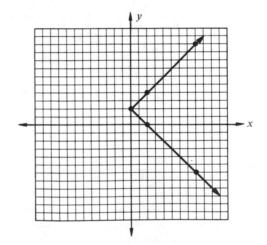

J. 32. D: {x | 1, 2, 0, −4}    R: {y | 5, −3, −1}
   33. D: {x | x is any real}    R: {y | y ≥ 0}

K. 34. $f(0) = -5$
   37. $g(1) = 4$

35. $g(-2) = -2$
38. $g(a) = a^2 + 3a$

36. $f(3) = -2$
39. $f(u + 2) = u - 3$

L. 40. $x + y = 17.$
   $x - y = 5$
   The numbers are 11 and 6.

41.    $x + y = 6000.$
   $0.07x + 0.05y = 384.$
   $4200 is invested at 7% and
   $1800 is invested at 5%.

**Answers to Module 6 Review Problems, Contd.**

42.   $\{(x, y)|x - y \geqslant 2\}$

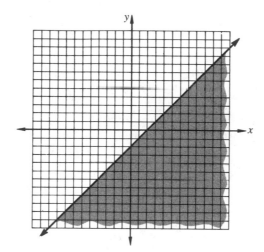

43.   $\{(x, y)|y \leqslant 3x\} \cap \{(x, y)|x + y \geqslant 5\}$

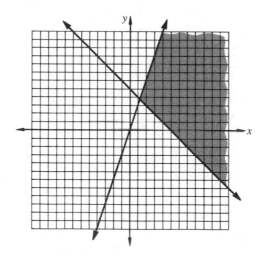

# Appendices

# Completing the Square and Derivation of the Quadratic Formula

☐ Objectives                                                                                          (1)

By the end of this appendix you should be able to solve quadratic equations by completing the square, and you should understand the derivation of the quadratic formula.

☐ Perfect Square Trinomial                                                                            (2)

$x^2 + 6x + 9$ is a *perfect square trinomial* because $x^2 + 6x + 9 = (x + 3)^2$.

**Examples:** 1. $x^2 + 8x + 16 = (x + 4)^2$
2. $x^2 + 4x + 4 = (x + 2)^2$
3. $x^2 - 10x + 25 = (x - 5)^2$

☐ Relationship of the Coefficient of $x$ to the Constant Term                                         (3)

1. $x^2 + 6x + 9 = (x + 3)^2$                      2. $x^2 + 8x + 16 = (x + 4)^2$

$\left(\frac{1}{2} \cdot 6\right)^2$                $\left(\frac{1}{2} \cdot 8\right)^2$

3. $x^2 + 4x + 4 = (x + 2)^2$                      4. $x^2 - 10x + 25 = (x - 5)^2$

$\left(\frac{1}{2} \cdot 4\right)^2$               $\left(\frac{1}{2} \cdot 10\right)^2$

This relationship is valid only when the coefficient of $x^2$ is 1.

☐                                       *Study Exercise One*                                           (4)

Fill in the blanks so that each trinomial is a perfect square.

1. $x^2 + 12x +$ _____                           2. $x^2 + 20x +$ _____
3. $x^2 + x +$ _____                             4. $x^2 + kx +$ _____, where $k$ is a constant

5. $x^2 + \frac{b}{a}x +$ _____, where $\frac{b}{a}$ is a constant

☐ The Square Root Property for Solving Equations                                                      (5)

If $y^2 = k$, where $y$ is the variable and $k$ is a nonnegative constant, then $y = -\sqrt{k}$ or $y = \sqrt{k}$.

**Proof:** 1. $y^2 = k$
2. $y^2 - k = 0$
3. $(y + \sqrt{k})(y - \sqrt{k}) = 0$
4. $y + \sqrt{k} = 0$, or $y - \sqrt{k} = 0$
5. $y = -\sqrt{k}$, or $y = \sqrt{k}$
6. Since both $-\sqrt{k}$ and $\sqrt{k}$ will check in the original equation, the solutions are $-\sqrt{k}$ and $\sqrt{k}$.

☐ Using the Square Root Property                                                                      (6)

**Example 1:** Solve $x^2 = 4$.

**Solution:**

*line (a)*  If $x^2 = 4$, then $x = -\sqrt{4}$ or $x = \sqrt{4}$.

*line (b)*                    $x = -2$  or  $x = 2$.
*line (c)*  The solutions are $-2$ and 2.

**Example 2:** Solve $(x + 3)^2 = 6$.

   **Solution:**

    *line (a)* If $(x + 3)^2 = 6$, then $x + 3 = -\sqrt{6}$   or   $x + 3 = \sqrt{6}$.

                                   $\downarrow$                   $\downarrow$

    *line (b)*                                 $x = -3 - \sqrt{6}$  or  $x = -3 + \sqrt{6}$.

    *line (c)* The solutions are $-3 - \sqrt{6}$ and $-3 + \sqrt{6}$.

**Example 3:** Solve $x^2 + 10x + 25 = 3$.

   **Solution:**

    *line (a)*  $x^2 + 10x + 25 = 3$

    *line (b)*  $(x + 5)^2 = 3$

    *line (c)*  $x + 5 = -\sqrt{3}$, or $x + 5 = \sqrt{3}$

    *line (d)*  $x = -5 - \sqrt{3}$, or $x = -5 + \sqrt{3}$

□                               *Study Exercise Two*                        **(7)**

Solve the following equations using the square root property.

1.  $x^2 = 25$                   2.  $(x + 6)^2 = 7$             3.  $x^2 + 4x + 4 = 5$

□  Solve $x^2 + 5x + 2 = 0$ (not a perfect square trinomial).                   **(8)**

## □ Completing the Square                                            **(9)**

  *Step (1):* Obtain all terms containing a variable on one side and all constant terms on the other.

    *line (a)*  $x^2 + 5x + 2 = 0$

    *line (b)*  $x^2 + 5x = -2$

  *Step (2):* Turn the left member into a perfect square trinomial.

    *line (c)*  $x^2 + 5x = -2$

    *line (d)*  $x^2 + 5x + \dfrac{25}{4} = -2 + \dfrac{25}{4}$

$$\left(\frac{1}{2} \cdot 5\right)^2$$

  *Step (3):* Use the square root property for solving equations.

    *line (e)*  $x^2 + 5x + \dfrac{25}{4} = -2 + \dfrac{25}{4}$

    *line (f)*  $\left(x + \dfrac{5}{2}\right)^2 = -2 + \dfrac{25}{4}$

    *line (g)*  $\left(x + \dfrac{5}{2}\right)^2 = \dfrac{17}{4}$

    *line (h)*  $x + \dfrac{5}{2} = -\sqrt{\dfrac{17}{4}}$, or $x + \dfrac{5}{2} = \sqrt{\dfrac{17}{4}}$

    *line (i)*  $x + \dfrac{5}{2} = \dfrac{-\sqrt{17}}{2}$, or $x + \dfrac{5}{2} = \dfrac{\sqrt{17}}{2}$

    *line (j)*  $x = \dfrac{-5}{2} - \dfrac{\sqrt{17}}{2}$, or $x = \dfrac{-5}{2} + \dfrac{\sqrt{17}}{2}$

    *line (k)*  $x = \dfrac{-5 - \sqrt{17}}{2}$, or $x = \dfrac{-5 + \sqrt{17}}{2}$

The solutions are $\dfrac{-5 - \sqrt{17}}{2}$ and $\dfrac{-5 + \sqrt{17}}{2}$.

## □ Solving $2x^2 - 6x - 3 = 0$ by Completing the Square (10)

*Step (1):* Obtain all terms containing a variable on one side and all constant terms on the other.
line (a)   $2x^2 - 6x - 3 = 0$
line (b)   $2x^2 - 6x = 3$

*Step (2):* Turn the left member into a perfect square trinomial.
line (c)   $2x^2 - 6x = 3$

line (d)   $x^2 - 3x = \dfrac{3}{2}$

line (e)   $x^2 - 3x + \dfrac{9}{4} = \dfrac{3}{2} + \dfrac{9}{4}$

$$\left(\frac{1}{2}\cdot 3\right)^2$$

*Step (3):* Use the square root property for solving equations.

line (f)   $x^2 - 3x + \dfrac{9}{4} = \dfrac{3}{2} + \dfrac{9}{4}$

line (g)   $\left(x - \dfrac{3}{2}\right)^2 = \dfrac{3}{2} + \dfrac{9}{4}$

line (h)   $\left(x - \dfrac{3}{2}\right)^2 = \dfrac{15}{4}$

line (i)   $x - \dfrac{3}{2} = -\sqrt{\dfrac{15}{4}}$, or $x - \dfrac{3}{2} = \sqrt{\dfrac{15}{4}}$

line (j)   $x - \dfrac{3}{2} = -\dfrac{\sqrt{15}}{2}$, or $x - \dfrac{3}{2} = \dfrac{\sqrt{15}}{2}$

line (k)   $x = \dfrac{3}{2} - \dfrac{\sqrt{15}}{2}$, or $x = \dfrac{3}{2} + \dfrac{\sqrt{15}}{2}$

line (l)   $x = \dfrac{3 - \sqrt{15}}{2}$, or $x = \dfrac{3 + \sqrt{15}}{2}$

The solutions are $\dfrac{3 - \sqrt{15}}{2}$ and $\dfrac{3 + \sqrt{15}}{2}$.

## □ Study Exercise Three (11)

Solve the following quadratic equations by completing the square.

1.  $x^2 + 5x + 6 = 0$         2.  $x^2 + 4x - 7 = 0$         3.  $2x^2 - 6x - 5 = 0$

## □ Derivation of the Quadratic Formula (12)

Solve $ax^2 + bx + c = 0$, where $a, b, c$ are constants and $a \neq 0$, by completing the square.

1.  $ax^2 + bx + c = 0$
2.  $ax^2 + bx = -c$
3.  $x^2 + \dfrac{b}{a}x = \dfrac{-c}{a}$
4.  $x^2 + \dfrac{b}{a}x + \dfrac{b^2}{4a^2} = \dfrac{-c}{a} + \dfrac{b^2}{4a^2}$

$$\left(\frac{1}{2}\cdot\frac{b}{a}\right)^2$$

5. $\left(x + \dfrac{b}{2a}\right)^2 = \dfrac{-c}{a} + \dfrac{b^2}{4a^2}$

6. $\left(x + \dfrac{b}{2a}\right)^2 = \dfrac{-4ac + b^2}{4a^2}$

7. $\left(x + \dfrac{b}{2a}\right)^2 = \dfrac{b^2 - 4ac}{4a^2}$

8. $x + \dfrac{b}{2a} = -\sqrt{\dfrac{b^2 - 4ac}{4a^2}}$, or $x + \dfrac{b}{2a} = \sqrt{\dfrac{b^2 - 4ac}{4a^2}}$

9. $x + \dfrac{b}{2a} = -\dfrac{\sqrt{b^2 - 4ac}}{2 \cdot |a|}$, or $x + \dfrac{b}{2a} = \dfrac{\sqrt{b^2 - 4ac}}{2 \cdot |a|}$

10. $a$ may be either positive or negative, but this may be discounted because the right members of each equation are opposites or additive inverses. Therefore, the absolute value symbols are not necessary.

11. $x + \dfrac{b}{2a} = -\dfrac{\sqrt{b^2 - 4ac}}{2a}$, or $x + \dfrac{b}{2a} = \dfrac{\sqrt{b^2 - 4ac}}{2a}$

12. $x = \dfrac{-b}{2a} - \dfrac{\sqrt{b^2 - 4ac}}{2a}$, or $x = \dfrac{-b}{2a} + \dfrac{\sqrt{b^2 - 4ac}}{2a}$

13. $x = \dfrac{-b - \sqrt{b^2 - 4ac}}{2a}$, or $x = \dfrac{-b + \sqrt{b^2 - 4ac}}{2a}$

The solutions are $\dfrac{-b - \sqrt{b^2 - 4ac}}{2a}$ and $\dfrac{-b + \sqrt{b^2 - 4ac}}{2a}$ or, for convenience, the quadratic formula is usually written as $x = \dfrac{-b \pm \sqrt{b^2 - 4ac}}{2a}$.

**(13)**

The quadratic formula is analyzed and used in Unit 25. Therefore, no problems are given here. However, in preparation for Unit 25, the formula should be memorized.

## REVIEW EXERCISES

A.  Fill in the blanks so that each trinomial is a perfect square.

    1.  $x^2 + 14x +$ \_\_\_\_        2.  $x^2 - 30x +$ \_\_\_\_        3.  $x^2 + \dfrac{1}{2}x +$ \_\_\_\_

    4.  $x^2 + \dfrac{3}{4}x +$ \_\_\_\_        5.  $x^2 - \dfrac{1}{3}x +$ \_\_\_\_

B.  State the square root property for solving equations.

C.  Use the square root property to solve the following equations.

    6.  $x^2 = 36$          7.  $x^2 = 1$          8.  $x^2 = 7$
    9.  $(x - 5)^2 = 9$      10.  $x^2 + 2x + 1 = 11$

D.  Solve the following quadratic equations by completing the square.

    11.  $x^2 + 2x - 15 = 0$        12.  $2x^2 - x - 3 = 0$
    13.  $x^2 - 5x + 3 = 0$         14.  $2x^2 + 7x + 4 = 0$

E.  Using $ax^2 + bx + c = 0$, where $a$, $b$, $c$ are constants and $a \neq 0$, try to derive the quadratic formula without looking at Frame 12.

## Solutions to Review Exercises

A.  1.  $x^2 + 14x + 49$, since $\left(\frac{1}{2} \cdot 14\right)^2 = 49$

2.  $x^2 - 30x + 225$, since $\left(\frac{1}{2} \cdot 30\right)^2 = 225$

3.  $x^2 + \frac{1}{2}x + \frac{1}{16}$, since $\left(\frac{1}{2} \cdot \frac{1}{2}\right)^2 = \frac{1}{16}$

4.  $x^2 + \frac{3}{4}x + \frac{9}{64}$, since $\left(\frac{1}{2} \cdot \frac{3}{4}\right)^2 = \frac{9}{64}$

5.  $x^2 - \frac{1}{3}x + \frac{1}{36}$, since $\left(\frac{1}{2} \cdot \frac{1}{3}\right)^2 = \frac{1}{36}$

B.  See Frame 5.

C.  6.  $x^2 = 36$
$x = -\sqrt{36}$, or $x = \sqrt{36}$
$x = -6$, or $x = 6$. Solutions are $-6$ and $6$.

7.  $x^2 = 1$
$x = -\sqrt{1}$, or $x = \sqrt{1}$
$x = -1$, or $x = 1$. Solutions are $-1$ and $1$.

8.  $x^2 = 7$
$x = -\sqrt{7}$, or $x = \sqrt{7}$. Solutions are $-\sqrt{7}$ and $\sqrt{7}$.

9.  $(x - 5)^2 = 9$
$x - 5 = -\sqrt{9}$, or $x - 5 = \sqrt{9}$
$x - 5 = -3$, or $x - 5 = 3$
$x = 2$, or $x = 8$. Solutions are 2 and 8.

10.  $x^2 + 2x + 1 = 11$
$(x + 1)^2 = 11$
$x + 1 = -\sqrt{11}$, or $x + 1 = \sqrt{11}$
$x = -1 - \sqrt{11}$, or $x = -1 + \sqrt{11}$. Solutions are $-1 - \sqrt{11}$ and $-1 + \sqrt{11}$.

D.  11.  $x^2 + 2x - 15 = 0$
$x^2 + 2x = 15$
$x^2 + 2x + 1 = 15 + 1$
$(x + 1)^2 = 16$
$x + 1 = -\sqrt{16}$, or $x + 1 = \sqrt{16}$
$x + 1 = -4$, or $x + 1 = 4$
$x = -5$, or $x = 3$. Solutions are $-5$ and 3.

12.  $2x^2 - x - 3 = 0$
$2x^2 - x = 3$
$x^2 - \frac{1}{2}x = \frac{3}{2}$
$x^2 - \frac{1}{2}x + \frac{1}{16} = \frac{3}{2} + \frac{1}{16}$
$\left(x - \frac{1}{4}\right)^2 = \frac{25}{16}$
$x - \frac{1}{4} = -\sqrt{\frac{25}{16}}$, or $x - \frac{1}{4} = \sqrt{\frac{25}{16}}$
$x - \frac{1}{4} = -\frac{5}{4}$, or $x - \frac{1}{4} = \frac{5}{4}$
$x = -1$, or $x = \frac{3}{2}$. Solutions are $-1$ and $\frac{3}{2}$.

13.  $x^2 - 5x + 3 = 0$
$x^2 - 5x = -3$
$x^2 - 5x + \frac{25}{4} = -3 + \frac{25}{4}$
$\left(x - \frac{5}{2}\right)^2 = \frac{13}{4}$
$x - \frac{5}{2} = -\sqrt{\frac{13}{4}}$, or $x - \frac{5}{2} = \sqrt{\frac{13}{4}}$
$x - \frac{5}{2} = -\frac{\sqrt{13}}{2}$, or $x - \frac{5}{2} = \frac{\sqrt{13}}{2}$
$x = \frac{5 - \sqrt{13}}{2}$, or $x = \frac{5 + \sqrt{13}}{2}$. Solutions are $\frac{5 - \sqrt{13}}{2}$ and $\frac{5 + \sqrt{13}}{2}$.

## Solutions to Review Exercises, Contd.

14. $\quad 2x^2 + 7x + 4 = 0$

$$2x^2 + 7x = -4$$

$$x^2 + \frac{7}{2}x = -2$$

$$x^2 + \frac{7}{2}x + \frac{49}{16} = -2 + \frac{49}{16}$$

$$\left(x + \frac{7}{4}\right)^2 = \frac{17}{16}$$

$$x + \frac{7}{4} = -\sqrt{\frac{17}{16}}, \text{ or } x + \frac{7}{4} = \sqrt{\frac{17}{16}}$$

$$x + \frac{7}{4} = \frac{-\sqrt{17}}{4}, \text{ or } x + \frac{7}{4} = \frac{\sqrt{17}}{4}$$

$$x = \frac{-7 - \sqrt{17}}{4}, \text{ or } x = \frac{-7 + \sqrt{17}}{4}. \text{ Solutions are } \frac{-7 - \sqrt{17}}{4} \text{ and } \frac{-7 + \sqrt{17}}{4}.$$

E.  See Frame 12.

## SUPPLEMENTARY PROBLEMS

A.  Fill in the blanks so that each trinomial is a perfect square.

     1.  $x^2 - 3x +$ _____          2.  $x^2 + 5x +$ _____          3.  $x^2 - 4x +$ _____

     4.  $x^2 + \frac{b}{a}x +$ _____, where $\frac{b}{a}$ is a constant          5.  $x^2 + 6x +$ _____

B.  Use the square root property to solve the following equations.

     6.  $x^2 = 100$          7.  $x^2 = 64$          8.  $x^2 = \frac{9}{4}$

     9.  $(x + 8)^2 = 1$          10.  $(2x - 3)^2 = 5$          11.  $x^2 + 6x + 9 = 13$

     12.  $4x^2 + 20x + 25 = 7$

C.  Solve the following quadratic equations by completing the square.

     13.  $x^2 + x - 2 = 0$          14.  $2x^2 + x - 10 = 0$          15.  $3x^2 - x - 4 = 0$

     16.  $2x^2 + x - 21 = 0$          17.  $x^2 + 3x + 1 = 0$          18.  $3x^2 - 7x + 3 = 0$

     19.  $2x^2 + 3x - 7 = 0$          20.  $x^2 - 5x - 1 = 0$          21.  $x^2 + x - 1 = 0$

     22.  $5x^2 - 2x - 3 = 0$          23.  $x^2 - 3x + 2 = 0$          24.  $x^2 + 4x - 21 = 0$

D.  Do as directed.

     25.  Try to prove the square root property of solving equations without looking at Frame 5.

     26.  Show that $\dfrac{\pm\sqrt{b^2 - 4ac}}{2|a|} = \dfrac{\pm\sqrt{b^2 - 4ac}}{2a}$ no matter if $a$ represents a positive or a negative real number.

## ☐ Solutions to Study Exercises                              (4A)

### Study Exercise One (Frame 4)

1.  $x^2 + 12x + 36$, since $\left(\frac{1}{2} \cdot 12\right)^2 = 36$.          2.  $x^2 + 20x + 100$, since $\left(\frac{1}{2} \cdot 20\right)^2 = 100$.

3.  $x^2 + x + \frac{1}{4}$, since $\left(\frac{1}{2} \cdot 1\right)^2 = \frac{1}{4}$.          4.  $x^2 + kx + \frac{k^2}{4}$, since $\left(\frac{1}{2} \cdot k\right)^2 = \frac{k^2}{4}$.

5.  $x^2 + \frac{b}{a}x + \frac{b^2}{4a^2}$, since $\left(\frac{1}{2} \cdot \frac{b}{a}\right)^2 = \frac{b^2}{4a^2}$.

## Solutions to Study Exercises, Contd.

☐            *Study Exercise Two (Frame 7)*          **(7A)**

1. $x^2 = 25$
$x = -\sqrt{25}$, or $x = \sqrt{25}$
$x = -5$, or $x = 5$. Solutions are $-5$ and $5$.

2. $(x + 6)^2 = 7$
$x + 6 = -\sqrt{7}$, or $x + 6 = \sqrt{7}$
$x = -6 - \sqrt{7}$, or $x = -6 + \sqrt{7}$. Solutions are $-6 - \sqrt{7}$ and $-6 + \sqrt{7}$.

3. $x^2 + 4x + 4 = 5$
$(x + 2)^2 = 5$
$x + 2 = -\sqrt{5}$, or $x + 2 = \sqrt{5}$
$x = -2 - \sqrt{5}$, or $x = -2 + \sqrt{5}$. Solutions are $-2 - \sqrt{5}$ and $-2 + \sqrt{5}$.

☐            *Study Exercise Three (Frame 11)*          **(11A)**

1. $x^2 + 5x + 6 = 0$
$x^2 + 5x = -6$
$x^2 + 5x + \dfrac{25}{4} = -6 + \dfrac{25}{4}$
$\left(x + \dfrac{5}{2}\right)^2 = \dfrac{1}{4}$
$x + \dfrac{5}{2} = -\sqrt{\dfrac{1}{4}}$, or $x + \dfrac{5}{2} = \sqrt{\dfrac{1}{4}}$
$x + \dfrac{5}{2} = -\dfrac{1}{2}$, or $x + \dfrac{5}{2} = \dfrac{1}{2}$
$x = \dfrac{-5}{2} - \dfrac{1}{2}$, or $x = \dfrac{-5}{2} + \dfrac{1}{2}$
$x = -3$, or $x = -2$. Solutions are $-3$ and $-2$.

2. $x^2 + 4x - 7 = 0$
$x^2 + 4x = 7$
$x^2 + 4x + 4 = 7 + 4$
$(x + 2)^2 = 11$
$x + 2 = -\sqrt{11}$, or $x + 2 = \sqrt{11}$
$x = -2 - \sqrt{11}$, or $x = -2 + \sqrt{11}$. Solutions are $-2 - \sqrt{11}$ and $-2 + \sqrt{11}$.

3. $2x^2 - 6x - 5 = 0$
$2x^2 - 6x = 5$
$x^2 - 3x = \dfrac{5}{2}$
$x^2 - 3x + \dfrac{9}{4} = \dfrac{5}{2} + \dfrac{9}{4}$
$\left(x - \dfrac{3}{2}\right)^2 = \dfrac{19}{4}$
$x - \dfrac{3}{2} = -\sqrt{\dfrac{19}{4}}$, or $x - \dfrac{3}{2} = \sqrt{\dfrac{19}{4}}$
$x - \dfrac{3}{2} = \dfrac{-\sqrt{19}}{2}$, or $x - \dfrac{3}{2} = \dfrac{\sqrt{19}}{2}$
$x = \dfrac{3 - \sqrt{19}}{2}$, or $x = \dfrac{3 + \sqrt{19}}{2}$. Solutions are $\dfrac{3 - \sqrt{19}}{2}$ and $\dfrac{3 + \sqrt{19}}{2}$.

# Word Problems Using

# Equations and Inequalities

## ☐ Objectives      (1)

By the end of this appendix you should know the meaning of a mathematical model and be able to use mathematical models to solve word problems concerning:

- numbers
- geometric objects
- distance, rate, and time
- coin collections
- mixtures
- inequalities

## ☐ Mathematical Models      (2)

A *mathematical model* is an expression, equation, or inequality which describes a written or a verbal situation.

## ☐ Variable Expressions Used as Mathematical Models      (3)

**Example 1:** Word phrase: The sum of a number and 15
*Mathematical model:* $n + 15$

**Example 2:** Word phrase: 6 more than twice a certain number
*Mathematical model:* $2n + 6$

**Example 3:** Word phrase: The sum of a number and three times itself
*Mathematical model:* $n + 3n$

**Example 4:** Word phrase: The sum of two consecutive integers
*Mathematical model:* $n + (n + 1)$

**Example 5:** Word phrase: An integer subtracted from the square of the next consecutive integer
*Mathematical model:* $(n + 1)^2 - n$

## ☐      *Study Exercise One*      (4)

A. For each of the following phrases, give a variable expression as a mathematical model. Use $n$ as the variable.

1. The sum of a real number and 6.
2. 8 less than 4 times a certain number.
3. The sum of three consecutive integers.
4. The sum of three consecutive even integers.
5. The sum of an integer and 7 times its square.
6. The absolute value of the difference of a number and 5 times the next consecutive integer.

## ☐ More Examples Using Variable Expressions as Mathematical Models      (5)

**Example 1:** The sum of two real numbers is 24. If $x$ represents one addend, represent, in terms of $x$, the other addend.

**Solution:** $24 - x$, because $x + (24 - x) = 24$.

**Example 2:** The sum of two real numbers is 18. If $n$ represents the larger number, represent, in terms of $n$, seven times the smaller number.

**Solution:** The larger addend is $n$. Therefore the smaller addend is $18 - n$. Hence, the solution is $7(18 - n)$.

**Example 3:** Represent in cents the value of each of the following sets of coins:

(a) 6 nickels     **Solution:** $5 \cdot 6$ or 30 cents
(b) 3 dimes     **Solution:** $10 \cdot 3$ or 30 cents
(c) 5 dollars     **Solution:** $100 \cdot 5$ or 500 cents
(d) 7 quarters     **Solution:** $25 \cdot 7$ or 175 cents
(e) $x$ nickels     **Solution:** $5x$ cents
(f) $y$ dimes     **Solution:** $10y$ cents
(g) $(n + 3)$ dollars     **Solution:** $100(n + 3)$, or $(100n + 300)$ cents
(h) $(z + 2)$ quarters     **Solution:** $25(z + 2)$, or $(25z + 50)$ cents

478

Appendix 2

## Study Exercise Two (6)

Write a variable expression acting as a mathematical model for each of the following.

1. The sum of two real numbers is 73. If $x$ represents the smaller number, represent in terms of $x$:
   (a) the larger number.  (b) twice the larger number.  (c) five times the larger number.

2. Represent in cents the value of each of the following sets of coins:
   (a) $x$ quarters  (b) $(n + 6)$ dimes  (c) $(3y + 2)$ dollars  (d) $2z$ nickels

## □ Solving Word Problems (7)

*Step (1):* If possible, draw a picture describing the problem.
*Step (2):* Write variable expressions representing the word phrases.
*Step (3):* Relate these variable expressions in terms of an equation or inequality (*mathematical model for the problem*).
*Step (4):* Solve the equation or inequality.
*Step (5):* Interpret the solution in terms of the original problem.

## □ Examples of Word Problems Concerning Numbers (8)

**Example 1:** The sum of a certain integer and 25 is equal to six times the integer. What is the integer?

**Solution:** Let $n$ represent the integer.

*Mathematical model:* $n + 25 = 6n$
Solve the equation: $25 = 5n$
$5 = n$
The solution of the equation is 5.
The integer we seek is 5.

**Check:** The sum of 5 and 25 is equal to $6 \cdot 5$.

## □ Example 2: Find three consecutive integers whose sum is 261. (9)

**Solution:** Let $x$ represent the first integer. Then $x + 1$ and $x + 2$ represent the next consecutive integers.

*Mathematical model:* $x + (x + 1) + (x + 2) = 261$
Solve the equation: $3x + 3 = 261$
$3x = 258$
$x = 86$

The solution of the equation is 86.
The three consecutive integers are 86, 87, and 88.

**Check:** The sum of 86, 87, and 88 is equal to 261.

## □ Study Exercise Three (10)

Solve the following word problems.

1. A certain integer is four times another. Their sum is 135. Find the integers.
2. Find four consecutive integers whose sum is 206.
3. The sum of the squares of two consecutive integers is 25. Find the integers.

## □ Examples of Word Problems Concerning Collections of Coins (11)

**Example 1:** A collection of nickels and dimes has a value of $7.25. How many nickels and dimes are in the collection if there are 38 more dimes than nickels?

**Solution:** Let $x$ represent the number of nickels. Then $x + 38$ represents the number of dimes.

| Value of nickels in cents | + | Value of dimes in cents | = | Value of collection in cents |
|---|---|---|---|---|
| $5x$ | + | $10(x + 38)$ | = | 725 |

479

*Mathematical model:* $5x + 10(x + 38) = 725$
Solve the equation: $5x + 10x + 380 = 725$
$$15x = 345$$
$$x = 23$$

The solution of the equation is 23.
There are 23 nickels and $23 + 38$ or 61 dimes in the collection.
**Check:** $5 \cdot 23 + 10 \cdot 61 = 725$

**(12)**

**Example 2:** A man has $4.55 in change, consisting of five more quarters than nickels. How many nickels and quarters does he have?

**Solution:** Let $x$ represent the number of nickels. Then $x + 5$ represents the number of quarters.

| Value of nickels in cents | $+$ | Value of quarters in cents | $=$ | Value of collection in cents |
|---|---|---|---|---|
| $5x$ | $+$ | $25(x + 5)$ | $=$ | $455$ |

*Mathematical model:* $5x + 25(x + 5) = 455$
Solve the equation: $5x + 25x + 125 = 455$
$$30x = 330$$
$$x = 11$$

The solution of the equation is 11.
There are 11 nickels and $11 + 5$ or 16 quarters in the collection.
**Check:** $5(11) + 25(16) = 455$

### Study Exercise Four
**(13)**

Solve the following word problems.

1. A collection of quarters and half dollars has a value of $8.75. How many quarters and half dollars are in the collection if there are 8 fewer halves than quarters?

2. A man has $7.08 in pennies, nickels, and dimes. There are 102 coins in all. How many of each coin does he have, if there are twice as many dimes as pennies?

### ☐ Word Problems Concerning Geometric Objects
**(14)**

**Example 1:** When each side of a square is decreased by 6 inches, the area is decreased by 72 square inches. Find the length of each side of the original square.

**Solution:** Draw a picture of both squares.

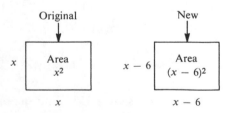

*Mathematical model:* $(x - 6)^2 = x^2 - 72$
Solve the equation: $x^2 - 12x + 36 = x^2 - 72$
$$-12x + 36 = -72$$
$$-12x = -108$$
$$x = 9$$

The solution of the equation is 9.

Each side of the original square was 9 inches.

**Check:** Area of original square was $9 \cdot 9$ or 81 square inches. The area of the new square is $3 \cdot 3$ or 9 square inches. Therefore, the area of the new square has decreased by $81 - 9$ or 72 square inches.

□ **(15)**

**Example 2:** The length of a rectangle is 6 feet greater than its width. The perimeter is 44 feet. Find the dimensions.

**Solution:** Draw a picture where $x$ represents the width and $x + 6$ represents the length. The perimeter is the sum of the four sides.

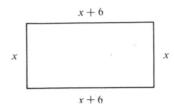

*Mathematical model:*  $x + x + (x + 6) + (x + 6) = 44$
Solve the equation:                    $4x + 12 = 44$
                                                      $4x = 32$
                                                        $x = 8$

The solution of the equation is 8.
The width is 8 feet and the length is $8 + 6$ or 14 feet.
**Check:**  $8 + 8 + 14 + 14 = 44$

□ *Study Exercise Five* **(16)**

Solve the following word problems.

1. When each side of a square is increased in length by 3 inches, the area is increased by 51 square inches. Find the length of each side of the new square.
2. The length of a rectangle is 4 feet more than its width. If the perimeter is 56 feet, find the dimensions.
3. An 84-foot rope is cut into three pieces so that the length of the first piece is twice the second, and the length of the second is one-third as long as the third piece. Find the length of each piece.

□ **Word Problems Concerning Mixtures** **(17)**

**Example 1:** How many pints of a 20% salt solution should be added to 30 pints of a 50% solution in order to obtain a 40% salt solution?

**Solution:**

| Pure salt in 20% solution | + | Pure salt in 50% solution | = | Pure salt in 40% solution |
|---|---|---|---|---|
| 20%(x) | + | 50%(30) | = | 40%(x + 30) |

*Mathematical model:*  $0.2x + 0.5(30) = 0.4(x + 30)$
Solve the equation:        $2x + 5(30) = 4(x + 30)$
                                        $2x + 150 = 4x + 120$
                                                    $30 = 2x$
                                                    $15 = x$

The solution of the equation is 15.
15 pints of the 20% salt solution must be added.

**Check:**  $20\%(15) + 50\%(30) = 40\%(15 + 30)$

☐ **(18)**

**Example 2:** How many ounces of an alloy containing 40% aluminum must be melted with an alloy containing 70% aluminum in order to obtain 20 ounces of an alloy containing 45% aluminum?

**Solution:**

$$\boxed{\begin{array}{c}\text{Pure aluminum}\\\text{in 40\% alloy}\end{array}} + \boxed{\begin{array}{c}\text{Pure aluminum}\\\text{in 70\% alloy}\end{array}} = \boxed{\begin{array}{c}\text{Pure aluminum}\\\text{in 45\% alloy}\end{array}}$$

$$40\%(x) \quad + \quad 70\%(20-x) \quad = \quad 45\%(20)$$

*Mathematical model:* $0.40x + 0.70(20 - x) = 0.45(20)$

Solve the equation:
$$40x + 70(20 - x) = 45(20)$$
$$40x + 1400 - 70x = 900$$
$$-30x = -500$$
$$x = \frac{50}{3}, \text{ or } 16\tfrac{2}{3}$$

The solution of the equation is $16\tfrac{2}{3}$.

$16\tfrac{2}{3}$ ounces of the 40% solution must be added.

**Check:** $40\%(16\tfrac{2}{3}) + 70\%(3\tfrac{1}{3}) = 45\%(20)$

☐ **(19)**

**Example 3:** Two investments produce an annual income of $910. $5600 more is invested at 8% than at 6%. How much is invested at each interest rate?

**Solution:**

$$\boxed{\begin{array}{c}\text{Interest from}\\6\%\end{array}} + \boxed{\begin{array}{c}\text{Interest from}\\8\%\end{array}} = \boxed{\begin{array}{c}\text{Total}\\\text{interest}\end{array}}$$

$$6\%(x) \quad + \quad 8\%(x + 5600) \quad = \quad \$910$$

*Mathematical model:* $0.06(x) + 0.08(x + 5600) = 910$

Solve the equation:
$$6x + 8(x + 5600) = 91000$$
$$6x + 8x + 44800 = 91000$$
$$14x = 46200$$
$$x = 3300$$

The solution of the equation is 3300.

$3300 is invested at 6%; $3300 + 5600$ or $8900 is invested at 8%.

**Check:** $6\%(3300) + 8\%(8900) = 910$

☐ *Study Exercise Six* **(20)**

1. How many ounces of a 30% acid solution should be added to 20 ounces of a 60% acid solution in order to obtain a 50% acid solution?
2. How many ounces of an alloy containing 10% titanium must be melted with an alloy of 25% titanium in order to obtain 40 ounces of an alloy containing 15% titanium?
3. Two investments produce an annual income of $3090; $13,000 more is invested at 9% than at 7%. How much is invested at each interest rate?

☐ Word Problems Concerning Distance, Rate, and Time **(21)**

**Formula:** $d = rt$

*Distance equals rate multiplied by time.*

**Example 1:** A man made a trip at an average speed of 50 miles per hour. A second man made the same trip in one hour less time at an average speed of 60 miles per hour. What was the distance of the trip?

**Solution:** The first man traveled a distance of $50t$. The second man traveled a distance of $60(t-1)$. Both men traveled the same distance.

*Mathematical model:* $\quad 50t = 60(t-1)$
Solve the equation: $\quad\quad 50t = 60t - 60$
$$60 = 10t$$
$$6 = t$$

The solution of the equation is 6.
The distance traveled was $50 \cdot t$, or $60(t-1)$; $50t = 50 \cdot 6$, or 300 miles, or $60(t-1) = 60 \cdot 5$, or 300 miles. Therefore, each man traveled a distance of 300 miles.

☐ **(22)**

**Example 2:** A jet airliner travels 500 miles in the same time a bus travels 40 miles. If the airliner travels 470 miles per hour faster than the bus, find the rate of each.

**Solution:** Let $r$ represent the rate for the bus. Then $470 + r$ represents the rate of the jet airliner. The times for the bus and the airliner are the same, and $t = \dfrac{d}{r}$.

$$\boxed{\begin{array}{c}\text{Time for}\\\text{airliner}\end{array}} = \boxed{\begin{array}{c}\text{Time for}\\\text{bus}\end{array}}$$

*Mathematical model:* $\quad\quad \dfrac{500}{470 + r} = \dfrac{40}{r}$
Solve the equation: $\quad 40(470 + r) = 500r$
$$18{,}800 + 40r = 500r$$
$$18{,}800 = 460r$$
$$\frac{18{,}800}{460} = r, \text{ or } \frac{940}{23} = r$$

The solution of the equation is $\dfrac{940}{23}$ or $40\frac{20}{23}$.

The approximate solution is 41.
The rate of the bus is approximately 41 miles per hour.

☐ *Study Exercise Seven* **(23)**

Solve the following word problems.

1. Two test rockets are fired over a 5600-mile range. One rocket travels twice the speed of the other. The faster rocket covers the distance in two hours less time than the slower. Find the speed of each rocket.
2. Two planes leave New Providence, Iowa, in opposite directions. One plane averages 60 miles per hour faster than the other. At the end of 5 hours they are 1550 miles apart. Find the rate of the slower plane.

☐ Word Problems Involving Inequalities (24)

**Example 1:** A student must have a grade average of 80% to 90% to receive a B. His grades on the first three tests were 76%, 82%, and 72%. What grade on the fourth test would assure him of a B?

**Solution:** Let $x$ represent the percentage on the fourth test.

*Mathematical model:*
$$80 \leq \underbrace{\frac{76 + 82 + 72 + x}{4}}_{\text{average of 4 tests}} \leq 90$$

Solve the inequality:
$$320 \leq 76 + 82 + 72 + x \leq 360$$
$$320 \leq 230 + x \leq 360$$
$$320 - 230 \leq x \leq 360 - 230$$
$$90 \leq x \leq 130$$

Any grade greater than or equal to 90% would assure him of a B. Notice that the upper limit of 130% in the model is not relevant to the problem because the percent could not exceed 100.

☐ (25)

**Example 2:** A bank offers two types of checking accounts, plan A and plan B. Plan A charges a flat 15¢ per check per month. Plan B charges $1.00 per month and 10¢ per check. After how many checks will the monthly charge on plan A be greater than plan B?

**Solution:** Let $x$ represent the number of checks written per month. The monthly charge on plan A in cents is $15x$. The monthly charge on plan B is $100 + 10x$.

*Mathematical model:* $15x > 100 + 10x$
Solve the inequality: $5x > 100$
$x > 20$

If more than 20 checks were written per month, the charge for plan A would exceed the charge for plan B.

☐ *Study Exercise Eight* (26)

1. A student must have an average of 60% to 75% on six tests in a course to receive a C. His grades on the first five tests were 58%, 72%, 62%, 80%, and 82%. What grade on the sixth test would assure him a C?
2. A car rental agency has two rental plans. Plan A charges $25 plus 15¢ a mile. Plan B charges 25¢ a mile. After how many miles would the charges for plan B exceed the charges on plan A?

REVIEW EXERCISES

For each problem, use $x$ as the variable:

(a) Write the mathematical model.
(b) Find the solution set.
(c) Interpret the solution to the given problem.

1. The sum of two integers is 47. One of the integers is 17 larger than the other. Find the integers.
2. The sum of two integers is 76. One of the integers is three times the other. Find the integers.
3. If a certain number is increased by 6 it will be 2 less than twice as large as before. What is the number?
4. A man has 45 coins consisting of nickels and dimes. The total value is 350 cents. How many of each are there?

## REVIEW EXERCISES, Contd.

5. A store owner sells nickel and dime candy bars. In one day, he sold 109 candy bars for $9.40. How many of each kind were sold?

6. How many pounds of walnuts at 49 cents per pound should a grocer mix with 20 pounds of pecans at 58 cents a pound to give a mixture worth 54 cents a pound?

7. A 20-quart solution of acid and water is 30% acid. How many quarts of pure acid must be added so that the solution will be 65% acid?

8. A car leaves Los Angeles for San Francisco, 420 miles away. At the same time, another car leaves San Francisco for Los Angeles. They meet at the end of 4 hours. Find the rate of each car, if one car travels 15 miles per hour faster than the other.

9. Two airplanes start from the same airport at the same time, one flying north, the other south. The ground speed of the first airplane is 200 miles per hour less than the ground speed of the other airplane. After 2 hours they are 1680 miles apart. What is the speed of each airplane?

10. Find the dimensions of a rectangle of perimeter 126 inches whose length is two and one-half times the width.

11. The perimeter of a rectangle is 7 times its width and the length is 2 inches more than twice the width. What are the dimensions of the rectangle?

12. The product of 3 and a certain number is less than one. Find the number.

13. To be eligible for the Math Club at a certain school, a student must maintain an overall average of 85% to 100%. His first math course score was 83%, second was 91%, and third was 78%. What grade must he receive in the fourth course to be eligible for the club?

## Solutions to Review Exercises

1. (a) $x + x + 17 = 47$
   (b) $x + x + 17 = 47$
   $2x + 17 = 47$
   $2x = 30$
   $x = 15$
   (c) The integers are 15 and 32.

2. (a) $x + 3x = 76$
   (b) $x + 3x = 76$
   $4x = 76$
   $x = 19$
   (c) The integers are 19 and 57.

3. (a) $x + 6 = 2x - 2$
   (b) $x + 6 = 2x - 2$
   $x + 8 = 2x$
   $8 = x$
   (c) The number is 8.

4. (a) $5x + 10(45 - x) = 350$
   (b) $5x + 10(45 - x) = 350$
   $5x + 450 - 10x = 350$
   $450 - 5x = 350$
   $450 = 5x + 350$
   $100 = 5x$
   $20 = x$
   (c) 20 nickels, 25 dimes

5. (a) $5x + 10(109 - x) = 940$
   (b) $5x + 10(109 - x) = 940$
   $5x + 1090 - 10x = 940$
   $1090 - 5x = 940$
   $150 = 5x$
   $30 = x$
   (c) 30 nickel candy bars; 79 dime candy bars.

6. (a) $49x + 58(20) = 54(x + 20)$
   (b) $49x + 58(20) = 54(x + 20)$
   $49x + 1160 = 54x + 1080$
   $49x + 80 = 54x$
   $80 = 5x$
   $16 = x$
   (c) 16 pounds of walnuts.

7. (a) $0.30(20) + x = 0.65(x + 20)$
   (b) $0.30(20) + x = 0.65(x + 20)$
   $30(20) + 100x = 65(x + 20)$
   $600 + 100x = 65x + 1300$
   $100x = 65x + 700$
   $35x = 700$
   $x = 20$
   (c) 20 quarts of pure acid.

## Solutions to Review Exercises, Contd.

8. (a) $4x + 4(x + 15) = 420$
   (b) $4x + 4(x + 15) = 420$
   $$4x + 4x + 60 = 420$$
   $$8x + 60 = 420$$
   $$8x = 360$$
   $$x = 45$$
   (c) Rate of first car is 45 miles per hour; rate of second car is 60 miles per hour.

9. (a) $2x + 2(x + 200) = 1680$
   (b) $2x + 2(x + 200) = 1680$
   $$2x + 2x + 400 = 1680$$
   $$4x + 400 = 1680$$
   $$4x = 1280$$
   $$x = 320$$
   (c) Speed of first airplane is 320 miles per hour; speed of the second airplane is 520 miles per hour.

10. (a) $2x + 2(2.5x) = 126$
    (b) $2x + 2(2.5x) = 126$
    $$2x + 5x = 126$$
    $$7x = 126$$
    $$x = 18$$
    (c) Width is 18 inches; length is 45 inches.

11. (a) $2x + 2(2x + 2) = 7x$
    (b) $2x + 2(2x + 2) = 7x$
    $$2x + 4x + 4 = 7x$$
    $$6x + 4 = 7x$$
    $$4 = x$$
    (c) Width is 4 inches; length is 10 inches; perimeter is 28 inches.

12. (a) $3x < 1$
    (b) $3x < 1$
    $$x < \frac{1}{3}$$
    (c) All real numbers less than $\frac{1}{3}$.

13. (a) $85 \leq \dfrac{83 + 91 + 78 + x}{4} \leq 100$

    (b) $85 \leq \dfrac{83 + 91 + 78 + x}{4} \leq 100$

    $$340 \leq 83 + 91 + 78 + x \leq 400$$
    $$340 \leq 252 + x \leq 400$$
    $$88 \leq x \leq 148$$

    (c) Any grade greater than or equal to 88%. The upper limit of 148% is not pertinent because the percent would never exceed 100.

## SUPPLEMENTARY PROBLEMS

For each problem, use $x$ as the variable:

(a) Write the mathematical model.
(b) Find the solution set.
(c) Interpret the solution in terms of the given problem.

1. A boy has 75 cents in pennies, nickels, and dimes in his pocket. There are 3 more pennies than nickels and three times as many dimes as nickels. How many of each type of coin are in his pocket?

2. A school bookstore sells ballpoint pens for 15 cents and packages of notebook paper for 25 cents. In a certain week the store sold 10 more than twice the packages of notebook paper as pens and took in at least $15.50 from these sales. What was the minimum number of pens sold?

## SUPPLEMENTARY PROBLEMS, Contd.

3. A man made a trip at a rate of 30 miles per hour. A second man made the same trip in two hours less time at a rate of 50 miles per hour. What was the distance of the trip?

4. What number added to 34 gives a sum which is 2 more than 5 times the original number?

5. There are 28 students in a certain mathematics class. The number of students who do not wear glasses is 4 less than three times the number of students who do wear glasses. How many students wear glasses?

6. If the length of a rectangular plot of ground is 28 feet more than its width and the perimeter is 296 feet, what are the dimensions of the plot?

7. A man wishes to purchase a new automobile that has a window-sticker price of $5725.00. If the dealer gives a 15% discount off the sticker price and taxes and license are 6% of the discounted price, how much does the man pay for the automobile?

8. How much acid must be added to 12 quarts of a 10% solution of acid and water to make it a 20% solution?

9. A square has $\frac{1}{2}$ the area of a rectangle whose length is 8 feet more than a side of the square and whose width is 4 feet more than a side of the square. Find the side of the square.

10. In one season a Little League team played 32 games. They lost two more than twice as many games as they won. How many games did they win and how many did they lose?

11. Find two integers such that the larger integer is 11 more than the smaller integer and their sum is three more than three times the smaller integer.

12. Tom is 3 times as old as his son. The sum of their ages is 52 years. How old is the son; how old is Tom?

13. A man has an amount of money in savings at 5% and another investment at 6% simple interest. The amount invested at 6% is $2000 more than that invested at 5%. The total annual interest is $395.00. How much money is invested at each rate?

14. The warranty book for a certain new car states that the cooling system should contain a minimum of 40% antifreeze for proper corrosion protection. If the radiator has a capacity of 17 quarts, what is the minimum number of quarts of antifreeze to be added?

15. The label on a particular gallon of exterior paint claims a coverage from 200 square feet to 400 square feet. If a block wall around a certain housing tract is 8 feet high and 1200 feet long, then what are the minimum and the maximum number of gallons of paint to cover the wall?

16. The tickets for the circus cost $2, $3, or $4. There were twice as many $2 tickets as $4 tickets sold, and three times as many $3 tickets as $4 tickets. If the total receipts were $1581, how many tickets at each price were sold?

17. A man has $4000 invested at a certain rate of interest and $3000 invested at 1% more than the interest rate for the $4000. The annual interest of the investments totals $380. Find the rates.

18. How much water must be added to 30 quarts of a 75% solution of acid to reduce it to a 25% solution?

19. Two automobiles start from the same point and travel in opposite directions. The first automobile averages 45 miles per hour and the other averages 55 miles per hour. In how many hours will they be 935 miles apart?

20. If it requires 140 feet of fence to completely enclose a rectangular garden plot which is 20 feet wide, how long is the plot?

21. One number exceeds another by 2. Five times the smaller exceeds four times the larger by 9. Find the numbers.

22. An estate of $18,500 is to be divided among a mother, a son, and a daughter. The daughter is to receive $1500 more than the son, and the mother is to receive twice as much as the daughter. Find the amount that each will receive.

23. Find three consecutive numbers such that when the first is subtracted from three times the second, the result exceeds the third by 18.

24. A 100-ft rope is cut into two pieces. One piece is 16 ft longer than the other. How long is each piece?

## SUPPLEMENTARY PROBLEMS, Contd.

25. Oil tank A has a capacity twice that of tank B. Tank C has a capacity of 100 gal more than tank B. Together the tanks have a capacity of 3700 gal. Find the capacity of each tank.

26. A jet airliner made a trip at an average speed of 400 miles per hour. A second jet airliner made the same trip in two hours less time at an average speed of 600 miles per hour. What was the distance of the trip?

27. Six times a positive number when added to the square of the number will produce 16. Find the number.

28. The length of a rectangle is 10 feet more than the width. The area of the rectangle is 24 square feet. Find the length and the width.

29. A dealer sold a certain number of radio sets at $24 each. He would have taken in as much money had he sold 6 fewer sets at $36 each. How many sets did he sell at $24 each?

30. Admission to a movie theater is $2.25 for orchestra seats and $1.75 for balcony seats. The total receipts from the sale of 350 seats were $672.50. Find the number of orchestra seats sold.

31. A boy's grades on three tests were 87, 91, and 83. What was his grade on a fourth test if his average on the four tests was 86?

32. A jar contains dimes, quarters, and nickels having a total value of $4.15. The number of dimes is three times the number of nickels; the number of quarters is 7 more than the number of nickels. How many of each coin are there?

33. The sum of two numbers is 66. The larger number is 6 more than three times the smaller number. Find both numbers.

34. A rope 50 feet long is cut into two pieces. One piece is 8 feet longer than the other. How long is each piece?

35. An electric current of 23 amperes is branched off into three circuits. The second branch carries three times the current of the first branch. The third branch carries 2 amperes less than the first branch. Find the amount of current carried in each branch.

36. A collection of dimes and quarters has a value of $10. How many dimes and quarters are in the collection if there are 12 fewer dimes than quarters.

37. A man bought some 15-cent stamps and some 10-cent stamps costing a total of $2.55. If he bought 3 more 10-cent stamps than 15-cent stamps, how many of each kind did he buy?

38. The greater of two numbers is 8 more than the smaller. Five times the greater exceeds six times the smaller by 20. Find the two numbers.

39. A toy bank has $5.20 made up of nickels and quarters. If there are 40 coins, how many nickels and how many quarters does the bank contain?

□ **Solutions to Study Exercises** (4A)

### Study Exercise One (Frame 4)

1. $n + 6$
3. $n + (n + 1) + (n + 2)$
5. $n + 7n^2$

2. $4n - 8$
4. $n + (n + 2) + (n + 4)$, where $n$ is even
6. $|n - 5(n + 1)|$, or $|5(n + 1) - n|$

□      ### Study Exercise Two (Frame 6)      (6A)

1. (a) $73 - x$      (b) $2(73 - x)$      (c) $5(73 - x)$
2. (a) $25x$ cents      (b) $10(n + 6)$, or $(10n + 60)$ cents
   (c) $100(3y + 2)$, or $(300y + 200)$ cents      (d) $5(2z)$, or $10z$ cents

## Solutions to Study Exercises, Contd.

### Study Exercise Three (Frame 10)      (10A)

1. *Mathematical model:* $\quad 4x + x = 135$
$$5x = 135$$
$$x = 27$$
One integer is 27 and the other is $4 \cdot 27$, or 108.

2. *Mathematical model:* $\quad n + (n+1) + (n+2) + (n+3) = 206$
$$4n + 6 = 206$$
$$4n = 200$$
$$n = 50$$
The four integers are 50, 51, 52, and 53.

3. *Mathematical model:* $\quad n^2 + (n+1)^2 = 25$
$$n^2 + n^2 + 2n + 1 = 25$$
$$2n^2 + 2n - 24 = 0$$
$$(2n - 6)(n + 4) = 0$$
$$n = 3, \text{ or } n = -4$$
If $n = 3$, then $n + 1 = 4$. If $n = -4$, then $n + 1 = -3$.

### Study Exercise Four (Frame 13)      (13A)

1. *Mathematical model:* $\quad 25x + 50(x - 8) = 875$
$$25x + 50x - 400 = 875$$
$$75x = 1275$$
$$x = 17$$
17 quarters and $17 - 8$ or 9 halves.

2. *Mathematical model:* $\quad 1x + 5(102 - 3x) + 10(2x) = 708$
$$x + 510 - 15x + 20x = 708$$
$$6x = 198$$
$$x = 33$$
The collection consists of 33 pennies, $102 - 3 \cdot 33$ or 3 nickels, and $2 \cdot 33$ or 66 dimes.

### Study Exercise Five (Frame 16)      (16A)

1. *Mathematical model:* $\quad (x + 3)^2 = x^2 + 51$
$$x^2 + 6x + 9 = x^2 + 51$$
$$6x = 42$$
$$x = 7$$
The length of each side of the new square is $7 + 3$ or 10 inches.

2. *Mathematical model:* $\quad x + x + (x + 4) + (x + 4) = 56$
$$4x + 8 = 56$$
$$4x = 48$$
$$x = 12$$
The dimensions of the rectangle are 12 feet by $12 + 4$ or 16 feet.

3. *Mathematical model:* Let $x$ represent the length of the third piece. The length of the second piece is then represented by $\frac{1}{3}x$ and the first by $2\left(\frac{1}{3}x\right)$.

$$2\left(\frac{1}{3}x\right) + \frac{1}{3}x + x = 84$$
$$\frac{2}{3}x + \frac{1}{3}x + x = 84$$
$$2x + x + 3x = 252$$
$$6x = 252$$
$$x = 42$$

The length of the first piece is $2 \cdot \left(\frac{1}{3} \cdot 42\right)$ or 28 feet.

The length of the second piece is $\frac{1}{3} \cdot 42$ or 14 feet.

The length of the third piece is 42 feet.

## Solutions to Study Exercises, Contd.

☐                                 *Study Exercise Six (Frame 20)*                            **(20A)**

1. *Mathematical model:*
$$0.30x + 0.60(20) = 0.50(20 + x)$$
$$3x + 6(20) = 5(20 + x)$$
$$3x + 120 = 100 + 5x$$
$$20 = 2x$$
$$10 = x$$

10 ounces of the 30% solution should be added.

2. *Mathematical model:*
$$0.10x + 0.25(40 - x) = 0.15(40)$$
$$10x + 25(40 - x) = 15(40)$$
$$10x + 1000 - 25x = 600$$
$$-15x = -400$$
$$x = \frac{400}{15}, \text{ or } 26\frac{2}{3}$$

$26\frac{2}{3}$ ounces of the 10% alloy need to be added.

3. *Mathematical model:*
$$0.07x + 0.09(x + 13,000) = 3090$$
$$7x + 9(x + 13,000) = 309,000$$
$$7x + 9x + 117,000 = 309,000$$
$$16x = 192,000$$
$$x = 12,000$$

$12,000 is invested at 7% and 12,000 + 13,000 or $25,000 is invested at 9%.

☐                                 *Study Exercise Seven (Frame 23)*                          **(23A)**

1. *Mathematical model:* The rate of the faster rocket is twice the rate of the slower.
$$\frac{5600}{t - 2} = 2\left(\frac{5600}{t}\right)$$
$$\frac{5600}{t - 2} = \frac{11,200}{t}$$
$$5600t = 11,200(t - 2)$$
$$5600t = 11,200t - 22,400$$
$$22,400 = 5600t$$
$$4 = t \text{ or } t = 4$$

The rate of the slower rocket is $\frac{5600}{4}$ or 1400 miles per hour.

The rate of the faster rocket is $\frac{5600}{4 - 2}$ or 2800 miles per hour.

2. *Mathematical model:* The sum of the distances traveled in 5 hours is 1550 miles
$$5r + 5(r + 60) = 1550$$
$$5r + 5r + 300 = 1550$$
$$10r = 1250$$
$$r = 125$$

The slower plane averages 125 miles per hour.

☐                                 *Study Exercise Eight (Frame 26)*                          **(26A)**

1. *Mathematical model:*
$$60 \leq \frac{58 + 72 + 62 + 80 + 82 + x}{6} \leq 75$$
$$60 \leq \frac{354 + x}{6} \leq 75$$
$$360 \leq 354 + x \leq 450$$
$$6 \leq x \leq 96$$

The student must receive a test score from 6% to 96% in order to be assured of a C.

2. *Mathematical model:*
$$2500 + 15x < 25x$$
$$2500 < 10x$$
$$250 < x \text{ or } x > 250$$

After 250 miles, the charge for plan B would exceed the charge for plan A.

# Answers to Odd-numbered
# Supplementary Problems

# Unit 1

A.   1.  $\{n, i, g, h, t\}$            3.  $\{m, i, s, p\}$           5.  $\{6\}$

B.   7.  $A$ and $B$ match. $C$, $D$, and $E$ match.

C.   9.  $\{f, g, h, i, j\}$       11.  $\{k, m, n, o\}$      13.  $\varnothing$             15.  $\{f, g, h\} = A$

     17.  $\varnothing$               19.  True          21.  False

D.  23.  8         25.  1            27.  3            29.  8           31.  0

E.  33.  False      35.  True

     37.  False                  39.  False                 41.  True

# Unit 2

A.   1.  $5 + 7 = 12$                  3.  $7 + 0 = 7$

B.   5.  $1 + 1 = 2$                  7.  $0 + 0 + 0 + 0 + 0 = 0$

C.   9.  $4 \cdot 6 = 24$          11.  $0 \cdot 13 = 0$          13.  $1 \cdot 11 = 11$

D.  15.  Yes                17.  No                  19.  Yes

E.  21.  31, 22

F.  23.  18                       25.  12 or $18 - 6$

G.  27.  6

H.  29.  No            31.  Yes          33.  No           35.  Yes

I.  37.  18          39.  29          41.  47          43.  3         45.  9

     47.  5            49.  2            51.  8           53.  5

J.  55.  $\overset{④}{2} \cdot [\overset{②}{3} + \overset{③}{6} - (\overset{①}{1} + 2)]$      Basic product       57.  $\overset{②}{3} \cdot (\overset{①}{7} - 4)$      Basic product

     59.  $\overset{②}{15} \div \overset{③}{3} \cdot (\overset{①}{5} - 2) \cdot \overset{④}{3}$      Basic product

K.  61.  $3 \cdot (2 + 2) \cdot 5 = 60$             63.  $3 \cdot 2 + 2 \cdot 5 = 16$      No grouping symbols needed.

     65.  $6 \cdot (5 - 4 \div 2) = 18$

     67.  $60 - 3 + 4 \cdot 8 \div 2 = 73$      No grouping symbols needed.

L.  69.  10,045           71.  13,220          73.  367,455         75.  25,725

# Unit 3

A.   1.  Yes                3.  No, cannot divide by zero.       5.  No, $m$ could represent zero.

     7.  Yes                9.  Yes                           11.  No, need an operation.

B.  13.  $4 + 2 = 6$           15.  $5 \cdot 4 - 3 \cdot 2 + 0 = 14$       17.  $3 \cdot 4 + 3 \cdot 2 = 18$

     19.  $2 \cdot 4 + 3 \cdot 2 + 4 \cdot 0 = 14$      21.  $5 \cdot [4 + 2(2 - 0)] = 40$

     23.  $2(4 + 2) - 3 \cdot 0 = 12$

     25.  $4[(4 + 2) - (2 + 0)] + 3 \cdot 2 = 22$

C.  27.  Basic sum               29.  Basic product          31.  Basic difference

     33.  Basic product          35.  Basic sum

D.  37.  $x - 6$               39.  $2b - 10$             41.  $7 - x$

E.  43.  All whole numbers      45.  7                47.  3

     49.  6                       51.  0                53.  No solutions

F.  55.  Conditional             57.  Identity             59.  Conditional

     61.  Conditional

G.  63.  Symmetric             65.  Symmetric          67.  Substitution

     69.  Addition

H.  71.  $236(1054 + 561) = 381,140$

     73.  $3 \cdot 1054 - 2 \cdot 236 + 4 \cdot 561 = 4934$

     75.  $(1054 - 236) \cdot [1054 - (561 - 236)] = 596,322$

# Unit 4

A.   1.   apa             3.   clpm           5.   mult. ident.         7.   mult. ident.
     9.   cpa           11.   cpm          13.   cpm             15.   mult. by 0
    17.   dpma, or dpma and mult. ident.     19.   mult. ident.

B.   21.   $(3 + 1) + 4 = 4 + 4 = 8$ or $3 + (1 + 4) = 3 + 5 = 8$
    23.   $[(2 + 1) + 0] + 5 = [3 + 0] + 5 = 3 + 5 = 8$
         or $(2 + 1) + (0 + 5) = 3 + 5 = 8$
    25.   $[(2 \cdot 5) + (3 \cdot 2)] + 1 \cdot 4 = [10 + 6] + 4 = 16 + 4 = 20$
         or $2 \cdot 5 + (3 \cdot 2 + 1 \cdot 4) = 10 + (6 + 4) = 10 + 10 = 20$

C.   27.   $3 \cdot (6 + 2) = 3 \cdot 6 + 3 \cdot 2$
                  $= 18 + 6$
                  $= 24$
    29.   $(10 + 13) \cdot 3 = 10 \cdot 3 + 13 \cdot 3$
                        $= 30 + 39$
                        $= 69$
    31.   $12(3 + 1) = 12 \cdot 3 + 12 \cdot 1$
                 $= 36 + 12$
                 $= 48$

D.   33.   $3x + 3z$         35.   $y \cdot 6 + 12$       37.   $3xy + 3xw$       39.   $7t + 7$

E.   41.   $3(m + n)$        43.   $a(b + c)$        45.   $9(m + 1)$        47.   $6(t + 3)$
    49.   $4(3y + 2)$

# Unit 5

A.   1.   Base is $y$, exponent is 6.      3.   Base is $x$, exponent is 2.      5.   Base is $(x + 4)$, exponent is 5.

B.   7.   "$y$ squared" or "$y$ to the second"      9.   "the group $(a + 2b)$ to the sixth"

C.   11.   $y^4$          13.   $(a + 2)^2$       15.   $(xy)^3$        17.   $(x + 5y)^2$

D.   19.   5         21.   2       23.   4       25.   8       27.   13

E.   29.   Addition property of exponents     31.   Distributive property of exponents
    33.   Power to a power property

F.   35.   $x^8$   [Addition property of exponents]     37.   1    [Zero power property]
    39.   $8x^3$   [Distributive property of exponents]     41.   $(m + 3n)^{11}$    [Addition property of exponents]

G.   43.   $10n^2$       45.   $24x^6$       47.   $6a^6b^3c$       49.   $3x$
    51.   3        53.   $2x^3y^2z^3$      55.   $5ab^2$

H.   57.   4096         59.   34,328,125          61.   39,062,500
    63.   10,218,313      65.   5148

# Unit 6

A.   1.   positive                  3.   neither

B.   5.   south                   7.   loss

C.   9.   $+3$                     11.   $-6$

D.   13.   $-2$                  15.   0

E.   17.   7 or $+7$        19.   1 or $+1$       21.   1 or $+1$
    23.   $a$ or $+a$       25.   13 or $+13$      27.   0
    29.   0           31.   12 or $+12$      33.   23 or $+23$

F.   35.   $-20$           37.   0          39.   $+10$

G.   41.   True          43.   True         45.   False
    47.   True          49.   True         51.   True

H.   53.   7      55.   $-3$      57.   $10, -10$      59.   $-3$      61.   2

I.   (a)   opposite of or additive inverse of     (b)   add     (c)   negative or opposite of or additive inverse of
    (d)   subtract                    (e)   same as     (f)   add
    (g)   positive or same as

# Unit 7

A. 1.

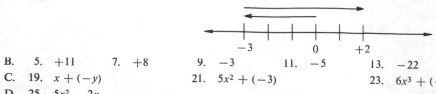

3.

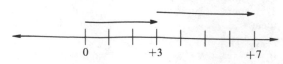

B. 5. +11    7. +8    9. −3    11. −5    13. −22    15. −26    17. −4
C. 19. $x + (−y)$    21. $5x^2 + (−3)$    23. $6x^3 + (−5x^3)$
D. 25. $5x^2 − 2x$
E. 27. positive    29. negative
F. 31. −13    33. 16    35. −22    37. 2    39. −7
G. 41. 0    43. −6    45. 0    47. −10    49. −9
   51. −8    53. 18    55. −7    57. −2    59. −2
H. 61. 415    63. −15,996    65. −20,466

# Unit 8

A. 1.

3.

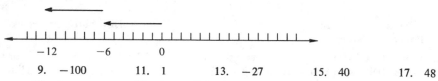

B. 5. 0    7. −20    9. −100    11. 1    13. −27    15. 40    17. 48
C. 19. −3    21. 9    23. 1    25. impossible    27. 3
D. 29. −4    31. −32
E. 33. −9    35. 4    37. −2    39. −8
F. 41. (c)    43. (b)
G. 45. 345    47. −237,403    49. 2

# Unit 9

A. 1. $−xy$    [Property one]    3. $−m^2$    [Property one]    5. $a^2$    [Property two]
B. 7. $8x$    9. $35x^2$    11. $12x^3y^3$
   13. $−24x^3y^7z^3$    15. $−2a^2$    17. $−3x$
   19. $2a^2$    21. $2x − 10$    23. $−8m^3n^2 + 10m^2n − 4mn^2$
   25. $5x^3 − 5xy$    27. $3m^3n − 12m^2n − 3mn$
C. 29. $9(x − y)$    31. $3m(n + 3p)$    33. $5(x − 2)$    35. $2(x + y + z)$    37. $5xy(xy + 2x − 1)$
D. 39. The variables are different.    41. The exponents are different.
E. 43. $7x$    45. $−2a$    47. $15xy$    49. $−5m^2n$
   51. $6ab − 7a + 2b + 8mn$    53. $6x^2 − 10x − 3$    55. $13x^2 − 3x − 1$    57. $x^2 − 12$
F. 59. $6x + 3$    61. $−2x + 6$    63. $−a$    65. $5a − 4$    67. $−7a − 2b$

## Unit 10

A.  1. Yes                    3. No                    5. Yes

B.  7. Yes                    9. Yes

C. 11. Conditional          13. Identity            15. Conditional

D. 17. Subtraction          19. Multiplication

E. 21. The solution is 3        23. The solution is 1
    25. The solution is 0        27. The solution is −5
    29. The solution is 9        31. The solution is −12
    33. The solution is 3        35. The solution is 11
    37. The solution is 5        39. The solution is 5
    41. The solution is 1        43. The solution is 1

F. 45. 10 and 28            47. 2 and 13            49. 15 and 51
    51. 6                    53. 5                    55. 7 cm and 13 cm
    57. 10 in and 14 in                              59. 11 ohms, 16 ohms, 23 ohms
    61. 100 liters/min, 300 liters/min, 400 liters/min     63. 60 nickels, 10 quarters and 9 half dollars
    65. 11,100 reg, 5200 box

## Unit 11

A.  1. False    3. False    5. True    7. True    9. False    11. False    13. True    15. False

B. 17. $\dfrac{1}{-8}$ or $-\dfrac{1}{8}$      19. $\dfrac{1}{1}$ or 1      21. $\dfrac{1}{\frac{2}{7}}$      23. $\dfrac{1}{-n}$ or $-\dfrac{1}{n}$

C. 25. 0.05        27. 2.2

D. 29. Rational      31. Rational      33. Rational      35. Irrational      37. Irrational

E. 39. **cpa**          41. Symmetric property of equality          43. **add. inv.**
    45. **dpma**        47. **mult. by zero**                        49. **clpm**

F. 51. Addition property of exponents          53. Distributive property of exponents
    55. Zero power property                    57. Definition of subtraction
    59. Definition of absolute value           61. Removing grouping symbols

G. 63. Any number which can be written in the form, $a \div b$ or $\dfrac{a}{b}$, where $a$ and $b$ are integers and $b \neq 0$. Alternate definition:

    Any number which can be symbolized as either a terminating or a repeating decimal.

    65. Any number which can be symbolized by a decimal numeral

H. 67. −1782.823          69. 153.100          71. −0.440
    73. 132.671          75. 498.112

## Unit 12

A.  1. Numerator is $3a$; denominator is $5b$          3. Numerator is $(2a - 7)$; denominator is $-3a$.

B.  5. $\dfrac{2a}{a - 4} = (2a) \div (a - 4) = 2a \cdot \dfrac{1}{a - 4}$

C.  7. $\dfrac{3y}{y + 4}$          9. $\dfrac{2x + 1}{7}$

D. 11. $a$          13. 1

E. 15. True                    17. False

F  19. True                    21. False

G. 23. The solution is 3        25. The solution is 4          27. The solution is $-\dfrac{5}{2}$

H. 29. $\dfrac{20}{24}$                    31. $\dfrac{8m^2 n}{6mn^2}$

## Unit 12, Contd.

I. 33. Yes      35. No      37. No      39 No

J. 41. $\dfrac{4}{5}$    43. $\dfrac{-2}{3}$    45. $\dfrac{5}{2}$    47. $\dfrac{-3a}{2}$    49. $\dfrac{x}{6y}$

   51. $2y$    53. $\dfrac{1}{2}$    55. $\dfrac{5}{2}$    57. $y + z$    59. 3

K. 61. 0.699    63. 8.260    65. 6.934
   67. 2388.975    69. 6.478

## Unit 13

A. 1. $\dfrac{1}{15}$    3. $\dfrac{1}{24}$    5. $\dfrac{1}{8a^2b^4}$

   7. $\dfrac{22}{9}$    9. $\dfrac{3}{5}$    11. $\dfrac{6x^3}{y^3}$

   13. $\dfrac{6a^3b^4}{c^4}$    15. 1    17. $\dfrac{x}{8a}$

   19. $\dfrac{a(a + b)}{bx}$ or $\dfrac{a^2 + ab}{bx}$    21. $\dfrac{3m^2(m^2 + 2)}{2(m^2 + 4)}$ or $\dfrac{3m^4 + 6m^2}{2m^2 + 8}$

B. 23. $y$    25. $\dfrac{15}{4x}$    27. 1    29. $\dfrac{4b^2}{3}$

   31. $\dfrac{8}{a + b}$    33. $\dfrac{3}{2}$    35. $\dfrac{3}{4}$    37. 3

   39. $ac$    41. $\dfrac{2m^2n^2}{27}$    43. $\dfrac{16x^3}{9y^2}$    45. $\dfrac{3}{20x}$

   47. $3a^3$    49. $\dfrac{r}{3s}$    51. $\dfrac{21}{10}$    53. $\dfrac{9}{2a}$

   55. $\dfrac{r}{3s}$

## Unit 14

A. 1. Prime    3. Prime    5. Composite    7. Composite

B. 9. $2^2$    11. $3 \cdot 5$    13. $2^3 \cdot 5$    15. $2^4 \cdot 3 \cdot 5$

C. 17. 360    19. 180    21. $(x + 3)(x - 2)$    23. $b(b + 1)$

D. 25. $\dfrac{7}{9}$    27. $\dfrac{-3}{7}$    29. $\dfrac{-5m}{n}$    31. $\dfrac{2a - 7}{2b}$    33. $\dfrac{11}{8}$    35. $\dfrac{4b + 3a}{ab}$

   37. $\dfrac{4r + 3}{9}$    39. $\dfrac{4a - 5b}{6}$    41. $\dfrac{13a - 4}{4a^2}$    43. $\dfrac{4y + x}{y}$    45. $\dfrac{5a - 3}{10a^2}$

   47. $\dfrac{5m + 5n + 2}{(m + n)^2}$    49. $\dfrac{3a^2 + 5ab - 2b^2}{(a - b)(a + b)}$

   51. $\dfrac{4x + y}{6}$

E. 53. $-\dfrac{21}{2}$    55. $\dfrac{19}{10}$    57. $\dfrac{97}{8}$

F. 59. $-2\dfrac{7}{8}$    61. $3\dfrac{3}{4}$    63. $16\dfrac{3}{5}$

## Unit 15

A.   1.   Not a polynomial

3.   Polynomial

5.   Not a polynomial

B.   7.   4

9.   12

C.   11.   $35x^2$

13.   $12x^3y^3$

15.   $-24x^3y^7z^3$

17.   $-21a^3 + 15a$

19.   $-6x^3y^2 + 9x^4y - 12x^2y^3$

D.   21.   $2a^3 + a^2 - 26a + 15$

23.   $m^4 - m^3 - 7m^2 - 7m - 2$

E.   25.   $a^2 + 5a + 6$

27.   $6x^2 + 5x - 6$

29.   $2x^2 + 7x + 3$

31.   $a^2 + 6a + 9$

33.   $4x^2 - 20x + 25$

35.   $20x^2 - 7x - 6$

37.   $4a^6 - 25b^4$

39.   $3x^2 + 13x - 10$

41.   $x^2 - x - 20$

43.   $6x^2 + 11x - 10$

45.   $x^2 + 12x + 36$

47.   $9r^2 + 24x + 16$

49.   $4x^4 - y^4$

51.   $a^2 - \dfrac{4}{9}$

53.   $x^2 - 2xy + y^2$

55.   $6 - 7x + 2x^2$

57.   $a^4 - b^4$

59.   $x^2 + x - 6$

61.   $8m^3 - 27$

F.   63.   $-4a$

65.   $-3x^2$

67.   $-1$

69.   $-5x^3y^3z^2$

71.   $-6m + 3$

73.   $-3x^3y^2 + 4xy - 2y^2$

75.   $m + n$

G.   77.   889.633

79.   $-5.317$


## Unit 16

1.   $5y(3 - x^2y)$

3.   $5abc(3a^2b - 2ac^2 + 1)$

5.   $(x + 2y)^2$

7.   $(a + 4)(a - 1)$

9.   $3(a + 3)(a - 3)$

11.   $(3x + 4)(x + 1)$

13.   $(2a - 3)(3a - 2)$

15.   $(5x + 2)(x - 1)$

17.   $(2a - b)(a + 3b)$

19.   $(3x + y)(x + 2y)$

21.   $2(x + 2)(x + 3)$

23.   $3m(m + 1)(m - 1)$

25.   $3m(2mn - 1)(mn - 3)$

27.   $x(y + z - w)$

29.   $2ab(1 - 2ab - 4a^2b^2)$

31.   $(3r - 7s)^2$

33.   $3rs^2(r + 1)^2$

35.   Not factorable

37.   $7h(m - 1)$

39.   $5x(2x^2 + 4x - 11)$

41.   $y^4(y + 1)$

43.   $(3x + 40)(3x - 40)$

45.   $(m^3 + 5n^5)(m^3 - 5n^5)$

47.   $\pi R(R + 5)(R - 5)$

49.   $(m + 3)(m + 16)$

51.   $(c - 15d)(c - 2d)$

53.   $2y(y - 4)(y + 1)$

55.   $3m(1 + m^6)(1 + m^3)(1 - m^3)$


## Unit 17

A.   1.   The solution is 7

3.   The solution is 7

5.   The solution is $-1$

7.   The solution is 5

9.   The solution is $-4$

11.   The solution is 4

13.   The solution is $-1$

15.   identity

B.   17.   The solutions are 3 and $-3$

19.   The solutions are 0 and 2

21.   The solution is 1

23.   The solutions are 4 and $-3$

25.   The solutions are $-2$ and 1

27.   The solutions are $\dfrac{1}{2}$ and $-1$

29.   The solutions are $\dfrac{9}{2}$ and 8

C.   31.   5

33.   3 ft, 5 ft

35.   14 ft, 8 ft

37.   10 in.

39.   125 mi/hr

41.   $-2$ amps, $-6$ amps, 8 amps

43.   2

45.   2 sec

# Unit 18

A. 1. All real numbers    3. All real numbers except $-3$

B. 5. $\dfrac{8xy^2z}{12y^3z^2}$    7. $\dfrac{9m^2 - 4}{6m^2 - m - 2}$

C. 9. $\dfrac{b^2}{2a}$    11. $\dfrac{b - c}{b + c}$    13. $\dfrac{-5}{7}$

15. $\dfrac{x + 1}{x - 1}$    17. $\dfrac{a - 2}{a - 3}$    19. $\dfrac{x - 1}{x - 3}$

21. $\dfrac{x - 2y}{x + 2y}$

D. 23. $-\dfrac{1}{32}$    25. $\dfrac{16a^4}{81}$    27. $\dfrac{27a^6b^3}{8c^9}$

E. 29. $\dfrac{y}{45x}$    31. $2x^2y^5$    33. $\dfrac{9}{y + 2}$

35. $\dfrac{m - n}{9}$    37. $\dfrac{-y^2}{2}$    39. $\dfrac{x}{x + 2}$

41. $\dfrac{x + 7}{x - 3}$    43. $\dfrac{x - 1}{x + 7}$    45. $\dfrac{(x - 3)^2}{(x + 2)^2}$

47. $\dfrac{x^2(x + 1)}{2(x + 3)^2(3 - x)}$

F. 49. .802    51. .590

# Unit 19

A. 1. $\dfrac{17}{36m}$    3. $\dfrac{y^2 + 2xy - x^2}{x^2y^2}$    5. $\dfrac{3 + 5a^2 - 2ab}{a^2b}$    7. $\dfrac{-1}{3(x + 1)}$

9. $\dfrac{3 - a - b}{3(a + 2b)}$    11. $\dfrac{12a - 46}{(a - 5)(a + 2)(a - 3)}$    13. $\dfrac{-2}{(m + 1)^2(m - 1)}$    15. $\dfrac{10x + 7}{2(x + y)}$

17. $\dfrac{2m - 3n - 1}{(m - n)(m + n)}$    19. $\dfrac{t^2 + 8t + 3}{(t + 3)(t - 3)(t + 7)}$

21. $\dfrac{5a^2 - 17a}{(a - 5)(a + 3)(a - 1)}$    23. $\dfrac{2(t^2 + 5t + 2)}{(t + 3)(t + 2)(t + 1)}$

25. $\dfrac{2m^2 - 10m + 13}{(2m + 1)(m - 2)(m - 3)}$    27. $\dfrac{y^2 + 6y - 3}{(y + 3)(y - 3)(y + 7)}$

29. $\dfrac{2(m^2 + 3mn + 4n^2)}{(m + n)^2(m + 3n)}$    31. $\dfrac{y^2 + 6y + 1}{(y - 1)(y + 1)^2}$

33. $\dfrac{5}{4}$    35. $\dfrac{a^2 - 1}{a^2 + 1}$ or $\dfrac{(a + 1)(a - 1)}{a^2 + 1}$

37. $\dfrac{3rt - r^2}{3rt - t^2}$ or $\dfrac{r(3t - r)}{t(3r - t)}$    39. $\dfrac{2}{x}$    41. $\dfrac{m}{n}$

43. $\dfrac{b(3a + 2b)}{6(a + 5b)}$    45. $\dfrac{x}{2}$    47. $\dfrac{x - 3}{x + 3}$    49. $\dfrac{a}{4}$

51. $\dfrac{m^2}{m - 2}$    53. $\dfrac{x - 5}{x - 4}$    55. $\dfrac{x - 2}{x + 2}$    57. $\dfrac{2}{-3}$

59. $\dfrac{a + 1}{a(2a + 1)}$

# Unit 20

A.  1.  The solution is $\dfrac{5}{2}$  3.  The solutions are 0 and 3

5.  The solutions are $-5$ and 2  7.  The solution is $\dfrac{3}{2}$

9.  The solution is 6  11.  The solution is 3

13.  The solutions are 0 and $-7$  15.  The solution is $\dfrac{14}{15}$

17.  No solution, since $x \neq 3$  19.  The solution is 1

21.  The solution is 5  23.  The solution is $\dfrac{4}{3}$

25.  The solution is 1  27.  The solution is 1
29.  No solution, since $x \neq 2$  31.  The solutions are 1 and $-3$
33.  The solutions are 6 and $-6$  35.  No solution
37.  No solutions

B.  39.  $b = \dfrac{2A - hc}{h}$ or $b = \dfrac{2A}{h} - c$  41.  $q = \dfrac{pf}{p - f}$

43.  $m = \dfrac{Fgr}{v^2}$  45.  $r = \dfrac{Sl - a}{S - l}$

47.  $D = \dfrac{Tl + 12d}{12}$ or $D = \dfrac{Tl}{12} + d$

49.  8 and 10  51.  24 and 25
53.  24  55.  1 ohm

57.  20 quarts  59.  $13\dfrac{1}{3}$ lbs.

61.  \$2500 @ 5% and \$4500 @ 6%  63.  \$12000 @ 7% and \$25000 @ 9%

# Unit 21

A.  1.  True  3.  Open
B.  5.

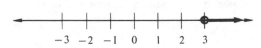

7.

9.

C.  11.  $\{y \mid y > -3\}$  13.  $\{t \mid t > -3\}$

15.  $\{x \mid x \leqslant -2\}$  17.  $\{n \mid n > \dfrac{5}{-2}\}$

19.  $\{m \mid m \leqslant -2\}$  21.  $\{x \mid x \leqslant 2\}$

23.  $\{n \mid n < \dfrac{25}{3}\}$  25.  $\{t \mid t > -5\}$

27.  $\{y \mid y \geqslant 3\}$  29.  $\{m \mid m \leqslant -2\}$
31.  $\{x \mid x > 0\}$  33.  $\{a \mid a < 3\}$

35.  All real numbers  37.  $\{y \mid y \geqslant -\dfrac{1}{2}\}$

## Unit 21, Contd.

39. $\{y|y < 3\}$

41. $\{m|m < 5\}$

43. $\{m|m \geqslant \frac{10}{9}\}$

45. $\{b|b \leqslant \frac{15}{2}\}$

47. $\{x|x \leqslant -2\}$

49. $\{m|m < -1\}$

51. $\{y|y < 3\}$

53. $\{x|x \leqslant 2\}$

55. $\{x|x < \frac{-3}{11}\}$

57. $\{x|x < 4\}$

59. $\{t|t \geqslant -\frac{1}{6}\}$

D. 61. False  63. True  65. False

## Unit 22

A.  1. $\frac{1}{27}$  3. $\frac{1}{32}$  5. $\frac{1}{10}$ or 0.1  7. $\frac{16}{9}$

B.  9. $\frac{1}{3x^2y}$  11. $\frac{m^5n^2}{3}$  13. $\frac{c^4}{a^2b^3}$  15. $\frac{b+a}{ab}$  17. $\frac{n^3 - m^3}{4m^3n^3}$  19. $\frac{3}{(x+y)^2}$

C. 21. $\frac{1}{m^7}$  23. $\frac{1}{x^6}$  25. $5x^7$  27. $\frac{-108a^2b^3}{c^2}$

D. 29. 0.121  31. 4650

E. 33. $2.03 \times 10^{-3}$  35. $6.39 \times 10^1$

F. 37. $9.12 \times 10^6$  39. $3 \times 10^2$ or 300  41. $2 \times 10^{-2}$ or 0.02

G. 43. 0.119  45. 0.466  47. 0.001  49. 0.010

## Unit 23

A.  1. Each number has exactly one cube root. A square root must be unique—see frames 6, 7, and 18.

B.  3. True  5. False  7. False  9. True  11. False

C. 13. $-7$  15. $\frac{1}{2}$  17. 3  19. $\frac{1}{4}$

21. $m$  23. $|k|$  25. $-2m$

27. $-64$  29. $\frac{1}{64}$  31. 1  33. 9

35. $-1$  37. 1000  39. 100  41. $\frac{1}{8}$

43. 16  45. $-32$  47. $\frac{8}{27}$  49. $\frac{8}{27}$

D. 51. $\frac{7}{\sqrt{m+n}}, (m+n) > 0$  53. $2\sqrt[5]{x^3}\ \sqrt[8]{y}$ or $2(\sqrt[5]{x})^3\ \sqrt[8]{y}, y \geqslant 0$

55. $\sqrt{a} - \sqrt{b}, a \geqslant 0, b \geqslant 0$

E. 57. $k^{\frac{1}{2}}, k \geqslant 0$  59. $11(x+y)^{\frac{1}{2}}, (x+y) \geqslant 0$

61. $a^{\frac{1}{3}} - b^{\frac{1}{3}}$

F. 63. 1.530  65. 10.440  67. 2.393

69. 12.498  71. 10.563  73. 6.878

Appendix 3

## Unit 24

A.  1. $2\sqrt{2}$  3. $3\sqrt{2}$  5. $3x\sqrt{2x}$  7. $2a^2\sqrt{3a}$  9. $-2$  11. $mn\sqrt[3]{m}$

B.  13. $8\sqrt{2}$  15. $-2\sqrt[3]{5}$  17. $4\sqrt{3}$  19. $12\sqrt[3]{2x}$
    21. $15\sqrt{3}$  23. $13\sqrt{2}+11\sqrt{3}$  25. $12\sqrt{3x}+2\sqrt{2x}$  27. $64x\sqrt{x}+38x\sqrt{2}$

C.  29. $\sqrt{42}$  31. $\sqrt{xy}$  33. $12\sqrt{15}$  35. $\sqrt[3]{6}$  37. 24
    39. $x\sqrt{3}+\sqrt{6}$  41. $-1$  43. $25a-9b$  45. $38-12\sqrt{10}$  47. $46+16\sqrt{21}$

D.  49. $\dfrac{\sqrt{3}}{3}$  51. $\dfrac{3\sqrt{2}}{2}$  53. $\dfrac{\sqrt{15}}{7}$  55. $\dfrac{-2\sqrt[3]{10}}{15}$  57. $\dfrac{\sqrt[3]{4x}}{3}$  59. $\dfrac{6\sqrt{14}+70}{-157}$

E.  61. $\dfrac{7\sqrt{2}}{2}\approx 4.949$  63. $\dfrac{\sqrt[3]{2}}{2}\approx 0.630$

F.  65. 16.941  67. 18.452  69. 11.619
    71. 0.749  73. 2.810  75. $-1.414$

## Unit 25

A.  1. The solutions are $-2$ and 4  3. The solutions are 3 and $-3$
    5. The solutions are 0 and $\dfrac{7}{3}$  7. The solution is $-3$
    9. The solutions are 2 and $\dfrac{-2}{3}$

B.  11. The solutions are 3 and 1  13. The solutions are 3 and $\dfrac{-11}{5}$
    15. The solution is $\dfrac{1\pm\sqrt{7}}{2}$ or the solutions are 1.823 or $-0.823$
    17. No solution
    19. The solution is $\dfrac{5\pm\sqrt{145}}{6}$ or the solutions are 2.84 or $-1.18$

C.  21. The solution is 8  23. The solution is 7
    25. The solution is 6  27. The solution is 5; 2 is extraneous

D.  29. 9 and 6  31. 8 ft.

E.  33. There would be no real solutions  35. Two real solutions

F.  37. No solution  39. The solutions are 2 and $-\dfrac{1}{6}$
    41. The solution is $\dfrac{-1\pm\sqrt{19}}{6}$  43. The solutions are $-1$ and $-2$
    45. The solutions are 2 and 9  47. The solutions are $\dfrac{3}{2}$ and $-4$

G.  49. The solutions are 1.661 and $-.946$  51. The solutions are 1.239 and $-.670$
    53. No solution

## Unit 26

A.  1. $x$ is the independent; $y$ is the dependent.  3. $r$ is the independent; $A$ is the dependent.
    5. $t$ is the independent; $s$ is the dependent.  7. $s$ is the independent; $A$ is the dependent.

B.  9. 35, 15, 3, $-1$, 3, 15, 35  11. 6, 5, 4, 3, 2, 1, 0, 1, 2

C.  13. Abscissa is $-5$; ordinate is 1.  15. Abscissa is 3; ordinate is 0.  17. Abscissa is 2; ordinate is 3.

D.  19. $(3, -6)$  21. $(4, -1)$  23. $(0, 0)$

E.  25. I  27. IV  29. No quadrant

501

Unit 26, Contd.

F.  31.

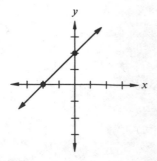

33.

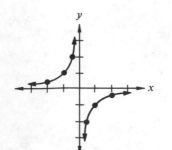

35.

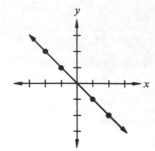

37.

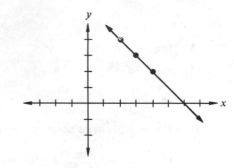

39.

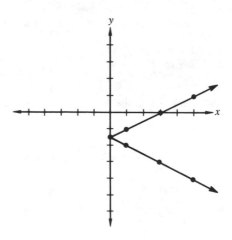

41.

G.  43.  10 in³

45.  10 lb/in²

47.  Decrease

# Unit 27

A. 1. $y = x$

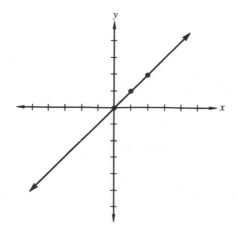

3. $y = x + 4$

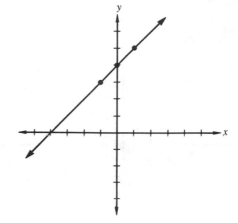

5. $y = 2x + 3$

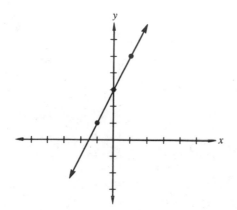

7. $x + y = 3$

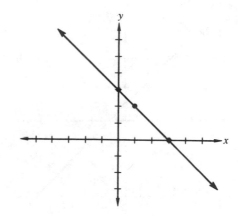

9. $2x - 5y = 10$

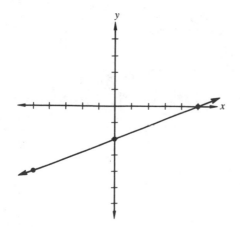

## Unit 27, Contd.

B.  11.  $y = x - 2$

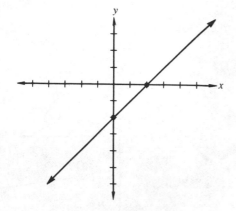

13.  $3x - 4y = 12$

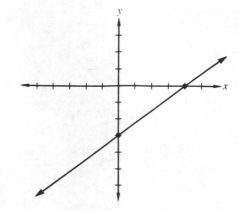

C.  15.  $x + y = 1$
slope $= -1$

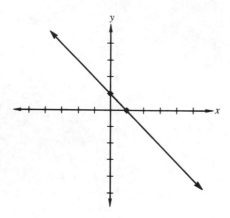

17.  $5x + 2y = 10$
slope $= -\dfrac{5}{2}$

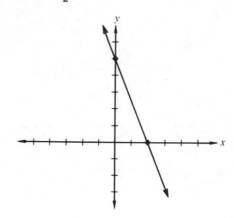

D.  19.  $y = -x^2$

21.  $y = x^2 - 1$

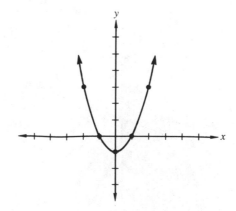

## Unit 27, Contd.

23.  $x = y^2 + 1$

25.  $x = y^2 + 2y - 8$

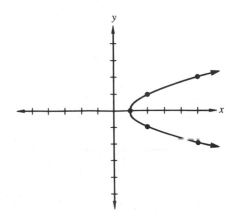

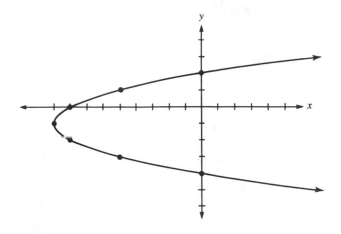

E.   27.  $(2,0)$ and $(-2,0)$     29.  $(5,0)$ and $(-\frac{1}{2},0)$

F.   31.  True          33.  False          35.  True          37.  False          39.  False

G.   41.  Any equation that has a form equivalent to $y = mx + b$, where m and b are constants.
     43.  The first element of an ordered pair.
     45.  The point named by $(0,0)$.

## Unit 28

A.   1.

3.

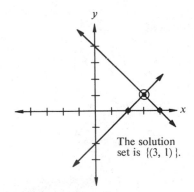

The solution
set is $\{(3, 1)\}$.

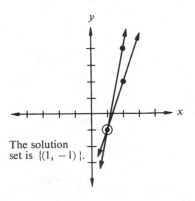

The solution
set is $\{(1, -1)\}$.

5.

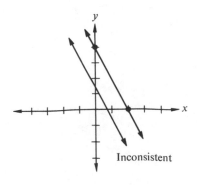

Inconsistent

## Unit 28, Contd.

B.  7.  {(4, 7)}           9.  Dependent          11.  Inconsistent

C.  13.  $\left\{\left(\dfrac{3}{4}, \dfrac{1}{16}\right)\right\}$      15.  {(0, 0)}        17.  {(2, 1)}          19.  Dependent

D.  21.  {(−2, 1)}    Consistent        23.  $\left\{\left(\dfrac{-3}{2}, -4\right)\right\}$  Consistent

25.  Inconsistent                  27.  Dependent

29.  {(0, −3)}    Consistent          31.  $\left\{\left(-\dfrac{1}{2}, \dfrac{5}{2}\right)\right\}$  Consistent

E.  33.  38 and 15          35.  $2500 at 7% and $1500 at 8%    37.  $26\frac{2}{3}$ oz
    39.  7.5 mi/hr and 1.5 mi/hr      41.  12 qt              43.  19 and 57
    45.  15 ohms and 5 ohms

F.  47.  Two straight lines which are parallel and therefore do not intersect

G.  49.  {k, c, o}                51.  ∅

## Unit 29

1.

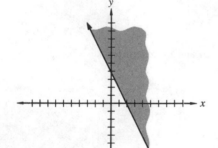

3.

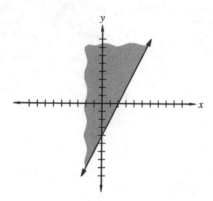

5.

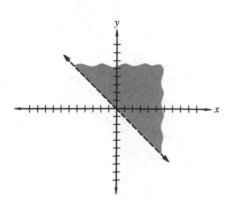

7.

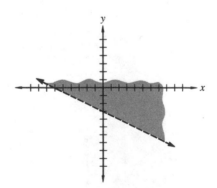

# Unit 29, Contd.

9.

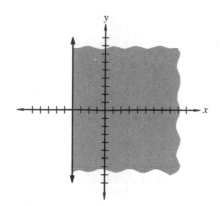

11.

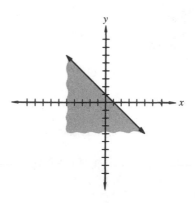

13.

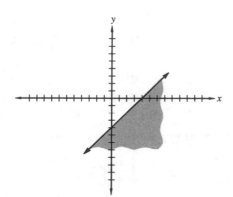

15.

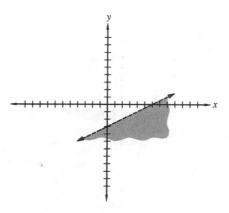

17.

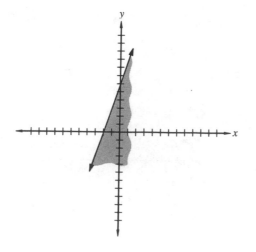

19.

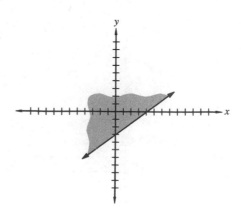

# Unit 29, Contd.

21.

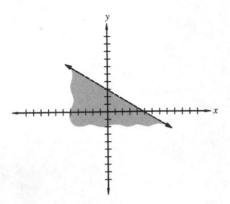

23.

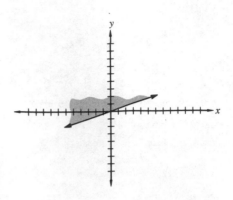

25.

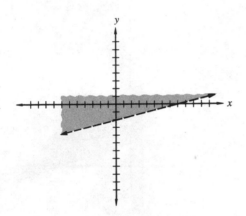

27.

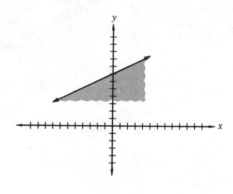

29.

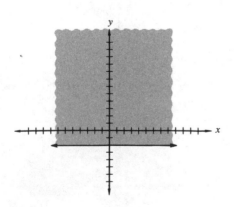

31.

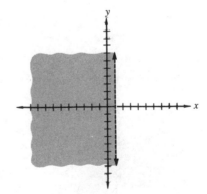

# Unit 29, Contd.

33.

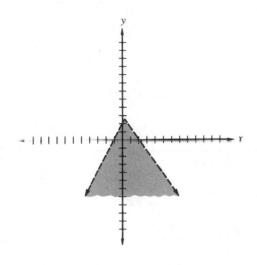

35.

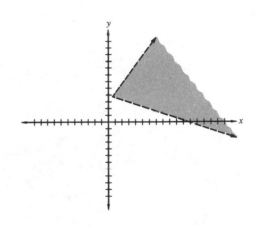

37.

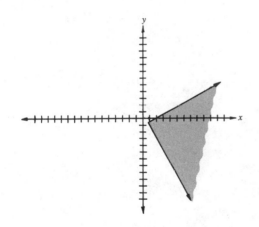

39.

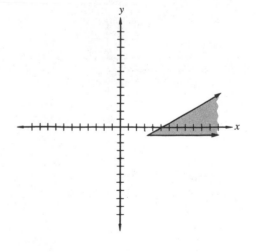

41.

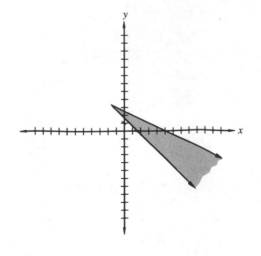

43.

Unit 29, Contd.

45.

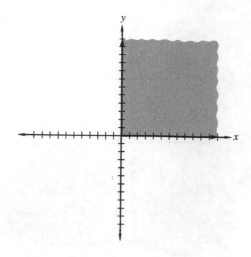

## Unit 30

A.　1.

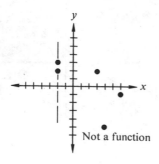

3.

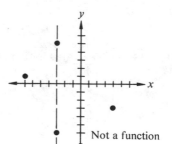

5.

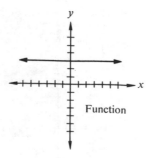

7.

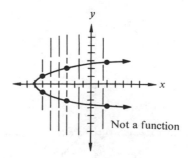

## Unit 30, Contd.

9.

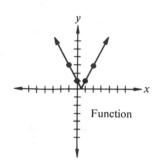

Function

11.

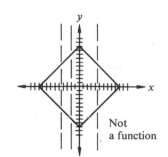

Not a function

B. 13.

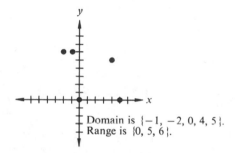

Domain is $\{-1, -2, 0, 4, 5\}$.
Range is $\{0, 5, 6\}$.

15.

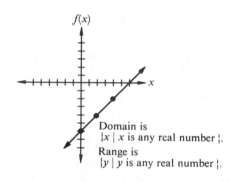

Domain is
$\{x \mid x \text{ is any real number}\}$.
Range is
$\{y \mid y \text{ is any real number}\}$.

17.

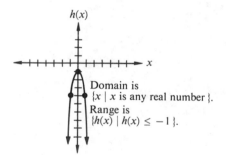

Domain is
$\{x \mid x \text{ is any real number}\}$.
Range is
$\{h(x) \mid h(x) \le -1\}$.

19.

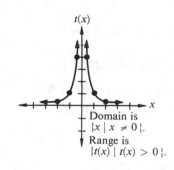

Domain is
$\{x \mid x \ne 0\}$.
Range is
$\{t(x) \mid t(x) > 0\}$.

C. 21. $-3$   23. 9   25. 1   27. 4
29. $2a + 5$   31. $|a + 6|$   33. $8a^2 - 10a - 3$

## Appendix 1

A. 1. $\dfrac{9}{4}$   3. 4   5. 9

B. 7. The solutions are $-8$ and $8$.
  9. The solutions are $-7$ and $-9$.
11. The solutions are $-3 \pm \sqrt{13}$.

C. 13. The solutions are $1$ and $-2$.
  15. The solutions are $\dfrac{4}{3}$ and $-1$.

17. The solution is $\dfrac{-3 \pm \sqrt{5}}{2}$.
  19. The solution is $\dfrac{-3 \pm \sqrt{65}}{4}$.

## Appendix 1, Contd.

21. The solution is $\dfrac{-1 \pm \sqrt{5}}{2}$.

23. The solutions are 2 and 1.

25. See Frame 5.

## Appendix 2

1. (a) Let $x$ = number of nickels, $1(x + 3) + 5x + 10(3x) = 75$
   (b) $x = 2$
   (c) 2 nickels, 5 pennies, and 6 dimes

3. (a) Let $T$ = number of hours first man, $30 \cdot T = 50(T - 2)$
   (b) $T = 5$
   (c) $(30)(5) = 150$ miles

5. (a) Let $N$ = number of students who wear glasses
       $N + (3N - 4) = 28$
   (b) $N = 8$
   (c) 8 students wear glasses, 20 do not wear glasses.

7. (a) Let $P$ = price of automobile
       $P = .85(5725) + .06[.85(5725)]$ or
       $P = 1.06[.85(5725)]$
   (b) $P = 5158.225$
   (c) $5158.23

9. (a) Let $S$ = side of square
       $$S^2 = \frac{1}{2}(S + 8)(S + 4)$$
   (b) $S = 6 \pm 2\sqrt{17}$
   (c) The side of the square is $6 + 2\sqrt{17}$ feet.

11. (a) Let $x$ = the smaller integer
        $x + (x + 11) = 3x + 3$
    (b) $x = 8$
    (c) The integers are 8 and 19

13. (a) Let $A$ = amount invested at 5%
        $.05A + .06(A + 2000) = 395$
    (b) $A = 2500$
    (c) $2500 at 5%, $4500 at 6%

15. (a) Let $N$ = number of gallons to cover wall
        $N = \dfrac{8 \times 1200}{200}$ or $N = \dfrac{8 \times 1200}{400}$
    (b) $N = 48$ or $N = 24$
    (c) Minimum of 24 gal, maximum of 48 gal

17. (a) Let $R$ = rate for $4000
        $(4000)R + 3000(R + .01) = 380$
    (b) $R = .05$
    (c) $4000 at 5%, $3000 at 6%

19. (a) Let $H$ = number of hours of first auto
        $45H + 55H = 935$
    (b) $H = 9.35$
    (c) 9.35 hr or 9 hr 21 min

21. (a) Let $x$ = larger number, $x - 2$ = smaller number
        $5(x - 2) = 4x + 9$
    (b) $x = 19$
    (c) The numbers are 17 and 19

## Appendix 2, Contd.

23. (a) Let $x$ = first number, $x + 1$ = second number, and $x + 2$ = third number.
$3(x + 1) - x = (x + 2) + 18$
    (b) $x = 17$
    (c) The numbers are 17, 18, and 19

25. (a) Let $x$ = capacity of tank B
$2x + x + x + 100 = 3700$
    (b) $x = 900$
    (c) Tank A is 1800 gal, tank B is 900 gal, and tank C is 1000 gal

27. (a) Let $x$ = the number
$6x + x^2 = 16$
    (b) $x = -8$, $x = 2$
    (c) The positive number is 2

29. (a) Let $N$ = the number at $24
$24N = 36(N - 6)$
    (b) $N = 18$
    (c) 18 sets at $24

31. (a) Let $G$ = grade on fourth test

$$\frac{87 + 91 + 83 + G}{4} = 86$$

    (b) $G = 83$
    (c) Score on fourth test is 83.

33. (a) Let $x$ = smaller number, $66 - x$ = larger number
$3x + 6 = 66 - x$
    (b) $x = 15$
    (c) Smaller number is 15, the larger is 51

35. (a) Let $x$ = amount of current in first circuit
$x + 3x + (x - 2) = 23$
    (b) $x = 5$
    (c) 5 amps, 15 amps, 3 amps

37. (a) Let $x$ = number of stamps at 15 cents
$10(x + 3) + 15x = 255$
    (b) $x = 9$
    (c) 12 stamps at 10 cents, 9 stamps at 15 cents

39. (a) Let $x$ = number of nickels, $40 - x$ = number of quarters
$5x + 25(40 - x) = 520$
    (b) $x = 24$
    (c) 24 nickels, 16 quarters

## Table A.1

### Powers and Roots

| $n$ | $n^2$ | $n^3$ | $\sqrt{n}$ | $\sqrt[3]{n}$ | $n$ | $n^2$ | $n^3$ | $\sqrt{n}$ | $\sqrt[3]{n}$ |
|---|---|---|---|---|---|---|---|---|---|
| 0 | 0 | 0 | 0.000 | 0.000 | 50 | 2 500 | 125 000 | 7.071 | 3.684 |
| 1 | 1 | 1 | 1.000 | 1.000 | 51 | 2 601 | 132 651 | 7.141 | 3.708 |
| 2 | 4 | 8 | 1.414 | 1.260 | 52 | 2 704 | 140 608 | 7.211 | 3.733 |
| 3 | 9 | 27 | 1.732 | 1.442 | 53 | 2 809 | 148 877 | 7.280 | 3.756 |
| 4 | 16 | 64 | 2.000 | 1.587 | 54 | 2 916 | 157 464 | 7.348 | 3.780 |
| 5 | 25 | 125 | 2.236 | 1.710 | 55 | 3 025 | 166 375 | 7.416 | 3.803 |
| 6 | 36 | 216 | 2.449 | 1.817 | 56 | 3 136 | 175 616 | 7.483 | 3.826 |
| 7 | 49 | 343 | 2.646 | 1.913 | 57 | 3 249 | 185 193 | 7.550 | 3.849 |
| 8 | 64 | 512 | 2.828 | 2.000 | 58 | 3 364 | 195 112 | 7.616 | 3.871 |
| 9 | 81 | 729 | 3.000 | 2.080 | 59 | 3 481 | 205 379 | 7.681 | 3.893 |
| 10 | 100 | 1 000 | 3.162 | 2.154 | 60 | 3 600 | 216 000 | 7.746 | 3.915 |
| 11 | 121 | 1 331 | 3.317 | 2.224 | 61 | 3 721 | 226 981 | 7.810 | 3.936 |
| 12 | 144 | 1 728 | 3.464 | 2.289 | 62 | 3 844 | 238 328 | 7.874 | 3.958 |
| 13 | 169 | 2 197 | 3.606 | 2.351 | 63 | 3 969 | 250 047 | 7.937 | 3.979 |
| 14 | 196 | 2 744 | 3.742 | 2.410 | 64 | 4 096 | 262 144 | 8.000 | 4.000 |
| 15 | 225 | 3 375 | 3.873 | 2.466 | 65 | 4 225 | 274 625 | 8.062 | 4.021 |
| 16 | 256 | 4 096 | 4.000 | 2.520 | 66 | 4 356 | 287 496 | 8.124 | 4.041 |
| 17 | 289 | 4 913 | 4.123 | 2.571 | 67 | 4 489 | 300 763 | 8.185 | 4 062 |
| 18 | 324 | 5 832 | 4.243 | 2.621 | 68 | 4 624 | 314 432 | 8.246 | 4.082 |
| 19 | 361 | 6 859 | 4.359 | 2.668 | 69 | 4 761 | 328 509 | 8.307 | 4.102 |
| 20 | 400 | 8 000 | 4.472 | 2.714 | 70 | 4 900 | 343 000 | 8.367 | 4.121 |
| 21 | 441 | 9 261 | 4.583 | 2.759 | 71 | 5 041 | 357 911 | 8.426 | 4.141 |
| 22 | 484 | 10 648 | 4.690 | 2.802 | 72 | 5 184 | 373 248 | 8.485 | 4.160 |
| 23 | 529 | 12 167 | 4.796 | 2.844 | 73 | 5 329 | 389 017 | 8.544 | 4.179 |
| 24 | 576 | 13 824 | 4.899 | 2.884 | 74 | 5 476 | 405 224 | 8.602 | 4.198 |
| 25 | 625 | 15 625 | 5.000 | 2.924 | 75 | 5 625 | 421 875 | 8.660 | 4.217 |
| 26 | 676 | 17 576 | 5.099 | 2.962 | 76 | 5 776 | 438 976 | 8.718 | 4.236 |
| 27 | 729 | 19 683 | 5.196 | 3.000 | 77 | 5 929 | 456 533 | 8.775 | 4.254 |
| 28 | 784 | 21 952 | 5.292 | 3.037 | 78 | 6 084 | 474 552 | 8.832 | 4.273 |
| 29 | 841 | 24 389 | 5.385 | 3.072 | 79 | 6 241 | 493 039 | 8.888 | 4.291 |
| 30 | 900 | 27 000 | 5.477 | 3.107 | 80 | 6 400 | 512 000 | 8.944 | 4.309 |
| 31 | 961 | 29 791 | 5.568 | 3.141 | 81 | 6 561 | 531 441 | 9.000 | 4.327 |
| 32 | 1 024 | 32 768 | 5.657 | 3.175 | 82 | 6 724 | 551 368 | 9.055 | 4.344 |
| 33 | 1 089 | 35.937 | 5.745 | 3.208 | 83 | 6 889 | 571 787 | 9.110 | 4.362 |
| 34 | 1 156 | 39 304 | 5.831 | 3.240 | 84 | 7 056 | 592 704 | 9.165 | 4.380 |
| 35 | 1 225 | 42 875 | 5.916 | 3.271 | 85 | 7 225 | 614 125 | 9.220 | 4.397 |
| 36 | 1 296 | 46 656 | 6.000 | 3.302 | 86 | 7 396 | 636 056 | 9.274 | 4.414 |
| 37 | 1 369 | 50 653 | 6.083 | 3.332 | 87 | 7 569 | 658 503 | 9.327 | 4.431 |
| 38 | 1 444 | 54 872 | 6.164 | 3.362 | 88 | 7 744 | 681 472 | 9.381 | 4.448 |
| 39 | 1 521 | 59 319 | 6.245 | 3.391 | 89 | 7 921 | 704 969 | 9.434 | 4.465 |
| 40 | 1 600 | 64 000 | 6.325 | 3.420 | 90 | 8 100 | 729 000 | 9.487 | 4.481 |
| 41 | 1 681 | 68 921 | 6.403 | 3.448 | 91 | 8 281 | 753 571 | 9.539 | 4.498 |
| 42 | 1 764 | 74 088 | 6.481 | 3.476 | 92 | 8 464 | 778 688 | 9.592 | 4.514 |
| 43 | 1 849 | 79 507 | 6.557 | 3.503 | 93 | 8 649 | 804 357 | 9.644 | 4.531 |
| 44 | 1 936 | 85 184 | 6.633 | 3.530 | 94 | 8 836 | 830 584 | 9.695 | 4.547 |
| 45 | 2 025 | 91 125 | 6.708 | 3.557 | 95 | 9 025 | 857 375 | 9.747 | 4.563 |
| 46 | 2 116 | 97 336 | 6.782 | 3.583 | 96 | 9 216 | 884 736 | 9.798 | 4.579 |
| 47 | 2 209 | 103 823 | 6.856 | 3.609 | 97 | 9 409 | 912 673 | 9.849 | 4.595 |
| 48 | 2 304 | 110 592 | 6.928 | 3.634 | 98 | 9 604 | 941 192 | 9.899 | 4.610 |
| 49 | 2 401 | 117 649 | 7.000 | 3.659 | 99 | 9 801 | 970 299 | 9.950 | 4.626 |
|  |  |  |  |  | 100 | 10 000 | 1 000 000 | 10.000 | 4.642 |

# Index

517